Introduction
to Investments

McGRAW-HILL SERIES IN FINANCE
PROFESSOR CHARLES A. D'AMBROSIO
University of Washington
CONSULTING EDITOR

Introduction to Investments

GEORGE A. CHRISTY, Ph.D.
Professor of Finance
North Texas State University

JOHN C. CLENDENIN, Ph.D.
Professor of Finance, Emeritus
University of California, Los Angeles

SIXTH EDITION

McGRAW-HILL BOOK COMPANY

New York   St. Louis   San Francisco   Düsseldorf
Johannesburg   Kuala Lumpur   London
Mexico   Montreal   New Delhi   Panama   Rio de Janeiro
Singapore   Sydney   Toronto

34567890MAMM7987654

This book was set in Patina by University Graphics, Inc.
The editors were Jack R. Crutchfield and Edwin Hanson;
the designer was Ben Kann;
and the production supervisor was Thomas J. LoPinto.
The Maple Press Company was printer and binder.

Library of Congress Cataloging in Publication Data

Christy, George A
    Introduction to investments.

    In earlier editions, J. C. Clendenin's name
appeared first on the title page.
    Includes bibliographies.
    1. Investments. 2. Securities. I. Clendenin,
John C., joint author. II. Title.
HG4521.C455   1974   332.6   73-15710
ISBN 0-07-010825-0

Contents

Preface

This book is intended primarily as an introductory textbook for college-level classes in investments. However, its subject matter and its brevity should combine to make it useful for adult education classes and for individual reading as well. We have tried to include both sound investment philosophy and practical investment detail, in order to make the book broadly useful.

Like previous editions, this sixth one has been shaped by both authors' long experience with the field and teaching of investments. The book is therefore certain to reflect many of the ideas and prejudices which we have accumulated through the years, both in the choice of subject matter and in the conclusions reached. With respect to the latter, a conscious effort has been made in most passages to subordinate personal opinions to the conventional viewpoint, for we continue to believe that a beginning course in any field should be built around generally accepted philosophy and nomenclature. But in choice of subject matter and in mode of presentation, there has been less constraint. Like previous editions, this book is based on five central convictions.

In the first place, we are convinced that students make more progress in a course based on a readable textbook supplemented, as time permits, by periodical and other outside readings and by problems than they do by other methods. The book has therefore been kept simple and direct. Second, we find that more students are concerned with investments as a personal and family problem than with preparing for a specialized career with investment brokers or financial institutions. Accordingly, personal investment plans have been stressed along with policies and problems of the professional investor. Third, we believe that a broad perspective is more valuable to a beginner in investments than intensive coverage of a few highly professional or theoretical topics. We have therefore included a wide variety of subjects, among them life insurance, real estate, trusts, social security, tax planning, and savings institutions, in a book whose principal focus is on securities investments. The teacher may not have time to discuss all these topics in the classroom, but there will be time for the student to read the chapters in the book. The course will therefore provide an integrated survey of the many elements which fit into a modern investment program. Fourth, we consider market prices and their behavior to constitute one of the major problems of investment management. Consequently, the book makes a determined attempt to point the way to the evaluation of investment media. Fifth, we believe that a textbook on investments should provide a considerable amount of descriptive detail on market procedures, types of securities, and analytical mechanics. The student who does not know these details is usually uncertain and dissatisfied, and the instructor who must provide them in class is intolerably burdened. Accordingly, they have been included in the book, along with such critical, analytical, and explanatory comments as space permits. Issues of personal, institutional, and public policy, and of economic soundness, are raised in many brief remarks, in footnotes, and especially in the questions at the end of each chapter; the text should provide an adequate background for discussion of these issues.

Although these judgments pointed the way rather clearly to the material to be covered, they obviously did not solve all the problems of the book. To keep the volume at approximately the same readable length as previous editions, it was necessary to omit much more than seemed desirable by way of financial history, public policy issues, and analytical elaboration of key points. It was assumed that our readers would know something of corporate procedures and securities and a little of accounting, but the book does not assume a high degree of proficiency in either.

Although Dr. Clendenin, the senior author, did not work actively in producing this edition, the book continues to reflect overwhelmingly his insight, organizing skill, and concise writing. A conscious effort was made throughout the revision to preserve wherever possible the lucid, compact wording which has distinguished the style and readability of previous editions. The junior author, however, accepts full responsibility for all changes, blemishes, and omissions that appear in this sixth edition.

We gratefully acknowledge the aid and advice so generously given us in the preparation of this book. Our many friends, old and new, in the securities firms, banks, and stock exchanges throughout the country have provided us with a wealth of facts, ideas, and illustrative materials. Our colleagues in the teaching profession have given us needed advice and criticism on many points, as have numbers of students and other friends. To all these people we express our gratitude.

George A. Christy

Introduction
to Investments

part 1
Introduction

A book on investments must as its central function discuss the characteristics of various types of investments and the selection of suitable ones—at suitable prices—to serve investors' needs.

Before this central function can be discharged, however, it is necessary to consider the needs which must be served. There are investors whose financial circumstances or whose nervous systems are suited to certain choices and not others. There are investments which are ideal and risks which are not objectionable when included in a properly balanced plan. The introductory portions of an investments book ought to survey the field, define some terms, suggest some personal objectives, indicate the opportunities, point out the risks, and outline a systematic approach to a choice of investments. Chapter 1 does this in fairly broad terms, but it provides a definite framework of objectives around which an investor can make sensible decisions. Investors with special problems—for example, the businessman who must place all his resources in a speculative personal business or the widow who has a compulsive fear of securities—may find it difficult to live by the tenets of Chapter 1, but at least they can know what they are.

As everyone knows, prices in the investments field are always a problem. Stocks, bonds, homes, farms, mortgages, and many other things not only fluctuate in price; it is difficult to estimate what a typical or average value ought to be. However, investment valuations must be made, and Chapter 2 offers some concepts of practical economics and applied arithmetic which investors can use in many situations. Since these concepts are vital background for the study of investment values throughout the book, they are properly a part of the introduction. They deal mostly with the earning power of invested capital, interest rates, savings, and the demand for and supply of stocks and bonds in the markets.

INVESTMENT OBJECTIVES
AND RISKS

In the broad and customary sense of the term, an investment is any asset or property right acquired or held for the purpose of conserving capital or earning an income. This comprehensive definition does not distinguish between safe and hazardous investments, tangible and intangible investments, or between directly owned assets and institutionally managed ones, such as savings accounts and life insurance. It simply recognizes that savings accounts, bonds, mortgages, life insurance, corporate stocks, real estate, business equities, and other earning assets all fulfill the same basic function, that of employing their owners' funds. Furthermore, this definition does not limit the term investment to property intended to return a cash income or cash profit. Indeed, the most satisfactory investments held by many people are their homes, which yield their returns in family satisfaction and in exemption from rent payments.

The merit of this broad definition of investment will become clear when the problem of investment programming or portfolio planning is discussed. This discussion will show that the proper balancing of any investor's resources among various types of assets is a completely unified problem. Different kinds of investments serve different purposes. A savings account or a savings bond, for example, assures the owner of ready money for emergencies, while common stocks or real estate are better protection against inflation. Thus, in meeting the investor's full range of needs, sound policy will probably require an assortment of assets to provide overall balance.

SPECULATION VERSUS INVESTMENT

In a narrower sense, the term investment is sometimes used to suggest a commitment that is relatively free from certain risks of loss. High-quality bonds and stocks are said to be "of investment grade." In this sense, the label investment would be restricted to situations promising dependable income, relatively stable value, a modest rate of return, and relatively little chance for spectacular capital appreciation. People who seek high-income yields or large capital gains are therefore said to forsake investment for speculation.

Speculation means the deliberate assumption of risks in ventures which offer the hope of commensurate gains. The hoped-for gains may come in the form of larger incomes than a safe investment would supply. Or the speculator may hope that his "investment" will rise greatly in market price as its earning power increases or becomes more secure. More probably he expects its price (and that of the whole stock or real estate market) to go up because of favorable conditions or psychology. It is commonly said that speculators are more interested in price gains than in incomes from their properties, and the radical price variations in some speculative assets (50 per cent declines or 100 per cent increases in a year's time are not unusual) suggest that in most speculations, value of principal is of prime concern.

There is nothing immoral or undesirable about reasonable speculation. The difference between investment and speculation is only a matter of degree of risk, and few personal investment programs need be confined exclusively to ultrasafe items. Indeed, the nation would never have new industries or progress at all if speculators did not venture into untried projects. But sensible speculators do not gamble. They choose their ventures with care, they risk only what they can afford, and if possible they diversify their speculations enough to prevent errors in selection from resulting in burdensome losses. However, every investment dealer knows that many people "speculate" heavily on the strength of idle "tips" or gossip or plunge into situations which they do not understand. This is gambling, not speculation, even though the commitment is of reasonable speculative quality.

FEATURES OF AN INVESTMENT PROGRAM

While it would be foolish to assume that the investment needs of different families and institutions conform to any standard pattern, it seems clear that all investors have four tasks in common. First, they must determine clearly their investment objectives, including the combination of safety, income, and capital growth they are seeking. Second, they must decide upon the types of investments to be used and the proportions of each to be acquired. Third, they must select specific investments of the desired types, making sure that quality, stability, and other features are obtained as needed. Finally, they should study the long-run values of suitable investments and time their purchases and sales with due regard for the price behavior of characteristically unstable investment markets. The proper handling of this fourfold task is an assignment of no mean proportions. It demands technical knowledge, diligence, and some experience, but it is the essence of successful investment management for either an individual or an institution.

In choosing specific investments, the investor will need definite ideas regarding a number of features which his portfolio should possess. These features should be consistent with his general objectives and, in addition, should afford him all the incidental conveniences and advantages which are possible in his circumstances. The following eight features are suggested as the ingredients from which many successful investors compound their selection policies. They are not offered in any order denoting importance, except that the first is clearly the most vital.

1   Safety of principal   Although safety of principal does not necessarily require that the market prices of one's investments never shrink below their cost, it does require that the investor avoid unsound and profitless risks. It calls for careful review of economic and industry trends before choosing types of investments or the time to invest. It demands careful selection of the individual commitments. Finally, it recognizes that errors are unavoidable and requires extensive diversification.

Adequate diversification means assortment of investment commitments in five different ways—by industry, geographically, by management personnel, by financial type (that is, between dollar receivables and equities), and by maturities. If this is accomplished, losses due to the decline of any company or industry, to disaster in any geographic region, to error or defalcation by any management group, to changes in the price level, and to changes in interest rates would all be minimized. This is desirable, even if it also diversifies against fortuitous gains.[1] Since adequate diversification should balance fortuitous gains against fortuitous losses, it may justify a reasonable proportion of speculative stocks in the average portfolio—or better yet, the inclusion of investment company stocks with a reasonable proportion of speculative commitments.

Diversification can be wasteful if carried to extremes. Too many securities and real estate and mortgage holdings—possibly over 20 for the average individual—give him too many to watch, unless he makes a profession of supervising them or employs someone to do it for him. Too small commitments in securities are uneconomic because of excessive commission charges and other costs in transactions. Securities commitments, except for items of bed-rock quality such as government bonds, should probably range between $500 minimum and half a year's family income as a maximum.

2   Adequate liquidity and collateral value   Every investor requires a minimum, quick-recourse fund available to meet emergencies. Furthermore, a sound portfolio will look to the sure and quick availability of additional funds which may be needed for business opportunities, stock market opportunities, or estate taxes. Whether money raising is to be done by sale or by borrowing, it will be easier if the portfolio contains a planned proportion of high-grade and readily salable investments such as government or big-corporation bonds.

---

[1] This is a point on which violent difference of opinion exists. Most textbook writers, investment counselors, investment companies, and bank trust officers take the viewpoint indicated here, but some hold that safety lies in a few holdings carefully chosen and closely watched. One very successful investor argues that nearly all investments are subject to risk; that such investments fluctuate in price to an amount which overshadows any possible dividend or interest income; that careful and intelligent speculators can anticipate these price changes in a majority of cases; and that successive speculations, not widely diversified but always carefully studied, will employ funds more profitably than is possible through diversified investing. See G. M. Loeb, *The Battle for Investment Survival*, rev. ed., Simon and Schuster, Inc., New York, 1965.

3   Stability of income   This factor is important in arranging an investment portfolio for an individual who depends closely on the income; it is less important for others. Though income stability helps greatly in stabilizing the prices of corporate stocks, it can be found to a high degree only in certain industries, and insistence upon it therefore restricts the available choices. Probably stable income payers also cost a trifle more than other investments; hence, they should not be over-emphasized by those who do not need them.

4   Adequacy of income after taxes   There are really two problems involved here, one concerned with the amount of income paid by the investment and the other with the burden of income taxes upon that income. When the investor's income is small, he is often eager to obtain maximum cash returns on his investments and is prone to take excessive risks and to prefer immediate dividends to greater benefits at a later date. It is unfortunate to have to choose between adequate income and adequate security; but it is possible, to some degree, to seek out good stocks which pay practically all their earnings in dividends and real estate which nets its owner both real earnings and depreciation funds in cash.

The investor who is not pressed for cash income often finds that income taxes deplete certain types of investment incomes less than others, thus affecting his choices. For example, neither the rental value of an owner-occupied home nor the interest paid by a state or municipal bond is subject to federal income tax. Furthermore, corporate earnings which are not paid out in dividends are not taxable to the stockholders, even though, when used to add to the company's resources, they presumably enhance the value of the stock.

5   Purchasing-power stability   The price-level hazard needs no introduction to this generation of Americans. Suffice it to state the conclusion that the average personal or family portfolio is well balanced in normal times when it consists of one-third of dollar sum holdings, such as bank deposits, life insurance, and bonds, and two-thirds of ownership equities, such as real estate and common stocks. In making this computation some investors would regard mortgage and other debt as negative dollars—that is, as subtractions from the dollar sum investments.

From a purely theoretical viewpoint, it would appear that a portfolio consisting entirely of real estate and stocks would balance price-level changes more perfectly than the one-third–two-thirds program recommended. Perhaps it might, with luck, but the instability of equity prices, plus other considerations previously mentioned, commends the one-third–two-thirds choice in the average case. Obviously, such factors as the quality of the investments, the adequacy of insurance protection, the stability of personal earnings, family needs, and estate tax hazards could affect this ratio.

The indicated preference for a one-third–two-thirds balance between dollars and equities would not apply to an institution such as a bank or an insurance company, whose assets must be in dollars to offset obligations which are payable in dollars.

6 Possible appreciation It is neither necessary nor desirable, in making investments, to forswear hope for market profits in a search for safety. Both real estate and stock markets are highly irregular, and the individual who sticks closely to quality investments can still profit by choosing well, buying at the right time, and switching wisely from overpriced to underpriced items. Not many people will profit greatly by these devices, but reasonable acumen will be rewarded, and some of the inevitable losses can be offset. Ventures into speculative commitments may be similarly approached, with the expectation of more and greater losses which may be balanced by more and larger gains, if the investor has the diligence and skill which successful speculation demands.

7 Freedom from care The existence of important risks in every class of investment makes it impossible to "buy good things and forget them." Constant skilled supervision is necessary to avoid losses and to obtain good returns. But the pitfalls which await the uninitiated are much less dangerous in commitments of investment grade than in speculations. One who wishes to minimize the attention required by his investments should therefore make quality his watchword. Alternatively, a professional investment counselor or the investment management services of a trust company can be employed, at a cost approximating ½ of 1 per cent per year on sums of reasonably substantial size.

8 Legality Investments of trusts, estates, children, and incompetents must consist of types approved by trust instructions or by law. State laws and precedents vary, but in all cases the plans must include complete compliance with requirements.

RISKS OF INVESTMENT

The modern world is an exceedingly complex and dynamic one in which many forces affect the value and yield of investments. Careful investors try to identify these forces and profit from them if they can, or at least avoid losses from them. For example, the following economic and political factors were prominent during the years from 1950 through 1972: (1) basically prosperous conditions, underwritten by vigorous use of public expenditures and the Federal Reserve System's monetary powers; (2) occasional business recessions, to a considerable extent caused by public budget and monetary policy employed to counteract inflationary trends, but inevitably accompanied by some business distress and stock market weakness; (3) continuing inflation of the general price level, especially during periods of prosperity and full employment; (4) a persistent rise in interest rates from each business cycle to the next, reflecting an underlying demand for savings that repeatedly outran the supply, and a growing insistence by lenders that they be compensated for buying-power losses from inflation; (5) rapid scientific and technological progress, which resulted in large profits for some firms and obsolescence for others; (6) heavy property and income taxation; (7) the possibility of major war, which certainly would be accompanied by destruction, taxation, and price-level inflation; (8) increasing vulnerability of the domestic economy to international influences, highlighted by the gradual emergence of a balance of payments problem and eventual devaluation of the dollar; (9) growing confidence among investors that major depressions were no longer likely and that the government would be able to underwrite both continuing prosperity and an acceptable rate of economic growth; and (10) increased government intervention in business affairs, culminating in the early 1970s with new programs aimed at consumer and ecology protection, minority-group progress, and the direct control of prices and wage rates.

In considering economic and political factors, investors commonly identify four kinds of hazards to which their investments are exposed. Although popularly termed risks, these hazards never involve known probabilities or realistic opportunities for actuarial estimation. Literally, they are *uncertainties*. Some of these risk uncertainties scarcely exist at all in certain investments, and they vary greatly in intensity from one investment to another, but no investment is free of all of them. [2]

The first and most dangerous risk is the *business* or *functional risk*. Every business or piece of property is subject to the possibility that its earning power or usefulness may wane because of competition, change in demand, uncontrollable costs, managerial error, government action, or some similar circumstance. Likewise, any individual debtor may suffer a shrinkage in earning power or capacity to pay. Investments such as the bonds of the United States government or populous states, or the bonds of a far-flung and well-financed corporation such as the American Telephone and Telegraph Company, are little subject to this risk, at least in the foreseeable future. But the stock of the average business corporation, or real estate in a given neighborhood, or a farm whose money source is cotton or any other single crop—these are always vulnerable in greater or less degree. It is a major task of investment management to watch for business hazards and to take appropriate steps to avoid loss if the risk increases and to profit from the change if it decreases.

The second risk is the *market risk*. This hazard arises from the fact that market prices and collateral values of securities and real property may vary substantially, even when their earning power does not change. The causes of these price uncer-

---

[2] For a comprehensive discussion of investment risks see H. C. Sauvain, *Investment Management*, 3d ed., Prentice-Hall, Inc., Englewood Cliffs, N.J., 1967, Chaps. 5–7.

tainties are varied. At times many markets are simply "thin"—that is, buyers and sellers appear only intermittently. More commonly, investment prices vary because investors vacillate in their preference for different forms of investment, or simply because they sometimes have money to invest and sometimes have not. The extensive vagaries of the stock market, the uncertainty and slowness of real estate markets, and the irregular markets for mortgages and second-grade bond issues all illustrate the presence of market risk. Fluctuation in the market price of one's investments is not so damaging as the impairment of their earning power, if one does not have to sell them or borrow on them, but it is imperative to most investors that at least a part of their holdings be subject to quick liquidation without loss. The only investments which are completely exempt from the market risk are those which are always available in cash, such as savings accounts, Series E bonds, and life insurance reserves. However, U.S. government and top-grade corporate bonds have good resale markets and fluctuate very little in price except as a result of interest-rate changes.

The third risk, the *money-rate risk*, is really a compound one, a kind of dilemma that faces the purchaser of any investment of the debt type. The first part of this risk, the *capital-value* risk, affects the value of fixed-income securities of long or indefinite maturity, such as high-grade bonds, mortgages, and preferred stocks. It also applies in lesser degree to common stocks and real estate held for income purposes. Capital-value risk arises from the fact that long-term securities paying a fixed income (the standard $1,000 bond pays a fixed contractual rate of interest on its face value) are worth a premium if the interest rates on new issues decline, but are worth less if interest rates on new issues rise. For example, the Union Pacific Railroad in 1946 sold a large issue of 2½ per cent bonds due in 1991. These bonds are of thoroughly sound quality, and as long as interest rates remained low their market price remained close to their par value. But in later years a shortage of loan funds developed, and in 1969, borrowing corporations were selling new high-quality bonds paying as much as 9½ per cent interest. Since no investor would pay par value for a 2½ per cent bond when he could get 9½ per cent on comparable new bonds, the market price on the Union Pacific bonds dropped at one time to 46 per cent of par. This is a drastic decline—from $1,000 to $460—for a security which is almost free of the business risk. Of course, it can be argued that the owner of such bonds can hold them to maturity and complete the contract just as he originally planned it, but this does not alter the fact that his original commitment subjected him either to a capital loss or to an income below subsequently available rates for a long period of years. This hazard is theoretically balanced by the possibility of gain if interest rates fall instead of rise, but is nonetheless a source of concern to those interested in the market values of high-grade, long-term investments.

Selection of very short-term bonds and mortgages would minimize the effect of money-rate changes on value of the investment, since early maturity would release the funds for reinvestment at prevailing market rates; but this solution only confronts the investor with the other horn of the money-rate risk dilemma. This is the *income risk*, or chance that by the time a short-term investment matures, interest rates may have fallen so that less income can now be purchased with the same principal. For example, in February 1970, an investor could have bought a one-year treasury bill yielding 8¼ per cent. But during the next 12 months, interest rates declined drastically, and when his bill matured, new one-year bills were yielding less than 4 per cent. Income risks afflicting short-term debt securities can produce substantial losses over the years; the expense of frequent reinvestment can be considerable, and besides, interest rates on short-term investments ordinarily average lower than long-term ones.

The fourth hazard, the *price-level risk*, most seriously afflicts the traditionally conservative investments—government bonds, savings deposits, and life insurance—all of which are payable in fixed dollar sums. Receipt of the dollars is sure, but the buying power of those dollars in very uncertain. People who bought government bonds in 1950 had lost almost one-half their original purchasing power by 1972, though the bonds would still pay the same number of dollars at maturity. Price-level inflation has been present continuously over the past four decades, though its pace has varied widely, and most investors are acutely concerned with the real buying power of their investments and the income from them. There is no perfect solution to the problem, either, since investments which are theoretically protected against the price-level risk are frequently not so protected in fact and are, in addition, seriously subject to the business risk. It is usually argued that since real estate and common stocks represent tangible "commodities," their prices and earning power in dollars should rise and fall proportionally with all commodities and with the cost of living. This is probably vaguely true in the long run, if the real estate and stocks are wisely selected and widely diversified over many locations and industries. It is not likely to be true of individual stocks or real estate parcels, and it is most definitely not true over short periods of time.

MATERIAL OF INVESTMENTS

As already indicated, the commitments which may qualify as investments are large in number. Some are not even acquired voluntarily, since employers frequently require payment of savings into a retirement fund, and the United States government compels many people to invest in social security. The following 15 classes of investments do not enumerate all items employed by individual investors but they illustrate the significant types. Most of them will be discussed at greater length in later chapters, but the features which are most important to investors will be pointed out here. Note that investments which offer the greatest protection from the business risk tend to be stable in dollar value and dependable as a source of emergency cash but vulnerable to inflation, whereas those which promise compensation for price-level changes tend to be marked by business risk, market-price instability, and variable income returns.

1 Savings bank deposits Savings deposits are accepted by the savings departments of commercial banks and by mutual savings banks. Savings accounts are always payable in dollar sums, are extremely liquid (the deposit contract usually permits the bank to demand 30 days' notice of intent to withdraw the money, but payment is in most cases available instantly), and yield relatively low interest rates. During 1972 the maximum rate payable on savings deposits in commercial banks was 4½ per cent. Rates at mutual savings banks ranged as high as 5¼ per cent, averaging perhaps 5 per cent. The interest on these accounts is fully subject to income taxes, and the principal may be subject to property taxes to some extent.

2 Life insurance policies The typical individual (not group) life insurance policy is a combination of decreasing insurance protection plus increasing savings account. The insured pays into his company an annual premium which is sufficient to pay his share of the death benefits incurred by his age group, to pay his share of the operating expenses, and to contribute a definite sum to a reserve (or savings account) embodied in his policy. As this reserve grows, the savings component of his policy rises and the insurance feature declines. His savings also are increased through interest earnings on the accumulating reserve. A high-premium 20-year endowment or 20-pay life policy differs from a low-premium ordinary life policy in that the high-premium policy accumulates a large reserve more rapidly. High-premium policies are suitable for people who wish to use them as savings accounts, with insurance protection which diminishes as the savings are accumulated, and low-premium policies are suitable for people who wish chiefly insurance protection at a minimum cash outlay.

Life insurance policies are desirable investments when properly chosen to meet the insured's needs. They are poor investments if they result in the purchase of unneeded protection or in the assumption of high premium burdens which prevent other desirable investment. Since conventional policies involve fixed-dollar sums, they are subject to the price-level hazard, which has weakened their appeal as savings vehicles. However, *dollars* invested in life insurance reserves are very safe investments and usually earn between 2½ and 5 per cent for their owners. They are highly liquid, since almost the full reserve can be borrowed from the company at reasonable rates, at short notice, repayable whenever the insured chooses; or the policy can be canceled and the reserve recovered.

3 Savings and loan accounts Most communities have savings and loan associations which accumulate investors' savings and invest them in local mortgage loans. Since the associations are supervised by state or federal agencies, and since they are usually conservatively managed, their safety record is good. Most of them also insure the first $20,000 of each investor's account through membership in the Federal Savings and Loan Insurance Corporation. Interest-dividends paid on savings and loan accounts (technically, the investors in most of these organizations are shareholders and owners, not creditors) have usually exceeded the maximum rate legally payable on savings deposits in commercial banks. During 1972, most savings and loan associations paid dividends at a 5 per cent annual rate, the maximum permitted by federal regulations. Immediate liquidity of accounts is not guaranteed, since the associations employ most of their funds in long-term mortgages, but in practice, accounts can usually be withdrawn on demand or after short notice. Dividends are fully subject to income taxation. The property tax position varies but is not usually burdensome.

4   United States government securities   Marketable treasury bonds, notes, certificates, and bills, together with Series E and H savings bonds, represent the largest group of securities available to the American public and are almost certainly the group least subject to business risk. Maturities ranging from 90 days to 26 years were available during 1972. Interest yields vary, depending on the type of security and market interest-rate levels. Although business and market risks are negligible on government securities, the long-term marketable bonds fluctuate in price as a result of interest-rate fluctuations, and the price-level risk is as serious as for other investments collectible in fixed sums in dollars. Government obligations are exempt from state and local property taxes, and their interest payments are not subject to state or local income taxes. However, these securities are subject to federal and state estate, inheritance, and gift taxes, and interest is fully subject to federal income taxation. Like life insurance policies, government securities are so varied in their terms that a proper choice must depend on the needs of each individual investor.

5   State and municipal bonds   This category includes the obligations of scores of thousands of public agencies, including states, counties, cities, school districts, paving districts, sewer districts, and public business ventures, such as water departments or toll highways. Some of these borrowing agencies are rich and some are poor. Debt service (i.e., payment of interest and principal) may be promised from tax revenues, from public business revenues, from special assessments on real estate, or from a combination of these. Most public obligations are good quality, and many are top grade. All are payable only in dollars. Long-term bonds are subject to the money-rate risk, and many issues are subject to the market risk. Lower-quality issues are also subject to the business risk. Since state and municipal interest payments are exempt from the very heavy federal income tax, they are attractive to corporations and individuals in the higher tax brackets. This causes the bonds to sell higher and pay lower interest yields than corporate bonds of similar quality and maturity dates; the best ones yield less than taxable federal bonds, averaging perhaps 5½ per cent in 1972 on 20-year maturities. Each state usually exempts its own and its municipalities' bonds from income and property taxes within its borders, but the bonds are subject to federal and state inheritance, estate, and gift taxes.

6 Corporate bonds Corporate bonds are the debts of business concerns. They are usually sold to investors in $1,000 units. The bondholders, as creditors, usually have no voice in management and are entitled to little more than the regular payment of interest and the ultimate repayment on the principal, all in fixed-dollar sums. Corporate bonds vary widely in contract terms and quality but, in general, they are subject to the price-level and money-rate risks. Some issues have dependable markets and are of unquestioned quality; others are doubtful on both points. There are no significant tax exemptions available on corporate bonds as a class, but they are not usually subject to heavy property taxation. In 1972, the best-grade bonds yielded about one percentage point more than United States Treasury bonds of similar maturity.

7 Corporate stocks Stockholders are owners, and corporate stocks represent the residual ownership and control of corporations. The business risks inherent in the enterprise naturally fall with full force on the stockholder, who bears them because he may also hope for the extraordinary gains which success may bring him. The market risk is obviously high in stock ownership; the money-rate risk is an uncertain factor. As to the price-level risk, stock holding comprises indirect property ownership and ostensibly satisfies the objective of owning buying power instead of mere money. But no single stock is assured of fluctuating in close proportion to the price level; only an average of many stocks in many industries can hope to do this. Certain types of stocks, such as those of rate-regulated utilities, will not experience proportionate changes in dollar earning power when the price-level changes; these are of limited use as hedges against price-level inflation. And preferred stocks, which in general have accepted fixed dividends in return for a prior claim to dividends out of corporate earnings, are also poor price-level hedges. Good common stocks fluctuate considerably in price, and since the late 1950s a typical group has yielded a dividend return of between 2 and 5 per cent, depending on the particular stocks selected and on market conditions at the time of purchase. However, the investor's true yield on a common stock may also include an element of long-term capital growth, based on a sustained rise in the company's net earnings per share which may pave the way for increases in dividend payments and market price. Companies strive to promote "growth" in the value of their common shares by plowing back part of their earnings into the business, introducing new and more profitable products, or entering more promising lines of business. Corporate stocks and their dividends do not ordinarily receive any favorable tax treatment except a relatively minor income tax advantage provided in the Revenue Act of 1964 and the low-rate property taxation (or failure to assess) which is common to all intangibles.

8 Investment companies Investment companies are organizations which sell their own shares to the public and invest the proceeds in a diversified list of other securities. They thus enable investors to participate in professionally managed portfolios of diversified securities. After deduction of management fees and expenses, the investment company shareholder receives his prorata share of dividends or interest earned by the portfolio along with any capital gains realized from the sale of securities at a profit. Chapter 21 describes the rather bewildering variety of shares available to investors. Although investment in these companies can be quite profitable, the investor must exercise considerable judgment in selecting shares that meet his needs. Prices of investment company shares fluctuate with changes in the market value of the underlying securities portfolio.

9 Mortgages and loans Though this form of investment is utilized by thousands of individuals and institutions, the types of loans and the circumstances surrounding them are so varied as to preclude accurate generalizations. It is probable that skillful lenders find this type of investment very satisfactory, and the average uninitiated investor probably has better luck with mortgages than he has with corporate stocks. However, mortgages and loans are often too large to permit much diversification for small investors who use them. Mortgages and loans are often exempted from the property taxes, but the income from them is taxable.

10 Homeownership This investment, always popular with Americans, has received additional impetus in recent decades through the activities of the Federal Housing Administration. Homeownership is probably financially profitable to a family which finds a fixed location feasible and whose members can perform the small incidental functions of maintenance and repair. Otherwise, the case is doubtful, although psychic advantages of security, stability, and prestige may still weigh heavily for homeownership. From a strictly financial viewpoint, homeownership permits an investment from which substantial income in the form of free rent is assured, since the family's use of the premises is certain. A price-level hedge is thus obtained without the need for assuming heavy business risks. Market risks in real estate are always substantial. Homeownership affords an income tax advantage, since the family's occupancy of a home is not measured as taxable income. In general, it may be guessed that a properly chosen home investment, bought for a normal 80 to 120 times its normal monthly rental value, will yield the average family a tax-free 5 per cent return after allowing fair amounts for depreciation, property taxes, maintenance, and insurance.

11 **Real estate ownership**   Like mortgage lending, this form of investment takes so many forms that reasonable generalizations are impossible. Good results undoubtedly depend on skilled supervision and, in many cases, require the performance of incidental maintenance by the owner to keep costs down. Many owners find real estate ownership a convenient way of realizing both profit and a slow return of capital (out of depreciation allowances) in cash, when they are "living up" their estates after retirement. With respect to risk factors, general real estate ownership is similar to homeownership and also has the disadvantage of affording only fairly large individual parcels, thus precluding wide diversification. Profits from rental real estate are fully taxable.

12 **Business ownership**   Ownership of one's own business or farm is one of the great sources of psychic satisfaction in life. For many people, the investment is profitable in varying degree; for many others, perhaps for most, the financial commitment yields little more than an opportunity for self-employment at a modest wage. Risks are obviously specific to each case. The overriding claim of an investor-proprietor's own business on his financial resources may pose a serious problem when he attempts to diversify and balance his investment portfolio.

13 **Pension rights**   Many investors are now accumulating substantial pension and social security expectations in the course of their employment. These rights are extremely valuable and must be carefully included in the development of any investment plan. Since most of them are payable in dollars, they are clearly subject to the price-level risk, although both business pension plans and social security benefits are at times revised to offset price-level increases. Few are affected by the market risk or the business risk, and in many cases they enjoy very substantial tax advantages.

14 **Education and self-improvement**   Since payments for personal services — salaries, wages, commissions, and the like — account for the overwhelming part of most people's income, few individuals can afford to overlook the biggest investment opportunity of all — the chance to invest in themselves through additional education or other kinds of self-improvement. Today, as probably never before, technical training, college studies, and professional degrees are the keys to secure, well-paying positions in business, government, and elsewhere. Furthermore, the difference in earning power between those with and those without suitable education appears to be steadily widening. Extending one's education or personal skills may call for a considerable outlay of money, strenuous effort, and substantial sacrifices of family and social life, but almost invariably it more than repays these costs. The man who improves his earning power $2,000 a year through further education will receive as much additional income as he could obtain by investing $40,000 at 5 per cent. Money spent in overcoming defects of speech, hearing, or appearance can also be expected to produce returns far exceeding those of conventional investments.

15 Special ventures Wealthy individuals show increasing interest in limited-partnership or other shares in oil drilling, cattle raising, real estate development, and other special ventures. These investments hold out the lure of speculative profits plus tax-sheltered income based on accelerated depreciation, large deductions for interest payments, and occasional loopholes in the tax laws. However, commitments vary so greatly in type, quality, and reputability that generalizations concerning them are very difficult. Successful selection requires, at minimum, a thorough knowledge of the business invested in, careful legal advice concerning the investor's potential liabilities, an appreciation of the difference between profits and the mere return of cash, and most of all, rare luck. Such ventures are clearly beyond either the means or the competence of the average family man or professional worker.

THE INVESTMENT PROGRAM: PORTFOLIO SELECTION THEORY

Enough has been said in preceding pages about investment risks and needs to indicate that a systematic investment plan is in order. Whether the investor is an individual, an insurance company, or a bank, he must identify certain objectives to be reached and certain hazards to be met. He must measure his resources, present and prospective, weigh the economic and market conditions he expects to encounter, forecast the behavior of the various investments open to him, and carefully balance returns sought against risks to be incurred.

In recent years, a new theoretical framework for investment choices has been proposed, based on principles of mathematical programming and the goal of maximizing *risk-adjusted* returns.[3] This theory points out that a thoroughly rational investor will always aim at picking an "efficient"—or the best feasible—portfolio from the investments available and acceptable to him. An efficient portfolio is one that offers the largest return compatible with a specified degree of risk, or which minimizes the risk accompanying a sought-for level of return. Risks on a portfolio are diminished by selecting individual investments with opposite and offsetting patterns of expected fluctuation.

Chart 1-1 illustrates the meaning of "efficient-portfolio" selection. The horizontal axis measures the returns expected from various portfolios; the vertical axis shows the estimated risks incurred by these portfolios. Any portfolio can thus be represented by a point on the chart, the coordinates of which indicate the combination of return and risk which the particular portfolio is expected to offer. The

[3] See the Markowitz article cited in the bibliography of Chap. 28.

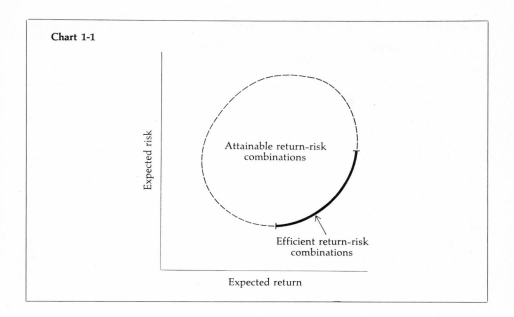

Chart 1-1

Attainable return-risk
combinations

Efficient return-risk
combinations

Expected risk

Expected return

dotted-line ellipse portrays the range of return-risk combinations an investor could hypothetically obtain by drawing all the different portfolios possible from a given list of investments. However, the heavy black line along the lower right-hand boundary shows the limited number of efficient portfolios he could achieve. Each portfolio on this boundary yields him either the highest expected return for a given level of risk, or the lowest risk he could expect for a given level of return. A "rational" investor would consider only these efficient portfolios and ignore the rest.

Although this mathematically based theory of portfolio selection may help clarify an investor's goals, it cannot assure him of wise or profitable choices. The investor himself must still decide his specific objectives and set limits on the risks he will accept. He must still forecast the returns and risks on each investment he is considering. Even the complicated computer programs available to professional portfolio managers can only sift and sort into possibly more meaningful patterns the unavoidably personal judgments incorporated in these inputs.

PLANNING A PERSONAL INVESTMENT PROGRAM

Although the first chapter of a book on investments is hardly the proper place for a discussion which must assume familiarity with the entire subject, it seems desirable at this point to stress the importance of a lifetime financial plan. It can perhaps be compared to a military campaign—the principal objectives are allowed for, and the whole procedure is kept sufficiently flexible so that contingencies may be met and opportunities may be seized.

An investor's financial aspirations are unquestionably his own affair. He may choose to emphasize complete family security and peace of mind, or he may make the upbuilding of his own business his major interest, or he may undertake to enhance his wealth by trading for profit in securities or real estate. In any case, the investor's hopes are likely to come closer to fulfillment if he is clear on what his desires are and if he has a systematic plan for reaching them.

This book will not undertake the thankless task of telling its readers what their investment objectives ought to be, though it may on occasion comment favorably or adversely on some of them. It will, however, offer a four-step plan for framing an investment program, which may help the reader to outline a comprehensive portfolio designed to attain his chosen goals. This will be supplemented in later chapters by discussions designed to aid in the choice of suitable individual investments and the timing of purchases and sales.

The four steps to be taken in organizing an individual's investment program call for the acquisition of (1) adequate life insurance, (2) a highly liquid emergency fund, (3) business and home investments, and (4) a general investment portfolio. These four steps might reasonably be considered and financed in the order named.

1 Necessary insurance   Life insurance protection on the family breadwinner is desirable to assure his family the savings he may not live to earn. This protection is often needed in largest amount when the family is relatively young, before much saving has been possible. Other life insurance to protect the family budget against death and readjustment expenses should be considered, and provision for business life insurance, estate tax liquidity, and peculiar personal estates such as life tenancies may also be needed. Again—and this is of outstanding importance —insurance providing disability income in case the breadwinner is sick or disabled for long periods should be provided. The amounts needed for all these purposes will often appear too great to be afforded in the average family budget, but account can be taken of social security, employer group insurance plans, and the available assistance from relatives in dire emergencies; and the passage of time and the accumulation of savings will ultimately bring resources closer to needs for most people.

2 A quick-recourse fund   Next on the high-priority list is the accumulation of a fund which will always be available for emergencies. For purely family use, readily available resources amounting to half a year's income, kept in insurance reserves, bank deposits, or government savings bonds, might suffice. Since this fund will doubtless be used and replaced a good many times in the history of the average family, it should be in a highly convenient form and location, and available without any delay, embarrassment, or heavy costs.

3 Investments to meet personal needs   Third on the priority list are the investments in a home and in a personal business, if needed. Modern installment financing makes it possible to control very substantial investments, especially in homes, without having to omit everything else.

4 General fund   This fund receives all sums not allotted to the preceding ones. In general, its function is a balancing and proportioning one to bring the entire investment program into line with sound principles. Its fundamental tasks are to provide safety through wide diversification and to bring about a reasonable balance between investments in dollar-value items and in property-ownership equities. The principles involved were discussed at length in the preceding section.

LEGAL OWNERSHIP AND TAX PROBLEMS

Investment plans and decisions are often affected by the legal aspects of property ownership and by tax problems involving both incomes and ultimate estates. For example, a plan for developing a number of living trusts for members of the family by making gifts into the trusts at annual intervals will require the planning of a whole series of independent portfolios. In another case, the decision of a high-salaried individual to retire from active business may justify switching extensively from tax-exempt to taxable income sources. Legal title and estate tax matters are most troublesome to people of substantial wealth, but every investor must deal with them to some extent, if only to decide if the joint tenancy laws of his state hold any advantage for him. Some of the principles involved are discussed in later chapters of this book.

INSTITUTIONAL INVESTMENT

Like individuals, financial institutions find it desirable to choose investments appropriate to their needs. Commercial banks, savings banks, life insurance companies, and savings and loan associations need investments which are almost exclusively payable in dollars. They must also have items which are very safe and free from excessive market-price fluctuation because their obligations customarily total between 90 and 95 per cent of their total assets and a relatively small shrinkage in asset values would endanger their solvency. Banks and savings banks, and to a lesser degree the life insurance companies, must also consider the ready marketability of a portion of their investments, since their customers have the right to demand the prompt return of the money in their custody, and it is important that such demands be met without the necessity of selling securities or property at a loss. Other institutions, such as endowed hospitals and colleges and trust companies administering the funds of others for a fee, are under less pressure to secure price stability but usually feel bound to obtain long-run security and, in an age of continual price inflation, a sufficient long-term rise in income and capital value to offset a depreciating dollar.

The investment policies of most financial institutions are regulated to some extent by public authority, and custom and precedent also exert great influence.

It must be concluded, therefore, that the investment policies of financial and endowed institutions are likely to vary greatly with the type of business conducted, the legal restrictions imposed, and the customs of the business, as well as with the preferences of their managements.

QUESTIONS AND PROBLEMS

1   Would you say that the stock of General Motors Corporation, which sold under 45 and above 110 in the years from 1962 through 1972, should be called a speculation?

2   Would the individual who carefully studied the prospects of General Electric Company in 1972 and estimated that the company's 1972–1974 earnings and dividends would average $3 per share and $1.60 per share, respectively, be investing or speculating if he bought the stock at 65?

3   Is it reasonable to say that a great progressive company and industry leader such as International Business Machines Corporation is significantly subject to the business risk? What could happen to it?

4   Is there any reason why one who is planning his investments today should be more concerned with future inflation than with possible depression? Could this lead to undue risk assumption? What kind of risk?

5   Would a well-diversified collection of residential properties have afforded an investor a satisfactory price-level hedge during the 1965–1972 period of inflation? Would farm properties have done so? Oil stocks? Will these precedents be followed during the next inflation? What would probably happen to these investments in a depression?

6   Why is life insurance enumerated as a form of investment?

7   Is there any real difference between the investment functions performed by savings deposits and by insured savings and loan accounts?

8   If you had $20,000 to invest in stocks, how many different stocks would you buy? What reasoning leads to your conclusion?

9   What explains the difference between the yields of corporate bonds and United States Treasury bonds? Why should there be a difference at all?

10   Why are public utility common stocks and nearly all preferred stocks regarded as poor price-level hedges?

11   Explain why homeownership yields a "tax-free" income. Would this be true of rental property?

12   Why is the money-rate risk unavoidable in making a fixed-income investment?

13   If you were retiring on social security plus employers' pensions totaling $300 per

month and had $75,000 in cash of your own, what types of investment would you regard as most suitable for your savings?

14 If you were an attorney aged 30, with a wife and two children, no relatives capable of giving financial support, no savings other than household furniture and office equipment, but with earnings now averaging $20,000 per year, how much life insurance and how much disability income insurance would you consider proper? (Assume that ordinary life insurance costs $20 per thousand per annum, of which half may be regarded as savings, and that total and permanent disability income coverage costs $60 per year for a disability income amounting to $100 per month.)

15 As you (the man just described) begin to accumulate savings, what should you do with the first $10,000, assuming you are saving $2,000 annually?

16 Would the purchase of a $40,000 home be advisable if the rental value was $250 per month, if the annual taxes were $600, average depreciation was $700, average maintenance costs were $400, and insurance was $80?

17 Assume that a physician, at 60, has no life insurance and no dependents except his wife, and that he continues in his profession earning $40,000 per year, with his $40,000 home fully paid for. You are asked to recommend investments for $200,000 cash which he has accumulated. What would you select? List amounts beside the following, and where corporations are involved, indicate how many different ones you would invest in: savings deposits, savings and loan, government bonds, telephone bonds, electric power company bonds, telephone stocks, electric power stocks, motor company stocks, electric equipment stocks, steel stocks, food stocks, chemical stocks, bank stocks, oil stocks, drug stocks, insurance stocks, office equipment stocks, residential (rental) property.

REFERENCES

American Research Council, Inc.: *Your Investments*, Rye, N.Y., semiannual.

Babson, Thomas E., and David L. Babson: *Investing for a Successful Future*, The Macmillan Company, New York, 1959.

Badger, Ralph E., Harold W. Torgerson, and Harry G. Guthmann: *Investment Principles and Practices*, 6th ed., Prentice-Hall, Inc., Englewood Cliffs, N.J., 1969, Chap. 6.

Bellemore, Douglas H., and John C. Ritchie, Jr.: *Investments*, 3d ed., South-Western Publishing Company, Incorporated, Cincinnati, 1969, Chap. 1.

Dougall, Herbert E.: *Investments*, 8th ed., Prentice-Hall, Inc., Englewood Cliffs, N.J., 1968, Chaps. 19–21.

Freund, William C.: *Investment Fundamentals*, American Bankers Association, New York, 1966.

Graham, Benjamin: *The Intelligent Investor*, 4th rev. ed., Harper & Row, Publishers, Incorporated, New York, 1973.

Hayes, Douglas A.: *Investments: Analysis and Management*, 2d ed., The Macmillan Company, New York, 1966, Chaps. 25, 26.

Sauvain, Harry: *Investment Management*, 3d ed., Prentice-Hall, Inc., Englewood Cliffs, N.J., 1967, Part 2.

Widicus, Wilbur W., and Thomas E. Stitzel: *Personal Investing*, Richard D. Irwin, Inc., Homewood, Ill., 1971, Chaps. 1, 2.

BASIC DETERMINANTS OF INVESTMENT VALUES

One of the most troublesome problems confronting investors is that of estimating the values to be paid or accepted for investment assets. The market prices for most types of investment vary considerably through the years, and some of the very important types, including real estate, common stocks, and bonds, fluctuate sharply as business conditions change. Because of the large sums involved, no investor can afford to ignore these price fluctuations, and many investors are interested in profiting from them if they can. An understanding of the basic factors affecting investment values is therefore of general interest.

Later chapters of this book will deal in detail with the values of specific types of investment. The task of the present chapter is to explore the fundamentals that affect all investment values. These fundamentals are pertinent to the determination of both long-run value trends and cyclical fluctuations in value.

In approaching this task, it is essential to realize that investment values are in the last analysis simply prices, and that prices are made by demand and supply. The real problem, therefore, is to explain how people arrive at their decisions to pay certain prices when they buy or to accept certain prices when they sell. Viewed in this light, it is clear that no answer can be complete, for a complete answer would have to explain the ideas of many people who buy and sell on impulse or as the result of faulty reasoning, in addition to the presumed majority whose decisions are informed and sensible. But if it is assumed that most investors are reasonably informed and sensible, it would appear that the major influences determining investment values can be identified with five fundamental concepts.

The first of these is a mathematical approach to the subject, which suggests that the prices people will rationally pay for an investment should be strongly influenced by their appraisals of the future dividends and other benefits which the investment may be expected to produce. This approach requires the estimation of future benefits, both in amount and time of receipt, and appraises them on a present-value basis by means of compound interest tables. The second concept involves an economic interpretation of capital supplies, profit margins, interest rates, the interrelations among them, and the impact of the whole upon investment values. The third concept stresses the fact that the demand for investment assets is greatly affected by the customs of financial institutions, the legal restrictions on institutional investment, and the portion of the nation's wealth which is invested by financial institutions. The fourth concept points out the great influence of public fiscal and monetary policy on investment results. Fiscal and monetary policy are major factors in the making of booms, recessions, inflation, interest-rate behavior, and even the fortunes of many industries. Fifth, it is clear that different types of investments—bonds, mortgages, stocks, properties—are offered for sale in quantities that bear little relationship to the quantities of each which investors desire, and that the result must inevitably be quasi-independent supply-and-demand markets for different types of investments. These five fundamental concepts are basic to the understanding of investment values. In addition, investors must deal with speculative instability in investment values, with the fluctuations occasioned by human reactions to economic uncertainties. These are highly important, but their effect is mainly seen in gyrations in prices, not the general level of values, and consideration of them is therefore deferred to a later chapter.

1 THE PRESENT-VALUE THEORY

It is often said that the reasonable present market value of any investment is the total of future benefits (whether as income or return of principal, in cash or in services, would not matter) expected from it, discounted down to the present at an interest rate consistent with the risk.[1] By this measure it could be computed that a share of stock deemed likely to pay $6 annually in dividends *forever* is worth $100 if the hazards justify a yield of 6 per cent on the bargain; or that a bond promising $60 per year interest plus a return of $1,000 principal after 20 years is now worth $803.70, if the risk is commensurate with an 8 per cent yield.[2] These statements appear to be fully logical. No investment is intrinsically worth more or less than the present value of the expected future benefits from it.

Experienced investors will immediately observe that at any given time the market value of an investment asset depends on demand and supply, which in turn

---

[1] In mathematical notation the present value of an investment can be generally represented as

$$V = \sum_{i=1}^{n} \frac{R_i}{(1 + r)^i}$$

where V stands for the present value of the investment, R_i for the dollar return from the investment in a given year and r for the rate at which returns are discounted for futurity, uncertainty, etc. The symbol $\sum_{i=1}^{n}$ refers to the summation of the discounted returns over all years in which the investment will pay, the years running from 1 to "n" in number, and i having a value of 1 for the first year, 2 for the second, 3 for the third, and so on.

[2] Table 2-2 indicates that $1 per year for the next 20 years is worth $9.82, if the appropriate discount rate is 8 per cent. Since the bond pays $60 per year, the total present value of 20 years' interest payments is $589.20 (60 × $9.82). The principal sum is to be repaid after 20 years: Table 2-1 indicates that a $1 sum due in 20 years has a present value at 8 per cent discount of $.2145, and the $1,000-bond principal must therefore have a present value of $214.50. The two present values, $589.20 on the interest payments and $214.50 on the principal, total $803.70.

reflect the estimates of a number of people concerning the future paying power of the investment and the degree of risk[3] involved. In other words, the market price is the result of a consensus about the future of the investment. This is unquestionably the proper viewpoint. But it must also be noted that, although this market consensus vacillates as people change their opinions about the future, it is certain to adjust itself to reflect the actual situation as the future unfolds. The individual who wishes to invest profitably must therefore base his decisions at least in part upon accurate appraisals of the income to be expected and the rate of discount which the risk requires.

It would appear that the first step in determining the dollar value of an investment must of necessity be to estimate the amount and timing of the benefits to be received from it from now until the end of time — unless, of course, it is appraised purely by guess. After all, the only advantages the owners will ever get out of an investment asset are the payments or services it brings them after expenses and taxes are deducted. It is immaterial, in making these estimates of future benefits, whether the investment in question is a contractual obligation such as a bond or an annuity, which promises fixed sums in dollars, or whether it is an equity item such as stock or real estate, whose payments might be irregular in amount and timing. In either instance the first step in valuation is to make the best possible forecast of future benefit receipts.

In many instances the future benefits expected by investors consist of attractive selling prices rather than long years of dividend or rental income. However, it may be argued that the most likely basis for expecting an increased selling price is the conviction that either the earning power or the safety of the investment is increasing and that the improvement will shortly be recognized by others and reflected in the price.[4] The underlying source of value is still the discounted value of expected future receipts.

It is clear that as time passes and differing aspects of the future appear, revisions of investors' estimates of benefits to come will cause continual changes in their appraisals of many investments. Obviously, those which wear out or become obsolete as time passes will have progressively smaller or fewer contributions to make in the future, and their values will decline progressively. Those which encounter severe competition or adverse political developments or any of a multitude of other hazards will also seem to promise less. And of course those

---

[3] The term should probably be *distaste* rather than risk, since an investor's insistence on a high-yield rate as an inducement to buy a certain investment may spring from his dislike of its long-term nature, of the supervision required, of its lack of marketability, or of any of a number of other factors.

[4] There are occasional irrational markets in which this is not true. For example, investors in 1929 borrowed money at 7 per cent and bought stocks at prices to yield 3 per cent, not in expectation of any dividend increase but rather in the hope of selling the already overpriced stock to "some other sucker" at a still higher price. Who cares about dividends when the principal appreciates 25 per cent per year? The same thing happened during the frenzied "bull" stock markets of 1966 and 1968.

whose advantages are ascendant will appear to offer more than was previously anticipated. All of this is clearly evident in the fluctuation of real estate and stock market values.

When the best possible estimates of future benefits have been made, it is next necessary to discount these estimates down to the present at a proper rate of interest to determine what they are worth. The proper rate of interest or discount is said to be a composite of two factors: the basic rate of interest on low-risk loans, which reflects chiefly the supply of and demand for funds, and the extra return which investors demand of an investment which they deem to be hazardous or inconvenient. Thus, long-term United States government bonds in mid-1972 yielded about 6 per cent, but good railroad bonds were regarded as sufficiently questionable to justify a 7½ per cent rate. (Both of these rates are before allowance for income taxes; the net returns would therefore be considerably less.) Investment values will obviously depend almost as much on the degree of hazard which investors believe attaches to a commitment as on the amount they believe it will earn; for a stock estimated to pay $4 per share per year into the indefinite future is worth $100 per share if its quality justifies a 4 per cent discount rate, but only $50 if uncertainty demands an 8 per cent yield. Furthermore, it is clear that the future of any investment will look less secure at certain times than at others. Business conditions, political conditions, and variations in public confidence will inevitably produce changes in the rate of compensation people will demand for bearing risks; and this means changes in the values they attach to their investments.

Tables 2-1 and 2-2 illustrate the ideas being presented here. These tables are small excerpts from very large tables which enable the investor to obtain at a glance the present-day theoretical value of sums which are expected to be paid in the future. Table 2-1 indicates the immediate value of *single* $1 payments to be collected in the future, allowing for various rates of interest over the time before the payment is due. Thus, the 5 per cent column shows that the present value of a $1 payment to be received 15 years hence is $.4810, if the appropriate interest rate is 5 per cent. Actually, this $.4810 is the sum which, if placed at 5 per cent compound interest, would accumulate to $1 in 15 years. An investor interested in evaluating a deferred payment would therefore find the sums in Table 2-1 to represent the correct present *per dollar* value of the deferred payment, allowing for the proper interest rate as shown in the table. The present value of any specified amount of deferred payment can be obtained by multiplying the amount of the payment by the proper *per dollar* value as shown in the table. The table can also be used in two-part calculations such as that in footnote 2.

Table 2-2 is a further development of the idea of Table 2-1. Table 2-1 shows the present values of *single* $1 payments at future dates; Table 2-2 simply adds up the present values of $1 payments made at the ends of first, second, third, and succeeding years, and states the *total* present value of many years of future *annual*

Table 2-1 *Present value of a single $1 payment to be collected at a future time, at specified rates of compound discount*

Years to payment date	2%	4%	5%	6%	8%	10%
1	$.9804	$.9615	$.9524	$.9434	$.9259	$.9091
2	.9612	.9246	.9070	.8900	.8573	.8264
3	.9423	.8890	.8638	.8396	.7938	.7513
4	.9238	.8548	.8227	.7921	.7350	.6830
5	.9057	.8219	.7835	.7473	.6806	.6209
10	.8203	.6756	.6139	.5584	.4632	.3855
15	.7430	.5553	.4810	.4173	.3152	.2394
20	.6730	.4564	.3769	.3118	.2145	.1486
30	.5521	.3083	.2314	.1741	.0994	.0573
40	.4529	.2083	.1420	.0972	.0460	.0221
50	.3715	.1407	.0872	.0543	.0213	.0085
60	.3048	.0951	.0535	.0303	.0099	.0033
80	.2051	.0434	.0202	.0095	.0021	.0005
100	.1380	.0198	.0076	.0029	.0005	.0001

payments. For example, the 5 per cent column of Table 2-2 states that $1 per year for 50 years has a total present value of $18.26. An annual payment of $2.50 (instead of $1) would be evaluated by multiplying the $18.26 for each $1 of payment by 2½ ($18.26 × 2½) to arrive at the correct value of $45.65.

Table 2-2 *Present value of a $1 annual payment for specified numbers of years, at various discount rates*

Years	2%	4%	5%	6%	8%	10%
1	$ .98	$ .96	$ .95	$ .94	$ .93	$ .91
2	1.94	1.89	1.86	1.83	1.78	1.74
3	2.88	2.78	2.72	2.67	2.58	2.49
4	3.81	3.63	3.55	3.47	3.31	3.17
5	4.71	4.45	4.33	4.21	3.99	3.79
10	8.98	8.11	7.72	7.36	6.71	6.15
15	12.85	11.12	10.38	9.71	8.56	7.61
20	16.35	13.59	12.46	11.47	9.82	8.51
30	22.40	17.29	15.37	13.76	11.26	9.43
40	27.36	19.79	17.16	15.05	11.92	9.78
50	31.42	21.48	18.26	15.76	12.23	9.92
60	34.76	22.62	18.93	16.16	12.38	9.97
80	39.74	23.92	19.60	16.51	12.47	9.99
100	43.10	24.50	19.85	16.62	12.49	9.99
Forever	50.00	25.00	20.00	16.67	12.50	10.00

Table 2-2 can be used to evaluate annual net rents or dividends which the investor expects to receive for a stated period of time. This is a practical idea; neither the rents from a building nor the dividends from a corporation can last forever, and the salvage value after the income ceases may not be great. As has been noted, the table indicates that the dividends from a stock expected to pay $1 per year for 50 years and to be valueless thereafter have a present value of $18.26, if the situation justifies a 5 per cent interest basis.[5] If the certainty of payment were significantly greater, so that the investor felt justified in accepting a 4 per cent return, the value of the expected dividends would be greater; the table shows the value of $1 per year for 50 years on a 4 per cent basis to be $21.48. A more uncertain case in which the investor demanded an 8 per cent return would permit a valuation of only $12.23.

One of the very significant aspects of investments valuation is the relative emphasis which must be attached to near-term dividends or other income as compared with the relative unimportance of receipts expected in distant years. For example, the dividends from a share of stock expected to pay a $1 dividend annually for 100 years (and to be valueless thereafter) are worth $19.85, if the risk is one which justifies a 5 per cent yield; yet the dividends for the first 20 years are worth $12.46, leaving a value of only $7.39 for those of the next 80 years. Other examples can be deduced from Table 2-2; it will be noted that the higher the yield rate expected, the greater the relative importance of the early receipts. Evidently an investor need not estimate the far-distant incomes from his investment with extreme accuracy; if he is right about what it can do for the next 20 years, his value conclusions can be substantially accurate. The importance of early receipts also emphasizes the investment weakness of idle land or non-dividend-paying stocks. Long-deferred incomes have only a limited current value, especially if the risk justifies a high discount rate. Table 2-1 illustrates the low present value of distant receipts.

Three more detailed aspects of present-value calculations should be noted. First, and most important, it is necessary to recognize that future cash receipts from any investment, whether it be a bond, a share of stock, a piece of real estate, or whatever, are not likely to come in regular annual amounts. A bond pays a series of fixed-interest payments plus a principal sum at the due date; a common stock may pay annual sums which tend to grow as the company develops successfully, or to decline as the company falls behind in the competitive race; an apartment house may pay less and less as obsolescence and maintenance costs reduce its net earnings. In these cases investors may appraise an asset by estimating its net cash earnings year by year (or possibly decade by decade), evaluating the

---

[5] Note that the $1 annual income exceeds 5 per cent on the $18.26 total value. The values are computed so that the investor gets his principal back out of the annual payments, in addition to his 5 per cent income. Conventional stock market computations, which measure the income "yield" on a stock as dividend divided by price, are assuming that the dividend payment will last forever, which may be slightly optimistic.

years or decades separately by the use of present-value tables, and adding up the separate values to obtain a total appraisal.

A second detailed aspect of present-value calculations involves the fact that near-term income expectations are often more certain of collection than far-distant ones and may therefore deserve to be valued at a lower discount rate. For example, if one estimated that General Motors common stock would produce an average of $4.25 in dividends annually for 50 years and thereafter produce nothing, the 50 years' payments at 5 per cent discount would have a present value of $77.60 (Table 2-2). But if the first 20 years' payments at $4.25 were deemed so sure that 4 per cent discount was sufficient, they alone would be worth $57.76; and if the remaining 30 years' payments were regarded as sufficiently uncertain to warrant 6 per cent discount, they would be worth $18.23. Adding the $57.76 and the $18.23 produces a present-value estimate of $75.99 on this basis.

The third detailed aspect of present values is based upon the fact that many investments seem very certain to produce a limited amount of dividends but are likely to produce much more. The more certain portion of the income may reasonably be evaluated at a lower discount rate than is applied to the remaining portions. For example, the 50-year $4.25 per share estimated income from General Motors stock need not all be regarded as of equal quality; possibly $2 per year is highly dependable, justifying a 4 per cent discount rate; perhaps $1 more is deserving of a 5 per cent rate; and the final $1.25 may be uncertain enough to justify a discount rate of 8 per cent. On this basis, Table 2-2 indicates that the income portions would have present values of $42.96, $18.26, and $15.29, respectively, to total to an appraisal of $76.51.

It is clear that complete realism would require that all three of these detailed aspects of present-value calculations—that is, the variation in annual incomes, the greater uncertainty of income expected in distant years, and the increasing uncertainty of marginal increments of expected income—should be considered together in all cases. The process might lead to unduly complicated arithmetic, more accurate in theory than in practice, but at least it is desirable to realize that sound logic commends the idea.

Calculations of the sort indicated here are seldom made by amateur investors, though they are common enough in connection with major real estate and bond transactions. Perhaps the reason amateurs do not make such calculations is that they dislike to "guesstimate" incomes for long periods into the unknown future and therefore prefer to choose in a more casual way between the values which the market provides. The simplified "rule-of-thumb" appraisal methods ordinarily used will be presented in later chapters.[6]

It is not to be expected that market prices, which reflect the current judgments

---

[6] These methods generally involve an attempt to predict average annual corporate profits and dividends per share of stock, and appraise the stock by multiplying the expected earnings and dividends by capitalization factors which past-value history indicates to be reasonable.

of fallible men, will at all times show accurate appraisals of investment assets. By the same logic, it is not to be expected that accurate appraisals by investors will always obtain immediate market profits. But there is hardly room for doubt that good judgment in appraising future earning power and in assaying economic hazards will have its reward in the long run. Even if market prices never reflect the values which the prescient investor identifies and acquires, the investor will obtain the income benefits which his wisdom enables him to foresee; and in most instances the market prices will sooner or later recognize the true situation. Market prices are often slow and erratic in arriving at logical levels, but they are forever searching for them.

The value of improbable possibilities   The theory that investment values may be appraised by capitalizing the best available estimate of future income receipts fails to work in cases in which the probable income is small but in which large gains are possible but unlikely. People are usually willing to pay good sums for such items as speculative oil land or doubtful-quality corporate stocks which probably will never pay any return but which may possibly produce large amounts. This speculative attitude also affects the price of some types of medium-grade real estate and stocks, for people are often willing to pay more than normal dividend capitalizations for assets with enticing additional long-shot possibilities.[7]

Although it is difficult to prove the point or to make any quantitative measures of the amounts, it seems reasonable to conclude that most real estate and stock values are based upon the capitalized values of estimated future incomes from them plus the speculative value attached to their improbable possibilities. It also seems reasonable to guess that the values of stable and profitable properties are mostly based upon capitalized anticipated incomes—this can be deduced from the fact that their values seem reasonably related to projected earnings and dividends—while the values of undependable or losing ventures are based mostly on their speculative possibilities. Finally, it is clear that values based on stable incomes are far more dependable than those based on vague possibilities, for the prices of productive real estate and steady-dividend-paying stocks fluctuate much less than those of their speculative counterparts.

On the strength of these deductions, it would seem wise for the investor in secure and stable properties to concentrate most of his attention on estimates of earnings and dividend distributions and for the owner of highly speculative

---

[7] It has been suggested by some writers that the real basis for these speculative prices lies in the mathematical probability that the contemplated dividend will be paid. Thus, if an oil-producing bonanza is a 1-chance-in-4 probability, the stock of the oil company ought to sell at about one-fourth the price it would bring if the bonanza were already a proven fact. The authors believe that the salability of bright dreams varies greatly from time to time, but that on the average they sell higher than true mathematical probabilities would justify. Hope springs eternal in the speculator's breast—and the net result is a pattern of stock and real estate prices which often makes speculative opportunities higher in price than they should be.

items to take special cognizance of market behavior. The values of extreme speculations often border on the irrational and are, consequently, extremely subject to market whims and fancies.

Sunk capital Most investments in business ownership, stocks, real estate, and to some extent mortgages and bonds represent interests in *sunk capital*. That is, these investments depend upon assets which, because of their nature or location, are definitely committed to one industry or type of service. If that industry or type of service produces a return, the investment will have value; if no returns can be had, the investment is a failure and will have only a speculative value based on the possibility of some future improvement in its position. The returns which investors obtain from their properties may consist of returns of capital or payments from net income or both.

For example, a poorly located apartment house costing $50,000 might enable its owner to pay all operating expenses and recover $1,000 annually for 50 years. No net income would be earned in this case; yet the apartment house would have a value based chiefly upon the discounted present value of $1,000 annually for the remainder of its useful life. Most buildings and many other "wasting asset" investments make returns consisting of recovered capital plus whatever net income is earned.

But a large percentage of business investments cannot make payments to their owners except out of real earnings, because of the necessity for constant modernization and improvement. The typical business finds that depreciation funds—the portion of cash receipts from sales which represent recoveries of original capital —must be steadily reinvested and even supplemented by outlays from earnings and new sales of securities, if competitive efficiency is to be maintained. Capital committed to such industries is forever "sunk" in them, and the investments must be evaluated largely on the basis of the distributions from earnings which can be expected.

These "sunk capital" situations explain why it is that securities experts emphasize earnings and dividends and often disregard book values or asset appraisals entirely when they evaluate corporation stocks. In these cases, investors can only get their money out of the enterprises by selling their stocks, and purchasers are disposed to pay prices which reflect the present values of probable future cash recoveries, not the cost of the companies' assets.

II EARNING POWER OF CAPITAL

The second basic determinant of investment values is the total supply of economic capital, its relative scarcity, and its consequent earning power. For this purpose, the term *capital* includes most of the man-made physical resources of the country, such as buildings, inventories, machinery, and the like, plus most of our economically developed land and mineral resources, plus certain intangibles such as patented processes and brand names.

As a beginning point, it seems clear that the earning power of invested capital depends importantly on how much capital the country has. Assuming that political conditions make private enterprise feasible and that a population exists to assure a labor supply and markets, competing capital owners (business firms) will undertake to produce and sell goods to earn a profit. If the capital supply is extremely short, there will be relatively few competitors in each industry, and profit margins should be high. If new areas and industries are being opened up, if new inventions offer opportunity for profitable employment of all available new capital, there will be little tendency for competition to become severe, and profit margins should continue high. On the other hand, if the nation is well supplied with competitors and capital equipment in every line of business, if new inventions and new industries are appearing so slowly that new savings provide capital for numerous competitors in every new field, profit margins will tend to be relatively low.

Of course, it is not to be expected that different businesses would have identical profit margins under any of these conditions. After all, skillfully managed concerns in all lines may be expected to do better than others. And it is to be expected that relatively secure lines of business, or those better known or easier to enter or easier to finance, may be somewhat more crowded and more competitive than the average. Logical differentials in earnings rates are certain to occur. Investors who are estimating the future dividend-paying power of a company must therefore consider both the general earning power of capital and the particular competitive position of the company and its industry.

As new savings become available for business use, their owners naturally tend to invest them in the industries in which future earnings seem likely to compensate most generously for the degree of risk involved. This is an individual and competitive process which tends to build up each industry competitively until its prospective average earnings rate matches all others, allowing for differences in risk and convenience. However, the profit-equalizing tendency does not work out perfectly; some industries seem always to earn above-average profits, whereas others, such as railroads and textiles, persistently fall below the average. Even so, the basic tendency to equalize profit rates seems to establish an average profit margin, or perhaps a group of related profit margins in different industries, and these margins provide a measure of the potential earning power of uninvested savings.

Chart 2-1 provides a general indication of the earning power of business capital in the United States. The chart shows the percentage earned each year on the *stockholders' equity* in large American manufacturing corporations. Although the figure fluctuates violently with business conditions, an average rate seems to be about 11.5 per cent per year, and from 1926 through 1972 there was no dis-

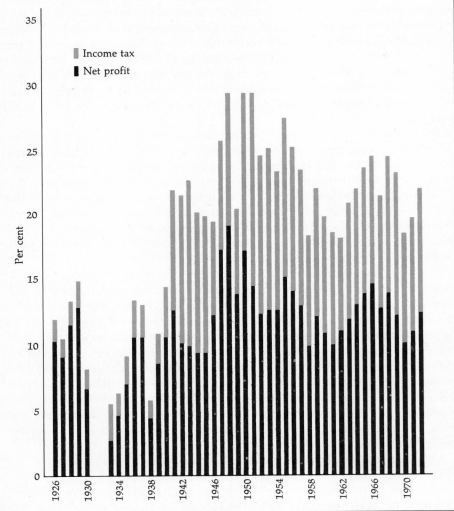

Chart 2-1   *The earning power of capital. The darker portion of the bars shows the percentage of total net earnings to total book net worth of leading manufacturing corporations in the United States. The earnings show no definite upward or downward trend from 1926 to 1972, although earnings have been much more stable since World War II. Notice that the increased income taxes in effect since 1941 have not reduced net earnings. Many of the years shown here are abnormal because of depression, war, inflation, and other factors. Corporate profits data, courtesy First National City Bank. Income tax estimated from Statistics of Income.*

cernible trend up or down. However, most of these business firms also use some borrowed money; if interest payments were added to net earnings and the total expressed as a percentage of net worth plus debt, the total earnings would average close to 8.5 per cent on total invested capital.

Because some owners of existing capital investments are always seeking to sell them, investors with free funds usually have a choice between the acquisition of existing properties and the construction of new ones. This is true whether the desired investments are in corporate stocks, small businesses, farms, residential real estate, or something else. As a rule, also, there are enough competing sellers and buyers in each field so that the prices paid for existing investments are reasonably related to the cost of constructing equally profitable new ones. This means that if the probable average earning power of new funds invested in business is 7 per cent, an existing business could be bought at a price upon which its average earnings would amount to a somewhat similar figure. To be more definite about it, if a new apartment house can be constructed at a cost upon which 7 per cent can be earned, a similar existing apartment house should bring a price upon which its earnings will approximate 7 per cent.

Investors may make two practical deductions from these facts. First, they may expect that the long-term average rate of business profits will tend to reflect the adequacy or shortage of the nation's capital supply as measured against its rate of growth and development. If the nation is able to save at a rate in excess of the sums needed to expand old industries and develop new ones, average profit rates will fall and the investor who holds long-term fixed-income bonds, preferred stocks, and mortgages, or who owns patent-protected or other monopolistic businesses, will retain a constant income, whereas the investor who depends on the diminishing profits of competitive enterprise will get less. If the nation's savings are small compared to the business opportunities available, the relative advantage will be reversed. The second deduction is that since the yield rates at which investment incomes of all sorts are capitalized will be related to the average rate of business profits, fixed-income investments will rise or fall in value as general profit rates change, while the value of a typical competitive investment will be subject to two offsetting influences: a tendency for profit rates and income capitalization rates to rise and fall together. For example, a decline in its profit rate from 8 to 6 per cent would not affect the investment value of a competitive enterprise if investors' savings increased in volume so that all comparable investment opportunities were crowded down to a 6 per cent basis. A $6 annual income capitalized at 6 per cent is worth as much as an $8 income capitalized at 8 per cent.

Although these deductions based upon capital supply and profit margins are true as general long-run tendencies, their effects are obscured and importantly distorted by other influences. Paramount among these influences are the economic disturbances known as business cycles, which affect all aspects of investment values, and the variations in investor preferences for different types of investments, which cause relative values to change sharply from time to time. These factors will be noted in succeeding sections.

Interest rates and stock yields[8] Among the many investment opportunities available to the owners of cash are the stocks of business corporations and the bonds or promissory notes of firms which wish to borrow funds for business use. Stocks represent an indirect and rather convenient form of property ownership through which investors obtain a dividend income. Historically, this dividend income has averaged about 60 per cent of the profits earned by the corporation; the balance is usually retained to strengthen and develop the corporation. Bond and note interest is paid regularly as a contractual obligation at whatever rate the parties have agreed upon. It is the purpose of this section to compare the cash incomes that are available to investors on stock and bond investments.

Since stock investment is an indirect form of business-property investment, carrying with it most of the major advantages and risks of business ownership, it is to be expected that the incomes available from stock ownership will be reasonably related to the profit rates on business assets, as shown in Chart 2-1. This is true, with two important qualifications: First, the dividends received by stockholders do not represent all of the corporate earnings; the stockholder usually expects to get additional profit in the long run from the undistributed earnings which are kept in the company to enlarge and strengthen it. Second, the percentage income return available on stocks depends on the *price* of the stocks as well as on the dividends paid, and the stock market is notorious for wide and almost irrational variation in stock prices. The effects of these price changes on stock yields are conspicuous in Chart 2-2.

With respect to bond and note yields, it is to be expected that they would average far less than the earning power of business net worth, as shown in Chart 2-1. No businessman would wish to pay as much for borrowed money as he could earn by employing it. Furthermore, bonds and loans are less subject to the business and market risks than property or stocks, so the investor can ordinarily afford to accept a lower rate of income. The historic tendency of bond yields to be lower than stock yields is apparent in Chart 2-2.

It would follow from all this that the yields on stocks would normally average much less than the earning power of business assets and that bond yields would normally average somewhat less than stock yields. However, as has been noted, these general tendencies have sometimes been overcome by unusual economic or speculative conditions. Furthermore, a permanent change in the thinking of investors and investing institutions—for example, a general preference for investing in stocks or business ownership instead of bonds and loans—might keep

---

[8] Yield may be defined roughly as the percentage of net income (dividend or interest payment) to the price of the security. More detailed definitions will be developed later.

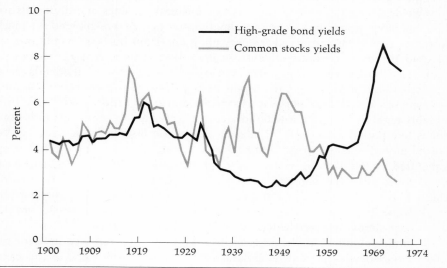

Chart 2-2 *Stock and bond yields compared. Data are based on annual average yields of high-grade bonds and representative indexes of common stocks. Note that bond yields have usually been below stock yields, that the yield trends have at times been parallel, and that stock yields fluctuate more than bond yields. Note also that the excess of bond over stock yields has been continuous since 1958 and has now reached its widest extent in the 73 years shown.*

bond yields relatively high and stock yields correspondingly low by limiting the money supply for bonds and loans and increasing the demand for stocks.

A 73-year history of average stock and bond yields is reproduced in Chart 2-2. Although a short review of this long period will permit only a few observations, these have significant lessons for investors.

It will be noted that the yields on both bonds and stocks tended to rise, with occasional cyclical interruptions, from 1900 until about 1923. This was a period of very great growth in the country, during which investment opportunities outran the supply of new savings, profit margins rose, and the yields on both bonds and stocks reflected the rising earning power of capital. The scarcity of capital at the end of this period was magnified by the wearing out of existing facilities during World War I. It will also be noted that stock yields tended to exceed bond yields by progressively wider margins during all of this period; this was before the day of wide public participation in the stock market, and it would appear that the nation's growing supply of common stocks could only be marketed at low prices and high yield rates.

The years 1923–1929 were prosperous years in which the capital supply of the country grew very rapidly. Bond interest rates drifted down slowly. Stock yields dropped rapidly, first in response to large-scale public buying of stocks as attractive investments, and in 1928–1929 as a reflection of the speculative mania which culminated in the crash of 1929.

The years 1930–1949 were in many respects diverse, but two things are clear: investors avoided stocks even at high yields and bought safe bonds willingly at low yields. During the depression decade, business earnings and dividends were low, but stock prices were correspondingly low—people remembered the market losses of 1929–1932, observed the prevailing uncertain business conditions, and ignored attractive stock investments. In 1943–1946 some recovery in stock prices took place, but even vigorous postwar prosperity and increased dividends did not attract enough stock buyers to sustain stock prices when corporations began to sell new stock to finance postwar expansion, and stock yields in 1947–1949 were notably high. By contrast, low bond yields reflected ample loanable funds during the whole period 1934–1949. While the depression lasted, the demand for borrowed money was not great, and both real savings and an ample credit supply generated by the banking system were offered at low interest rates. During the years 1942–1949 the banking system created great quantities of new credits; these, plus normal savings supplies, met all loan demands at low interest rates. In 1949 the low yield rates for bonds and very high yields for stocks provided a contrast almost unprecedented in prosperous peacetime years.

Beginning about 1950, the postwar business boom and renewed investor optimism coupled with price-level inflation set new forces to work in the capital markets. Promising business opportunities plus housing and other needs created a vigorous demand for loans. At the same time, inflationary price-level trends induced the banking authorities to limit the rate of bank-credit expansion. The increased demand for loans and the limited supply of available funds resulted in a rising trend in interest rates, which is reflected in Chart 2-2 in rising bond yields during the entire period 1950–1970. Meanwhile, stock yields fell rapidly until 1960. Good business, satisfactory profit rates, inflationary price trends, and a selling campaign by stockbrokers convinced investors that stocks were desirable holdings. Stock prices rose even faster than earnings and dividends, so that stock yields from 1959 through 1972 were significantly below bond yields.

Unfortunately, a review of history by means of Charts 2-1 and 2-2 does not provide a guaranteed measure of normal levels for stock and bond yields or of normal ratios between them. Most significant, seemingly, has been the tendency, deduced from Chart 2-2, for the *total* return to invested capital (both equity and borrowed funds) to gravitate across time toward approximately 8½ per cent. The persistence of this tendency throughout the multifarious business conditions and price-level trends of the past 73 years would suggest that when bond yields approach the 8½ per cent level, stock prices become vulnerable for two paramount reasons. First, the cost of borrowed funds exceeds the earnings which businessmen can expect from their employment, and the rate of profit, which stock prices usually reflect, declines. Second, the availability of unusually high yields on bonds prompts many investors to sell stocks and buy bonds.[9] Certainly, when bond yields reached 8 to 10 per cent levels in 1969–1970, stock prices fell heavily.

One more noteworthy observation may be made from Chart 2-2. The chart shows that the yields on stocks fluctuate much more than do those of bonds. The reasons are mostly matters affecting stock prices: (1) Stocks are more hazardous than bonds, hence tend to drop violently when investors are frightened by adverse business news; (2) bonds are to a greater degree held by institutions, whose finances and policies are more stable than those of individuals; and (3) stocks are subjected to speculative buying and selling to a much greater degree than bonds.

III THE IMPORTANCE OF INSTITUTIONS AND CUSTOMS

The third major economic force to be discussed in this chapter is the influence of our financial institutions on the investment markets. Since a continually increasing percentage of the funds available for investment in the United States is turned over to life insurance companies, banks, trustees, savings and loan associations, investment companies, and similar agencies and is invested by them, what they do with the money determines to a large extent both the demand for mortgages, bonds, stocks, and real estate and the prices and yields available on these.

The most important institutions for channeling savings into investment are the life insurance companies (230 billion dollars of assets at mid-1972), the savings departments of commercial banks (118 billion dollars), personal trusts in bank trust departments (around 145 billion dollars), savings and loan associations (225 billion dollars), mutual savings banks (96 billion dollars), trusteed corporate pension funds (105 billion dollars), mutual funds (58 billion dollars), and state and local government retirement funds (65 billion dollars). All of these have grown substantially in the past two decades, but the most phenomenal gains have been made by the savings and loan associations, which invest mostly in residential mortgages, and the corporate pension funds and the mutual funds which are important purchasers of stocks. However, other institutional changes have also taken place. Bank trust departments, endowment funds, and recently, life insurance companies, have begun to invest greater amounts in stocks; all institutions have started searching more aggressively for profitable investment outlets and techniques. To hedge purchasing-power risks during 1969–1970, insurance com-

---

[9] At 8 per cent yields, high-grade bonds sell 12½ times annual interest, which is virtually certain. This would at least raise a question whether common stocks as a class should sell for as much as 12½ times fluctuating, uncertain earnings.

panies and trust funds frequently required large mortgage borrowers to pay, in addition to conventional interest, a share of their profits or gross receipts. Keener competition among institutional investors has led also to an increasing emphasis on quick capital gains and a more exacting measurement of the way investment portfolios "perform" over relatively short periods of time. Since the middle 1960s, mutual funds and many of the bank trust departments that administer corporate pension funds have been buying and selling securities at much more frequent intervals than before; they have selected common stocks less for dividend yields and increasingly for their chances of capital growth and speculative gains.

Institutional investment to a large extent is controlled by law and custom, so that changes are usually made gradually. For example, commercial banks are usually limited by law to investments in bonds and loans, life insurance companies to bonds and mortgages plus relatively small amounts in stocks and real estate, and trust funds to generally conservative holdings; and the managements of these institutions are ordinarily reluctant to depart from precedent even when they are given the necessary authority. This means that institutional change is likely to come slowly, and that its effects in the investment markets are likely to be obvious and stable as well as important.

It is sometimes argued that people invest their savings through particular financial institutions because of the investment policies these institutions follow. But it seems more probable that investors pick their institutions mostly because of the service, income, liquidity, and tax advantages afforded, and because of the sales efforts made by the institutions. It follows, therefore, that the appeal to investors offered by the deposit accounts or other services of our major institutions is of great importance in establishing demand for our major types of investments. This demand will in turn affect the prices and relative yields of the investments. For example, since 1967, life insurance companies have begun offering *variable annuities* as an answer to the prolonged price inflation which has reduced the purchasing power of fixed-dollar amount annuities on which millions of people depend for their retirement income. An individual buying a variable annuity would pay dollar premiums into the life insurance company during his active lifetime; the money would be invested in common stocks. When he retired, his annuity would be based from month to month on a fair share of the common stock pool to which he had contributed. Presumably, a further price-level inflation would cause these stocks to rise in price, and the individual would receive a commensurately increased monthly payment. The variable annuity has encountered both regulatory and pressure-group obstacles, but the persistence of strong inflationary trends has caused a public demand for these to be cleared away. In years ahead, many people may buy variable annuities instead of conventional ones, and dollar sum life insurance may in some degree be replaced by *variable* life policies backed by equity investments. If so, *the relative flows of funds into stocks, bonds, and mortgages will be substantially altered.*

IV FISCAL AND MONETARY POLICY

During the past 40 years the intervention of governmental and quasi-governmental agencies into economic matters has grown increasingly influential. Government has become a major purchaser of goods, a vast lender of money, and a diligent manipulator of economic affairs. Its operations affect both the stability and the total performance of many investments. The impact of government is therefore the fourth major factor affecting investment values.

Although there are many statutes under which governmental and quasi-governmental agencies operate, space permits mention here of only two: the Employment Act of 1946 and the Federal Reserve Act. The Employment Act is a very simple statute which (1) sets up the President's Council of Economic Advisers, and (2) instructs all agencies of the government to undertake policies which will foster private enterprise, maximize employment and output, and maintain the general welfare. This is quite generally construed to mean that federal spending, lending, and loan guaranteeing should be increased and taxes decreased to counteract any tendencies toward recession or depression, and that contrary adjustments should probably be undertaken to combat inflationary booms. The activities of the federal government in this area will doubtless be a continuing subject for political debate, but they seem certain to increase and to exert a growing influence on investors' results.

The second statute in point here is the Federal Reserve Act. This is a comprehensive measure dating from 1913, but several times amended, under which the Federal Reserve banks are able to exert great influence over loan-fund supplies and interest rates. Although the Federal Reserve System operates under rather vague statutory instructions to "maintain sound banking conditions" and to "prevent excess use of credit," it regards itself as being subject to the Employment Act and therefore authorized to manipulate bank credit and interest rates to further the Employment Act objectives of prosperity and general welfare. The Federal Reserve System is thus primarily concerned with general economic affairs and only secondarily with the securities markets, but its activities inevitably exert a profound influence on securities prices.

Federal Reserve activities impinge upon the investment field in a number of ways, of which four may be specifically noted here. First, the System has the technical capacity to supply the commercial banks copiously with lendable funds or to cause a great scarcity of such funds. This power is obviously a major influence on the availability of bank loans and on the movement of short-term interest rates; it may have a considerable effect on business cash positions and on bond prices. The principal devices by which the System can affect bank lending are its open market operations, its power to change member bank reserve requirements, and its control of rediscount rates. Second, the Reserve System can to some extent influence high-class bond prices by open market dealing in government bonds. Extensive purchases of such bonds will keep them high in price and yielding relatively low rates; in consequence, private bond buyers seeking better yields will bid up corporate and municipal bonds, thus reducing their yields also. Obviously, sales by the Reserve System would cause government bond prices to drop, which would in turn drag down corporate bond prices and increase the interest yields available on all classes of bond investments.

The third sphere of Reserve authority which affects investors is its control over stock market credit. By specific statute the System is authorized to limit the percentage of value which any member bank may lend on stocks when the purpose of the loan is to finance the purchase or holding of such securities; and it is empowered to place similar restrictions on margin transactions in exchange-traded stocks or bonds when a securities dealer is the lender.[10] Rising markets have always made considerable use of credit financing, especially when large amounts of new securities are being sold. This credit control power appears to be very effective in restraining stock prices when new stock issues are being sold in quantities, even when large corporate earnings and dividends provide reason for higher prices. Corporate bond prices would probably be sensitive to it also, if they were not influenced even more by the money supply and interest-rate situation. The Reserve System uses its power over securities credit; it seems disposed to restrict stock market credit vigorously, even when it attacks inflationary credit expansion in no other way.

The fourth major application of Reserve authority upon investors is by means of moral suasion. Presumably, the Reserve System speaks mainly to the commercial banks when it comments upon business conditions, credit policies and banking practices, but its power over both banks and investment markets is so great that Reserve attitudes are always an influence in shaping private decisions on financial policy.

Although the great powers of the federal government and Federal Reserve may often benefit the economy, experience between 1965 and 1972 suggests that too much emphasis has been placed on maintaining maximum employment and near-term prosperity and too little on price-level stability and sound long-term conditions. In 1965–1966, and again in 1967–1968, expansionary monetary and fiscal policies were clearly followed too long and pushed too far; dangerously inflationary booms developed and had to be choked off with tight money and painfully restricted credit. Restraint was followed by slowdowns in business and by

---

[10] These powers were given the System by the Securities Exchange Act of 1934, which is discussed at some length in Chap. 12.

steep declines in the bond and stock markets. This tendency of the Washington authorities first to overstimulate the economy and then, as inflation accelerates, to restrain it harshly has been nicknamed "stop and go" policy. Along with probably slowing the nation's economic growth, it has been accompanied by increasing instability in both investors' expectations and securities prices.[11]

Clearly, almost every aspect of an investor's planning is affected by fiscal and monetary policy. Yields, selling prices, value growth, purchasing-power security, even near-term market prices are affected, and the investor must adapt his program to allow for the inevitable.

V SUPPLY AND DEMAND

Preceding sections of this chapter have noted logical basic relationships between bond yields, stock yields, and net earnings on real estate investments, but have also noted that these relationships do not remain constant. For example, bond yields may decline while stock yields rise and real estate yields remain unchanged. In the discussion of institutional and Federal Reserve policies, it was observed that these agencies may affect the prices and yields of various classes of investments by making heavy investment in one class and little or none in another.

But institutions are not the only unstable factors in the investment markets. Individuals, too, have their peculiarities. Their tendencies to change their investing policies radically, emphasizing reckless cupidity or unreasoning fear as business conditions are good or bad, are familiar to all. Less widely recognized but tremendously important are the tendencies of investors to give preference to temporarily favored industries or investment types and to neglect to invest in others; this may result, for example, in high prices for the stocks of growing industries which are much discussed in the press and relative weakness in others. And what is true of industries or investment types is even more true of individual companies' stock issues.

The essence of the matter is that there is a separate supply-and-demand market for each of many types of investments. In every case the supply consists of both old items—shares, bonds, or properties—offered for resale and new ones which may be issued or constructed. The demand is represented by new savings augmented by credit expansion, if any, and is expressed by institutions and individuals, each motivated by a separate set of convictions, expectations, and legal limitations, each preferring at the moment a particular type of investment, and each capable of changing his investment habits from time to time. In 1972, for example, the preference of institutional investors for high-grade growth stocks of the IBM and American Home Products variety produced a disproportionate

---

[11] Percentage swings in both stock and bond prices were much wider in the 1965–1972 period than in the preceding 20 years.

price rise in these equities while a majority of common stocks declined. In general, the pattern of demand for investment assets has shifted in recent years because steeply progressive taxes and government measures to redistribute the national income have changed the identities of the groups who have savings to invest.

Changing supplies also affect the price and yield of particular investments. During the 1950s, prosperous companies were reluctant to "dilute" their profits by selling new stock; this restricted the supply at a time when investors' demand for equities was growing rapidly and contributed to a tripling of industrial stock prices during the decade. At the same time, corporate managers' increasing preference for long-term debt financing helped swell the supply of bonds and forced their yields steadily upward. In 1971–1972, utility stock prices remained depressed at least partially because the companies sold record issues of new common stock to finance unexpectedly large construction programs and to keep already-strained bond-to-stock ratios from becoming excessive.

It is therefore not practicable to assume that there are exact permanent or normal relations between the yields available on bonds, stocks, real estate, or subclasses of these, nor between long-term and short-term money rates, nor between the yields on safe and speculative investments. Within reasonable limits, these relations may be expected to vary as supply and demand establish the various yields independently in quasi-separate markets.

MARKET FLUCTUATIONS

This chapter has thus far dealt with the general level of investment values and the rate of return upon them, and with the human and institutional preferences which account for differences in price and rate of return between different types of investments. It is now desirable to give brief attention to the *fluctuation* in these prices and percentage returns. The space devoted to this problem will be brief at this time because detailed treatment will be necessary later.

It is obvious that fluctuations in investment prices are the results of changes in the bids of buyers and the offers of sellers. Apparently either the buyers vary as the will-o'-the-wisp in their appraisals of the future, or they are engaged in frantic speculative attempts to outguess near-term market prices, or their actions are governed by their varying money supplies. Practically the same words could be said of sellers in the investment markets. The keys to current investment prices can therefore be found in the changing attitudes toward the distant future, in people's guesses on the price outlook for the next few months, and in the money supplies of business firms and investors.

Clearly, these situations will not be the same at all times—booms, recessions, politics, taxes, wars, inflation, new inventions, and other factors will intervene— so that neither various types of investments nor various industries nor specific geographic areas will retain their same relative desirability. And it is obvious that different kinds of investors—for example, bond-buying insurance companies and stock-buying families—are unlikely to have the same amounts or proportions of investible funds from one year to the next.

SUMMARY

The investor who would really appreciate the idiosyncrasies of the investment markets has a Herculean task on his hands. He must appreciate the intricacies of compound discount, grasp the relations between the rate of savings and the technical outlets for capital, understand the workings of the nation's institutional and credit and fiscal structure, follow the preferences and prejudices of the people who have money to invest, and translate the whole into a pattern of supply and demand for each separate type of investment. The whole of this task is preliminary, if the job of investing is to be done properly, to the two main functions assigned to this book—those of surveying the functioning of the investment markets and of reviewing the merits of the principal types of investments available in them.

QUESTIONS AND PROBLEMS

1   If you estimated that International Harvester Company stock would average $2 per year in dividends for the next 50 years and be valueless after that, how much would you pay for the stock if the risk justifies a 5 per cent yield?

2   If you estimated that General Electric would pay $2 per share in dividends for the next 10 years, $3 for the following 10 years, and $4 for the next 80 years, and if you thought that these payments should be discounted at 4 per cent, 6 per cent, and 8 per cent, respectively, what would the stock be worth?

3   Which of the two would be the better buy—General Electric at $60 or International Harvester at $30?

4   If you paid $100 for a stock whose dividends averaged only $2 annually over the first 10 years, what average dividend would the stock need to pay over the ensuing 30 years to provide you a 5 per cent return on your money, assuming that all dividends after 40 years' time were judged too nebulous to count?

5   Suppose you were offered an apartment house for $100,000, and you estimated that it would net you $7,000 per year after expenses and taxes (but before depreciation) for the next 30 years. Would it be a better investment than General Electric stock at $50? (Assume the premises of question 2.)

6   Would it be profitable to buy a vacant lot now for $6,000 which you could resell for $12,000 after 10 years, if your taxes and expenses would run $200 per year, and if your money could earn a 6 per cent annual return in other uses? (Ignore income taxes in working this problem.)

7   Find an example of a common stock whose value is based mostly on its improbable possibilities. What is the principle involved here? Do improbable possibilities exist in real estate? In bonds? Illustrate.

8 Would it be reasonable to say that a commitment justified by the discounted value of its most probable future dividend payments is an investment, while one justifiable only by its improbable possibilities is a speculation?

9 Would you call an electric utility sunk capital? What about a department-store chain owning chiefly inventory? Which is the better investment?

10 If a shortage of new inventions reduced the number of investment outlets in new industries, what would happen to the value of high-grade bonds? The value of rental properties? Common stock prices?

11 If the savings of the American people should diminish greatly during the next few years, while many new industries appeared, what would happen to bond values? To stock prices?

12 Does Chart 2-1 indicate that price inflation has added to corporate earning power? Does it suggest that common stocks are an effective inflation hedge? What issues are involved here?

13 If high-grade bonds yield 8 per cent, what would be a reasonable multiple of earnings for the price of good-quality stocks? Why?

14 If the public begins investing large sums in variable annuities and variable life insurance, would this activity change the long-term level of stock prices? Would it affect bond values? Mortgage interest rates?

15 How can the Federal Reserve System influence the prices and yields of corporate bonds? Can it keep bonds up and stocks down? How?

16 Why does the demand for stocks and real estate fall off in periods of depression? If new stocks are not sold and new houses are not constructed in depressions, why does the supply of these items for sale during depressions appear to be so large?

REFERENCES

Badger, Ralph E., Harold W. Torgerson, and Harry G. Guthmann: *Investment Principles and Practices*, 6th ed., Prentice-Hall, Inc., Englewood Cliffs, N.J., 1969, Chap. 8.

Bellemore, Douglas H., and John C. Ritchie, Jr.: *Investments*, 3d ed., South-Western Publishing Company, Incorporated, Cincinnati, 1969, Chaps. 5, 13.

Christy, George A., and P. Foster Roden: *Finance: Environment and Decisions*, Canfield Press, San Francisco, 1973, Chaps. 2–8.

Financial Handbook, rev. ed., The Ronald Press Company, New York, 1968, Secs. 1, 27.

Fredrickson, E. Bruce (ed.): *Frontiers of Investment Analysis*, International Textbook Company, Scranton, Pa., 1965, Part 2.

Institute of Chartered Financial Analysts: *C. F. A. Readings in Financial Analysis*, 2d ed., Richard D. Irwin, Inc., Homewood, Ill., 1970, Part 2.

Latané, Henry A., and Donald L. Tuttle: *Security Analysis and Portfolio Management*, The Ronald Press Company, New York, 1970, Chap. 8.

Sprinkel, Beryl W.: *Money and Stock Prices*, Dow Jones-Irwin, Inc., Homewood, Ill., 1964.

Williams, John B.: *The Theory of Investment Value*, Harvard University Press, Cambridge, Mass., 1938.

Wu, Hsiu-Kwang, and Alan J. Zakon: *Elements of Investments* (selected readings), Holt, Rinehart and Winston, Inc., New York, 1965, Part 2.

part 2
Corporate Securities

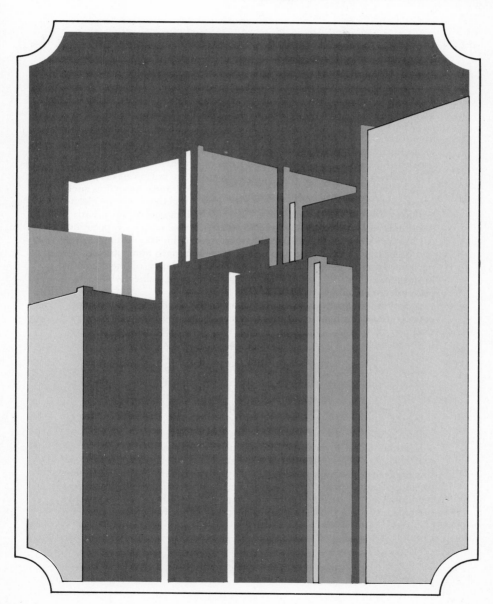

Corporation securities provide at least half the opportunities available to most investors and require two-thirds of the pages in a book which emphasizes securities investments. The topic occupies Chapters 3 through 7 to the exclusion of all else.

Chapter 3 deals with important corporation practices which affect investors. Dividend policy, stock splits, mergers, holding companies, recapitalizations, rights and warrants, state corporation codes, and articles of incorporation are among the essential items. With these basics out of the way, Chapters 4 through 6 consider the nature of corporate securities—common stocks, preferred stocks, and bonds, as well as such quasi-securities types as warrants and options—together with the essential factors which affect their value. The value of any corporate security is influenced by its legal and contractual position in the corporation—its priority over others, its opportunity for gain, its voting power, and other rights. Value is also affected by the strength and future prospects of the corporation, and by the market popularity of the security in question. These factors and the probable market values which they portend are examined in some detail.

Chapter 7 takes brief note of what happens when a corporation encounters serious financial trouble. This sort of thing has been less frequent in recent years, for many such situations are now resolved by hasty mergers in which strong corporations absorb the faltering ones and give the endangered securityholders their own securities in exchange. But there are still cases of insolvencies, forced recapitalizations, and corporate bankruptcies in which investors must consider the painful and slow procedures which resolve these difficulties. A description of these procedures is the task of Chapter 7.

Much of the content of Chapters 4 through 7 consists of reasonably orthodox ideas of corporate procedures and securities values, and considerations of how investors can adapt their affairs to the situations which exist. This is a sensible personal approach. But the authors of this book believe that a study of the investments field will show investor-citizens many instances in which the status quo in corporation law, regulatory policy, tax law, corporation policy, and the like could be advantageously reformed. Readers are urged to look for them.

3

CORPORATE PRACTICES
AND THE INVESTOR

The securities of business corporations represent the largest group of intangible investment values in America today. Corporation bonds and total debt outstanding at December 31, 1972, were estimated to total at least 370 billion dollars, and the value of outstanding corporate stocks in early 1972 ran well over a trillion dollars.[1] Approximately 32 million people owned corporate securities directly,[2] and a majority of the rest of the population had an indirect interest in them through their life insurance investments, bank deposits, and other holdings.

These impressive figures explain the preoccupation of investors with corporate affairs and justify the inclusion of a considerable discussion of corporate technicalities in any textbook on investments. The present chapter will therefore review certain corporate procedures which are of importance to investors, in order to provide an essential background for later discussions of the value of corporate securities.

NATURE OF A CORPORATION

A corporation may be defined as an artificial entity created by right of sovereign governmental authority and having the powers, privileges, and limitations stipulated by that authority.[3] Corporations usually have the right to own property, make contracts, sue and be sued, borrow money, employ people, and conduct their affairs much as a natural person would his own. In one sense the corporation is a sort of partnership of many people, who put their money into the venture and get back salable interests in it; but the investor does not own the corporation's property, nor is he responsible for its debts. The corporate entity owns the property and owes the debts. If the investor becomes a stockholder, he receives "shares" of stock in the corporation, is technically regarded as one of the owners

---

[1] Stocks listed on the New York Stock Exchange had a total value 742 billion dollars at the end of 1971. This value is reported regularly in the *Survey of Current Business*.

[2] Stockholders were estimated at nearly 31 million in 1970. See the 1972 *New York Stock Exchange Fact Book*.

[3] Compare the famous definition by Chief Justice Marshall in the Dartmouth College Case, 4 Wheat, 518 (1819): "A corporation is an artificial being, invisible, intangible, and existing only in contemplation of law. Being the mere creature of law, it possesses only those properties which the charter of its creation confers upon it either expressly or as incidental to its very existence. . . ."

of the business, and is entitled to such dividends, voting rights in selecting the management, and other privileges as the law and the corporation's financial progress may make possible. If the investor is a bondholder, he is a creditor of the corporation, not of its stockholders, and will receive the payments to which the bond contract entitles him if the corporation is able to pay them.

Business corporations are usually created under state law, though national banks and a few other specialized enterprises are federal creatures. General business corporations are permitted to incorporate (that is, to obtain a corporate identity) under the laws of any one state and then obtain "admission" to do business in any or all of the others. Admission is readily granted by all states to general commercial enterprises, which then become subject to the commercial laws and taxes of the states where business is done. However, the corporation laws of the incorporating state control the corporation in all matters affecting its corporate status, which would include stockholders' rights, dividends, borrowing of money, and many like items of concern to investors.

Each of the 50 states has a corporation law of some 100 to 200 pages which outlines that state's method of creating a corporation and the general rules under which it must operate. These corporation laws are much alike, but there are important differences among them despite the efforts of the American Bar Association to interest the states in uniform "model" codes. While incorporators often choose a state of incorporation with some care in order to obtain the most advantageous legal situation, investors as a rule seem little interested in their corporation's state of origin and the consequent controlling laws. However, there are occasions when the laws may make a difference to investors. They vary significantly, for example, on the following points:[4]

1   Methods by which corporations may amend their articles of incorporation
2   Classes of stock and par values which may be used
3   Protective features for preferred stock
4   Voting rights on all stock
5   Powers which must be conferred on directors, powers which may be conferred on directors, and powers which must be exercised by stockholder vote
6   Rights of stockholders
7   Right of the corporation to purchase and retire its own common shares
8   Definitions of surplus and eligibility to pay dividends
9   Method of authorizing new issues of securities and the prior rights of stockholders to buy them
10   Method of authorizing and consummating merger, reorganization, or dissolution and of safeguarding the rights of dissenting stockholders when these things are done

---

[4] The best comparative summaries of state laws on these and other corporate matters will be found in the United States Corporation Company's annual *Corporation Manual*, a large, two-volume reference work which is available in law and large general libraries.

Corporations come into being when chartered under the state code by the proper state official. This is done as a routine matter when the original incorporators file an application, together with the proposed *articles of incorporation*, certain other documents, and the necessary fee. This procedure is important to investors because the articles of incorporation (which may also be referred to as the corporation's *charter* when officially accepted for filing) constitute a contract between the state and the stockholders, outlining in considerable detail what the corporation is to do and the rights of the parties concerned. Each group of incorporators may write up a set of articles to suit themselves, subject only to the broad limitations of the law, and the investor who subsequently buys the stock automatically subscribes to these articles.

Amendments to a corporation's articles may usually be made by an affirmative vote at a stockholders' meeting, effective as soon as a formal notice is filed with the proper incorporation officials. However, the state codes usually stipulate the procedure which must be followed and often forbid changes adverse to the interests of any special group of stockholders, such as preferred stockholders, unless this group concurs in the action. Sometimes the corporate articles contain clauses which protect stockholders by forbidding certain types of amendments, as well as mergers and other similar actions, unless large majorities of each class of stockholders consent.

Some states (and the federal government in the case of national banks) prescribe standard charters for banks, insurance companies, and certain other classes of corporations. These prescribed charters may vary or be amended only in limited fashion—for example, to authorize large or small numbers of shares as needed.

The nature of corporate articles may be seen from the following outline, which is taken from the Nevada corporation code. Nevada was chosen because its law is typical and conveniently concise. The articles are required to state:[5]

1   The name of the corporation. . . .

2   The name . . . of the city . . . in which its principal office or place of business is to be located in this state. . . .

3   The nature of the business . . . to be transacted . . . by the corporation. [In writing this section, banks, insurance companies, and utilities usually indicate their intentions, but general corporations usually enumerate every transaction they can imagine and then add "all other lawful business."]

4   The amount of the total authorized capital stock . . . and the number and par value [including no par value] of the shares. . . . If the corporation is to issue more than one class of stock . . . a description of the different classes thereof [with regard to number of shares authorized, and to voting and other rights] . . . as to amount of preference . . . , rate of dividends, premium on redemption, conversion price, or otherwise. . . .

5   Whether the members of the governing board shall be styled directors or trustees, and the number. . . .

---

[5] Explanatory phrases in brackets are added by the authors.

6 Whether . . . stock . . . shall be subject to assessment. . . .

7 The names . . . of the incorporators. . . .

8 Whether or not the corporation is to have perpetual existence. . . .

9 The . . . articles . . . may also contain . . . provisions for the regulation of the business and for the conduct of the affairs of the corporation, and [on] the rights, powers or duties of the directors or stockholders, or any classes of stockholders, or holders of the bonds or other obligations of the corporation, or providing for the . . . distribution . . . of the profits of the said corporation; provided such provisions are not contrary to the laws of this state.

The importance of the corporate articles to investors can scarcely be over-stated, particularly in connection with items 4 and 9 on this list. Although prospective stockholders frequently believe that corporations are so orthodox in framing their articles that special investigations are unnecessary, this cannot be accepted as a sound conclusion. Important differences occur, and frequently. Since the outstanding features of all important corporations' articles are summarized in the investment reference manuals and in the prospectuses which offer new securities for sale, it is foolish for an investor to ignore this aspect of any prospective investment. Desirable and objectionable features in corporate articles will be discussed at several later points in this book.

ISSUANCE AND TRANSFER OF STOCK

The corporation laws of most states provide that new shares of corporate stock may be issued only when they are (1) authorized in the articles of incorporation, (2) approved for issuance by the stockholders, and (3) ordered sold and issued by the directors. In some cases new issues must also be approved by the corporation commissioner or some other regulatory agency. When all requirements have been met, the process of stock issuance in nearly all cases consists of filling out a stock certificate for the stockholder and entering the proper record on the stock ledger for the corporation.

A stock certificate is usually an engraved or lithographed document about 8 by 11 inches in size on which are entered the stockholder's name, the number of shares, and the date the certificate is issued. The face of the certificate will state the name of the corporation, the state of incorporation, the class of stock, and various other details about the company and stock. It will bear the printed signature of company officers and the manual signatures of a transfer agent and (usually) a registrar. On the reverse side of the certificate there is usually a verbatim copy of the portion of the corporation's articles outlining the features of the different classes of stock (this will be omitted if only one class is authorized) and a form for the stockholder to fill out when he assigns his stock to a purchaser, donee, or other transferee.

Corporations are careful about issuance of stock certificates. Due precautions are taken against forgeries, all certificates are numbered and recorded by number, and the number of shares is either engraved on the certificate or punched out in a forgery-proof manner. The transfer agent who issues new certificates may be a company official or employee, but most large corporations engage a bank or trust company to perform this service. The transfer agent is instructed not to issue new certificates unless certificates for a corresponding number of old shares are returned to him properly endorsed for reissue, or unless he has proper evidence that new shares are to be issued as requested. The registrar is always an officer of a bank or trust company and independent of both issuing corporation and transfer agent; his job is to countersign the transfer agent's new certificates if a corresponding number of old shares are canceled out or if evidence of the propriety of an additional issue is presented.[6]

When a stockholder sells his stock, or when for any reason he wishes to assign it or to have all or part of it reissued in another name, he must sign the assignment form on the back of the certificate. The certificate can then be sent in to the transfer agent, who will issue the new certificate(s) as instructed. However, large corporations do not find it convenient to keep signature files on their stockholders; so most of them decline to accept transfer instructions unless the stockholder's signature is guaranteed by the added endorsement of a bank, trust company, or securities broker.

Stockholders frequently wish to assign their stock certificates to banks or other lenders as collateral for loans. Since it is not desirable to endorse such a temporary assignment on a stock certificate, the banks have developed a separate assignment form for this purpose. When the note is repaid, this separate form can be destroyed, and the original certificate remains unimpaired. The corporation does not even need to be notified of the loan transaction. It continues to send corporate notices and pay dividends to the stockholder without interruption.

Lost stock certificates are not salable or negotiable by the finder, since they can be transferred only by the signed order of the stockholder of record or by his agent. However, transfer agents will usually refuse to issue replacements to holders who claim to have lost their certificates unless they are furnished with a surety bond which will indemnify the transfer agent if the "lost" instrument turns up in the hands of a legitimate holder.[7]

[6] Investors sometimes learn about these things in the hard way. In Los Angeles in 1927 the Julian Petroleum Corporation failed, after company officers had issued and sold over 3,000,000 preferred shares, of which only 600,000 were authorized. There was no registrar, or this could not have happened. In this case the catastrophe was compounded by the fact that there was also no audit by independent accountants, and someone managed to steal or dissipate most of the company's assets. At the present time, many corporations do not have stock registrars or adequate audits.

[7] Recently a typical corporate transfer agency reported that it replaced lost bonds and preferred stock when furnished with a perpetual surety bond in amount equal to 2 times the face value of the lost certificate; the premium on the surety bond would be 2 per cent of the amount of the surety bond. On a lost common stock or convertible bond, the perpetual surety bond had to be written for an indeterminant amount, at a pre-

The corporation's stock ledger will show at all times the name and address of each stockholder and the number of each certificate he holds, the date of its issuance, and the number of shares represented. A different stock ledger will be kept for each class of stock.

Since the stockholder list in most big corporations is constantly changing, it is necessary for dividends, stock purchase rights, voting privileges at stockholders' meetings, and other benefits to be assigned by the directors to stockholders "of record" at the close of business on stated days. These days are known as "stock-of-record" days. For example, if the directors of United States Steel Corporation decide at a meeting on March 1 that they wish to pay a dividend of $1 per share about April 1, they might order the treasurer to pay $1 per share on April 1 to stockholders of record at the close of business on March 20. The list of stockholders would be determined as of that date, thus giving the treasurer 11 days to prepare the checks before the designated mailing date on April 1.

However, a purchaser of the stock on the stock-of-record date would not be able to get the endorsed certificate from the seller and have it transferred to his name in time to obtain the dividend. So securities dealers designate a day 5 business days before the stock-of-record day as the *ex-dividend* day, the first day when a stock transaction does not also transfer the pending dividend. Since the purchaser on this day no longer obtains the dividend, he pays less for the stock.

These normal corporate procedures suggest a number of personal policies for wise investors. Clearly, it is unnecessary to invest in the stocks of corporations which do not employ disinterested registrars and competent external auditors to check on the issuance of stock; there are plenty of stocks available which have these protective devices. Second, it is important to guard securities from fire, theft, and misplacement by keeping them in a safe deposit box, in a good safe, or in the custody of an absolutely reliable securities broker. Third, it is neither necessary nor desirable to sign the assignment form on the back of a stock certificate until it is finally delivered for sale or transfer. Fourth, it is important to notify the corporation immediately if any security is lost or mislaid, so that sale or transfer to an innocent third party can be prevented.

DIVIDENDS: NATURE AND TYPES

Although the term *dividend* is ordinarily used to mean a cash payment to stockholders out of the past or present earnings of the corporation, it is also used on

---

mium cost of 6 per cent of the value of the lost certificate. These surety bond premiums were payable only once, but the loser of the certificate had to agree to reimburse the surety company if the surety ever had to pay a claim. If the surety company doubted the moral or financial integrity of the professed loser of a certificate, it simply declined to issue him a surety bond unless provided with collateral sufficient to absorb any possible claim.

occasion to designate distributions of stock, bonds, or property of various kinds. These latter distributions may be made out of earnings, but frequently are not. In view of the multitude of factors which may motivate noncash dividends, it seems best to discuss them separately under the headings Stock Dividends and Property Dividends and to confine the present section to the ordinary variety of cash dividends.

The great majority of successful American corporations pay four dividends yearly on each class of stock, at approximate quarterly intervals. A few pay monthly, semiannually, or annually, and a similar few make disbursements at irregular intervals. Concerns with erratic earnings obviously must pay when they can. These remarks apply equally well to both preferred and common stocks.

As respects the amounts paid on each successive distribution, corporate policies vary considerably. Preferred stocks usually get regular and equal periodic dividends, unless poor earnings, payments on arrears, or participations cause differences. Common stocks usually receive payments based on one of three identifiable plans:

1 *Regular dividends at infrequently revised rates.* Payments at a rate which can be maintained under normal conditions for months or years, though subject to growth or cyclical change. This is the policy of most substantial, well-established corporations. Examples: American Telephone, BankAmerica Corporation, General Foods, Safeway Stores.

2 *Moderate regular dividends plus extras as warranted.* Very widely used when a stable basic dividend is warranted but extra payments are desired as earned. Examples: General Motors, du Pont, U.S. Steel, Sears Roebuck.

3 *Amount and time of each dividend dependent on the situation.* Less popular with investors than other methods but used by some concerns in cyclical situations. Examples: Great Northern Iron Ore Properties, McIntyre Porcupine Mines, Pan American Sulphur Company.

DIVIDENDS: CORPORATE OBJECTIVES

Affirmative decisions with respect to dividend payments are made in practically all instances by the directors of the corporation. Neither preferred nor common stockholders have any contractual rights which entitle them to receive dividends. They will get them, in the order of preference as established in the corporation's articles, when and if the directors order the payments.

The fact that the corporation's directors have authority over dividend policy does not mean, of course, that an established and capricious board can refuse indefinitely to make payments when the corporation is in a position to pay. If a corporation should and normally would pay dividends, minority stockholders can get a court order which will compel payments.[8] But the directors' preferences are entitled to great weight in such matters, and the courts will not interfere unless the directors' attitude amounts almost to an abuse of discretion.

It is to be expected that directors will order dividend payments only after reviewing the interests of both the corporation and its stockholders. If the corporation has accumulated some surplus out of earnings,[9] if there is presently a more than adequate cash balance, and if the cash is not soon to be needed for working capital, plant expansion, debt retirement, or possible losses, dividends are in order. If the corporation is well equipped and virtually debt-free, as is National Biscuit Company, almost the entire current earnings may be distributed. If money for expansion is still needed, a corporation whose stock is widely held might find a liberal dividend policy advantageous because the attractive dividend would make the stockholders willing to buy new securities from the corporation at frequent intervals. The American Telephone and Telegraph Company is the outstanding exponent of this principle. However, a corporation whose stock is held in large blocks might find new prorata share offerings not acceptable to many of its large holders; such a corporation is likely to limit dividends and retain its earnings, if it needs money for expansion or debt retirement. Large stockholders are likely to prefer low dividends for another reason: dividends are fully subject to personal income taxes. If earnings are retained by the company and invested in expansion, the stockholder's personal income tax does not reach them, even though they cause his shares to rise in value; and if he ultimately realizes these gains in cash by selling some of his stock, he will pay only a relatively modest "capital gains" tax. These considerations, as well as others less commonly encountered, are likely to shape each corporation's dividend policy. The investor who understands such policies before buying stock may avoid unwelcome surprises.

DIVIDENDS: LEGAL AND CONTRACTUAL FACTORS

Attention has already been directed to the fact that cash dividend payments are usually made only out of accumulated earned surplus (prior earnings) or current earnings, since law and business practice discourage the payment of dividends out of paid-in funds. However, many states permit payment of preferred dividends from paid-in funds, and common stock payments may be made in some instances, if the directors feel that such action is advisable.

A second legal factor of note involves the corporation's own contractual commitments. It has become customary for bond indentures and bank loan agree-

---

[8] *Dodge v. Ford Motor Co.*, 204 Mich. 459 (1919).

[9] Accounting practice is now tending to substitute the term *retained earnings* for the historic term *surplus*. Since the latter is still used in corporation law, it will also be used in this chapter.

ments to forbid corporate dividends, especially those paid on common stock, when the corporation's cash holdings or net current assets fail to exceed a prescribed sum. Also, such agreements commonly require dividends to be paid only from earnings subsequent to the date of the loan or forbid them unless surplus exceeds a stated sum. In a few cases preferred stocks are protected by clauses in the corporation's articles forbidding dividends on common stocks except when similar cash and surplus conditions are fulfilled. Few of these restrictions have affected payments during the prosperous years from 1946 through 1972, but many could become significant if earning power declines in years ahead.

A third legal factor which has important bearing on corporate dividend practice is embodied in corporate tax law.[10] These influences are varied. For example, certain types of investment companies can escape *corporate* income taxes if they pay all of their net income out in dividends to their stockholders; consequently, most eligible ones do this. As an example with opposite effect, double taxation of subsidiary and parent corporations successively on the same income under certain conditions induces the parent company to cause the subsidiary to limit its dividends, thus reducing the parent's income and its capacity to pay. Another possible tax factor is found in the much-discussed Section 531 of the Internal Revenue Code. This measure imposes a heavy tax on "accumulated earnings," ostensibly to compel any earnings not actually needed in the business to be disbursed in dividends. However, it is legitimate to accumulate earnings for future debt repayment or for future expansion, so the Section is very difficult to enforce.

The fourth major legal factor affecting dividend policy is limited to public utilities, banks, insurance companies, and similar institutions whose finances are regulated by public authority. The regulatory agencies often have discretionary authority to order or to suggest firmly that dividend policy be subordinated to expansion or debt retirement. The corporation has little choice but to comply.

---

[10] At the rates effective in 1972, the federal corporate income tax absorbs 22 per cent of the first $25,000 of taxable corporate income and 48 per cent of any excess over $25,000. A deficit incurred in any year can be "carried back" into the 3 preceding years to offset the taxable income of those years and obtain refunds, or "carried forward" into the 5 succeeding years to cancel out future taxes. Net long-term capital gains on sale of equipment, real estate, or securities held as operating facilities or investments and not as inventories are taxed separately at a maximum rate of 30 per cent and are not included in taxable corporate income.

Taxable corporate income includes earnings from business operations after deduction of all proper expenses including depreciation, general taxes, state income taxes, and bond interest; plus interest earned on receivables, corporate bonds, and federal bonds; plus (approximately) 15 per cent of dividends received from domestic tax-paying corporations. Income from state and municipal bonds is not taxable. Holding companies and domestic subsidiaries may file a "consolidated return" (i.e., as though they constituted one corporation) if 80 per cent or more of the subsidiaries' common stocks are owned by the group; separate returns incur a small additional tax. Foreign income taxes paid by foreign branches or by foreign subsidiaries on earnings paid to the parent in dividends can normally be deducted from the domestic tax. Earnings of foreign subsidiaries are in most cases (but not always) exempt from domestic income tax until repatriated.

In addition to the federal taxes, corporations pay state income taxes averaging about 5 per cent. Since these are deductible in computing the federal tax, their effect is to add about 2½ per cent of taxable income to the total tax burden.

CASH DIVIDEND POLICY: SUMMARY

Since the dividend prospect is very important in establishing the value of a stock and in determining whether it is suitable for a given portfolio, it is important for an investor to review and understand the controlling factors in each case. Information can be had from the usual sources—prospectuses, annual reports, newspapers and periodicals, financial services—and facts not specifically stated may usually be deduced from the corporate history. The salient points to seek would appear to be:

1 Adequacy of net current assets and cash
2 Adequacy and stability of earnings
3 Requirements for expansion and debt retirement
4 Directors' policies regarding expansion and debt retirement
5 Directors' attitudes toward dividend payments
6 Preferences (or circumstances) of dominant stockholder groups
7 Adequacy of earned surplus
8 Contractual restrictions on dividends
9 Restrictions imposed by regulatory agencies
10 Effect of dividend policies on the corporation's own taxes

Although policies of individual corporations vary widely, the typical big American company pays out in an average year about 60 per cent of its earnings in dividends. This percentage rises in years of reduced earnings and falls in years when earnings rise because most companies prefer to pay stable dividends and increase their dividend rates only as they are confident they can maintain them. The percentage of earnings paid out is also affected by price-level changes; prolonged price inflation forces companies to retain more earnings to replace and expand their plant and equipment and to augment working capital.

At the beginning of 1973, a dividend reinvestment service was available to the stockholders of AT & T, Marine Midland, Crown Zellerbach, and about 200 other large corporations. This service permits an investor to reinvest his dividends in additional shares of the company's stock. A bank, usually the firm's transfer agent, handles the transaction for much less than a broker would charge. Since all shares purchased are held in trust by the bank, stockholders can buy fractional shares, computed to three or four decimal places, which also earn dividend income. The increasing popularity of this device, long available to mutual-fund shareholders, appeared to reflect both the resistance of small investors to rising brokerage commissions and the response of companies to shrinking stockholder lists.

STOCK DIVIDENDS

Stock dividends may be defined as prorata payments to common stockholders of additional amounts of common stock. Such payments increase the number of shares in each stockholder's hands but do not alter his aggregate investment in the corporation nor his prorata interest in it.

Stock dividends may be classified roughly into two groups: big ones and small ones. A big-percentage stock dividend, say from 10 per cent on up, will reduce the per share price of the stock, since the same corporate assets and earning power must now be divided among more shares. This may be desirable to the stockholders, since lower-price shares sometimes sell more readily and at a relatively higher price. Such a change may pave the way for a corporate offering of new stock by establishing a per share price which is within the reach of more prospective purchasers. Stock dividends may also be used to bring the value of the stock into equality or proportionality with that of another company, to facilitate a merger or combination by exchange of stock.

Small stock dividends, ranging from 10 per cent down, are generally used when an expanding corporation needs most of its cash earnings in the business or when loan agreements or regulatory limitations prevent disbursements of cash. For example, in 1972 the vigorously expanding Sun Oil Company and rapidly growing Papercraft Corporation were supplementing modest cash dividends with small stock dividends, while the holding companies which owned the stocks of several of the undercapitalized but profitable California savings and loan associations could pay out only stock dividends.

From the standpoint of pure logic, the prorata distribution of a few extra shares to stockholders who already own the corporation makes little sense. The holder who retains his new shares has still the same percentage ownership in the company, and the one who sells his stock dividend could have accomplished the same purpose by selling a few of his original shares. Yet the small stock dividend is popular with most stockholders, at least in prosperous years when stock ownership appears safe and profitable. Apparently the stockholders feel that the new stock is a valuable dividend which has the great merit of being tax-exempt, since common stock dividends paid in additional common stock are not taxable income. Stockholders who need cash can sell their dividend shares at moderate cost and obtain cash income which is taxable only to the extent that the cash realized represents a capital gain over the prorata cost of the shares sold. But there are disadvantages. Small stock dividends result in thousands of fractional-share claims; the company must either provide facilities through which the stockholders can sell these or buy matching fractions, or it must sell all the fractions in a bulk stock offering and remit the proceeds to the entitled stockholders. The total expenses involved in a small stock dividend will amount to $1 to $2.50 per stockholder. Furthermore, a small stock dividend is certain to allot one, two, or three shares each to many small stockholders who urgently need cash income. Sales in these quantities through stockbrokers are inconvenient and expensive, and the stockholders are likely to be unhappy unless the company subsidizes optional selling facilities for these shares also.

Stock dividends require the corporation to transfer an amount equal to the

market value of the new stock from its earned surplus account to its capital stock
accounts. This rule is intended to protect investors by making sure that companies declare stock dividends only out of past or current earnings.

DIVIDEND PAYABLE IN PROPERTY

Dividends payable in property usually fall into three categories: (1) those paid
in the bonds or preferred stock of the paying corporations, (2) those paid in the
securities of other corporations, and (3) those paid in merchandise. Ordinarily,
none of the three is common. In the past few years, however, the liquidation or
voluntary reorganization of many corporations has been accomplished by the
distribution of subsidiaries' stocks to the stockholders of the parent company.
A distribution which sets up a former subsidiary or business department as a new
independent company is termed a *spin-off*.

The procedures involved in the payment of property dividends are similar to
those followed in the payment of ordinary cash or stock dividends, with the addition of proper approval by stockholders if the dividend is a liquidating one. To
the receiving stockholders, the income tax situation could be quite complicated.
Generally speaking, securities received as a liquidating dividend or in a spin-off
are not taxable income but must be identified and recorded as representing a portion of the original investment, at a proper portion of the original cost. In most
other cases, property dividends are ordinary taxable dividend income, to be recorded at market value. Because of the complexity of these situations, corporations paying property dividends usually obtain rulings from tax authorities and
advise their stockholders on the proper accounting procedures.

STOCK SPLITS

The term *stock split* is applied to a case in which a corporation reduces the par
value or stated value of its stock and gives its stockholders a larger number of
shares having the same aggregate par value or stated value in exchange for their
old shares. For example, General Electric in 1971 split its $5 par common stock 2
for 1, giving each holder two new $2.50 par common shares for each $5 par share
previously held. Similarly, in 1970 Dr. Pepper Company split its no par stock 3
for 1 by issuing to stockholders two additional shares for each one previously
held without making any change in the aggregate stated value of its capital account. Thus stock splits increase the number of shares outstanding without in any
way affecting total capital or total net worth. The result is to reduce the per share
value of the stock accordingly. Indeed, this is the purpose of the split, for stock
whose value exceeds $70 or $80 per share is often neither as popular nor as salable
as its quality deserves. Stock splits are fairly common actions, especially in bull
markets or when new stock sales are contemplated. Frequently they are followed

by establishment of a new dividend rate which is proportionately greater than that paid before the split. As a rule, investors regard stock splits as bullish gestures reflective of expansion, good earnings, prospects for higher dividends, and hopes for higher share prices.

The additional shares received in a stock split are not regarded as taxable stockholder income. It is assumed that the total shares held after the split represent the same investment, whose cost must now be prorated over the larger number of shares.

ASSESSMENTS

Relatively few corporations now have legal power to impose assessments on their stockholders, and even in cases of insolvency the device is little used. Only in mining and small promotional concerns, where initial capital may need to be supplemented under possibly adverse operating conditions, is the assessment economically feasible. When state law and corporate articles permit assessments, the usual provision authorizes the directors to require the additional cash contribution on a per share basis on or before a date which they designate. Proper notice must be sent to the stockholders. In event of nonpayment, the defaulting shares may be seized and sold by the directors, the assessment deducted from the sales prices, and the balance (if any) remitted to the expropriated stockholder.

RIGHTS

Corporations frequently raise money for expansion by selling additional securities to their common stockholders. Usually the additional securities are common stocks, but preferred stocks or bonds are sometimes sold in this way also.[11] Since the common stockholders are the residual owners of the corporation, no injustice is done if the new securities are offered pro rata at a price below their market value. The low price will assure the sale of the securities, thus obtaining the money for the corporation, and the stockholders may even feel that the privilege of buying the new securities at a low price is analogous to a special dividend.

When stockholders are offered the privilege to subscribe pro rata to new securities, the privilege accruing to one old share is termed a *right*. If the offer permits the purchase of 1 new share for each 10 held, a stockholder owning 100 old shares

[11] A favorite device is to sell convertible bonds or preferred stock under rights. The bonds or preferred stock will be good grade, and if the conversion terms are attractive, they will be eagerly bought. Later, piecemeal conversion into common stock will complete the plan for ultimate common stock financing without the depressing effect on the stock market which the direct sale of the new stock might bring. The American Telephone and Telegraph Company is the foremost exponent of this technique, using, ever since World War II, debenture bonds convertible into common stock and, in 1971, a $1.4 billion issue of convertible preferred stock.

would receive 100 rights, which would entitle him to buy 10 new shares. The offering may be a large one, permitting the purchase of as much as one new share for each two held, or it may be a small one, such as one new for each 20 held.

Technically, rights are handled in a manner similar to dividends. Assuming that the charter properly authorizes additional stock and that a stockholders' meeting has approved it, the directors would then order rights to be sent to stockholders of record at the close of business on a stipulated date. The rights themselves would consist of transferable lithographed certificates entitling the holder to return them within the prescribed period (usually 2 or 3 weeks) accompanied by his check, to obtain the promised stock. Rights not exercised within the prescribed period usually "expire" and become valueless. Stockholders who do not wish to exercise their rights should consequently sell them promptly, so that the purchaser may have time to use them before they expire.

It is obvious that rights to purchase new stock below its market price would have value. The nature of that value may be illustrated as follows: Assume that the stock of the Example Corporation is selling at $30 per share on July 23, after announcement that stockholders of record July 30 will receive rights to subscribe to one new share at $24.50 for each 10 shares held. It may reasonably be calculated on July 23 that any 10-share block of stock now worth $30 per share, or a total of $300, is about to be supplemented by a $24.50 cash investment, making a total value of $324.50. This new total will, however, then represent 11 shares, or $29.50 per share. If the future value of the stock is to be $29.50 and the subscription price is $24.50 when accompanied by 10 rights, it is clear that the 10 rights save the subscriber just $5, or 50 cents per right. It is equally clear that the 50 cents per right, or a total of $5 needed to bring the new $24.50 share up to an equality of $29.50 with each of the other shares, will be raised by chipping 50 cents off each of the old $30 shares on the *ex-rights* date which, like the ex-dividend date described earlier, is usually set 5 days before the stock of record date.[12]

---

[12] The securities markets have a formula for the evaluation of rights to buy additional common stock, which is worked out as follows: Let M equal the market price of the stock, S the subscription price, N the number of rights needed to obtain the privilege of buying one new share, and R the value of a right. Before the ex-rights date,

$$R = \frac{M - S}{N + 1}$$

In the case of the Example Corporation, M is $30, S is $24.50, and N is 10. Consequently,

$$R = \frac{\$30 - \$24.50}{10 + 1} = \frac{\$5.50}{11} = 50 \text{ cents}$$

After the ex-rights date, the formula becomes

$$R = \frac{M - S}{N}$$

In this case the market price of the stock has already declined because the value of the right has been separated from it, but if no other market change has occurred, we would compute

$$R = \frac{\$29.50 - \$24.50}{10} = \frac{\$5}{10} = 50 \text{ cents}$$

The value of the right is therefore no mysterious bonus from Santa Claus; it is just a portion of the stockholder's original equity, which he can salvage only by exercise or sale.

Rights to purchase stocks which are actively traded on the public markets usually have an active market themselves. In most cases the prices on stock and rights will be mathematically related, since no careful purchaser would pay more for stock than a rights purchase plus a subscription would cost him, or vice versa. Obviously, the value of the rights will rise and fall in proportion to the difference between the market price of the stock and the subscription price for the new shares. Since the latter is usually a fixed sum, the rights must fluctuate as the market price of the stock fluctuates, and in much greater proportion.

When preferred stocks or bonds or the securities of subsidiaries are offered to stockholders under a rights arrangement, it is clear that the relationship between the value of the right and the value of the stock will not be necessarily close. The value of the stock will decline by something approximating the value of the right after the ex-rights date, but related market fluctuations cannot be expected.

In most cases a right is not regarded as taxable income when received by a stockholder from a corporation but represents, instead, a portion of his original investment.[13] This is true in nearly all cases where the right carries the privilege of buying additional common stock, bonds or preferred stock convertible into common stock, or the common stock of an important subsidiary. Rights to buy nonconvertible bonds or preferred stock are usually regarded as taxable income to the full extent of their value.

Although the rights technique frequently offers stockholders subscription privileges requiring investment of important sums of money on very short notice, the practice is popular with most investors. In fact, corporations like American Telephone and Telegraph Company and Pacific Gas and Electric Company, which have used this device again and again, are popular with many investors because they accept occasional additional investments in this way, free of brokerage charges and other incidental costs to the investor. And if the investor is unable or unwilling to exercise rights when they are sent to him, they are usually salable through brokers at a reasonable cost. The only real investment objection to the rights device comes from small investors whose few rights do not permit either economical subscription to whole shares or sale of rights in economical quantities and from holders of large blocks of stock who find the added investments asked of them to be burdensomely large.

Most companies using the rights device find that a fairly large percentage of

---

[13] If the stockholder sells his rights, the computed portion of the original cost of his stock is allotted to the rights and used in determining a capital gain or loss. If he subscribes to the new stock, he allots this computed portion plus the subscription price as the cost of his new stock, but no taxable gain or loss is realized unless he sells the new stock. If he lets the rights expire, his original cost remains with his original shares and he sustains no tax loss on the rights.

the rights cannot be exercised by the receiving stockholders and are therefore offered for sale. Furthermore, many stockholders receive numbers of rights which do not divide evenly into the numbers required to buy shares of stock; these stockholders need to sell their surplus rights or to buy a few. Finally, many small stockholders simply ignore their rights, permit them to expire, and sustain a loss thereby. These problems are met by the companies in various ways: most companies pay securities underwriters to buy rights in the markets and resell them to other investors who can be persuaded to exercise them; most companies also arrange to buy and sell small quantities of surplus rights for their stockholders free of charge; and various other expedients are used.

EXCHANGES OR RECAPITALIZATIONS

Occasionally corporations find it advantageous to retire certain outstanding securities in exchange for others, or to rewrite their articles to make major changes in their outstanding stocks, or to merge with subsidiaries in a manner which effects a major financial readjustment. Such action may be taken to eliminate securities with obsolete or undesirable features, or to simplify the group of securities comprising the capital structure, or to eliminate securities whose preferential rights prevent successful new financing, or to retire preferred stock with burdensome accumulated dividends attached, or possibly to scale down the entire capital structure to a size proportional to a shrunken earning power. In any of these situations, the usual procedure calls for the adoption of a "plan of reorganization" by the directors, the voting stockholders, and (usually) by each affected class of stockholders, voting separately. The plan will amend the corporate articles to authorize the desired new securities and order their issuance in exchange for the outstanding ones which are to be retired. Sometimes the plan will be binding upon all stockholders, once it is formally adopted. In other instances the exchange provided in the plan is optional to each stockholder; or there may be a choice of exchange offers.

Procedures of this sort are of great concern to the investor because they may result in either advantage or disadvantage to him. The state corporation laws and to a lesser extent the articles of incorporation should have provisions designed to prevent injustice in framing such plans. However, plans which inflict considerable sacrifice on classes of securityholders are possible in many states, if the proper majorities can be persuaded to vote for them. Investors owning stocks in weak corporations, and particularly the owners of preferred stocks, are vulnerable to this hazard. Such investors should be familiar with their rights under the state code and their own corporate articles.

An exchange or recapitalization ordinarily does not give rise to a taxable gain or loss to the stockholder, provided the corporation undertook it for normal business reasons. The new securities received by the stockholder would simply replace those surrendered by him, and for income tax purposes their cost to him would be the cost of his original holdings. However, plans which give an investor bonds in return for stock or a lesser amount of old bonds may result in taxable income.

REPURCHASE OF STOCK

Practically all corporations have the legal right to repurchase shares of their own stock from their stockholders. Such transactions must follow procedures authorized by the corporation laws of the state of incorporation, must of course be made at fair prices and under conditions which give all stockholders reasonable opportunity to participate in them, and the corporation must not expend so much on them that creditors or other stockholders are jeopardized. In addition, some states further discourage repurchase of common stock by requiring that sums so expended be charged against earned surplus. Large repurchases in such cases would soon exhaust the surplus and effectively prevent further dividend payments.

Stock repurchased by the corporation ceases to draw dividends or to vote while it is held in the corporate treasury. It may be resold by the corporation or reissued in exchange for the stock or property of other corporations; in either case, it again attains full status as outstanding stock.

Corporations buy their own stock for various reasons. During the stock market break of 1929, Transamerica Corporation bought large quantities of its own stock in an attempt to keep the market price up to what the officers regarded as the "true" value of the stock. In 1931, Pacific Finance Corporation bought quantities of its own stock at $15 per share, knowing that the corporate assets amounted to $25 per share and that every share retired at $15 netted a $10 gain to the remaining stockholders. During the years 1960–1963, the American Radiator and Standard Sanitary Corporation repurchased 1,693,000 shares of its stock, about 14½ per cent of the total, using cash no longer needed in the business. In 1970, Doric Corporation bought in about 8 per cent of its stock, at a price slightly below book value, to strengthen the future earning power of its remaining shares. And since 1960, hundreds of corporations have bought substantial quantities of their own stock in order to have it available for employee bonuses and stock purchase plans or for use in acquiring the stock or properties of other corporations.[14]

Corporate stock repurchases are most commonly made through a broker in the securities markets. Occasionally, a corporation may invite its stockholders to make "tenders" at prices of their choice; the corporation may then accept the

[14] The routine of authorizing new issues of stock and getting it "registered" with the Securities and Exchange Commission, getting it issued, and getting it listed on the stock exchanges is so cumbersome that the purchase of existing stock is more convenient. Besides, the price impact of judiciously timed purchases may be beneficial.

cheapest tenders. Or the corporation may offer to buy, from each stockholder who cares to sell, a stated fraction of his holdings at a stated price. If the stock in question is common stock, the corporation may not compel any stockholder to sell except by an elaborate process of stockholders' meeting, amendment of the articles, and recapitalization, which would affect every stockholder proportionately. If a preferred stock were involved, the situation would be the same, unless the preferred stock were subject to a sinking fund or to a redemption provision in the articles. These features of preferred stocks are discussed in Chapter 5.

Purchase or sale by a corporation of its own stock is chiefly significant to the investor because of its effect on the market price of his stock. However, such important matters as the company's cash position, its surplus position, and the remaining assets and earning power per share of stock may be affected by repurchases of stock.

ACQUISITIONS AND MERGERS

Two or more independent corporations frequently desire to combine for business or financial advantage. The object may be larger-scale operation, the unification of complementary product lines, or the integration of a raw-materials source with a processing operation. Or it may aim at improved diversification for the enterprises concerned: uniting a cyclical producer of capital goods with a manufacturer of stable consumer products, or joining a maker of defense items with a producer of civilian goods. Still other possible aims might be to employ the stagnating financial resources of a mature, nongrowing company in a new, rapidly expanding line of business, or for a growing but financially strained firm to unite with a company possessing large cash or borrowing-power resources. Sometimes the combination solves a management problem by enabling key individuals to serve the entire operation or by providing competent successors for officers who wish to retire.

The proposal to combine may originate with the management of the companies, with important stockholder groups, or in some other way; but however the idea may be initiated, it is likely to be brought finally to the majority of the stockholders as a well-developed proposal to which the managements and large stockholders have already agreed. Such proposals are usually about as equitable as two bargaining managements with diverse investor interests can make them, but they are unlikely to seem entirely fair to everyone concerned.

The procedures used for combining corporations are many and varied, but a firm that takes the initiative in acquiring another usually does so by employing one of three methods: (1) It purchases the *stock* of the acquired company, whose stockholders receive either cash or stock in the acquiring firm; (2) it buys the *assets* of the acquired firm, paying either cash or new stock which may then be distributed to the selling stockholders as a liquidating dividend; or (3) the acquired company is absorbed through merger, a statutory process which joins the identities, assets, liabilities, and stockholder interests of the predecessor firms into a single corporation.[15]

An acquiring corporation may obtain control of another by purchasing its stock in the open market. However, the purchasing company generally prefers not to buy any stock unless it can obtain almost the entire issue at a reasonable price. Consequently, the acquirer usually negotiates first with the management and large stockholders of the other company and, when agreement is reached, opens an escrow in a bank or trust company through which the same terms are offered to other stockholders. The escrow terms usually stipulate that no transaction will occur and the offer will be withdrawn unless the desired amount of stock reaches the escrow by a certain date. The offer-in-escrow may name a cash price, or more likely, it may propose payment in stock of the acquiring company. A cash offer obviously means that the selling stockholder may sustain a capital gain or loss; an exchange of stock for stock generally is a tax-free substitution. It is clear that there would be no way for a dissatisfied stockholder to keep others from selling their stock to an acquiring company, which could then elect its own officials and run the acquired company virtually as a division of its own business; but the dissenting holder could keep his own stock and obtain his usual prorata share of such dividends as the new management might disburse, as long as his corporation remained in business.

The sale of one company's entire assets to another usually requires the approval of the directors of both companies and a majority vote of the stockholders of the selling corporation. If the selling corporation is to be liquidated, the plans must include payment of all debts and the retirement of preferred stock before the final liquidating dividend is paid to the common stockholders; money for this must be provided or the acquiring corporation must assume the debts. When the sales proceeds are received in cash, the corporation will have no problem in financing the necessary payments to creditors and preferred stockholders, but the selling company will incur a tax on any capital gains which are realized, unless the sale is part of a total plan which involves prompt liquidation of the company. However, if liquidation follows after a cash sale, the common stockholders will presumably receive their liquidating dividend in cash; this could result in a taxable gain or loss to most of them. This complicated tax problem might be avoided if the selling corporation arranged to exchange its property for new securities in the purchasing corporation. Again, if prompt liquidation were a part of the plan, a taxable corporate gain or loss would be avoided, and a final liquidating distribution of the purchasing company's stock to the stockholders of the selling corporation would constitute a tax-exempt substitution of one security for another.

[15] Some financial writers reserve the term *merger* for a case in which one firm acquires the assets of the other and the latter loses its identity. Where two or more companies transfer their assets to a newly created corporation, these writers term the change a consolidation.

Mergers are worked out very exactly by contract between the merging firms, subject to all the restrictions imposed by law, and subject also to ratification by the voting stockholders. The process is roughly as follows: The directors of the firms to be merged work out a merger agreement which includes a complete set of articles of incorporation for the successor corporation[16] and a procedure for issuing stock in the new firm to the stockholders of each of the old ones. Bondholders need not be provided for; the new firm is automatically obligated on the debts of all its predecessors, and the merger process will not impair the validity of mortgages. The merger terms must satisfy the statutory requirements in each state in which any merging concern is incorporated. Large majorities of the voting stock of each merging corporation must usually approve the merger, and if state laws or corporate articles or bond indentures so require, the consent of majorities of preferred stockholders and bondholders may be necessary also. When all consents have been obtained, the merger may be declared consummated; but at this point many states, though not all, require that any dissenting preferred or common stockholder be given a reasonable time to refuse the merger and demand that his equity be appraised and paid to him in cash. The appraisal will not be generous, since it is usually based on an assumed liquidation of the company; but if the dissenter does not demand this option promptly, he will perforce participate in the merger on the terms thereof, for the original companies lose their identities and existence completely in the new one.

In general, it may be stated that few stockholders find it good business to demand cash payment as the means of avoiding participation in a merger. It is usually more profitable to sell the stock. Of course, the vast majority of stockholders do not disapprove proposed mergers. They usually agree with the managements that the mergers are desirable; and in the occasional instances in which vigorous stockholder opposition to a proposed merger develops, the deal is more than likely to be dropped. If a proposed merger plan is definitely unfair, an aggrieved stockholder can usually get the courts of the incorporating state to forbid it.

The terms of merger arrangements very commonly provide for the issuance of new securities, similar to those previously held, to the stockholders of the merging firms. That is, common stockholders usually get new common stock, and preferred stockholders usually get new preferred which is at least somewhat similar in privileges and dividend rights to their old stock. This practice naturally reduces resistance to the merger. However, it must be conceded that the combined firm will usually be different in size, nature of business, and capital structure from any of its predecessors; and in the process of framing new articles, many of the features of the old stocks may be dropped. Mergers are thus likely to change both the legal features and the quality of the securities held by some of the participants,

---

[16] The successor corporation might be one of the old firms, with its articles amended suitably, or it might be a new entity.

even when every effort is made to do justice to all concerned. Investors who chose the old securities to obtain these specific features and qualities may therefore be disappointed in the new arrangement; but an immediate financial loss is not often to be expected.

Ordinarily the securityholders involved in a merger will not realize a gain or loss for income tax purposes when they receive their new securities, since an appropriately planned merger is a tax-free reorganization under present federal law.

All these methods of combination have been used frequently since 1960, notably in the aggressive expansion of conglomerate-type, diversified companies. The most common method in 1971–1972 involved the purchase of the assets of one company by another, with the purchasing company assuming the debts of the seller and the selling company receiving common stock in the purchasing company for immediate distribution to its shareholders as a liquidating dividend.

HOLDING COMPANIES

Holding companies are concerns whose business includes investment in and control of other corporations through ownership of all or most of their common stock. The corporations thus controlled are called subsidiary companies. A portion of a subsidiary's common stock may be owned by outside shareholders, and these shares are termed the minority interest. Holding companies do not ordinarily own appreciable percentages of their subsidiaries' bonds.

Investors are interested in holding company problems because a large percentage of the nation's important corporations are holding companies and because the holding company form of organization poses certain financial problems which do not exist in a business operated by a single corporation. The problems center about the fact that all the corporations in a holding company system are still legally separate concerns. Their managements may be the same people and their policies may be coordinated, but their assets, incomes, and obligations are legally independent. Thus the cash holdings of a subsidiary are not available to the parent (holding) company unless the subsidiary pays a dividend, buys something from the parent, or makes a loan to it. Likewise, the parent's cash is available to the subsidiary only by means of a loan or other formal transaction. Dividends paid by a subsidiary are paid equitably (pro rata) on the stock held by the parent company and on that held by minority interests. If a subsidiary with substantial earnings is legally prevented from paying dividends (for example, by a provision in a bank loan agreement), the holding company has no means of obtaining these earnings as dividends, hence cannot credit them to its own earned surplus or add them to its cash account. Lacking cash and a surplus, it cannot pay dividends itself, even though its indirect earnings in the subsidiary are adequate. Obviously, a subsidiary without earnings or surplus cannot pay dividends, even though other subsidiaries of the same holding company and the holding company itself are prosperous. The debts of a subsidiary company are not the debts of the parent, and vice versa. To be sure, the parent company which permits a subsidiary to be forced into bankruptcy will probably lose its investment in the subsidiary, but the parent company is ordinarily under no obligation to throw good money after bad by paying the debts of an unsuccessful subsidiary which is not worth salvaging. Similarly, a sound subsidiary has no more duty to pay the debts of a faltering holding company than it has to pay those of any other stockholder.

This emphasis on the legal independence of different corporations should not, however, blind the reader to the fact that successful holding systems are usually substantially unified for both financial and operating purposes. For example, a cash-rich subsidiary can usually pay dividends to its holding company or make loans to it or to another subsidiary, and the holding company can use its dividend receipts or its own borrowings to assist any subsidiary. The whole resources of the group can thus be mobilized to finance the development of any member company, except in certain cases in the banking, public utility, and insurance fields where restrictive regulation may exist.

Holding companies often furnish their stockholders two sets of financial statements, one on a "corporate" basis and one on a "consolidated" basis. The statements on a corporate basis show the assets, liabilities, incomes, and expenses of the corporations separately, just as they legally stand. In that case the parent company's assets include the stocks it owns in the subsidiaries, and its income includes the dividends received from the subsidiaries. On the other hand, the consolidated statements show the entire group of companies as though they were one business.[17] On a consolidated balance sheet, all the companies' cash, receivables, and physical assets are shown as assets, and all the debt claims and stock owned by "outsiders," including the holding company's securityholders, are shown on the liabilities side of the statement; but intercompany debts and securities holdings are not shown, since they are meaningless if the companies are considered as one unit. On a consolidated income statement, all the companies' sales, expenses, and net incomes would be combined, except that intercompany payments would not be shown.

The following statements involving subsidiary corporations A and B and holding company H, though simplified, will illustrate the contrast between corporate and consolidated statements. In this case it is assumed that in addition to its own business, H owns 90 per cent of the common stocks of A and B but none of B's preferred. A and B each pay $1,000 per year in common dividends. The dividends paid by H are not shown, since they do not affect the consolidation. Examination of their statements will make clear the separate corporate positions of companies

---

[17] There are exceptions. "Consolidated" statements sometimes consolidate certain subsidiaries fully but treat the securities owned in others as investments. This is discussed in Chap. 14.

A, B, and H with respect to such vital matters as cash holding, debts, surplus, earnings, and the like. Their activities will be much influenced by these positions. But the aggregate position of the system as a whole, and particularly the scope of its earning power, will be shown by the consolidated statements. For example, it is only on the consolidated income statement that the entire $4,080 of earnings on the holding company stockholders' equity is clearly shown; and it is only on the consolidated balance sheet that their $29,300 of total equity ($25,000 stock account plus $4,300 surplus) is shown and compared with total system assets of $51,000. Most investors place particular stress on consolidated earnings as the

Corporate and consolidated balance sheet, December 31, 1972

	Subsidiary A	Subsidiary B	Holding Co. H	Consolidated companies
Assets:				
Cash	$ 1,000	$ 2,000	$ 500	$ 3,500
Other current assets	5,000	9,000	3,000	17,000
Fixed assets (net)	9,000	15,000	6,500	30,500
Stocks of subsidiaries at cost price			23,000	
Total	$15,000	$26,000	$33,000	$51,000
Liabilities:				
Debts, etc.	$ 3,000	$ 5,000	$ 1,000	$ 9,000
5 per cent preferred stock	0	6,000	4,000	10,000
Common stock	10,000	10,000	25,000	25,000
Minority interest in A and B common				2,700
Surplus (retained earnings)	2,000	5,000	3,000	4,300
Total	$15,000	$26,000	$33,000	$51,000

Corporate and consolidated income account, calendar year 1972

	Subsidiary A	Subsidiary B	Holding Co. H	Consolidated companies
Sales	$20,000	$45,000	$12,000	$77,000
Expenses and taxes	18,000	42,500	11,500	72,000
Dividend income	0	0	1,800	
Net income	2,000	2,500	2,300	5,000
Minority share (A and B common)				420
Preferred dividends	0	300	200	500
Earned for common	2,000	2,200	2,100	
Earned for H common				4,080

true measure of the earning power of a holding company investment, on the theory that earnings retained for capital expansion by a subsidiary are just as advantageous to a holding company stockholder as they would be if paid into the holding company and retained by it.

Holding company securities and the securities of their subsidiaries are not unsound or otherwise dangerous to investors, as a rule. There are, as has been noted, some legal intricacies in the use of multiple corporations which may make the shifting of cash through the system a little more difficult than in the case of a single corporation. This is especially true if the subsidiaries are publicly regulated utilities in which intercompany loans and dividends are subject to the approval of the regulating commissions. Also, minority holders of subsidiaries' common stocks may sometimes find that the plans and objectives of the holding company are not entirely in their best interests. Finally, there are certain regulatory measures, especially in the public utility and banking fields, which discriminate against the holding company form of organization. However, these factors do not seem important enough to justify the rejection of otherwise satisfactory investment choices.

JOINT VENTURES

The joint venture is another type of corporate operation which has appeared in great numbers in recent years, mostly because of the emergence of new products which require complementary technologies from several industries or which serve as markets or raw materials for several industries. For example, Dow Chemical Company and Corning Glass Works operate a jointly owned company, Dow Corning Corporation, which utilizes both chemical and glassmaking technologies in producing silicone products and hyper-pure silicon. The advantages of these joint ventures are obvious. The principal disadvantage seems to be a hostile attitude by the federal antitrust authorities; however, this has not yet resulted in many court prosecutions.

QUESTIONS AND PROBLEMS

1 Could California businessmen incorporate a corporation in Delaware and cause it to do all its business in Colorado? If they did so, which state laws would govern it with respect to its power to pay dividends, repurchase its stock, or merge with another corporation? With respect to the meaning of its contracts for the sale of merchandise?

2 Would a uniform federal incorporation law have significant advantages for corporations and investors? Would there be disadvantages?

3 If you had stock in a Maryland corporation and the management proposed a merger plan which seemed unfair to you, where could you ascertain your rights under the law?

4 Should stock dividends be free of income tax? What if a prosperous company desires to retain its cash for expansion and therefore pays a 5 per cent annual stock dividend, but employs a securities dealer to buy all proffered fractional and one- or two-share dividend certificates at market price for the shareholders without charging a commission, and resell them through a public offering?

5 Should corporation codes make it difficult for a company which is short of surplus (retained earnings) to pay dividends and/or repurchase its own stock, if creditors are not jeopardized and the action sustains the price of the stock in an adverse market?

6 Investigate and evaluate the dividend policies of several corporations, for example, Acme Markets, Bethlehem Steel, du Pont, Eastman Kodak, Commonwealth Edison, Beckman Instruments, Exxon, First Charter Financial, Dr. Pepper Company.

7 Enumerate several reasons for omission or limitation of corporate dividends. Are all these signs of corporate weakness?

8 Why are stock splits more common than large stock dividends? What is the difference?

9 If you held stock in a successful corporation which needed all its earnings in the business, would you advocate **(a)** no dividends, **(b)** small stock dividends, or **(c)** sale of additional stock under rights, with cash dividends continued? Why? Which system would keep the price of the stock the highest? What does American Telephone do in this regard? Why?

10 Should dividend policy, stock splits, and other corporate policies be aimed at maximizing the value of the stock, or solely at the corporation's strength and growth?

11 Do you advocate a corporation law which gives corporations maximum freedom to sell securities, pay dividends, repurchase stock, merge, etc., or do you advocate a law which attempts to define standards and procedures closely?

12 Why is it difficult to work out a merger which does not disappoint at least some of the stockholders? If outstanding bonds were left unchanged in their contractual features, but through the merger became the obligations of the new corporation, could they be improved or weakened in quality by the change? Explain.

13 If your stock in a local manufacturing company had cost you $10 per share in 1950 but is now worth $50, if this company's property cost $1 million but is now worth $5 million, and if American Can Company wishes to combine this plant into its own system, what process of combination would suit you best? Would your answer be the same if you were a $50,000 executive, the indispensable key man in the enterprise and owner of 25 per cent of the stock, and if you were 67 years old?

14 Investigate the terms and procedures of the following corporate combinations: **(a)** Plough and Schering, in 1971; **(b)** Glen Alden Corporation and Schenley Industries, in 1971; **(c)** International Utilities and Pacific Intermountain Express, in 1971; **(d)** Philip Morris and Miller Brewing, in 1970; **(e)** Warner Lambert and Parke, Davis, in 1970; **(f)** Xerox and Scientific Data Systems, in 1969.

15 Do you agree that investors in holding companies will find consolidated financial statements more illuminating than corporate ones? Are the latter needed at all?

16 Would you like to be a minority stockholder in a subsidiary which the controlling company wishes to expand greatly by use of reinvested earnings? Why?

17 On what factor does the interest-paying power of the bonds of a nonoperating holding company depend? Investigate the interest sources of the bonds of General Public Utilities Corporation. How are these bonds rated? Why?

REFERENCES

Financial Handbook, rev. ed., The Ronald Press Company, New York, 1968, Secs. 12, 13, 18, 20.

Guthmann, Harry G., and Herbert E. Dougall: *Corporate Financial Policy*, 4th ed., Prentice-Hall, Inc., Englewood Cliffs, N.J., 1962, Chaps. 2–4, 25–28.

Husband, William H., and James C. Dockeray: *Modern Corporation Finance*, 7th ed., Richard D. Irwin, Inc., Homewood, Ill., 1972, Chaps. 2, 3.

Securities and Exchange Commission: *Special Study of Securities Markets*, Washington, 1963, Part 3, Chap. IX of Part 5.

United States Corporation Company: *Corporation Manual*, New York, annual.

COMMON STOCKS
AND THEIR VALUE

This chapter is mostly concerned with the investment characteristics of common stock and with its value for long-range investment purposes. Although many investors seem more concerned with the volatile behavior of stock prices than with the normal values the stocks represent, it is important to successful investing to have a clear understanding of the basic values around which price fluctuations occur. That is the immediate task.

Common stock may be defined as the residual ownership of a corporation, which is entitled to all assets and earnings after the other limited claims have been paid and which has the basic voting control. In short, common stock is the fundamental ownership equity. No private business corporation is without common stock; most corporations draw the major portion of their funds from their common stockholders, and nearly all are managed basically in the interests of the common stockholders.

The investor in common stock thus occupies a position directly comparable to that of the owner of a farm or a factory. Successful operation means in either case good income from the business and increased value for the investment; losses mean the opposite. Common stock bears the main burden of the risk of the enterprise and also receives the lion's share of the advantages of success; it is the potent and dynamic element in corporate financing and the one which commands the highest concentration of investor interest.

Since the common stockholders usually control the corporation, it is to be expected that corporate policies will be developed to further their interests. Such corporate actions as dividend payments, stock dividends, stock splits, recapitalizations, mergers, expansion, sale of new securities, and use of rights are normally planned by management with particular reference to their effect on the common stock. Bondholders and preferred stockholders are not disregarded, of course; but it is assumed that they will be content with the exact preferences and advantages stipulated in the bond indenture and the corporate articles, so that management discretion may be applied chiefly in the interests of the common stock.

INVESTMENT CHARACTERISTICS

Before proceeding further with the study of common stocks, it will be desirable to summarize the investment features usually attributed to them. These features are in several cases generalizations which are subject to exceptions, but on the whole a common stock may be said to have the following characteristics:

1 It normally has control of the corporation and will exercise that control in its own interests.

2 It has unlimited ownership rights to the remaining gains from the business, after other securityholders have received their (usually) limited contractual payments.

3 It bears the principal hazards of the business, since other securityholders, creditors, and employees usually have prior claims, and its quality depends importantly on the amount and nature of the prior claims.

4 Common stock may be sold by its holder to any willing buyer, but in the ordinary course of business it does not come "due," hence need never be redeemed by the corporation; nor may the corporation ordinarily "call" it for redemption or force the stockholder to surrender it against his wishes. (A formal recapitalization or merger or final liquidation may be an exception.)

5 The earnings on the common stockholders' equity may be unstable. Not only will the corporation's total earnings fluctuate as business conditions change and its own affairs progress, but creditors and preferred stockholders must be allowed prior rights, thus making the residual share more unstable than the total.

6 Dividends may fluctuate. Dividends must depend on earnings, cash position, surplus position, expansion needs, debt situation, and management policy. Even if management desires a stable dividend rate, it may not always be feasible, for expansion, debt retirement, and cash accumulation are often more important to the corporation.

7 Dividends are normally less than the earnings on the common stockholders' equity; hence the value of that equity should grow as a result of the investment of the undistributed earnings in the business.

8 The earnings and dividends on a firm's common stock, and hence the stock's value, may grow very greatly if successful product development or successful sales promotion or skillful cost control outdistances competitors and earns more per dollar of invested capital and builds toward a promising future. The earnings and dividends and stock values in an unprogressive firm can decline even if present earnings are being used to enlarge the firm's resources.

9 Common stocks in general are a price-level hedge. That is, they tend to earn, pay dividends, and bring market prices at levels which are vaguely related to the general commodity price level. However, this is only a long-run overall tendency subject to numerous exceptions, as will be noted later.

10 Common stock prices fluctuate extensively. These fluctuations are so extreme that even in high-grade stocks the timing of purchases and sales is a major investment problem. Large profits or losses on such investments are therefore commonplace.

11 Good-quality common stocks can always be sold quickly and for cash, an advantage over real estate, owner-operated businesses, or art collections. Prices can be read daily in the newspapers, and the various laws passed for investor protection generally require company managements to inform stockholders of important developments that may affect the value of their shares.

Investors in common stocks are thus afforded commitments which are interesting, useful, potentially profitable, and hazardous. The selection of such commitments requires more than average care and competence, but is not so difficult that a careful investor should not attempt it. In fact, the average investor needs common stocks to create a balanced investment program. He must therefore either learn to select them himself, place that task in the hands of a thoroughly knowledgeable friend, an investment counselor, or some other informed person, or rely on the managers of an investment company whose shares he may buy.[1]

STOCK PRICES

Shares of stock of ordinary investment types range in price between $10 and $200 per share. A few sell higher, and a number of good issues mingle with the more speculative types valued between $1 and $10 per share. The average value of the shares listed on the New York Stock Exchange normally ranges between $30 and $50, but great numbers of small and speculative corporations have shares worth less than $1 each. These low-priced stocks are usually not traded on the major stock exchanges.

It is conventional for shares selling in normal price ranges to be quoted in terms of dollars and eighths rather than dollars and cents per share. Thus Ohio Edison was quoted at one time in 1972 at $22\frac{1}{8}$, meaning $22.12\frac{1}{2}$ per share, and Control Data Corporation at $63\frac{1}{2}$, meaning $63.50 per share. Pricing intervals smaller than eighths of a dollar are not often used in major markets except on stocks or rights priced below $1 per share. On prices below $1 per share, these markets use pricing intervals of $\frac{1}{16}$ or $\frac{1}{32}$ of a dollar, or even $\frac{1}{64}$ or $\frac{1}{128}$ in unusual instances. In other markets, including the Canadian and some of the important regional stock exchanges, certain classes of low-priced stocks are quoted in dollars and cents, with pricing intervals of 5 cents or 1 cent.

Shares of stock are always quoted at prices which contemplate transferring to the purchaser the ownership of the share and all future dividends or other disbursements except those already of record and in process of payment. Even accumulated back dividends on preferred stock are transferred from seller to buyer. The price of the stock must be determined with this in mind.

---

[1] An investment company is an organization which sells its own shares to the public and invests the proceeds in a diversified list of other securities. The investments are bought and sold as conditions warrant. See Chap. 21.

FUNDAMENTAL CALCULATIONS

Investors in common stocks make constant use of four basic calculations for gauging the merit of a common stock and testing the reasonableness of its price. These calculations are in no sense final determinants of quality or value, but they are convenient preliminary indicators which, taken in conjunction with the investor's general knowledge of the industry and the company, tell whether the stock is worthy of further investigation. Although the actual arithmetic is usually done by securities analysts, so that the investor may take the figures directly from securities manuals and analytical reports, it seems best to review the processes briefly. The calculations in question determine (1) the earnings per share, (2) the net asset value (or book value) per share, (3) the price-earnings ratio, and (4) the yield.

In computing earnings per share, assets per share, and other such measures, it is customary to divide the appropriate sum of earnings or assets by the number of shares *outstanding*, that is, owned by the stockholders. The corporate articles may authorize additional shares which have never been issued, and reacquired shares may be held as treasury stock by the corporation. But these shares do not receive dividends and would not share in the assets in the event of liquidation, hence need not be included in the per share calculations.

Earnings per share   Since the common stock is the lowest-ranking security and the residual claimant to the earnings of a corporation, it is usually possible to compute its earnings per share by taking the net corporate profit after expenses, interest, and taxes, subtracting the preferred dividend requirement for the period (whether paid or accumulated unpaid would not matter), and dividing the remainder by the number of common shares outstanding. This may be illustrated by reference to the 1971 income statement of Bristol-Myers Company. In that fiscal year the company had a profit of $75,767,000 after deductions for all expenses, interest, and taxes. Preferred dividend requirements for the year were $2,562,000. The remaining $73,205,000 divided by the average of 29,878,000 common shares outstanding during 1971 gave earnings of $2.45 per share. Earnings per share are computed in the same manner for quarterly or semiannual periods when the data are available.

If the company does not earn enough to cover the full preferred dividend for the time period in question, the amount of the deficiency is regarded as a deficit to the common stock. For example, if Bristol-Myers had had a profit of only $500,000 in 1971, it would have been $2,062,000 short of covering its preferred dividend requirement of $2,562,000. Dividing this $2,062,000 sum by 29,878,000, the average number of common shares, would indicate a deficit of 6.9 cents per common share. If this imaginary situation had been worse—for example, if there had been a $2,000,000 *loss* after deduction of all expenses— the deficit to the common stockholders would have been $2,000,000 plus the

$2,562,000 preferred dividend requirement. The total of $4,562,000 divided among 29,878,000 common shares would show a deficit of 15.3 cents per common share.

Investors generally place very great emphasis upon earnings per share and the trend of earnings per share, arguing that both present and future dividends are dependent upon earnings. This is a reasonable position if the earnings statements are studied to make sure that they are fairly presented and free from distortions due to nonrecurring incomes or expenses and if proper attention is given to other developments in the company or the industry which are not yet reflected in the earnings figures.

Earnings backed by realistic depreciation allowances and other conservative accounting practices, low-debt capital structures, and decline-resistant earning power are said to be of high *quality*. Prudent investors weigh the quality of earnings per share as well as their magnitude and trend.

Net asset value per share The net asset value per share, commonly referred to as the book value per share, attempts to measure the amount of assets which the corporation has working on behalf of each share of common stock. It is arrived at by taking the net (after allowance for depreciation and depletion) balance sheet value of the corporate assets, subtracting the face value of creditors' and preferred stockholders' claims, and dividing the remainder by the number of outstanding common shares. Bristol-Myers at December 31, 1971, had total assets carried at $796,431,000, after allowances for depreciation and bad debts. Debts and preferred stock amounted to $434,306,000. The remaining $362,125,000 indicated a net asset value of $12.05 for each of the 30,059,612 shares outstanding at this date.

Students of accounting will observe that this method of calculating net asset value per share makes no deduction from assets for such balance sheet credit items as contingency reserves, inventory value reserves, and self-insurance reserves. The reason is that these items are usually tantamount to appropriated surplus and thus truly a part of the stockholders' net worth, unless there is definite reason to regard them as offsets to assets which are likely to be lost in the near future.

In any business in which available assets are a good measure of earning power, the asset value per share may be highly significant. However, it must be conceded that (1) corporate book values are usually based on cost, not earning power; and (2) intangible assets not on the books may be more significant than book values in determining earning power. Asset value figures should thus not be overstressed, though the solid dependability of good assets in assuring future earnings should not be belittled.

Because most corporations with patents, trade names, goodwill, and other intangible assets do not show them on their financial statements at all, it has become customary in recent years to base net asset values on tangible assets alone. This practice sometimes results in very small book values per share for some highly valuable stocks, but in other cases it avoids distortion by excluding the dubious intangible values which a few corporate statements contain.

In computing book values for holding company stocks, consolidated balance sheets are generally used. If minority interests exist, they are allotted a proper share of subsidiary net worth.

Although the basic idea of earnings or assets per outstanding share seems very simple, many complications ensue when analysts undertake to compute figures which are truly meaningful. Four of the complications should be noted here:

1   When a corporation issues new stock for property or cash during a business year, the new assets contribute to earnings during only part of the year. In such cases analysts often compute earnings per share on the weighted average number of shares outstanding, rather than on the total number outstanding at year-end. The Bristol-Myers earnings computed earlier illustrate this procedure.

2   When there are participating preferred stocks or special classes of common stocks outstanding, whose share in the earnings varies with the amount of earnings or the size of the common dividend, it is sometimes necessary to devise special calculations to determine the proper per share allocations of earnings. The nature of such calculations must obviously depend on the rights to earnings as established in the corporate articles.

3   If the stock considered is that of a holding company, of a company with large investments in other companies, or of a participant in joint ventures, earnings per share may be computed from either the corporate or the consolidated income statement. The earnings of the corporate statement will include the dividends received by the company from its subsidiaries or affiliates, plus the profits from its own operations; this may be a measure of the company's capacity to pay dividends from current earnings. Earnings per share computed from a consolidated statement will show the per share profits of the business as a whole, whether the subsidiaries and affiliates paid dividends or not. This is the calculation most commonly used by investors because most investors wish to measure as earnings per share the total earned increment accruing on their investment in both the principal and related companies. Accounting rules effective in 1972 require companies to consolidate earnings in their published reports; along with earnings from its own operations, a company must include its proportionate share of earnings or losses in all other corporations of which it owns 20 per cent or more of the voting stock.

4   In calculations which appraise stock value on a per share basis, the investor must make allowance for any situation which threatens to dilute his per share earnings or assets. This dilution problem often occurs when corporations sell bonds or preferred stocks which are convertible into common or have stock purchase warrants or options outstanding which permit their holders to buy new stock at a fixed price. Usually the conversion of bonds or preferred stock into common stock will reduce the senior claims to income by a relatively modest amount. Stock purchase options may call for prices which add relatively little to the earning assets of the corporation. In either instance, therefore, the number of outstanding common shares might increase greatly while the total earnings available for the common stock increased very little. The result would be a decline in per share earnings. The American Institute of Certified Public Accountants now requires companies to report their earnings per share on both a current and a fully diluted basis, the latter showing what earnings would have been if all warrants and conversion rights had been exercised.

Price-earnings ratio The price-earnings (P/E) ratio is simply the market price of the stock expressed as a multiple of the per share earnings (EPS) of the corporation. Thus, General Motors stock would be selling for 16 times earnings if it sold for $80 per share when the annual earnings were $5 per share. The price-earnings ratio is a conventional and highly regarded measure of stock value because it gives an indication of stock prices measured against the earning power of the stock.[2]

As an indication of typical price-earnings ratios on investment-grade stocks, Chart 4-1 has been compiled to cover the period 1947–1972 inclusive. Ten stocks are charted; in each case the average stock price for the year is divided by the earnings per share for the year, to obtain a measure of the prices investors might be willing to pay. The chart shows an almost unbelievable divergence of price-earnings ratios; even if extreme figures are disregarded as mathematical freaks (years of abnormally low or high per share earnings could cause this), it appears that certain high-quality stocks can in most years be bought for as little as 10 times earnings while other stocks readily bring as much as 30 times earnings.

There is, of course, an explanation for all this. The high-quality, dependable stocks which can be purchased in normal times for 10 to 14 times earnings will usually be those of steady, unspectacular companies in which earnings growth is slow and dividend increases are rare. Such stocks should increase in value slowly over the years, but there is little prospect of big profits. On the other hand, some companies seem to be continuously involved in expansion and new-product development which promise rapid increase in earnings and dividends. Stockholders will pay high multiples of present earnings for these "growth" stocks because they expect larger earnings and dividends in the future. The

---

[2] Instead of the commonly used price-earnings calculations, some writers invert the ratio and compute the *earnings yield*—that is, the percentage which the annual per share earnings figure bears to the price of the stock.

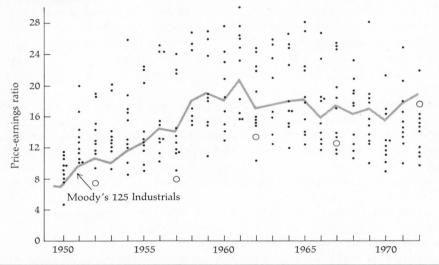

Chart 4-1 *Price-earnings ratios on 10 important high-grade industrial stocks and on Moody's Index of 125 Industrials. Each dot represents the ratio of the year's average price to the year's earnings per share. The same stocks are used throughout. Some are growth stocks: some are not. A few dots are freakish because of temporary situations. The large circles in the 1952, 1957, 1962, 1967, and 1972 years show an average price-earnings ratio for 10 medium-grade stocks of large companies which pay dividends and seem to promise a satisfactory future.*

stocks priced at 15 to 30 times current earnings are almost always stocks with significant growth prospects—the faster and more durable the growth trend, the higher the price.

Chart 4-1 also contains a line graph showing the average price-earnings ratios (at the average price for each year) of the 125 stocks comprising Moody's Industrial Stock Index, and five circles showing an average price-earnings ratio for 10 stocks of lesser quality, in the years 1952, 1957, 1962, 1967, and 1972. In addition to the wide range of price-earnings ratios among these stocks, the chart shows that high-grade stocks sold around only 7 to 12 times earnings before 1958 but have averaged 16 or 17 times earnings since that date. Because the long-time norm has been close to 14 times earnings, today's investor has a puzzling problem when he undertakes to appraise common stocks.

The purpose of studying the history of price-earnings ratios is, of course, to provide a means for estimating the average future market values for stocks. For example, if International Harvester Company appears able to earn an average of $3 per share on its common stock, and if the stock is classed as a high-quality, slow-growth type worth about 13 times earnings, an average valuation of $39 per share would be indicated.

Price-earnings ratios are baffling or meaningless unless the earnings figures used are normal and typical. In Chart 4-1, the companies represented are all large and stable, but it is necessary to disregard freak ratios resulting from unusually large or small earnings in abnormal years. For the same reason, price-earnings studies of stocks of either small or speculative companies or of companies with erratic earnings records do not provide dependable data upon which to base valuation estimates.

Yield   The yield refers to the percentage which the annual dividend bears to the current price of the stock. If General Motors stock pays dividends at the rate of $4 per annum and sells at $80, the yield is 5 per cent. The yield is one of the most definite indicators of the reasonableness of a stock's price, if the dividend figure used is a normal prospective annual rate.

Chart 4-2 presents the yield history of the same stocks whose earnings are studied in Chart 4-1. In addition, the yield record of a group of high-grade bonds is shown. In Chart 4-2, each dot on the chart represents a percentage yield rate

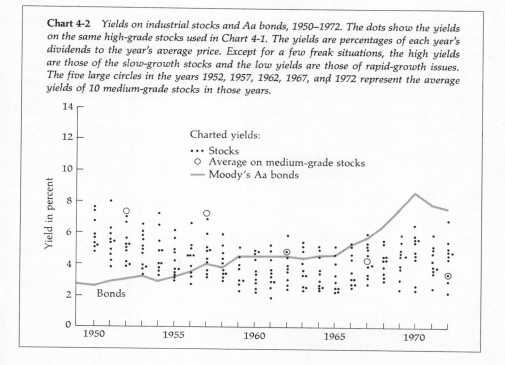

Chart 4-2   *Yields on industrial stocks and Aa bonds, 1950–1972. The dots show the yields on the same high-grade stocks used in Chart 4-1. The yields are percentages of each year's dividends to the year's average price. Except for a few freak situations, the high yields are those of the slow-growth stocks and the low yields are those of rapid-growth issues. The five large circles in the years 1952, 1957, 1962, 1967, and 1972 represent the average yields of 10 medium-grade stocks in those years.*

obtained by dividing the dividend paid during the year by the average price of the stock during the same year. As in Chart 4-1, some of the dots are freaks, either because the year's dividend was abnormally small or large or because the stock was priced at abnormal levels during the year. If the freaks are disregarded, it appears that the yields normally available on these high-quality stocks range from about 2½ per cent to about 5 per cent. This is a situation similar to that encountered in Chart 4-1. The slow-growth or nongrowth stocks yield as much as 5 per cent, while the ones promising a growing dividend in the future may yield only 2 or 3 per cent at the moment.

In addition to the dots representing the high-grade stocks, Chart 4-2 shows five large circles representing the average yields of 10 medium-grade stocks in the years 1952, 1957, 1962, 1967, and 1972. These are the same stocks whose price-earnings ratios appear in Chart 4-1. The average yields on the medium-grade stocks are noticeably higher than those on the high-quality stocks.

As in the case of price-earnings ratios, the principal purpose in studying stock yield history is to obtain a basis for stock valuation. If the dividend to be paid by a stock can reasonably be estimated, and if the normal yield on such a stock is known, an evaluation is a matter of simple arithmetic. For example, if slow-growth International Harvester pays a $1.80 per share annual dividend, and if a stock of this quality might normally yield about 5 per cent, dividing the $1.80 by .05 obtains a valuation estimate of $36. The fact that this is lower than the estimate obtained in the previous section by capitalizing Harvester's earnings does not signify lack of accuracy; some divergence in these estimates is normal, and both should be considered and perhaps averaged in reaching a final judgment.

Two further yield factors are suggested by Chart 4-2. First, it is apparent that stock market price fluctuations can force most yields to abnormal levels, sometimes for periods of several years. A long-term chart would show conspicuous low-yield periods centering in 1929, 1946, and 1965, along with high yields in 1932, 1942, and 1949. Second, the relative yields afforded by stocks and bonds vary as market conditions change. In the years 1928–1929 and 1959–1972, for example, high-grade bonds yielded a higher return than most stocks. On the other hand, high-grade bonds yielded less than most stocks during the long period of low bond yields between 1936 and 1952. It is difficult to define any "normal" relation between stock and bond yields. The greater safety inherent in bonds' prior claim and unconditional contractual rights to payment would perhaps justify a yield lower than that available on most stocks. However, the dividends on most good stocks usually increase with the passage of time, especially if the general price level rises, and it might be reasonable to accept a stock yield lower than a bond yield if the dividends were expected to increase within a reasonable time. So far as Chart 4-2 is concerned, it is clear that high-grade bonds have tended to yield less than the slow-growth type of high-grade stocks but definitely more than the most vigorous growth stocks.

TOTAL INVESTMENT GAIN

Major corporations ordinarily distribute between 40 and 75 per cent of their earnings as dividends and retain the balance to add to their net worths. This practice permits them either to pay down debts or to add to operating resources out of earnings, and normally results in a slow growth in per share earnings and stock prices. However, not all industries and companies enjoy the same profit characteristics. There are some whose earning power and stock prices seem to rise by more than their undistributed earnings would account for, while others reinvest substantial amounts of earnings in the business without seeming to add anything to earning power. Although it must be assumed that the new assets acquired by this latter class of static-profit companies are profitable and that the older assets are deteriorating, the fact remains that in these companies investors are rewarded only by the cash dividends. The reinvested earnings are not represented by increases in the earning power or market value of the stock.

This line of reasoning suggests that the true returns realized by long-term stockholders in any company consist of dividends plus market value increases plus (less importantly) occasional valuable perquisites such as nondiluting rights to subscribe to new stock. The approach may be illustrated as follows: Chart 4-3 indicates that in the 25-year period 1947–1972, the earnings per share on the 125 stocks in Moody's Industrial Stock Index have maintained an average growth

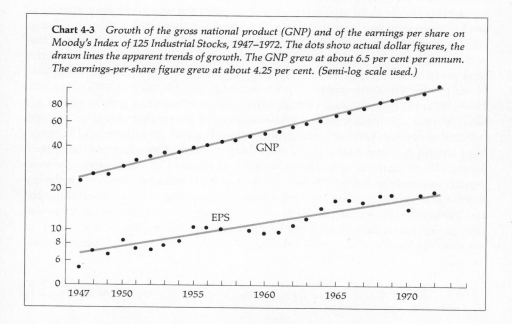

Chart 4-3 *Growth of the gross national product (GNP) and of the earnings per share on Moody's Index of 125 Industrial Stocks, 1947–1972. The dots show actual dollar figures, the drawn lines the apparent trends of growth. The GNP grew at about 6.5 per cent per annum. The earnings-per-share figure grew at about 4.25 per cent. (Semi-log scale used.)*

trend of about 4.25 per cent per annum. Although at least one-third of these dollar gains must be ascribed to price-level inflation, the fact remains that the average major industrial corporation has been able to increase its dollar earnings per share (and presumably its dividends and stock prices) at the 4.25 per cent rate for the past quarter-century, and there is no strong indication of any early change. The long-term investor who holds a diversified group of industrial shares has therefore come to expect an average stock price growth of about 4.25 per cent, in addition to a typical dividend yield of 3 to 4 per cent.

At this point it is desirable to refer again to Chart 2-2, which shows that common stock yields since 1959 have been extraordinarily low. There are several causes for high stock prices and low yields since 1959, but one of them is certainly the fact that earnings growth since 1947 has been twice as fast as its average during the preceding 75 years.

In those earlier years an investor who desired a typical 7½ per cent return on his stock investments,[3] and who expected an average value growth of about 2 per cent per year, had to buy at relatively moderate stock prices in order to obtain a dividend yield of 5½ per cent; but if he now gets a value growth of 4.25 per cent, he needs only 3.25 per cent in dividend yield in order to complete his 7½ per cent total, and he is therefore justified in buying stocks at relatively high prices. Rising income taxes and the preferentially low rates applied to capital gains have encouraged investors to substitute this expected "growth yield" for part of their dividend return.

Lest this simple yield arithmetic appear to point the way to an easy method of stock valuation, a few further facts are in order. (1) Although the 20-year earnings growth trend for the average corporation as depicted in Chart 4-3 seems clear and stable, it should be noted that neither stability nor certainty exists in shorter time periods; very rapid growth in such periods as 1952–1955 and 1961–1965 seems to alternate with nongrowth or decline in periods such as 1957–1961 and 1966–1971. (2) In individual concerns the long-term earnings growth trends are not so dependably persistent and stable as those of the market averages; industry conditions change, products and product lines flourish or decline, and management decisions have their effects over long periods. Consequently, long-term projections of earnings and price growth are unreliable. (3) Furthermore, in individual concerns the *short-term* periods of earnings gain and decline are often very intense and very irregular; they reflect not only general business conditions but also factors developing within the firm or its industry. Consequently, past growth records are not reliable indicators of earnings and price gain in the next 1 to 3 years. (4) Finally, the whole calculation is technically faulty because it as-

[3] In an article entitled "Stock Values and Stock Prices," published in the May–June, 1960, issue of *Financial Analysts Journal*, Nicholas Molodovsky presents data to show that this has been the approximate average return realized by stockholders over three generations.

sumes that a stated percentage gain in earnings will always cause a similar percentage gain in price, regardless of whether the existing price is high or low; this is a dubious assumption when applied to stocks. For all these reasons, investors are skeptical of the total investment gain concept, and seem to prefer the traditional price-earnings and yield calculations. Whether these are any better, or even as good, is open to doubt; but they are simple and familiar and therefore used.

It also should be noted that farsighted stock buyers must think in terms of *real*, or constant-dollar, returns rather than of conventional ones expressed in current dollars only. In eras of price inflation, for example, yields measured in purchasing power are much lower than those reckoned in money. An investor may earn 10 cents annually in dividends plus price appreciation on each dollar's worth of stock held, but if the general price level rises 5 per cent per year, his $1.10 will buy only as much as $1.05 would have bought at the year's beginning; his real rate of return will be only about 5 per cent.

The large rise in bond yields between 1965 and 1972 made it evident that bond investors had awakened to the money-rate risk and were demanding higher current-dollar yields as compensation. Although the long-term rise in stock prices weakened after 1965, neither dividend yields nor the ratios of earnings to common stock prices rose in anything like the proportion of bond yields. This persistence of relatively low yields and historically high price-earnings ratios on stocks almost certainly reflected stockholders' confidence that corporate earnings growth would eventually accelerate to match any increase in the rate of price-level inflation. However, logic would suggest that if these expectations were disappointed, stockholders—like bond buyers—would demand sharply higher current-dollar returns on their investments, an outcome which would involve a rise in yields and a fall in price-earnings ratios and prices.

GROWTH STOCKS

It was noted in the preceding section that most successful corporations increase their per share net worths out of earnings and in consequence are able to increase per share earnings and dividends slowly. But there are always certain industries in which technological progress or rapid growth of sales opportunities affords, for a span of years, a chance for aggressive concerns to do exceptionally well. A new patented product, for example, may permit a firm to grow phenomenally. Or a rapidly growing demand may eliminate the need for sharp price competition and make generous profits possible for a whole industry; the favored firms can then build up large and efficient resources to assure future earnings. During such a growth period it is also possible to develop brand names, specialized products, and customer loyalties. Better yet, a period of technological progress makes it possible for research-minded concerns to make tremendous profits out of a constant stream of new products and processes. In the past two decades, the computer and health-care industries, among others, have been conspicuous as growth industries.

But spectacular growth is not confined to industries exploiting new technologies. Aggressive and pioneering managements have produced great growth by developing new methods and greater efficiency in chain-store management, electrical equipment manufacturing, food packaging, and other industries for their companies. The essential characteristic of a growth situation, then, is a generous and rising earning power which is building up the resources and trade position which will contribute to large earnings and dividends in the future. Such a situation is almost certain to be accompanied by improving quality (i.e., assurance of future strength) in the company as well. It is obvious that the stock market should respond vigorously to evidence of increasing earnings coupled with increasing stock quality. Stocks of established companies in those situations often rise in price rapidly until they sell for 20 to 30 times current earnings and yield only 2 to 3 per cent on their current dividends, and promising new ventures with small current earnings sell at even higher ratios. As the expected growth builds up the earnings and dividends, the high stock price should ultimately be justified by normal price-earnings and yield ratios at the higher level.

Rapid growth often continues for a long time, but in a competitive economy it can hardly be expected to be a perpetual phenomenon in any company or industry. Initial demands are met, new products appear, competition becomes substantial and vigorous. Consequently, the investor who pays a high price-earnings ratio for a growth stock must be convinced that the growth will continue long enough to justify the price he is paying and to compensate for the low initial rate of dividend. The investor who buys into a growth situation before the impending growth is fully reflected in the price will of course obtain this ultimate increase in the dividend and, in addition, a very handsome increase in the price of his stock, but the investor who pays a price which fully allows for the expected growth will find little profit in it, even though the growth subsequently develops as he expected.[4]

The reasonable value of a growth stock is very baffling to estimate, since both the future speed and the duration of earnings growth are involved. Furthermore, future price-level inflation which may increase the earnings and dividends of the future would produce an effect somewhat similar to real growth. The evidence of Chart 4-3 establishes 4.25 per cent per year as an average earnings growth rate for major industrial firms, but Table 4-1 shows that growth rates ranging from 10

---

[4] The tardy buyer at a high price may still profit at the expense of his gullible fellows. If the buyer pays 30 times earnings after his stock has enjoyed several years of earnings growth at 10 per cent per annum, the market is likely to continue to pay 30 times earnings for the increasing level of earnings until it becomes abundantly clear that growth has slowed down or ceased. When that becomes obvious, a lower price-earnings multiple will result. But our late buyer would doubtless be astute enough to sell out before the price-earnings multiple declined.

Table 4-1 *Yields and price-earnings ratios, recent growth rates, and beta coefficients for common stocks of different qualities and features*

Stock	Average price 1971* (1)	Price-earnings ratio 1971* (2)	Yield 1971* (3)	Percentage growth rate per annum		Beta† (6)
				1966–1971† (4)	1956–1971† (5)	
Glamor type, high grade:						
Avon Products	97	51	1.2	15.3	21.1	.73
International Business Machines	325	34	1.6	16.9	18.1	.89
Polaroid	96	52	0.3	2.0	23.9	1.17
Xerox	106	39	0.7	20.2	44.2	.93
Investment type, growth:						
Dow Chemical	64	19	2.7	4.7	7.9	.72
General Electric	57	22	2.4	− 2.7	3.1	.76
Proctor & Gamble	69	23	2.0	10.0	8.9	.71
Sears, Roebuck	90	25	1.7	7.6	8.1	.73
Investment type, income:						
American Telephone	47	12	5.5	3.1	5.1	.49
Exxon Corporation	75	11	5.1	4.3	5.2	.53
General Motors	82	13	4.1	− 7.2	5.0	.72
Nabisco, Inc.	53	16	4.2	− 1.5	5.7	.41
Intermediate quality, growth:						
Baxter Laboratories	32	42	0.3	23.0	19.3	1.28
Combustion Engineering	59	17	2.3	8.9	8.7	1.16
Lucky Stores	20	19	2.4	24.3	16.4	1.02
Southern California Edison	30	12	5.0	6.8	4.2	.77
Intermediate quality, income:						
Lone Star Gas	26	12	5.0	9.1	4.0	.52
Phelps Dodge	38	10	5.5	8.8	3.6	.95
Southern Pacific	41	10	4.8	− 1.5	4.3	.96
Timken Company	39	11	4.6	− 5.1	5.6	.65
Semispeculative						
Certain-Teed	37	12	2.2	− 4.8	− 3.1	1.70
Kaiser Aluminum	27	22	3.3	3.3	1.5	1.00
Syntex Corp.	62	28	0.6	− 2.2	42.8	1.03
Textron, Inc.	28	15	3.2	8.7	12.1	1.24

* Figures based on 1971 earnings, dividends, and average prices.
† Figures taken from *Value Line Investment Survey.*

per cent to nothing at all or even declines may persist for 5 to 10 years; and Table 4-1 also suggests that such trends frequently change and often reverse direction. Great wisdom and great caution are obviously necessary in choosing stocks whose value depends largely on a rapid growth rate, for growth appears to be a very volatile thing. Judging from past market price history, it would appear that 25 times earnings or a 2½ per cent yield basis, as suggested in Charts 4-1 and 4-2, would determine a prudent maximum price under ordinary conditions for the stocks of established companies.[5]

Because of the melodrama popularly attached to growth situations, which of course stems from recognition of the enormous gains made by those who bought in time into such stocks as Polaroid and International Business Machines, investors and brokers are much attracted to them. The attraction is increased by the fact that income taxes are levied on capital gains only if the stock is sold, and even then only at the low capital gains rates. This eagerness to participate in growth results in rather high prices for many growth stocks, with consequent risks of disappointment for people who buy them. As in many another dynamic situation, therefore, it must be conceded that the opportunities and the pitfalls in this area are both substantial.

[5] As an attempt to demonstrate the rationality of high market prices for growth stocks, the following table has been computed. This table is not an empirical study; it is only an exercise in arithmetic, to demonstrate the growth rates and growth periods necessary to justify certain levels of stock prices. The table is based on four assumptions: (1) that the stock of a large, well-established industrial company with *average* growth and dividend performance will be valued at about 15 times its earning power in future markets; (2) that growth and inflationary conditions will continue to resemble those of the 1947–1972 period; (3) that the typical stock can best be valued by assuming that it will revert to an average growth performance and price-earnings ratio after a few years which can be predicted; and (4) that the average investor desires a 7½ per cent return on his stock investments. The price-earnings values shown in the table are based on arithmetical present values of the computed stock valuations at the end of the growth period plus the present values of assumed dividends at 60 per cent of earnings during the growth period.

The growth rates assumed in this table are of about the same magnitude as most of those shown in Table 4-1. There are a few in real life which grow faster and a few which seem to retrogress, and a few whose oustanding growth records have already lasted much longer than those shown in this table.

Suitable present price-earnings ratios for high-grade stocks whose earnings are expected to grow at the indicated rates for the indicated period of years and thereafter to grow at average rates

Initial rate of growth per cent	Initial growth period in years			
	5	*10*	*15*	*20*
0	13.0	11.5	10.3	9.4
2	14.1	13.5	13.0	12.4
4	15.5	15.8	16.3	16.7
6	16.9	18.7	20.7	22.6
8	18.5	22.2	26.3	31.0
10	20.3	26.7	34.7	44.3

ONLY THE FUTURE IS SIGNIFICANT

Yields and price-earnings ratios are commonly computed by investors either to judge whether a given stock price is high or low or to determine which stocks in a given list are the highest or lowest. In making these computations, the investor will naturally use the current price, since this is the one he must pay or accept if he buys or sells. But the dividend and earnings rates which will prove him wise or unwise are those of the next few years, not the current ones, and certainly not past ones. Consequently, it is important to compute the price-earnings ratios and yields that guide investment decisions on the basis of current normal or average earnings and dividends, which presumably bear a reasonable relation to those of the next few years.[6]

In most professional investment literature, the yields and price-earnings ratios are calculated using the present dividend rate and the rate of earnings as shown by some recent financial report. This avoids confusing the investor by giving him estimates whose source he does not understand, and this method is certainly sound if current earnings and dividends are at typical levels and provide an accurate clue to the future; but it gives absurd results when the immediate present is far out of line with future expectations. For example, the Ford Motor Company in 1958 earned $1.75 per share and in the fourth quarter was maintaining a dividend rate of $1.60 per annum. In late December the stock was selling at $50 per share, "at 28.5 times earnings and yielding 3.2 per cent." Such computations neglected the fact that Ford's earnings over the past several years had been averaging well over $4.50 per share, that its dividends had averaged $2.40, and that a resumption of these rates was reasonably in prospect.

To the investor who in 1958 conservatively estimated Ford's future earning power at $4 and probable dividend at $2.40 (a normal 60 per cent payout of earnings), the $50 stock price would have meant 12½ times earnings and a yield of 4.8 per cent. These ratios would justify the immediate purchase of a high-quality and promising stock such as this one if other factors were favorable, whereas 28.5 times earnings and a 3.2 per cent yield would suggest a dangerously high price.[7]

To repeat: yields and price-earnings ratios must be based on estimated normal dividends and earnings, or possibly on estimates of future average dividends and earnings, if they are to be meaningful in indicating which stocks are most attractively priced. Past and current actual dividends and earnings are chiefly significant as indexes of what can be expected in the all-important future.

[6] As an alternative approach, the following rule of thumb for comparing fast-growth, slow-growth, and nongrowth stocks is suggested: Estimate the earnings per share and the dividend per share for each stock as they will be 10 years hence. Using these estimates and today's stock prices, compute price-earnings ratios and yields. The lowest price-earnings ratio, or the highest yield, marks the best buy. If you don't know enough about the stock's probable future to make 10-year estimates, can you justify buying it?

[7] Actually, Ford's earnings and dividends far exceeded the pre-1958 figures in 1959 and later years, and the stock in 1963 earned $4.42 per share *after a 2-for-1 stock split in 1962!*

QUALITY AND PRICE

Because investors do not all prefer stocks with identical characteristics, it is not feasible to define quality with mathematical exactness. Many investors, for example, do not require that a stock pay large or regular dividends. To others such a dividend practice is the exact measure of desirability. But all will agree that a high-quality stock must of necessity represent a profitable and an enduring equity. For present purposes, therefore, a high-quality common stock is one upon which the corporation appears able to earn and pay reasonable (though not necessarily completely regular) dividends into the indefinite future, while maintaining its financial strength, its competitive position, and the vigor of its business. This definition implies that a public utility stock with very stable earnings and dividends, such as Pacific Gas and Electric Company common, may be similar in quality to an industrial like General Motors Corporation, whose earnings are less stable but appear equally sure into the long-run future. A low-quality stock, by obvious contrast, is one whose future contributions to its owners' welfare are uncertain because of weaknesses in the industry, the business, or the corporation's finances.

A second vital quality feature is the capacity to increase earnings and dividends as a result of growth. The growth capacity is so important that many financial writers do not even include it under the general heading of quality but speak of quality and growth capacity as two separate features which bear upon the values of stocks. Table 4-1 illustrates a typical use of quality and growth classifications and the price-earnings and yield ratios which occurred in these stocks.

There are two general approaches which an investor may make in appraising quality. First, he may assemble all available information on the industry and the company and undertake a comprehensive and technical study covering stability, growth, profit margins, costs, capital structures, and many other such items. This is not an impossible task even for an amateur, though it requires time, patience, and for accuracy, some experience. Security analysts regularly study and compare corporate prospects along these lines, to determine both quality and the probable amounts of future earnings and dividends. Some of the techniques and criteria employed will be suggested in a later chapter.

For the present, it will be sufficient to suggest that a high-quality common stock is likely to be found in a well-entrenched and profitable large concern which has a low-leverage capital structure[8] and which operates in an enduring and preferably growing industry. If the stock is really high quality, net profits will

---

[8] A low-leverage capital structure occurs when debt and preferred stocks represent relatively small portions of the corporation's funding and the common stock equity is a relatively large portion. The prior claims against the firm's assets and earnings are thus relatively small, the concern's credit is relatively good, and the fluctuation in common stock earnings is minimized. A high-leverage capital structure implies a high ratio of debt and preferred stock funding. If the company's earnings on such senior capital are more than the interest and dividends paid on it, the excess earnings will cumulate as additional earnings on the

have been reported in each of the past 10 years, dividends will have been paid regularly, and both earnings and dividends will have increased rapidly enough to offset purchasing-power losses from price-level inflation. Obviously, the company and its industry must be promisingly situated for a prosperous future.

Two further observations respecting quality and stock prices are perhaps useful at this point. First, it is to be expected that a low-quality stock will normally fluctuate more violently in price than a high-quality one. It will be less highly secure, less well reputed, and less acceptable under adverse conditions than will a higher-grade stock—yet in good times, when all companies prosper, the weaker stock may sell for a good price. Second, the volatile price behavior of low-quality stocks is a function of their *quality*, not of their price. Speculators often say that greater market fluctuations occur in low-priced stocks, hence one who desires speculative excitement should look among low-priced stocks. As a statistical matter this is true—because there are more low-quality stocks than high-quality ones among the low-priced issues. However, careful studies show that on a percentage-of-average-price basis, high-quality stocks which sell in the low price ranges (because of stock splits or low assets per share) do not fluctuate much more than other high-quality stocks.

If the investor has not the time or the facilities for conducting his own investigation into the qualities of stocks, he may with reasonable safety employ the conclusions of others. Financial advisory services, financial periodicals, and brokers all prepare lists in which stocks are classified or otherwise labeled as to quality and which may also contain "guesstimates" respecting future earnings and dividends. Because the prediction of the future is an uncertain process, the conclusions reached by different analysts may differ, but they should be sufficiently alike to confirm one another to a satisfactory degree. Some analysts report their quality findings by assigning very candid and comparable "grades," such as A, B, C, to the stocks studied; others use word terms, such as "investment grade," "good quality," or "speculative"; still others use less categorical but more illuminating descriptive paragraphs. In any event, it will not be difficult for the inquiring investor to obtain a consensus of informed opinion as to the quality of any well-known stock in which he is interested. This consensus may then be checked against his own conclusions or accepted as a guide to action.

MARKET FACTORS

Though earning power, dividends, growth prospects, and quality are the major factors determining the value of a stock, there are market factors which may cause its price to depart extensively from a long-run norm. These market factors

---

common stock; if earnings are poor, the shortfall may cumulate as a deficit on the common stock. High leverage thus offers a speculative potential accompanied by risk, while low leverage implies relative stability and security.

are numerous. They may affect all stocks, or an entire industry, or an individual
stock issue. The most important market factors, of course, are the great economic swings which are grounded in boom or recession, easy money or tight
money, federal deficit or surplus, and like forces; these impinge forcefully on both
the demand for securities and the supply offered for sale, and thus upon prices.
But other forces are important too. For example, a reduction in margin requirements might provide enough additional buying demand to drive the general
stock market upward; or an exceptionally heavy expansion program by the
electric utilities might deluge the markets with so much new utility stock that
such stocks would be in great oversupply and therefore weak; or extensive discussion of space exploration in the public press might interest people in the
companies making spacecraft and supplies, and cause a demand for their stocks;
or an attempt by a large stockholder to liquidate a block of his company's stock
might find few buyers, hence depress the market for that particular stock.

Another group of market factors which cause violent fluctuations in the
prices of individual stocks seems to center in the short-sighted impetuousness
of many investors. These people are prone to regard any reported increases or
decreases in per share earnings as permanent changes in earning power or as
changes in long-term growth trends, even when the earnings changes are obviously caused by transient circumstances. Changes in dividend rate or the payment of extra dividends are given similar exaggerated importance. These im-
petuous investors, with the help of market speculators who regularly exploit
such news, cause stock prices to gyrate extensively above or below the "normal"
appraisals upon which this chapter is focused.

These market factors are so important in the study of common stocks that
they must be mentioned at this point, though a more complete discussion of
them is reserved for Chapter 10.

COMPARING STOCKS FOR INVESTMENT

Most careful investors find it convenient to select common stocks for investment by comparing price-earnings ratios, yields, growth prospects, and market
price records in the light of available information on quality and market factors. Since there are thousands of issues available for consideration, some systematic method of choice is a practical necessity. Probably the best first step
is a review of the stocks already in the portfolio, in order to choose the industries
in which added holdings would be most appropriate and to determine the most
desirable quality. Other preferences, such as the desire for stability of dividend
rate, for the stock of a large concern, for a low-priced stock, for a listed market,
or for a certain geographic location might further guide the selections.

A knowledge of the economic and financial behavior of industries is in-
valuable at this point. Familiarity with the capital structures, earnings and

dividend stability, and stock market reputations of such diverse industries as electric power, banking, steel production, oil refining, and the like will assist the investor in determining his needs. Knowledge of the relative importance of various cost factors, such as labor, fuel, and materials, and of the sales opportunities available will make his judgments more accurate. Some introduction to these industry factors will be provided in later chapters of this book, and further sources of information will be cited; for the present, it is sufficient to note that an acquaintance with industries will assist in making basic decisions.

Having decided upon the quality and detailed features of the desired stock, the investor may next look for issues which meet his specifications. The most convenient source of inspiration will probably be the "recommended" lists of financial advisory services, investment periodicals, and securities brokers, which, as was previously noted, are likely to include data on quality and other statistical information. Other suggestions can no doubt be drawn from quotation sheets, well-informed friends, and the investor's own broker. From these numerous sources it should be easy to select several stocks which appear to be suitable and attractively priced. These may then be compared, to arrive at a final choice.

The final step is, obviously, one of comparing values. If the investor is so minded, this may become an elaborate task, involving extensive economic and financial research. If the investor is disposed to spend his money on another's recommendation, the job can be done very simply yet reasonably well by reviewing a good analyst's summary of each stock and making a decision based on the summaries plus a very few fundamental statistical measures. The most vital convenient statistical measures are:

1   The price-earning ratio between the present price per share and the normal current earning power per share

2   The yield of the stock, based on the present price and a normal current dividend rate

3   The average annual growth rate in earnings during the past 5 or 10 years

4   The price-earnings ratio between the present price of the stock and the probable earnings per share 5 or 10 years hence

5   The range (high and low) or the stock's price during each of the past several years

6   The probable price 5 or 10 years hence

7   Expected investment gain—dividend yield plus average percentage price gain

This list of judgment criteria would probably seem frightening to most securities analysts. Five of the seven items require judgment estimates, and three of these call for estimates of future earnings and prices. Doubtless, many well-informed people will say that such estimates are little better than guesses. However, future earnings and prices are the measure of investment success, and surely the best available foresight in such matters is better than none.

Table 4-2 illustrates a compilation of statistics and estimates which would

Table 4-2 *Comparison of four stocks at May 1, 1972*

		Goodyear Tire	Safeway Stores	Schering- Plough	Phelps Dodge
1.	Price per share	31	39	100	41
2.	3-year average EPS, 1969–1971	$2.10	$2.62	$1.98	$4.47
3.	Price-earnings ratio on 3-yr. EPS	14.8	14.9	50.0	9.2
4.	Indicated 1972 dividend	$ .88	$1.35	$ .93	$2.10
5.	Current yield, per cent	2.8%	3.5%	0.9%	5.1%
6.	Average annual earnings growth, 1960–1961 to 1970–1971	8.3%	5.9%	15.4%	10.9%
7.	Past growth rate plus current yield	11.1%	9.4%	16.3%	16.0%
8.	Price range, 1971	35–27	40–32	90–60	48–28
9.	Price range, 1969–1970	34–21	34–22	63–38	56–34
10.	Estimated price, 1974–1976	48	55	92	79
11.	Estimated EPS, 1974–1976	$3.20	$4.20	$3.85	$6.60
12.	Price-earnings ratio on present price and 1974–1976 EPS	9.7	9.3	28.6	6.2
13.	Estimated EPS growth rate, 1970–72 to 1974–1976	9.0%	10.0%	13.5%	8.0%
14.	Current yield plus average estimated price growth, 1972–1975	18.5%	15.9%	— 1.4%	29.5%

This table presents certain figures but does not attempt to gauge stock quality or current economic status. In 1972 Goodyear confronted an unexciting tire market, Safeway was enjoying steady progress, Schering-Plough was benefiting from a great boom in its Garamycin antibiotic, and Phelps Dodge looked bad by comparison with a high earnings period in 1969–1970. Items 10 and 11 were taken from *Value Line Investment Survey*, which regularly publishes such estimates.

be very useful to an investor comparing the four stocks listed in the table. The first nine of the criteria used require figures which are readily available from financial papers and securities reference manuals. Only one of them, the 10-year average growth-rate figure, requires any exacting calculation. Items 10 and 11 might involve some thoughtful effort on the part of the average investor, but carefully prepared figures are available in at least one of the major analytical services and can be used instead of, or to confirm, personal estimates. Items 10 and 11 as used in Table 4-2 were taken from this analytical service.

APPRAISING A COMMON STOCK

An appraisal is a valuation which will be justified by future earnings, dividends, and stock prices. It establishes a figure which fluctuating markets may surpass or fall below, but which, as a purchase price, would not result in loss or abnormally low income returns to an unhurried long-term investor.

Such a valuation should guard against the error of buying a stock at an excessive price just because it is the best of a popular or prosperous group. It should encourage purchase when all stocks are cheap, and comparative appraisals should help in choosing the stocks whose prices stand farthest below ultimately realizable values. But appraisals are of only incidental help in choosing stocks which may appreciate sharply in short-term speculative trading. Such trading follows patterns established by public interest and current affairs, and is not always closely related to the long-run development of investment values.

Appraisals of common stocks are usually based on the same factors which were considered as criteria for comparing stocks in the preceding section. The most fundamental factors in the appraisal are earnings and dividend and growth estimates, which must be capitalized in some fashion by the use of price-earnings ratios and yields seemingly appropriate for the quality and market attractiveness of the stock being considered. Market price histories and net asset values can then be used to confirm or modify the appraisals based on earnings and dividend capitalizations. Although an appraisal is intended to establish logical values, not to rationalize present or past market prices, many analysts place great emphasis on a stock's actual historical price-earnings ratios and yields over a period of several years. These analysts argue that an appraisal based on a price-earnings ratio which the markets refuse to pay is simply wrong. This is doubtless true; yet the appraiser must also consider whether the markets will continue at a price-earnings level which is no longer justified by the facts.

This section will present four simple appraisal techniques which the users may accept, modify, or combine as the occasion requires. More sophisticated formulas are available, but elaboration of these simple ones to meet occasional needs seems a better approach than initial complexity. The four techniques are:

1 Determine the current normal earning power and dividend rate per share, capitalize these at appropriate price-earnings and yield rates, and average the results. Determining normal earning power and dividend rate for the current year of course calls for examining and perhaps averaging the two or three most recent years' figures, comparing these with the trends of the past decade, considering the outlook for the future, and arriving at a "representative normal" for the present year. The appropriate price-earnings and yield rates are equally a matter for judgment; Charts 4-1 and 4-2 show that large corporation common stocks sell in an average market at 10 to 25 times earnings and on a 6 per cent to 2½ per cent yield basis, depending on quality and growth promise. An average high-quality stock growing at about 4 per cent per annum seemingly sells in an average market for about 15 times earnings and yields about 4 per cent. It is clear that the wide disparity in these capitalization ranges is due far more to growth variation than to quality variation; a study of the price-earnings estimates shown in footnote 5 may help the investor to arrive at proper capitalization rates, or a study of actual historical price-earnings ratios and yields may suggest usable rates for the stock in question, but there is no clear and obvious method of selection in all cases. Finally, an appraisal arrived at by capitalizing earnings and another obtained by capitalizing dividends are likely not to agree perfectly. The happy solution is to average them, but this results in an unreasonably low appraisal in many of the best growth stocks. Such stocks often pay low dividends and retain most of their earnings to finance growth, a policy which in many such cases does not hold down the price of the stock.

As a case in point, the Goodyear Tire and Rubber stock may be considered. Table 4-2 indicates that earnings per share, which averaged $2.10 in 1969–1971 (and were about $2.65 in 1972), were expected to rise at about 9 per cent per year to about $3.20 in the 1974–1976 period. Thereafter, Goodyear's entrenched position and superior management should do at least as well as the average, and probably better. An average price-earnings multiplier of 15 times earnings would be too small in this case; the estimate in footnote 5 suggests that 19 times earnings would be more defensible. If the 1969–71 average earnings of $2.10 per share are multiplied by 19, an appraisal of $39.90 per share results. However, this is based on earnings alone; Goodyear's 88-cent annual dividend is an unusually small payout, probably because large reinvested earnings are needed to finance growth. A normal yield for a stock selling for 19 times earnings, based on a 60 per cent dividend payout, would be 3.16 per cent. If Goodyear's 88-cent dividend rate is capitalized at 3.16 per cent ($.88 ÷ .0316), the result is an appraisal of $27.85. This is far removed from the earnings appraisal of $39.90, and requires reconciliation by averaging the two divergent figures and also a further consideration of other items, such as those shown in Table 4-2. A simple average of the two appraisals would produce $33.88, which falls in the upper part of the depressed price range of 1969–1972.

2 The second appraisal process is similar to the first except that the price-earnings and yield ratios are computed from past history rather than determined by judgment. That is, price-earnings and yield figures are computed for each of the past, say, 5 years, and averaged. Appraisals are then made by capitalizing the normalized current earnings and dividends at these past price-earnings and yield rates. This process has the alleged merit of basing an appraisal in part on actual past market experience, instead of on the appraiser's judgment; this could also be a source of error.

3 The third appraisal process is simple in concept, though it may be somewhat difficult in execution. It requires simply *(a)* an estimate of the earnings-per-share rate the stock will have attained 10 years hence, *(b)* the multiplying of this earnings-per-share figure by 15 to arrive at a valuation at that time, and *(c)* the computation of the appraisal as the sum of the present value of the future stock valuation at 7½ per cent compound interest plus the present value at the same rate of all the dividends expected during the 10 years. This concept assumes that a 10-year earnings forecast is not impossible, though it will be a rough estimate; that most major company stocks will be alive and strong at the end of 10 years, but should be regarded as being average in growth outlook at that time, since economic and competitive conditions beyond that point cannot be visualized; and that stock investors want a 7½ per cent return on their investments.

4 The fourth appraisal process is very direct and simple. It is founded on the same concept as the third, but is modified for simplicty in execution. The process requires two steps: *(a)* Estimate the probable earning power per share 10 years hence and the *average* annual dividend during these 10 years, and add them; and *(b)* multiply this total by 7. This rather mystifying process is a very rough approximation of the third appraisal method described in the preceding paragraph; it works because the earnings multiplier (15) used on the "earning power 10 years hence," when combined with the present value at 7½ per cent of a valuation 10 years away, reduces to (roughly) 7; and the present value at 7½ per cent of a 10-year series of dividends falls in the general area of 7 times the average dividend. Thus the formula approximates the present value of the stock 10 years hence plus the present value of the intervening dividends.

A very brief example may be based on the Goodyear data of Table 4-2, as follows: The estimated earnings per share of $3.20 for 1974–1976 will grow by 1982 (at a "normal" 4.25 per cent rate) to $4.28 per share. A normal dividend rate of $2.57 can be expected out of such 1982 earnings; and an average of this $2.57 and the present 88 cents amounts to an expected average dividend of $1.72 for the whole period 1972–1982. Adding the ultimate earnings rate of $4.28 and the average dividend of $1.72 produces a total of $6, and multiplying this total by 7 produces an appraisal—as of 1972—of $42. This appears high, but a glance at the last five lines of Table 4-2 will show why any forward-looking appraisal of Goodyear based on these data will appear high. The table anticipates very

rapid earnings growth in the immediate future, but the 1969–1972 stock prices
are relatively low and seemingly unaffected by growth prospects.

MARKET LEVELS

The preceding section suggested that investors appraise stocks by estimating
their normal current earnings and dividends and capitalizing these by price-
earnings ratios and yields which were in turn based on the average or normal
price-earnings ratios of comparable stocks (and the market averages) in prior
years. But the higher price-earnings ratios and low yields in the period 1959–
1972 have posed a new (or perhaps a recurrent) problem for the investor.

This problem may be illustrated by reference to the level of stock prices
during 1972. Throughout the year the major indexes of industrial stock prices
fluctuated around 15 to 17 times the corresponding indexes of earnings, and
dividend yields averaged only 3.2 to 3.5 per cent. Inasmuch as these same indexes had shown average price-earnings ratios of 13 or 14 times earnings and
average yields of about 5 per cent in most "normal" years of the past generation,
the price levels of 1972 looked rather high. Furthermore, during the whole period
1904–1972, stocks had yielded more than bonds except in the peak year of 1929
and in the 1959–1972 period; yet, in 1972, stocks were so high that the indexes
yielded little over 3 per cent while good bonds were yielding more than 7 per cent.
It was clear that any appraisal based on the average standards of a generation
or longer would indicate stock values well below existing market prices. But it
was equally evident that the 13-year departure of stock prices from their pre-
1959 valuations was no random fluctuation, and that it might reflect the dominance of new forces in both the economy and investors' preferences.

In vindication of higher market appraisals, investor-optimists argued that
(1) saving in America was steadily increasing in amount and required investment outlets; (2) institutional investors, including pension funds, investment
companies, trusts, endowed agencies, and insurance companies, were using
stocks in increasing quantities and bidding against other investors to get them;
(3) government intervention in 1970–1971 had again held economic recession
within moderate bounds, stabilizing business and investment risks; (4) corporate
earnings had resumed their historic upward trend in 1971–1972 after declining
moderately in 1969-1970; and (5) an ongoing business recovery promised to
raise earnings 10 per cent or more annually for several years, reinforcing stockholders' 3 to 3½ per cent yields with substantial capital gains. To rebut this
favorable assessment, the skeptics of current market levels pointed out that (1)
in contrast to the 1960s, corporations were offering increased quantities of new
stock for sale, adding rapidly to supply pressures on market prices; (2) individual
investors, increasingly disenchanted by past speculative losses and rising com-

mission costs, were showing less enthusiasm for common stock investment; (3) inflation, which had led in the late 1960s to profit-crippling rises in labor, construction, and money costs, had not been reduced below a 3 per cent annual rate; (4) high-grade bond yields had not fallen below 7 per cent and would clearly offer stocks increasing competition as rising stock prices further reduced already-low stock yields; and (5) the increasingly political control of prices, wages, and corporate profit margins might slow and limit the earnings recovery which stock prices appeared, in part at least, to be discounting.

In large degree, future investment values in common stocks appeared to hinge on whether investors could expect inflation rates to fall below 3 per cent and bond yields below 7 per cent. If they could not, then a serious question would arise whether the stock of a well-established but not rapidly growing company would yield the investor a sufficient *real* return at 15 times normal earnings. From the experience of the preceding 25 years, the investor might expect common stocks bought at these levels to yield 3 per cent in annual dividends and about 4.25 per cent in long-term earnings and market-price growth. Yet against a 3.25 per cent rate of price-level inflation, this 7.25 per cent dividend-plus-growth return in current dollars would provide *a return on purchasing power* of only 4 per cent before taxes and, for the average investor, perhaps only 2 to 2½ per cent after taxes.

Increasingly, the portfolio preferences of large financial institutions suggested that many professional investors were looking to stocks with much above-average rates of earnings growth for an answer to the problems of inflation and a possible slowdown in rising corporate profits. These investors were willing, as they had been throughout the 1960s, to pay very high multiples of earnings for stocks which in the past 5 to 10 years had increased their earnings per share regularly by 10 per cent or more annually. (Note Schering-Plough in Table 4-2.) A study of footnote 5 will indicate that 10 per cent growth rates, successfully maintained over periods of 10 years or more, do indeed justify very high multiples of current earnings. Yet, as experience has continually demonstrated, the projection of existing growth rates even a short distance into the future can prove highly uncertain and liable to error; and if projections err badly, huge losses can be suffered when earnings multiples unexpectedly collapse.[9]

It seemed clear that investors in 1972 continued to face dilemma choices. Between fear that slow-growing stocks would prove unrewarding in a new market climate, and the large market and business risks present in buying rapid-growth stocks at astronomical multiples of earnings, it did not appear that a generation of well-sustained national prosperity had materially eased the uncertainties present in common stock selection.

---

[9] For specific examples, consider the stocks referred to in question 17 at the end of this chapter.

COMMON STOCKS AS PRICE-LEVEL HEDGES

During the inflationary years from 1941 through 1972, investors were much concerned to know whether common stocks actually live up to their theoretical capacity to serve as a price-level hedge. For a number of years during and immediately after World War II, they failed to do so—dividends and stock prices both lagged behind the advancing cost of living. However, the tide seemingly turned about 1949 or 1950, and since that time common stock owners have fared very well.

It seems reasonable, in considering this issue, to conclude that a common stock might give evidence of service as a price-level hedge if (1) its price rose or fell permanently with a change in the price level, or (2) its earnings per share changed with the prive level, or (3) its dividends changed with the price level. A really good price-level hedge would have to do all three.

Table 4-3 presents some statistical evidence upon which judgments may be based. It compares the post-1941 increases in stock prices, earnings, and divi-

Table 4-3 *Common stocks as price-level hedges—indexes of per share prices, earnings, and dividends compared with indexes of price levels (1940–1941 average = 100%)*

	1947	1952	1957	1962	1967	1972
Consumer price index	156	185	196	211	232	290
Wholesale price index	179	214	218	221	235	279
Moody's 125 Industrials						
Prices	153	250	475	656	938	1174
Earnings per share	192	259	346	374	578	730
Dividends per share	134	241	340	370	517	571
Moody's 24 Utilities						
Prices	135	162	225	418	462	371
Earnings per share	127	154	201	278	384	443
Dividends per share	105	128	162	199	295	333
Dividends—selected examples						
American Telephone	100	100	100	120	150	181
Chase Manhattan	143	143	216	247	314	427
Consolidated Edison	84	105	126	158	190	190
General Mills	163	180	218	261	348	433
General Motors	80	213	320	480	648	759
International Harvester	136	222	222	267	400	311
Marcor	126	126	189	84	84	101
Minnesota Mining	124	334	800	1600	2600	3850
Mobil Oil	200	400	625	590	925	1325
St. Paul Companies	162	225	392	454	646	985
Swift & Co.	154	147	166	118	176	112
Union Pacific	100	200	267	267	333	333

dends with the increases in wholesale and cost-of-living price indexes. In order to have a stable basis for comparison, all the data are stated as percentages of their 1940–1941 averages. In reading this table, it seems reasonable to estimate that ordinary asset growth from reinvested earnings should have accounted for at least 100 per cent dividend growth in the 31 years from 1941 to 1972; therefore, a stock which performed well as an inflation hedge would have to exceed the 1972 consumer price index figures by 100 points, to a total of about 390. Most of the nonregulated industrial stocks exceeded this. The utilities fell behind because of rate regulation. Among the individual stocks in the table there are several—Marcor and Swift, for example—which would naturally have been expected to be good inflation hedges and which have not gained satisfactorily. Others, such as Mobil Oil, have done extraordinarily well. Some of these differences are doubtless due to abnormalities in the figures of the particular years, but in large part they result from fundamental but unpredictable differences in the growth and profits of the industries and companies. And an examination of the year-by-year record of these companies discloses that in most cases, the *timing* of the stock price and dividend increases did not coincide with the price-level rises, but instead tended to occur later and in the less inflationary years between periods of accelerating inflation.

The sensible conclusion, which coincides with theory and previous experience, is that the common stocks of most nonregulated competitive industries are potentially good price-level hedges, but that a widely diversified collection of stocks would be needed in order to assure reasonably typical results, even in the long run.

DOES COMMON STOCK OWNERSHIP PAY?

The answer to this question is not an unequivocal one. The people who manage their stock investments with diligence and skill should ordinarily find them profitable. Others who invest without either knowledge or luck probably do very badly. Though they have no adequate data to support their belief, the authors are under the impression that the average small stockholder fares badly most of the time. The reasons lie mainly in his choice of mediocre-quality stocks and in poor timing of purchases and sales. Amateurs are notorious for buying stocks when market prices are high (they have surplus money during prosperous years and this is the time when booming stock prices come to their attention) and for selecting doubtful promotions or historically successful concerns whose futures are unpromising. And it must be admitted that the market choices at nearly all times include large numbers of stocks which will not prove to be good investments.

But there is no doubt that many corporate ventures do very well. The good stocks included in the well-known stock market indexes have given satisfactory results both in the aggregate and as individual stocks. So have many others. Some have gained spectacularly in earnings and market value. Most of the time in recent years it has been possible to buy good common stocks which pay as much as savings accounts and whose earnings are far in excess of the dividends paid. These are surely potentially profitable. Even if it be admitted that the re-invested earnings have not always added pro rata to corporate stock values as reflected in market prices, they have nevertheless had a pronounced effect on both stock prices and earning power.

Careful statistical studies made by a number of persons indicate that holders of diversified stock investments in relatively large American corporations (such as those listed on the New York Stock Exchange) have fared very well if their stocks were held on a long-range basis.[10] Even lists chosen at random under varying conditions of prosperity and depression were usually more profitable than bond holdings, if retained for a reasonable span of years and sold under any conditions except those of deepest depression. These results reflect, in the main, (1) the dividend yields obtained on the stocks, (2) the growth due to reinvested earnings and business development, and (3) the gains attributable to price-level inflation.

The conclusion to be drawn from this and other evidence is that common stocks should be profitable to those who diversify wisely, identify quality and value correctly, and succeed in avoiding calamitous errors. However, errors are possible; predicting the future is not an exact science, and even the economic expert may be wrong. And the chances for error as well as the damage an error may cause increase in geometric proportion as the investor forsakes quality for the speculative grades of stocks.

One other factor which lends some attractiveness to dividend-paying stocks is embodied in the federal personal income tax law. The Revenue Act of 1964 provides that in 1965 and later years each taxpayer may exclude his first $100 of dividends from his taxable income; this makes the first $100 of dividends to an individual or $200 to a married couple free of federal income taxes. This tax advantage is certainly enough to justify almost any investor in making sure that he has at least his full quota of tax-free dividend income.

PERSONAL POLICY IN STOCK INVESTMENT

For the great majority of reasonably well-informed and financially middle-class investors, the best possible stock investment policy could be summed up in three simple rules: First, buy only good-quality stocks; second, buy stocks only when

---

[10] See L. Fisher and J. H. Lorie, "Rates of Return on Investments in Common Stocks," *Journal of Business,* January 1964; or Chelcie C. Bosland, *The Common Stock Theory of Investment,* The Ronald Press Company, New York, 1937; or Edgar L. Smith, *Common Stocks as Long Term Investments,* The Macmillan Company, New York, 1928.

they can be had at attractive prices; third, diversify well. More detailed ideas on procedure will be presented in another chapter, but these are the essentials. The choice of good-quality stocks is stressed because they grow and yield almost as much as speculative stocks and offer much greater security. It is to be assumed that middle-class investors are too much preoccupied with other things to devote constant attention to speculation and that they should not risk serious losses. Some minor speculation through the medium of investment company shares might be an exception to the rule. The reasons for stipulating attractive prices and adequate diversification are obvious.

For the investor whose stake in the stock market must be small, say under $5,000, adequate diversification is a difficult problem. The solution may be found in investment company shares, provided the investment companies in turn confine themselves for the most part to conservative stocks. The investor of limited means has no occasion to risk his funds in other than quality commitments which are most carefully selected for assured future and attractive price.

QUESTIONS AND PROBLEMS

1 Are some common stocks better-quality investments than some bonds? Why?
2 Would a small investor obtain good value in stocks by refusing to buy a stock yielding less than 5 per cent? Would it be a better rule to refuse to buy any stock unless the Standard & Poor's Industrial Stock Index yielded at least 4 per cent?
3 Why would a middle-class small-investor family want to own common stock? When the hazards and the necessary effort of supervision are considered, is it worthwhile?
4 If high-grade bond yields remain in the 7 to 8 per cent range, will a $7\frac{1}{2}$ per cent discount factor prove too low for realistically discounting common stock earnings?
5 If earnings growth is an irregular, fluctuating thing, should it be ignored or given limited weight in attempting to gauge the value or desirability of a stock? Can you improve on the stock comparison or appraisal methods offered in the text?
6 If earnings growth averages 4.25 per cent per year and dividends average 3.50 per cent, is not stock ownership satisfactorily profitable? If all stocks suddenly doubled in price, how much would this reduce the stockholder's rate of return? Is this total investment gain a sound measure of stock pricing? Is there a better way?
7 Could you measure the stockholder's rate of return by adding the normalized current dividend and the average annual growth of earnings in cents per share multiplied by 15, and expressing this total as a percentage of the current price? Why use 15 as the multiplier?
8 Do retained earnings (corporate earnings not distributed in dividends) cause earnings per share and stock prices to rise by related amounts? If not, is a price-earning ratio a sensible calculation?
9 General Cable Corporation (a leading producer of copper wire and cable) at year-end 1971 had assets of $332,770,450, debts of $163,167,415, no preferred stock, and 14,269,186 common shares (20 per cent of which were owned by a large British cable concern). The common stock at year-end 1972 was paying a regular dividend of 80 cents per year, maintained since 1970 after dividends of $1 to $1.20 in 1967–1969. Earnings in 1972 were about

$1.30 per share. Between 1968 and 1971 they averaged $1.12; between 1964 and 1967 they averaged $1.79. Sales in 1970 through 1972 were 3 per cent less than for the 1967–1969 years but exceeded those of 1964–1966 by 10 per cent. The company's current ratio at year-end 1971 was 1.18. The market price of the stock had moved between 12¼ and 55¾ over the previous 9 years, and the price-earnings ratio between 11 and 45 times. Appraise this stock.

10 Is it true that a growth stock is likely to go up in price at least as fast as its earnings grow and faster than slow-growth stocks, and hence is a better buy at any reasonable price? How would you identify a growth stock and estimate its speed of growth? How gauge its duration of growth? How determine a reasonable price?

11 Could you develop a method of speculating in high-class stocks which permitted purchases only when both the general market and the individual stocks appeared reasonable in price? How would you time the sales?

12 Would it not be more profitable to speculate in medium-grade and speculative stocks, because they fluctuate more and the profits could be greater? Why do not all investment professors get rich by doing this?

13 What is meant by market factors? What kind of market factors could cause General Cable common stock to sell at a price out of line with similar stocks?

14 If you should want to compare the stocks of Allis-Chalmers, International Harvester, Caterpillar Tractor, and Westinghouse Electric as respects quality, but do not have time for extensive study, where could you get information?

15 Are all common stocks good price-level hedges? What kinds are not? Would a high-leverage stock have any advantages in a time of inflation? Of deflation? How about an investment company stock?

16 In a competitive economy, would it be feasible for leading stocks to continue indefinitely to sell at 15 times earnings and at twice their book values when net worth on capital employed in business earned an average of 10 per cent?

17 Do investors often pay undeservedly high prices for expected growth? Investigate Bausch & Lomb, Levitz Furniture, and New Process in 1972, Litton Industries between 1967 and 1972, Scott Paper between 1962 and 1972, and NL Industries (formerly National Lead) from 1955 to 1970.

18 Between 1962 and 1972 the debt ratios of nonfinancial corporations rose sharply, and interest payments as a percentage of profits-plus-interest payments increased from 27 per cent to 47 per cent. Has this development been beneficial or desirable from the common stockholder's standpoint?

19 Investment analysts use the term *horizon* to denote how far ahead investors look in trying to forecast earnings, dividends, and speculative market currents. How far ahead do you think they look? Do horizons differ as between investors and speculators? Small investors and financial institutions? Investors during booms and investors during recessions?

REFERENCES

American Research Council, Inc.: *Your Investments*, Rye, N.Y., semiannual.

Amling, Frederick: *Investments*, 2d ed., Prentice-Hall, Inc., Englewood Cliffs, N.J., 1970, Chaps. 6, 16.

Bellemore, Douglas H., and John C. Ritchie, Jr.: *Investments*, 3d ed., South-Western Publishing Company, Incorporated, Cincinnati, 1969, Chaps. 11–14.

Bernhard, Arnold: *The Evaluation of Common Stocks*, Simon and Schuster, Inc., New York, 1959.

Bosland, Chelcie C.: *The Common Stock Theory of Investment*, The Ronald Press Company, New York, 1937.

Cohen, Jerome B., and Edward D. Zinbarg: *Investment Analysis and Portfolio Management*, rev. ed., Richard D. Irwin, Inc., Homewood, Ill., 1973, Chap. 5.

Francis, John Clark: *Investment Analysis and Management*, McGraw-Hill Book Company, New York, 1972, Chaps. 9–11.

Graham, Benjamin, David L. Dodd, and C. Sidney Cottle: *Security Analysis*, 4th ed., McGraw-Hill Book Company, New York, 1962, Part 4.

Institute of Chartered Financial Analysts: *C. F. A. Readings in Financial Analysis*, 2d ed., Richard D. Irwin, Homewood, Ill., 1970, Part 3.

Lishan, John M., and David T. Crary: *The Investment Process*, paperback ed., International Textbook Company, Scranton, Pa., 1970, Part 2.

Wu, Hsui-Kwang, and Alan J. Zakon: *Elements of Investments* (selected readings), Holt, Rinehart and Winston, Inc., New York, 1965, Part 3.

OTHER EQUITIES AND
THEIR VALUE

The investor who wishes to acquire an equity, or ownership, position in a corporation need not always confine himself to the common stock. Other types of marketable equity claims are often available. Although these claims are more restricted, more contingent, or more perishable than those inherent in common stock, they may at times better serve the needs of particular investors or speculators. This chapter therefore assumes the task of describing in turn four major classes of further equity claims: (1) preferred stocks, including those with convertible, participating, or warrant-bearing features; (2) guaranteed stocks; (3) long-term stock purchase warrants; and (4) options, including puts, calls, and straddles.

Corporate managements have learned that some stock-buying investors prefer the type of fundamental ownership equity represented by common shares, and that others prefer to accept limited rights to dividends and other corporate benefits in exchange for the greater security afforded by a prior claim. Preferred stocks have been devised for the benefit of the investor who wants priority. Preferred stocks are ownership shares which typically are entitled to a limited annual dividend out of available earnings before the common stock gets anything, and in case of liquidation, to a limited sum out of the assets before the common stock gets anything. Some corporations create more than one class of preferred stock; such classes may rank in sequence (first, second, third, etc.) in priority of claim, or they may be equal in this respect.

Since preferred shares are definitely a part of the ownership, their claims are inferior to those of bondholders and other creditors. Furthermore, the corporation does not *owe* them anything; they may be entitled to receive dividends before other stocks get them, but the dividends will be available only if the directors declare them, and this should be done only if the corporation can afford the payment.

The investment merits of any class of stock in a corporation issuing more than one class will depend importantly on the special features and privileges granted to that class by the articles of incorporation. Preferred shares are not all alike; aside from the question of priorities, they may be voting, callable, convertible, cumulative, and participating, or they may have some of these features, or none of them; and still other features may or may not be present. Investors in preferred stocks need to be thoroughly familiar with their rights and privileges under both the articles of incorporation and the corporation code of the chartering state. However, the state codes are lengthy, technical, and inaccessible documents;

so most investors assume that the law will be fair and just and confine their inquiries to the corporate articles. The important provisions in the articles are summarized in official prospectuses and in the major financial reporting services, such as Moody's or Standard & Poor's. These sources are usually adequate.

AUTHORIZED STOCK

The quality of preferred shares may be strongly affected by the number of shares outstanding or authorized by the articles. Prior rights to earnings or assets can assure a high degree of safety if the number of shares enjoying the priority is small and if the articles limit the number which may be issued. In checking the number of authorized and outstanding shares, it is desirable to note all the classes of stock which the articles permit, since several classes with equal or varying preferences could be authorized.

DIVIDEND PROVISIONS

Preferred stocks nearly always have some sort of preference as to dividends. The usual provision calls for quarterly dividends which must be paid up to date before a dividend may be paid on any lower-ranking preferred or common stock. Most modern issues are also cumulative; that is, preferred dividends which are not paid cumulate and must be paid up in full before dividends may be resumed on the lower-ranking stocks. Issues on which dividends are noncumulative never get their payments if the corporation is forced to omit them at the regular payment time. A few preferreds have special variations, such as the provision that unpaid dividends cumulate up to a limited amount only or to the extent earned but no more; these provisions are designed to forestall the possibility of excessive accumulations which might embarrass the company.

When corporations issue preferred stocks which rank sequentially—that is, a First Preferred, a Second Preferred, etc.—the First Preferred is usually entitled to all accumulated and current dividends before any payments may be made on the Second Preferred. The Second Preferred will then have similar preferences over the next-ranking issue. Sometimes a junior or lower-ranking preferred will be noncumulative when the senior (high-ranking) preferred is fully cumulative.

Clearly, a cumulative preferred is a more satisfactory investment vehicle than a noncumulative one. There are times when even strong corporations must omit preferred dividends temporarily, and it is better for the investor that these be merely deferred rather than lost. Furthermore, there is greater incentive for the management to try to pay dividends regularly if unpaid ones cumulate; for cumulated dividends presumably must be paid sometime, whereas unpaid noncumulative dividends embarrass no one but the unpaid stockholder.

When preferred dividends have accumulated unpaid, they are regarded as being attached to the stock. If the stockholder sells his stock, the purchaser obtains title to the dividend accruals. If the corporation itself acquires the stock, the dividend rights are retired.

Preferred stocks are ordinarily entitled to their preference dividends and no more. They seldom receive rights or other special disbursements. Exceptions are found in the case of participating preferreds, which will be discussed later.

ASSET PREFERENCES

Most preferred stocks are preferred as to assets. That is, if the firm is liquidated, they receive their par value or a stated sum plus all cumulated unpaid dividends, plus a premium or bonus in some instances, before lower-ranking stock gets anything. Very commonly the articles specify that in case of involuntary liquidation (under compulsion of law or because of insolvency), the asset preference is limited to par or stated value plus cumulated dividends, but that if the liquidation is voluntary, a premium must be paid also. This premium may vary from nothing to 25 per cent, but it is generally between 5 and 10 per cent. These three items— par or stated value, possible premium, and cumulated dividends if any—are all that most preferreds are entitled to receive.

VOTING POWER

Preferred stock issued prior to 1930 usually has no vote on ordinary management matters or the election of directors. This feature was probably written into the articles in most cases by men who regarded preferred shareholders virtually as creditors, with limited risk and limited rights. There is at the present time a pronounced trend toward full voting rights for preferred shares. However, it must be admitted that common shares usually far outnumber preferred shares, so the usual one vote per share provision will not give the preferred holders much power; and it must be further conceded that most of them will not be much interested in voting anyhow.

Preferred stockholders are much more likely to take an interest in management when they do not receive dividends than when they do. Consequently, the considerable number of corporations which give unpaid preferred holders (1) the right to elect certain directors, or (2) the right to elect a majority of the directors, or (3) some other significant voting power are placing their preferred stockholders in a position where they can at least become vocal in self-defense. This is a sound provision. The preferred stock will seldom undertake to displace a management which is conscientiously battling adversity, but neglect and fraud can be summarily chastened. The usual provision giving preferred stockholders these powers makes them effective only after omission of several consecutive quarterly payments or when total payments are 2 or 3 years in arrears.

Even more important than a vote on management matters is the preferred stock's right, voting as a single class of stock, to veto certain types of proposals. The veto power should extend to all such matters as (1) amendment of the articles to change the preferred stock's own privileges, (2) amendment of the articles to authorize more preferred or higher-ranking preferred, (3) issuance of bonds or preferred stock, and (4) mergers or substantial change of business. Action adverse to its interests on these matters could greatly weaken a preferred stock without at all injuring the common. State laws in a number of states specifically give each class of preferred stock a veto on some of these matters, but not all states do so. Stronger protection is afforded in the articles of many corporations.

Since there are many preferred shares on the market, the wise investor will merely choose among those whose voting and veto powers are adequate. There is no point in being unnecessarily vulnerable.

CALL FEATURES

Most modern preferred stock is callable or redeemable. That is, the corporation reserves the right to pay it off at prices specified in the articles and retire it. Many old preferreds are noncallable (N.C.), however, because the articles either say so or do not mention redemption at all.

Usually the stockholder must be given 2 or 3 months' notice prior to the call date. The call price, which is specified in the articles, consists of par or a stated value, plus a possible premium, plus all cumulated unpaid dividends. The premium is usually the same as that payable in voluntary liquidation, any amount from nothing to 25 per cent, but generally between 5 and 10 per cent. Sometimes the call premium declines or rises with the passage of time.

A call feature in a preferred stock is seldom of advantage to an investor, but it enables a prosperous corporation to retire high-rate preferreds. The call price thus limits the advantage an investor can gain by purchase of preferreds in corporations whose financial standing is improving, for it is clear that the market price is unlikely to go very far above the call price. Investors are understandably reluctant to pay much more than the call price for any callable preferred, even if it is of high quality.

The absence of a call feature in a preferred stock is not a positive assurance that an investor can keep it indefinitely, for mergers or recapitalizations may result in the substitution of a new security which may be callable. Such mergers and recapitalizations may be done only under the terms of the state corporation code and the company's own articles, which may protect the preferred by (1) requiring the approval by vote of a heavy majority of the preferred, voting as a separate group; or (2) providing that dissenting shareholders must be paid a fair appraised amount in cash; or (3) some other safeguard. In addition, the courts will enjoin an unjust plan.

Among firms which eliminated noncallable preferreds in this way during the 1960s were Bethlehem Steel, U.S. Steel, International Harvester, and Eastman Kodak. However, most of these plans were generous to the preferred shareholders. For example, when U.S. Steel retired its $7 dividend preferred by recapitalization in late 1965, it gave the stockholders $175 per share in 4⅝ per cent bonds due in 1996; these bonds were worth about $166 per preferred share, and provided annual interest amounting to $8.10 per preferred share.

PAR VALUES

Most preferreds have par values, even when the issuing company's common stock is no par. In such cases the asset preferences, call prices, and dividend rights are usually calculated as percentages of the par value. But there is no necessary relationship between these basic rights and par values. For example, Union Electric Company has a no par preferred which is entitled to cumulative dividends of $3.50 per annum, is callable at $110, and would receive $100 in involuntary liquidation. However, in mid-1972 these preferred shares sold at $48, and it seems reasonable to conclude that par values are not fundamentally significant investment attributes.

SINKING FUNDS

A considerable number of preferred issues obligate the corporation to purchase and retire some of the shares annually. The amount to be retired may be fixed at a definite sum, or it may depend on the sales volume or earnings. It may be a large amount or a relatively small one. Usually there is provision for selecting shares by lot, to be redeemed at a stated call price, if the corporation cannot buy stock on the open market at or below the call price. Sinking funds are important to the investor because they progressively reduce the number of preferred shares outstanding and thus improve the security behind those remaining. Sinking-fund purchases also help both to stabilize and to keep up the price of the stock on the market, because the purchase of shares which are offered for sale will remove them from the market.

The corporation is not under any inflexible legal obligation to pay into a preferred stock sinking fund. The usual provision in the articles requires the stipulated sinking fund to be provided after payment of the preferred dividend but before payment of dividends on any lower-ranking class of stock. Unpaid sinking-fund installments may or may not cumulate.

RESTRICTIONS ON COMMON DIVIDENDS

In recent years it has become common practice to write into the corporate articles certain limitations on cash dividends to common stock and on disbursements to repurchase common stock, to be effective during the time that the preferred stock is outstanding. These limitations usually forbid such outlays except when (1) the corporate working capital exceeds a stated amount and (2) the accumulated earned surplus exceeds a stated amount. Such restrictions add substantially to the quality of the preferred stock, for they prevent the weakening of the business by payment of ill-advised cash dividends on the common. Stock dividends are not usually restricted.

ACCUMULATED PREFERRED DIVIDENDS

When a corporation is compelled to omit preferred dividends for several years, the amount of unpaid accumulations is often large enough to pose a serious problem. Efforts to pay current dividends and several years' arrears in a short period would drain working capital severely; and a conservatively slow payment program would tax the patience of junior preferred and common stockholders. Corporate managements are therefore likely to try to settle large dividend arrearages by offering the stockholders new securities, if an acceptable plan can be found. Small arrearages are usually paid up in cash.

If a substantial dividend arrearage is to be settled by issuance of new securities, it is usually not best to do it by simple declaration of a dividend payable in the new securities, for two reasons. In the first place, such a dividend need not be accepted in lieu of cash by any stockholder who does not wish to do so, and inevitably some would refuse; thus not all the arrearages could be cleared. Second, the value of the new securities distributed as a dividend would be taxable income to the stockholders.

The method of settling large preferred arrearages commonly involves some such procedure as the following: (1) After earning power is sufficiently recovered to make the project feasible, a formal "plan of recapitalization" is adopted by directors and stockholders. (2) The corporate articles are amended to create a new class of preferred stock superior in priority to the existing preferred. (3) Dividend payments are announced on the new prior preferred but not on the old preferred. (4) Old preferred holders are offered the option to exchange their shares for an equal amount of new prior preferred plus some extra new preferred or common to compensate for the accrued dividends attached to the old stock. They will do this because (a) they want dividend-paying stock, (b) the extra stock received in lieu of back dividends is not taxable as income, and (c) the new preferred will be prior in claim to the old. (5) After a year or two, when the exchanges have been largely completed, the arrears can be paid up on the remaining old preferred, and regular dividends may then begin on it and the common.

Sometimes the recapitalization is not consummated by voluntary exchange of stock but, instead, becomes mandatory upon all stockholders when approved by the requisite majorities. In general, recapitalization plans during the past few years have been approved by heavy majorities of preferred stockholders. The plans have seldom been generous to preferred holders, but usually they have not been excessively harsh.

FUNDAMENTAL CALCULATIONS

There are four basic calculations ordinarily used in indicating the investment merit of a preferred stock and gauging the reasonableness of its price. These calculations determine (1) the earnings per share, (2) the adequacy of dividend coverage on the overall basis, (3) the asset coverage per share, and (4) the yield.

Earnings per share   The earnings per share as ordinarily computed on preferred stocks show the number of earned dollars per share out of which the preferred dividend may be paid. The figure does not purport to show how much could legally be paid to the preferred shares. For example, if a corporation having 100,000 preferred shares outstanding has $1,000,000 in profits left after paying all expenses, interest, and taxes, the earnings per preferred share would be $10. If the annual preferred dividend rate is $5 per share, that is the dividend rate which would be paid; the $10 earnings figure merely indicates that $10 was available where $5 would suffice.

When corporations have more than one issue of preferred stock outstanding, it is customary to divide the available profits by the total number of such shares if the two issues are of equal priority. For example, General Motors at year-end 1971 had 1,000,000 shares of $3.75 dividend preferred and 1,835,644 shares of $5 dividend preferred. The corporation had $1,935,709,000 in profits in 1971; divided among the 2,835,644 preferred shares, this indicated earnings of $628.63 per preferred share.[1]

But corporations frequently have issues of preferred stock which rank successively rather than equally. In such cases it is customary to regard all the profits as available to the First Preferred; dividing total profits by the number of outstanding First Preferred shares produces the desired figure of earnings per share. The profits available to the Second Preferred are those remaining after the First Preferred dividend requirements are subtracted from total profits; this remaining sum is then divided by the number of Second Preferred shares. The process may be illustrated by the figures of Northwest Industries, Inc. This company in 1971 earned profits in the amount of $47,747,000. There were outstanding, at the year-end, 3,035,068 shares of $4.20 dividend convertible prior preferred, and 876,641 of Series A 5% $100 par convertible preferred and 669,276 shares of Series C $5 convertible preferred, which ranked equally after the prior preferred. Earnings

---

[1] Despite the difference in dividend rate, these General Motors shares are regarded as being equal in claim, since both are no par and their call prices are not far apart. However, when two equal-ranking preferreds of substantially different income rights are involved, special arithmetic techniques are required.

per share on the prior preferred were computed by dividing the $47,747,000 of earnings available by 3,035,068, which gave the $15.73 reported. Earnings available for the two junior preferred issues were next calculated by subtracting the $12,747,000 actually needed for the prior preferred from the total profits of $47,747,000: this left $35,000,000. Taken together, the Series A and Series C issues comprised, 1,545,917 shares of $5 dividend preferred. Dividing the 1,545,-917 shares into the $35,000,000 available gave earnings of $22.64 per share on the second-ranking preferred stock.

The technical weakness in the earnings-per-preferred-share calculation is apparent in the Northwest Industries illustration. Because the number of second-ranking preferred shares is small, the earnings appear to cover the junior preferred dividends by a wider margin than they do the prior preferred requirement. Such is not the case, since it is clear that the prior preferred has an absolute first claim. The truth of the matter is that an earnings-per-share figure is a reliable index of earnings adequacy on preferreds only when the corporation has no interest-bearing debt and when the calculation is applied to First or Prior Preferreds only. Despite these limitations, earnings-per-share figures on preferreds are generally reported in leading analytical services.

Dividend coverage on the overall basis Analysts desiring a better measure of preferred stock quality than the earnings-per-share figure have developed a figure generally referred to as "times dividend earned, overall basis." In the authors' opinion, this computation should be made by dividing a company's *profit before interest and taxes*[2] by the total amount of interest and preferred dividend requirements plus income tax due on the earnings out of which the preferred dividend must be paid. For ease of calculation, this divisor ordinarily consists of the interest charges plus *twice* the preferred dividend, since with a corporate income tax of about 50 per cent, a company must earn roughly $2 before taxes to support each $1 of preferred dividends. Thus, if a corporation had $4,000,000 of earnings left after paying all operating expenses but before interest and taxes, and if its bond interest required $500,000 and its preferred dividend $750,000, a total of $2,000,000 would be required to meet all prior requirements and the preferred dividend would be earned 2 times. If a Second Preferred required another $250,000 of annual dividends, then $500,000 more would be added to prior requirements. The new sum of $2,500,000 divided into the $4,000,000 available would indicate a coverage ratio of 1.6 times for the Second Preferred as compared with 2.0 times for the First.

The logic of this method is supported by two considerations. First, it invariably

---

[2] We favor this method as opposed to the prevailing practice of dividing the posttax earnings by the total amount of interest and preferred dividend requirements, since the latter calculation treats the entire income tax as an expense prior in claim to bond interest.

shows a higher rate of dividend coverage for a senior preferred. This will remain true however small the junior issues may be in relation to prior ones. Second, the fractional *inverse* of the times-coverage figure obtained will truly reflect to the investor the percentage to which a company's operating earnings, i.e., its earnings before interest and taxes, can shrink before it fails to earn its preferred dividend. In the example of the First Preferred just given, the coverage figure of 2 indicates that earnings before interest and taxes could fall to one-half their reported level before the preferred dividend would be uncovered. This inversion of the times-covered figure gives a correct result because $2,000,000 before interest and taxes would leave $500,000 for interest, $750,000 for the preferred dividend, and $750,000 for the related income tax.

In comparing the quality of preferred stocks in similar concerns in similar industries, the "times dividend earned" figure is a good one. In comparing preferreds in different industries, however, it is necessary to bear in mind that the amount of available earnings fluctuates far more in some industries than others. In the electric power industry, a preferred whose requirements are earned 2 times overall in the average year is of investment grade; but in the steel or railroad industry, such a preferred would be rated only fair, for the earnings would doubtless fall below the preferred dividend requirement in bad years.

Assets per share   A figure showing net assets per preferred share, or book value per preferred share, is of value in some instances. It is computed by taking the net assets after depreciation and other allowances, subtracting all debts, and dividing the remainder by the number of preferred shares outstanding. The result indicates the book value of the net assets available to support each preferred share. The computation may be adapted to a situation involving more than one class of preferred stock by procedures similar to those used in computing earnings per share. The book value idea is useful in indicating whether earnings depend on solid assets or chiefly on the intangibles of good will and going-concern value, and it is highly significant in investment companies and other concerns dealing in securities and receivables; but it is open to all the criticisms noted in connection with the book value of common stocks.

Yield   The yield of a preferred stock, measured by expressing the annual dividend rate as a percentage of the price of the stock, is fundamental in gauging its attractiveness for investment. In fact, the yield and the quality of the stock are the main determinants of its attractiveness. In the case of common stocks, it is customary to give great attention to undistributed earnings, which are reinvested to improve future earnings, and to the possibility of market profits; but since these factors are not usually of prime importance to preferred holders, the yield and quality (certainty of payment) factors receive greater emphasis.

Table 5-1 indicates the relation between quality, as evidenced by overall divi-

Table 5-1   *Comparison of industrial preferreds*

Stock, annual dividend, call price	Times dividend earned, overall basis, 1971	Yield on market price, 12/1/72	Price range 1970– 1971	Standard & Poor's quality rating
Armstrong Cork $3.75 ($102.75)	10.48	6.8	68–47	AA
Owens-Illinois $4.00 ($101.75)	4.78	5.4*	79–62	AA
Standard Brands $3.50 ($100.00)	3.56	6.5	63–47	AA
American Can $1.75 (N.C.)	2.91	7.0	31–22	A
Getty Oil $1.20 ($25)	14.49	6.2	21–16	A
Amstar $.68 (N.C.)	7.01	7.5	11–8	BBB
Celanese $4.50 ($100)	2.52	7.8	70–49	BBB
Uniroyal $8.00 (N.C.)	2.10	7.8	135–91	BBB
Armour $4.75 ($101)	3.34	7.5	76–50	BB

These nine preferreds are arranged in order of rated quality. Note that company strength and stability are at least as important as earnings coverage, that a preferred which has no bonds or prior preferred ahead of it is better than a junior issue, and that no one year's earnings coverage will be completely typical for all companies. Rental charges are regarded as operating expenses, not fixed charges, in these calculations. Should they be?

* The low yield of the Owens-Illinois preferred reflects the operation of a sinking fund which requires the company to repurchase $2 million of this stock each year, provided the market price is less than $100. Only about one-third of the original issue was still outstanding in 1972.

dend coverage, and yield. The statistics in the table are not perfect, since they are based on 1971 earnings without any reference to future prospects; nevertheless, their implication is clear.

INVESTMENT POSITION OF PREFERRED STOCKS

The better grades of preferred stocks are chiefly sought by insurance companies, endowed institutions, trustees, and other conservative large holders who want security and a reasonable income. They are especially attractive to income-tax-paying corporations, such as fire insurance companies, because 85 per cent of dividend income is exempt from a second corporate income tax in the receiving corporation.[3] Lower-grade preferreds are mostly held by members of the general public who are willing to bear speculative risks for a somewhat higher return.

[3] In order to avoid taxing the same income at full rates successively in two or more corporate layers, the tax law provides that any corporation which receives either common or preferred dividends from another taxpaying corporation must add only 15 per cent of such dividends to its taxable income. This 85 per cent

Although preferred stocks seem to enjoy a satisfactory market, they are relatively less used as a corporate financing device than they were before 1941. In these days of high income taxes a typical corporation must earn $2 to $2.20 before state and federal income taxes in order to have $1 left for dividends, whereas earnings used for bond interest are not taxed. Consequently, corporations find it economical to sell bonds rather than preferred stocks, and the supply of preferreds is thus ordinarily restricted. Public utility companies are the largest issuers of preferred stocks because regulatory commissions typically require them to use a certain proportion of preferred in their capital structures and allow them high enough rates to pay income taxes on their preferred-share earnings without reducing net per share on the common stock.

The best preferred stocks are almost as secure and as sure of regular income as high-grade bonds.[4] They do not fluctuate seriously in price because of business risks. However, substantial fluctuations in interest rates such as have occurred since 1958 do produce major price changes in high-grade preferreds, as Table 5-1 shows. Because preferred stocks have no maturity dates, a market-induced change in their yields causes a relatively drastic change in their prices. Medium-grade preferreds are affected both by company earnings and market interest rates; often these have compensating effects. Lower-grade preferreds are competitive with common stocks as well as with bonds, are very sensitive to the issuing company's affairs, and are especially sensitive to any situation which seems to threaten the preferred dividend.

The yield records in Table 5-2 indicate that preferred stock yields have risen less since 1947 than bond yields, and that since 1962 the better grades of preferreds yield less than bonds of similar quality. This is undoubtedly the result of the tax situations previously noted, but the fact clearly reduces the attractiveness of preferreds for personal investment.

CONVERTIBLE OR WARRANT-BEARING PREFERREDS

About one-third of all preferred shares are originally convertible into the common stock of the company at the option of the individual stockholders. This privilege permits the preferred holder to participate more fully in the company's success if it succeeds but to retain his preferred position if it does not.

---

exclusion applies to income from all preferred stocks except those of public utility operating companies. On "new money" utility preferreds, meaning those issued on or after Oct. 1, 1942, to raise net new funds, the 85 per cent dividend exclusion applies. On "old money" preferreds, those issued prior to Oct. 1, 1942, or for the refunding of bonds or preferred stocks issued prior to that date, only 60.8 per cent of the dividends are excludable from taxable corporate incomes.

[4] Very high-grade preferred stocks are often called "money preferreds" because of their tendency to fluctuate only with changing interest rates.

Table 5-2 *Comparison of average yields on bonds and stocks, per cent*

Year	Aa bonds*	High-grade preferreds†	Medium-grade preferreds	Industrial common stocks*
1947	2.70	3.79	5.12	5.06
1952	3.04	4.13	5.86	5.55
1957	4.03	4.63	5.88	4.11
1962	4.47	4.50	5.63	3.39
1967	5.66	5.46	5.72	3.11
1970	8.32	7.29	7.53	3.60
1972	7.49†	6.85‡	7.11‡	2.66‡

* From Moody's Investors Service.
† From Standard & Poor's.
‡ Preliminary.

Corporations sell convertible preferreds in order to attract money at lower dividend rates than would otherwise be possible. Also, this may be a means of obtaining new common stock capital in the long run, for the preferred stock will tend to be converted into common whenever conversion offers an opportunity to obtain higher dividends in stock having at least as much market value or a higher market value with no reduction in dividend income. Convertible preferreds have been particularly popular with investors since 1965, for the combination of senior rights to income plus opportunity to convert to common stock in case of price-level inflation seems to meet a definite need. In fact, this popularity is so great that preferreds with options to convert into common stock at prices far above current market values usually sell at higher prices and yield much less than comparable ordinary preferreds.

In theory, a convertible preferred share should sell at the higher of two prices: (1) its value as a dividend-paying security, or (2) its value when converted into common stock. Its value as a dividend-paying security can be found by dividing its annual dividend by the yield obtainable on nonconvertible preferred stocks of the same investment quality. For example, Flintkote Company Series B cumulative convertible 2nd preferred pays an annual dividend of $2.25 and carries a quality rating of BBB by a leading statistical service. In April 1972, when nonconvertible preferred stocks of BBB quality ratings yielded 7.3 per cent, the Flintkote share, valued on its dividend alone, was worth $2.25 divided by .073, or $30.82. This figure represents the lowest price at which this preferred stock could possibly have sold as long as nonconvertible shares of equal quality yielded 7.3 per cent. However, this "floor" price did not prevail because this issue of Flintkote preferred was convertible at any time into 1.111 shares of the company's common stock, which was selling at $31. The value-in-conversion of each preferred share was therefore 1.111 times $31, or $34.44.

Inquisitive readers will note that neither of these prices prevailed in the stock market. In April 1972, the Series B Flintkote preferred sold at about $44 per share, well above its calculated value-in-conversion. It is usual for convertible preferred stocks (and for convertible bonds as well) to sell somewhat above their calculated values; this margin is called the *speculative premium*. When the common stock is below the price at which conversion of the preferred is profitable, the speculative premium measures the value which investors attach to their chance of sharing in a future price rise by the common stock; this estimate is sometimes realistic, sometimes excessive, but in principle justified. However, the further the common stock rises above the profitable conversion price, the more difficult it becomes to justify any speculative premium on the preferred. Some investors argue that the "floor" price set by the capitalized dividend and the *long-range* value of the conversion privilege gives the preferred stock better protection against the business and market risks than the common shares enjoy. But this is not true if the preferred price reflects a large advance in the common stock; if the common declines, the preferred will drop proportionately—for many points at least—before any "floor" is reached. Over this price range, an investor might as well own the common. Consequently, conversion premiums tend to disappear as convertible preferreds rise greatly in price. For example, American Home Products $2 preferred, convertible into 1.5 shares of the company's common stock, had a value-in-conversion, during April 1972, some 5 times its capitalized $2 dividend. It sold at 144, exactly 1.5 times the $96 common price.

The number of common shares for which a preferred is exchangeable is indicated in the corporate articles. In most instances the conversion ratio—the number of common shares received for each preferred share—is such that immediate conversion of new preferreds would not be profitable, for the common shares so obtained would pay less in dividends and be worth less than the preferred. But rising earnings and dividends on the common could soon change that. However, the articles often provide that the conversion ratio decreases through the years, and in some instances the conversion right lapses altogether after a time. If the stock is both convertible and callable, the stockholder may usually exercise his conversion option after he receives notice of a call but before the payment date. Obviously, a corporation can use the call feature to force conversion of a preferred selling to reflect the conversion privilege.

Conversion rights should be protected against *dilution*. The corporation's articles should specify that if the value of the common stock is altered by splits, stock dividends, mergers, or rights, the conversion terms will be proportionately adjusted. Sometimes the problem of rights is solved by offering them to convertible preferred stockholders and to common stockholders simultaneously.

Instead of making a preferred issue convertible, some corporations have attached common stock purchase warrants to their preferred certificates. These can be detached and submitted with a check for the indicated amount to buy new common stock. When such warrants are valuable, contracts for the purchase and sale of preferred must stipulate whether the stock is to be transferred *with warrants* or *ex-warrants*.

PARTICIPATING PREFERREDS

A few preferred issues are made participating, which means that in case other stockholders get large dividends or special benefits, the preferred participates in them also. For example, the Southern California Edison Company's Original Preferred has a preferential right to a 5 per cent cumulative dividend; but in case any other stock issued by the company gets a larger dividend or a special disbursement (including rights), the Original Preferred gets an equal rate. This preferred is noncallable. Other provisions of varying nature are found in other companies' participating preferred issues, since the corporate articles may be written to provide almost any reasonable features desired. For example, the participating preferred may get its basic dividend *plus* any payments made on the common; or the participation may be limited to a stated maximum amount per year.

Participation occasionally extends to the matter of asset distribution if the corporation is liquidated, but this is much less common and normally much less important than dividend participation.

GUARANTEED STOCKS

The railroad, telegraph, and certain other industries afford investors a considerable number of "guaranteed" stocks. These are stocks whose dividend payments are either guaranteed by a parent or affiliated company or contractually paid as a lease rental by the guarantor corporation. The latter type is the most common. In these cases the guarantor has leased the entire property and business of the lessor concern and has agreed to pay as a lease rental all operating expenses, maintenance costs, taxes, interest, and a stipulated dividend on the lessor's stock. The legal arrangements vary greatly in technical details and duration, but most such leases run for very long periods.

If the guarantor is financially strong and the contract has many years to run, any guaranteed stock is of good quality. Otherwise, its future depends on the earning power of the property. Most guaranteed stocks are products of the railroad and telegraph merger era, from 1875 to 1914. By modern standards they are relatively small issues.

STOCK PURCHASE WARRANTS

Along with convertible securities, long-term stock purchase warrants have become popular with both investors and issuing corporations during recent years.

A stock purchase warrant[5] is a marketable option, tradable like a share of stock; it entitles the holder to buy from the company a specific amount of authorized but unissued stock at a set price during a prescribed period, ordinarily several years. For example, American Telephone and Telegraph Company warrants, issued in May 1970, entitle the holder of each warrant to buy one share of the company's common stock at a price of $52 through May 15, 1975. Warrants pay no dividends, include no voting rights, and become worthless at expiration if the common stock is below the exercise price. Most warrants run 3 to 5 years, although some have 10- to 20-year lives, and a few, including those of the Tri-Continental and Alleghany Corporation, are perpetual and noncallable. Corporations attach warrants to new stock and bond issues as "sweeteners" to raise their price and lower their yield, and conglomerate companies frequently issue warrants in partial exchange for the securities of acquired firms. In early 1972, more than 300 issues of warrants were actively traded on the New York and American Stock Exchanges and in the national over-the-counter market. Companies with warrants outstanding included such important names as Avco Corporation, Carrier, Mobil Oil, and Commonwealth Edison.[6]

Because warrants lack income and an assured value at maturity, they are usually the domain of the speculator rather than the investor. Speculators making successful commitments in warrants usually prefer to sell their warrants rather than exercise their right to purchase stock. Warrants held longer than 6 months qualify for long-term capital gains or losses, but if they are exercised, a new holding period begins on the common stock the cost basis of which is the cost of the warrant plus its exercise price.

Warrants are popular with speculators because ordinarily their price rises and falls at a faster rate than the price of the related common stock. Over certain price ranges, this is necessarily true because the *intrinsic value* of the warrant (common share price less exercise price of the warrant) changes in larger proportion than the stock price. For example, when a stock is selling at $25, a warrant to buy it at $20 per share will have an intrinsic value of $5. If the common stock moves up $10, or 40 per cent, the intrinsic value of the warrant would rise to $15 ($35 minus $20), or 200 per cent. In this oversimplified example, the warrant would advance at 5 times the rate of the stock. Of course, this "price leverage" works both ways, and the intrinsic value of the warrant also will decline by a greater percentage in a falling market.

The foregoing example is oversimplified, however, because a warrant does not

[5] The term *warrant* is also used in the securities business to mean the piece of paper which evidences the ownership of rights, fractional shares of stock, or some other claim or privilege which does not quite attain the stature of a security.

[6] A cynic might label the reappearance of warrants in large numbers the sign of a dangerously speculative investment atmosphere. Warrants were popular in the frenzied markets of the 1920s, but from 1930 until the middle 1960s they were largely ignored by both investors and corporate issuers.

sell in the stock market on the basis of its intrinsic value, but at a changing speculative premium *above* this value. The premium is the difference between the warrant's market price, which is always positive, and its intrinsic value, which is frequently negative. Thus, if the stock in the previous paragraph sold at $15, and the
warrant at $3, the premium would be $8—it would take a $3 warrant plus $20
cash to buy a common share that could be bought in the stock market for $15.
Premiums are typically large when stocks are below the exercise price of their
corresponding warrants, often around 40 per cent when the stock sells at the exercise price, and nominal or nonexistent when the stock reaches twice the exercise
price or more.

The reader may develop some feeling for the comparative movements of
market prices, intrinsic values, and speculative premiums by considering changes
occurring in Tenneco Corporation securities during the period 1970–1972. In
November 1970, the common stock sold at $19⅜, and the warrants, exercisable
at $24¼ until November 1975, were quoted at $3. The intrinsic value of the warrants was then —$4.87, and their speculative premium amounted to $7.87. By
February 1972, when the common had risen to $28½, the warrant had climbed to
$10¼. Its intrinsic value had meanwhile increased to $4¼, while the speculative
premium had declined to $6.

It should now be evident that the trader in warrants confronts a more difficult
task than the common stock buyer because he faces two major problems, not one:
he must concern himself not only with prospective movements of a company's
common stock but also with fluctuations in the speculative premium on its warrants. In contrast to intrinsic value, the speculative premium cannot be calculated
from other known magnitudes; it is derived by a market process from a changing
mix of not-precisely-measurable influences. In general, premiums tend to narrow
as a warrant's remaining life shortens, as the outlook for the common stock
deteriorates, as the temper of the stock market itself grows less speculative, and as
the proportion of warrants to common shares increases. Large warrant issues are
unattractive because their conversion into stock will substantially dilute common
share earnings and so retard the stock price. In 1972, for example, the conversion
of National General Corporation's 10 million outstanding warrants would have
reduced the expected net earnings per common share from $3.80 to $2.40. Finally,
in theory at least, high dividend payouts diminish the premium on a company's
warrants by reducing the growth rate of retained earnings on which an advance
in the common stock price depends.

One basis for comparing the values offered by different warrants is to calculate
the multiples by which the associated common stocks would need to rise to make
each warrant a more profitable holding upon expiration than its stock would be.
These multiples can be calculated by dividing the exercise price of each warrant
by the current price difference between the stock and the warrant (though the
computation must be modified for warrants which authorize purchase of more or

less than single shares.) Thus, if a stock is selling at $20 and a warrant exercisable at $30 is selling for $10, the stock must rise to $30/($20 — $10), or 3 times its present price—$60[7]—before the warrant would be *intrinsically* more profitable than the stock. The less the related stock needs to rise to make a warrant a better investment by its expiration date, the more favorably a trader may consider the warrant. Obviously, other factors, such as the warrant's time to expiration, the likelihood of a rise in the stock price, and the number of outstanding warrants, must also weigh in the investor's final comparison and judgment.

Warrants may prove to be profitable investments when bought in low, quiet markets, when common stocks generally are underpriced. Between 1962 and 1966, United Air Lines warrants rose from $4\frac{1}{2}$ to 126. Tri-Continental Corporation warrants rose from $\frac{1}{32}$ in 1942 to $5\frac{5}{8}$ in 1946 and to $75\frac{3}{4}$ in 1969. But warrants have also brought correspondingly large losses to investors who acquired them in speculative markets or when the related common stocks were selling at historically high levels. Between 1968 and 1970, Ling-Temco-Vought warrants fell from 83 to $2\frac{1}{4}$. Between February 1966 and their expiration date the following September, Mack Trucks warrants fell from $33\frac{1}{2}$ to zero.

The low and volatile prices of warrants clearly invite their purchase for speculation and often even for gambling. For this reason, it seems likely that warrants ordinarily sell at speculative premiums which reflect the "improbable possibilities" discussed in Chapter 2. They are clearly unsuitable commitments for beginners, and even experienced investors of ample means should approach them with caution and moderation.

OPTIONS

In New York and other financial centers, there is an active over-the-counter market in *options* to buy or sell stocks. Most options are initially made for 30, 60, or 90 days or 6 months, and stipulate a price at which the option holder may make a purchase or sale transaction within that period. Both new and existing unexpired options are bought and sold by members of the Put and Call Brokers and Dealers Association, Inc. The standard option contract covers 100 shares of stock, generally an active and well-known stock, and usually names a price reasonably close to the market price at the original date of the option.

An option to buy stock is termed a *call*. It is useful to one who expects the stock to rise, or who has sold short and wishes to hedge against an unexpected rise. An option to sell stock at the contract price is a *put*. It is of interest to one who expects the stock to fall, or who wishes to hedge against a decline in a stock

---

[7] In rising $40, from 20 to 60, the stock would have appreciated 200 per cent. The warrant, bought at $10, would have an intrinsic value of 30 when the stock reached 60; this would also amount to a 200 per cent gain. At 70, the stock would have risen 250 per cent, but the warrant would then have an intrinsic value of 40, up 300 per cent.

now held but which cannot conveniently be sold. An option entitling the holder to either a put or a call is termed a *spread* or a *straddle*. It is a speculative position desired by one who expects violent fluctuation in the market but is not sure whether the major change will be up or down.

The purchasers of options are in the most part speculators who wish to take substantial market positions on a small cash outlay or to hedge speculative positions carried on margin. Statistical studies indicate that the majority of speculators who use calls as long-side speculations and puts as the equivalent of short sales do not profit on them. As Table 5-3 indicates, the options themselves are costly. If a call is exercised, the actual total purchase cost to the long-side speculator will be the option purchase price plus the cost of the option. On a put, the seller's actual net realization is the sale price minus the cost of the option. And in

Table 5-3 *Options advertised to writers and buyers by a leading New York stock exchange member, March 5, 1973*

Stock	Type of option	Option price per share	Number of shares	Life of option	Cost of option	Market price of stock 3/5/73
For writers (options wanted)						
Houston Oil & Mineral	Call	Market	100	6 months 10 days	$450	27½
Denny's, Inc.	Put	Market	100	65 days	$112.50	15¼
Control Data	Call	Top limit 48	100	95 days	$412.50	48
MGIC Investment	Put	Lower limit 72	1,000	6 months 10 days	$900	74½
Massey-Ferguson	Straddle	Market	100	6 months 10 days	$375	22
For buyers (options offered)						
Acme-Cleveland	Call	Market	100	September 10	$387.50	43
Braniff Airways	Call	Market	in volume	13 months	$300	13
Robbins (A. H.)	Call	Top limit 69	100	6 months	$750	70½

Options sold at market have an exercise price equal to the stock price at the moment the option is sold. Two calls in the table have upper price limits, and one of the puts has a lower price limit. Most options wanted or offered are for 100 shares, but the call wanted on MGIC Investment is for 1,000 shares, and the call offered on Braniff is designated "in volume," meaning that a call will be sold for several thousand shares at least. The brokerage firm advertising these options served as an intermediary between clients desiring to buy options and those wishing to sell them.

either case there will be a standard brokerage commission to pay to the broker who procures the option and later attends to the process of exercising it.

The nominal makers of stock options are usually well-known brokers. They represent the real makers, individual or corporate investors who will contract to buy or sell stock at the option prices in return for the option fee. If a call is exercised, the option maker receives the option price for his stock in addition to the amount previously paid him for the call. If a put is exercised, the maker buys at the option price but he may also keep the amount he previously received for the put. And if the option is not exercised, the amount for which it was sold becomes income to the maker.

The prices paid for options obviously depend on the purchase or sale price guaranteed in the option, the duration of the option period, and the outlook for the market. In a low and rising market, calls are high and puts are relatively cheap, whereas, in a high and shaky market, calls are cheap and puts are high. In either case the option requires the delivery of dividends which go ex-dividend during the option period as a part of the contract—actually, the seller credits these against the option price. Calls ordinarily seem to sell higher than puts, perhaps because speculators have more use for them and investors are more reluctant to sell them.

Obviously, the holder of an option will lose what he paid for it if he does not exercise the option before it expires. A put will always be exercised before it expires if the market price on the last day is more than a small fraction below the option. A call will be exercised if the market is similarly above the option.

Once issued, options may be bought and sold like other securities, although their short life, variety of makers, and frequent nonstandard terms have confined trading in them to informal markets. In early 1973, however, the Chicago Board Options Exchange, an affilliliate of the Chicago Board of Trade, received authorization from the Securities and Exchange Commission (SEC) to inaugurate experimental trading in call options on about 30 major-company stocks. If this experiment proved successful, it seemed likely that calls on other companies, along with puts, would be added to the approved trading list, and that other exchanges also would seek to list these recurrently popular speculative instruments.

QUESTIONS AND PROBLEMS

1 Do you see possible disadvantages to buying shares in a very small preferred issue if it is of high investment quality and has a good yield?

2 Look up the essential charter provisions of Flintkote Co. $2.25 Series B Preferred, Tenneco, Inc. 4.92% Second Preferred, American Telephone and Telegraph $4 Preferred, Santa Fe Industries, Inc. $0.50 Preferred, Empire District Electric Company Preferred, and Union Pacific Preferred. Do you think that investors should ever buy preferred stocks without studying the charter provisions?

3. Why would anyone ever pay more than the call price for a preferred stock? Which one would fluctuate the most in price, a high-grade bond or an equally good preferred stock?

4. If you held 100 shares of a 1,000,000-share preferred issue which you knew to be high quality, would you regard a sinking-fund provision requiring the company to retire 10,000 shares annually as of any particular importance?

5. What kind of dividend restrictions might be imposed on common stock for the benefit of the preferred? Why is this done?

6. Would you regard a chance to buy a medium-grade preferred with 4 years' accumulated back dividends at 70 per cent of par as a bargain?

7 The 1971 earnings on Ohio Edison Company 4.56% preferred ($100 par value) were reported as $76.27 per share. Does this suggest that the company's earnings could shrink to approximately one-fifteenth of their reported level and still leave the dividend on this preferred intact? Discuss the principle at issue.

8 Assume that Imaginary Corporation earned $1,000,000 in 1972 after payment of all expenses except interest and federal income taxes at 50%. If it had outstanding $10,000,000 of 5 per cent bonds, a 50,000-share issue of $3 dividend First Preferred, a 20,000-share issue of $2 dividend Second Preferred, and 10,000 common shares, what were the earnings per share on the First Preferred? On the Second Preferred? Which is the better-quality stock? Prove your statement.

9 Would it be economically desirable to make preferred dividends tax-deductible, as bond interest is, so corporations could use them as financing devices?

10 List a number of criteria, both legal and economic, which would enable you to classify a preferred stock as high quality.

11 Which is the stronger security, a guaranteed stock or the preferred stock of the guarantor?

12 Do you agree with the critics of preferred stocks who say that they have neither the unconditional promise of a bond nor the speculative possibilities of a common stock but that they have the major disadvantages of both types?

13 Look up the Cleveland & Pittsburgh Railroad 7 per cent guaranteed stock. How has the guarantee worked out? Why? What future do you foresee for this stock?

14 Under what circumstances can a convertible preferred stock fairly be said to represent both a safer investment than the related common and an equal attraction for speculative price gains? In your opinion, are these circumstances attained frequently or rarely? Why?

15 Investigate speculative premiums on the following convertible preferred stocks in July 1972, and explain why they were relatively large or small: Libby-Owens-Ford $4.75 Preferred, Commonwealth Edison $1.425 Preferred, Foote Mineral Company $2.20 Preferred, Litton Industries $3 Preferred, R. J. Reynolds $2.25 Preferred, Lincoln National Corporation $3 Preferred.

16 In April 1972, the $0.60 Convertible 'A' Preferred of National Industries sold to yield only 4.1 per cent, while the $1.25 Convertible 'B' Preferred yielded 8.6 per cent. What explains this apparent discrepancy?

17 Investigate the price and provisions of Ryder System, Inc. warrants in April 1972. Were these warrants in your opinion soundly valued? Why or why not? What issues do these questions raise?

18 Which would have been the better holding for a speculator between December 15 and year-end 1971: American Telephone common? The preferred? The warrants? From January

1, 1972, to July 31? How do you explain the percentage moves of each security during
the two intervals under discussion?

19 Investigate and explain the price moves of Atlantic Richfield Company warrants
issued in mid-1969. What main lessons for warrant traders do you read in this experience?

20 Would an investor ever have occasion to buy an option? Would a large investor who
was willing to sell just a little above the current market ever find it advantageous to sell
calls? Could he ever find it advantageous to sell puts?

REFERENCES

Amling, Frederick: *Investments*, 2d ed., Prentice-Hall, Inc., Englewood Cliffs, N.J., 1970,
  Chap. 5.

Badger, Ralph E., and Paul B. Coffman: *Investment Analysis*, McGraw-Hill Book Company, New York, 1967, Chap. 5.

Cohen, Jerome B., and Edward D. Zinbarg: *Investment Analysis and Portfolio Management*, rev. ed., Richard D. Irwin, Inc., Homewood, Ill., 1973, Chaps. 9–11.

Donaldson, Elvin F., and John K. Pfaul: *Corporate Finance*, 3d ed., The Ronald Press
  Company, New York, 1969, Chaps. 5, 9.

Filer, Herbert: *Understanding Put and Call Options*, paperback ed., Popular Library Inc.,
  New York, 1966.

Graham, Benjamin, David L. Dodd, and C. Sidney Cottle: *Security Analysis*, 4th ed.,
  McGraw-Hill Book Company, New York, 1962, Chaps. 28, 29.

Guthmann, Harry G., and Herbert E. Dougall: *Corporate Financial Policy* 4th ed., Prentice-Hall, Inc., Englewood Cliffs, N.J., 1962, Chap. 9.

Husband, William H., and James C. Dockeray: *Modern Corporation Finance*, 7th ed.,
  Richard D. Irwin, Inc., Homewood, Ill., 1972, Chaps. 5, 17.

CORPORATE BONDS AND THEIR VALUE

In essence, corporate bonds are the promissory notes of a debtor corporation. They are called bonds instead of notes or mortgages chiefly to indicate that they are part of a mass borrowing arrangement, termed a bond issue, through which the corporation borrows the sum it needs. Corporate bond issues normally range in amount from $100,000 to $250,000,000; smaller or larger ones are not unknown.

All bonds of the same issue are part of a single elaborate bond contract and will therefore be similar or identical in their terms. Thus, all the Texas Company 3⅝s of 1983, which were sold in the amount of $150,000,000, have the same interest rate, maturity date, protective covenants, and other features.[1] Individual bonds are usually of $1,000 denomination, though an issue may include some units as large as $100,000 and some as small as $100. Interest is usually payable semiannually, though quarterly or annual payments are sometimes found.

Most bonds sold before 1964 were issued in *bearer* form, that is, payable to bearer. Such bonds do not show the owner's name and may be transferred to a new owner by the simple act of delivery. At each interest date, the owner clips the appropriate printed and dated coupon from his bond and collects it through his bank, which handles the coupon in a manner somewhat similar to that used in collecting checks. Since 1964, nearly all new corporation bond issues have been sold in *registered* form, which means that they are issued to specific named bondholders and must be returned to a transfer office for reissue when acquired by a new owner. Holders of registered bonds receive interest by check. Bonds *registered as to principal only* represent a compromise between the bearer and the fully registered forms; in this case the bond bears the owner's name and the principal will be payable only to the registered owner, but interest coupons payable to bearer are attached to the bond.

As might be expected in a field in which borrowers and lenders are free to contract on any basis they desire, bonds vary greatly in their terms. With respect to maturity, the choice ranges from perpetual bonds, which never come due, to the early maturities of equipment obligations, which have a term of only a few months. With respect to pledged security, some bonds are secured by liens on real property, some by pledge of collateral or chattels, and some are unsecured. With

---

[1] The name of the debtor company has been changed to Texaco, Incorporated, but the bonds retain their original title. This is common practice.

respect to investment quality, some bonds are superbly certain and others are highly dubious. With respect to special contractual features, such as the right of the bondholder to have his bond converted into stock or the right of the debtor to pay off the bond before maturity, bond contracts are so diverse that an entire section of this chapter must be devoted to an enumeration of commonly used devices.

Bondholders are creditors, with rights and privileges which are definitely fixed in the bond contract. They ordinarily have no voice in the management of the debtor enterprise, and they usually receive only stipulated interest earnings and the return of their principal at maturity. Since they are in no sense owners or partners, their rights are contractual and enforcible at law. If the proper payments are not made or if other agreements are not fulfilled by the debtor, the bondholders' representatives may take action in court. Remedies may include a court order forcing the debtor to perform, appointment of a receiver to administer the business for the benefit of creditors, bankruptcy proceedings, or a foreclosure and sale of property belonging to the debtor.

New bond issues are usually bought as a block by groups of securities firms and sold at retail by them. Thereafter, individual bonds or blocks of bonds offered for resale are most commonly purchased by dealers, who then offer them for sale. Bonds from some of the larger corporation bond issues are also traded on the New York Stock Exchange or the American Stock Exchange. The retailers of new issues, and to some extent the over-the-counter (resale) dealers, are sometimes inclined to regard 5 or 10 bonds as normal "round lots," and to be reluctant to buy or sell lesser quantities. However, the standard unit of stock exchange trading is one bond; the over-the-counter wholesale dealers will generally handle any quantity desired, and even new issues are obtainable in single bonds except when the issue sells exceptionally well.

THE CORPORATE BOND CONTRACT

There are three parties to a corporation bond contract, the borrowing corporation, the bondholders, and the trustee. The trustee is a bank or trust company, which is chosen and paid by the corporation but serves mainly to protect the bondholders.[2] The trustee's functions usually include (1) countersigning the bonds to assure authenticity, (2) collecting interest and principal payments from the debtor and distributing them to those entitled, (3) acting as mortgagee or collateral holder if the bonds are secured, (4) verifying the performance of the debtor corporation's promises on behalf of the bondholders, and (5) taking legal action

---

[2] Most bond indentures also provide for a cotrustee who is a natural person in whose name certain types of legal action may be taken, but the corporate trustee usually performs all the trust duties.

on behalf of the bondholders if necessary. Obviously, the bondholders cannot usually be parties to the framing of the bond contract, but they adopt its provisions when they choose to acquire bonds.

The contract itself, known as the *bond indenture*, is a complete, lengthy legal document which constitutes the agreement between the parties. The bonds themselves are certificates of participation in this contract. In the indenture, the corporation promises to pay principal and interest, promises to pay the trustee, promises to pay its taxes and other debts, and promises to maintain its property and conduct its business prudently. It will usually also agree not to enter a merger, sell its property, or change its business greatly, except under certain conditions; and it may agree to make sinking-fund payments, to limit its indebtedness, and to limit its dividend payments. The trustee will promise to fulfill his functions faithfully throughout the entire life of the bond issue. The bondholders agree to allow certain grace periods in event of default, to abide by majority rule in certain situations, and to look only to the corporation's assets, not to the personal assets of directors or stockholders, for their payments.

The bond indenture will contain many other provisions, including: (1) the total amount of bonds authorized to be issued under the indenture or a statement that the amount is *unlimited;* (2) a statement that additional bonds may be issued in the future *(open indenture)* or that the first issue will be the only one permitted *(closed indenture);* (3) statement of the purposes for which additional bonds may be issued, such as for construction or acquisition of property; (4) stipulation that all bonds must be identical in terms or that a *series* of issues, possibly having different interest rates, maturity dates, and call prices, may be sold under the basic indenture[3] (in the latter case each series issue would have a supplemental indenture detailing its special features); (5) details of the collateral or mortgage security to be provided; (6) mechanics of interest payments, registration of bonds, and principal repayments; (7) terms of special features such as sinking funds, call provisions, and conversion options.

During the depression of the thirties there was complaint to the effect that bond indentures did not sufficiently protect the bondholders' interests and that bond trustees were too slow in acting when defaults occurred. Under the provisions of the Trust Indenture Act of 1939, which is one of the series of federal reform measures known as the Securities Acts, new bond issues must avoid these faults. The trustee must be financially independent of the debtor, and vigilance and positive action must be made obligatory on the trustee by the terms of the indenture.

---

[3] Pacific Gas and Electric Company recorded its First Refunding Mortgage indenture and sold the Series A under it in 1920. Series A through K and Series O have now been retired. Except for Series O, the successive series L through Z and Series AA through WW, all issued after 1943, were outstanding in December 1972. They all have separate interest rates, call provisions, and maturity dates.

SECURED AND UNSECURED BONDS

Creditors often find it advantageous to have a legally enforcible lien on the property of a corporate debtor so that, in case of default, they may have prior rights secured by that property. Such liens have no function unless default occurs, hence add little to the attractiveness of bonds sold by very strong borrowers, for example, the American Telephone and Telegraph Company. However, the economic turbulence of the thirties demonstrated that moderately good borrowers can quickly become weak ones, in which case a prior claim is superior to an unsecured one.

In modern practice a corporate enterprise is seldom liquidated when business disaster forces it to default on its debt. Instead, the corporate properties are placed temporarily in the possession of a trustee in bankruptcy while the corporation is "reorganized." Reorganization consists of (1) determining what amount of bonds and stocks the future earning power of the firm will support, and (2) distributing these new securities to the old securityholders in order of priority. Creditors who have liens on a sufficient amount of valuable and profitable corporate property will get full value in new securities. Creditors who have liens on property of insufficient value, or who have second liens, may get lower-grade securities in whole or part. Unsecured creditors, preferred stockholders, and common stockholders will get progressively less favorable treatment, each group in turn, and some groups may get little or nothing.

A second advantage in a well-secured position is experienced if the corporation pays interest during the bankruptcy proceedings. Sometimes a corporation is placed in bankruptcy because it cannot meet a large maturing debt or because it cannot pay all of its interest and rent obligations during a time of poor earnings. In that case, even while the bankruptcy trustee is in charge, there may be earnings sufficient to pay some interest. If interest is to be paid, however, it will be paid only to claimants who are so well secured that the ultimate bankruptcy adjustment would have to pay them anyhow. Such situations are not uncommon.

In the event that it seems best to liquidate a defaulting corporation instead of reorganizing it, lien-protected bondholders will have first claim to the sale proceeds of the property covered by their liens and a prorata share with other creditors in a general claim against all corporate assets for any uncovered balance. In this case the bondholder will often be better off if his lien covers assets which are not single-purpose assets but, instead, are generally useful to other firms and other industries, hence salable at a good price.

All the preceding circumstances indicate that, other things being equal, a well-secured bond is preferable to an unsecured one in the same corporation. However, other things may not be equal. Secured bonds often cost more or yield less than unsecured ones, yet it is likely that all the bonds of a company which gets into serious financial trouble will decline painfully in price or even default altogether. Some investment experts argue that it is better to buy the unsecured junior-ranking bonds of a company too strong to default rather than the well-secured senior bonds of a company which also has a burdensome amount of lower-ranking debt. It seems best to concede both sides of the argument; it is admittedly not wise to buy, at normal prices, any bond in a shaky company; but if trouble comes, or if one speculates in a troubled situation at a depressed price, the priority afforded by a secured position is valuable.

Mortgage security   The most common method of providing security for a bond issue is to mortgage some or all of the corporation's property for the purpose. This is accomplished by a trust deed, which gives the bond trustee a lien on the property. Bondholders formerly preferred mortgage-secured bonds issued under a closed indenture which permits the indenture to secure only the original issue of bonds and no more, but experience has shown that this leads to an undesirable proliferation of indentures and liens and occasionally to difficulties in financing expansion, if all available property is already encumbered. Also, the problem of determining the quality and relative priorities of bond issues secured by different portions of the same corporation's properties was frequently a baffling one.

The modern trend is toward large open indentures secured by mortgages covering all or most of the debtor corporation's property. Each indenture may then provide for successive series of bonds to be issued under it when the corporation needs the money. All series issued under the same indenture would have equal priority. If bonds of different qualities are desired, any number of open indentures ranking in sequence may be created, for example, one secured by a first mortgage, one secured by a second mortgage, and one unsecured.

Mortgage-secured open indentures usually also carry an *after-acquired property clause*, which obligates the corporation to bring under the mortgage all property acquired subsequent to the date thereof. This clause is intended to assure the bondholders that their lien will cover new and added property as it is acquired, not just the depreciating original assets. Although clever attorneys have devised ways to defeat the clause—for example, property can be bought subject to an existing mortgage, or subsidiaries can be set up to acquire and mortgage the new property, or a purchase-money mortgage can be created,[4] or after a merger the successor corporation can deny that the clause applies to it—most corporations comply with it faithfully. Also, modern indentures often specifically obligate the debtor corporation not to use these evasive devices.

In order to prevent reckless issuance of bonds under an open indenture, the

[4] A purchase-money mortgage is one which is given to the seller as part of the payment for newly purchased property or one which is given to a lender who provides the money to pay the seller. In either instance the purchasing corporation acquires the property subject to the purchase-money mortgage, hence cannot give its old bonds a first mortgage on it.

Chart 6-1 *Cover page of prospectus offering first mortgage bonds for sale. The bonds of this General Public Utilities Company subsidiary are rated only Baa and carry a relatively high rate of interest. The 5-year limitation on redemption of the bonds by refunding them at a lower effective interest cost is typical of bonds issued in relatively high-interest periods. This prospectus contained 42 pages, about 50 per cent more than the average.*

PROSPECTUS

$25,000,000

JERSEY CENTRAL POWER & LIGHT COMPANY

FIRST MORTGAGE BONDS, 8% SERIES DUE 2002

The Bonds will be redeemable at the option of the Company at prices set forth herein, provided that, prior to August 1, 1977, no such redemption may be made at the regular redemption price through certain refunding operations at an effective interest cost to the Company of less than 7.85% per annum.

Interest payable February 1 and August 1 **Due August 1, 2002**

THESE SECURITIES HAVE NOT BEEN APPROVED OR DISAPPROVED BY THE SECURITIES AND EXCHANGE COMMISSION NOR HAS THE COMMISSION PASSED UPON THE ACCURACY OR ADEQUACY OF THIS PROSPECTUS. ANY REPRESENTATION TO THE CONTRARY IS A CRIMINAL OFFENSE.

	Price to Public(1)	*Underwriting Discounts and Commissions(2)*	*Proceeds to Company(1)(3)*
Per Unit	101.75%	1.182%	100.568%
Total	$25,437,500	$295,500	$25,142,000

(1) Plus accrued interest from August 1, 1972 to date of delivery.

(2) In the Purchase Agreement the Company has agreed to indemnify the Purchasers against certain civil liabilities, including certain liabilities under the Securities Act of 1933.

(3) Before deduction of expenses payable by the Company, estimated at $100,000.

The above Bonds are offered by the several Purchasers named herein subject to prior sale, when, as and if issued and accepted by them and subject to the approval of counsel; and the Purchasers reserve the right, in their discretion, to reject any orders for the purchase of the Bonds, in whole or in part. It is expected that the Bonds will be ready for delivery on or about August 24, 1972.

BLYTH EASTMAN DILLON & CO.
INCORPORATED
HALSEY, STUART & CO. INC.

SALOMON BROTHERS

MERRILL LYNCH, PIERCE, FENNER & SMITH
INCORPORATED

The date of this Prospectus is August 16, 1972

authorization of new bonds is often forbidden except (1) to obtain money to retire equally secured or better-secured bonds, (2) to finance not over 75 per cent of the cost of new property, and (3) to obtain a very limited amount of working capital. This latter provision is for use in emergencies. Additionally, the new bonds are often forbidden in any case unless the corporate earnings during the past 3 or 5 years have been adequate to cover the total proposed interest charges by a safe margin.

Mortgage bonds are said to have either *senior* or *junior* liens, depending on the priority of their claims. The senior liens are those which have the most advantageous positions. They include *first mortgage* bonds, such as the Chicago and North Western Railway First 3s of 1989; *purchase-money mortgage* bonds, which take senior rights against property acquired with the bond proceeds, even though another indenture contains an after-acquired property clause; and *prior lien* bonds, such as the Northern Pacific Railway Prior Lien and Land Grant 4s of 1997. It is also customary to class as senior bonds certain apparently junior issues which are really well secured because of the adequacy of the mortgaged property, because the preceding lien is small in amount, because prior liens previously outstanding have been retired, or because the issue in question has a junior lien on part of the property and a first lien on other parts.

Junior bonds are those whose claim is subordinate to a first lien on the property. They may be either secured or unsecured. The lien status of junior bonds is often clearly defined in the bond title, as is that of the Chicago, Indianapolis & Louisville Railway Second 4½s of 2003. But corporations often dignify the position of junior issues by other labels such as *general*, or *consolidated*, or *first refunding*, or *first leasehold*. All refunding mortgages are likely to be originally junior mortgages; their function is to secure new bonds which will provide money as needed for expansion and for retirement of existing senior bonds. They may eventually become senior bonds, but the wise investor will appraise them on the basis of their immediate position rather than on their expectations.

One form of junior bond which should be understood by all bond buyers is the *leasehold mortgage* bond. Such bonds are commonly used to finance the construction of office buildings, hotels, apartment buildings, and other structures *erected on leased land*. The debtor corporation first leases the land at long term from a fee owner, agreeing to pay all taxes plus a lease rental; then it mortgages its lease plus the building it plans to erect, as security for *first leasehold mortgage* bonds. If the rental income from the building proves sufficient to pay the expenses, taxes, land rental, and principal and interest on the bonds, all will be well; but if the building earns less than expected, the bondholders may lose, for operating expenses and taxes must be paid, and *if the landowner is not paid he can repossess his land and the attached building together*. Thus a leasehold mortgage is clearly a junior lien. If trouble develops, the bondholders may have to forgo their interest, take over the ownership, or even pay the ground rent, to save their investment.

Collateral security   Bonds which are secured by deposit of other bonds and stocks are termed *collateral trust notes* or *collateral trust bonds*. The pledged securities are generally assigned and delivered to the trustee of the collateral trust bonds, but the rights to receive the income and to exercise the voting powers of the pledged securities are usually retained by the debtor corporation. The pledged collateral may consist of (1) stocks and bonds of subsidiary and affiliated corporations, (2) stocks and bonds held as investments, or (3) portions of closed or limited senior issues of the borrowing corporation. In every instance, the relative quality of a collateral trust bond will be judged by the adequacy and quality of the deposited collateral.

Collateral trust bonds as a class did not perform very satisfactorily for investors between 1925 and 1935, chiefly because the device was ideal for use in much of the reckless and ill-advised finance of that period. Loosely drawn indentures permitted the withdrawal or substitution of good collateral, collateral was sometimes vastly overvalued, and indenture terms were not carefully observed. But previous misuse of a sound device is not necessarily a good reason for mistrusting it now; many completely satisfactory collateral trust issues are outstanding, such as the Potomac Edison Company 9⅛s of 2000 and the Northern Pacific Railway 4s of 1984. All in all, the collateral trust method seems as reliable a method of providing security as any other.

Chattel security   The only common use of chattels for bond security is found in the widespread practice of financing locomotives, railway cars, aircraft, buses, large trucks, and similar equipment by selling serial notes or certificates secured by them. Equipment obligations, as such securities are called, have an enviable record for soundness and are usually bought by banks and insurance companies on a low-yield basis.

The usual equipment purchase transaction requires the purchasing concern to make a down payment of 15 to 25 per cent of the cost. The balance is financed by the sale of equipment obligations which are secured by the equipment itself. The equipment obligations will be arranged to mature a few at a time over the next 5 to 15 years, so that interest and principal can be paid conveniently as the equipment is used. Maintenance of the equipment is the obligation of the purchaser.

There are two well-known legal arrangements for handling equipment obligations. Under the most common *Philadelphia*, or *equipment lease*, plan, the legal title to the equipment is placed in the trustee. The equipment obligations are not bonds, but certificates of beneficial interest, each entitled to semiannual dividends and to principal repayment at a stated date. The trustee leases the equipment to the purchaser for a rental sufficient to meet the scheduled dividends and

Chart 6-2 *Circular offering equipment obligations for sale. Note that many of the standard features of this type of security are pointed out here.*

New Issue

Circular

$13,800,000

Southern Railway

Equipment Trust No. 6 of 1972 Certificates

7% Equipment Trust Certificates
(Non-Callable)

To be issued under The Philadelphia Plan

To be dated December 1, 1972

To be due annually $920,000 from December 1, 1973 to December 1, 1987, inclusive.

Principal and semi-annual dividends (June 1 and December 1) payable at the office of the Trustee in New York City. Not redeemable prior to maturity. The Trust Certificates are to be issued as bearer Trust Certificates, with dividend warrants attached, in the denomination of $1,000, registrable as to principal, and as fully registered Trust Certificates in the denomination of $1,000 and any multiple thereof. Trust Certificates with dividend warrants and fully registered Trust Certificates are exchangeable, as provided in the Equipment Trust Agreement. Request for fully registered Trust Certificates should be made to Merrill Lynch, Pierce, Fenner & Smith Incorporated on or prior to December 11, 1972.

Trustee: First National City Bank

These Trust Certificates are to be issued under an Equipment Trust Agreement dated as of December 1, 1972, which provides for the issuance of an aggregate of $13,800,000 principal amount of Trust Certificates to be secured by the following new standard-gauge railroad equipment estimated to cost not less than $17,295,363:

535—70-ton 50' 6" Box Cars, Pullman Incorporated (Pullman-Standard division), builder,

299—70-ton Bulkhead Pulpwood Cars, Greenville Steel Car Company, builder, and

8—SD40 Diesel-Electric Locomotives, General Motors Corporation (Electromotive Division), builder.

The aggregate principal amount of these Trust Certificates will not exceed 80% of the actual cost of the specifically described equipment and of any substituted or additional equipment, other than passenger cars and work equipment, subject to this Trust.

Under the Agreement the equipment referred to above will be leased to Southern Railway Company for a term of 15 years from and after December 1, 1972. During the period of the lease, title to the equipment is to be vested in the Trustee and the rental due from Southern Railway Company under the lease is to be sufficient to pay, when due and payable, the principal and dividends on the Trust Certificates.

MATURITIES AND YIELDS
(plus accrued dividends)

1973	5.50%	1978	6.50%	1983	6.90%
1974	5.90	1979	6.60	1984	6.90
1975	6.10	1980	6.75	1985	6.95
1976	6.20	1981	6.80	1986	7.00
1977	6.30	1982	6.85	1987	7.00

These Trust Certificates are offered when, as and if issued and received by us and subject to prior sale, to withdrawal, cancellation or modification of the offer without notice. Issuance and sale of these Trust Certificates are subject to authorization of the Interstate Commerce Commission. Delivery will be made at the office of Merrill Lynch, Pierce, Fenner & Smith Incorporated, One Liberty Plaza, 165 Broadway, New York, N. Y. 10006.

Merrill Lynch, Pierce, Fenner & Smith
Incorporated

The information contained herein has been carefully compiled from sources considered reliable, and while not guaranteed as to completeness or accuracy, we believe it to be correct as of this date. This circular does not constitute an offer to sell or a solicitation of an offer to buy any of these Trust Certificates in any jurisdiction to any person to whom it is unlawful to make such offer or solicitation.

November 28, 1972

maturities, and upon retirement of the last certificates, the equipment is given unconditionally to the purchaser. Under the *New York,* or *conditional sale,* plan, the trustee receives the equipment from the manufacturer and sells it to the purchasing corporation in return for a series of equipment trust notes. These notes are interest-bearing and of serial maturities; when sold to investors they provide the money to pay the manufacturer. When the notes are paid off by the purchasing corporation, the conditional sale becomes final and complete.

The good record of equipment obligations is probably due to (1) the fact that the equipment is essential and must be retained at any cost by the purchaser; (2) the mobility of the equipment, which makes repossession easy; (3) the favorable legal position of equipment obligations, which assures the right to repossess; (4) the gradual improvement in the security, since the debt is liquidated faster than the property depreciates; and (5) the ready salability of repossessed equipment. Receivers and bankruptcy trustees usually pay interest and principal installments on equipment obligations even when mortgage bonds are in default.

Debentures   Debentures are bonds which are not secured by any kind of lien or pledge. Such bonds would ordinarily be the lowest-ranking obligations of a company which also had secured bonds outstanding. For example, in late 1967 the Ohio Power Company's two issues of debentures totaling $60,000,000 were junior to 11 issues of mortgage bonds totaling $366,000,000. But not all debentures are inferior in rank. The United States government, most of our states and municipalities, and many of our strongest corporations issue no bonds except debentures. Some very large corporations—such as Mobil Oil Company, Exxon (formerly Standard Oil Company of New Jersey), and Texaco, Inc., to name but three—prefer to finance with debentures to avoid the nuisance of property mortgages, but they assure debenture holders of seniority by either (1) agreeing not to mortgage their property while the debentures are outstanding, or (2) promising to secure the debentures equally under any mortgage which may be created. This latter promise, which is known as the *equally secured* or *ratably secured* clause, sometimes results in an issue of debentures acquiring mortgage security and ultimate seniority over other bonds.

FEATURES OF BOND CONTRACTS

Reference has already been made to the multitude of features which appear in bond contracts. Several of these are discussed in ensuing paragraphs. In addition, it seems desirable to review certain fairly common situations in which bonds are issued jointly by several debtors, guaranteed by corporations other than the debtor, assumed by successor corporations, or extended or adjusted by joint agreement between debtor and bondholders.

Maturity provisions   Most bond issues have definite maturity dates on which all outstanding bonds are due and payable. These maturity dates are unconditional and may ordinarily be deferred only by individual agreement between the bond-holder and debtor or by a bankruptcy adjustment. However, a few bond inden-tures may obligate bondholders to accept majority rule in "amending" the indenture to extend the maturity date, if extension is requested by the corpora-tion.

Since World War II the normal life term provided in new corporate bond issues has ranged from 10 to 50 years. The longer maturities have been sold by well-established railroad and utility companies and have usually been high quality, either mortgage bonds or covenant-protected debentures. The Southern Pacific Railroad First Mortgage Series F 2¾s of 1996, which were sold in 1946, and the Southwestern Bell Telephone Company Debenture 5⅜s of 2006, which were sold in 1966, are good examples. However, the majority of recent rail and utility bond offerings have ranged from 25 to 35 years' term. Industrial bonds usually have shorter terms; from 10 to 25 years would be typical. Of these, the shorter maturi-ties may represent debt which the companies hope to repay out of earnings or convertible bonds which are expected to be exchanged for stock at an early date; or they may be low-quality bonds which would not sell advantageously at long term.

During the high-yield years of 1969–1972, bonds with 5- to 8-year maturities became popular with utility, industrial, and financial corporations and with many investors. Short maturities offered companies the chance of refunding their borrowings at substantial savings if interest rates should decline in the next few years. Short bonds also appealed to investors who were uncertain about price-level inflation and future interest rates and preferred not to commit their funds for overly long periods.

Outstanding issues also include old bonds of very long maturity, many of them issued prior to 1925 or created in corporate reorganizations, which do not mature until long after the year 2000. Examples are the New York Central 5s of 2013, the Northern Pacific Railway 3s of 2047, and the West Shore Railroad 4s of 2361. Rather unusual situations are represented by the Canadian Pacific Perpetual 4s and certain British and Canadian government bonds which never come due.

On a minority of bond issues, but usually on equipment obligations, building bonds, and municipal bonds, the maturities are made *serial*. That is, the bonds mature in installments over the life of the issue. Each bond has its own def-inite maturity date and bears interest up to that date, but by paying each batch of bonds as they mature, the debtor is able to pay off the entire issue in installments planned to suit his own convenience. Serial bonds are regarded as ideal for bor-rowing municipalities which wish to amortize debts out of tax revenues and for corporate debtors who expect to pay out of the earnings of the financed property. Serial maturities also afford the bond buyer a chance to select a repayment date which is exactly to his taste. However, they have two patent disadvantages: (1) The small number of identical bonds (same maturity) outstanding limits the market and tends to reduce the salability of the bonds; and (2) the inflexibility of pre-arranged maturities sometimes embarrasses the debtors when business conditions are bad. Despite these disadvantages, the serial maturity idea seems to have gained a little in popularity since the 1940s, especially among industrial concerns seeking funds for expansion. Serials may be secured or unsecured, high quality or speculative.

Call provisions Bond issues which may be paid off before maturity at the option of the debtor are said to be *callable* or *redeemable*. Most corporate bond issues are callable, as are most of the newer state and municipal issues. United States government long-term bonds are usually callable during the last 2 to 5 years of their terms, but not earlier.

Callable issues may be callable in part or only as an entire issue. Corporate bonds are usually entitled to a *call premium* of 3 to 10 per cent if called soon after issuance, but the premium often diminishes year by year and disappears entirely in the last years. This is desirable, since it permits necessary refunding to be done in advance of final maturity, which might occur during a depression when selling new bonds was impossible.

There is little advantage to an investor in having a call provision in his bond. If interest rates fall, the company may retire the bond at a premium, but he will have to reinvest at lower interest rates. If interest rates rise, the bond will not be called, but he will not gain anything. And always the call price remains as a virtual ceiling to the market value of a bond, a figure which a purchaser exceeds only at his peril. For example, the well-secured noncallable Great Northern Railway Series D 4⅛s of 1976 were selling in 1946 at 125; but the almost identical Series E 4⅛s of 1977 were selling at 108 because they were callable at 105. The Series E bonds were called later that year at 105, at a time when new bonds of equal quality were paying about 3 per cent.

When interest rates become unusually high, as they did in 1966 and 1969–1970, investors are unwilling to buy new bonds at prices close to par unless they are protected during the first 5 or 10 years by unusually high call prices or by a noncallable provision or other special feature.

Sinking funds About one bond issue out of every eight provides for a sinking fund. This is an arrangement under which the debtor pays annual or semiannual contributions into a fund designed to retire some or all of the bonds before maturity. Obviously, this arrangement is not used on serial issues.

Sinking-fund provisions usually require the debtor to make annual or semiannual payments to the trustee. Each payment may be a definite sum, or it may be a percentage of the debtor's gross sales, a percentage of his net earnings, or some other sum based upon his ability to pay. The payment may be required in cash, or it may be optionally in bonds which the debtor has purchased in the open market. The trustee is usually required to purchase bonds if he receives cash payments, in order to reduce the outstanding debt; and if the bonds are not available at a fair price, the trustee is authorized to select certain bonds by lot. These will then be retired by payment of face amount plus a small premium, probably not exceeding 3 per cent.

Sinking funds are found on both high-grade and speculative bond issues. They may be designed to retire all or a large portion of the issue by the maturity date, or they may retire only a small percentage of it. In various situations, the sinking funds are intended (1) to retire the bonds as rapidly as the debtor's finances will permit, (2) to increase the security behind the bonds by a steady retirement program, (3) to retire the bonds as minerals or other resources essential to their welfare are used up, or (4) to keep the market buoyant by sending the debtor or the trustee out to purchase bonds for the sinking fund. Small sinking-fund requirements are sometimes attached to long-term utility and railroad bonds by regulatory commissions in order to compel the company to reduce its indebtedness out of earnings.

Investors generally are inclined to regard sinking funds as advantageous to them. However, there are exceptions. Occasionally a sinking fund may drain the debtor corporation of working capital at a time when liquid resources are badly needed. More often, individual investors are hurt when convertible or high-coupon bonds selling at high prices are selected by lot for sinking-fund retirement at par or slightly above. Sinking-fund call prices are usually lower than the regular call prices and are often not very generous. See, for example, the Columbia Gas System 9s of 1994, which were marketed in the high-interest period of 1969 and sold at 112 in mid-1972 but were callable for sinking-fund retirement at 100½ beginning in 1974.

Conversion Convertible bonds are those which may be exchanged for stock at the option of the holder. About 1 issue in 10 contains a conversion option. Nearly all conversion options provide for conversion into common stock. Convertible bonds are sold to investors who believe that the corporation's stock may rise in price and who therefore hope to profit from future sale or conversion of the bond, or to people who prefer bond security but who wish the option of taking stock if inflation reduces the buying power of bond dollars. Corporations sell convertible bonds because they find that they sell more readily or at a lower interest rate than equally well secured ordinary bonds, or because they hope to get the bonds converted into stock the next time the stock market is high. Convertible bonds are often of medium- or lower-grade quality.

Bonds may be convertible during the entire life of the issue, but more often the conversion option expires after a 10- or 15-year period. Usually a conversion option permits the exchange of each $1,000 bond into a definite number of shares of stock, but variations are found; the American Telephone and Telegraph Company has on several occasions sold debentures which had to be supplemented by a substantial additional cash payment in order to convert them into stock. It is also common practice to provide in the indenture that the number of shares obtainable per $1,000 bond shall decline as time passes. For example, a bond may be convertible into 40 shares during the first 5 years, 30 shares during the second 5 years, and 20 shares thereafter. In most cases the conversion terms are such that conversion is unattractive at the time the bonds are sold but would be profitable if the stock rose sharply in price; but there is no uniformity on this point. Consequently, some convertibles are always on the point of being converted, and some are never near it. Conversion often takes place at a rapid rate when the total market price of the shares into which a bond is convertible is greater than the value of the bond *as a bond;* but if the stock is not paying a dividend or appears to be unduly risky, bondholders will often delay conversion.

It should be noted that convertible bonds have the priorities and contractual rights common to all bonds, hence should remain valuable in a depressed market in which stocks decline sharply. On the other hand, the bonds at all times have the option of conversion into stock, will seldom sell below the market price of the stock into which they are convertible, and will usually rise in price if the stock goes up. In fact, convertible bonds on which the conversion privileges have several years to run, and which do not appear likely to be called, often sell 10 to 20 per cent above their value either as ordinary bonds or as stock because they have the virtues of both and the disadvantages of neither. The price itself may be a disadvantage to an investor who must decide whether to pay a high figure for what is in effect an ordinary bond worth much less than the quoted price, plus an option to exchange the bond for stock which may or may not be worth the quoted price sometime during the conversion period. However, the convertible bond will probably pay a reasonable interest income, and the chances of temporary or even permanent growth in the value of the stock over a long period are often attractive.

Conversion options are usually elaborately protected against dilution. That is, the indentures provide that if the company splits its stock, pays a stock dividend, issues stock under rights, or merges, an appropriate adjustment will be made in the conversion terms. Investors who buy convertible bonds should make sure that the dilution provisions are adequate.

Mention should be made of two devices, somewhat related to the conversion privilege, which are infrequently used with bond issues. The first is to attach a *warrant* to the bond. This warrant entitles the bondholder to purchase for cash a certain number of shares of stock in the company at his option, at times and prices stated in the warrant. The warrant may be detachable, in which case the bondholder could sell it and retain his bond; or it may be exercisable only by the bondholder himself. The second device is to make the bond *participating*, so that it would get larger interest payments in case the company had large earnings or paid large dividends.

Income bonds   Income bonds are bonds on which the payment of interest is mandatory only to the extent of current earnings. If earnings are sufficient to pay only a portion of the interest, that portion usually is required to be paid, but if the corporation is able to pay the unearned balance out of its cash resources, it is of course free to do so. Income bonds are not often offered for sale as new financing, but are often issued in reorganizations or recapitalizations to replace other securities. This is especially true in cases involving railroads and building corporations.

A number of income bonds have been issued since 1950 in recapitalization plans designed to reduce the burden of corporation income taxes. The typical business corporation pays federal and state income taxes of over 50 per cent on its *net income after interest payments*. Net income used for preferred dividend payments is fully taxable. However, if the preferred stockholders can be given long-term income bonds in exchange for their preferred stock, their dividends will become *interest* payments which are deductible in computing taxable income. And long-term income bonds are not onerous burdens to the company. Companies which have issued income bonds to retire preferreds include Armour and Company (now a subsidiary of Greyhound Corporation), St Louis–San Francisco Railway Company, and Gulf, Mobile & Ohio Railroad.

Income bonds vary in their details. Many of them are convertible into common stock. Sometimes a portion of the interest is mandatory and a portion is contingent upon earnings, as in the Baltimore and Ohio Railroad 2s-5s (2 per cent mandatory, 5 per cent if earned) of 1995. Usually any unpaid portion of the contingent interest accumulates and is payable if and when earned in the future, though there are many and various exceptions. Frequently, interest on income bonds is paid only once a year. The income bond has the merit of being a realistic instrument which will not force a concern with intermittent or limited earnings into bankruptcy, yet will definitely compel payment when earnings are available. It is probable that many of the income bonds arising out of reorganizations between 1935 and 1945 will prove to be good investments. They are now parts of acceptable capital structures, have sound indentures, and many have mortgage security. [5]

---

[5] The Atchison, Topeka & Santa Fe Railway Adjustment 4s of 1995 were issued in 1906; they have worked out well. Similar hopes may be entertained for later issues, such as Chicago, Milwaukee, St. Paul & Pacific 4½s of 2019; the Gulf, Mobile & Ohio 5s of 2015; the Wabash 4s of 1981; and the Denver and Rio Grande Western 4½s of 2018.

SUBORDINATED BONDS OR DEBENTURES

In recent years an increasing number of bond issues, usually debentures and often convertible issues, have been specifically issued as *subordinated* securities. This means that the company may contract other debt—bonds, debentures, or bank loans—which will have prior rights against the company's earnings or property. Subordinated bonds or debentures may thus remain the company's lowest-ranking debt even though other debts are retired and new ones are incurred.

Obviously, investors buy subordinated debt securities only when they believe that the risk is not excessive and when the interest rate, conversion option, or other indenture features are attractive.

DEBT-LIMITING AND DIVIDEND-LIMITING COVENANTS

Among the features often found in corporate bond indentures are covenants in which the corporation binds itself not to incur additional long-term debt nor to pay dividends except under certain conditions. Debt-limiting covenants usually do not prohibit bank loans or other short-term debt, but they often limit new bond issues to 75 per cent of amounts required to buy or build new fixed assets and require that total debt be limited to a sum whose interest charges would have been amply covered by recent earnings. Sometimes covenants attached to the indentures of senior bonds do not limit additions to junior issues. Any covenant is likely to apply to the subsidiaries of a covenanting corporation as well as to the corporation itself.

Dividend limitations usually take the form of prohibiting cash payments except from earnings accumulated since the date of the bonds and at any time when the remaining net working capital would be less than a stipulated sum. Variations on these limitations are numerous. Sometimes the limitations apply only to dividends on common stock and sometimes to all dividends.

Debt-limiting and dividend-limiting covenants are seldom damaging to corporate efficiency, though they might be if they were too severe. They do afford the bond investor protection against a speculatively minded corporate management and must be regarded as valuable to bondholders. However, stockholders who prize continuity of dividends may not appreciate this bondholder's advantage.

MODIFICATION OF INDENTURE

Considerable numbers of bond indentures now carry provisions permitting modification of the bond indenture when proposed by the company and consented to by two-thirds or three-fourths of the outstanding bonds. Usually these majority-rule modifications may not alter the principal sum, interest rate, or due dates of either principal or interest. They are most commonly used to release from the mortgage property which the corporation wishes to sell, to increase the amount of bonds issuable under the indenture, to release the corporation from its promise not to incur other debts or pledge its property, to modify dividend restrictions or sinking-fund provisions, and for similar purposes.

However, any provision of any bond contract may be altered by private agreement between debtor and creditor. Corporations frequently propose changes in bond contracts when there are no indenture provisions permitting the changes. These changes often *extend* the maturity date for mutual advantage, or they may make interest payments contingent upon earnings for a time in order to avoid defaults. Such private agreements affect only the bonds which consent to them. The bonds are usually overprinted to evidence the changes and are subsequently known as *extended* bonds, *stamped* bonds, *assented* bonds, etc.

ASSUMED BONDS

When a debtor corporation sells its assets to another, the successor firm may as part payment *assume* the debtor's bonds as its own debt. If the debtor is merged into the successor corporation, the assumption is automatic. In either case the bonds will continue to bear the name of the original debtor, but they are fully binding upon the successor for payment. If the bonds are secured by lien, the sale of the property or a merger will not affect the lien; it remains in full effect. Thus the Pere Marquette Railway First 3⅜s of 1980 are now the obligation of the Chesapeake and Ohio Railway, a successor by merger; but they retain their original title and their original lien.

GUARANTEED BONDS

A considerable number of corporate bonds, especially in the railroad field, have been guaranteed by firms other than the debtors. Some of the guaranties assure payment of both principal and interest, some assure interest only. The guaranty may be extended to enable the guarantor's subsidiary to borrow at lower interest rates, as has been done for the bonds of the Cincinnati Union Terminal by the railroads which own the terminal company's stock; or it may be extended as part consideration for a lease of the debtor's property, as in the case of the New York & Harlem Railroad 3½s of 2000, guaranteed by the Penn Central Transportation Company. An effect somewhat similar to a guaranty is achieved when a lessee company agrees to pay a long-term rental which is more than sufficient to service the lessor's bonds; this was illustrated by the Northern Central Railway 5s of 1974, serviced from lease rentals paid by Penn Central.

A guaranty or a lease contract will add strength to a bond if the guarantor or lessee is financially powerful. However, the legal effects of guaranties and lease contracts are not usually so potent as those of outright assumptions, and an assumption undertakes only an unsecured obligation. Consequently, many guaranteed or lease-assured bonds are strong because of their own lien security rather than because of guaranty or lease.

BOND TERMINOLOGY

Corporate bond issues are commonly given titles which undertake to describe the terms of the contract. Thus, promissory instruments running 5 years or longer are bonds or debentures; shorter maturities are *notes*. An equipment obligation (Philadelphia plan) may be a *trust certificate*. To identify the type of lien, the words *mortgage, leasehold mortgage, collateral trust*, and *secured* are used; for further clarification, adjectives such as *first, second, refunding, consolidated, general, divisional, prior*, and *adjustment* may be used singly or in combination. To describe the pledged property, such words as *bridge, terminal*, or *equipment* may be included. Additionally, such descriptive terms as *income, sinking fund, purchase money, extended, series, serial, participating*, and *convertible* are used.

Since a bond title conventionally includes the corporate name, interest rate, and maturity date, a not unusual bond is described as *Chicago and Northwestern Railroad Second Mortgage Convertible Income 4½s of 1999*. Another is *Shawinigan Water and Power Co. First Collateral Trust Sinking Fund Series N 3s of 1971*.

COMPUTATION OF BOND YIELDS

As has been previously noted, the yield on any investment is one of the determinants of its attractiveness. This is especially true of bonds. Yet the concept and the calculation of bond yields are both difficult.

A bond usually promises payment of a definite principal sum on its due date, plus interest at a stated rate on that maturity value during the interim. Thus, a 6 per cent $1,000 bond due in 1985 would pay $60 interest per year until 1985 and $1,000 principal at that time. There is a further possible complication in that the bond may be called for redemption at a premium (that is, at a price in excess of face value) before 1985. These circumstances lead bond investors to compute, on occasion, at least four types of yields: the nominal yield, the current yield, the yield to maturity, and the yield to call date.

The *nominal yield* is simply the percentage which the annual interest payment bears to the face of the bond, in brief, the rate named in the bond, otherwise known as the *coupon rate*.

The *current yield* is the percentage the annual interest payment bears to the price of the bond. Thus, the current yield on a 6 per cent $1,000 bond price at $900 would be measured as $60 divided by $900, or 6.67 per cent. The current yield is commonly used in appraising speculative bonds whose repayment at maturity is doubtful. It is not much used on good bonds.

The *yield to maturity* is the most common measure of yield on good bonds. For purposes of approximation it may be visualized as follows: Assume that a bond due in exactly 20 years is priced at $900. The purchaser who holds that bond to maturity will obtain an annual cash income of $60, plus an average annual appreciation of $5 on his principal, as the bond rises from its present value of $900 to its maturity value of $1,000. The combined annual gain is therefore $65. The average investment in the bond during the 20 years consists of the midpoint between the $900 cost and the $1,000 maturity value, or $950. (This assumes that the $5 annual appreciation adds itself to the principal in daily installments during the whole 20 years.) The yield to maturity is the percentage which the *combined annual gain* bears to the *average investment*—in this case $65 divided by $950, or 6.84 per cent.

If the bond is bought above par, the formula is the same: yield equals combined annual gain divided by average investment. Assume a $1,000 bond due in 15 years, paying an 8 per cent coupon rate, and priced at $1,090. The combined annual gain would be $80 cash interest minus $6 annual depreciation (one-fifteenth of the $90 premium), or $74. The average investment would be $1,045, the mean of $1,090 and the $1,000 maturity value. The yield to maturity by this (approximate) method is therefore $74 divided by $1,045, or 7.08 per cent.

In commercial practice the yield to maturity is computed, by a slightly different method, as the discount rate which, compounded semiannually, will reduce all future interest and principal payments to a present value equal to the quoted price. Since this is rather difficult to compute by arithmetic, yields to maturity are usually taken from *bond tables*, which are published in great detail and in a number of forms. Excerpts from bond tables are shown in Tables 6-1 and 6-2. All the tables show the bond price as a *percentage of face value*, the number of years remaining before the bond matures, the nominal or coupon interest rate of the bond, and a yield rate based on semiannual compounding. Though the tables are usually detailed enough to permit an approximate yield or bond value to be read directly from the columns, it is sometimes necessary to interpolate—that is, estimate a figure part way between two shown in the table—if fractional years or fractional bond prices are involved.

Since the compound-interest calculations embodied in the bond tables are the conventional ones, bond yields should be computed from the tables if possible.[6]

---

[6] Because others will do so. However, a conventional bond yield calculation reduces a series of semiannual interest collections plus a long-term capital gain or loss at maturity to a composite average percentage yield. The capital gain portion of this yield is taxable at reduced rates and no portion of it is contractually available until the bond matures, and on long bonds the annual market price fluctuations amount to several times as much as any assumed amortization of premium or discount on bonds bought far above or below par.

Table 6-1   *Bond price at which a bond due after 20 years will produce indicated yields*

Yield to maturity, %	Nominal interest rate paid					
	4%	5%	6%	7%	8%	9%
6.00	76.89	88.44	100.00	111.56	123.11	134.67
6.20	74.98	86.35	97.73	109.10	120.47	131.84
6.40	73.14	84.33	95.52	106.72	117.91	129.10
6.60	71.36	82.37	93.39	104.41	115.42	126.44
6.80	69.63	80.48	91.32	102.17	113.01	123.86
7.00	67.97	78.64	89.32	100.00	110.68	121.36
7.20	66.36	76.87	87.38	97.90	108.41	118.92
7.40	64.80	75.15	85.50	95.86	106.21	116.57
7.60	63.29	73.49	83.68	93.88	104.08	114.28
7.80	61.83	71.87	81.92	91.96	102.01	112.05
8.00	60.41	70.31	80.21	90.10	100.00	109.90
8.20	59.05	68.80	78.55	88.30	98.05	107.80
8.40	57.72	67.33	76.94	86.55	96.16	105.77
8.60	56.44	65.91	75.38	84.85	94.32	103.79

Source: Excerpted from Financial Publishing Company, *Expanded Bond Values Tables*, 1970.

Table 6-2   *Bond prices at which a 7 per cent bond will produce indicated yields*

Yield to maturity, %	Years to maturity				
	18	19	20	21	22
6.00	110.92	111.25	111.56	111.85	112.13
6.20	108.60	108.86	109.10	109.32	109.54
6.40	106.36	106.54	106.72	106.88	107.03
6.60	104.18	104.30	104.41	104.51	104.61
6.80	102.06	102.12	102.17	102.22	102.27
7.00	100.00	100.00	100.00	100.00	100.00
7.20	98.00	97.95	97.90	97.85	97.81
7.40	96.06	95.95	95.86	95.77	95.69
7.60	94.17	94.02	93.88	93.75	93.64
7.80	92.33	92.14	91.96	91.80	91.65
8.00	90.55	90.32	90.10	89.91	89.73
8.20	88.81	88.54	88.30	88.07	87.86
8.40	87.12	86.82	86.55	86.29	86.06
8.60	85.48	85.15	84.85	84.57	84.31

Source: Excerpted from Financial Publishing Company, *Expanded Bond Values Tables*, 1970.

However, the arithmetic approximation is reasonably accurate if the bond price is between 90 and 110 and the maturity date is within 10 years. Less accurate but still significant results can be had for prices between 80 and 120 or maturities up to 20 years, provided one of these values remains within the narrower range noted in the previous sentence.

A *yield to call date* is the percentage rate which will discount future interest and principal payments back to the present quoted price, assuming the bond to be called for redemption at a definite future date. If the call price at the assumed date is the par value of the bond, the yield calculation is easy; a bond table will provide the answer if "years to call date" is substituted for "years to maturity." However, if the call price is above par, the yield must be either approximated by the arithmetic method or estimated by proportioning in bond tables. A formula for this process is included in many bond tables.

TRANSACTIONS IN BONDS

Corporation bonds and most public bonds are quoted in *percentages of par value*. That is, a $1,000 bond selling for face value would be quoted at 100; if it were to sell for $900 it would be quoted at 90. The rule would also hold for $500 or $100 bonds; at a price of 90, a $500 bond would sell for $450 and a $100 bond for $90.

When it is desired to quote bonds in percentages *and fractions*, it is conventional to use *eighths*. Thus, Columbus and Southern Ohio Electric 9s of 1999 were quoted at 107⅝, meaning $1,076.25 for a $1,000 bond, and Sun Oil 4⅝s of 1990 were quoted at 74½, meaning $745 for a $1,000 bond. Quotations in United States government bonds are an exception in the matter of fractions; they are traded in percentages and *thirty-seconds*. Certain short-term federal bonds and most municipal issues are commonly quoted by yields instead of quoted price; that is, a bond might sell on a 3.25 per cent basis. The actual price would be computed as the one which would allow a 3.25 per cent yield to maturity.

It is also conventional in the securities markets to assume that the quoted price for a bond covers only the principal of the bond. A purchaser would pay extra for any interest which had accrued since the last interest date. Thus a 4 per cent $1,000 bond bought 3 months after the last semiannual interest payment at a price of 90 would cost the purchaser $910 — $900 for the principal and $10 for 3 months'

Since most individuals and family trusts are likely to hold bonds for limited periods rather than to final maturity, the authors of this book believe that on long bonds bought away from par—the Southern Pacific 2¾s of 1996 bought in 1972 at 45, for example—the current yield of 6.11 per cent is a more realistic measure than a bond table reading of 7.89 per cent to a maturity 24 years away. This Southern Pacific Bond ranged in price from 39 to 70 during the years 1960–1972; and it is rather obvious that a medium-term holder will realize a current yield plus a capital gain or loss which is indeterminable at the time of purchase and very little related to the .85 point per year amortization of discount which the bond table assumes during the first 2 years.

accrued interest. If, at the end of another 3 months, the corporation failed to pay the 6 months' interest, that would be the purchaser's misfortune. He could not get his $10 back from the seller.

An exception to the "price plus accrued interest" rule is made in the case of bonds which are already defaulting their interest payments and on income bonds which may not be able to pay at the next interest date. Such bonds are traded *flat*, that is, with the understanding that no accrued interest will be added to the stated price. It is customary to mark a flat quotation with a small letter "f" or some other identifying mark.

Whether a coupon bond is traded flat or "and interest," the seller is expected to deliver it with all unpaid coupons attached; past due and unpaid coupons and all future ones become the property of the buyer. No question can arise if the bond is registered; transfer of ownership will automatically transfer all subsequent payments of every sort.

In order to compute the accrued interest on corporation bonds which are traded, certain standard rules are followed. They are as follows: (1) A bond coupon or interest check pays the interest through the day of its due date. (2) The period from an interest date through the corresponding numbered day of the next month is one full month, and is counted as 30 days, regardless of actual elapsed days. Each successive month is similarly counted. (3) The seller receives and the buyer pays interest for days elapsed in addition to full months since the last interest date, up to but not counting the day when the buyer's broker pays for the bond. (4) In prorating a year's interest, a year is assumed to be 360 days. For example, if a 7 per cent $1,000 bond which pays interest on February 1 and August 1 is traded on May 13 but payment is to be made on May 20, accrued interest for 108 days would be computed; 3 months or 90 days would accrue through May 1, and May 2 to 19 inclusive would add 18 more. The accrued interest would be 108/360 of $70, or $21.

INVESTMENT POSITION OF BONDS

Except for the relatively few issues which are convertible or which bear stock purchase warrants, bonds entitle their holders to stipulated income and principal payments in dollars, and nothing else. Such an investment is obviously a speculation on the general price level. If the price level rises, the bond dollars will buy less; if it falls, they will buy more. Bondholders who buy long-term bonds also speculate on the future of interest rates; if interest rates rise, a fixed-interest bond will decline in value; if interest rates fall, such a bond will tend to rise, unless limited by a call price.

Despite these uncertainties, bonds have long been regarded as the most conservative type of securities investment. They are creditor instruments, enjoying a creditor's seniority of position. Good bonds have records of consistent payment and freedom from trouble which cannot be equaled in stocks, real estate, or mortgages.[7] They provide investment outlet for 42 per cent of life insurance funds, 22 per cent of commercial bank funds, 23 per cent of mutual savings bank funds, and a probable 50 per cent of endowment and trust funds.

Of course, not all bonds are good bonds. One authority estimates that in the middle thirties, interest payments were suspended on 6 per cent of the outstanding utility bonds, 16 per cent of the railroad bonds, 38 per cent of the foreign bonds, and 2 per cent of the municipals. Most of these were the obligations of over-bonded railroads, speculatively financed building corporations, pyramided holding companies, and foreign public projects. Careful investigation would have disclosed their speculative nature; in fact, it did, for those who took the trouble to study the subject. However, even the reckless or blundering bondholder usually salvages something, for reorganizations or adjustments are much less severe on creditors than on the lower-ranking stockholders.

OWNERSHIP OF CORPORATE BONDS

Corporation bonds range in quality all the way from near-perfection to long-shot speculations. The best issues have often yielded only one-fourth of a percentage point more than United States government bonds of similar maturity. The poorest may yield more than 10 per cent or default their payments entirely.

Obviously, bonds of such diverse qualities would not appeal uniformly to all investors. The better grades, those yielding 7½ per cent and less in the 1972 markets, are held in huge sums by insurance companies, endowment funds, pension funds, trust funds, savings banks, commercial banks, and conservative private investors. The bulk of these holdings are in fairly large blocks and would appear to be in strong hands—that is, they are not in the possession of people likely to be forced to liquidate them. Commercial bank holdings consist largely of short-maturity obligations.

High-quality bonds, especially the corporate issues, are bought in very large quantities by trust funds and mutual savings banks whose bond investments are restricted by law to issues which meet very high, legally prescribed standards. Commercial banks, insurance companies, and many nonregulated investors also choose from bonds which meet the "legal list" requirements of leading states, thus further augmenting the demand for these bonds. Many analysts believe that the heavy demand for "legal list" bonds causes them to sell higher and to yield less than they should, even admitting their high quality. Chart 6-3 illustrates the tendency for superior corporate bonds (the first two grades, in particular) to sell well above lesser ones.

---

[7] On the performance of bonds, see W. B. Hickman, *Corporate Bond Quality and Investor Experience*, National Bureau of Economic Research, New York, 1956.

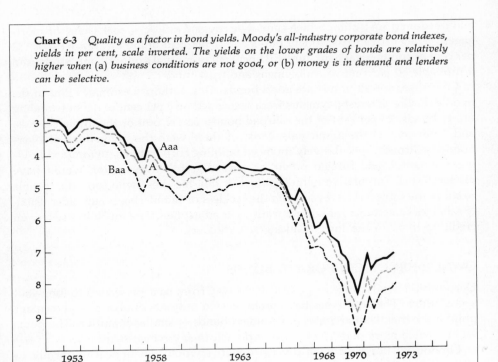

Chart 6-3 *Quality as a factor in bond yields. Moody's all-industry corporate bond indexes, yields in per cent, scale inverted. The yields on the lower grades of bonds are relatively higher when* (a) *business conditions are not good, or* (b) *money is in demand and lenders can be selective.*

The speculative grades of bonds are much more widely scattered in owner-ship and are generally held by individual investors and investment companies who are more interested in price than income. These bonds therefore respond not only to changes in business conditions and the fortunes of the issuing companies but also to variations in stock market prices and speculative psychology.

The heavy demand for good long-term corporates by life insurance companies and pension and endowment funds reflects the fact that such investors have (1) legal or contractual limitations on type and quality of their investments, (2) a de-sire for maximum income with minimum administrative costs, (3) relatively slight emphasis on liquidity, and (4) little or no income tax liability. They are able to choose between long-term government bonds and high-grade corporates, with risk and yield as the factors controlling their choices. Consequently, the highest-grade corporates follow a yield pattern very similar to that of government bonds. Slightly lower-grade corporates are influenced by this pattern, but each succes-sive lower grade is more sharply affected by business risks and speculative attitudes.

Individual investors, largely indifferent to corporate bonds from 1920 through

1964, have become important buyers of these securities since 1965. Factors attracting an increased flow of personal funds into bond investment have included (1) the large rise in bond yields to the 7 to 9 per cent range, (2) the commanding advantage of these bond yields over the 3 to 4 per cent dividend yields obtainable on investment-grade common stocks, (3) the failure of stock prices to rise as robustly since 1965 as before, and (4) the much higher yields available on bonds than on savings-type deposits. In tight-money years like 1969, individual demands have been the balancing factor in the market for new corporate bond issues, and bond yields have been forced upward to levels sufficient to attract small investors as "residual buyers."

BOND YIELDS

Because of the peculiar effects of length of term on the prices of bonds, their values are perhaps best shown in terms of yields. Table 6-3 presents a comparison of corporate bond yields with other leading forms of conservative investment. As shown by the table, the best long-term corporate bonds have sometimes yielded little more than long-term United States government bonds. Yields on the "good" category, which are the weakest bonds considered suitable for banks and other conservative institutions, are substantially greater than those on the "best" bonds and often greater than those on high-grade preferred stocks. Bonds lower in quality than those in Table 6-3 usually offer generous yields but must be regarded as unstable in price and subject to a moderate degree of business risk.

Table 6-3 *Percentage yields on selected investments (bond yields are on a yield-to-maturity basis)*

| | | | | | End of year |
Investments	1948	1958	1964	1969	1972[e]
3-year U.S. bonds*	1.49	3.70	4.15	8.41	5.87
Long-term U.S. bonds†	1.84‡	3.79	4.18	6.81	5.52
Long-term municipal bonds†	2.26‡	3.84‡	3.15‡	6.91‡	5.11‡
Best (Aaa) corporate bonds*	2.79	4.08	4.44	7.72	7.09
Very good (A) corporate bonds*	3.16	4.42	4.56	8.21	7.50
Good (Baa) corporate bonds*	3.53	4.85	4.81	8.65	7.94
High-grade bank stocks*	4.74	4.00	2.96	3.82	3.17
Industrial common stocks†	6.21	3.23	2.90	3.22	2.63
High-grade preferred stocks†	4.15	4.63	4.23	7.19	6.92

[e]Estimated from data available Dec. 15, 1972.
*From Moody's Investors Service.
†From S & P's Trade and Securities Service.
‡Exempt from federal income tax.

Table 6-3 serves to emphasize two aspects of yield-rate fluctuations. First, the contrast between the yields in easy-money times, such as the 1948 and 1964 year-ends and the high-rate dates of 1927 and 1969, is marked. As Chapter 2 pointed out, interest rates can be quite low when borrowing demand is low and when real saving, plus bank credit expansion, provides a generous supply of loan funds; but they can also be high when periods of business expansion give rise to a demand for loan funds and at the same time induce the Federal Reserve System to limit the bank credit supply as an inflation-control measure. For obvious reasons, the prices on old bonds fall when tight money requires high interest rates on new bonds, and vice versa, so that the yield rates on all bonds tend always to reflect the money-market conditions of the moment.

Table 6-3 also distinguishes between the yields of United States Treasury securities of 3 years' maturity and longer-term bonds. In 1927, 1959, 1966, and 1969, when all interest rates were relatively high, the yields on 3-year treasury securities at times exceeded those on long-term bonds; but in years when all yields were low, the long-term yields were higher. This is normal. Short-term interest bargains can be made at very high or very low rates under extreme market conditions, for neither borrower nor lender will be burdened with an onerous arrangement for very long; but long-term bond transactions establish yields which may endure for many years, hence they are not ordinarily made at extremely high or low rates.

The influence of risk on bond yields is illustrated in Chart 6-3. The chart shows the yields of various classes of corporate bonds through 21 years of varying interest rates and varying degrees of corporate prosperity. The most impressive lesson to be gained from Chart 6-3 is that all bonds tend to look good when money is plentiful and business is good. If this happens at a time when lenders have ample funds, the second-quality bonds will rise in price and their yields will approach those of high-grade bonds. Chart 6-3 shows that this happened in 1952–1956 and again in 1963–1965. But either uncertain business conditions or limited money supplies will cause lenders to prefer high-quality bonds, and the weaker issues will decline both absolutely and relatively. This can be seen in Chart 6-3 in 1957–1962, in 1966, and most notably in 1970 when the Penn Central Railroad's bonds shook investors' confidence by defaulting on their interest payments. The moral to be pointed is this: Second-grade bonds may be good speculative vehicles when bought at a major discount by an expert, but when business is good and bond yields are low, it is unwise to compromise on quality when the objectives are safety and price stability. The wise investor will get the very best; the yield will be almost as good, and the risk will be small. The price of any bond is subject to basic changes in interest rates, but this hazard is small compared to the price risk on a mediocre bond.

Secular moves in bond yields   Besides changing cyclically in response to business and monetary conditions, bond yields have been characterized by much longer-term shifts in their general level. The solid black line in Chart 6-4 depicts the course of bond yields over approximately the past century. Although the impact of successive business cycles is visible, yield levels are clearly dominated by four giant long-term trends: a declining tendency from roughly 1870 to 1899, a rising trend from 1899 to 1920, a prolonged fall from 1920 to 1946, and a long-term or secular rise from 1946 into the early 1970s. Chart 6-4 suggests that it has not been unusual for bond yields either to double in amount or to fall to half their former level over a 20- or 30-year interval, with inverse—and almost proportionate—effects on bond prices.

Three points about these secular moves in bond yields deserve special emphasis. First, it should be obvious that the secular trend of yields basically shapes the bond investor's chance of profit or loss. The man who buys bonds when yields are

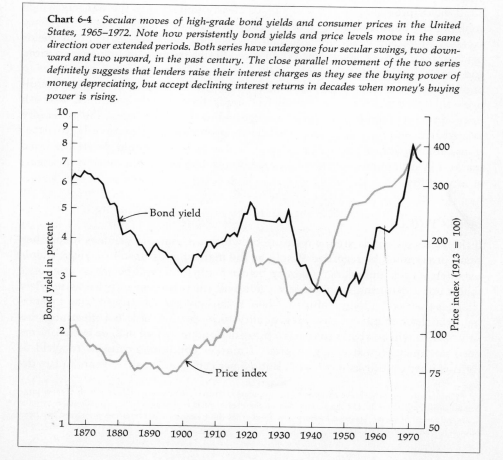

Chart 6-4 *Secular moves of high-grade bond yields and consumer prices in the United States, 1965–1972. Note how persistently bond yields and price levels move in the same direction over extended periods. Both series have undergone four secular swings, two downward and two upward, in the past century. The close parallel movement of the two series definitely suggests that lenders raise their interest charges as they see the buying power of money depreciating, but accept declining interest returns in decades when money's buying power is rising.*

rising secularly (as they were in the 1950s) is in effect buying into a prolonged bear market; he is almost certainly fated to see his bonds decline in value from one business cycle to the next. By contrast, buying bonds when yields are falling secularly means that the investor is riding a favorable underlying trend and so can expect ultimate profits as bond prices rise from cycle to cycle. Second, although other influences[8] undoubtedly help shape secular swings in bond yields and other interest rates, their primary determinant appears to be the course of commodity prices and living costs. As the shaded line in Chart 6-4 indicates, long-term swings in interest rates are almost perfectly correlated with long-term trends in prices and the buying power of money. Indeed, a growing number of economists believe that bond yields can always be explained as consisting of a basic 3 per cent rate plus an add-on equal to the expected rate of inflation. Thus, bond yields in 1970 averaged 8 per cent, 3 per cent plus the year's 5 per cent rate of inflation, which bond investors feared would continue. Third, the record level of bond yields prevailing in the early 1970s clearly underscores the dangers which confront the bond and other fixed-income-securities markets if the inflationary excesses of recent years are not sharply reduced. In 1969–1970, bond yields reached their highest levels since the United States became an industrial nation, and bonds purchased at the lower yield figures of earlier years fell sometimes to one-half or less of their original prices. It seemed evident that if intemperate additions to the nation's money supply and budgetary deficits continued to push prices upward, interest rates could be expected to rise accordingly; the possibility existed that bond yields might reach levels prohibitively expensive to corporations, municipalities, and other issuers, or that investors could desert the bond markets in such numbers that long-dated bonds, at least, might become unsalable at any yields.

BOND PRICES

If the yields on bonds are the measure by which the market evaluates them, then bond prices must be regarded simply as the mathematical result of yield, nominal interest rate, and years remaining before maturity. It will be apparent at once that a bond maturing within a few years will fluctuate less in price as its yield changes than will a long maturity. There is thus greater security for one's principal in a short maturity, assuming quality to be good. Table 6-4 illustrates this principle. It will be observed that a 5 per cent bond maturing in 2, or even 5, years need not fluctuate extremely in price if market conditions cause it to yield as little as 3 per cent or as much as 7. But a 5 per cent bond with 30 years to run de-

---

[8] Particularly the occurrence of inventions, population growth, and wars, each of which creates large demands for capital funds. On the supply side of the capital market, changes in rates of saving may have some influence; however, statistical evidence suggests that the fraction of national income saved has been relatively steady over the years.

Table 6-4 *Bond prices necessary to permit a 5 per cent bond to produce indicated yields*

Yield %	2	5	10	Years to maturity 20	30
2.0	105.85	114.21	127.07	149.25	167.43
3.0	103.85	109.22	117.17	129.92	139.38
4.0	101.90	104.49	108.18	113.68	117.38
5.0	100.00	100.00	100.00	100.00	100.00
6.0	98.14	95.73	92.56	88.44	86.16
7.0	96.33	91.68	85.79	78.64	75.06
8.0	94.56	87.83	79.61	70.31	66.06
9.0	92.82	84.17	73.98	63.20	58.72
10.0	91.14	80.70	68.84	57.10	52.68

preciates drastically if it must yield 7 per cent. In view of the recent tendency for bond yields to fluctuate widely, it is especially important that long-term bonds be good ones. To add the hazard of higher yield because of poor quality to the obvious hazard of a rise in basic interest rates would seem to belie any interest in security of principal.

It is perhaps desirable at this point to emphasize again the money-rate risk inherent in a "safe" investment in a long-term bond. Two examples will serve. The first is the Treasury 3⅛s of 1990, sold in early 1958 at par. Within the next few months, because of low interest rates occasioned by the recession of 1957–1958, the bonds sold as high as 107¼. Thirteen months later, as a result of high interest rates incident to the 1959 boom, the bonds had declined 17 per cent to a price of 89! Obviously these Aaa-rated, perfectly safe bonds are not perfectly safe repositories for ready cash which may be needed in a year like 1959. A second case is even more striking: the Aaa-rated Southern Bell Telephone 6s of 2004 were sold in September 1966 at about 100¾; between then and 1972 they sold as high as 106¼ and as low as 68; in the first half of 1972, they ranged between 82 and 86. Truly, high-grade bonds are not necessarily price-stable bonds.

Speculatively minded investors often argue that bond yields tend to be high and bond prices low when business is booming and stock prices are high. Conversely, bond yields are low and bond prices high when business is dull and stocks are depressed. Therefore, it follows that one should sell stocks at high prices at the peak of each boom and immediately buy bonds at rock-bottom prices. As soon as the boom has passed, the bonds will bring top prices, and the sagacious investor can buy stocks "on the bottom." In a few more months he can repeat the process—providing, always, that he correctly identifies the tops and the bottoms, that he picks always the right stocks and bonds, and that his theoretical economic pattern always runs true to form! It is worth noting that this theoretical economic pattern does not always fit the picture. For example, stocks and bonds were both high in 1963–1964, as the result of an "easy-money" program pursued by government during a time when business was reasonably good. They were both depressed throughout much of 1969–1970 when a prolonged application of tight money was required to throttle a stubborn inflationary boom.

Table 6-4 illustrates another interesting feature of bond markets. It has already been noted that bonds of long maturity are likely to fluctuate more in price than equally good bonds of short maturity. This feature is distasteful to many bond investors, and, in consequence, long-term bond issues must normally pay a somewhat higher interest rate than shorter ones of equal quality. But as a high-quality long-term bond becomes a shorter-term bond with the passage of time, it becomes acceptable to more holders and has a tendency to sell on a lower-yield basis. Table 6-4 indicates that a 30-year 5 per cent bond with only 10 years left before maturity would bring a price of 85.79 if it sold on a 7 per cent yield basis; 5 years before maturity, it would bring 95.73 on a 6 per cent basis. Naturally, the possibility of a call before maturity would affect these figures. But it is clear that the

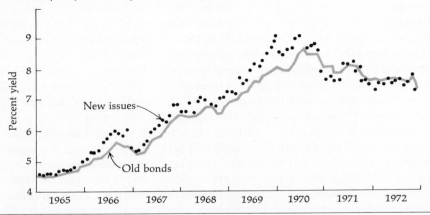

Chart 6-5 *Yields on new bond issues compared with yields on outstanding bonds of the same grade. The solid line shows the monthly average yield on Moody's Aa bond index. The dots represent the average yield at public offering prices of new nonconvertible Aa bonds offered during the month. Other good bonds (Aaa to Baa) show similar relationships. Over a long period of years it seems that (a) new bonds in normal periods are priced to yield a little more than outstanding ones, to facilitate quick sale; (b) new bonds yield much more than old ones when large-scale bond buyers are short of funds, as in late 1966, late 1969 or mid-1970; and (c) new bonds may even yield less than old ones when large-scale investors have surplus funds, as in early 1971 and throughout much of 1972. Note that a yield concession of .1 per cent is worth about $15 (1.5 points) on the price of a 30-year bond. Data adapted from Moody's Bond Survey.*

investor who is willing to ignore possible price fluctuations in long-term bonds will often have a chance to sell them at a good profit in the years preceding their final maturity. This practice, which is sometimes possible in shorter-term government securities as well, is known as *playing the pattern of rates*.

Still another interesting feature of the bond markets results from the twin facts that bonds are generally first brought to market in large issues but thereafter are mostly held by institutions and other strong investors who seldom need to sacrifice them. In consequence, the original marketing prices for new issues are usually slightly lower than the going prices for similar-quality bonds previously marketed, as Chart 6-5 shows. This assures a ready sale for the new issue. The prices on new bonds are *relatively* much lower if the new bonds must be offered in tight-money periods when buyers' money is in limited supply, as was notably the case in 1966 and 1969. Conversely, in early 1972, when bond buyers' funds were abundant, new bonds temporarily brought higher prices than old ones.

INTEREST COVERAGE

One of the important criteria by which analysts judge any bond is the adequacy of its interest coverage—i.e., how many times the necessary interest payment has been earned. This is measured by dividing the annual interest requirements into the business earnings after all expenses but before income taxes. If its bonds are to be classed as good, the typical utility or railroad must earn its fixed-interest charges 3 times; a typical industrial must earn them 6 times or more in the average year. It is very important that interest charges be small enough so that poor years' earnings will usually cover them, or at least so that unearned interest charges will not deplete working capital disastrously.

If the corporation has two or more issues of bonds which are successive in priority, it is significant to compute the coverage for the first lien bonds by dividing their interest alone into the available earnings. A high ratio of coverage would of course indicate a well-secured first lien. The coverage for the second lien is then computed on the overall basis, by dividing its interest plus that of the senior issue into the earnings. Coverage for a third lien could be similarly figured. However, this process of computing interest coverage on successive liens has one weakness: it may show a senior bond as being amply covered by earnings, hence quite secure, when the junior bonds are not even fully covered. It must be remembered that if any mandatory bond interest is defaulted, a bankruptcy proceeding could ensue. Bankruptcy might cause temporary suspension of interest payments and declines in the prices of well-secured senior bonds.

When a corporation such as a railroad operates both owned and leased properties, its fixed charges will consist of interest and lease rentals. In some cases the lease rentals exceed the bond interest in amount. Interest coverage on railroads is computed as "coverage for fixed charges," with fixed charges including both interest and lease rentals. Usually it is not easy to determine whether the lease rentals should be regarded as prior to, equal to, or junior to the bond interest.

When interest coverage on holding company bonds is being considered, it should be remembered that subsidiary bonds, subsidiary preferred stock, and possibly subsidiary income taxes will be senior to holding company bonds, if the holding company derives its income from subsidiary common-stock dividends.

CRITERIA OF QUALITY

Quality in a bond might well be defined as certainty of payment. A high-quality bond is one in which there seems little chance of difficulty but which is amply protected by lien and indenture terms if difficulty should arise. Quality of a bond is further enhanced if it seems likely to be stable in price, readily salable, and useful as collateral.

The principal tests by which experienced bondmen appraise corporate bonds are as follows:

1 Adequacy of earnings to cover interest and charges, in average years and poor years.

2 Lien protection, including priority, adequacy of amount of property under lien, durability of value of property, provisions regarding additional bonds, and provisions for release or substitution of lien.

3 Indenture provisions, especially on limitations on new debt, dividends, repurchase of stock, merger, sale of business, and amendment of indenture.

4 Nature of the industry, including its permanence, growth, earnings stability, competitive situation, labor problems, and relations with government.

5 Strength of the company, competitively and financially.

6 Marketability of the bonds, including size of the issue, market in which traded, sinking fund if any, eligibility for banks, legality for savings banks and trustees.

The individual who is thoroughly familiar with the bond features discussed in this chapter, and who is willing to make point-by-point comparison of these features as they occur in different bond issues, will have no trouble in classifying bonds into quality groups. The yields available on bonds of similar maturity and quality may then be compared and checked against the bond yield indexes published by the financial services. However, the individual investor will probably find it easier to accept the guidance of the quality ratings and the bond analytical summaries prepared by leading financial services such as Moody's or Standard & Poor's. These are well done and will also provide price and yield comparisons for convenient study. Good dealers' and brokers' surveys may serve the same purpose.

High-grade corporation bonds—those classified as Aaa, or Aa, or A by Moody's Investors Service or as AAA or AA, or A by Standard & Poor's—are obviously useful to conservative investors. Such bonds offer the investor ultimate safety of his dollar principal, a modest but dependable income, and relative freedom from any need to supervise them. The larger issues are highly salable, and the cost involved in buying or selling standard $1,000 bonds of major companies is small, usually $2.50 to $5 per bond. The longer maturities usually yield more than treasury bonds, savings bonds, or savings accounts, and a capital gain on them is distinctly possible. Temporary price depreciation of 10 to 20 per cent may occur during periods of high interest rates. Short-term corporation issues are more profitable than savings accounts when interest rates are high and also offer a reasonable degree of price stability. High-grade corporation bonds may thus serve as a conservative dollar-type income-producing segment of a permanent investment program, as a temporary investment (in short-term bonds), and as a quasi speculation for the investor who has funds to invest when interest rates are high and who may wish to buy stocks or real estate in some future period of business recession.

For investors to whom income and estate taxes pose a problem, the large numbers of long-term low-coupon bonds marketed between 1945 and 1956 may be useful. Low-coupon bonds paying $2\frac{1}{2}$ to $3\frac{1}{2}$ per cent per year in nominal interest usually sell far below par, and a large part of the yield on these bonds consists of their progressive appreciation in value from purchase date to maturity. But this appreciation is not taxable until the bond is sold or collected and even then it is a low-taxed capital gain. Furthermore, if the investor dies before selling or collecting his bond but after it has appreciated greatly in value, the bond will go to his heirs at the appreciated value and no income tax will be paid on this gain.

Convertible bonds range in quality from the superb to the speculative; some offer conversion terms which would be profitable after only a small rise in the price of the stock, and some would not be profitable unless the stock doubled or tripled. In practically all cases a convertible bond sells higher than either a similar ordinary bond or the stock into which it is convertible—10 to 20 per cent would be common excess—so investors using them must pay generously for the speculative potential or the inflation insurance which they provide.

Fixed-interest bonds in the B categories (Baa, Ba, and B) range from the reasonably good to the definitely speculative. In almost all cases, however, they should be watched as carefully as the typical common stock, for their value is not so free from impairment as that of the A groups. In good times these bonds may yield little more than high-grade bonds of equivalent maturity date, but in bad times their price declines may be drastic, as indicated in Chart 6-3, and the bonds are not free from the chance of permanent loss. Since medium-grade income bonds can often be had at prices which yield more than ordinary medium-grade bonds, and since income bonds do not burden the company with inflexible fixed charges in bad years, it would seem that they should often be considered instead of medium bonds. Definitely, medium-grade bonds do not afford the safety, price stability, and freedom from care which are sought in the superior bonds, but the generous income and the chance for price appreciation which they often afford when depressed in price make them interesting and enticing.

Finally, the case of speculation in bonds may be considered. Bonds rated B, Caa, and Ca may be expected to fluctuate widely in price, and the investor who buys them "right" may make money on them. This is particularly true of issues in default of interest or in danger of defaulting, and of income bonds. The latter, particularly, may fluctuate sharply when interest omission is not imminent, and it should be noted that temporary omission on an income bond is not damaging to a corporation, since it does not force bankruptcy proceedings. Bonds of these types, held strictly as speculations, are often more appropriate to individual portfolios than the Baa and Ba grades of fixed-interest bonds.

QUESTIONS AND PROBLEMS

1   How do price fluctuations compare for a *callable* high-coupon bond of recent issue date versus a low-coupon bond issued years ago? Why?

2   Is it true that short-term bonds fluctuate more in yield than long-term ones but that the long-term ones fluctuate more in price? Why?

3   Should interest and principal payments on bonds be geared to some index of the dollar's purchasing power—say the Consumer Price Index—to make bonds inflation-proof?

4   Why are bond buyers interested in lien security? May a debenture issue have any of the advantages of lien security? How?

5   Are open indentures as satisfactory to the bondholder as closed ones? Why? What special added feature is important to make sure that the lien always covers ample property, if the indenture is open?

6   Suppose that a $100,000,000 corporation has three bond issues, one a $20,000,000 first mortgage on half of its property, another a $5,000,000 first mortgage on the second half of its property, and the third a $10,000,000 second mortgage on the second half of its property. Rank these bonds in order of quality.

7   Under what conditions might a leasehold mortgage bond be high grade?

8   Explain how a forecast that interest rates would rise should affect choice of maturities for a bond investor greatly concerned with making capital gains and avoiding capital losses. What strategy should this investor follow re maturities if a fall in interest rates is foreseen?

9   Why is the Philadelphia plan for financing equipment regarded as stronger legally than a simple chattel mortgage on equipment to which the debtor has received title?

10   Would you want the 60-year bonds of a merchandising firm owning chiefly inventory and doing business in leased premises? Why would a railroad or telephone bond be different? Or would it?

11   Would serial bonds be a good choice for an individual investor? Who would want them?

12 What are the advantages of a sinking fund to the investor? Are there any possible disadvantages?

13 Would you ever buy a bond above its call price? How far above?

14 Would a policy of investing in high-grade convertible bonds be a means of combining investment safety with inflation insurance?

15 What advantage could mortgage security have for an income bond maturing in 2015?

16 Which would you choose for purchase, an 11-year 4 per cent bond priced at 77¼ or a 7 per cent bond priced at par, if both were rated Aaa?

17 If you were preparing a list of high-grade long-term bonds from which to choose, what price and yield and quality data would seem essential as a basis for choice?

18 According to a bond table, a 14-year 2¾ per cent bond priced at 70 yields 5.93 per cent. Since the cash interest is obviously 3.93 per cent on the price of 70, would it be correct to conclude that the extra 2 per cent represents capital gain and is equal to 3 per cent of ordinary income to a holder in a 50 per cent tax bracket?

19 Assume that a 6 per cent bond pays interest on March 1 and September 1. You bought the bond at 94 on June 10, and the transaction settlement date was June 17. Disregarding commissions, taxes, and mailing costs, how much was your total payment?

20 Why does deterioration in the quality of a long-term bond cause a drastic change in its price? Would a gradual rise in the general level of interest rates have the same effect?

21 Why do fixed charges as reported on railroad statements include lease rentals?

22 The effective brokerage commission to buyers and sellers on stock exchange transactions in bonds runs $2.50 to $7.50 per bond and on stocks (in modest quantities) 1½ to 2 per cent of market price. Since brokers' salesmen are usually paid a percentage of the commissions they generate, would they recommend bond purchases to their customers? Is this situation good public policy? Why does it exist?

23 What implications would you see for bond yields if common stocks in a relatively stable economy offered well-assured dividend yields of 4 per cent and strong prospects of 4 per cent per year dividend growth?

24 If stocks are selling 14 times annual earnings, and if risks on them are deemed low, what should bonds yield to be in equilibrium with stocks? Why?

REFERENCES

Badger, Ralph E., and Paul B. Coffman: *Investment Analysis*, McGraw-Hill Book Company, New York, 1967, Chaps. 3, 4.

Bellemore, Douglas H., and John C. Ritchie, Jr.: *Investments*, 3d ed., South-Western Publishing Company, Incorporated, Cincinnati, 1969, Chaps. 9, 10.

Cohen, Jerome B., and Edward D. Zinbarg: *Investment Analysis and Portfolio Management*, rev. ed., Richard D. Irwin, Inc., Homewood, Ill., 1973, Chaps. 9, 10.

Financial Handbook, rev. ed., The Ronald Press Company, New York, 1968, Sec . 14, also Sec. 27, pp. 45–54.

Financial Publishing Company: *Expanded Bond Values Tables*, Boston, 1970.

Francis, John Clark: *Investment Analysis and Management*, McGraw-Hill Book Company, New York, 1972, Chap. 8.

Graham, Benjamin, David L. Dodd, and C. Sidney Cottle: *Security Analysis*, 4th ed., McGraw-Hill Book Company, New York, 1962, Parts 3, 5.

Guthmann, Harry G., and Herbert E. Dougall: *Corporate Financial Policy*, 4th ed., Prentice-Hall, Inc., Englewood Cliffs, N.J., 1962, Chaps. 10–12.

Hayes, Douglas A.: *Investments: Analysis and Management*, 2d ed., The Macmillan Company, New York, 1966, Chap. 4.

Hickman, Walter B.: *Corporate Bond Quality and Investor Experience*, Princeton University Press, Princeton, N.J., 1956.

Homer, Sidney: *The Bond Buyer's Primer*, Salomon Brothers & Hutzler, New York, 1968.

Homer, Sidney, and Martin L. Leibowitz: *Inside the Yield Book*, Prentice-Hall, Inc., Englewood Cliffs, N.J., and New York Institute of Finance, New York, 1972.

EMBARRASSED OR
INSOLVENT CORPORATIONS

When a corporation encounters financial difficulties, its securities may offer both a problem and an opportunity. The bad news will usually cause both stocks and bonds to decline sharply in market price, thus forcing the owners to choose between painful losses and the further hazards involved in waiting for a possible future recovery. Speculatively minded purchasers, on the other hand, may buy the securities at prices far below long-run values, if they can correctly anticipate the outcome of the situation. The securities markets usually continue to trade in the stocks and bonds of an embarrassed or bankrupt concern; so decisions to buy or sell can be implemented without difficulty.

EMBARRASSMENT AND INSOLVENCY

Financial embarrassment exists when the corporation is so short of liquid assets that it finds constant difficulty in meeting its obligations, or when its earnings are so deficient that debt service (i.e., the regular contractual payment of interest and sinking fund and principal maturities if any) tends to impair its cash position, or when large-scale debt maturities are impending and must be refunded in markets where bonds are difficult to sell. Financial embarrassment thus presents a situation in which the corporation is not bankrupt and is still meeting its obligations, and in which the stockholders are still in control, but in which some emergency adjustment of the corporation's affairs is needed. Such an adjustment may be made in various ways, including (1) sale of some part of the firm's property or business, or (2) merger with another firm, or (3) a voluntary agreement between the corporation and its major creditors, or (4) an agreement between the corporation and its bondholders acting as a group.

Insolvency exists when the corporation is definitely unable to pay currently maturing debts or when its property at a fair valuation is worth less than the amount of its debts. Insolvency might possibly be cured by a voluntary adjustment between a corporation and its creditors, but when matters have reached this critical stage, it is usually necessary to resort to court supervision through receivership or bankruptcy proceedings. Court supervision prevents the corporate assets from being seized piecemeal by unpaid creditors while negotiations are proceeding, sees that a fair adjustment is planned, and often induces or compels claimants to cooperate in a fair plan.

FINANCIAL PROBLEMS

Corporate financial troubles have many causes, including such diverse ones as management incompetence, embezzlement, depression losses, loss of markets, errors in financial planning, and simple inability to sell securities in adverse markets. The necessary corrections are also diverse in nature. If the concern is so ineffective that little hope for successful operation exists, a plan to liquidate the assets or to sell operating units to other concerns will be best. If the problems include both frozen assets and depleted net worth, as they often do when finance companies or insurance companies get into difficulties, a merger in which the common stockholders get a relatively poor bargain may be inevitable. If inadequate or frozen working capital is the source of the trouble, present creditors may be persuaded as a group to defer or subordinate their claims so that new borrowings or credit purchases will be possible. If impending bond maturities constitute the difficulty, the bonds must be extended or exchanged for others maturing at a later date. If inadequate earning power is the source of trouble, it may be necessary to convert bonds into income bonds or stock and to reduce or eliminate the old stockholders' equity in accordance with the probable real net worth remaining in the company.

In relatively few instances will it be advantageous to liquidate a large-scale corporate enterprise. Sale of the assets in most cases would net so little that almost any alternative is preferable. The obvious solution is to correct the concern's present financial troubles and try again.

The details of corrective plans developed in different cases vary considerably, but the general procedures and the methods of evaluating the rights of the securityholders in an embarrassed corporation are now quite definite. Investors who are familiar with these matters and who are capable of appraising the potentialities of an embarrassed corporation's business are therefore able to obtain a fair idea of the outcome of the average situation.

PROTECTIVE COMMITTEES

When securityholders learn that a corporation is encountering serious difficulties, they sometimes form protective committees to consult with the management and to participate in court proceedings if any occur. Protective committees are self-appointed and usually develop around interested investment bankers and a few large holders of the securities. Normally a committee represents only one class of securityholders—i.e., first mortgage bondholders, debenture holders, preferred stockholders, etc.—so there may be a different committee for each class and, quite possibly, two or three competing committees for some classes. Such committees often collect proxies or powers of attorney from all securityholders who will join them. A protective committee which has the authority to speak for and commit a large group of securityholders is obviously a potent force in planning any corporate adjustment, for it can provide many assenting votes to a plan it approves or an almost insurmountable block of dissenting votes if it disapproves.

When a protective committee enters into extensive negotiations, securityholders are often asked to deposit their securities with the committee and to authorize expenditures for legal and other costs by the committee. If the negotiations are successful, the corporation or its successor will probably pay the committee's expenses, but this is not always the case. While the negotiations are in progress, the depositing securityowners will possess the committee's deposit receipts instead of their bonds or shares. These deposit receipts are transferable but are usually not so easy to sell as the original securities would be. In general, it may be concluded that an investor will risk distinct disadvantages if he deposits his securities too hastily; but, on the other hand, he may help to delay the solution of his problems if he withholds his cooperation too long.

The contumacious attitude of many protective committees during the financial troubles of the early thirties, and the excessive expenses which many of them incurred, led Congress in 1935 and 1938 to limit the activities of protective committees in federal bankruptcy cases. These legal limitations have greatly reduced the scope of committee activities but have not eliminated them.

VOLUNTARY ADJUSTMENTS ON BONDS

Embarrassed corporations often believe that they can avoid defaults and expensive court proceedings if their bondholders will accept temporary reductions in interest rates, or conversion of their bonds into income bonds, or deferments of maturities on early-maturing bonds, or some other change of bond terms which will help to solve the immediate problem. Proposals along these lines are commonly advanced by managements after consultation with representative bondholders or protective committees. From the standpoint of the bondholders, it is worthwhile to make reasonable concessions to avoid the expense, delay, and probable cessation of interest payments which a corporate bankruptcy would entail. It is important to make sure, however, that the proposed adjustments are fair, that they can actually be consummated, and that they will save the situation if consummated.

Most bond indentures provide that certain changes may be made in the indenture if the holders of a large proportion (possibly 75 per cent) of the outstanding bonds agree, but the permitted changes seldom include matters affecting principal sums, maturity dates, or interest payments. Adjustments on these matters must therefore be made between the corporation and each bondholder individually. There are two ways of doing this: The corporation may offer to exchange new securities having the desired features for those currently outstanding, or it may

ask the bondholders to send their bonds back to the trustee to be stamped to show
that the owners agree to the desired modifications of the original indenture.

Under either of these two procedures, only the consenting bondholders will
be bound, and if their sacrifice is successful, they will assure full and prompt
payment to the noncooperating minority, who will continue to have a legal right
to collect on the original basis. Because these facts are well known, it is often difficult to persuade bondholders to join in a voluntary adjustment; each holder
would prefer to profit as a member of a noncooperating minority. Corporations
meet this problem by making the proposed adjustments as attractive as possible—
for example, if an extension of a bond maturity is sought, a cash bonus of 1 to 5
per cent may be paid to bondholders who consent to the change. The proposal
will be vigorously urged upon all bondholders in advertisements, by mail, and by
the use of salesmen.

It is usually not best to rush to comply with a corporation's request for voluntary adjustment. Even though the bondholders are merely asked to deposit their
bonds in escrow, with no exchange or stamping permitted unless enough bonds
are obtained to assure success, the depositing bondholder has surrendered his
freedom of action. And after the exchange or stamping is completed, the new or
stamped bond is a new security, unlike the old, and salable or pledgeable only as
a new issue. There is usually plenty of time, after mature consideration and consultation with others, to accept a sound exchange or modification plan. Such
proposals are generally analyzed at length in investment periodicals and advisory
services; these should be consulted before any plan is accepted or rejected.

ADJUSTMENT BY MAJORITY RULE

Corporations whose financial troubles are limited to embarrassment may sometimes obtain adjustments which are binding on all the affected classes of creditors,
providing the requisite majorities can be persuaded to approve them.

As noted in the preceding section, corporate bond indentures commonly provide that indenture terms relating to sinking funds, working capital, limitation
of debt, nonpledging of property—in fact, almost anything other than principal
sums, interest payments, and maturity dates—may be altered by request of the
corporation and approval of two-thirds or three-fourths or some similar fraction of the bonds. This type of indenture modification is binding on all the bonds,
since the indenture itself provides the method for doing it. In the proper circumstances, relief from sinking funds or freedom to borrow needed working capital
might make the difference between surviving a crisis and becoming insolvent.

A second though infrequently used device for obtaining financial adjustments
by majority rule is found in Section 102 of the Delaware Corporation Laws. This
Section permits a Delaware corporation to include in its articles a clause providing that any financial adjustment agreed to by certain majorities of its stockhold-

ers and creditors and approved by a Delaware court of equity shall be binding upon all. As a part of the corporation's very existence, this clause thereafter is a part of every contract the corporation may make and is automatically accepted by every stockholder and every creditor.

The third procedure under which creditors' claims may be adjusted by majority rule is applicable only to railroads. Under the so-called Mahaffie Act, which the President signed in April 1948, a railroad may propose a readjustment of the terms of any or all of its outstanding securities, or an exchange of existing securities for new ones of a different nature, in order to forestall financial difficulties. The proposal must first be addressed to the Interstate Commerce Commission, which will investigate to see if the plan is equitable and in the best interests of all concerned. If the ICC decides affirmatively, the proposal is submitted for the approval of each class of securityholders affected by it. If 75 per cent of the holders approve, the ICC may then order the adjustment placed in effect. Dissenting securityholders may carry an appeal to the courts, alleging that the plan is inequitable or improper, but there can be no bargaining advantage gained by refusing to cooperate in a fair plan.

The Mahaffie Act procedure may also be tried by railroads which are already in receivership or bankruptcy, if the supervising judge approves the attempt.

The Mahaffie Act is a streamlined revision of Chapter XV of the Bankruptcy Act, which was placed on the statute books experimentally in 1939–1940 and again in 1942–1945. The most important readjustment handled under the original Chapter XV was that of the Baltimore and Ohio Railroad Company, which was completed in 1945, approximately 2 years after the plan was first undertaken. The Mahaffie Act procedure was used in 1956 to readjust the entire financial structure of the Missouri Pacific Railroad and has also been used for partial readjustment of smaller roads.

EQUITY RECEIVERSHIP

When a corporation is insolvent or unable to pay its obligations, it becomes important to prevent creditors from dismembering it to their own and others' ultimate disadvantage by attaching portions of its property or commencing foreclosure suits. The corporation or a friendly creditor may accomplish this by requesting a federal or state court to appoint a receiver to take over the corporation's properties. The function of a receiver is to conserve the properties and to operate the business, if that is the best method of conserving it, while the stockholders, the creditors, and the judge seek a sound method of settling the corporation's affairs.

Prior to 1933 most corporate insolvencies were corrected through equity receiverships. After the receiver took charge, a court hearing was held to determine whether the debtor company should be liquidated or reorganized. If liquidation appeared best, the judge would order the sale of the properties and the distribution of the proceeds to creditors and stockholders in order of priority. If substantial majorities of the claimants wished to establish a suitable successor corporation, accept its securities in satisfaction of their claims, sell new securities to raise necessary cash, and "buy" the assets of the old company at a foreclosure sale, the equity court judge would approve their plan and assist in carrying it out.

However, the equity court procedure had serious weaknesses. It could not compel dissenting claimants to accept securities in the successor corporation, and it was obligated to "sell" the assets of the old company for a fair price and see that the nonparticipating claimants got their share in cash. This made equity reorganizations very difficult and slow, for the reorganization plan had either to please practically all claimants, so that they would accept settlement in securities of the new company, or to include a method of raising a large amount of cash to pay off the dissenters. Even when all the protective committees supported a reorganization plan—and that itself was unusual—many independent security-holders were likely to dissent.

Since 1933 most large corporate insolvencies have been handled in federal bankruptcy courts, for the bankruptcy courts have been given the power to compel recalcitrant minorities to share in equitable reorganization plans; this supposedly speeds up the reorganization, for minorities cannot demand special advantages as the price of cooperation, cash to pay dissenters does not have to be raised, and the sale of the property is unnecessary. Equity procedures are still used in small corporate insolvencies handled in state courts when no serious dissents arise.

It is important to note at this point that equity reorganizations and bankruptcy reorganizations are available only in cases of actual insolvency, in which the corporation definitely either cannot pay its immediate obligations or has assets worth less than the amount of its debts. A corporation which is merely short of funds or which foresees insolvency at some future date may try to work out an adjustment as outlined in preceding sections, but it cannot resort to equity or bankruptcy reorganization until insolvency is actually upon it.

RAILROAD BANKRUPTCY REORGANIZATIONS

An insolvent railroad may be reorganized under Section 77 (Chapter VIII) of the federal bankruptcy law. Section 77 was enacted in early 1933 in the hope that it might expedite the reorganization of a large number of railroads which were in trouble at that time. It has since been amended into its present form.

Either the insolvent railroad or a creditor may initiate reorganization proceedings under Section 77. If the judge hearing the case is satisfied that the facts justify procedure under the Section, he will appoint a bankruptcy trustee to operate the properties until reorganization is completed. Plans for reorganization may then be submitted to the ICC by the debtor railroad, by the trustee, by groups of stockholders or bondholders, and by protective committees; and the commission must ultimately recommend one of these plans or one of its own to the judge, who will then hold hearings to review its practicability and fairness. A plan consists simply of a proposed capital structure which is suitable to the future earning power of the corporation, plus an equitable apportionment of the new securities to each class of old creditors and stockholders, plus any necessary provision for raising cash and meeting reorganization costs. The plan must recognize the prior rights of secured creditors and other senior claimants by giving them better securities or more securities than lower-ranking claimants receive. If the judge believes the plan to be proper, he will order it submitted to each class of creditors and stockholders who are entitled to participate (that is, whose claims are high enough in priority to share in the assets), and if two-thirds in amount of each class of claimants approves, the judge will order the plan carried out by delivery of the new securities to all claimants. Even if the desired two-thirds majorities cannot be had, the judge may in his discretion order a plan carried out.

During and after the Great Depression, reorganizations under Section 77 typically required 5 to 7 years to complete. This was due in part to the debtors' complicated financial structures; because of the interlacing of first, second, and third liens on different portions of property, collateral, and equipment, it was very difficult to determine which securities were entitled to priorities. A second reason for delay in reorganizations was found in earnings experience during the years from 1934 through 1948. Neither depression, war, nor postwar boom gives a dependable indication of future normal earning power, either to plan a capital structure or to measure the value of a lien on a given portion of a railroad,. Shortages of cash did not delay Section 77 reorganizations. When cash was scarce, the trustees simply suspended interest and sinking-fund payments on all but the best secured claims and used the earnings to improve the properties and the railroads' cash positions.

In order to guard Section 77 reorganizations against the delays and multiplied expenses which excessive protective committee activity would entail, the law forbids such committees to solicit proxies or deposits of securities except with the consent of the ICC. This is generally withheld until the official plan is ready for acceptance or rejection. Small groups of 25 or fewer securityholders may form their own protective committee at any time if they do not engage in general solicitation of proxies or deposits.

INDUSTRIAL AND UTILITY REORGANIZATIONS

Bankruptcy reorganizations for general corporations may be conducted under Chapter XI or Chapter X of the federal bankruptcy act. General corporations may be defined as corporations which are not doing a railroad, banking, insurance, or savings-and-loan business. Chapter XI is intended for the simpler cases in which adjustments on only unsecured debts are required. In Chapter XI cases, the debtor initiates the proceedings by admitting insolvency and proffering a reorganization plan to the court. The judge must investigate the situation and consult with the creditors, and may appoint a receiver or a bankruptcy trustee if that appears necessary. If a majority in number and amount of each affected class of creditors accepts the debtor's plan, and if the judge finds it equitable and feasible and otherwise proper, it may be made binding on all concerned.

Where secured creditors are affected by the insolvency, resort must be had to a Chapter X reorganization. Under this Chapter the proceedings may be initiated by either the debtor corporation or its creditors. The judge will appoint a trustee to manage the property and prepare a plan or reorganization. Creditors and stockholders may confer with the trustee as he prepares his plan and may prepare plans of their own. After hearings on the plans, the judge must ask the advice of the Securities and Exchange Commission, if the corporation is a large one, and may do so in any event. Finally, the judge must approve a plan as being equitable and feasible and order it submitted to the claimants. If two-thirds in amount of each class of creditors and a majority of each (participating) class of stockholders approve, the judge confirms the plan and orders it carried out.

Chapter X limits the activities of protective committees in a manner somewhat similar to Section 77. Committees are forbidden, unless by consent of the judge, to solicit any approval or disapproval of any plan or to collect any proxies along such lines, until the judge orders the official plan submitted for the acceptance of the securityholders. Furthermore, the judge may in some cases invalidate proxies or deposit agreements empowering the committees. Under these circumstances, protective committees do not exist at all in many cases and develop only as small groups representing a few large claimants in others. Only when opposition to a submitted plan is undertaken by determined groups will there be any extensive protective committee work under Chapter X.

The average Chapter X reorganization is completed in 2 to 3 years though complicated cases have taken 5 or 6.

ADJUSTMENT AND REORGANIZATION PLANS

Because of the noncompulsory nature of most nonbankruptcy adjustment plans, their terms cannot be made severe. Consequently, most of them feature such mild expedients as 2- to 10-year extensions of maturing bonds, conversion of interest payments to an income bond basis for a limited period, or modification of indentures to eliminate sinking-fund payments or to permit other borrowing. Usually these voluntary adjustment plans are not operative unless a minimum of 80 to 90 per cent of affected bondholders will consent. Typical cases include the

Laclede Gas Light Company's 1934 plan for a 5-year extension of its 5s of 1934, in which cooperating bondholders received a cash bonus of $21.60 per $1,000 bond; the Associated Gas and Electric Company's 1933 plan for exchanging new income debentures for old fixed-interest bonds; the Baltimore and Ohio Railroad Company's 1938 plan for placing part of its fixed charges on an income basis for 8 years and deferring certain maturities; and the New York, Chicago and St. Louis Railroad Company's 1932 plan for extending its 6s of 1932, which involved payment of 25 per cent in cash and the balance in 6s of 1935.

Bankruptcy reorganizations are commonly made of sterner stuff. A corporation which becomes bankrupt should emerge from the reorganization with a sturdy capital structure which reflects the real earning power and value of its properties, even if this means that old stockholders are dropped out entirely and old bondholders have to become stockholders. A drastic reorganization of this sort is often resisted by the claimants but must be sought by the court and commissions under the terms of the bankruptcy laws.

Any bankruptcy reorganization should be planned with the following criteria in mind:

1   The capital structure of the new concern must be such that (a) fixed-interest requirements can be met easily, (b) income bond interest and preferred dividends can be paid most of the time, and (c) there is at least a possible equity in earnings for the common stock. A speculative possibility of increased earnings may be reflected in the amount of common stock authorized.

2   Priorities in the old capital structure must be strictly observed—creditors must be fully compensated in new securities (at potential, not current, market values) before any stockholder is allotted anything, and all the preferred stockholders are fully compensated ahead of the common. Secured creditors are given preference over other creditors according to the earning power or importance of the property pledged to them.[1]

[1] To illustrate this principle: Assume that a corporation financed by $4,000,000 of mortgage bonds, $3,000,000 of unsecured debt, and $6,000,000 of stock has failed because of inability to meet its obligations when due. Bankruptcy appraisal shows that the business can earn $150,000 of dependable income annually, another $150,000 most of the time, and an average of $300,000 more intermittently; this is held to justify a new capital structure consisting of $2,000,000 in bonds, $2,000,000 in preferred stock, and $3,000,000 in common stock. Appraisals indicate that the mortgage bonds covered a portion of the property which earned all the dependable income, half the "most of the time" income, and half the intermittent income. In the reorganization, the new bonds would be allotted first; the old bondholders would get all or nearly all of them, since the old mortgage covers all the property from which the bond-quality income is derived. In allotting the preferred stock, half of it must be set aside at once for the old bondholders, since their lien covers half of the income sources upon which the new preferred depends. The other $1,000,000 of new preferred goes pro rata to the next-ranking claims, which consist of the remaining $1,000,000 of old bond claim plus the $3,000,000 of unsecured creditors; the division is therefore $250,000 and $750,000. The $3,000,000 of new common is next divided: the old bondholders have a lien priority to half of it, but $750,000 of it pays them up in full; that leaves $2,250,000 of common to meet the remaining unsecured creditors' claims of exactly that amount. The old stockholders therefore get nothing.

3 Unpaid interest usually is added to the bondholder's claim. If the company has earnings to spare during the bankruptcy period, and if senior creditors are certain to be paid in the long run anyhow, the trustee may pay such interest regularly.

4 Well-secured senior bonds which receive interest during bankruptcy may be permitted to continue undisturbed as the obligations of the reorganized company. This happened to most equipment obligations and to some first mortgage bonds when the debtor railroads failed during the thirties.

A good example of a bankruptcy reorganization is that of Paramount Publix Corporation in 1935, which continued $57,000,000 of subsidiary and senior debts undisturbed, allowed $59,000,000 of holding company creditors 50 per cent in new debentures and 50 per cent in new preferred stock, and allowed each old share of stock one-fourth of a share of new stock plus warrants for the purchase of extra preferred and common stock at attractive prices. Another typical example is that of the Associated Telephone Utilities Company, a holding company which failed in 1933. Two years later the bondholders of the old company received all the common stock of the successor General Telephone Corporation, investigation having proved the subsidiaries' debt to be so heavy that senior securities in the holding company were undesirable. A third example is that of the Denver and Rio Grande Western Railroad Company, whose bankruptcy period extended from 1935 to 1947. In this case the equipment obligations were continued without default; one well-secured old bond issue was fully compensated in cash and new bonds; less adequately secured old bonds got new fixed-interest bonds, income bonds, preferred stock, and common stock in varying proportions; and an issue of debentures got a small amount of new common stock. The old stockholders got nothing.[2]

BANKRUPTCY REORGANIZATIONS AND THE INVESTOR

In most modern bankruptcy reorganizations, the small investor is strictly a bystander. Large investors may enter protective groups and consult with trustees

---

A recapitulation of this example indicates that the $4,000,000 of old bonds got $2,000,000 in new bonds, $1,250,000 in new preferred, and $750,000 in new common. Each bond received $500 in new bonds, $312.50 in new preferred, and $187.50 in new common.

In this example, extreme emphasis has been laid upon the future earning power of specific properties, on the assumption that no great sums could be realized by selling these properties to other concerns. It must be noted, however, that the unsecured creditors in this reorganization could have claimed better treatment if the unmortgaged properties in the example had been salable at a good price to outside interests.

[2] Complete descriptions of these plans will be found in the appropriate Moody's Investors Service manuals for the year of consummation. For an unbelievably fantastic story of a bankruptcy case, investigate the history of the Missouri Pacific Railroad, which failed in 1933 and was in 1954 still embroiled in litigation and confusion over bankruptcy reorganization plans, though its business had been solidly prosperous for many years. The Mo Pac was reorganized under the Mahaffie Act in 1956.

or the court, but the small holder is usually well advised to avoid such groups, watch what goes on, and retain his position or sell out as the situation warrants. As a rule, he should also stay out of groups which form to contest official reorganization plans or to press for modifications. There are a number of reasons for this. In the first place, protective committee efforts are expensive, and depositing securityholders may have to pay for them. Second, controversies involving protective committees are likely to drag on for years; the large holders who control a committee may prefer to contest a minor point rather than compromise. Third, protective committee deposit receipts are usually less salable than free securities and usually bring a lower price, if the holder subsequently decides to sell. Fourth, a feasible and equitable reorganization plan is likely to be developed and confirmed without the services of a protective committee, and in less time. Finally, most protective committee efforts to resist or modify reorganizations are fruitless, anyhow.

The best sources of general information on the progress of reorganizations will be the financial reporting services, the financial newspapers and periodicals, and the daily newspapers. When plans are submitted to securityholders for final approval or rejection, a complete presentation of the situation will accompany the forms.

QUESTIONS AND PROBLEMS

1   Investigate the troubles of Douglas Aircraft Company in early 1967 and the terms of its merger into McDonnell-Douglas Corporation. Was this a fair plan?

2   What happens to the prices of its securities when a concern fails? Why would these securities be likely to fluctuate in price during the bankruptcy period?

3   How long does a bankruptcy reorganization take? Do you approve of the Mahaffie Act? Is there a counterpart to the Mahaffie Act which may be employed by general corporations? Should there be, if the purpose is to coerce unwilling creditors into a compromise of their property rights?

4   If you hold a bond which is due to mature in 6 months, and if the corporation writes you saying that it can pay the interest but not the principal at this time and requests you to agree to a 5-year extension of maturity, should you comply? Under what conditions?

5   If a protective committee writes you about the situation in question 4, requesting that you give it your bond so that it may negotiate effectively with the management, would you do it? Why?

6   Why was the equity receivership procedure inadequate to deal with corporate insolvencies during the depression of the early thirties?

7   What is the procedure followed in a Chapter X reorganization?

8   What are the guiding principles upon which bankruptcy reorganizations are based?

9   Assume that an established meat-packing corporation has just sustained very severe losses as a result of inventory price declines, is unable to meet the principal of a bond issue which is currently due, and is therefore in bankruptcy under Chapter X. It needs $10,000,000 of additional working capital, which can be obtained at 8 per cent by selling

new bonds secured by a first mortgage on its two packing plants. At present the corporation's assets consist of two packing plants and $10,000,000 of other assets; their total earning power is estimated for the future at $1,500,000 per year after all taxes and is credited in equal portions (thirds) to the two plants and the other assets. With the new working capital added, earning power will average about $2,500,000; of this, $1,000,000 will be very dependable, $750,000 will be available 4 years out of 5, and $750,000 will be irregular. The old capital structure consisted of a $15,000,000 first mortgage at 4 per cent on the two packing plants, $10,000,000 of unsecured debt, and 1,000,000 shares of stock. Recommend a reorganization plan.

10 Investigate the financial troubles of the New York, New Haven, and Hartford Railroad in 1961 and later years. Are its bondholders being fairly treated?

11 Investigate the problems involved during 1972 in settling the claims of bondholders of the Jersey Central Railroad. (See especially the item in *The Wall Street Journal*, December 5, 1972, p. 20.) Are such problems typical and likely to recur in other bankruptcy cases? Does this suggest a principle for guiding bond investment?

REFERENCES

Financial Handbook, rev. ed., The Ronald Press Company, New York, 1968, Secs. 21, 22.

Guthmann, Harry G., and Herbert E. Dougall: *Corporate Financial Policy*, 4th ed., Prentice-Hall, Inc., Englewood Cliffs, N.J., 1962, Chaps. 29–31.

Husband, William H., and James C. Dockeray: *Modern Corporation Finance*, 7th ed., Richard D. Irwin, Inc., Homewood, Ill., 1972, Part 7.

Investment Bankers Association of America: *Fundamentals of Investment Banking*, Prentice-Hall, Inc., Englewood Cliffs, N.J., 1949, Chaps. 14, 15.

MacLachlan, James A.: *Handbook of the Law of Bankruptcy*, West Publishing Company, St. Paul, Minn., 1956.

Securities and Exchange Commission: *Report on the Study and Investigation of the Work, Activities, Personnel, and Functions of Protective and Reorganization Committees,* ..Washington, 1936–1940.

Stanley, David T., Marjorie Girth, and Vern Countryman: *Bankruptcy*, The Brookings Institution, Washington, 1971.

Weston, J. Fred, and Eugene F. Brigham: *Managerial Finance*, 4th ed., Holt, Rinehart and Winston, Inc., New York, 1972, Chap. 24.

part 3
The Securities Markets

This is a vital and controversial topic. The American securities markets assemble about one-half the new savings of the country for investment in the new securities of industries and governments. They provide resale facilities for many billions of existing securities and thus assure the liquidity which makes the financing of business transactions, home purchases, and consumer durables possible.

Obviously, the securities markets must function smoothly and equitably. They must be used confidently by both the issuers of securities and the investors who buy and sell securities.

But the securities markets are gigantic marketplaces in which supply and demand are largely independent of each other and in which buyers and sellers often insist on nearly instantaneous transactions. Prices are thus almost forced to fluctuate. And price fluctuations tend to be accentuated by the always uncertain future of the national economy.

The securities business provides facilities and procedures for handling transactions in new and old securities, and there are also facilities which provide investors with a great deal of investment information and advice. However, the market facilities are elaborate and technical, market price fluctuations follow complicated patterns, and the available securities information is often difficult to procure and interpret. Investors can usually do much better if they make expert use of the facilities which are available. Chapters 8 through 11 undertake to introduce investors to the market machinery and methods, market behavior patterns, and information sources which they need to understand.

It is to be expected that a business which handles vast sums would occasionally have both dishonest practitioners and unintended disasters, and that these would lead to public regulation. Given the bias toward detailed public intervention which dominates this generation, it is not surprising that securities market regulation seems bent on burgeoning and proliferating. Chapter 12 discusses existing and proposed regulation.

Part 3 is thus a review of dozens of practices and situations in which an investor-citizen must repeatedly ask himself, "How do I meet this situation?" and "Is this practice economically sound?" and "Is this a proper use of regulatory authority?" No doubt most readers will find greatest interest in learning to utilize market techniques to their personal advantage, but a critical attitude toward market practices and public policy among informed citizens should in the long run yield important benefits in improved markets.

SECURITIES MARKET
ORGANIZATION

The securities markets of the United States function through some 5,000 security houses or firms, a number of trade associations, 11 active national securities exchanges and several other informal ones, and a number of banks which deal in public bonds. These agencies handle or participate in investor transactions which, in 1972, almost certainly exceeded 300 billion dollars, exclusive of dealings in short-term government securities.

From the investor's viewpoint, the functions of the securities business can best be analyzed by classifying them as (1) investment banking, which has to do with procuring money for corporations and government bodies by marketing new securities; (2) dealing in securities, which means making a market in them by buying and selling securities as merchandise with a firm's own money; and (3) brokerage, which means handling transactions as the customer's agent, strictly on a commission basis. Many securities firms engage in all three of these functions, and practically all the others engage in two. In fact, it is often difficult to determine where one function leaves off and another begins.

The three functions just described correspond closely with the three major divisions of the securities markets. (1) The *new issues market* is a wholesale market in which business corporations or governmental bodies sell entire issues of newly created securities to the investing public, largely through the medium of investment bankers who provide underwriting, marketing, advisory, and other services to the issuers. (2) The *over-the-counter market* is a nationwide network of approximately 5,000 dealer firms, closely linked by telephone and by computer-based market-quotation services, which make "bid and asked" markets in more than 12,000 publicly held securities. (3) The *organized stock exchanges* are centralized, auction-type markets in which brokers and dealers who hold exchange memberships buy and sell some 5,800 "listed" stocks and bonds, largely as agents for their customers. This chapter and the next will present a unified treatment of the organization, functions, and trading procedures of these three markets. Chapter 8 discusses the new issues and over-the-counter markets, and Chapter 9 deals with the stock exchanges or listed markets.

As might be expected, there are both statutes and industry organizations which attempt to enforce sound practices in the securities field. Most of the states require all securities firms and personnel to be licensed and have enacted antifraud and regulatory statutes. The federal government has nine major statutes in force in this area. These measures regulate many aspects of corporate practice and control practically all phases of the securities business, insofar as honesty, full publicity, and fair dealing are concerned. Although a thorough study of securities regulation will be deferred to Chapter 12, it will be necessary to include certain of its aspects in the present description of the securities business itself.

INVESTMENT BANKING

Investment banking has been defined as the business of obtaining money for corporations or government bodies by marketing their new securities. The definition should perhaps say "assisting in marketing . . . ," for few houses do the entire job of marketing even a small new issue, except when the issue is sold in a private transaction to a few large buyers, such as insurance companies. The investment banking function is usually accomplished in one of three ways, which may be called (1) standby underwritings, (2) purchasing-distributing, and (3) agency marketing.

Standby underwritings   When corporations undertake to sell stock or bonds to their existing securityholders on a "rights" or similar basis, they naturally want to make sure they receive the money which a successful sale would provide. To guard against failure, a group of investment bankers is often asked to *underwrite* the offering—that is, to agree in advance to buy at a stipulated price all the securities which the original offerees or their assigns do not take. The investment bankers would then organize a sales campaign to dispose of any stock which they might buy pursuant to the underwriting agreement.

A successful rights offering usually attracts subscriptions to 95 per cent or more of the proffered securities.[1] However, reasonable certainty of success with an offering will require most or all of the following circumstances: (1) an offering price at least 5 per cent below market value on stocks, or 3 per cent below on bonds; (2) a reasonably stable securities market during the offering period; (3) an offering which does not exceed in value 15 per cent of the offerees' existing investment in the company; (4) a well-distributed group of stockholders, so that subscription will not exceed the buying capacity of too many of the stockholders, as it would if the stock were held in large blocks; and (5) a seasoned group of stockholders who have faith in the company. It is often possible for an offering to be successful with one or more of these requirements unfulfilled, but each departure adds to the hazard. The entire problem is accentuated by the fact that any new offering of a security inevitably adds to the supply offered for sale on the market during the offering period and ensuing weeks, thus tending to depress the price.

The fee which underwriters obtain for assuring the success of a rights offering

---

[1] The technique of a rights offering is described in Chap. 3.

generally ranges between 1 and 3 per cent of the value of the issue if the stock is well known and of good quality. Obviously, the fee will vary with the quality and popularity of the stock, the condition of the stock market, the ability of the stockholders to subscribe, and the amount by which the market price exceeds the offering price. Sometimes the underwriting fee is a flat sum per share or a percentage on the whole value of the offering; more often it is a flat sum per share plus a second fee per share on all shares actually purchased by the underwriters; and still more detailed arrangements are common.

Two cases may be cited. In November 1972, the Wisconsin Power and Light Company offered its shareholders 1 new share for each 10 held. The subscription price was $18.60 per share, $1.40 below the prevailing market price of $20. Marketing conditions were ideal, and underwriters accepted a below-average fee of $107,092, or 17 cents per share on the whole 629,954-share offering, for agreeing to buy all the unsubscribed stock at the $18.60-per-share subscription price. The second example involves the Philadelphia Electric Company offering of 1,382,472 shares in October 1967. Shareholders were offered 1 new share for each 20 held at a price of $27.50; the market price was $30.38. In this case the underwriters obtained a fixed fee of 14 cents per share on the whole offering, plus 55 cents per share extra on all shares obtained by them through exercise of rights which they might purchase as well as on unsubscribed shares which they were required to purchase. Finally, the underwriters agreed to give the company 50 per cent of any profits they might make by selling the unsubscribed stock purchased by them.

The securities firms which underwrite a rights offering do not stand idle during the offering period. They often undertake to persuade large stockholders to exercise their rights, and to induce nonstockholders to buy rights and exercise them. They may buy rights and exercise them themselves, and then attempt to sell the stock to their customers. And they will most certainly buy stock if necessary to prevent the price from declining seriously during the offering period. In the Philadelphia Electric Company offering just described, the underwriters bought rights and subscribed for 167,988 shares, and also purchased 51,379 shares which were not subscribed for during the offering period. During the offering period they sold 244,917 shares to their customers. The 25,550 shares by which the underwriters' sale exceeded their purchases represented a "short" position deliberately established by the underwriters, as is legally permitted. To obtain these 25,550 shares, already sold to their customers, the underwriters were obligated to enter the open market and buy additional stock, thus augmenting the demand and helping to assure a firmer price in the days following the offering.

Although both investors and corporate managers may be impressed with the heavy cost of underwriting services, the advantages should also be apparent. If the corporation needs the money, the partial failure of a securities offering may leave the concern in a position in which its existing investment is imperiled. Whether the new offering is made on a rights basis or through investment banking firms, it is important for an investor to consider the possible consequences, if the transaction is not underwritten. As an alternative to the relatively costly underwriting process, some corporations endeavor to enlist the cooperation of the entire securities business in a rights offering by paying a small per share fee to any securities firm which forwards a subscription. However, a good many rights offerings are conducted without any arrangements of any kind with securities firms.

Purchasing-distributing A major portion of the investment banker's business is concerned with purchasing entire new issues of securities from the issuing corporations and reselling them to investors. This process is also known as underwriting, and the purchasing group of investment bankers are called underwriters. This is the common method of marketing bonds and preferred stocks and is also used extensively when better grades and large issues of common stocks are to be sold.

Securities issues offered for marketing in this manner may range in size from $500,000 to $500,000,000 or more. Most of the important ones will exceed $10,000,000, and $250,000,000 is not uncommonly large. These sums are so vast that few investment bankers find it either convenient or prudent to buy entire new corporate issues for their own accounts. Instead, they form *purchasing syndicates* consisting of several firms willing to share the responsibility. A separate syndicate is formed for each issue, though securities firms commonly ally themselves in cooperating groups which handle one issue after another.[2] Small issues may be underwritten by two or three firms; large ones may require fifty to a hundred. In each case the syndicate members will indicate the portion of the entire issue for which they take responsibility; that is, one member may take 10 per cent, another 5 per cent, etc. A purchase group agreement among the participating firms outlines the syndicate's plan of procedure and delegates authority to one firm to act as agent for the group in making the purchase and organizing the selling effort.

When the purchasing syndicate has been formed, the corporation and the syndicate enter into a formal *agreement to purchase and sell*. Under this agreement the details of the security to be sold are outlined, and the corporation agrees to print the securities, pay the cost of audits and other surveys required for the registration statement, "register" the issue with the Securities and Exchange Commission, obtain clearances with state securities commissions, and provide descriptive prospectuses for distribution to interested investors. Sometimes the corporation's officers and leading stockholders will agree not to sell their stock for a period of months and to assist in electing a representative of

---

[2] Because the leading firms tend always to form their syndicates among their own groups, it is difficult for a new or "outside" firm to compete effectively in the business. In the years 1948–1952 a number of firms were prosecuted under the antitrust laws because of this situation, but were adjudged not guilty.

the underwriters to the board of directors. The commitment of the underwriters is usually somewhat less positive; they agree to make the purchase if no legal barriers to the issuance and sale of the securities develop and if no substantial adverse changes in the condition of the corporation or the securities market appear before the date for the public offering. Sometimes the exact price of the security is left for last-minute determination on the basis of market conditions.

If an issue is expected to sell readily to a few large insurance companies or other major investors, the purchasing syndicate members may feel that no extensive sales campaign is necessary. Possibly the syndicate manager can sell the entire commitment by telephone in a few hours. If he can do so by offering the securities to a relatively few potential buyers, so that it is a private and not a public offering, a significant saving in time and money can be had because registration under the Securities Act of 1933 will not be required. If a public offering is necessary, it may still be possible for the syndicate members to find buyers for the entire issue through their own sales forces. But if the issue is very large, or if it consists of common stock or medium-grade securities which must be sold widely to individuals, it will be necessary to have many firms and many salesmen participate in the sales campaign. This calls for a *selling group*—an organized group of securities firms with substantial sales forces and clientele to which the securities can be sold. The purchasing syndicate's manager usually organizes and directs the selling group. He plans the sales program, furnishes the literature and advertising, sets the date of the offering and the price, and offers the proposed members of the selling group "allotments" of securities which they may obtain at a "concession" below the public offering price. The selling group members must usually commit themselves definitely to purchase their allotments, but they may and do share their allotments and their price concession with other firms which assist them in selling the securities promptly. The retail sales effort is made simultaneously by the firms in the original purchasing syndicate and those enlisted through the selling group agreement.

On new issues offered to the public by organized selling groups, the price per share or per bond will be the same to all purchasers and no commission will be charged. However, investors who ask firms which are not members of the selling group to obtain the securities may be charged a commission, and they assuredly will be if the purchasing broker must buy the security on the secondary (resale) market instead of from the original offerors. There is usually an active secondary market in new issues during and for a few days after a new offering, approximately at the public offering price during the time the syndicate remains in operation and at a free-market price thereafter. The secondary market is commonly able to supply odd lots (less than 100 shares or less than 5 bonds), whereas the original offerors are often reluctant to accept such orders if the securities can be readily sold in larger lots.

One of the essential elements in a successful public offering is *price stabiliza-*

tion. It is therefore customary for the issuing corporation or the underwriting manager to stabilize prices by buying or selling in the open market any securities of the corporation whose prices might conceivably affect the success of the new offering. These transactions would be fraudulent if they deliberately manipulated the prices of the securities in question, but if they merely stabilize them, the process is legitimate. With respect to the new securities, the selling group manager will sustain the market price during the sales campaign by purchasing any of them which are offered on the market below the established price. The selling group members will be under obligation not to cut the price on any new securities offered by them during the selling period, which may extend for 30 to 60 days. When the selling effort is complete, both the purchasing syndicate and the selling group will be dissolved, unsold securities will be turned over according to agreement to the members of the syndicate, and all securities prices will be free to seek their own level.

Investors sometimes feel that new issues are priced high when offered by a selling group and that purchases can be made to better advantage later when "the pressure is off." There are good reasons why this might be true on occasion, for it is to be expected that corporations will try to make their new offerings when the market is high, to get the best possible prices; and everyone knows that after the original sale, many securities tend to drift about on the market until they "find homes" where they are respected and cherished. However, it is hardly to be expected that selling group members would make a consistent policy of selling overpriced securities to their regular customers, if careful analysis could discover the excessive pricing; nor is it reasonable that underwriters would hazard their capital in buying issues which they believed to be overpriced. In fact, underwriters often need to price new issues reasonably in order to obtain quick and economical sale.

Chart 6-5, in Chapter 6, indicates that from 1965 until 1971, new bond issues were consistently priced below the levels prevailing in the resale markets for older bonds, whereas, in 1962 and 1963, new bonds had been priced higher. The reason lies in the fact that institutional bond buyers, whose large unit purchases can only be supplied in the new-issue markets, had relatively more funds available (and fewer alternative outlets) in 1962–1963 than in later years of tighter money and stronger demands for long-term funds.

The gross profit margin between the price of new securities to the investor and the price received by the corporation is known as the *underwriting commission* or *spread*. The amount of this margin varies. On an issue of $100,000,000 7½ per cent bonds due 1999 marketed in 1973 by Philadelphia Electric Company, the commission was $3.84 per $1,000 bond—less than $\frac{4}{10}$ of 1 per cent. On the other hand, 20 per cent is not an unprecedented figure if the offering consists of common stock in an untried venture. Table 8-1 indicates the amount of the underwriting commissions on several important offerings in 1972. None of the items listed in Table 8-1 represents financing by a new or untried concern, but it is clear from the size of the commissions on several of the common offerings that the underwriters were concerned about the risks and sales problems involved. The size of the spread obviously will depend on the risk the underwriter takes, considering the quality of the issue; on the condition of the markets; on the extent of the selling effort which will be required; on the size of the issue; and on the intensity of the competition for business between underwriters. The first, second, and third of these factors are the most important.

Agency marketing   Instead of purchasing and reselling a new securities issue, an investment banker may merely market it as the agent of the issuing corporation. In this instance the investment banker bears no financial risk and the cor-

---

Table 8-1   *Size of underwriters' commissions on large purchase-distribution ventures in 1972*

Issue	Commission as per cent of public offering price
$350,000,000 American Telephone and Telegraph Company 7⅛% Bonds, 2003	.88
$150,000,000 American Telephone and Telegraph Company 6½% Notes, 1979	.60
$25,000,000 Ohio Power Company 7¾% Bonds, 2002	.78
$40,000,000 General Telephone Company of the Southwest 7½% Bonds, 2002	.80
$100,000,000 Province of Ontario (Canada) 7.70% Bonds, 2002	.88
$100,000,000 Caterpillar Tractor Company 6⅞% Bonds, 1992	.88
$60,000,000 J. Ray McDermott & Company, Inc., 4¼% Convertible Debentures, 1997	1.25
$10,000,000 Circle K Corporation 4½% convertible, subordinated debentures, 1997	1.50
$5,000,000 Houston Oil & Minerals Corporation 6¼% convertible, subordinated debentures, 1987	5.70
$35,000,000 Gulf State Utilities $7.56 Preferred	.64
$20,000,000 Tampa Electric Company 7.44% Preferred	1.00
$14,566,500 Iowa Electric Power & Light Company Common	3.12
$33,200,000 The Clorox Company Common	3.61
$35,100,000 Smith, Kline & French Laboratories Common	3.85
$3,375,000 Allied Telephone Company Common	4.44
$4,631,250 Dillard Department Stores, Inc. Common	5.96
$3,500,000 Benham, Blair & Affiliates	8.00

poration gets its money only if the banker succeeds in selling the securities. The commission or fee to the banker will therefore range between one-third and one-half the fee for underwriting and marketing similar securities.

Agency marketing is usually undertaken under one of three conditions. Either the corporation feels that it can safely economize on the cost of underwriting by having a banking firm make a public offering on an agency basis; or the securities are so speculative that no underwriter cares to buy them, though he will sell them for a commission; or the corporation asks the investment banker to find a few major buyers who will take the entire issue after details have been arranged by negotiation.

On small promotional ventures of every sort—brickyards, canneries, stores, small industrial plants generally—the cost of underwriting services on stocks would be prohibitive. Consequently, many such local issues are marketed by investment bankers on a sales commission ranging from 7 to 20 per cent. Such marketings are often called "best-efforts deals." Very commonly the corporations are ones in which the investment banker has a continuing interest as promoter, heavy stockholder, or holder of stock purchase options.

Investment bankers are frequently asked to find a limited group of institutional investors, usually life insurance companies, who will buy an entire issue of new bonds or stock. This is not difficult to do if the issue is of good quality, for the growth of insurance companies, trust funds, and endowments makes single investments of $1,000,000 to $50,000,000 readily salable. A small group of such investors can absorb a large issue. For example, the weekly *Investment Dealers' Digest* of December 12, 1972, announced four major private sales, including $25,000,000 of National Airlines bonds placed by Smith, Barney & Company, and $92,000,000 of Plychamp Montana Corporation bonds placed jointly by Goldman, Sachs & Company and Blyth Eastman Dillon. These and similar issues were not and will not be offered to the general public. The issuers therefore need not undertake the task of registering with the SEC, preparing a suitable prospectus, and qualifying with state blue-sky-law commissions. Other expenses incident to a sales campaign are also avoided, and the investment banker who finds the buyers and handles the negotiations bears no financial risk and need receive only about .25 per cent of the sum involved. This economical form of agency marketing is known as *private placement*. It is popular with corporations, certain securities houses, and large insurance companies and is used in marketing large numbers of bond issues, but it is regarded rather bitterly by smaller institutions and private investors, who are denied access to such issues.

COMPETITIVE BIDDING

Corporations in competitive lines of business typically decide the nature, terms, and prices of their new securities issues through a process of negotiation with their investment bankers. Many large industrial corporations maintain continuing banker-client relations with investment houses which handle all their business as a matter of course. On the other hand, the Federal Power Commission, SEC, ICC, and a number of state regulatory commissions require public service companies to sell their new securities issues to the highest bidder. This rule does not usually apply to securities sold to existing stockholders on a rights basis, nor to the underwriting of such an issue, but it normally does apply on issues sold to bankers or placed privately by them. State laws also commonly require municipalities, school districts, road districts, and other public issuers to plan bond issues having statutory features and to sell these bonds to the highest bidder.

It is still possible, through discussions undertaken while a stock or bond issue is being planned, for the investment banker who hopes to bid on a public utility or railroad issue to have some voice in the terms of the security to be offered. It is also possible for an investment banker to interest a group of insurance companies in a forthcoming utility bond offering, and by entering a bid, to obtain the entire issue for private placement with them. However, it must be conceded that competitive bidding makes private placements much more difficult and awkward.

Controversy over the merits of competitive bidding has continued ever since its widespread adoption during the 1930s. Although some evidence suggests that direct competition of this sort may be keeping underwriting margins in the utility field slightly below those obtained in the less competitive industrial field, from the investor's standpoint the difference appears to be insignificant.

REGULATION OF SECURITIES OFFERINGS

New securities offerings are regulated mainly by the states under their *blue-sky laws* and by the federal government under the Securities Act of 1933. These laws are considered more extensively in Chapter 12, but their impact on investment banking will be noted briefly here.

The state blue-sky laws are antifraud statutes in the main, designed to forbid the sale of doubtful or improperly presented securities and to exclude dishonest firms or personnel from conducting a securities business. The usual enforcement methods require (1) that the issuing corporation obtain a permit or file explanatory data before any new securities are offered for sale in the state, and (2) that each securities firm and each securities salesman obtain a license before entering the business. The commissioner in charge of enforcement is given substantial discretion in the issuance of permits and licenses.

The Federal Securities Act of 1933, sometimes called the truth-in-securities act, was designed to obtain full and complete disclosure of pertinent information about new corporate securities when they are offered publicly. Government, state, municipal, bank, railroad, and certain other securities are exempted, and relatively small issues are subjected to less-detailed procedures. The act requires *registration* of any nonexempt new issue of stock or bonds with the SEC. Registration consists of filing a large mass of data about the corporation and the proposed security and the preparation of a *prospectus* which summarizes the registration data for public use. If within 20 days (or in less time with the positive consent of the commission) the commission does not object to the registration statement or prospectus, the securities may then be offered for sale. Every investor who is offered any of the securities by the corporation, an underwriter, or any dealer must also be handed a copy of the prospectus.

During the period preceding the date when a security may legally be offered for sale, no orders may be taken for it and no promises for its delivery may be made. However, information as to the nature of the forthcoming security may be circulated, and a tentative "red-herring" prospectus may be given to investors for their consideration. It is also legitimate to record investors' "indications of interest" in the forthcoming security, to obtain an active prospect list for the actual offering.

Needless to say, corporations and underwriters are very careful about the facts and figures included in the prospectus. Very little editorial opinion and no excited praise about either company or security will be included. In fact, a prospectus comes close to being a voluminous compilation of dry facts. Nevertheless, the facts are there for one who has the diligence and the capacity to interpret them.

Neither the state blue-sky laws nor the Securities Act of 1933 can prevent an incompetent individual or a lazy one from buying hazardous securities. They are not intended to; speculative business ventures are needed and must be financed. These laws do deter fraud and misrepresentation, however, and they see that substantial information is available on the issues which are subject to their jurisdiction. Competence to judge that information and the diligence to study it are up to the individual investor.

INVESTMENT BANKERS AND THE PUBLIC

Investment banking firms are of many types, ranging from the austere big-money institutions which specialize in large-scale purchases to the small firms which function exclusively in retail distribution. The typical firm would be one which operates chiefly at retail and also does some business as broker and over-the-counter dealer.

Most firms are keenly interested in maintaining customer good-will and in building a reputation for sagacity in selecting only good issues for their representatives to sell. This does not mean that they will avoid speculative securities, but they will try to avoid unpromising ones and ones which are unsoundly priced. However, there are situations which induce well-intentioned investment bankers to suppress their doubts at times. Corporations depending upon the banker for financial assistance and advice may need funds at unpropitious times. Other investment houses with which the banker works may need his assistance in purchasing or selling groups, and he may wish to retain their goodwill. Or his own organization may be in need of a job to do. This conflict of interests is in no way unique to the business of investment banking. It is a situation which every manufacturer or retailer meets constantly and which must be resolved in accordance with the policies of the firm.

In most instances the ordinary investing public will deal with investment bankers through the banking firms' salesmen, who must be *registered representatives*. A registered representative is a salesman who has passed a proficiency test and signed a code of ethics prescribed by the National Association of Securities Dealers. The larger firms also have statisticians or technical investment advisers who are available for consultation without charge to the investor, and statistical and financial service libraries are available in all offices. The personnel in most houses are competent and sincere. They will furnish available information candidly and will add personal opinion and advice when solicited. However, investors should realize that investment house salesmen are not omniscient, nor are they professional securities analysts. They must of necessity depend on the opinions of the firm's analysts and those of the purchasing group.

Salesmen naturally have a desire to make sales, for their compensation depends upon it. Some of them may therefore urge their wares upon the prospect with greater enthusiasm and in greater suggested amounts than the situation warrants. Others are very temperate on these points. Many salesmen keep records of their clients' portfolios and suggest additions and changes needed to maintain proper balance; this is helpful to the investor if the salesman is competent. However, it is a well-known fact that a salesman may utilize his knowledge of a client's holdings to suggest shifts from present holdings into whatever the salesman is offering at the moment. The firm for which the salesman works might or might not be aware of such an abuse of trust. On such matters the investor should make his own studies and act accordingly.

The conclusion to be drawn is that in dealing with investment bankers, the investor may rely substantially on their facilities and on their advice, but the responsibility for sound decisions rests fundamentally upon himself.

MARKETING OF INVESTMENT-FUND SHARES

Investment banking of a unique type is found in the marketing of the shares of open-end *investment funds*. These funds are institutions which invest their assets in diversified lists of stocks and bonds, thus providing their own shareholders with a diversified and competently managed securities investment in a single package. Most of them continuously sell new shares and also continuously redeem existing shares in cash if any shareholder so requests. Technically, each sale of a fund's shares is a new offering of securities, and SEC rules require that fund buyers receive a prospectus describing the fund shares purchased.

Since new shares are sold continuously by the open-end funds, it would not be feasible for syndicates to buy and resell them. Instead, a single investment banking house—possibly one which does nothing else—functions as a perpetual selling wholesaler operating on an agency basis. The wholesaler will allow a "concession" from the public offering price to any other broker or dealer who may sell some of the shares. The shares are priced daily at the net asset value per share of the fund's assets, plus a fee of 4 to 9 per cent which covers selling costs. Shares are redeemed upon request at approximately net asset value, computed at the date of redemption.

SECONDARY DISTRIBUTIONS, EXCHANGE DISTRIBUTIONS, AND SPECIAL OFFERINGS

When a large block of a security already in public hands must be resold by the holder, the task is similar to that of marketing a new issue. A simple offering of the stock or bonds on the market would depress the price and defeat its purpose. The situation requires an organized sales effort which will create an additional demand and place the securities, just as a selling group would so with a new issue. Two techniques are used: (1) the secondary distribution, in which a firm or selling group follows very closely the procedure which would be used with a new issue; and (2) the exchange distribution or the special offering, in which the members of a stock exchange are invited to solicit their customers' orders in the security at a stated price, out of which the member would be paid a concession somewhat larger than the regular commission.

The stock or bonds to be placed through one of these offerings may come from a single large stockholder, an investment company, an estate, a trust, an insurance company, or a holding company. They may be purchased by the investment banker making the offering, or they may be offered on an agency basis. If the securities come from the holdings of an influential stockholder or a holding company, they may have to be registered with the SEC just as though they constituted a new issue.

If the investment bankers controlling the offering are not members of a prominent stock exchange upon which the security is listed, the secondary-distribution technique is certain to be used. A selling group will be formed if needed, a definite offering price and offering date will be set, and ethical securities houses generally will be given an opportunity to submit orders for their customers and earn a concession for themselves. Even if stock exchange firms and a listed stock are involved, a secondary distribution is likely to be made if very large amounts are to be sold.

Exchange distributions and special offerings are organized selling efforts in a listed security conducted from the stock exchange floor. Approval of the exchange must be obtained, but this will be granted if it appears that the quantity to be sold is too large to be placed by regular trading methods. An exchange distribution is a process by which a member broker may sell formally a block of listed stock to buyers solicited by himself at prevailing stock exchange prices. The special offering is an offer to sell, announced by a member of the exchange during regular trading hours, at a definite selling price, less a concession to any exchange member who produces a buying order. The stated selling price is net to the purchasing customer; the concession paid by the seller to the member firms submitting orders is their compensation.

Obviously, secondary distributions and exchange offerings would not succeed if the offering prices were any higher than the familiar everyday quotations in the security. It seems probable that most of them are made at prices fractionally lower than the regular market would have recorded on the same day if no unusual sales were in prospect. However, it must be remembered that firms planning these organized sales are permitted to stabilize the market, and they may also choose their offering dates to get the best possible prices. No one can say that in the long run an investor either gains or loses as a result of buying on these offerings instead of on the everyday markets. Probably there is not much difference despite the oft-expressed fear that facilities for block selling enable institutions and insiders to "unload" overpriced or deteriorating securities on the general public.

DEALERS AND THE UNLISTED MARKET

The unlisted or over-the-counter market is the very extensive resale market maintained by dealers who buy and sell securities as merchandise. In this market the participating firms buy stocks and bonds which are offered for sale by the general public and resell them to others who wish to buy. Any security may be bought or sold by any securities firm which cares to do so. Actually, the bulk of such business is done in securities which are not actively traded on the stock exchanges, by a relatively limited group of dealers who have elected to carry inventories and "make" both buying and selling markets in the securities in which they specialize, and by brokers who act as agents for their customers in buying from, or selling to, the dealers.

MECHANICS OF THE MARKET

The fundamental cog in the over-the-counter market is the *dealer* who elects to make a market in a given security or group of securities. The firm acting as dealer is prepared to buy for its own account at its "bid" price any reasonable quantities of the security offered to it by the public or other securities houses, and it will sell in the same manner at its "asked" price. The difference between the bid and asked prices is the firm's "spread," or gross profit margin.

In most cases the individual investor who buys over-the-counter securities does not seek out a dealer. Instead, he relies on his regular stockbroker to find a suitable dealer and arrange the transaction. When a broker buys unlisted securities for a customer, he usually buys from the dealer, acting as the customer's agent; he charges the customer the dealer's asked price plus a commission, increasingly the standard New York Stock Exchange commission for the size of order in question. Less frequently, he will buy from the dealer and resell to his customer at a "net" price which will include a small profit to himself. If the customer is selling, he may receive the dealer's bid price minus a brokerage commission to his own broker, or his broker may buy from him at less than the dealer's bid price and then immediately resell to the dealer. Where the broker buys or sells the security for his own account, he is bound to disclose this fact to his customer, either orally in negotiating the order or in writing on the customer's bill for the transaction.

Brokerage commissions on over-the-counter stocks typically range from around ¾ of 1 per cent on orders amounting to $5,000 to about 3½ per cent on orders for $500 worth of stock. Markups average about 1½ per cent and are proportionately larger on low-price stocks than on more expensive ones. The rules of the National Association of Securities Dealers prohibit markups in excess of 5 per cent except where they are necessary to compensate the broker for unusual expense or effort in completing the transaction. Markdowns on purchases by brokers from customers are typically smaller percentages than the markups charged on sales by brokers to customers.

Besides paying a commission or markup, the over-the-counter investor also must bear the cost of the spread between the bid and asked prices of the stock he buys. Spreads will be discussed in detail a few paragraphs further on, but it may be observed here that the asked price which a buying customer is charged typically runs from ½ of 1 per cent up to 5 per cent more than the bid price which he would receive by selling the same stock to the dealer. It should be clear, therefore, that if the customer pays a 1 per cent commission and the spread amounts to 2 per cent, his stock must then rise approximately 3 per cent to cover his purchase cost. A further rise of 1 per cent would also be needed to meet the cost of the selling commission.

It is obvious that no dealer could make a market or even trade in all the thousands of unlisted securities which the market handles. Dealers therefore specialize either by type of security, such as municipal bonds, bank stocks, or utility preferreds, or in the local securities of a particular community, or in a given list of securities. Their advertisements and quotations quickly familiarize other dealers and brokers with their intentions and attract business in their chosen specialties. Such dealers may from time to time also trade in securities other than their specialties, and investment bankers and brokers who ordinarily do not function as dealers at all may buy and sell as opportunity offers.

In addition to at least 4,000 more important issues on which dealers' markets are continuously available, the over-the-counter market handles numerous transactions in more than 8,000 smaller issues. In many instances, dealers familiar with the concern or with the industry will buy lesser-known securities at a negotiated price and then list their holdings for resale on quotation sheets which are widely circulated among dealers and brokers. In other instances, dealers will decline to commit their funds to slow-moving securities but will take options on them or act as agents in an attempt to market them. Brokers or dealers interested in obtaining lesser-known securities often find them by telephoning other dealers or by publishing offers in the quotation sheets.

The over-the-counter market is well equipped mechanically to do its job. The larger dealers maintain trading rooms in which their traders are connected by private telephone lines with other dealers and brokers in the same city. Teletype facilities on which bids or offers can be dispatched to a number of dealers simultaneously, either locally or on an inter-city hookup, are widely used. A nationwide, computer-based automatic quotation service provides up-to-the-second bid and asked prices throughout the trading day on about 3,500 major stocks. Leading dealers also circulate daily or weekly "want-and-offer" sheets detailing their active bids and asks. One nationwide reporting service, the National Quotation Bureau, makes a business of collecting dealers' bids and offers on a nationwide basis and reporting them, along with the dealer's names, on properly classified daily and weekly quotation sheets. Similar local quotation services operate in the principal cities. Newspapers and magazines carry quotations on the more active over-the-counter securities.

The heart of the over-the-counter trading process is the National Association of Securities Dealers Automated Quotation system (known as NASDAQ). This centralized, instant-quotation arrangement unites the entire unlisted market in a single, computer-based trading network. The dealers in each regularly quoted stock key-punch their changing quotations into a central computer memory. When a dealer wishes to know the "market" on a given stock, he presses a few buttons and all bids and offers in that stock are flashed simultaneously on an electronic screen, together with the identities of the dealers making them. The inquiring dealer, if he wishes, may punch another code and have either bids or offers arrayed in order of price. The NASDAQ system thus induces keener competition among dealers and operates to reduce both spreads and interdealer differences in the over-the-counter market.

SECURITIES TRADED

The over-the counter market operates chiefly in government bonds, state and municipal bonds, corporation bonds, bank stocks, insurance company stocks, and issues too small, too local, too inactive, or too closely held to have successful stock exchange markets. These latter include serial bonds, building corporation bonds, utility preferred stocks, and issues of small corporations generally. There is also an active over-the-counter market in many bond and preferred stock issues which are listed on the stock exchanges. Large blocks of corporate bonds or preferreds which could hardly be sold on the listed markets without breaking the price are often sold on the over-the-counter market.

The bonds of the United States government are listed on the New York Stock Exchange, but the bulk of the business in them is done over the counter. This is probably because the commercial banks of the country and a few other large dealers make very good markets in federal bonds, and their huge inventories plus their close contact with Federal Reserve policy enable them to dominate the market. Other dealers in governments perforce deal with and follow these leaders. State and municipal bonds are seldom listed on the stock exchanges because (1) many of them are serial, and in serial issues there are usually not enough identical bonds to make a satisfactory listed market; (2) such bonds do not change hands often, so a listed market would be too dull to be efficient; and (3) commercial banks trade in this market also. Dealers and banks together can make an excellent market in these bonds, providing bids and offers when asked on almost any bond of satisfactory quality.

PRICE BEHAVIOR ON THE UNLISTED MARKET

Experience shows that prices on active over-the-counter securities do not fluctuate much from hour to hour, since dealers absorb irregularities in the timing of public orders by adding to or reducing inventories. However, any substantial day-to-day or week-to-week fluctuations in the listed stock market have their repercussions in public bids and offers in the unlisted market and thus compel dealers to adjust their prices. From an inspection of long-term price ranges recorded by listed and unlisted securities, it would appear that actively traded securities of comparable qualities fluctuate about as much in one market as they would in another. Table 8-2 shows recent price ranges of four groups of widely traded stocks, two on listed and two on unlisted markets.

It would be impossible to prove or disprove the oft-repeated statement that prices on the unlisted market average a little lower than those on the listed market. When securities are traded in both markets, arbitrage transactions naturally keep the prices at the same level. On actively traded securities of similar type and quality, little difference is apparent, though listed securities usually have somewhat greater collateral value. On inactive securities, no sure generalization is possible, for on either listed or unlisted markets a determined effort to buy or sell in large quantities may distort prices considerably. However, because of the existence of many very inactive securities in the unlisted market, because these securities are little known and therefore not regularly sought by buyers, and be-

Table 8-2 *Comparison of price fluctuation of listed and unlisted stocks*

Stock	*Market*	*Price range* 1971	1972
Investment type:			
General Electric	NYSE	66½–46½	73–58¼
Texaco	NYSE	39⅝–29⅝	39⅛–29½
Eastman Kodak	NYSE	100–72	149¾–93¼
International Business Machines	NYSE	365¾–283¼	426¾–331¾
Chase Manhattan	NYSE	61¾–47⅞	66¾–52
INA Corporation	NYSE	57½–34⅞	54⅞–38⅝
BankAmerica	Unlisted	35⅜–30⅛	50¾–34⅜
Southwestern Life	Unlisted	37⅜–27½	47–30½
Republic National Bank, Dallas	Unlisted	33½–22⅛	40–26¼
St. Paul Companies	Unlisted	74¾–52¾	109½–61¾
Wider price movement:			
American Airlines	NYSE	43⅞–21⅞	49⅞–22½
McDonald's Corp.	NYSE	39–14¾	77⅜–37⅛
Texas Instruments	NYSE	129–79½	190–117¼
Yellow Freight System	Unlisted	35⅞–15⅝	47–26½
Snap-On Tools	Unlisted	29⅜–14¾	56¼–28½
Russell Stover Candies	Unlisted	22¼–14⅝	30½–21⅝

cause such securities lack marketability and collateral value, it is a fair guess that in these categories the unlisted market may at times offer better-quality securities for less money than can be had on the listed markets.

PRICE MAKING IN THE UNLISTED MARKET

The bid and asked prices in the unlisted market are established from moment to moment by the dealers who make the market. However, these prices must be set at levels which will result in the dealers' purchases roughly equaling their sales, unless the dealers wish to increase or decrease their inventories for speculative reasons. Usually dealers do not change their inventories much for speculative reasons; so it can be said that their prices are set approximately at levels where public demand equals public offering. If a dealer's inventory rises or falls by reasonable amounts from hour to hour but balances out over a few hours' time, he will regard his price as being right; and even if he has an excess of sales over purchases or vice versa, he will consider his prices right if other dealers have contra balances and will buy or sell with him. However, if dealers generally find that they are buying more than they are selling of a particular security, they will reduce both their bid and asked prices; and if they are selling more than they are buying, both figures will be raised.

Dealers in the unlisted market must not only establish the level of prices in each issue traded, they must also determine the spread between the bid and asked price. To the dealer, the spread represents the gross profit margin out of which he must pay his expenses and earn his living. To the customer, it is a differential which makes his probable selling price somewhat lower than the best available buying price. In general, it appears that four factors govern the size of the spread a dealer establishes.

1 *Activity of the security.* If the dealer's inventory can be turned over rapidly, thus earning the regular gross profit at frequent intervals, the profit on each transaction can be low.

2 *Quality of the security.* If the security is of high quality, or if for any other reason a decline in its value is improbable, a dealer can afford to handle it at a low gross profit, for he is not likely to sustain a severe inventory loss.

3 *Dividend or interest payments.* If the security pays dividends or interest regularly, its inclusion in inventory does not hold the dealer's capital idle and he can afford a lower margin than otherwise.

4 *Competition.* The over-the-counter market is sharply competitive, and a dealer's expenses consist largely of overhead costs. He cannot afford to let other dealers take his business by making closer markets—that is, by paying slightly more and asking slightly less—and he will establish his spreads accordingly.

It is customary, when a dealer is asked for a market price on a security, for him to quote his bid and asked prices and indicate the quantities he will trade without knowing whether the inquiring broker wishes to buy or sell. The "market" quoted by the dealer then becomes the basis for negotiations. It is usually the dealer's final price on transactions ranging between a few hundred and a few thousand dollars; no better or worse prices are made on large or small transactions unless the amounts involved are extreme. However, a dealer is a principal, and if he can be persuaded to pay a little more or sell for a little less in a given instance, that is his privilege. He does not have to treat everyone alike.

On securities in which the dealer does not maintain a regular market, or in which a good market does not exist, any dealer or broker may offer to buy from or sell to a customer at a price satisfactory to himself. If the broker or dealer knows that his asking price is higher or his bid price is lower than a fair competitive price, he is duty-bound to say so to a nonprofessional customer; he is in a position of trust in such a case. However, a great many over-the-counter securities do not have steady and close markets; this forces both dealer and investor to negotiate as best they can.

Investors obtain price quotations on unlisted securities from their newspapers;

from dealers' printed or mimeographed circulars, from the daily reports of the quotation services, and from their brokers. Such quotations are always in "bid and ask" form. Quotations appearing in published lists are regarded as approximate or *nominal*; they are not binding offers to buy or sell. To get a *firm* quotation which is legally binding on a dealer, it is necessary to ask him personally for a quotation. All firm quotations by dealers are understood to hold good for the sale or purchase of at least 100 shares of stock or 5 bonds. The only exception occurs where the dealer attaches some qualifying word, such as "subject," "work-out," or "small," to his price quotation.

Newspaper quotations on over-the-counter securities generally include only issues in which there is an active local interest. In most cases the price figures are current bids and offers by local dealers. Table 8-3 shows a sample of over-the-counter quotations on a variety of securities. Note that the dealers' spreads range from less than ½ of 1 per cent on active bonds and common stocks to more than 10 per cent on one inactive preferred stock.

INVESTING IN UNLISTED SECURITIES

For the investor who buys securities for income or long-term gain, the facilities of the unlisted market are as satisfactory as those of the listed market, if he finds securities appropriate to his needs. The dealer's spread on the inside market is

Table 8-3   *Over-the-counter quotations, March 2, 1973*

Issue	Bid	Ask
American Telephone 2⅝s, 1986	61½	61¾
Duke Power 4⅞s, 1982	81	82½
Standard Oil of California 7s, 1996	98⅜	98¾
Arden Mayfair $3 Pfd.	25	28
Shoprite Foods $2.04 Conv. Pfd.	24¾	25¾
Tucson Gas & Electric $8.25 Pfd.	106⅝	107
American Reinsurance	42⅝	43⅛
Franklin Life	26¾	27⅛
Southwestern Life	40¾	41¼
BankAmerica	43⅞	44¼
Cleveland Trust Company	85¾	86½
Republic National Bank, Dallas	39¾	40¼
American Express	59¾	60¼
American Greeting Card	47	47¾
Harper & Row	8	8½
Pabst Brewing	67	67½
El Paso Electric	14⅛	14½
Indianapolis Water	19¾	20¼

not usually great enough to do any harm, brokerage commissions are about the same as on the listed markets, price ranges are about the same, and values appear to be established at about the same level. Purchases and sales are made on a dealers' stabilized market and can be negotiated to a definite figure, and there are no odd-lot differentials for small investors to pay. For short-term traders, the unlisted market is slightly less advantageous; the steadier hour-to-hour prices limit the chances for adventitious bargains, and the dealer's spread cuts down the chances for quick profits from small changes in the market.

Investors buying or selling anything other than the most active over-the-counter securities can often save a little money when dealing through a broker by asking that broker to "shop around" among competing unlisted dealers. The dealers are often a fraction of a point apart in their bid or asked prices, and the broker who is willing to make the effort can find the best price.

Investors' transactions in unlisted corporation securities are mostly handled by firms which are members of the National Association of Securities Dealers. In these firms, customers' orders must be handled by registered representatives operating under NASD rules, just as in the special cases of new issue and secondary offerings. In firms which also belong to stock exchanges, the same sales personnel will be required to pass another test and accept a code of ethics prescribed by the exchange, thus becoming registered representatives under exchange rules also. Although the interests of the firms and the preferences of the individual representatives often lead these salesmen to specialize in one form of sales effort, most registered representatives can serve the whole breadth of the average investor's need, in new issues, in existing unlisted issues, and in securities listed on the exchanges, with reasonable proficiency and under standard procedural and ethical rules.

QUESTIONS AND PROBLEMS

1   Do you think that retail broker-dealer firms—that is, firms which have individual investors as customers—should be forbidden by law to sell to their customers securities which they own as dealers or underwriters? In other words, would it be feasible or advantageous to require that all retail-customer transactions be on a brokerage basis?

2   Under what conditions do you believe a rights offering should be underwritten? When is this not necessary?

3   Would a selling group be formed to distribute 500,000 shares of new common stock which an underwriting group was purchasing from a public utility holding company? Why?

4   Do you think price stablization should be forbidden by law? Why, or why not?

5   Would it be desirable or feasible to forbid private placement by law?

6   How much would the Commonwealth Edison Company of Chicago have to allow as commissions if it sold a $100,000,000 bond issue to underwriters? What would the cost be on a preferred stock issue? What determines these rates? Do these represent the entire cost of obtaining needed funds?

7 Would you be willing to invest in a new bond or stock issue just being marketed by an underwriting group? Why, or why not? Where could you get adequate information about the quality of a new issue?

8 As an investor, would you feel assured of better value in buying an issue which the underwriters had obtained by competive bidding, or would you prefer one on which the price was negotiated?

9 Do you think that the blue-sky laws and the Federal Securities Act of 1933 are properly designed to protect the investor? Should they require that every security be labeled A, B, C, etc., or in some other manner to identify its quality? Should the price of new offerings be subject to veto by a regulatory authority?

10 Would you trust a securities salesman who recommended sale of a stock which you held and purchase of another now being offered by his firm? Would a good salesman ever make such a proposal?

11 What action would a dealer probably take if, in a stock he was trading, he was buying two shares for every one he sold? Would it be likely that a dealer might deliberately buy two shares for every one sold over several days' time? Why? Could the opposite happen?

12 Does the dealer's "spread" constitute a significant price disadvantage to the investor who considers unlisted stocks? Why?

13 How does a broker who wishes to sell a bank stock for a client find a buyer?

14 Why can the over-the-counter market absorb an offer to sell 100 Union Pacific bonds when there might be danger that such an offering would depress the stock exchange price?

15 If you were a stockholder in CNA Financial Corporation, would you want the company to withdraw its stock from the New York Stock Exchange and depend upon the unlisted market exclusively?

16 Is it likely that the actively traded insurance stocks (see Table 8-2 and 8-3) would sell any higher, on the average, if they were listed on the stock exchanges? Would the less actively traded ones have as good markets as they now have?

17 Why is the spread on Harper & Row so much larger proportionately than on Republic National Bank (see Table 8-3)?

18 Why do underwriting commissions on the two preferred stock issues shown in Table 8-1 average far less than commissions on common stock issues and approximate the commission charges on high-grade bond offerings?

REFERENCES

Bellemore, Douglas H., and John C. Ritchie, Jr.: *Investments*, 3d ed., South-Western Publishing Company, Incorporated, Cincinnati, 1969, Chap. 2.

Cooke, Gilbert W.: *The Stock Markets*, rev. ed., Schenkman Publishing Co., Inc., Cambridge, Mass., 1969, Chaps. 2, 3, 4, 6, and Part 4.

Dougall, Herbert E.: *Investments*, 8th ed., Prentice-Hall, Inc., Englewood Cliffs, N.J., 1968, Chaps. 15, 16.

Eiteman, Wilford J., Charles A. Dice, and David K. Eiteman: *The Stock Market*, 4th ed., McGraw-Hill Book Company, New York, 1966.

Financial Handbook, rev. ed., The Ronald Press Company, New York, 1968, Secs. 9, 10.

Friend, Irwin, and others: *The Over-the-counter Securities Markets*, McGraw-Hill Book Company, New York, 1958.

Investment Bankers Association of America: *Fundamentals of Investment Banking*, Prentice-Hall, Inc., Englewood Cliffs, N.J., 1949, Chaps. 16–18, 20.

Leffler, George L., and Loring C. Farwell: *The Stock Market*, 3d ed., The Ronald Press Company, New York, 1963, Chaps. 24, 25.

Loll, Leo M., and Julian G. Buckley: *The Over-the-Counter Securities Market*, Prentice-Hall, Inc., Englewood Cliffs, N.J., 1973.

Sears, Marian V., and Irving Katz: *Investment Banking in America*, Harvard University Press, Cambridge, Mass., 1970.

Securities and Exchange Commission: *Special Study of Securities Markets*, Washington, 1963, Parts 1 and 5.

Waterman, Merwin H.: *Investment Banking Functions*, University of Michigan, Bureau of Business Research, Ann Arbor, 1958.

Widicus, Wilbur W., and Thomas E. Stitzel: *Personal Investing*, Richard D. Irwin, Inc., Homewood, Ill., 1971, Chap. 3.

BROKERAGE AND
THE STOCK EXCHANGES

Practically every firm engaged in the securities business does some brokerage. Some firms do little else. A broker's business consists of searching out buyers when his customer wishes to sell and sellers when his customer wishes to buy and arranging transactions in accordance with his customer's instructions. Usually those transactions are arranged with other brokers representing their customers. The brokers do not function as principals in these transactions; they are agents only. A broker charges a commission on each purchase and each sale which he executes, but he ordinarily gets nothing unless he can complete a transaction.

In order to fulfill his function and earn commissions, a broker must develop his business along three lines: First, he must provide an office with adequate financial information sources, current quotation facilities, and salesmen-advisers' to enable investors to make the decisions upon which they act. Second, he must know where to find the best unlisted markets for his customers and how to obtain new securities currently being offered by underwriters and distributors. Third, he must arrange memberships in or contacts with the principal stock exchanges of the country, for a very large percentage of all securities buying and selling is done on the stock exchanges. He must also offer his customers incidental services in the financing of their transactions and in the storage of their securities. Brokers need not be investment bankers, over-the-counter dealers, or even stock exchange members, but they find great advantage in being stock exchange members, and their close contact with investment bankers and dealers encourages them to participate in these functions also.

NATURE OF A STOCK EXCHANGE

A stock exchange is an association of brokers formed to provide improved facilities for the execution of customers' orders. The main function of an exchange is to operate a trading room to which all the brokers may bring their orders in a given list of securities. With a large number of customers' buying and selling orders thus brought together, it is expected that many transactions can be completed. Selling and buying orders can usually be matched without the intervention of a middleman, the customers will get good service, and the brokers will earn commissions.

Stock exchanges conduct trading in both bonds and stocks. However, only the New York Stock Exchange and the American Stock Exchange have any significant amount of business in bonds, and all exchanges do most of their business in stocks. To avoid cluttering their facilities with futile attempts to do business in inactive stocks, the exchanges limit their operations to a stated list of securities in which their members hope to have a reasonable number of orders.

Each brokerage house which belongs to an exchange has the privilege of placing a trader and assisting clerks on the trading floor and operating a private telephone line from the floor to the brokerage office. A brokerage firm handling a very large business may hold several memberships or "seats" on the same exchange, which permit a corresponding number of the firm's officers or partners to execute orders on the exchange floor. All the business on the trading floor is done by the brokers, as the exchange is a facilitating agency only. The expenses of the exchange are defrayed by monthly dues paid by the member brokers, plus sums collected as fees for services done for the brokers and the corporations whose stocks are listed on the exchange.

Although closely regulated by various government agencies, a stock exchange is a private association with a closed membership. In order to obtain a membership a brokerage firm usually must buy one from a member who is willing to sell. A membership on a successful stock exchange is an expensive asset. In 1972 a New York Stock Exchange membership cost about $200,000, an American Stock Exchange membership about $120,000, and the regional exchange memberships varying but generally lesser amounts. When a membership has been arranged for, the prospective member must next apply for admission. If the governing board of the exchange finds the applicant's financial stability and business reputation acceptable, he will be admitted to full privileges. Successful brokers often have memberships on many stock exchanges and branch offices scattered throughout the country.

Stock exchanges generally have visitors' galleries from which visitors are permitted to watch activities on the trading floor. However, no business may be transacted from such galleries, nor does any exchange accept trading orders from any visitor. Orders must be placed with brokers at their brokerage offices for transmission to the exchange floor.

Every stock exchange has extensive rules governing the business practices of its members and the methods of trading on its floor. Many of these rules are intended for the protection of the public, whereas others are chiefly valuable to protect and develop the exchange and its members. The floor trading rules are highly technical, but in general they provide for a well-organized routine in which all orders are handled equitably. Exchange members are permitted to trade on the floor for their own accounts as well for customers, but their "professional" trading is limited to keep it from dominating the market or taking unfair advantage over customers' orders. Brokerage practices and stock exchange operations are subject to the supervision of the Federal Securities and Exchange Commission, under the terms of the Securities Exchange Act of 1934.

THE STOCK EXCHANGES

The New York Stock Exchange and the American Stock Exchange are national in their scope. They conduct trading in securities which are nationwide in ownership, their broker members have offices from coast to coast, and their members also execute orders forwarded to them by banks and nonmember brokers everywhere. Most of the New York Stock Exchange members are also members or associate members of the American Stock Exchange. The securities traded on these two exchanges are all different; no stock or bond is traded on both. The New York Stock Exchange usually has the securities of the larger, older, and stronger corporations, and the American has the others. However, there are conspicuous exceptions; the big board (New York Stock Exchange) has some very poor issues while the American has such solid successes as Carnation Company and George A. Hormel, Inc., to name but two, as well as some distinguished Canadian stocks.

The other stock exchanges are properly called *regional* exchanges, for their principal service is to provide trading markets for local brokers and investors. The most important of these exchanges are located in Boston, Chicago, Los Angeles–San Francisco, and Philadelphia–Baltimore–Washington. The regional stock exchanges not only provide markets for local stocks but also trade in the stocks of nationally owned corporations which originated in their regions or are closely affiliated with them, even when such stocks are traded in New York. In addition, they often trade in the stocks of national corporations which have enough local stockholders to enable the local exchange to maintain a market. The members of the regional exchanges are mostly local brokers with local offices and customers, but every regional exchange has members who also hold memberships in the New York and other exchanges. The country's leading stock exchanges, with value and number of securities traded, are listed in Table 9-1.

The rapid growth of the Canadian economy since 1945 has attracted the interest of investors in the United States as well as Canada. This growth has induced important outlays in Canadian branches by corporations originating in the United States, but it has also brought about extensive purchases of Canadian securities both by Canadians and by citizens residing south of the border. With the growth of Canadian securities has come a corresponding growth in Canadian over-the-counter and stock exchange markets. The Toronto Stock Exchange, the Montreal Stock Exchange, and the Canadian Stock Exchange (also in Montreal) are now important stock exchanges.

Table 9-1 *Value and number of securities traded, leading United States stock exchanges*

Exchange	Value of securities transactions, year ended 12/31/70, millions of dollars		Number of issues traded, 6/30/71	
	Stocks	*Bonds*	*Stocks*	*Bonds*
American	14,366	394	1,292	184
Boston	892	*	653	13
Midwest	4,943	1	658	16
New York	103,063	4,328	1,925	1,831
Pacific Coast	4,986	36	924	47
Philadelphia– Baltimore– Washington	2,629	3	982	57
All registered exchanges	131,126	4,763	3,691	2,036
All other exchanges	8	*	49	5

*Less than $500,000.
Source: Data from the 1971 *Annual Report* of the Securities and Exchange Commission.

LISTED STOCKS AND BONDS

A stock exchange must have an understanding with the corporate issuer of each stock or bond in which it trades, regarding such matters as the transfer of securities, the timely announcing of dividends and rights, and the publication of data about the corporation's affairs. These and other matters are often covered in a *listing* contract between the corporation and the exchange. The leading exchanges try to impose good corporate practices—for example, the use of registrars for stock certificates and the publication of audited financial statements—as conditions precedent to listing. The New York Stock Exchange, as a gesture of disapproval, even goes so far as to refuse to list nonvoting common stocks and preferred stocks without adequate contingent voting power.

The American Stock Exchange and the regional stock exchanges have formal listing contracts with many corporations, but a considerable number of their "listings" are traded without benefit of a contract. In these instances the corporation usually consents to the trading procedure and cooperates in furnishing information and handling transfers, but does not sign any formal agreement. The securities traded without listing contracts are said to be "traded unlisted," but the trading is handled in exactly the usual manner, and most people do not know or need to know the difference.

Stock exchange trading methods are not usually satisfactory even on a regional market in issues having less than 300 to 500 stockholders, for a good listed market requires enough interested people to maintain a constant flow of bids and offers to the trading floor. If there are enough holders, however, the stock exchange market is usually preferred by both investors and corporations. The publicity given to stock exchange markets widens interest in the stock, the prestige of the market enhances its collateral value, and the supervision of exchanges and regulatory agencies usually brings good corporate and trading practices.

The Securities Exchange Act of 1934 undertakes to enforce sound conditions relating to annual audits, publication of financial reports and other data, proxy systems, "insider" trading in securities, and similar topics as conditions precedent to listing or trading on the exchanges.[1] The SEC makes rules to implement the statute and must approve the addition or dropping of any security by any of the exchanges. Though there have been conflicts, the exchanges have generally welcomed government enforcement of sound corporate practices. The smaller exchanges had been unable to compel corporations to adhere uniformly to good rules prior to passage of the act, for the only sanction available to an exchange was suspension of trading in the security, and this often hurt the exchange members more than it did the corporation.

Since 1929 many of the regional exchanges have at times found it difficult to obtain enough total business to maintain their facilities. Several reasons help to explain this. First, the amount of speculative trading declined for many years, and the decline was especially marked in the securities of local corporations. Second, many of the larger local corporations found that the trading boom of 1927–1929 caused their stocks to scatter widely over the country. They therefore obtained listed or unlisted trading markets in New York, and local trading in their stocks diminished. Third, the over-the-counter markets have been greatly improved, so that they now offer many moderate-sized issues closer and steadier markets than the exchanges can provide.

The SEC wishes to maintain the effectiveness of the regional exchanges and has endeavored to do so by encouraging them to expand unlisted trading in nationally owned stocks which have large numbers of stockholders in their regional areas. As a result, leading stocks are traded on many exchanges; in 1972, General Motors and RCA were each listed on eight exchanges in the United States, American Telephone was listed on seven, and General Electric and International Business Machines on five each. The purpose of sustaining the regional exchanges as useful local markets is a sound one, for their services are needed to widen public interest in the securities of growing local concerns and to develop the marketability of such concerns' stocks. The regional exchanges also serve as economical

---

[1] The Securities Exchange Act and other measures for the protection of investors are reviewed in Chap. 12.

local markets for nationally known securities, especially in small quantities (odd lots). Although it might be argued that the efficiency and stability of the market in a nationally known security would be improved by collecting all the bids and offers on it in one market place, it must be remembered that many of the bids and offers appearing on the local exchanges exist because local brokers have encouraged their customers' interest in the stocks. Local trading therefore cannot be said to consist exclusively of business diverted from a central market place. Arbitrage transactions, through which profit-seeking brokers buy on one exchange and sell on another, keep the prices on different exchange markets virtually uniform and have the effect of synthesizing the bids and offers on all markets into a single resultant price.

EXCHANGE-FLOOR TRADING

The "post trading" system now used by most stock exchanges is a continuous auction arrangement under which any security may be traded at any time while the exchange is open. Basically, the plan provides for the assignment of the securities to a number of different posts or areas on the trading floor. When any broker has an order to buy or sell a security, he goes to the assigned area, calls out his bid or offer, and hopes for an acceptance from another broker who has a corresponding order to sell or buy. When a number of brokers are interested in the same security, each will be desirous of buying at a low price or selling at a high price for his customer. Competitive raising of bids and lowering of asking prices should then produce transactions at prices representing truly free markets. All bidding, offering, and accepting is done by audible word of mouth. When a transaction is completed, the two brokers note each other's names on their "buy" and "sell" order tickets, turn these over to their clerks for bookkeeping purposes, and send reports to their offices by telephone. Meanwhile, stock exchange employees at the post report the number of shares and the price to the exchange's ticker and reporting system; so the transaction can be reported immediately in financial offices everywhere via the ticker tape and other devices.

The stock exchanges adhere to the general practice of quoting stocks in dollars and eighths per share and bonds in percentages and eighths of par value. No splitting of eighths is permissible, with two exceptions. United States government bonds are quoted in percentages and thirty-seconds, since that is the accustomed practice elsewhere, and very low-priced stocks and stock subscription rights are allowed smaller trading intervals than eighths of a dollar. The New York Stock Exchange trades rights in fractions as low as sixty-fourths; some of the regional exchanges trade low-priced stocks in dollar and cent quotations, using 5- and 1-cent intervals.

To avoid confusion in floor transactions, the exchanges require that regular trading be done only in standard quantities, termed *board lots* or *round lots*.

The round lot in stocks is usually 100 shares, though 50-share, 25-share, and 10-share round lots are established when investigation shows that those units would accommodate buyers and sellers to best advantage. The standard bond unit is one $1,000 bond. Small numbers of shares, *odd lots*, are handled by a separate process through an odd-lot dealer.

The post trading system poses two problems which require the facilitating services of a *specialist*. A specialist is a stock exchange member who stays continuously at one post and watches all trading in certain stocks. Brokers who have business to handle at other posts may hand him their orders for execution at his post, especially if the orders specify prices remote from the ruling market price and therefore cannot be filled immediately. The specialist gives priority to the highest bids and lowest selling offers, with orders at the same price ranked in sequence of arrival. The specialist usually has a considerable number of orders in his possession and is likely to figure in a large percentage of the transactions at his post. When he completes transactions for other brokers, he is paid a share of the commission. A second major function of the specialist is that of preventing "needless fluctuations" in market prices. Since customers' bids and offers arrive on the trading floor at irregular intervals, auction prices based entirely on them would doubtless fluctuate violently. The specialist is obligated by agreement with the exchange to buy or sell for his own account when necessary to prevent meaningless price irregularities. Obviously he cannot prevent major market changes or eliminate all short-term fluctuations, but he can help materially.

A specialist can often judge the strength of the market in his stock by the number of buying and selling orders accumulated in his "book." This is top-secret information. The specialist can and will disclose the highest bid and the lowest offer in his possession and may indicate the number of shares bid for or offered at those prices, but that is all he can say. Detailed rules prevent him from profiting from this inside information by trading excessively for his own account.

The specialist system is criticized at times because the specialist is often able to buy on customers' selling offers and sell to customers' bids at prices virtually set by himself, when these are market orders and no adequate bids or offers from other customers are available at the moment. The exchanges all have rules which attempt to command certain standards of specialist performance and which forbid specialists to trade at all except to help stabilize the market or to liquidate the long or short positions that accumulate as a result of stabilizing transactions. But it seems clear that some discretionary latitude must inevitably remain in the specialists' hands.[2] No alternative system comes readily to mind, if the exchanges are to continue the present continuous auction method of trading.

[2] Allegations of misconduct by specialists on the American Stock Exchange in 1961 resulted in an extensive public investigation. See *Securities and Exchange Commission: Staff Report on Organization, Management, and Regulation of Conduct of Members of American Stock Exchange*, U.S. Government Printing Office, Washington, 1962.

The larger exchanges have a limited number of members called *floor brokers* who do not maintain brokerage houses, but instead make a business of executing buy or sell orders handed to them by other members who have more business than they can handle. For this service the floor broker receives a share of the commission. On all exchanges it is permissible for a member who does not have a trader on the floor at the moment to route his orders through another member firm which will then share the commission.

Although the New York and American Stock Exchanges do a total annual sales volume of around 6 billion dollars in some 2,000 different bond issues, there is no formal specialist system at their bond posts. Incoming bids or offers which cannot be immediately filled are entered on cards which remain available for inspection by other brokers; as additional orders arrive, the highest bids and lowest offers on the cards are filled in order of receipt, if price limits permit. The unit of trading is one bond; there is no formal odd-lot system.

DELIVERY AND SETTLEMENT

Transactions in stocks and bonds require a clear understanding of the time for transfer and payment. Stock exchange rules are rather elaborate on these points, but it suffices here to say that transactions are usually made on one of three bases: (1) *cash*, requiring settlement on the day of the contract; (2) *regular way*, requiring settlement on the fifth full business day thereafter; and (3) *seller's option*, requiring settlement within 60 days but as specified in the contract. Over-the-counter transactions involve similar understandings. The primary obligations to meet delivery and payment dates rest upon the brokers or dealers involved, but their customers must of necessity fulfill their commitments on time.

The most critical problems concerned with delivery of securities involve transfers of stocks or bonds before the record dates for distribution of dividends, interest, rights, or other privileges. When it appears that delivery of a stock can be had in time for a transfer before a forthcoming dividend, the stock is said to sell *with dividend* at a price which both buyer and seller regard as inclusive of stock and dividend. On a date believed too late to permit a purchaser to get the dividend, the stock sells *ex-dividend*, usually at a lower price which reflects the fact that the dividend is not being transferred. Stock exchanges are accustomed to set the dates on which stocks will be quoted ex-dividend, ex-rights, or ex-distribution.

RIGHTS, WARRANTS, WHEN-ISSUED CONTRACTS

Both stock exchanges and over-the-counter markets have occasion to trade in these instruments. Rights, as has been noted in previous chapters, are short-term privileges for the purchase of securities. Warrants are more difficult to define, for the term is used in the securities business in two ways: in a technical sense, a warrant is a piece of paper which evidences the ownership of rights, fractional shares of stock, or some other claim or privilege which does not quite attain the stature of a security. However, the term warrant is also used to mean a long-term right, usually one whose purchase privilege is valid for several years; it is this meaning which is implied when the securities markets report transactions in Tri-Continental Corporation warrants, for example. When-issued contracts are agreements for the future delivery, at the price named in the contract, of pending rights or securities which have been authorized but are not yet issued. Securities traded on a when-issued basis include those to be issued in connection with mergers, recapitalizations, reorganizations, and liquidations, and newly marketed ones which have not been physically delivered.

Because of their short lifetime, rights are often sold or bought on a when-issued basis before the certificates (warrants) evidencing them are mailed out by the company. A seller on this basis simply contracts to deliver his expected rights when he receives them. His broker may require him to make a cash or securities "margin" deposit to guarantee that he will actually provide the rights, since the broker obligates himself to deliver them to the purchaser's broker. Similarly, the purchaser of the rights makes a margin deposit with his broker. When the rights become available, all when-issued contracts are settled by payment and delivery, and subsequent transactions in rights are made the regular way or on a cash basis.

Trading in when-issued securities is quite common on both over-the-counter and stock exchange markets. However, when-issued contracts of all types are invalidated if the right or security is not issued substantially as expected. This factor, coupled with the margins required and the uncertainty of the time element in reorganizations, frequently results in when-issued contract prices which are inconsistent with the prices of other securities. For example, at one point after the announcement of a 2-for-1 split of W. T. Grant stock in May 1966, the when-issued stock was selling at 28 and the old stock at $53\frac{1}{4}$. An arbitrager could have bought 100 shares of the old stock and sold 200 when-issued shares for a profit (before commissions) of $275.

BROKERAGE ORDERS

Brokers receive a number of different types of buying and selling orders from their customers for execution either on the exchanges or the over-the-counter market. Brokerage orders vary as to the price at which the order may be filled, the time for which the order is valid, and contingencies which affect the order. In addition, the customer may further specify how his order is to be handled—for example, he may instruct the broker to function as an agent only, not as a principal, if the transaction is over the counter; or he may designate the exchange to which the order is to be sent, if the security is traded on several. The customer's desires are followed explicitly.

Market orders are instructions to a broker to buy or sell, as the case may be, at the best reasonable price obtainable. The broker will regard a market order as evidence that the customer wishes a transaction completed within a few hours at most and is leaving the price to the broker's discretion in order to be sure that the deal can be made. The broker should not abuse his discretion by paying too much or selling for too little, if the market is obviously abnormal, but the emphasis is on completing the deal, not on bargaining for price. On stock exchange orders, where the presence of a specialist can be assumed to protect the investor against totally unreasonable prices, market orders are usually executed at once at the best price available. Market orders are commonly used by investors when trading in active stocks or when a desire to buy or sell is urgent; but they can be damaging in "thin" markets in which a temporary absence of either bids or offers could result in a market order being executed at an extreme price.

Limit orders are instructions to a broker to buy or sell at a stated price "or better." If a customer instructs his broker to buy General Motors at 80 or better, the broker will buy at a lower price if one is immediately available, but he will bid up to 80 if necessary, since the customer specifically authorized that figure. If the order is to sell Union Carbide at 53½, the broker will try for more, but if he does not get it he will offer on down to 53½ in search of a buyer. If the limit makes an immediate trade impossible (i.e., a limited bid is too low or a limited offer is too high), the broker will leave the order with the specialist (or dealer, if the market is over the counter) with instructions to execute it if the opportunity occurs. A limit order protects the customer against paying more or selling for less than he intended, but it may cause disappointment if it results in a desired purchase or sale being missed by a trifling margin.

Open or *GTC* orders are orders which are "good till canceled" by the customer. Limit orders to buy at a low price or sell at a high one may be left indefinitely on this basis; the senior author saw a specialist on the old Los Angeles Stock Exchange fill an open buy order in 1930 which had been handed to him in 1927. Most stock exchanges require that brokers send customers a monthly memorandum of outstanding open orders, and most of them automatically reduce the limit on an open bid by the amount of the dividend each time the stock sells ex-dividend. Instead of an open order, the customer may give his broker a "day" order, only valid for one day, or a "fill or kill" order which is to be tried immediately and either filled or canceled. Needless to say, these time specifications are most important when they are in conjunction with orders which are limited as to price.

Stop orders (sometimes called *stop-loss orders*) are orders which are not effective until another transaction takes place at an indicated price. The stop order then becomes a market order. For example, a stockholder who held Standard Oil of Indiana when the market price was 55 might hope to get 60 for it, but might also want to sell out quickly if the market started down. He could place a stop order to sell at 51. This would instruct his broker to sell the stock at market if ever a regular trade took place at 51 or less. If the desired sale at 60 could be made, the customer would cancel his stop order. Stop orders are also used on the buy side of the market. A customer might wish to buy Union Oil because he anticipated a major rise in its price. If the current price was 58, he might still hope to buy at 56 or 57 within a few days; but to guard against being left out on the rise, he might enter a stop order to buy at 61. If a regular transaction took place at 61 or higher, his buying stop order would become a market order and would soon be filled at the lowest price his broker could obtain.

Stop orders are useful to both speculators and investors. Stop orders to sell can be used (1) to sell out holdings automatically in case a market drop deemed large enough to indicate the beginning of a major decline takes place; (2) to sell short if the ominous market drop occurs; or (3) if placed close to the market, to assure ultimate sale of stock which is now offered on open sell order just above the market. Stop orders to buy can be used (1) to limit possible losses on a short position; (2) to buy if a market rise seems to indicate a major upswing; or (3) if placed close to the market, to assure purchase of a stock which is being sought on an open bid just below the market. It will be noted that item 3 in each case requires entering two selling orders or buying orders when only one transaction is desired. However, the chance of two executions is fairly remote, for each order can be made subject to an automatic cancellation if the other is filled.

Stop orders can sometimes be assured of execution at their effective price by a process known as "stopping stock." If, for example, a stock exchange specialist has several bids for Standard Oil of Indiana at 51 when the market is 55, he may be willing to earmark one of his bids to cover a selling stop order at 51. He can then assure the broker placing the stop order that, unless the bidders should withdraw their bids or unusual situations creating priority rights should arise, the stop sale at 51 is guaranteed as soon as the first regular sale takes place at that price. By a similar process, an above-market selling offer may be earmarked to cover a stop-buying order.

ODD LOTS

Thousands of stockholders own listed stock in quantities smaller than the standard round lots, and between 5 and 10 per cent of the buying and selling done on stock exchanges is in these so-called *odd lots*. Because the odd lots appear in definitely odd quantities—8 shares, 10 shares, or 15, 20, 28, 35, whatever the customer wants or has—it would be almost impossible to match buying and selling orders in them. Also, the confusion arising from verbal trading in odd lots would lead to errors. The problem has been solved by permitting designated members of the stock exchanges to operate as dealers in odd lots. These odd-lot dealers agree to buy odd lots which other members have for sale and to sell odd lots which other members need to buy. If the dealer buys more than he sells or sells more than he buys, he can clear his position by engaging in round-lot transactions.

Stock exchange firms who receive odd-lot orders in listed stocks send them immediately to an odd-lot dealer. Each time a round-lot transaction takes place, the odd-lot dealer in that stock is obligated to buy all odd-lot offerings in his book which are offered below the round-lot price, at a transaction price exactly one-eighth below the round-lot price. Simultaneously, he must fill all odd-lot buying orders willing to pay more than the round-lot price, at one-eighth above the round-lot price. For example, when a round lot in Columbia Gas System stock sells at 28, all customers' odd-lot bids at market or at 28⅛ or higher are filled by the dealer at 28⅛, and all customers' odd-lot offers at market or 27⅞ or lower are bought at 27⅞. The odd-lot dealer's privilege of buying below the market and selling above it affords him a margin for expenses and profit.

Investors who use limit orders in odd lots should understand that neither a buying nor a selling order at "28 or better" would be filled after a round-lot sale at 28. Since the price limit set by an odd-lot customer in his order is the price limit at which his transaction may take place, not that at which the basic round-lot transaction takes place, the odd-lot dealer can fill an odd-lot limit buying order only after a round-lot transaction below the customer's buying limit, and he can complete a customer's odd-lot limit selling order only after a round-lot transaction above the customer's limit.

The foregoing description indicates that odd-lot purchasers pay more for their shares than round-lot purchasers do and sell them for less. However, the differential is not large enough to be significant except on very cheap stocks, and few people need to resort to odd-lot transactions in them.

Another sort of odd-lot service provided for small investors is the Monthly Investment Plan (or some other such label) which is intended to permit the frequent investment of small stated sums in shares and fractions of shares of a single stock. The transactions are handled by stock exchange member brokers in the usual course of their business. The plans vary a little on the different exchanges, but typically, each monthly or quarterly investment of $40 or more is charged an 8.4 per cent or smaller brokerage commission, after which the balance is applied to buy shares and fractions of shares from the odd-lot dealer at the next odd-lot transaction price. Dividends are credited to the buyer's account, and when the arrangement is finally terminated, any existing fraction of a share is cleared by purchase or sale of a fraction, and the buyer obtains his accumulated purchases in whole shares.

Over-the-counter stocks, some of the inactive stocks on regional exchanges, and bonds are not on an odd-lot basis. Over-the-counter dealers usually trade in shares or bonds at the same price regardless of quantity taken or at an individual negotiated price in each case. Odd lots of inactive stocks on regional exchanges and the $500 and $100 bonds which appear on the New York exchanges are simply offered and bid for in the quantities which appear. Brokers who buy and sell for their own accounts frequently trade in these issues. There is no assurance that odd lots in such securities will have a market price closely related to the round-lot prices.

SHORT SALES

One who sells short sells something he does not own in the hope of buying later at a lower price and delivering the later purchase against his short sale. Obviously, it would be profitable to sell a stock short at 50 and obtain the stock to deliver to the buyer by a later purchase at 40.

The fact that securities sales customarily require delivery within a few days introduces a slight mechanical complication for one who sells short. In order to deliver on the short sale, the seller must have his broker *borrow* stock for the purpose. The broker will either provide the stock from his own or his customers' holdings or get it on loan from another broker. In either instance, the borrowing customer must (1) provide cash equal in value to the stock, to be delivered to the lender as collateral for the loan of the stock;[3] (2) make good to the lender the value of any lost dividends or rights or other disbursements; and (3) pay any daily rental or "premium" which may be agreed on if the borrowed stock is scarce. Most stocks usually loan "flat"—that is, the use of the money collateral is regarded as a fair rental for the stock—but a premium of $1 or $2 per day per 100 shares is not uncommon on some issues. On infrequent occasions when stock is plentiful but money is scarce, the lender of stock may pay a small interest rate on the money collateral in addition to lending the stock without premium.

In order to prevent undue pressure on weak markets, the SEC has issued an order forbidding short sales in round lots in listed securities except at a price at least as high as the preceding sale and higher than the last (preceding the proposed short sale) regular-way sale which brought a price different from the proposed short-sale price. Some of the exchanges also require short sales in odd lots to be based on round-lot transactions which conform to these rules. Every selling order which is sent to the floor of a stock exchange must be identified as "long" or "short," so that proper trading procedure may be followed. Subject to the rules, orders to sell short may be market orders or limit orders, open orders or time-limit orders.

Before the rule forbidding short sales on declining markets, it was conceded that speculative short selling sometimes drove securities prices down to unreasonably low levels with disastrous speed. However, it was also argued that spec-

---

[3] The cash proceeds of the short sale are used for this purpose, but the short seller must also deposit adequate margin in cash or other securities, to assure his broker against loss and to meet margin requirements.

ulative short selling in normal markets would prevent bullish enthusiasm from driving prices up too high and that in any case "short covering" (the purchase of stock by short sellers to close out their positions) would support falling prices at reasonable levels. At the moment, questions regarding the merits and demerits of unrestrained short selling would seem to be moot, but it is still significant to note that issues in which a large short interest is outstanding have potential market strength, for the short sellers must cover eventually. The total of member and customer short positions outstanding in offices of New York Stock Exchange firms is published monthly for each listed stock.

MARGIN TRADING

For many years it has been customary for brokers and dealers to handle some of their customers' securities transactions *on margin*. In a margin account the customer does not provide enough money to finance his account completely; he provides enough to absorb any probable loss, and the broker lends him the balance. For example, if a customer purchases $10,000 market value of stocks and bonds, the customer might provide 60 per cent margin, or $6,000, and the broker would lend him the remaining $4,000, holding the securities as collateral. The chief purpose of the arrangement is usually to enable the customer to speculate by holding an extra amount of securities on credit, but it also permits the customer to make bargain purchases on credit when opportunity offers or to borrow cash from the broker when he needs it, provided he has ample securities collateral in his account.

Brokers charge their customers interest on the debit balances in their accounts. The rate is usually 1 to 3 per cent above the bank loan rate which the brokers themselves pay. A customer who buys on a margin is required to authorize the use of the securities as collateral for the broker's borrowings from banks. Dividends and interest on such securities are credited to the customer's account.

It is obvious that a severe shrinkage in the value of the securities held in a margin account would compel the broker to ask his customer for more margin (which could be provided either in cash or securities), and that if the customer failed to produce the margin, some or all of the securities in the account would have to be sold. To minimize the number of forced sales during market declines, the stock exchanges usually require their member brokers to keep customers' equities (net margin) above 25 per cent of the market value of corporate securities carried, and the brokers themselves are reluctant to permit a customer's equity to decline below 35 or 40 per cent on corporate securities.

As a further restrictive measure, the Securities Exchange Act of 1934 permits securities firms to extend credit only on listed stocks and bonds, unlisted corporate securities approved by the Federal Reserve authorities,[4] federal govern-

---

[4] In 1972 about 500 unlisted stocks were eligible for margin purchase.

ment securities, and state and local securities, and directs the Board of Governors of the Federal Reserve System to make additional rules limiting the use of margin credit on corporate securities. Since 1934 the Board has specified an *initial margin percentage*—that is, a net equity percentage which should be present in a margin account after each purchase transaction—but has not required that additional margin be provided if the securities decline in value between transactions. However, withdrawals of stock or cash are *restricted* while the account equity is below the initial margin percentage. Sales from a restricted account are permitted, and also new purchases which are not in excess of simultaneous sales. Since 1934 the Board's initial margin requirement has been set, at various times, as high as 100 per cent and as low as 40 per cent. In November 1972, it was raised from 55 per cent to 65 per cent.

Margin accounts may be used to finance both round lots and odd lots in listed stocks and bonds, and short sales in listed securities. They can also be used with margins as low as 5 per cent to finance government bonds, or with margins of 15 to 25 per cent to finance municipals. Most brokers welcome substantial margin accounts trading in good-quality securities. The New York Stock Exchange requires a $2,000 minimum equity to open a margin account and a subsequent equity, or *maintenance margin*, of at least 25 per cent.

In order to prevent evasion of margin requirements through the use of bank loans, the Board of Governors limits the percentage a bank may lend on any listed or unlisted stock to (usually) the same percentage which a broker could advance on stock in a margin account, *if the purpose of the bank loan is to purchase or carry stocks.* Bond-secured bank loans (except on convertibles) are not subject to this rule. The banks are thus permitted to make loans on many unlisted corporation bonds or stocks upon which a broker can lend nothing. However, bank loans in lieu of margin accounts are not wholly convenient to many stock buyers unless the loan is to be liquidated from income or other funds. Bank loans, unlike brokers' advances, usually have definite maturity dates; sale of the securities and acquisition of others is less convenient; and banks usually demand evidence of capacity to repay by some means other than sale of the collateral.

Substantial loans on securities collateral by finance companies and other large-scale lenders remained free of regulation until early 1968. At that time a new Federal Reserve regulation under the Securities Act of 1934 brought these lenders under rules similar to those under which the banks operate.

Margin transactions were a very important part of the securities business in the robust markets of 1928–1929. They were of substantial importance also in 1935–1937. However, they have been moderate in amount since the 1930s. Institutional investors have become more important in the stock market, and most institutions do not trade on margin. Furthermore, margin requirements have usually been held at 70 per cent or higher and the leverage available on 70 per cent margin is not great enough to elicit much interest. Experience indicates that margin requirements below 60 percent generally result in a steady growth in the use of margin credit, with a bullish impact on market prices, and that requirements above 70 per cent have an opposite tendency.

COMMISSIONS

The stock exchanges customarily adopt schedules of minimum commission rates to which their members are obliged to conform on stock exchange transactions. In practice, the prescribed minimum is usually the actual amount charged. Each exchange has its own minimum commission schedule, but the variations between them are not usually great. Brokers may charge any reasonable commission rate for their services on over-the-counter transactions, but they usually follow a schedule similar to that adopted by one of the exchanges. When banks or non-member investment houses originate brokerage orders which must be executed on an exchange, they sometimes charge the customer service fees of their own, in addition to the regular commissions which are paid to the broker. However, many nonmember brokers and dealers do not do this. Instead, they send their stock exchange business through a friendly member firm which will reciprocate by extending favors in its over-the-counter and new-issue business.

In 1972 the New York and American Stock Exchange schedules of commissions were summarized as follows.

Stocks, rights, and warrants selling at $1 per share and above

A   100 share orders and odd-lot orders:

Money value	Commission
$100 to $799	2% plus $6.40
$800 to $2,499	1.3% plus $12
$2,500 and above	.9% plus $22

Odd lot—$2 less on each transaction.

B   Multiple round-lot orders: $6 per round lot for the first round lot to the tenth, $4 per round lot for the eleventh and above, *plus* in each case the following:

Money value	Additional charge
$100 to $2,499	1.3% plus $12
$2,500 to $19,999	.9% plus $22
$20,000 to $29,999	.6% plus $82
$30,000 to $300,000[5]	.4% plus $142

(The commission per round lot within a multiple round-lot order must not exceed the single round-lot commission as computed for a 100-share order.)

---

[5] The SEC in 1972 had set a tentative target of reducing this figure to $100,000 by April 1974.

C Special case: For orders involving more than $300,000,[6] the commission is to be negotiated between the exchange member and his customer without regard to the foregoing rates.

Stocks, rights, and warrants selling below $1 per share

Money value	*Commission*
Under $1,000	8.4%
$1,000 to $9,999	5% plus $34
$10,000 and above	4% plus $134

Bonds
Commission per $1,000 bond (excepting governmental, short-term, or called bonds)

Selling at less than $10 (1%)	$0.75
Selling at $10 (1%) and above but under $100 (10%)	1.25
Selling at $100 (10%) and above	2.50

OTHER COSTS

In addition to the commission charges on transaction, buyers will encounter a postage and mailing charge, ranging from 20 cents to $1 on typical transactions. Sellers will have to bear a postage and mailing charge and in many instances a transfer tax. The federal government no longer taxes security transactions, and state transfer taxes reach only transfers or sales made within the state. Only a few states have transfer taxes, but New York is among them. New York State transfer tax rates in effect for New York residents during 1972 were as follows:

$.01¼ per share selling under $5
$.02½ per share selling at $5 but under $10
$.03¾ per share selling at $10 but under $20
$.05 per share selling at $20 and over

Stock sales by nonresidents were to be taxed at 65 per cent of these rates through mid-1973 and at 50 per cent of these rates thereafter.

A federal "registration fee" of 1 cent per $500 of transaction value is also levied on sellers using the facilities of a national securities exchange.

These commission and tax rates are modest costs to an investor who operates a stable investment program. However, they are large enough to burden one who trades excessively, unless he has more than average skill in obtaining market profits. It will be noted that commission costs are a larger percentage of the sums involved in stock trading than in bond trading and are higher on low-priced, as compared with high-priced, stocks.

[6] This figure also is scheduled by the SEC for reduction to $100,000 by April 1974.

BROKERAGE FACILITIES

Brokers and dealers offer the public many services, which may be grouped conveniently as information and advice, trading facilities, and general service.

Investors in securities have need for much information about corporations and their capital structures, earnings, dividend policies, and prospects. They need to know about economic events and what they portend, and they often need information and advice about taxes, portfolio planning, and investment management. Brokers and dealers can provide a good deal of help on these matters. In the first place, they equip their offices with expensive financial services, financial periodicals, and files of prospectuses and annual reports. Second, they prepare advisory literature and analyses which are often valuable. Third, they have registered representatives who are competent to assist customers with most of their problems.[7] Fourth, they have analysts and investment experts to whom difficult problems can be taken. Fifth, some of them operate investment advisory departments where detailed investment supervision can be had for a fee. Except for the most detailed and continuing type of personal service, all these information and advisory services are provided without charge.

Trading facilities offered to customers vary considerably. Brokers who cater to stock exchange traders always provide a "board room" where customers may sit and watch reports of current transactions from the exchange floor. These are transmitted by a stock ticker which flashes ticker symbols (abbreviations of company names), quantities, and prices for a few seconds in a moving stream across an electronic quotation board. (An example is shown in Chart 9-1.) A well-equipped board room will have electronic stock tickers to report New York and American Stock Exchange transactions, plus older types of devices to report transactions from the local stock exchange and the several commodity exchanges; typically, these will consist of telegraph tickers that print out transactions on cellophane or paper tapes, and electrically operated quotation boards that automatically post the latest prices. A Dow-Jones newsticker, which teleprints a laconic version of the day's corporate and financial news as it happens, is standard equipment. Needless to say, the registered representatives will be on hand, ready to take orders or discuss the market with those present or with anyone who telephones in. They can obtain the quotation and last price of any New York or American Stock Exchange stock (and of many over-the-counter issues) simply by punching out a code on a set of push buttons. Other quotations, plus statistical information and opinions from the firm's research department, will be speedily available by telephone or teleprinter request. The board room also will have reasonably direct telephone or teleprinter connections with the exchanges it

---

[7] The stock exchanges for some years have required all new sales personnel in member firms to take training courses, pass proficiency examinations, and accept a code of ethics before doing any selling. Acceptable candidates are then "registered" by the exchange.

Chart 9-1 *Specimen quotations from the New York Stock Exchange electronic ticker. These sales took place March 7, 1973. All sales are in 100-share round lots unless otherwise noted. The upper row reports a sale in Eastman Kodak at 144¾, five lots of Texas Gulf Inc. at 23⅝, 100 shares of Abbott Laboratories at 75⅝ and 500 more at 75½, 10 lots of Caterpillar Tractor sold at one time at 64½ (a single transaction or a group of related transactions totaling 1,000 shares or more is printed in full on the tape), and a 25,000-share block of Texaco traded at 36½. The lower row reports 100 shares of International Minerals and Chemical traded ex-dividend at 29⅛, 100 shares of Atlantic Richfield $2.80 convertible preferreds (a company's different issues of preferred stock are designated A, B, C, etc., on the ticker), 20 shares of Pennsylvania Power & Light 4.40% preferred (two 10-share round lots), 500 American Telephone warrants at 6⅜, and 1,000 Pacific Gas and Electric rights traded on a "when-issued" basis at ⁵⁄₆₄. Odd-lot transactions do not appear on the ticker screen.*

$$\text{EK}_{144\frac{3}{4}} \quad \text{TG}_{5s23\frac{5}{8}} \quad \text{ABT}_{75\frac{3}{8}.\,5s\frac{1}{2}} \quad \text{CAT}_{1000s64\frac{1}{2}} \quad \text{TX}_{25.000s36\frac{1}{2}}$$

$$\text{IGL. XD}_{29\frac{1}{8}} \mid \text{ARC Pr C}_{52} \mid \text{PPL PrA}_{20\,\substack{S\\s}\,59\frac{1}{2}} \quad \text{T.WS}_{5s6\frac{3}{8}} \quad \text{PCG}\,\substack{R\ W\\I\ I}\,{}_{1000s5.64}$$

serves, so that an obliging representative can speedily obtain the specialist's report on the number of orders on hand at the prevailing bid and ask quotations or the specialist's reaction to a request to "stop stock." A market order in a reasonably active stock can be originated in Los Angeles, forwarded to New York, executed on the stock exchange, and reported back to the Los Angeles board room in less than 5 minutes.

Brokers and dealers who serve an investment-minded clientele frequently do not have board rooms. A market ticker and a news ticker may be in evidence, but possibly not. Quotations may be obtained by telephone. The financial services and periodicals will be on hand. Customers meet the salesmen in the calm and privacy of an office or by appointment in their own homes or offices. This type of organization is likely to stress new issues or over-the-counter securities, rather than listed ones.

A broker or dealer is often willing to provide free storage for a customer's securities if the customer trades often enough to give the firm some revenue from the account. The securities can be kept in the broker's name, with interest and dividends being credited to the account or remitted to the customer as received;[8] the broker can then execute telephoned orders without the customer's signature.

---

[8] Customer cash and securities deposited with a broker or dealer are now insured up to a maximum of $50,000 (provided the cash does not exceed $20,000) by the government-backed Securities Investor Protection Corporation. For further information on the SIPC, see Chap. 12.

Brokers can also lend money to customers on their securities collateral, either
for securities trading or general business purposes, at low rates and without
maturity date, subject to the federal margin regulations only if the loan is for
the purpose of buying or carrying securities. This service is sometimes a highly
convenient one, especially if the broker's own loan practices are generous.

In choosing a brokerage connection, each individual should seek out the type
of establishment which best serves his need. One who makes little use of analytical publications need not search for the firm with the best library. An investment-
minded individual who is not technically skilled himself might do well to find
a house with a capable and accommodating analyst. In any event, it will be wise
to find a congenial and diligent salesman; a friend who will trouble to obtain
quotations before entering orders, who will shop around for the best market
over the counter, or who will telephone his customer when interesting news
appears, is worth having. Other bases for discriminating choice, including reputation for fairness, financial strength, accurate bookkeeping, and prompt, correct
stock transfers, will no doubt suggest themselves.

BROKERAGE ACCOUNTS

Because of the substantial sums involved, brokers are very careful of their accounts. Each new customer is carefully identified before his orders are accepted.
His account is correctly labeled with his full name or established as a joint account between himself and his wife. If a customer and his wife have both separate
and joint holdings, three accounts are generally used, for transfer of either securities or money from one account or name to another cannot be accomplished
without a written order from the transferor.

When an account is opened, the customer may choose between one which is
available for cash transactions only and one which is designed to permit either
cash or margin operations. The broker will prefer the latter, for it paves the way
for all possible transactions without committing either customer or broker to
undertake them. The broker will ask his customer to fill out a signature card
and a personal data card, for identification purposes; a margin card, which accepts the terms of the margin account, authorizes the broker to hold the securities
as collateral, and permits the securities to be used as collateral for the broker's
debts; an authorization to solicit his margin business by telephone; and written
instructions for the transfer or custody of securities which are to be acquired.
These documents will be needed for each account. When the accounts are those
of trustees, executors, attorneys-in-fact, or corporations, the legal ramifications
may be extensive.

Instructions to a broker or dealer to make transactions are commonly given
by telephone, after the account is established. When the account is regarded as

reliable, the instructions are carried out even if the account has no credit balance. A few days' grace, usually about 5, are allowed the customer to get sold securities or a cash purchase price into the office. The cash proceeds of a sale are available to a customer in 5 days, provided they are not required as margin in his account.

Brokers or dealers may be given *discretionary* accounts, in which the firm is authorized to use its own discretion in buying or selling for the account. The stock exchanges generally disapprove of this practice; the New York Stock Exchange does not permit a member firm to accept a discretionary account unless an officer or partner of the firm supervises it. However, the exchange does not object if an employee is instructed by a customer to buy or sell a specific amount of a specific security at a time and price which are left to the employee's discretion.

THE THIRD MARKET

The last few years have witnessed a sharp rise in the over-the-counter trading of common stocks listed on the New York Stock Exchange. This so-called third market in securities is conducted by a score or so of nonmember firms, mostly located in New York, who maintain inventories of listed issues and specialize in trading large blocks of listed stocks among mutual and pension funds, foundations, banks, and insurance companies. These broker-dealer firms specialize in seeking out large-scale buyers and sellers; they often buy or sell large blocks for their own accounts (hence are able to moderate the price impact which large-scale public bids or offers might cause); and they often charge relatively modest commission rates in large transactions. Third market volume is ordinarily concentrated in a relatively few large or unusually active issues. In 1971 it amounted to 7 per cent of the total New York Stock Exchange volume.

RECENT TRENDS IN BROKERAGE AND STOCK EXCHANGES

The securities business is changing rapidly, and this reflects the accelerating emergence of new financial needs, mechanical improvements, and business problems. Several recent developments will be reviewed in detail in Chapters 10 and 12, but five of them directly involve matters discussed in this chapter and deserve brief mention in closing.

1 Market unification. Both the SEC and the securities industry itself have planning committees and other groups studying ways and means of unifying the various stock exchanges and over-the-counter markets into a single, completely interlinked system. This arrangement would contemplate the automatic routing of each customer order to the most advantageous market and a single reporting tape showing transactions for each stock in all markets in which it is traded.

2 Market liquidity. The role of the stock exchange specialist has been based on the traditional 100-share-order market, and if the exchanges are to digest with minimal price disturbance the 10,000- to 300,000-share blocks of stock bought and sold daily by financial institutions, both the financial resources and the trading methods of the specialists must be augmented. This is being accomplished through a variety of new rules and procedures.

3 Brokerage-house diversification. To reduce an often excessive dependence on stock exchange commission business, many brokerage firms are diversifying into such other fields of financial endeavor as life insurance sales, real estate syndication, and personal estate planning, as well as increasing their activities in such traditional brokerage-related lines as securities dealing, investment banking, and commodities trading. A leading brokerage firm in 1972 advertised 29 different ways in which a client might invest through its facilities.

4 Improved operations. To reduce paperwork confusion, loss of securities or failure to deliver them, and mix-ups on customers' accounts (such as plagued many stock exchange firms in the 1968–1970 period), brokerage houses generally are paying increased attention to routine operations and back-office procedures. The introduction of computerized record-keeping, accounting, and stock-transfer methods is not only keeping down the operating costs of securities firms, but it also is opening new careers for computer programmers and systems analysts in the securities business.

5 Brokerage commissions. Brokerage commissions on trades ranging from odd lots up to several hundred shares have risen steeply during recent years. At least part of this increase has resulted from the expense which brokerage houses incur in providing investor advice, research departments, safekeeping facilities, margin accounts, and other services which only a minority of customers may use. This has produced some demand by investors that brokers "unbundle" their services, reduce commission charges to cover basic buying and selling operations only, and allocate the cost of special services to the customers who use them. As noted earlier in this chapter, very large orders executed on the stock exchanges no longer pay fixed fees.

QUESTIONS AND PROBLEMS

1 Can a brokerage business be done by a firm which owns no stock exchange memberships?

2 Why do nonmember firms not organize stock exchanges of their own?

3 Since they appear to hold quasi-monopolistic positions in an important industry, should the stock exchanges be compelled to admit all competent and solvent brokerage firms to membership?

4 Why would the New York Stock Exchange and the American Stock Exchange not trade in the same stocks?

5 Why would an investor prefer a listed stock to an unlisted one? Are there any advantages to the corporation in having a listed market?

6 What would happen to the price of Bethlehem Steel stock if, for no good reason, most of the day's buying orders reached the stock exchange in the morning and most of the selling orders came in the afternoon? Would stock exchange members interested in trading for their own accounts help or hinder in this case?

7 What sort of techniques would a specialist establish to govern his own participation in the market for one of his stocks, assuming that **(a)** exchange rules permit him to trade only to help stabilize the market or to liquidate inventories or short positions accumulated in stabilization operations, **(b)** he cannot accurately anticipate either hour-to-hour or longer-term market trends, and **(c)** he will occasionally encounter very large-sized bids or offers from institutional investors, which must somehow be absorbed?

8 Does the continuous auction system of stock exchange trading as now used produce fair and stable prices? Would it be better to open each stock for trading for about 15 minutes every second day, so that the accumulated bids and offers would have a better chance to balance?

9 Would a stock exchange ex-dividend date fall before, on, or after the corporation's stock-of-record date for the dividend?

10 What is a when-issued contract? Why would investors want to buy or sell rights on a when-issued basis? Is there any real need for when-issued trading?

11 Stock exchanges receive more market orders than limit orders. Why?

12 What securities market techniques would be appropriate to liquidate 20,000 shares of Xerox Corporation for an estate? or 300,000 shares for a large investment company? How would a large investment company go about buying a holding of that size?

13 Would you expect limit orders to be open orders or day orders?

14 As a practical investment matter, should one whose funds are limited try to select stocks in which he can afford round lots or should he invest freely in odd lots?

15 Which is the largest sum, the commission on 100 shares of $9 stock, or the commission on 10 shares of $90 stock plus an odd-lot differential on 10 shares?

16 Can an odd lot be bid for by means of a market order? By means of a limit order? By an open order? Can it be bought on margin? Can an odd lot be sold short?

17 Explain the SEC rule limiting short selling. How does this prevent "bear raiding"? Is there any economic justification for short selling?

18 May an investor—as distinguished from a speculator—ever have occasion to sell short?

19 Explain how a margin purchase works. Would an investor ever have occasion to buy on margin? Which would you prefer, if you were investing money due to be paid to you in two months: a margin purchase using your own free securities as margin, or a purchase with money borrowed from your bank?

20 What brokerage facilities would seem most important to you as an investor in securities?

21 By 1974 it is planned to abandon fixed commissions on all stock exchange transactions amounting to $100,000 or more. Why should not all commissions—even those on 100-share and odd-lot orders—be subject to negotiation? Would this arrangement not be fairer to customers? Would it force brokers to become more efficient?

REFERENCES

Bellemore, Douglas H., and John C. Ritchie, Jr.: *Investments*, 3d ed. South-Western Publishing Company, Incorporated, Cincinnati, 1969, Chap. 4.

Bogen, Jules O., and Herman E. Krooss: *Security Credit*, Prentice-Hall, Inc., Englewood Cliffs, N.J., 1960.

Cooke, Gilbert W.: *The Stock Markets*, rev. ed., Schenkman Publishing Co., Inc., Cambridge, Mass., 1969, Part 3.

Eiteman, Wilford J., Charles A. Dice, and David K. Eiteman: *The Stock Market*, 4th ed., McGraw-Hill Book Company, New York, 1966.

Leffler, George L., and Loring C. Farwell: *The Stock Market*, 3d ed., The Ronald Press Company, New York, 1963.

Lishan, John M., and David T. Crary: *The Investment Process*, paperback ed., International Textbook Company, Scranton, Pa., 1970, Part 4.

New York Stock Exchange: *New York Stock Exchange Fact Book*, New York, annual.

Petrillo, H. V., and C. L. Bullock: *Processing Securities Transactions*, The Ronald Press Company, New York, 1969.

Robbins, Sidney M.: *The Securities Markets: Operations and Issues*, The Free Press of Glencoe, Inc., New York, 1966.

Schwartz, Robert J.: *You and Your Stockbroker*, The Macmillan Company, New York, 1967.

Securities and Exchange Commission: *Special Study of the Securities Markets*, Washington, 1964, Part 2; Part 3, Chap. 10; Part 5.

Widicus, Wilbur W., and Thomas E. Stitzel: *Personal Investing*, Richard D. Irwin, Inc., Homewood, Ill., 1971, Chap. 3.

10

BEHAVIOR OF THE
SPECULATIVE MARKETS

All common stocks and the lower grades of preferred stocks and corporate bonds may be classed as speculative in greater or less degree. As has been stressed in previous chapters, this does not mean that they are not fit commitments for thoughtfully planned investment portfolios. The contrary is true. But it does mean that these securities carry a significant degree of business and market risk and that their prices will fluctuate substantially, and often rapidly, over the years.

In final analysis, the prices of all securities, speculative and nonspeculative alike, are products of the familiar forces of supply and demand. However, the demand for speculative securities is affected not only by the savings people have to invest in them and the competitive attractiveness of other investments, but also by the margin credit available, the business outlook, and the speculative enthusiasm of the moment. The supply of speculative securities is at all times potentially large, for a very large amount of existing stock is capable of becoming "supply" if its holders lose faith in business prospects or the immediate future of stock prices or have urgent need of money for other purposes. To this resale supply must be added at times the very considerable amount of new stock which industry must often sell when expansion programs are under way.

The stocks of every industry and every company are affected by some of the forces which act upon the stock market. Changes in margin credit rules, for example, make it easier to own more stock or more difficult to do so, hence affect the buying or selling pressures in many issues. And boom or recession in important groups of securities naturally communicates itself to others; buyers in a rising market naturally seek the undervalued issues, thus raising them also, and sellers in a weak market tend to sell those not yet depressed, thus driving them down. As a matter of experience, it can be said that the ups and downs of the stock market are experienced in varying degree by nearly all industries and individual stocks.

The investor in stocks is confronted by a number of problems and a number of choices. He needs an investment policy which will guide him in choosing and timing his commitments. Should he attempt to take advantage of the major swings in the market by buying when the market appears to be at a cyclical low spot and selling when it appears to be high? Should he attempt to ferret out the industries and companies which have "growth" prospects and confine his investments to them? In view of the uncertainty of market prophecies, is it ever justi-

fiable to sell a promising holding just because the market appears high or to buy
an unpromising one just because it or the market is low? Which is easiest for
the layman, to pick good industries and good stocks, or to pick profitable times
to buy and sell? Is it not sensible investing for a layman to buy a good stock in
a good industry when the price-earnings ratio and yield prospects are right and
to ignore market behavior?

These and other policy questions could be answered easily if the investor were
omniscient in the matter of forecasting market movements. Unfortunately, not
even professionals are good at that. Most of them have to work as investment
bankers or stockbrokers or investment counselors to make a living, which pretty
well proves the point. And the constant study which market trading requires
would consume time beyond the nonprofessional trader's ability to afford it.
The problem, then, has no easy answer.

MEASURES OF MARKET BEHAVIOR

Because securities prices often seem to rise or fall concertedly in response to
"general conditions," investors and speculators have developed great interest
in index numbers or "averages" which measure these general market-price movements. These indexes are valuable, and their use is essential to any study of securities market behavior. But it is equally essential to note their limitations. They
are at best only *averages* based on the prices of certain securities, and the prices
of individual securities rarely if ever conform to the average movement. Individual security prices reflect differences in attractiveness between companies,
between industries, between large and small concerns, between high- and low-
grade issues, and in many other ways. One who compares a specific situation
to an average must always take care.

The most widely used securities indexes are simple price index numbers which
show the composite rise and fall in price of a selected group of issues.[1] The leading common stock price indexes are accompanied by related indexes of per share
earnings and dividends which make it possible to compute price-earnings ratios
and yields for the index as a whole. On bonds and preferred stocks, both price
and *yield* indexes are published, but the yield indexes are the most widely used.

Stock price indexes are compiled and published by many sources and on a
number of bases. Indexes representing the whole market, computed either from

---

[1]The technical problems presented in compiling these indexes are byond the scope of this book but should
be studied by anyone making serious use of the indexes. There is, for example, the problem of weighting.
Another problem is posed by the fact that a daily or hourly total will never catch all the stocks at peak or
bottom simultaneously; therefore the average will have a smaller range than most or all of the constituent
stocks. In preparing a bond price average, should one compute yields to maturity, average them, and re-
convert this average yield to a price for an assumed coupon and maturity? Or is it better to average the prices
of somewhat similar bonds?

a limited group of representative stocks in diverse industries or by use of a very large number of stocks, are available. Indexes representing groups of industries with certain common characteristics, such as industrial or utility, are compiled; and there are detailed price indexes by industries, such as telephone, steel, meat packing, and chain stores. Some indexes are classified by quality of security, though this is more common in bond than stock computations, and there are indexes of growth stocks, low-priced stocks, over-the-counter stocks, and many others.

The most famous indexes of stock prices are those compiled by Dow, Jones & Co., Inc., publishers of *The Wall Street Journal* and other financial services. The Dow-Jones Industrial Average consists of the total market price of 1 share each of 30 representative stocks, divided by a denominator, which was originally 30. Through the years it has been necessary to substitute stocks in the list for various reasons or to make adjustments because of stock splits and similar changes. Continuity of the index has been maintained when these changes occur by adjusting the denominator by which the total is divided; in August 1972, this denominator was 1.661. The second well-known Dow-Jones index is the Transportation Average consisting of 20 representative railroad, airline, and motor freight stocks, compiled by the same system as the Industrial Average. Dow-Jones also computes an average of 15 utility stocks and a composite average of 65 stocks, but these have not caught the public fancy as the others have done.

A broader measure of New York Stock Exchange fluctuations is provided by the Exchange's own series of five stock price indexes, each weighted by the market values of the stocks it includes and related to a base set at 50 as of December 31, 1965. The Common Stock Index is a composite of all common stocks listed on the Exchange, while separate indexes are computed for industrial, transportation, utility, and financial-company shares. The American Stock Exchange publishes a price level index which reflects the average dollars-and-cents change in the price of all common stocks and warrants traded on the Exchange, and the National Quotation Bureau publishes a daily average of over-the-counter industrial stocks based on the bid prices of 35 issues. The broadly based NASDAQ industrial index of some 1,800 over-the-counter stocks was established by the National Association of Security Dealers and Analysts in February 1971, so it cannot yet serve in long-term comparisons.

The most comprehensive collection of stock price indexes is the one that is maintained by Standard & Poor's Corporation and published in its *Trade and Securities Service*. The principal indexes in this collection—industrials, rails, utilities, and composite—are based on large numbers of stock prices and appropriately weighted. The S & P service also maintains a large number of stock price averages by specific industries. A somewhat less ramified but carefully compiled collection of stock price averages is maintained by Moody's Investors Service. Another good collection is maintained by Barron's, a subsidiary of Dow, Jones

& Co., Inc. Other organizations, including the SEC, contribute to the voluminous literature in this field.

Bond and preferred stock averages are usually maintained on both a price and a yield basis. Bond indexes are classified by quality, time to maturity, and groups of issuers, such as industrial, rail, utility, municipal, and federal government. The best collections of indexes are published by the agencies already mentioned.

STOCK PRICE MOVEMENTS

The most obvious stock price movement apparent in a long-term chart of industrail stock prices, such as Chart 10-1, is a general upward growth trend averaging some 4.7 per cent per year. This growth trend is for the most part the product of reinvested earnings and price-level inflation. However, it progresses at a modest average rate which is overshadowed by the sharp fluctuations which occur in stock prices.

Consequently, when stock traders speak of stock price movements they usually ignore the modest underlying growth trend and speak of three shorter-term types of market movements. First, there is the intermediate-term tendency, presumably conforming to business cycle stages in normal times, for the market to move in a general upward or downward direction for 6 months to 3 years at a time. Market analysts usually refer to this as the *basic trend* or the *primary trend*, and assert that this trend determines whether a bull or a bear market exists at the moment. Chart 10-1 clearly shows bull markets, for example, in the periods 1949–1952, 1954–1957, 1962–1966, and 1967–1968. Bear markets appear in 1953, 1957, 1962, 1966, and 1969–1970. The 1946–1949 period shows an unusually long sidewise movement or *line*.

Superimposed on the primary trend are frequent shorter cycles of 3 months' to a year's duration, during which the averages may fluctuate 5 to 15 per cent in value. These short-range cycles also show clearly on the chart; for example, the low points in August 1971 and November 1971 interlace the high spots in April 1971, September 1971, and April 1972. The up, down, and sidewise movements of the averages in forming these shorter cycles are termed *secondary*, or *short-term*, *trends*.

A third type of market movement is observable in the day-to-day fluctuations of the averages. For example, in the week ending July 21, 1972, the Dow-Jones Industrial Average fell 7.30 points on Monday, fell 3.34 points on Tuesday, gained 4.97 points on Wednesday, fell 6.24 points on Thursday, and gained 10.00 points on Friday. On every single day the range of fluctuation within the day exceeded the net change for the day. This is typical. No cyclical pattern can be found for these hour-to-hour, day-to-day, and week-to-week fluctuations, except to suggest that extremely sharp gains or declines for a few hours or days seem usually to be "corrected" by rebound movements in the opposite direction.

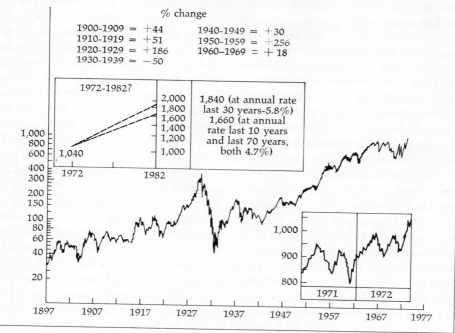

Chart 10-1 *Seventy-six years of the Dow-Jones Industrial Average. This chart shows the progress of the Average through wars, booms, inflations, and depressions, and the 76-year, 4.7 per cent per annum growth rate shown here is a product of all these. The chart is on a semi-logarithmic scale, which would cause a constant percentage growth to appear as a straight line. The box at the upper left shows the average rate of growth maintained for certain past periods and the results if such growth should continue to 1982. The box at the lower right presents a close-up picture of secondary moves in the Industrial Average during 1971 and 1972.*

% change

1900–1909 = +44	1940–1949 = +30
1910–1919 = +51	1950–1959 = +256
1920–1929 = +186	1960–1969 = +18
1930–1939 = −50	

1972–1982?

2,000
1,800
1,600
1,400
1,200
1,000

1,040

1972   1982

1,840 (at annual rate last 30 years–5.8%) 1,660 (at annual rate last 10 years and last 70 years, both 4.7%)

It must be emphatically stated that in recognizing these three types of market movements, and in identifying some apparent periodicity in them, no conclusions can be drawn respecting the extent and timing of market changes. Such factors as wars, inflation, taxes, labor problems, and economic conditions generally are far too complex to permit the mechanical forecasting of stock prices. However, some knowledge of typical market behavior and its causes may help in avoiding obvious mistakes and in making an occasional sound decision.

Primary trends Primary trends are the result of fairly fundamental forces in economic affairs. They must be, for market trends and price levels which prevail for years in a logical and competitive market must have substantial foundation. There are five interrelated groups of forces which contribute to the primary trend. In the apparent order of importance, they are (1) the outlook for business activity and stability, (2) the outlook for business profits, (3) speculative attitude and expectations, (4) the availability of money for stock investment, and (5) the amount of money removed from the stock market by investors who need it elsewhere and by business for expansion.

Little argument is needed to demonstrate the importance of items 1 and 2 to any student of the investment markets. Most of the space in financial periodicals is given over to painstaking study of business activity and business profits, and investment policies are constantly shaped by the conclusions reached. Although the investor's emphasis is constantly on the *outlook* for business, it appears that major securities market changes are mostly somewhat ahead of variations in business conditions. However, most of the major periods of business uptrend or downtrend in the past 50 years have also been periods of parallel stock market uptrend or downtrend; and although the stock market has tended to move ahead of business, the peaks and bottoms of stock market and business cycles have seldom been separated by more than a few months. It may therefore be concluded that primary trends in the stock market are in large part reflections of the movements of the business cycle.

Primary trends are also vitally affected by item 3, speculative attitude and expectations. There is a very large group of investors who are more interested in market profits than in future dividends. They are therefore constantly studying economic history and market patterns in the hope of recognizing coming events in time to profit from them. When they conclude that price-earnings ratios are too high or that economic and monetary conditions suggest a coming depression, as they seemed to in 1966, their action can greatly influence the market trend. And the decline of the market in 1962 was doubtless due in large part to a belief that the steel price controversy of early 1962 indicated governmental hostility to business and investors. More examples to the same effect could easily be cited.

Item 4, the availability of money for stock investment, is also an important factor in establishing the primary trend. The amount of money seeking investment in stocks is affected chiefly by the size and distribution of the national income; the volume of liquid funds in the hands of individuals, businessmen, and other investors; the attractiveness of competing investments such as corporate and tax-exempt bonds, life insurance, savings accounts, and real estate; and the availability of credit for stock purchases. In these respects, the 1946–1949 period contrasted sharply with the 1953–1965 years. Though the well-to-do and professional classes had satisfactory earnings in 1946–1949, high progressive taxes reduced their surpluses for investment to modest amounts, and the substantial incomes going to farmers and wage earners did not find their way to the stock market. Life insurance, home investment, and savings acounts were popular competing outlets for savings, and many people were using their funds to build up their own businesses. Credit for the stock market was almost a thing of the past. And the 1946–1949 stock market did not advance despite prosperity, profits, and dividends. The period 1953–1965, in contrast, was characterized by a strongly rising stock market. This was a period in which the money demand for stocks was very great, for several reasons: first, institutional investors, especially corporation pension funds, began to invest large sums in stocks; second, a successful sales promotion campaign by securities firms attracted thousands of new stock buyers; third, many stock-buying families completed their planned postwar improvements to their homes and family businesses and began to divert larger sums to stock investment; fourth, many conservative investors turned to stocks as a hedge against inflation; and fifth, during most of this period 50 per cent margin credit was available. The importance of the available funds aspect of the stock market was particularly noticeable in 1954 and 1958; although the business situation in these years did not promise increased profits or dividends, people had substantial incomes and somewhat less-than-average need for money for consumption and capital goods uses. They therefore bought stocks, and the stock market rose vigorously.

Item 5, the withdrawals from the stock market, represents two separate influences on the stock market trend. First, there are always people who must sell their stocks to finance their businesses and their personal affairs. The market must find replacement money to finance these retirements. Second, business corporations frequently must sell new stock to finance expansion or debt repayment. This financing removes from the market substantial amounts which otherwise would bid for existing stocks. Unless margin credit or unusually large amounts of new savings or both are available, the market has difficulty in advancing while absorbing new corporate financing. This factor contributed importantly to the 1946–1949 doldrums. However, the increased demand for stocks during the whole 1949–1972 era absorbed a large volume of new stock sales without serious effect on the advancing market trend.

Secondary movements   It seems probable that most of the secondary movements in the stock market can be attributed to hasty speculators who "overdo it" in attempting to take advantage of impending price changes and who then overdo it in the opposite direction in attempting to correct their errors. After all, speculative advantage can be had by identifying the bit of news which indicates that the market should go up or down and acting upon it substantially and quickly. Perspective is limited when time is of the essence, and it is not unlikely that many reversals of opinion will take place. Also, people are very prone to become accustomed to a market level in a few weeks' time. If the natural trend of the market is up, they are inclined to seize quick profits by selling after a few weeks of rising prices. This will reverse the direction of movement, stampede panicky speculators, and "touch off" an extensive market "correction." Presently the natural rise will be resumed, with another correction to be expected in due time. Market declines show the same phenomena in reverse.

The existence of secondary movements can unquestionably be laid to the fact

that the forces shaping primary trends are difficult to evaluate except in retro-
spect. In attempting to appraise them prospectively, the market blunders and
vacillates. The vacillations themselves—the secondary movements under consideration—are very likely to be set off by news events whose significance is
exaggerated by current prominence. Because of their infinite variety and scope,
it is extremely difficult to anticipate the behavior of secondary movements to
any extent. There is a saying that a typical secondary decline in a rising market
will retrace 30 to 70 per cent of the gain since the last secondary bottom, and
that the following advance will gain 1½ to 3 times as much as the secondary decline lost. In a declining market the ratios are reversed. However, not many
secondary movements are typical, a fact which helps to make the way of a
prophet somewhat similar to that of the proverbial transgressor.

Day-to-day movements   Stock prices often fluctuate sharply from hour to hour,
day to day, and week to week. These gyrations are usually not at all predictable,
except that "spot" news of considerable moment, such as the threat of war, the
outcome of a presidential election, the settlement of a critical strike or a dividend
increase by an important corporation, is almost certain to elicit a response. The
listed market's daily and hourly quotations are produced by the flow of bids
and offers to the trading floor. Any news which halts or accelerates either of
these flows will change market prices. If, after an hour or so of reflection, traders
come to the conclusion that the news was not so important after all, its effects
will soon die out. If the impression created by the news disturbs the balance of
bids and offers for several days, the market effect will last just that long. Of
course, any impetus of this sort may be the beginning of a substantial secondary
movement. But the day-to-day movements themselves, constituting indexes of
the accidental or transitory impressions of buyers and sellers for fleeting hours,
do not seem to be of fundamental importance.

The Dow theory   There are many authors with many ideas for anticipating stock
market movements and profiting from them. By far the best-known system is
built around the Dow theory, a doctrine developed by the editors of *The Wall
Street Journal* in the early years of the century and much elaborated by others
since.[2] First, the Dow theory proceeds on the assumption that if profits are to
be made in the stock market, they must be made by taking advantage of the
primary trend, not by resisting it. Since a primary trend "usually" lasts 1 to 4
years and produces changes of 25 to 90 per cent or even more in the market aver-

[2]The theory is not clear in its original form and has been expounded and often distorted for half a century. Highly regarded presentations, at some length, are found in W. P. Hamilton, *The Stock Market Barometer*, 1922; Robert Rhea, *The Dow Theory*, 1932; and G. W. Bishop, Jr. (ed.), *Charles H. Dow, Economist*,
Dow Jones & Company, Inc., Princeton, N.J., n.d.

ages, there is ample time and ample room to make profits, for well-selected individual stocks should move farther than the averages.

The next fundamental assumption in the Dow theory is that when the primary trend is up, each secondary cycle will produce a peak higher than the last preceding one, and a trough higher than the last preceding one. Conversely, when the primary trend is down, each secondary peak and trough will be lower than the preceding ones. If these facts are usually correct, they provide a basis for determining the direction of the primary trend, for every secondary rise which surpasses the previous peak will clearly *signal* a rising basic trend, and every secondary decline which drops lower than a preceding trough will signal a basic downward trend. In cases in which the market averages have made no significant progress up or down for several months, a decisive movement out of the recent price range in either direction is also regarded as a signal indicating the direction of the primary trend.

The third fundamental assumption of the Dow theory is that any true indication of primary trend will be "confirmed" by similar action in different stock price indexes within a short time. The Dow-Jones Industrial Average and the Transportation Average are usually used for this purpose. If the Industrial Average signals the beginning of a bull market, the faithful wait to see what the Transportation Average will do. If it shortly produces a bull signal also, they mortgage the old homestead and buy every stock in sight. A bear-market signal by either average must similarly be confirmed by the other before it is regarded as authentic.

The earlier Dow theorists seem to have regarded the secondary swings as too unpredictable to be profitable in themselves but as very useful in indicating the primary trend. Some of the less-conservative later writers have attempted to use day-to-day and week-to-week market fluctuations as indications of the continuation or reversal of secondary trends, thus corrupting the Dow method to a different purpose. Although some good logic on market behavior has been mustered in support of this idea, it does not seem to be so well grounded as the original doctrine.

Critics of the Dow theory argue that the theory is ineffective even if correct, for it usually fails to signal a change of primary trend until a distinct breakthrough of a preceding peak or trough has been made by two averages. This means that the trend will have changed weeks or months before. The criticism is true; but the proponents' rejoinder is that the typical primary trend is generous in scope and of long duration; so signals which are quite late can still salvage most of the cyclical gain or avoid most of the loss. An equally serious criticism is found in the fact that the Dow theorists have difficulty in identifying the key peaks or troughs which must be surpassed or broken through; the secondary movements are not clean-cut, and the interpreters of the theory disagree as to whether given peaks, troughs, or movements are primary or secondary, and as to whether given breakthroughs are decisive enough to be significant. Finally, the theory does not always work; it gives a considerable number of false signals, and several of the correctly identified primary trends of the postwar period proved so short that users of the theory incurred losses.

Regardless of the issues of dependability and practical usefulness, however, there are two reasons why the Dow theory may have elements of merit. In the first place, a great many people believe it and will act upon it. In acting upon it they can help to cause the upward or downward trend the theory predicts. The second reason for the appeal of the Dow theory is that it has a sensible core of hard logic. It is a familiar and reasonable fact that stock market moves often precede and announce the ups and downs of business, which usually take some time

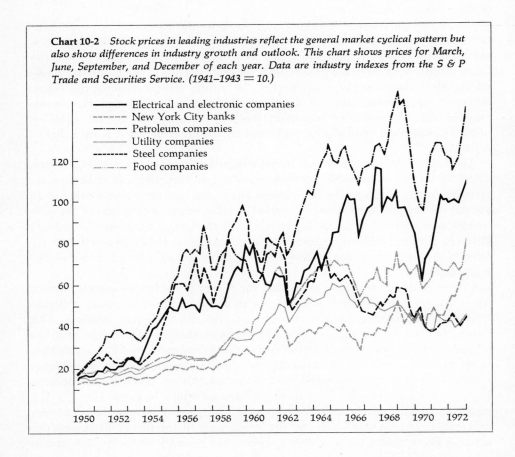

Chart 10-2 *Stock prices in leading industries reflect the general market cyclical pattern but also show differences in industry growth and outlook. This chart shows prices for March, June, September, and December of each year. Data are industry indexes from the S & P Trade and Securities Service. (1941–1943 = 10.)*

Electrical and electronic companies
New York City banks
Petroleum companies
Utility companies
Steel companies
Food companies

to work themselves out.[3] The major swings of the business cycle are related to the primary trends of the market. The secondary trends of the market merely reflect the excesses of human nature superimposed on and following the primary trend. That successive secondary peaks and troughs should follow the direction of the primary trend is obvious; if most of them did not, there would be no primary trend.

STOCK PRICES IN DIFFERENT INDUSTRIES

Previous paragraphs have noted that the primary, secondary, and day-to-day market fluctuations all have noticeable effects on the stocks of every industry. General movements are well-nigh universal. On a day when the Dow-Jones Industrial Average drops 15 points, there will usually be sharp declines in railroad, electric power, bank and insurance stocks, both listed and over the counter. Full-scale secondary and primary trends are similarly widespread. Charts 10-2 and 10-3 illustrate the situation. On each chart the major gains of the periods 1953–1955, 1963–1964, and 1967–1968, and the declines of 1962, 1966, and 1969–1970, are in some degree common to all industries and all stocks. The shorter secondary swings—for example, those of 1965 and 1971—are also shown to be general in scope.

The reasons for this are pretty clear. Stock market credit conditions, speculative psychology, changes in the tax laws, labor legislation, foreign relations, the distribution of national income, the level of prosperity—these are factors which affect the supply and demand for all stocks. Only an industry or a stock influenced by very powerful unique circumstances can "buck the market trend."

However, Charts 10-2 and 10-3 both show that some stocks and some industries have improved their position through the years, while others have made little progress. This is proper and reasonable. The stock market superimposes its general cyclical swings on all stocks and all industries, but underlying values are not ignored. If an industry is prosperous and growing, its stocks will drop less in market declines and gain more on advances than the average and may even gain considerably while the average suffers a net loss, as the soap stocks did in 1966–1967. A weak stock or industry will do the opposite, as instance the utility companies from 1967 through 1972.

An industry whose stocks do better than the general market at any time will probably be one which (1) is enjoying relatively good earnings, or (2) seems to

---

[3]Long-standing studies by the National Bureau of Economic Research find that between 1879 and 1958, stock prices were among the most reliable "leading" indicators of the business cycle. See Geoffrey H. Moore, *Business Cycle Indicators*, Vols. I and II, Princeton University Press, Princeton, N.J., 1961; or Julius Shiskin, "Signals of Recession and Recovery," Occasional Paper 77, National Bureau of Economic Research, New York, 1961.

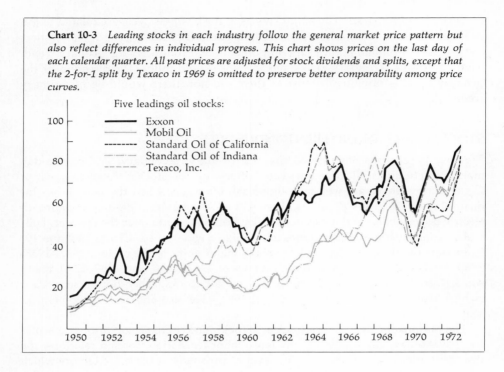

Chart 10-3 *Leading stocks in each industry follow the general market price pattern but also reflect differences in individual progress. This chart shows prices on the last day of each calendar quarter. All past prices are adjusted for stock dividends and splits, except that the 2-for-1 split by Texaco in 1969 is omitted to preserve better comparability among price curves.*

Five leadings oil stocks:

——— Exxon
———— Mobil Oil
-------- Standard Oil of California
—·—·— Standard Oil of Indiana
— — — Texaco, Inc.

have promise of an unusually good future, or (3) has a vogue among stock buyers, or (4) is comparatively free of financing problems. In 1972, examples of industries whose stocks were high because of good current earnings were drugs, electrical equipment, soft drinks, and tobacco companies. An industry enjoying a vogue among stock buyers was the mobile home industry; similar vogues for electronics firms in 1961, airlines in 1964–1965, conglomerates in 1967, and computer software companies in 1968–1969 colored the markets in those years. Financing problems in 1971 and 1972 were especially conspicuous for the effect they had on electric utility stocks. An excessive quantity of stock was being offered for sale because new issues were needed to finance expansion at a time when utility companies were unable to sell bonds in the desired amounts. The market, however, did not want so much utility stock, and the prices sagged.

Some industries, such as electric power, banking, and insurance, are sometimes said to be "noncyclical," that is, less subject to business cycle and general stock market trends than others. Very high-quality stocks of all types are often considered to be in this category. The truth of the matter is that these stocks are mostly in industries or companies in which the earnings are both stable and predictable. With earnings and dividends stabilized, stock price fluctuations are lessened both because people understand more clearly the long-run values inherent in the stock and because they are assured of continuity of earnings and dividends in the short run. However, these stocks must not be thought immune to primary and secondary movements; usually they are relatively stable, but speculators sometimes run them to extravagant prices, as they did food and soap stocks in 1961; the ensuing relapse to more normal price levels may prove extremely painful to incautious investors who bought in at the market highs.

PRICES OF INDIVIDUAL STOCKS

What has been said of whole industries applies with equal force to individual stocks. Good quality and stable earning power will tend to limit the scope of price fluctuations. Regardless of quality, good current earnings, promise of future prosperity, a vogue or a following among stock buyers, and freedom from need to sell new stock will all help to sustain the price of a stock. Opposite influence will exert depressing effects. Aside from these factors and the familiar influences of dividend policy, stock dividends, splits, and the like, there are several *market* elements which contribute to the price behavior of a stock. These include:

1 *Accumulation and distribution.* Important financial interests, including investment companies, trusts, pension funds, corporate officers, and major stockholders, frequently undertake to acquire or dispose of substantial amounts of a stock. This may be done on over-the-counter markets, on the regular exchange markets, by special or secondary offering, or through the block-trading procedures of the interinstitutional market. But regardless of the channel used, the amount of stock for sale to the public will be affected, and unless the transactions are handled with great skill, there may be immediate effects on the market price. The market price effects may be present for months, for if accumulation mops up the "floating supply" of a stock, or if distribution adds to it greatly, it may be a long time before the disturbed supply-and-demand relationship is adjusted. The floating supply is the portion of the stock which is likely to appear for sale on either a market rally or a decline, because its holders regard it as a trading position rather than as a permanent investment. A stock with a small floating supply is likely to be buoyant; and excessive floating supply will cause market weakness.

2 *Stockholder confidence.* There are many stocks, for example, General Electric and Kraftco Corporation, whose holders have confidence in them because of their long records and good reputations. These holders are disinclined to sell on market declines and are disposed to buy "bargain" offerings if the price drops. If such stocks as these are widely distributed in many hands, and if few excessive concentrations exist to give rise to frequent secondary distributions, the market price should be relatively steady. On the other hand, stocks whose earnings performances or market price histories have not earned their holders' confi-

dence, stocks of new concerns or corporations recently reorganized in bank-ruptcy, and those in industries subject to adverse gossip are likely to be unstable under selling pressure and to be unable to advance as fast in a rising market as their intrinsic merit would justify. The opinions of professional portfolio managers who manage the multimillion-dollar stock accounts of financial institutions greatly affect the price behavior and trends of most stocks in today's large-volume markets.

3 Market sponsorship. Individual stocks can be kept in stronger position marketwise if large floating supplies are not allowed to accumulate and if urgently offered stock is bought up and resold to new holders by use of security salesmen. This is undertaken by dealers and underwriters in some instances and by company managements and interested stockholders in other cases. It is not illegal manipulation if the transactions are carried out with stabilization rather than deception in mind. A stock will also enjoy greater price stability if block-trading firms are willing to absorb temporarily large numbers of shares which are suddenly offered by institutional holders and for which some hours or days may be required to find buyers at a fair price.

4 Publicity and endorsement. The demand for the stocks of companies and industries is greatly affected by what prospective stock buyers read and hear. Stocks which are recommended by brokers and investment advisory services are likely to sell higher than they would otherwise. Furthermore, stocks which receive publicity, if it is not grossly unfavorable, are called to the attention of prospective stock buyers with advantageous results.

5 Profit and tax factors. Stocks whose market values change sharply in a short time may be vulnerable to several types of buying and selling adjustments. First, a stock or group of stocks showing a definite improvement or decline in value is likely to be carried too far in the sweep of speculative enthusiasm, thus paving the way for a "correction." Second, a substantial rise will create paper profits for holders who will be eager to "take" them and who will hastily sell when a correction appears. The short sellers who gain on the down side will be similarly quick to buy in when a correction halts its decline. Third, any stock which has experienced a sharp decline during any calendar year, especially in the last half of the year, and most especially in a year when many people have capital gains, will be a target for tax selling.

Because both industry and individual stock features affect the market for each stock, it is unlikely that all stocks will fluctuate in parallel fashion throughout a stock market cycle. Some will reach their "peaks" ahead of the averages, and some later; and the same will be true of "bottoms" as well as of "climbs" and "declines." Furthermore, this timing will not necessarily be consistent either from one cyclical phase to another or from one cycle to another.

Beta How rapidly a stock has tended to move up or down relative to the general market is indicated by its *beta coefficient*. Beta is a statistical ratio derived by plotting a stock's rates of change during a number of past time periods against corresponding changes in some stock market average. The result is a percentage figure which compares the variability of the individual stock with that of stocks in general. For example, in 1972 the *Value Line Investment Survey* showed the following beta coefficients: American Telephone, .51, Globe Union, Inc., 1.01, and Fairchild Camera, 1.98. These ratios signified that in previous years the percentage price swings in American Telephone had been only about half as wide as fluctuations in the Value Line's 1,400 composite stock average; Globe Union had fluctuated about as widely as the average, and Fairchild Camera about twice as widely.

Aggressive speculators have always sought to own fast-moving stocks in excitedly rising markets and to sell them in declining or doubtful ones. Beta coefficients provide traders with an easily understood measure of relative price variability in different stocks. However, betas are not always stable across time, and coefficients for the same stock based on different past periods sometimes diverge widely. The investor has no assurance that new factors may not drastically alter a stock's market price behavior; for example, discovery of the Timmins ore body in 1964 changed Texas Gulf Sulphur from a steady-priced dividend payer into a speculator's football. Beta is sometimes termed a measure of the *market risk* in common stocks. However, risk and variability are not identical concepts. A stock's market risk depends not only on its inherent price variability but also on where it is selling within its probable price range. Even low-beta stocks may entail large risks when bought at excessively high prices or at extravagant multiples of earnings.

It should be noted that beta measures only a stock's tendency to fluctuate with the market. Price swings contrary to the market can be measured, but other statistical devices such as the standard deviation are then employed. Such swings are broadly ascribed by beta enthusiasts to "nonmarket" influences. Finally, over long periods a stock may tend to rise or fall relative to stocks in general. The ratio of a stock's long-term rate of price change to that of the general market is called its *alpha*. Both beta and alpha coefficients may be based either on changes in market price alone or on changes in overall return: price fluctuations plus dividends and other distributions.

INVESTOR POLICY

Much of what has been said about market movements emphasizes the fact that it is more profitable to take advantage of them than to resist them. Even the careful selection of companies and industries cannot afford so much gain as relatively casual selections will if bought and sold at the right times. Of course, no sensible investor will make his selections casually, but he can add to careful selection some diligent effort to time his purchases and sales for profit.

Just what an investor should do about market timing is a hard-to-answer question. One possibility is to do nothing except to limit new commitments to times when market prices are reasonable and the outlook appears promising. A second possibility, somewhat more aggressive in nature, is to increase portfolio holdings of good stocks when market conditions appear promising, and to retire to the security of bonds, savings accounts, or United States Treasury bills when the outlook is adverse. A third and still more aggressive policy suggests the purchase of "dynamic" stocks—high-leverage or second-quality issues which fluctuate very widely in price—when the outlook is promising, and a shift to "defensive" securities—bonds and treasury bills—when conditions are uncertain. The pursuit of an aggressive policy would require the investor to study market and economic conditions and risk his future on his findings. This would be a sound decision if the investor could be sure that, with reasonable effort, he could be right.

But therein lies the rub. Economic affairs respond to so many stimuli that forecasts of coming events are little better than guesses. Despite time and money spent endlessly on the study of the subject, even the best-informed investors must depend chiefly on investment selection and diversification for preservation of their savings. Market studies are not dependable enough to serve as the major framework of investment policy.

BASES OF SELECTION AND TIMING

Investors or traders in securities must make two crucial decisions. They must select issues suitable to their particular objectives. Then they must time their purchases and sales effectively. In making these decisions, they may employ either valuation or forecasting approaches.

1   The valuation approach   Many investors analyze stocks in order to arrive at appraised values. A typical appraisal is made by estimating the expected net earnings per common share and multiplying this figure by a price-earnings ratio that reflects the company's anticipated stability, growth rate, dividend payout, and other features. The investor then buys a stock only if it is selling below its appraised value by some predetermined "margin of safety." Conversely, he sells a stock whenever it exceeds its appraised value by a certain percentage.

Applied with patience and common sense, the valuation approach offers the investor a good chance of getting his money's worth. It reduces his risk by confining his purchase to stocks that are selling at reasonable multiples of expected earning power and, ordinarily, near the lower limit of their price range in recent years. On this basis, an alert investor in 1970 might have bought American Home

Products around 55 or Texaco under 25. Even if these stocks had not advanced, the "margins of safety" implicit in these low purchase prices would almost certainly have protected him against serious loss.

Two difficulties, however, beset the buyer for value. First, even though stocks are acquired at sound prices, they may fail to advance, owing to adverse news, investor prejudice, or lack of fashionable appeal. In 1971, for example, the leading domestic oil companies offered reasonable values and good growth prospects, but investors shunned them in favor of greater "glamor" in drug or office equipment issues. Second, valuation standards are usually a less reliable indicator of when to sell than of when to buy. If a company's fortunes and popularity are on a major upswing, it is easy for the value-conscious investor to sell too soon. This is particularly true if his appraisals are based on an industry's or a company's past performance. Many investors, for example, found it plausible to sell American Home Products around 90 in early 1972 on the ground that it had far exceeded its old high and had become overpriced. In general, both authors of this book can testify from long personal experience that when to sell is almost always a much more difficult problem than when to buy.

2 Forecasting approaches Since market trends and underlying values often diverge for considerable periods, a valuation approach rarely meets the needs of the short-term trader. His foremost task is timing purchases and sales to fit the briefer swings of the market and of individual stocks. For guidance he may look to either fundamental or technical data.

In relying on *fundamental analysis*, the trader studies the trend of the economy; the background of particular industries; and the prospective sales, costs, and profit expectations of individual companies. If he can foresee developments that will affect stock prices with greater clarity than other traders, a superior timing of purchases and sales will bring him large profits.

By contrast, the advocate of *technical analysis* downgrades the importance of economic or business information available to the general public. By the time such facts and figures have been released, he believes, their effect on stock prices has already been discounted through the buying and selling of insiders and other "knowledgeable" traders. In his eyes, therefore, the stock market must serve as its own barometer. He is convinced that the underlying patterns of demand and supply, and the trader-investor psychology that shapes them, can be read in the movements, statistics, and character of the market itself.

Over the years, many theories, generalizations, and rules of thumb have developed, based on the interpretation of seemingly significant indicators. Although the logic which supports most of these doctrines is clear and sensible, none of them appears to be vital enough or dependable enough to serve as a market forecaster. Collectively, however, they serve as interesting but not infallible vehicles for market analysis. Among the better-known doctrines are:

1 Price-volume relation It is often said that a market movement accomplished on a large or rising volume of trading reflects the consensus of the whole market and is therefore substantial, unlikely to be retraced, and likely to continue in the same direction. If the market moves up or down on small or diminishing volume, the move is likely to be ephemeral because the majority of traders is not concurring.

2 Support and resistance points A support point, below the existing price, is one at which a decline in price is expected to encounter heavy buying. A resistance point is a price above the existing price at which an advance in price is likely to be "resisted" by heavy selling. Such points are said to exist both in single stocks and in the whole market as exemplified in the market averages. They are usually alleged to center about a convenient round-number price, or possibly at the extreme point at which a previous price rally or slump was turned back, because these would be logical points at which open orders would be concentrated. Stocks are considered to show strength by rising through resistance points or by holding their support prices; they are deemed weak if they turn back at resistance or break support.

3 Lines A line is a prolonged sidewise movement, that is, a lack of substantial rise or decline, which has continued for weeks or months. A line may occur either in the market averages or in a single stock. Since it is held that business conditions and the market outlook are constantly changing, the line simply marks a period of delay in adjusting the market to fundamental values. The longer the line continues, the more substantial will be the change when a breakout finally occurs. Needless to say, the line will consist of a series of small fluctuations; the breakout will consist of a significant rise or fall away from the "trading range" which constitutes the line.

4 Advances and declines The ratio of the number of stocks advancing in price to the number declining on any one day is rarely significant, but cumulative totals of advances and declines maintained over an interval of several days or weeks may connote important strength or weakness in the general market. If an excess of advances over declines widens, or an excess of declines over advances narrows, these movements in the cumulative totals would suggest that the market was getting stronger. Conversely, a widening of declines over advances, or a narrowing of advances over declines, would signify that the market was weakening.

5 New highs and lows When individual stocks reach new high or low prices for the year (or other significant periods), many traders believe they have overcome important resistance or support. Consequently, the average ratio of new highs to new lows over periods of several days to a few months is interpreted by many traders as a significant sign of market strength or weakness. Like the index of cumulative advances and declines, this ratio is often used by traders to see whether or not, under cover of strength in the market averages, a majority of stocks are beginning to change trend.

6   Leadership   The issues with the highest trading volume for the day, week, or month comprise the market leaders, and many traders attach great significance to the *quality* of this leadership. If during a market rise the most active stocks are high-priced, investment-grade issues, such "good" leadership is said to reflect substantial buying by important interests and to forecast continuing market strength. On the other hand, "poor" leadership by unseasoned, low-priced issues would signify speculation by the uninformed public and suggest that the rise was unstable and likely short-lived. Similarly, a decline headed by good leadership would indicate liquidation by large investors and prolonged market weakness and poor leadership on a decline would suggest emotional selling by frightened or overextended speculators that would soon run its course.

7   Breadth of market   Many traders feel that stock market movements which are participated in by many stocks are more significant than those which represent only a part of the market. They therefore watch the daily reports of the number of issues which were traded on the New York Stock Exchange, and the numbers of these which rose, declined, or remained unchanged in price. An advancing market in which half or more of the traded issues advance each day is regarded as a strong market.

8   Reaction to news   The market's reaction to announced news is often regarded as a sign of underlying strength or weakness. According to this doctrine, a strong market will advance on good news and resist selling on bad news. A weak market will break on bad news and fail to rally on good news. This would be true if news were always news, but if special groups already know or have correctly guessed what will be announced, then stock prices may already have moved in anticipation of the announcement. In this case, knowledgeable traders who bought early may take their profits by "selling when the good news is out," causing the market to drop; or when bad news is forthcoming, they may buy in previously established short positions, causing the market to rise. Bad news that no one can foresee or discount—such as the Israeli–Egyptian war in 1967—will always drop the market as surprised traders sell out and stand aside until the situation clears. Overall, the market's reaction to news does not appear to be a reliable indicator of its future movement.

9   Demand-supply pressure   This approach recognizes that demand and supply make price, and that a correct indication of impending demand-and-supply pressures will provide an indication of probable future prices. There are many indicators available. New issues brought to market, secondaries, and the volume of trading itself are clues to supply; the state of the money market, the amount of customer indebtedness on margin accounts, the amount of customers' free cash balances in brokerage accounts, and the income levels being enjoyed by professional men and entrepreneurs, bear on the probable demand; and the trend of the market itself with reference to some of these demand-and-supply factors provides a measure of their current effectiveness. A few market advisory services attempt to measure the strength of supply and demand directly by plotting the daily share-volume in stocks that decline against daily volume in those that rise. Typically, the volume in each direction is weighted with the average price change in that direction; the weighted upside and downside volumes over a given period are cumulated, and conclusions about the relative strength of supply and demand forces are drawn by comparing these totals. Measuring demand-and-supply pressures on the market requires the synthesizing of a number of these factors plus a great deal of guesswork; probably the results are not too reliable because of the unavoidable omission of many more factors which are equally relevant but not easy to measure.

10 Weak and strong hands This variant of the "public is always wrong" idea asserts that the market's outlook is improved when stock passes "from weak to strong hands." This line of argument suggests that many stockholders are not courageous enough or financially able to hold their stock when conditions are adverse, but that financial institutions and large stockholders can do so. Consequently, evidences of institutional buying, of the liquidation of margin accounts, and of odd-lot sales in excess of purchases are all welcomed as signs that stock is drifting into strong hands which will not offer it for resale. The weak-and-strong-hands analysis is applied either to single stocks or to the whole market.

11 Theory of contrary opinion This theory argues that not only individual stockholders, but securities dealers, institutional portfolio managers, and investment advisers as well, become excessively optimistic when conditions are good and excessively pessimistic when conditions are bad. Therefore sales should be made when optimism is highest and purchases made in times of deepest gloom. There is doubtless much truth in this logic, but its application poses difficulties. How can one be sure that today's optimism will not be followed by a more optimistic tomorrow, or that today's gloom will not be followed by a much darker tomorrow? There have been many highly optimistic periods during the long market rise between 1949 and 1972, and no periods of truly deep gloom; should one have sold out in bright 1950 and never bought in again?

12   Odd-lot index   It is widely believed that odd-lot traders are always wrong at major turns in the market, and that the market is due to fall when odd-lot purchases greatly exceed odd-lot sales, and vice versa. It is argued that odd-lot stockholders are an unsophisticated group who are likely to become interested in stocks after a market rise or at the top of a bull market, and to become disillusioned and inclined to sell after a period of adversity when stocks are low. They are also more likely to have money to invest during boom-time conditions when stocks are high, and to need to sell stocks to raise money when conditions are bad and stocks are cheap. This reasoning, buttressed by many statistical tests, has given rise to the cynical rule of thumb just noted, and to a well-known market advisory service which relies heavily on the idea. There is doubtless some truth in the approach, especially when it is given a proper setting as part of a comprehensive market analysis; but as a single and separate indicator of market performance, it is discredited by numerous exceptions: for example, odd-lot investors bought more shares than they sold at the market lows of 1970, a time when large institutions were predominantly sellers.

13   The short interest   Although short selling is severely limited by regulations imposed under the Securities Exchange Act of 1934, it is still possible for short sellers to take substantial short positions in buoyant stocks. Although short selling undoubtedly adds to the offers and tends to restrain price while short sales are being made, the existence of a larger-than-average short position in any stock is a clear indication that these accounts must become purchasers within a reasonable time. In order to indicate the possible impact of short covering on prices, market analysts compute the *short interest ratio*, which is the ratio of the outstanding short interest in the stock in question to the most recent month's average daily sales volume. A short interest exceeding 1.5 days' trading on the market as a whole or 2 days' trading in a single stock is considered mildly significant. The New York and American Stock Exchanges report the outstanding short interest in their listed stocks as of the fifteenth day of each month.

14   Tax selling, tax-payment dates, long-term points   These are three income tax factors which bear significantly on market behavior. When a stockholder holds a stock in which he has a substantial unrealized loss, he may be able to save on the current year's income taxes by selling the depreciated stock, thus recording a deductible loss. If he reinvests in another stock, or in the same stock after a lapse of 31 days, he will have been a net seller and a contributor to market weakness for a period of time, at least. Tax selling occurs in considerable volume after any general market decline and in specific stocks after declines in those stocks, and is likely to concentrate in November and early December as people begin to foresee the end of the income tax year. Late December is most often dominated by reinvestment purchases, and is thus typically buoyant rather than depressed.

Tax selling may not occur except in isolated stocks in a year when the fourth-quarter markets are buoyant for other reasons, and it may on occasion be offset by buying orders from disappointed short sellers who are taking tax losses on short positions. This happened, for example, in 1971. In that year many people sold short in the summer and fall, expecting that the dollar's troubles abroad would bring still lower stock prices in late 1971 or early 1972. However, a world currency agreement was reached in November, the stock market rose, and in December seasonal tax selling was replaced by seasonal short covering (buying).

The federal personal income tax payment dates are January 15, April 15, June 15, and September 15. On these dates, and especially on April 15, individual taxpayers are deprived of enormous amounts of money. It is said that the buying demand for stocks is affected by this, especially between March 15 and May 1.

Long-term points are the dates when stock or bond holdings have been held for 6 months and thus become long-term for income tax purposes. Reportedly, much of the buying demand at the bottom of stock market declines — for example, in August and November, 1971 — is professional and speculative, with quick profits in mind. If the market subsequently rises, the speculators have great incentive to hold their positions for 6 months in order that their profits be taxed as long-term gains. After the 6-month point, the market is thus vulnerable to profit-taking sales in considerable volume. Although this line of reasoning is often discussed, clear examples are hard to find except in a few cases of individual stocks and in some large issues of government bonds. Because a new issue of government bonds is huge in quantity and is usually offered at a mildly attractive price in order to stimulate sales, large blocks are purchased by investing institutions and individuals with ultimate resale in mind. These holdings are often resold after they become long term, and the term-point date may be followed by enough selling offers to have a mild effect on the price.

15 Seasonal strength or weakness Stock market literature is replete with references to the "traditional August rally," the "January reinvestment demand," and similar terms. Studies of changes in the major market indexes show that certain months have shown gains in most years, and other months have shown declines in a majority of years. However, these seasonal tendencies are small, amounting to less than 2 per cent for the month in most cases, and they are thus small enough to be overcome by other market factors and too small to make it profitable for speculators to exploit them. Explanations for this slight seasonal pattern are not hard to find. Seasonal reinvestment demand in January and July is financed by bond maturities at the ends of half-years; by savings-account money available at the ends of interest periods, by pension-fund money deposited with trustees, and by similar sources; August is strong because new securities issues are seasonally not plentiful; November and April are weak because of tax factors; and others could be cited.

It is likely that periods of seasonal strength or weakness offer advantages to small-scale investors who would be making transactions at such times anyway. It is especially likely that certain individual stocks—for example, one being depressed in November by tax selling *because it is already at a low level* at which many holders have losses in it—may be opportunely priced.

16 Mutual-fund position The net sale or redemption of mutual-fund shares, reported monthly by the Investment Company Institute, measures the flow of new cash to closed-end investment companies, which in 1970 accounted for an estimated 13 per cent of New York Stock Exchange volume.[4] The ratio of mutual funds' cash to total assets indicates the liquidity of their portfolios and is reported at quarterly intervals by the Securities and Exchange Commission. A large excess of fund share sales over share redemptions, or a cash ratio approaching 10 per cent, suggests that the funds will be substantial purchasers of stock, since, rather clearly, investors do not expect them to sit with idle cash. Conversely, an excess of share redemptions or an uncomfortably low cash ratio of say 5 per cent suggests that the funds may need to liquidate stocks.

17 Other "technical" doctrines A few other rules of thumb for market forecasting may be cited briefly without comment. Since the American Stock Exchange is generally considered to list a higher proportion of speculative issues than the New York Stock Exchange, increased volume on the ASE relative to the NYSE may suggest that the overall stock market is becoming more speculative and fundamentally weaker. Some observers believe that when American Exchange volume reaches 40 per cent or more of New York Exchange volume, a major decline in stock prices will soon follow. Other oft-cited indicators of coming stock market weakness include a rising number of secondary offerings, a heavy predominance of stock sales over purchases by corporate insiders (officers, directors, and very large stockholders), large-volume trading in low-priced stocks, and feverish activity and rapid price rises in the market for new stock issues.

CHARTING

Line and vertical-bar diagrams on either arithmetic or semi-logarithmic scales are widely used by all types of investors and speculators. They can depict the trends of earnings, dividends, stock prices, short interest, or any other factor capable of numerical expression.

[4]Computed from the Exchange's 1971 *Fact Book*, p. 53 as follows: Institutions contributed 56 per cent of the year's publicly originated share volume, and mutual-fund trading constituted 23 per cent of this.

But the stock market also serves a special cult of enthusiasts known as "chartists." A chartist is an individual who believes that hour-by-hour or day-by-day movements of stock prices on a chart will produce graphic configurations which are reliably followed by predictable market price changes. Dozens of these "chart formations"—double tops, triple tops, triangles, head-and-shoulders—are identified by their various enthusiasts and used as the basis for predicting price movements in either individual stocks or the whole market. Sometimes the alleged predictive values of the formations are established empirically by repeated observation, and sometimes they are developed logically by analysis of the market situations they depict. In either instance the chartists purport to use the market's own behavior as the predictive device, instead of relying on interpretations of a multitude of causal forces such as earnings, dividends, and the technical factors discussed in the preceding section.

In general, the chartists are a group apart. The securities analysts who devote themselves to the "fundamentals" of earnings, dividends, money supply, and general economic forces are inclined to see the believing chartist as a sort of voodoo-worshiper who can harm no one but himself, while the chartist sees the fundamentalist as one who is too conventional to accept a good thing in a new form. There is quite possibly some truth in each creed; certainly there are many individuals who resort to both forms of analysis.

THE STOCK MARKET—A RANDOM WALK?

Some academic authorities have questioned whether chartist or technical methods have *any* value in predicting stock prices. These writers cite mathematical studies which show that successive price changes in individual stocks are statistically independent; thus stock price fluctuations form a "random walk" similar to the aimless steps of a blind-drunk vagrant. It this is so, then past price movements are useless in predicting a stock's future swings; the in-and-out trader who uses charts or other technical methods cannot hope to do better in the long run than the investor who simply buys and hold good stocks. Random-walk partisans buttress this argument by citing computer-based simulation studies which show that mechanical trading rules based on stock price moves yield generally lower profits than buying and holding the stock used in the tests.[5] The random-walk

[5]Rules used in these simulation tests may be of interest to investors since they apply well-known principles used by stock traders long before the computer era. First, moving averages of various lengths were tested, the computer being instructed to buy if the stock price rose above its average price over the past X weeks or months; to sell, if the price fell below the moving average. Second, "filters" (or per cent reversal rules) were utilized, for example, telling the computer to buy the stock only after it had risen, say 10 per cent from some previous low price, to sell it if it fell 10 per cent from some previous high. In general, tests of moving averages ranging in length from 3 days to 2 years, and of filters ranging from 1 to 25 per cent, have shown these rules to yield lower profits in level or rising markets than a "naïve" investment policy or buying and holding the same stocks. The tendency of mechanical rules to yield better profits than buy-and-hold investing on declining markets still does not overturn the random-walk hypothesis, since the trend of stock prices is predominantly upward through time.

theorists do not deny that better knowledge, greater ability to assess fundamentals, or superior access to news may bring the trader better-than-average results. In fact, an important part of their theory holds that the stock market is an "efficient" market in which new information is digested so quickly that stock prices as a rule are accurate estimates of intrinsic values.

Although debate continues, so far traders, investors, and security analysts have overwhelmingly rejected the random-walk hypothesis. Most professionals remain convinced that stocks do move up and down in consistent trends, difficult though such trends may be to forecast. Furthermore, many erratic moves that take place in stock prices do not appear consistent with an "efficient" market in the sense claimed by the random-walk theory. In 1961–1962, for example, IBM stock rose from 387 to 607, then fell abruptly to 300 despite an uninterrupted rise in the company's sales and earnings. To say that IBM's *intrinsic* value changed this much seems nonsense. A simpler and more plausible explanation for this price move—and others even more extravagant—is excessive speculation and its subsequent collapse.

THE 1967–1972 STOCK MARKET

Unsteadying forces gripped the stock markets in the years 1967–1972. Externally, war boom and inflation and a prolonged tight-money ordeal were followed by the first business recession since 1961. Along with price controls, dollar devaluation, and a delayed business recovery, these influences produced wide swings in investor sentiment and common stock prices. Net purchase or sale of United States stocks by foreigners increasingly affected the supply-demand balance in the nation's stock markets and fluctuated in considerable degree with both the country's business outlook and the dollar's wavering fortunes. Measured by the Dow-Jones Industrial Average, investment-grade stocks proved barely able to surpass their record high prices of 1966, while stock price declines between 1968 and 1970 were the largest, percentagewise, since the 1930s.

Internal changes also foreshadowed less stable markets. Financial institutions and block-trading continued to displace the small investor and the 100-share transaction as dominant forces in the daily turnover. By 1970, mutual funds, bank trust departments, pension and profit-sharing trusts, college and university endowment funds, insurance companies, and other large-scale buyers and sellers accounted for almost 60 per cent of the New York Stock Exchange's publicly originated volume; single transactions of 10,000 or more shares comprised more than 15 per cent of the year's turnover. This growing concentration of market power in fewer and larger hands brought occasional warnings that future markets might prove less liquid for lack of widespread small-buyer support. Goaded by mounting competition to attract funds, many institutions sought larger market profits in more venturesome trading methods. They concentrated their portfolios in fewer and ostensibly more promising issues, bought and sold at quicker intervals, and "ganged up" both in buying popular stocks and in selling unpopular ones; active stocks with thin capitalizations or small floating supplies might rise or fall 10 per cent in a single day. Even in broad markets, bad news sometimes forced trading in particular issues to be halted altogether. High-quality stocks showed unjustifiable weakness during the 1969–1970 bear market, suggesting that institutions, forced to raise cash, were obliged to sell their better stocks because second-grade holdings had become unsalable in appreciable amounts. In strong markets such as that of 1972, the institutionally favored growth and glamour stocks soared in excited trading while traditional industrial and utility issues did little or nothing—a contrast which led brokers and investment advisers to speak of there really being "two stock markets."

The spreading influence of institutions and professional portfolio managers brought revolutionary experiments in investment thinking and techniques. Avowed efforts were mounted to make investing more "scientific." Brokerage firms and leading institutions spent heavily on researching answers to prevailing issues: how risks and returns from stocks should be measured, whether larger returns could be obtained by accepting larger risks, how "performance" should be measured and/or adjusted for the risks taken, and how consistent the price gains in a stock were likely to be from one time period to the next. Portfolio management became increasingly mechanized and geared to quick decisions. The nanosecond speed and vast memory capacity of electronic computers were programmed to assist—or even replace—decision making by human portfolio managers or brokerage-house advisers. Among other uses, computers were employed to comb markets for undervalued issues, to calculate the money outlays or share volume needed to lift a stock's price, to detect accumulation and distribution patterns in particular stocks, and to test the effectiveness of different trading methods through machine simulations using historical market prices. In Wall Street, computer-trained analysts rose rapidly in price, even when their recommended issues failed to follow suit. There seemed little doubt that the institutional investors' horizon—the time they looked ahead for market results—was tending to shorten, and that this accounted in part for the increasingly "hairtrigger" tendency of many stocks to leap or collapse. Whether the new emphasis on scientific method and mathematic analysis was really bringing improved foresight or keener judgment to the investment process was, as experienced investors might have predicted, a moot question as 1973 began.

TRADING THE MARKET

Theoretically, the trader in stocks can earn larger profits than an investor. He can enlarge his profits by doing three things: (1) buying and selling during the market's shorter swings; (2) shifting from one stock or group of stocks to another to "get where the action is"; and (3) selling short to profit from price declines. A trader may deal in either conservative securities or risky ones. Some astute professionals confine their trading to high-grade bonds, which frequently show worthwhile fluctuations. The annual price swings on the blue-chip stocks found in the Dow-Jones Industrial Average are ordinarily large enough to yield handsome profits to the trader who buys them near the year's low and sells them near its high. Venturesome traders, willing to accept larger risks, prefer issues with wider price swings: glamor stocks, growth stocks selling at high price-earnings ratios, "feast or famine" cyclical issues, highly leveraged stocks, equities in new companies, and stocks with a small number of outstanding shares and, consequently, a "thin" market.

In practice, a majority of stock traders either lose money or wind up making considerably less than they could have made as investors. Common sense would predict such a result, for if stock market speculation could be reduced to a systematic science, brokers, investment advisers, and others close to the market would retire early with comfortable fortunes instead of working on to age 65, as most of them are obliged to do. Successful trading not only requires great skill in selecting and timing purchases and sales; it also calls for unusual degrees of patience, emotional stability, and self-discipline in the trader's personal makeup. The authors, in their combined experience, have known only a few traders whose profits over the years have approached what these same people could have earned with less effort as long-term investors. These men and women have varied widely in occupation, background, age, and education, yet their trading habits showed something of a common pattern. All were willing to spend many hours each week studying the market and individual securities. Whether buying for a rise or selling short, they selected their stocks carefully. They refrained from buying or selling until they were sure the market was moving their way. They abandoned a position quickly if their judgment was wrong; often they took a whole series of small losses. However, if they were right, they resisted the temptation to settle for a small gain; they held their position and let their profits run.

The precepts implied by the preceding paragraph are those which most stock market writers accept as key rules for successful trading. However, these principles are easier to grasp in theory than to apply in practice, and the strain of uncertainty on the trader's nerves and emotions will lead inevitably to some wrong judgments. The amateur who aspires to trade must also recognize that he is pitting himself against full-time professionals, fund managers, corporate insiders, and other experts who are looking for the same opportunities. The presence of professional competitors does not guarantee that the amateur trader will fail, but it substantially raises the odds against his success.

FORMULA PLANS

Because forecasts are uncertain, a number of investment managers in the period 1935–1950 attempted to develop *formulas* which would automatically manage an investment portfolio by limiting or reducing stock holdings in high markets and buying stocks in low markets. The stocks for purchase or sale were to be carefully chosen, but the timing and quantities of the transactions were to be established by logical, unemotional formulas. Most formula plans were developed under the assumption that stock market fluctuations would continue to be substantial but that permanent up or down trends would be moderate. Consequently, the plans were designed to profit from fluctuations, and in most instances were not designed to perform well in a prolonged market rise such as that of 1949–1972. A considerable number of formulas were developed, but only one — dollar-cost averaging — has had appreciable use in recent years.[6]

Dollar-cost averaging Dollar-cost averaging is a very simple system intended to make sure that the stock investor who is accumulating stocks out of income will buy them at less than the average market price. First, the prospective investor chooses a definite dollar sum which he proposes to invest in common stocks at regular periodic intervals, possibly every 3 or 6 months. Excess savings go into a bank account or bonds, to make sure that the budgeted stock investment will be available each time as planned. Second, the periodic stock investment may always be made in the same stock, or, alternatively, in whatever stock seems most attractive at the time. Instead of choosing individual stocks, the investor might "buy the whole market" by investing his periodic installments in investment company stocks. Third, switches from one stock to another more promisingly situated can be made at any time.

Over a long period, this system assures that the investor will buy his stocks at a very favorable average price unless the chooses poorly or unless the market trends down continuously. Consider, for example, what happens if the market in the long run proves cyclical, trending neither up nor down, and if the investor buys average stocks. If he invests $300 quarterly, each market "cycle" might give him two investments (one on the way up, one on the way down) at an average price, say $10 per share; perhaps another two at high prices, say $15 per share; and another two at low prices, say $5 per share. At $10, he would buy 30 shares on each purchase, or 60 shares in all. At $15, he would buy 20 shares twice, or 40 shares in all. At $5, he would buy 60 shares twice, or 120 shares in all. His total cost would be 6 times $300, or $1,800; his purchases would total 220 shares; and his average cost would be $8.18 per share, or $1.82 below the average price. The mathematical legerdemain here stems from the fact that the constant sum buys more shares at low prices than at high ones. This holds down the average cost per share.

Dollar-cost averaging is a more sensible plan than that followed by most people, if pursued over a long period of years, for it will prevent the bulk of the

---

[6]For further descriptive details concerning other types of formula plans, see the fifth and earlier editions of this book, Chap. 10.

investments being made in high markets. It is not fantastically profitable—the 18 per cent saving in the example is much too large to be typical and would be the product of a several-year period, not a single year—but even a small gain is better than a loss. The plan does not guarantee against poor choices of investments, and it cannot prevent a long downtrend in the market, but it does not cause these things either. Dollar-cost averaging will of course be unprofitable if the low-cost investments in the depression years are not made, but its average investment budget is the best possible guarantee that the money will be available to make the low-cost purchases.

Many investment companies will sell their shares on periodic investment plans designed to make use of dollar-cost averaging. The stock exchange plans for monthly or quarterly investment in a single stock, or in rotation among several stocks, are similarly designed.

QUESTIONS AND PROBLEMS

1 Would a good-grade common stock fluctuate in price as much as the Dow-Jones Industrial Average? Why? How much does the Average vary during a 10-year period?

2 What elements contribute to the demand for stocks? To the supply?

3 Why do most stocks participate in a primary market upswing or decline? Why are there significant differences in the extent to which stocks participate, in any particular case?

4 Assuming that the market doctrine associated with the theory of contrary opinion had validity in the past, does it appear likely to be valid in markets dominated by institutional investors and professionally trained portfolio managers?

5 What are the basic causes of primary stock market movements? Is it possible for a business boom to proceed while the stock market remains unchanged? Why?

6 Would it be reasonable for an investor to try to avoid purchases at secondary highs or sales in secondary troughs? How?

7 Could the Dow theory possibly work out in a period in which business news and prospects are chiefly concerned with political policies and wars? Would it be sound to follow Dow theory "signals" which call for the buying of stocks only when the market seems generally undervalued and those calling for selling only when stocks seem overvalued?

8 Is it wise to buy stocks which seem to be definite bargains at a time when the general market appears to be weak?

9 Would you recommend that an individual who believes business conditions to be deteriorating should sell all his stocks or merely shift from dynamic to defensive types?

10 Explain tax selling. Why is early December often a bargain season for stock investors?

11 If you want to try dollar-cost averaging, how would you select your stocks? Would commissions and odd-lot differentials obliterate any possible gain? Would you buy dynamic stocks in low markets and defensive ones in high markets?

12 How large are the short-term risks in secondary stocks selling at high multiples of earnings? Investigate 1972 price declines in Levitz Furniture, Wang Laboratories, New Process, and Handleman Company. Why did these stocks rise to high price-earnings ratios? What accounted for their rapid price declines?

13 Why should the average person expect to do better as a long-term investor than as an in-an-out trader?

14 Can computers be programmed to make investment judgments and decisions as well as to process data concerning possible investments? How would you distinguish between a decision, a rule, and a judgment?

15 If the rapid growth of a company seems assured, can the investor ever pay too much for its stock? Won't growth eventually justify whatever price the investor must pay now?

16 Does it seem that stock market fluctuations are dominated more by the values involved or by speculators' attempts to sell and buy when they think market movements down or up are impending? Are there other important market influences?

17 Should laws be enacted limiting the amount and frequency of stock purchases and sales by the large trading funds? Why, or why not?

18 Do you believe that the individual investor's participation is important to stock market liquidity? Can liquidity be preserved if individual investors quit the market in large numbers?

REFERENCES

Badger, Ralph E., and Paul B. Coffman: *Investment Analysis*, McGraw-Hill Book Company, New York, 1967, Chaps. 10–13.

Cohen, Jerome B., and Edward D. Zinbarg: *Investment Analysis and Portfolio Management*, rev. ed., Richard D. Irwin, Inc., Homewood, Ill., 1973, Chaps. 12, 13.

Cooke, Gilbert W.: *The Stock Markets*, rev. ed., Schenkman Publishing Co., Inc., Cambridge, Mass., 1969, Chaps. 7–9.

Cootner, Paul H. (ed.): *The Random Character of Stock Prices*, The M.I.T. Press, Cambridge, Mass., 1964.

Drew, Garfield A.: *New Methods for Profit in the Stock Market*, 4th ed., Fraser Publishing Company, Wells, Vt., 1966.

Edwards, Robert D., and John Magee: *Technical Analysis of Stock Trends*, John Magee, Springfield, Mass., 1957.

Eiteman, Wilford, J., Charles A. Dice, and David K. Eiteman: *The Stock Market*, 4th ed., McGraw-Hill Book Company, New York, 1966, Chaps. 19–23.

Elton, Edwin J., and Martin J. Gruber: *Security Evaluation and Portfolio Analysis*, Prentice-Hall, Inc., Englewood Cliffs, N.J., 1971, Part 1.

Friend, Irwin, Marshall Blume, and Jean Crocket: *Mutual Funds and Other Institutional Investors*, McGraw-Hill Book Company, New York, 1971.

Goodman, George J. W. ("Adam Smith"): *The Money Game*, Random House, Inc., New York, 1968.

Granville, Joseph E.: *New Key to Stock Market Profits*, Prentice-Hall, Inc., Englewood, Cliffs, N.J., 1963.

Keynes, John M.: *The General Theory of Employment Interest and Money*, Harcourt, Brace & World, Inc., New York, 1936, Chap. 12.

Krow, Harvey A.: *Stock Market Behavior*, Random House, Inc., New York, 1969.

Latané, Henry A., and Donald L. Tuttle: *Security Analysis and Portfolio Management*, The Ronald Press Company, New York, 1970, Chaps. 14, 20.

Leffler, George L., and Loring G. Farwell: *The Stock Market*, The Ronald Press Company, New York, 1963, Chaps. 29–35.

Lishan, John M., and David T. Crary: *The Investment Process*, paperback ed., International Textbook Company, Scranton, Pa., 1970, Part 3.

O'Connor, William P., Jr.: *Techniques for Maximum Market Profits*, Prentice-Hall, Inc., Englewood Cliffs, N.J., 1964.

Robbins, Sidney M.: *The Securities Markets: Operations and Issues*, The Free Press of Glencoe, Inc., New York, 1966, Chap. 2.

Securities and Exchange Commission: *Institutional Investor Study Report*, Washington, 1971.

Tomlinson, Lucile: *Practical Formulas for Successful Investing*, Wilfred Funk, Inc., Publishers, New York, 1953.

Vaughn, Donald E.: *Survey of Investments*, Holt, Rinehart and Winston, Inc., New York, 1967, Part 4.

Widicus, Wilbur W., and Thomas E. Stitzel: *Personal Investing*, Richard D. Irwin, Inc., Homewood, Ill., 1971, Chap. 13.

Willet, Edward R: *Fundamentals of Securities Markets*, Appleton-Century-Crofts, Inc., New York, 1971.

11

INVESTMENT INFORMATION
AND ADVICE

Probably no other industry or type of business is as abundantly supplied with trade literature and reference materials as the securities business. Periodicals, books, and special reports by experts are available on every hand. The quantity and quality of the available information are almost incredible to newcomers in the business. It is not possible to say that any reasonable question about any prof-fered security can be answered, but it is possible to say that adequate information can be had on so many topics that there is no reason to invest where reasonable questions remain unanswered. It does not follow, of course, that an amateur in-vestor or a careless one can obtain information which will guard him from loss, for even an experienced and diligent man must expect some error in a field where every transaction involves a forecast of the future. But the diligent amateur can, with the assistance of a modicum of professional help and knowledge, make very practical use of most of these materials.

For those who do not care to undertake the study which sound securities in-vesting requires, there are several varieties of professional investment counsel which may be obtained. Much free advice can be had from brokers and dealers, both on securities selections and on personal portfolio problems. There are also commercial advisory publications which undertake to report the results of their staffs' analytical work in condensed form to their clients. For clients who prefer personal consultations, professional investment advisers and bank trust depart-ments offer consulting or investment management services for a fee. Since all these types of services are varied and combined in many forms, an investor has a wide choice of services available to his needs.

Because there is no clear line of demarcation between the purveyors of invest-ment information and the investment advisers who sell their clients a service of investment analysis and advice, this chapter will present the two functions as related and overlapping, as indeed they are.

TYPES OF INFORMATION

The information available to investors falls readily into two classifications, that dealing with general economics, market behavior, and industries, and that dealing with specific corporations and public debtors and specific securities. The investor must be interested in both types. If he holds Certain-Teed Products Corporation convertible preferred stock, he is interested in general prosperity, the trend of commodity prices, the market for convertible preferred stocks, and the outlook for the building and construction industries; but he must also watch Certain-Teed's profit progress, working capital position, dividend policy, and the position of its preferred and common stocks.

The sources of investment information used may also be divided into two groups, according to their reporting practices; one group presents facts as dispassionately as possible, leaving all interpretation to the investor, while the other presents an analysis which offers interpretations and conclusions. Uncolored facts are demanded by an analyst who is seeking specific information or testing a hypothesis of his own, but most investors like to read arguments and opinions which they can then accept or reject. After all, it is easier to review the conclusions of others than to formulate one's own. Also, the editors of an analytical report can be expected to call attention to the most important factors in the situation, thus assisting the reader to make his own decision.

Decisions by individual investors or their investment advisers will still be necessary, however. The editors of investment literature are not so infallible that their advice can be followed without hesitation. In fact, they often do not agree with one another; two leading advisory services recently published lists of the 50-odd stocks they rated the best buys chosen from the same 3,600 stocks. Only six stocks appeared on both lists. Very few of the selections favored by one service were given low ratings by the other, but the divergences are nevertheless significant. Investors must also base their choices to a considerable extent on their own needs for stability of income, quality standards, diversification in certain industries or areas, and other matters of which the editor of an advisory publication can have no knowledge.

SOURCES OF INFORMATION AND ADVICE

Investors in securities obtain information and advice from a great variety of sources. However, it seems desirable to classify these sources for brief review into seven groups and to discuss each in turn. The first group consists of the publications of the two large financial publishers, Standard & Poor's Corporation and Moody's Investors Service. These firms sell a number of informational and advisory publications, most of which are quite expensive. Many investors subscribe to them, but most people use them without cost in brokerage offices or public libraries. The second important group of sources consists of a number of investment advisory publications which offer printed investment advice in condensed form, based on extensive analytical work, for a rather high annual subscription price. A third group of sources provides help through personal consultation and counsel, rather than advice in printed columns; the service may be free or it may cost a fee; it is provided by brokers, banks, attorneys, accountants, and professional investment counselors. The other important source groups, which will be discussed in detail later, are (4) newspapers and periodicals; (5) annual reports and prospectuses; (6) literature provided by brokers and dealers; and (7) certain specialized sources and reference works.

Standard & Poor's corporation   Standard & Poor's Corporation, one of the leading financial publishing firms, offers 16 major financial reporting services and several minor ones. Subscribers include securities firms, banks, insurance companies, corporations, libraries, and private investors, among others. Since the services are sold separately and overlap to some extent, few subscribers buy them all. The major services are quite expensive, ranging up to $590 per year for *Corporation Records*, which is the basic informational service published by S & P.

   Corporation Records consists of six large loose-leaf manuals in which descriptions of all important corporate and many public issuers of both listed and unlisted securities are maintained. Each description is revised annually, and later information is added by a monthly supplement and a daily supplement which are indexed separately. The *Corporation Records* coverage is very broad. On the smaller concerns, the material presented is somewhat sketchy, but very comprehensive descriptions of important concerns are offered. They include the firm's address, state of incorporation, officers and directors, business history, property and business, important provisions of articles and bylaws, bond indenture provisions, comparative financial statements, financial ratios and per share figures, and market price history of each issue. The descriptions in the *Corporation Records* are completely factual and without editorial comment of any kind, except that most of the bonds are given a quality rating.

   The next most extensive S & P services are the *New York Stock Exchange Reports*, the *Over-the-counter Stock Reports*, and the *American Exchange Stock Reports*. Each of these services consists of a set of advisory reports on more than 1,000 important securities. The individual reports are revised two to four times annually, to keep them up to date. Each report is on two sides of a single page and consists of certain statistical data on sales, earnings, dividends, market history, and financial position, coupled with a description of the company, its business, and, for New York Stock Exchange (NYSE) companies, its prospects and an appraisal of the market outlook for the issue. The stock report is a candid editorial opinion throughout and includes a summary comment on the stock's attractiveness at the current market price relative to other stock prices.

   Another major S & P service, and one of paramount significance to careful investors, is the *Trade and Securities Service*. It consists of three loose-leaf volumes, one of which is given over to business and financial statistics, including a fine collection of securities price and yield indexes. The other two volumes—sometimes sold separately as the *Industry Surveys*—contain treatises on the history, status, and prospects of 46 important industries—steel, petroleum, chain stores, banking, insurance, and the like. These industry descriptions are designed to acquaint the investor, in 15 to 30 concise pages, with the important features of each industry which make for stability, profitableness, and growth. These factors are then reviewed in appraising the current outlook for the industry. The presentations include brief comments and comparisons of the leading companies in each industry and are critical and advisory throughout. The loose-leaf sections are frequently revised to keep them up to date.

Other S & P services include *The Outlook*, a weekly market letter or bulletin which serves as an investment advisory service. It carries articles on market behavior, the outlook for various industries, important individual issues, lists of securities on which purchase or sale is recommended, and suggested groups of stocks and bonds which are deemed suitable as complete portfolios. The *Outlook*, at $87 per year, is much less costly than S & P's major services and is intended for individual investors. S & P also compiles monthly a *Stock Guide* and a *Bond Guide*, which are 150- to 200-page books in which all important corporation securities are listed. The books show earnings, dividend, yield, capital structure, working capital, and market price data; and they rate stocks as to attractiveness for purchase and bonds as to quality and eligibility. These books may be purchased on subscription but are often distributed free to customers by brokers and dealers. S & P has several other publications which are bought chiefly by brokers and dealers. In addition, it offers a personalized service in planning and supervising portfolios for both individuals and institutions.

Moody's investors service   The principal Moody published service consists of three parts: the big reference manuals, the manual supplements, and the stock and bond surveys. The manuals are six large bound books of 1,500 to 3,500 pages each, one on listed industrials, one on over-the-counter industrials, one on utilities, one on transportation companies, one on governments (all public issuers), and one on financial (bank, insurance company, investment company, real estate company and real estate investment trust) issuers. They are published annually and contain analytical descriptions and histories of all important issuers, covering business, properties, financial statements, securities, earnings, dividends, and securities prices. In addition, each manual has a special features section which includes valuable summaries of industry history, legislation, standard financial ratios, and other material. The manuals are completely factual and nonadvisory except that most bonds are given a quality rating and an opinion is expressed as to their eligibility for institutional investment. Each manual is brought up to date twice weekly [weekly for over-the-counter (OTC) industrials] by an accompanying manual supplement, which is a loose-leaf volume containing factual information subsequent to the date of the manual.

Moody ventures into the printed opinion and advisory field in two loose-leaf volumes entitled *Moody's Stock Survey* and *Moody's Bond Survey*. Each volume addresses itself in weekly releases to general business and securities market conditions and predictions concerning them. Additional articles discuss the problems and prospects of individual industries and express opinions concerning specific corporations and their securities. Lists of recommended securites are included, and suggestions for switches from one stock or bond to another are commonly made. New securities offerings and recapitalization proposals are discussed, the securities are appraised as to quality, and suggestions as to purchase or rejection are made. On the whole, the Moody opinions give the impression of a relatively conservative editorial outlook which places great emphasis on quality and growth.

Moody's also publishes a twice-weekly *Dividend Record* containing information on declared dividends and dividend meeting dates; a quarterly *Handbook of Common Stocks* which gives statistics and price graphs on nearly 2,500 stocks; and a monthly *Bond Record* giving interest dates, call prices, yields to maturity, price ranges, ratings, and other data on more than 19,000 bond issues.

Moody's is also one of the major rating agencies for corporate and municipal bonds and for commercial paper, rating both outstanding debt and new issues prior to placement.

Other published services   Investors are offered other publications and services almost too numerous to mention. Most of them have merit, though some are apparently based on theories of stock market performance which are almost as fantastic as the economic panaceas which were so common a few years ago. These services can be roughly classified into four groups: First, there are several whose main contribution is to chart the price history of selected stocks, usually comparing price with dividends, earnings, other stocks in the same industry, and certain market averages. From these graphic and tabular presentations the investor is expected to draw his own conclusions. Second, there are several, of which *Value Line Investment Survey* is the best known, which employ technical and mathematical formulas to analyze both general market positions and fundamental values for specific stocks. The results are integrated with conventional research and published periodically as loose-leaf pages, to form a concise but substantial advisory and reference service. Third, there are a number of services which report the results of economic and investment studies to their subscribers in highly condensed printed letters. These letters usually offer advice both on market policy and on individual stocks. Typical of these would be the Babson, Holt, and United Business and Investment services.

Finally, there are many services which offer, by means of secret formulas or the personal prescience of the staff, to determine for the investor when the next rise or fall in the market will occur and how far it will go. Sometimes the stocks which will move farthest and fastest are also indentified. These mystic auguries are distributed by air mail or telegram in time to permit the subscribers to profit greatly in the market. Strangely, the possessor of the crystal ball continues to eke out a paltry sustenance in the publishing business.

A survey of these services leaves the impression that most of them are primarily concerned with attempts to gain stock market profits, since the advertisements frequently feature such offerings as "our list of ten fastmoving stocks for the next rise" or "our supervised list which consistently out-performs the general market." However, the better-grade services usually present well-developed opinions on (1) the position of the general market, (2) the positions of individual industries, (3) stocks and bonds recommended for profit or for income or for price stability, and (4) portfolio policy and selections for investors of different means and tastes. Some of the services, for example, Value Line, provide their subscribers with condensed analytical studies of industries and the leading companies in them. Other services merely mention their investment selections by name in their advisory letters, leaving the subscriber to investigate elsewhere if he chooses, or to accept their advice on faith.

Many services offer supplementary personal accommodation to subscribers desiring it. This extra service, which usually costs an extra fee, may range all the way from answering questions by letter to complete portfolio management. Without supplementary accommodation, the services range in cost from $50 to $200 per year; including personal consultation, the fee is usually much higher.

Personalized investment advice   An investor in securities needs to procure or to supply at least six types of investment supervision. He must keep his securities physically safe from fire or other loss; he must give them a mechanical supervision which will take care of rights, conversion and exchange options, maturing bonds and coupons, and similar matters; he must have accounting records for income tax and other purposes; he should have an estate plan which will allow for adequate liquidity and divisibility; he needs a general portfolio policy incorporating his estate plan but allowing also for other objectives, such as diversification, general liquidity, price-level protection, and price appreciation; and he must make the selections of individual securities. These six functions must be performed either by the investor or by persons paid to perform them. Parts or all of these functions may be obtained from brokers, investment service organizations, investment counselors, banks, and accountants or attorneys.

Brokers are accustomed to give all their clients a considerable amount of free advice on selection of securities, estate and portfolio planning, and tax matters. They also furnish library facilities which will contribute to an investor's efforts to solve his problems for himself. Finally, they often provide free safekeeping for securities held in customers' accounts. For large accounts, brokers often do considerably more; for example, one typical firm announces its willingness to accept custody of portfolios aggregating $50,000 or more, to assist the customer in planning the portfolio to his needs, to keep accounting records on it, to handle such details as rights and exchanges after consultation with the customer, and to review the portfolio occasionally and recommend changes in conformity with market conditions and the customer's expressed policy. All this is done without a service charge, in the expectation that the occasional commission revenues will make the account profitable. Other firms make various charges which may total .2 to .5 per cent of the principal per year for such services.

The publishers of printed investment services offer a wide variety of personalized advice. The less costly types are usually limited to an annual or semiannual review of the client's portfolio in the light of his desires and needs as disclosed by his answers to a questionnaire submitted to him. The client is usually also entitled to submit occasional letters of inquiry about his policies or his holdings. More elaborate personal service may include detailed portfolio planning in accordance with the client's needs, continuous supervision of his holdings by the organization, day-by-day recommendations to him, and return reports by him to the organization. The most elaborate of these services may include management supervision of a portfolio in the custody of a broker or a bank by the advisory organization, which will order purchases and sales under a power of attorney and perhaps maintain the accounting records itself. The cost of thorough supervisory service is likely to range between 1/3 per cent and 1 per cent of the principal per annum on amounts under $1 million, with a minimum of $5,000 to $10,000. Such services are often used by small insurance companies and endowed institutions as well as by individuals.

The term *investment counsel* is applied to investment advisors whose services are sold to the public on a personal basis, not in conjunction with a publication which is regarded as a vital part of the service. Investment counselors render a service very similar to the more elaborate types furnished by the publisher-advisers described in the preceding paragraph, for the same types of clientele, at about the same cost. Because most investment counselors are local professional men serving local clients, there is often a more intimate contact with clients than is possible to nationwide publishing organizations. Most investment counselors find it impractical to accept clients with portfolios under $50,000, although some undertake to service small accounts by recommending "standard" portfolios or by operating open-end investment companies into which such funds may be directed.

Banks have developed several types of services which investors may use. The simplest of these, which is sometimes termed the *custodian account,* obligates the bank to maintain physical care of the securities, keep accounting records, collect income, call the owner's attention to such matters as rights and bond maturities, and execute transactions at the owner's request. No advice or counsel is included; the annual fee is about ¼ of 1 per cent of the market value of the portfolio, with a minimum fee of $120. A second and somewhat more elaborate type of bank service may be termed the *limited management agency.* It includes all the services of the custodian account and in addition, obligates the bank to review the holdings periodically and to make recommendations for changes if needed. Because the bank accepts some responsibility for choice of investments, these accounts are usually not desired if the customer insists upon speculating extensively. The annual cost of this service will range between ¼ and ½ of 1 per cent of the principal involved, with a minimum fee of $150 specified, although the exact sums will depend on the amount of service promised. A third type of service is termed the *full management agency*. In this case the bank offers all the custodian services, promises continuous investment supervision upon the basis of agreed policies, and undertakes to buy and sell securities as needed for the account under a power of attorney. This is not a trust, but the cost approximates that of a trust service, ranging between ³⁄₁₀ and ¾ of 1 per cent per annum, typically. A fourth service furnished by a few banks is that of *investment supervision without custody*, similar in nature to the service of an investment counselor. This service seems to be intended mainly for conservative institutions such as insurance companies, hospitals, and schools. Finally, banks offer *investment supervision in connection with their trust functions*. Funds or property may be delivered to a bank as trustee under the terms of a voluntary deed or a will; the bank takes title as trustee, manages the property as directed in the deed of trust or will, bears responsibility for proper custody and supervision, and pays out income and principal when and as directed in the trust instrument. This arrangement is normally more stable and enduring than an agency contract, and the cost is very little more than that of a full management agency. Trusts are sometimes accepted in amounts much smaller than the $50,000 minimum usually desired for an agency account. Small trust funds are now pooled by many banks in "common trust funds" which afford diversification as well as professional selection and management. All bank investment policy appears to lean definitely to the conservative side, at least in the matters of proportioning holdings between bonds and stocks and restricting commitments to high-quality issues.

Accountants and attorneys are often in a position to render investment services to clients, particularly in relation to tax matters, estate planning, and portfolio planning. Their contributions are too varied to permit any adequate description here.

Public regulation of investment advice   Abuses of trust by investment advisers led the Congress to enact the Investment Advisers Act of 1940,[1] which undertakes to impose sound principles of conduct upon persons who sell investment advice and to bring their activities under the supervision of the SEC. Many states have laws with a similar purpose. These laws ordinarily do not apply to banks and brokers, who are separately regulated, or to newspapers and magazines of general circulation, or to attorneys, accountants, and certain others. Also, the statutes do not attempt to assure the competence of the advisers or the accuracy of their conclusions; public responsibility ends with the prevention of fraud and deception.

---

[1] This act is examined in more detail in Chap. 12.

Appraisal of investment advice A number of attempts to tabulate the results of "buy" and "sell" instructions to clients by leading advisory services have led the tabulators to the conclusion that the clients would have done as well if they had merely held diversified portfolios of good securities throughout the period and had made no effort to improve results by buying and selling as the experts suggested. The experience of many investment companies, whose carefully managed portfolios have just about paralleled the performance of the market averages over many years, lends considerable support to this view, though it should be noted that in the 1963–1972 period a number of aggressively managed funds "beat the averages" by substantial margins. On balance, the investment experts have made both good and bad decisions; those with the greatest widom or luck seem to have found it easier to select profitable stocks than to prognosticate successfully on the future of economic affairs or the trend of the general market.

However, there are other factors to be considered. Investment portfolios do not appear, ready-planned, as gifts from heaven; they have to be developed to suit the individual need. Furthermore, investment securities which will at least parallel the general market in performance must be chosen; it would be easy to do much worse than the general market, as many investors have learned to their sorrow. Again, the relative certainty and peace of mind which should accompany the use of competent professional investment management is worth having, and the long successful history of some endowments and similar funds under professional management suggests that success is at least possible. Finally, the technical administration and record keeping which some investment supervision embraces is a worthwhile service for the preoccupied or the uninitiated.

In general, it is easier to have faith in investment advice which is primarily concerned with the conservation of capital, and only secondarily interested in attempts to make market profits, than in advice geared to an ambition to "beat the stock market." It is easier to choose profitable, enduring investments than it is to find securities that will quickly rise in price, and less risks need be taken in pursuing the objective. But it must be admitted that stock market fluctuations are often the logical results of ascertainable causes, and even here an expert ought to be right more often than he is wrong. Experts ought to have better performance ratings than rank amateurs. Consequently, good logic will not permit the decrying of investment advice of any type which is soundly conceived and not too reckless.

All this leads inevitably to the conclusion that good investment advice or supervision may be in order for many people. The type of service each person should have and the identification of the good adviser whose services should be chosen are problems deserving careful thought; but they are not problems which should burden an intelligent man unreasonably. The investor must inevitably shoulder at least this responsibility.

Newspapers and periodicals Most metropolitan daily newspapers include a financial section of fair quality, and some of them, like the *New York Times*, contain very good ones. Good daily financial sections include sales quotations from the New York, American, and local stock exchanges, a limited number of quotations from the unlisted markets, earnings and dividend announcements by major corporations, a report on the market averages, highlights from the business news, editorial or syndicated commentaries on market and business affairs, and announcements of new securities offerings. Except for the very best ones, it is probably fair to say that newspaper financial sections do a better job of reporting securities market affairs than they do of acquainting their readers with the progress of industries and economic affairs. American finance also enjoys the services of an outstanding daily financial newspaper, *The Wall Street Journal*, which is printed simultaneously in a number of cities in order to assure timely delivery in all parts of the country. The *Journal* does a somewhat more elaborate job of reporting stock and bond quotations than the general newspapers do, but its outstanding sphere of excellence is that of reporting news of corporations, industries, products and commodities, financial affairs, taxes, labor, public policy, and foreign relations from a financial viewpoint. Much of its reporting is interspersed with interpretation, to give the reader perspective on the significance of the news. Daily reading of a financial newspaper by a nonprofessional investor is a time-consuming task, but the contribution which such study can make to a grasp of financial and business affairs is substantial.

Seven general-purpose financial periodicals are best known to investors. The *Commercial and Financial Chronicle* is a combination magazine and financial newspaper. One of its two weekly issues is chiefly used for articles on business and financial affairs. The articles include many on securities markets and industries but also place heavy emphasis on Federal Reserve policy, public finance, labor, and other public policy matters. The second of the two weekly issues is a financial newspaper which provides an excellent coverage of both stock exchange and unlisted quotations, as well as condensed news of corporations, industries, and business affairs. *Barron's* is a weekly investment magazine published by Dow, Jones & Co., publishers of *The Wall Street Journal*. It contains extensive editorial commentaries on investment and financial affairs; articles on corporations, industries, and products from an investment point of view; excellent tabular reports on stock exchange quotations; other stock and bond price data; and limited over-the-counter reports and business news notes. *Financial World* is a weekly investment magazine which carries editorial comment and articles on industries and individual investment. It offers specific advice to investors on policy and individual investment, features brief sketches of corporations and quality ratings on their securities, but does not carry quotations. Subscribers also receive an annual descriptive reference manual on leading stocks and a monthly pocket statistical manual which rates listed stocks according to quality. *The Magazine of Wall Street* is published on alternate weeks. Like *Financial World*, it carries no quotations but does an excellent job as a purveyor of financial information and investment advice to its readers. The investment advice is definite and specific. *Forbes* is a business and financial magazine, with only a portion of its pages given to finance and investments. It is published twice monthly. Its comments on the investments field are both informative and advisory. *United States Investor— Eastern Banker*, a weekly publication, devotes its issues mostly to general articles and brief advisory comments on investments and insurance. Subscribers to the *Investor* may also subscribe to a supplemental weekly *Investment Edition*, which carries detailed recommendations on portfolio policy and individual securities and industries. Finally, *The Money Manager* (formerly *The Weekly Bond Buyer*) presents authoritative articles on a wide range of economic, business, and financial topics, along with weekly summaries of United States and foreign securities markets, a comprehensive schedule of new corporate security offerings, and extensive tables of bond and money-market yields, particularly on United States government securities.

These financial and investment periodicals are widely read and are of good quality. Their subscription prices range from $12 to $90 per year. The investor who buys and reads one or more of them regularly will obtain many sound suggestions and increasing competence as an investment manager, at a cost of a moderate amount of money and a considerable amount of time.

Specialized sources   The specialized sources of information available to the investor and actually studied by many professionals in the investment field are almost too numerous to mention. Almost every trade journal, such as *Steel*, *Railway Age*, and *Oil and Gas Journal*, has information and statistical data which are of value. A long list of trade associations and research organizations, such as Edison Electric Institute, American Petroleum Institute, F. W. Dodge Corporation, and Automobile Manufacturers' Association, furnish ideas and data. Government sources such as the ICC, the U.S. Department of Commerce, and SEC have much that is pertinent and helpful. The Federal Reserve System supplies much material relating to money markets, credit, and finance.

A considerable number of specialized information sources are regarded as the outstanding reference centers in their particular fields. For example, the Alfred M. Best Company is the most eminent publisher of manuals on fire insurance stocks, casualty insurance stocks, life insurance companies, and insurance statistics. In addition, the firm has an insurance stock reporting service and two monthly journals on property insurance and life insurance. No other source provides as extensive material on insurance finance. Arthur Wiesenberger & Co., New York securities dealers, has developed its annual volume *Investment Companies* until it has become an institution in its field. The volume carries information on legislation, taxes, and administrative policies in the field, has comprehensive statistical comparisons of leading companies, and describes each one separately. Between issues the Wiesenberger firm is a prolific source of news and figures about investment companies. Walker's *Manual of Western Corporations and Securities* is an annual reference manual after the manner of Moody's, but on a much smaller scale. Monthly supplements (a separate service) are also available. In view of the more detailed coverage of large business concerns in other reference sources, the significance of Walker's is greatest as a convenient reference source covering approximately 1,500 publicly financed corporations headquartered in the West, including many described in no other single source or not adequately described elsewhere. The firm also publishes an excellent weekly news-letter which is devoted chiefly to analytical reports and studies of Western securities, based largely upon data obtained in personal interviews with corporate managements.

Annual reports and prospectuses   Corporate annual reports plus the proxy reports, digests of annual meetings, and special interim reports which companies send to stockholders are often extremely illuminating. Modern reports to stockholders are becoming quite comprehensive. Financial statements in the better reports are thorough and well explained, operating policies are outlined, hopes and problems are defined. Though much of this material gets into the securities manuals, a great deal does not. A careful investor would do well to study annual reports obtained from the company or borrowed from brokers before buying stock, and he most certainly should study them when he receives them as a stockholder.

Prospectuses are issued by corporations as descriptive literature in connection with the sale of new securities. Most of them are now issued under SEC regulations, in compliance with the Securities Act of 1933. The better ones are gold mines of information, containing corporate history, description and appraisal of property, descriptions of current problems and affairs, descriptions of securities, and other matters. Prospectuses are issued only when securities are sold, so are not kept up to date, but subsequent data can be had from other sources. Prospectuses may also be difficult to obtain except on loan from dealers' files after the initial offering period has passed.

Brokers' and dealers' literature   Some of the best and some of the worst investment literature is provided by brokers and dealers. Securities firms generally are eager to enhance their own prestige by offering their customers good analytical work and sound advice. They may on occasion be biased through a desire to sell their own wares, but poor literature and advice seem more commonly to stem from haste or incompetence than from selfish interest. It is difficult to tell good literature from bad unless the subject matter is intimately known to the reader, but the reputation of the firm and the quality of its personnel should afford a clue.

Investment house literature can be divided for present purposes into three types, which may be called (1) specific analyses, (2) statistical comparisons, and (3) pamphlets on industry or market conditions. Any of these may be elaborately printed or very inexpensively mimeographed, as the firm's plans may dictate. Specific analyses are discussions of the position and prospects of individual securities. These analyses may contain definite statements of opinion that the security is attractive for investment, or the presentations may avoid giving advice. In most cases firms will not bother calling their customers' attention to a security unless an express or implied recommendation of some sort is intended. Statistical comparisons of the stocks of similar or competing concerns are among the interesting contributions which securities firms make to investment literature. Such studies may tabulate types of property held, capital structures, sales, expenses, earnings, dividends, price history, and other items. Outstanding examples of this type of work are found in comparisons of bank, insurance, investment company, public utility, and oil company securities. Investment house letters and pamphlets about industry conditions or securities market conditions range from brief notes suggesting a course of action to extensive treatises presenting the state of the nation and the comparative condition of all industries. Most investment house literature is distributed free to clients and other inquirers. However, a number of investment houses, especially those which specialize in certain industries such as public utilities or petroleum, have elaborate analytical departments and maintain published services which they sell to other dealers and the public. Houses that serve institutional clients must prepare long and particularly searching studies of individual companies and industries to obtain the confidence and business of professional portfolio managers. Individual investors rarely have access to these carefully prepared materials.

READING THE FINANCIAL PAGE

Although much of the material presented on a newspaper financial page is direct and simple, the hieroglyphics used in some of the statistical tables usually require explanation. The forms are conventional and not always adequately explained in the headings used. While there are many tables shown in a comprehensive financial section, five of them will serve to illustrate most of the commonly used devices. The following examples are all taken from a newspaper dated February 27, 1973.

The most conspicuous statistical tables in any financial section are those used to report stock exchange transactions. A segment of the New York Stock Exchange report in this case appeared as follows:

| 1972–1973 | | Stock and | P-E | Sales | | | | Net |
High	Low	dividend rate	ratio	100s	High	Low	Close	change
42½	22¼	Paprcft .60b	11	3	22⅞	22⅞	22⅞	+ ¼
38	29½	PrkHan 1.04	13	x12	29⅞	29⅝	29⅞	+ ⅜
17⅞	6½	Penn Fruit	—	20	7	6¾	6¾	− ¼
98½	67⅛	Penney 1.08	34	130	92⅞	91½	92	−1¼
67½	59	PaPL pf 4.50	—	z40	61	61	61	—
79	53	PetrieS .40a	39	41	72⅞	72¼	72⅞	+ ½
25⅝	17½	Petrlm 2.10e	—	16	22	21¾	42¾	− ¼

The 1972–1973 columns list the highest and lowest per share prices paid for round lots of stock during the two years prior to the publication day. The Stock and Dividend Rate column names the stock and the apparent annual dividend rate; if the annual rate appears uncertain, as in the Petroleum Corporation case, a footnote tells why. In this instance, footnote "e" states "declared or paid in preceding 12 months." The symbol "a" following the regular 40-cent cash dividend paid by Petrie Stores indicates that one or more extra dividends are also paid, and the symbol "b" associated with Papercraft Corporation's 60-cent cash dividend indicates that a stock dividend also is paid. If no dividend is being paid, as was the case with Penn Fruit, the dividend space is left blank. The Sales Column in the table lists the number of 100-share transactions which took place, except that only 40 shares of Pennsylvania Power & Light 4.50 preferred were traded; the "z" footnote shows that sales are printed in full. The "x" designation preceding sales of Parker-Hannifin indicates that the stock was selling ex-dividend the current payment on this date for the first time. The price-earnings ratio column is self-explanatory, except that ratios are not calculated for Pennsylvania Power & Light because it is preferred stock; for Penn Fruit, which has reported a deficit for the past year; or for Petroleum Corporation of America, which is an investment trust. Some newspapers show dividend yields rather than price-earnings ratios. The High, Low, and Close columns indicate the per share price of the highest, lowest, and last sales of the day respectively. The Net Change column shows the difference in price between the last sale on this date and the last on the preceding day, except that in the case of a stock selling ex-dividend, the net change is adjusted for the amount of the dividend; a blank space means no change.

Corporate bond transactions on stock exchanges are reported in similar fashion. Sales are reported in units of $1,000 bonds, and the bonds are identified by corporate name, coupon rate, and maturity date. Prices are quoted in percentages and eighths. The February 27, 1973, newspaper included the following in its NYSE bond sales report:

1972–1973 High	Low	Bonds	Sales	High	Low	Close	Net change
113⅜	108	SW Bell Tel 8¾s	22	109	108¾	109	+ ¼
89⅞	84½	Std Oil Cal 5¾s92	1	85½	85½	85½	−1¾
76	60⅛	St Pkg cv 5¼s90	10	60	57⅛	57⅛	−3
96	82¾	TWA 6½s78f	400	91¾	91	91¾	+ ⅛
83⅞	78½	U Carbide 5.30s97	10	80¾	80	80¾	+ ¾

The foregoing bond quotation should be clear to the reader except for two items. The designation "cv" identifies the Standard Packaging bonds as "convertibles"—bonds convertible into the company's common stock. The small "f" shown in connection with the TWA 6½ of 1978 means that by stock exchange rule the bond sells "flat"—that is, no accrued interest is added to a sale price, and the quoted price thus pays for both principal and accrued interest.

Government bond transactions are mostly over the counter, and quotations usually appear as bids and asks rather than as sales reports. Portions of the quotations from February 27, 1973, appeared as shown below:

Treasury bonds

Bonds	Bid	Asked	Bid change	Yield
3½s, 1980, November	81.26	82.10	−.10	6.45
7s, 1981, August	102.28	103.12	−.8	6.48
3¼s, 1978–83, June	75.8	76.8	−.14	6.44
4⅛s, 1989–94, May	74.24	75.24	−.10	6.20

Treasury bills

Maturity	Bid	Asked
March 15, 1973	5.61	5.15
May 31, 1973	5.81	5.61
September 25, 1973	5.93	5.71

The treasury bonds are normally quoted in percentages and thirty-seconds, rather than in percentages and eighths as are corporate bonds. For convenience in typesetting, the fraction is normally set after a dash or a decimal point: thus, the

Treasury 3¼s of 1978–83 shown here are quoted as 75%₃₂ bid, 76%₃₂ asked. Treasury bonds often are identified with two "maturity" dates: the first is the date the bond becomes callable at par (until then it is noncallable), and the second is the final maturity date.

Treasury bills are promissory short-term notes which do not bear interest. They are sold at a discount below par, mature a few months later at par, and are quoted in terms of the interest yield which the bidder demands and which the seller is willing to yield. The bid yield is greater than the ask yield, which means that the bid price must be lower than the ask price.

Except for state and municipal securities, which are usually also quoted in terms of yields, other over-the-counter quotations in newspapers are relatively easy to interpret. Usually no information is given except the name of the security and a bid and asked price. Over-the-counter quotations are usually grouped into reasonably homogeneous groups—e.g., bank stocks, insurance stocks, industrial and utility stocks, mutual funds, corporation bonds, public authority bonds—in the quotation tables. Over-the-counter quotations in newspapers must be interpreted in the light of the trading and quotation methods explained in Chapter 8.

One of the very vital news items on any financial page concerns corporation dividends. The February 27, 1973, newspaper included the following dividend reports.

Company	Period	Amount	Payment date	Record date
Alcon Labs	Q	c.04	April 27	April 13
American Precision Ind		.05	March 30	March 15
Beneficial Corp $4.30 Preferred	S	2.15	March 31	March 9
Dominion Fndrs & Stl	Q	b.22½	April 1	March 12
Fin Federation Inc	Stk	5%	April 10	March 9
Richard D. Irwin	Q	.08	April 16	April 2
Richard D. Irwin	E	.03	April 16	April 2
Ryan Homes Inc	In	.05	April 10	March 15

Dividend tables are not so uniform in their construction as quotation tables, but they are much alike in content. This table names the stock, identifies the periodic nature of the dividend, states the amount per share, and lists the dates of payment and the stock-of-record date to which the dividend applies. When the company calls the dividend a "quarterly" dividend, a "Q" in the table notes the fact. Other symbols indicate special features of dividends announced. In the foregoing table, for example, "c" denotes an increase in the quarterly rate, "S" indicates a semiannual dividend, "b" tells that the dividend is payable in Canadian funds, and "E" identifies an extra dividend. Similarly, the abbreviation "Stk" designates a stock dividend and "In" the initial once paid by that company.

Financial pages also report corporate earnings in condensed or tabular form. The form used varies greatly, but the reported earnings or deficit figures usually cover a stated time period and are expressed on a per share basis. Comparisons with preceding periods are commonly given.

QUESTIONS AND PROBLEMS

1 In considering Monsanto Chemical Company stock for investment, would you prefer a factual description or an editorial presentation? What would be the worst hazards in the former? In the latter?

2 What materials and services would you want to consult before investing your money in Monsanto? Are all of these concerned with the company and its affairs?

3 Where would you find investment-minded comments on the state of the nation and on the position of the stock market? Are these proper topics for investment analysts to ponder?

4 Would it be feasible to choose promising securities by selecting only those recommended by several published services? How would you go about this?

5 If a busy professional man should ask your opinion, would you advise employing an investment counselor to manage a $100,000 fund? Why, or why not?

6 If a middle-aged widow, unskilled in business, informs you that she is considering having her bank manage her $100,000 fund, would you recommend a limited management agency, a full management agency, or a trust? Why?

7 Why are annual reports and prospectuses highly prized by investors who supervise their own investment?

8 Obtain a newspaper financial page and examine every table of figures on it. If United States Treasury bills were quoted 4.80 per cent bid, 4.70 per cent asked, would this mean that someone was offering to pay more than someone else was asking for the bills? Explain.

9 If a table headed Dividends Announced contained the data "Adams Express Company $.50 June 22–July 2," what would it mean?

10 If you should decide you can afford to spend $150 annually for reading information to be used in supervising a moderate-sized portfolio, what publications would you subscribe to, and why?

REFERENCES

Bellemore, Douglas H., and John C. Ritchie, Jr.: *Investments*, 3d ed., South-Western Publishing Company, Incorporated, Cincinnati, 1969, Chap. 15.

Cohen, Jerome B., and Edward D. Zinbarg: *Investment Analysis and Portfolio Management*, rev. ed., Richard D. Irwin, Inc., Homewood, Ill., 1973, Chap. 3.

Cooke, Gilbert W.: *The Stock Markets*, rev. ed., Schenkman Publishing Co., Inc., Cambridge, Mass., 1969, Chaps. 5, 12.

Dougall, Herbert E.: *Investments*, 8th ed., Prentice-Hall, Inc., Englewood Cliffs, N.J., 1968, Chaps. 13, 14.

Eiteman, Wilford J., Charles A. Dice, and David K. Eiteman: *The Stock Market*, 4th ed., McGraw-Hill Book Company, New York, 1966, Chap. 8.

Francis, Jack Clark: *Investment Analysis and Management*, McGraw-Hill Book Company, New York, 1972, Chap. 7.

Latané, Henry A., and Donald L. Tuttle: *Security Analysis and Portfolio Management*, The Ronald Press Company, New York, 1970, Chaps. 5, 6.

Leffler, George L., and Loring C. Farwell: *The Stock Market*, 3d ed., The Ronald Press Company, New York, 1963, Chap. 38.

Widicus, Wilbur W., and Thomas E. Stitzel: *Personal Investing*, Richard D. Irwin, Inc., Homewood, Ill., 1971, Chap. 4.

Woy, James B. (ed.): *Investment Information*, Gale Research Company, Detroit, 1970.

PROTECTING THE INVESTOR

Although state authorities and the responsible elements in the securities business had attempted for many years to enforce reasonable ethical standards, the practices current in the late twenties left much to be desired. Misrepresentation and sharp practices were rife, and some of the activities permitted by the great organized markets were neither fair to their customers nor sound in their effects on the economy as a whole. As long as the markets were buoyant, there was little chance for reform; but when the stock market debacle of 1929–1933 inflicted great losses on investors, the demand for remedial action became too strong to be ignored. New laws were passed by states and by the federal government, new regulatory commissions were established, and industry agencies for self-policing were established or strengthened.

In general, it appears that the ethical tone of the securities business has been lifted to a significantly higher level. Fraud and deception have been largely eliminated, misleading or exaggeratedly optimistic sales presentations have been curtailed, and the old attitude of *caveat emptor* has been replaced by the viewpoint that securities firms occupy a position of trust in transactions with their clients. The better elements in the business are unquestionably dominant, and they now have powerful legal support in their attempts to suppress questionable practices.

Most of the measures developed to protect the securities investor have been intended to enforce honest and fair practices and have not been concerned with either the quality or the pricing of securities offered for sale. This is in accordance with American tradition; government does not deny its citizens the right to buy or sell as they choose, though it may insist on an honest description of the merchandise. However, this principle is coming to be disregarded at times, especially by the state authorities; some of them refuse to sanction admittedly honest securities transactions within their borders because they disagree with other legitimate company policies; and the federal government itself presumes to manipulate stock and bond values and to protect investors against themselves by limiting their use of stock market credit.

The modern investor is thus assured of a securities market whose mechanical functioning is reasonably fair and just and whose firms and personnel are in the main committed to high ethical standards. He has various channels of complaint and possible redress if he is unfairly treated. Some attempt may be made to keep reckless financial promotions from being offered to him, and he may be restrained from excessive speculative use of credit himself, but otherwise his choices of investments remain largely his own.

Measures taken for the protection of the public may best be reviewed by classifying them by sources—the securities business, the states, and the federal government. The federal activities in particular are extensive.

INDUSTRY MEASURES

The securities business has always had to cope with fraud and sharp practices within its ranks. The large amounts of money involved make the business an enticing one to practitioners with elastic consciences, and the greedy gullibility of the public makes protective measures difficult. Securities firms generally contribute freely to better business bureaus and similar agencies, which in turn keep a close watch on dubious promotions and questionable practice in the business. Complaints from the public are analyzed by the better business bureaus and sponsored with the proper prosecuting authorities if such measures are warranted. Frequently the intervention of the bureau can obtain adjustment of a dispute without legal steps. Needless to say, the prosecution of sharp practices by state or federal authority obtains the full sympathy and support of most elements in the securities business. Because of their fear of libel suits, the ethical securities firms will usually not advise or assist the injured clients of unscrupulous firms except to direct them to better business bureaus or prosecuting authorities, but they will cooperate quietly in any steps that these agencies take.

Stock exchanges have been increasingly vigilant in policing the activities of their member firms, for difficulties entangling these firms are likely to reflect upon an exchange and all its members. Every exchange has rules covering both floor trading and the members' relations with their customers, and member firms' accounts are audited to see that the firms both obey the rules and maintain standards of financial strength. Employees of member firms are required by the exchanges to pass proficiency tests and sign an agreement to follow certain standards of conduct, if they deal with the public. Complaints involving member firms are investigated by the stock exchanges, and infractions are punished by fine or suspension. The majority of the complaints concern either misunderstandings or technical violations of rules by employees, but in a large industry which has thousands of men dealing with the public, there are inevitably a few cases of fraud and sharp practices. These are usually dealt with firmly and promptly.

Trade associations, notably the National Association of Securities Dealers, constitute a third type of industry activity for the protection of the public. Such associations develop ethical codes and standards of procedure which must be adhered to by all members. The NASD has been especially effective in establishing written codes for the guidance of firms and their employees. Customers' dis-

putes with member firms will be investigated by either local or national offices of
the organization upon request.

The investing public thus has three powerful private agencies, the better business bureaus, the stock exchanges, and the NASD, to turn to in case of a dispute
with a securities firm. In most instances it will not be necessary to seek their help
in order to obtain fair treatment from a reputable firm, but they should be used,
and promptly, when needed. They make no charge for their services.

STATE BLUE-SKY LAWS

Though general statutes and common law in every state are available to punish
securities frauds, all the 50 states except Delaware have seen fit to enact special
legislation dealing with the securities business. The state of Kansas pioneered in
such legislation in 1911. Early discussion of this field made much use of a vernac-
ular phrase which characterized fraudulent securities as "pieces of the blue sky."
The term has stuck. State laws dealing with fraud prevention and punishment in
this field are universally known as blue-sky laws.

The blue-sky laws are composed, in varying proportions, of five types of provisions: (1) those establishing commissions or special functionaries in the office of
the secretary of state, attorney general, or corporation commissioner to administer this work; (2) those requiring licensing of securities firms and salesmen; (3)
those requiring the filing of data on new securities which are offered for sale;
(4) those requiring new securities to meet certain standards or to obtain official
clearance before offering is begun; and (5) those defining securities frauds and
specifying penalties. Nearly all of the states build their statutes around items
1, 2, and 3, with item 4 imposed upon securities of new corporations or of corporations having no securities listed on a national exchange. In a few states, notably
New York, no official permit is needed before an issue is offered to the public,
but an offering prospectus, making a full and fair disclosure of all material facts, is
required, and an explicit and vigorously enforced antifraud statute provides a
deterrent to objectionable practices.

Under many of the blue-sky laws, the enforcing authorities have a great deal
of discretionary power. The statutes commonly authorize denial of licenses to
firms or salesmen with objectionable records or doubtful competence. They also
authorize or require exclusion of securities when the expense of selling exceeds
a certain amount, when promoters or insiders receive large amounts for intangible
assets or services, when control is peculiarly distributed, and in various other
cases. Since 1960 a number of states—Wisconsin conspicuously—have taken a
markedly paternalistic stance; new issues and exchange offers have been banned
because the authorities disapproved the price of the new securities or the terms
of the proffered exchange or company policy on other matters, not because of

inadequate disclosure of facts or the presence of fraud. Application of state law often becomes a matter of judgment for the enforcing authorities.

It is probable that the blue-sky laws are stronger and more enforceable now than ever before. They serve as the exclusive regulatory device on securities offered solely within one state, for these are usually not subject to the federal securities acts. They supplement the federal activities on other matters. The state authorities are very conveniently located and empowered to handle investor grievances. In this they are probably less hampered by local politics than ever before, and if the problem has interstate aspects, they now have the aid of the SEC rather than the fetters of limited authority. Many of the blue-sky laws exempt numerous types of securities, but there is enough power in most of the laws to make the enforcing authorities very useful to the investing public.

Finally, it should be noted that state courts have become increasingly willing to entertain civil suits by investors against brokers and dealers chargeable with unethical practices. Grounds for damage awards, often substantial, have included unnecessary turnover of investors' accounts, failure to disclose risks when recommending highly speculative securities, and inducing clients to buy securities clearly unsuited to their age, financial condition, or investment objectives.[1]

THE FEDERAL SECURITIES ACTS

The federal securities acts consist of nine measures, eight passed between 1933 and 1940, with subsequent amendments, and the last in 1970. These statutes are not exclusively concerned with the regulation of the securities business, but they are all related to the subject of investments in one way or another. During the period 1933–37 it appeared to many that the federal legislation was conceived in bitterness and administered with a fervor that was more political than economic. However, attitudes on both sides have been tempered by experience and responsibility. The securities industry has discovered that the federal authorities will use their power to discourage unsound practices and encourage good ones; and the authorities have demonstrated their willingness to cooperate in businesslike fashion with the industry. There are still problems, to be sure, but few responsible leaders in the securities business would now be willing to see the securities acts repealed or materially weakened. The federal securities acts are administered by the Securities and Exchange Commission, which is generally known as the SEC.

Securities act of 1933 This measure, which is sometimes referred to as the truth-in-securities act, was the first of the federal securities acts. It is concerned chiefly with the requirement that new securities offered to the public be fully and clearly

[1] See "Of Love and Money," *Wall Street Journal*, April 21, 1972, p. 1.

described in the offering literature and sales presentation. The act does not attempt to control the quality of any issue, or the method of distribution, or any phase of corporate business practice. In this it differs from some of the state blue-sky laws under which securities may be disqualified from sale because of some of these factors. The principal features of the act may be summarized as follows:

1   The act applies to all new securities offered to the public by the issuer or by an underwriter or dealer, and also to substantial blocks of old securities offered from the corporate treasury or by major stockholders. It does not apply to securities offered privately to a limited number of institutions or people, whether the securities are new or old. Issues under $500,000 may be exempt from most of the provisions of the act with the consent of the SEC, which administers the law. The following are always exempt: *(a)* bonds of federal, state, and local governments and their agencies; *(b)* national and state bank stocks; *(c)* short-term commercial paper; *(d)* securities issued by nonprofit organizations; *(e)* savings-loan accounts and similar investments, and insurance policies; *(f)* securities of common carriers; *(g)* securities issued by a receiver or bankruptcy trustee; *(h)* securities issued after court approval in a corporate reorganization; *(i)* securities exchanged for others by the same issuer; and *(j)* securities sold wholly within one state by a locally incorporated and locally operating concern.

2   The act requires that nonexempt securities be "registered" with the SEC at least 20 days before they are publicly offered. Registration consists of paying a small fee and filing with the SEC a "registration statement" containing a mass of information concerning the legal, commercial, technical, and financial position of the issuer, together with a prospectus which summarizes this information for public use. The commission is required to delay or stop the public offering if any of the information is inadequate or misleading. It may shorten the 20-day waiting period before registration becomes fully effective, under certain conditions.

3   Until registration becomes fully effective, it is illegal to offer the securities for sale or to take subscriptions for them. After registration is effective, no offering may be made or subscription invited unless the offeree is handed a copy of the prospectus. However, a preliminary "red-herring" prospectus may be given to a potential buyer for his consideration before the effective date, and he may be asked if he is interested in the forthcoming issue.

4   Any purchaser of a registered security who sustains loss in it may sue for damages if the registration statement or prospectus contained false or misleading statements on material facts. Liability may fall upon the issuer, its officers, directors, accountants, engineers, appraisers, other experts, or any underwriter. However, anyone except the issuer may exonerate himself by proving that his own work in connection with the matter was performed with due care and diligence.

5   Severe penalties as well as civil liabilities are prescribed where the procedure of the act is violated or where fraud is committed in the sale of either registered or exempt securities.

The act as originally passed in 1933 was much more rigorous in imposing civil liabilities and more arbitrary in certain administrative details than the present law. Amendments in 1934 made the liability sections more moderate, and other changes in 1940 enabled the SEC to accelerate the effective date of registration or to accept supplements to registration statements without delaying the effective date. In its original form the act was regarded as extremely hazardous to directors, underwriters, accountants, appraisers, and others, and some refused to have any part in the distribution of registered securities. However, this attitude no longer exists. Registration is still expensive because of the extensive descriptions, legal opinions, appraisals, engineering reports, audits, and printing costs entailed; but analysts are glad to have the information, and the ultimate advantage to the public is probably substantial. The improvement in reported financial statements is especially noteworthy. The Commission has insisted on reasonably detailed statements using standard or fully defined accounting methods with adequate explanatory notes and auditors' certificates.

As was noted in a previous chapter, the prospectus developed in connection with a new issue is not only a source of valuable information to an investor who considers purchasing the new security, it is a reference source for years to come. Its thoroughness and dispassionate presentation make it more than ordinarily useful for one who wishes to study his investments carefully. The prospectuses used during the first 15 years of the Securities Act were especially voluminous and led many investors to complain that they were excessively tedious and dry. In fact, many people believed that the lengthy prospectus defeated its own end because investors would not read it. Since 1950 there has been a noticeable trend toward shorter and simpler prospectuses, mainly at the urging of the SEC. However, many underwriters and corporate officers hesitated to shorten the prospectuses, for fear of the lawsuits which might develop if any material facts were omitted.

Securities exchange act of 1934   In this act, Congress extended federal regulation of the securities business to include all phases of trading in existing securities. Including amendments added in 1964, the act contains the following principal features:

1   The SEC, consisting of five members appointed by the President with the consent of the Senate, was established to administer this and other related measures. Until the SEC was established, the Securities Act of 1933 was administered by the Federal Trade Commission.

2 All stock exchanges of substantial size are required to "register" with the SEC as national securities exchanges. The SEC is given authority over *(a)* listing or delisting of securities; *(b)* short selling; *(c)* floor trading techniques, including trading by members, specialists, and odd-lot dealers; and *(d)* general rules and practices of the exchanges.

3 Corporations whose securities are listed on any exchange and most others having 500 or more stockholders must file registration statements and financial data with the SEC and must keep these up to date by periodic supplementary reports.

4 Each officer, director, and major stockholder of a registered corporation must file an initial report disclosing the amount of stock he owns, and thereafter, monthly reports of any changes in his holdings of the stock. If any such person makes a profit in the stock on a transaction which is completed entirely within a 6-month period, the profit is considered to be due per se to inside information and must be surrendered to the corporation if it or any stockholder sues to compel such surrender. No officer, director, or major stockholder may sell the stock short.

5 Proxy requests and other consents solicited by management from owners of registered corporations are subject to SEC rules. Such requests must give stockholders an opportunity to instruct their proxy holders how to vote on issues to come before the meeting. Any salaries or fees or other payments made to directoral candidates by the corporation, as well as their stock holdings, must be stated in the proxy material. Opposition proposals and candidates must be given space in the management's proxy material to present their case.

6 All securities brokers and dealers except those dealing exclusively in public bonds must register with the SEC whether affiliated with a stock exchange or not. They must all conduct their affairs in accordance with prescribed standards, must limit their borrowings to reasonable amounts, must keep certain records, and are subject to audit by the SEC.

7 In all securities transactions, the act forbids market manipulation, misrepresentation, deception, and any fraudulent practice.

8 The Board of Governors of the Federal Reserve System is authorized to fix the maximum credit which brokers or dealers may extend on margin transactions and which banks or other commercial lenders may extend by loan for the purpose of buying or carrying listed securities. In addition, the Board may regulate the extension of credit by securities firms on unlisted corporate securities and by banks on unlisted stocks. Loans on public bonds are not subject to these provisions, nor are bank loans on most corporate bonds.

Because this act is long, detailed, and inclusive of many topics, there are few people who endorse it completely. In the main, it is working well. Brokers and dealers both inside and outside the scope of stock exchange authority are controlled, and general standards within the industry have been improved. The control over margin credit is salutary. Some people have disputed the wisdom of driving "insiders" away from trading in their own corporation's stock, and many have questioned the desirability of the limitations imposed on short selling,[2] but few informed persons will deny that the act now accomplishes many of the good intentions of its framers.

Although the Securities Exchange Act of 1934 gives the SEC far-reaching regulatory powers, these powers have in the past been used mostly to press for equitable business methods and full disclosure of facts. Recently, however, the SEC has sought a multitude of detailed operational changes on such matters as trading by exchange members for their own account, specialists' finances and operating techniques, odd-lot operations and differentials, automation of stock exchanges, commission schedules, commission sharing between firms, member firm finances and back-office methods, negotiated fees on large transactions, exchange memberships for institutional investors, and the eventual unification of all securities markets. The approach has become managerial rather than one of stimulating full disclosure, honesty, and competition. However, the new attitude is fully compatible with the Securities Act of 1934.

Public utility holding company act of 1935 This act was the subject of bitter controversy in 1935. It was designed at that time to compel partial dissolution and extensive reorganization of public utility holding company systems and to subject them permanently to federal control. The resulting forced sales and other uncertainties were very costly to investors, but the industries ultimately emerged from their tribulations with stronger capital structures, better accounting systems, and a higher moral tone than they had had previously.

The growth of large electric and gas holding company systems in the 1920s actually came about because of technological progress, but the combining of small concerns into large systems in an era of "frenzied finance" resulted in many cases of overcapitalization, excessive indebtedness, complex capital structures, unsound accounting, evasion of state regulatory authority, and even outright fraud. State authorities often seemed unable to cope with far-flung holding company systems, yet reform was needed. Political considerations at the time called for federal intervention in a harsh manner, and the act was so written. Briefly, its provisions are these:

---

[2] The stock market is unique in the degree to which its rules oppose and penalize short selling. In other major organized markets—notably commodity futures and foreign exchange—short selling is an accepted and valued function. In theory, it plays the same sort of role in opposing and limiting speculative price rises as margin buying does in fueling and overextending them. Many observers believe that if short selling were not hamstrung, extravagant and destabilizing rises in stock prices would be less widespread and dangerous.

1 Every operating electric or retail gas utility which is a subsidiary of a holding company operating interstate, and every holding company controlling such
subsidiary directly or indirectly, is required to "register" with the SEC. Subsidiary
or holding company status is measured by the ownership of 10 per cent or more
of the voting stock, regardless of the factor of control.

2 Registrants come immediately under the regulatory authority of the SEC
on matters relating to capital structure, issuance of securities, expansion, dividends, intercompany loans and investments, intercompany contracts, business
methods, and accounting.

3 Every holding company system is required to be reduced to a single geographically integrated and unified system of a size not so large as to "impair the
advantages of localized management, efficient operation, or the effectiveness of
regulation." This has frequently been held to require restriction of the system's
operation to one service (electricity or gas), but in appropriate cases an additional
system or incidental business may be permitted.

4 Simplification of the corporate systems and capital structures is required,
to assure sound financing, to distribute voting power equitably, to eliminate unnecessary corporations, and to reduce the "corporate layers" to not more than
three — operating companies, intermediate holding companies, and top holding
company.

The Holding Company Act in the mid-seventies effectively discourages interstate consolidations of similar services and often compels uneconomic separation
of electric, gas, water, and other services in the same locality. It imposes bureaucratic control which duplicates state regulation in many instances and other federal
regulation in others. It is, perhaps, a solid barrier against a recurrence of the holding company abuses of the 1920s, but the circumstances which led to that situation are gone and the prohibition of complex multicorporate structures could
doubtless exist without regulating procedures.

Maloney act of 1938   This measure, an amendment to the Securities Exchange
Act of 1934, authorizes the formation of national associations of brokers and
dealers for the purposes of establishing fair trade practice rules and maintaining
self-discipline. Such associations must register with the SEC and accept its regulatory supervision, but they enjoy special privileges also. Only one such organization, the National Association of Securities Dealers, has been formed. In 1972 it
had as members about 88 per cent of the nation's registered securities firms, including most of the large ones. It maintains its authority by means of a rule which
forbids any member to allow a dealer's concession to be given to, or received
from, any nonmember firm on any new issue or secondary offering or over-the-
counter transaction. Since these transactions are vital to most firms' existence,
their memberships must be kept in good standing. New legislation, passed in 1964,

requires virtually all securities firms to join the NASD or a possible new organization or to submit to detailed direct supervision by the SEC.

The NASD functions principally along five lines. First, it has developed a written code of fair practices dealing with such matters as the fairness of prices quoted to customers, the profits or commissions taken in no-risk transactions, the disclosure of status when acting as principal, and deceptive or manipulative practices. Second, it has promulgated standard procedures in transactions between members, covering such matters as nominal and firm quotations, deliveries and settlements, interest computation, dividend adjustments, and the like. Third, it is attempting to organize the over-the-counter market for better service to the public. Salesmen of member firms are required to become "registered representatives" by filing personal data sheets, including a statement accepting the NASD rules of fair practice. New registered representatives must also pass a proficiency examination. Member firms must also accept all rules and are under pressure to finance themselves conservatively. On the technical plane, NASD initiatives have produced the NASDAQ, the automated stock quotation system described in Chapter 8, which has improved the speed, accuracy, and fairness of price quotations in the over-the-counter market. The NASD also seeks greater publicity for over-the-counter quotations and provides daily trading volume figures on NASDAQ-quoted stocks. Fourth, the association undertakes to investigate and arbitrate disputes between members or between members and the public and to take disciplinary measures when justified. Fifth, the NASD undertakes, along with the Investment Bankers Association and other industry groups, to study and make recommendations on pending legislation in the securities field and on procedures being considered by the SEC and other public and private groups.

The NASD seems to be making progress. It is championed by important people in the securities business, its meetings and conventions are well attended, and its rulings are obeyed by its members. It has an important function to perform for the protection of the public in developing ethics and procedures on over-the-counter transactions and in publicizing over-the-counter quotations. There is also need to press for better standards of corporate practice on such matters as audits, adequate financial statements, proxies, information about the business, use of registrars, and the like by corporations whose securities are not traded on exchanges; but this does not seem to be a major objective of the NASD at the moment. Much of the association's energies are directed at systematizing relationships between securities firms and in enforcing its code of fair practices with respect to the public. The NASD has been sharply criticized by many firms, both member and nonmember, for an alleged tendency to establish rules of conduct which make transactions in little-known or speculative securities unprofitable, and for its rule which discourages transactions between members and nonmembers by forbidding the members to allow dealers' concessions to nonmembers. However, these and other conflicts which developed in the earlier years seem to be less sharply debated as time goes on, and the major work of the NASD remains noncontroversial.

Bankruptcy act of 1938   The Bankruptcy Act of 1938 made a general revision of federal bankruptcy laws as they related to the reorganization of general corporations. One portion of this act placed upon the SEC the task of advising the court on reorganization plans in all cases in which the scheduled liabilities exceed $3 million and in other cases when invited by the court. The SEC's statutory task is the rendering of an advisory report on the fairness and soundness of a proposed reorganization plan. Actually, it offers its advice on the preparation of the plan, on the selection of trustees and their counsel, on fee allowances to parties involved, and on matters pertaining to administration of the property pending reorganization.

The introduction of the SEC into bankruptcy reorganizations appears to have improved both the soundness and fairness of reorganization plans. Such plans had often tended to replace failed corporations with successors whose burden of debt had also been excessive or whose capital structures had been too complex. The SEC has persistently fought to obtain more severe and realistic reorganizations. It has also demanded and obtained more equitable plans than might otherwise have been developed.

Trust indenture act of 1939   This act regulates indentures and trustees of bond issues exceeding $1 million in amount which are to be registered under the Securities Act of 1933. Indentures effective prior to 1940 are not affected. The objectives of the act are to assure that the trustee serves the bondholders, not the corporation; to assure the competence of the trustee; and to require the inclusion of certain safeguards in all new bond indentures. The principal provisions of the act include the following:

1   The corporate trustee must have a capital and surplus of at least $150,000 and must not be affiliated with issuer or underwriter. If in the future any close relations exist between issuer and trustee, the trustee must resign or suffer removal.

2   The trustee must maintain a list of bondholders. It must report to the bondholders annually if certain adverse developments occur. It must notify them of all defaults within 90 days.

3   The indenture must contain provisions intended to assure vigilance, and necessary action on the part of the trustee, and certain other protective features must be included.

This is a sound law. A sharply literal interpretation of the requirement that no close relationships exist between a corporate issuer and a trustee at first made it difficult for large national corporations to find large banks eligible to serve as trustees, but this problem has been solved by a more sensible interpretation of the law. Because additional and more expensive duties are required of trustees under this law, large corporations with pre-1940 open indentures have tended to continue them in service, rather than to retire them and register new ones.

Investment company act of 1940   This act was passed by Congress in an attempt to prevent any repetition of the losses incurred by investors in investment company securities between 1929 and 1935. These losses were in part due to the depression and market slump, but in part they were due to bad management and outright dishonesty. Many investment companies were organized between 1925 and 1930 with unsound capital structures and no sensibly planned investment policies. Excessive debt and preferred stock financing left them vulnerable to business depression. Investment in speculative securities led to losses. Investment bankers controlling the companies abused their privileges by selling their own ill-advised investments into the investment companies. Excessive salaries and fees were paid. These and other bad practices added up to a situation which called for corrective legislation.

The Investment Company Act is a highly detailed statute which requires many sound procedures, forbids many unsound ones, and authorizes regulation by the SEC on a number of matters. The purpose of the Congress was evidently to make the investment companies, which can offer diversification and skilled management together in a single moderate-cost commitment, a safe place for the savings of small investors. The act is sane and sensible in view of its purpose and is firmly supported by the leading investment companies. Significant provisions include the following:

1   Directors must be elected by vote of the shareholders, except that Massachusetts trusts existing prior to the act may continue undisturbed, subject to power in the stockholders to remove trustees. Elected directorates must include persons who are neither officers nor employees, and only a minority may be investment bankers.

2   Officers, directors, and other insiders are closely limited in dealing with the company, employing its funds, or using its credit.

3   Shareholders must approve management contracts, selection of independent auditors, and any changes in company policy on investment objectives, diversification, specialization, participation in underwriting, and other important matters.

4   Company securities and cash must be deposited in the care of a bank or stock exchange firm, or kept safe as the SEC may require. The SEC may require any necessary fidelity or surety bonds.

5   The SEC has general supervision over accounting methods, semiannual reports to stockholders, use of proxies, selling methods, prospectuses, and other business methods.

6 Except for refunding issues, no new bonds may be sold unless covered by 3 times their amount in assets and no preferred stock unless covered twice on the over-all basis. New bonds and preferred stocks must have contingent voting rights and be protected by restrictions on common stock dividends and repurchases. New open-end funds may not have bonds or preferred stock in their capital structures.

7 Detailed regulation applicable to open-end companies, periodic payment plans, and face-amount certificate companies are provided.

The most recent amendment to the Investment Company Act, passed by Congress in 1970, incorporates three reforms long urged by the SEC. First, the amendment sets standards of fairness for the fees paid by investment companies to investment advisers. Second, it empowers the NASD to regulate the commissions charged purchasers of open-end shares. Third, the new law limits the first-year commissions paid by buyers of contractual savings plans to reasonable amounts. All these changes appear to be reasonable and fair to the parties concerned. In mid-1972, the SEC further persuaded the NASD to propose new rules prohibiting use of a mutual fund's own brokerage business to reward dealers for selling the fund's shares.

Investment advisers act of 1940   To protect the general public against investment advisers who might hire themselves out as expert counselors and then abuse the faith placed in them, the Congress passed the Investment Advisers Act of 1940. The act applies only to all those who serve the general public professionally as investment advisers, hence exempts lawyers, accountants, and others whose investment advice is incidental and professional advisers who serve only institutions or a limited clientele of fewer than 15 persons. Investment advisers subject to the act are required to register with the SEC, file data about themselves, and file reports about their business twice yearly. At June 30, 1971, there were 3,485 registrants. The SEC may not reject or revoke an adviser's registration because of incompetence or error; only ethical or legal infractions are punishable. Specific provisions of the act include:

1 Advisers must not be compensated by a share of market appreciation or realized profits; some other basis must be used.[3]

2 Advisers must not defraud their clients in any way or conceal material facts from them. Advisers must not trade as principals with their clients, or trade with their clients as the agent of another, without the clients' specific permission.

3 Advisers may not assign their contracts with clients.

[3] This rule applies strictly only to advisers of individual investors. The 1970 amendment to the Investment Advisers Act permits a limited compensation of the advisers of registered investment companies on the basis of portfolio performance.

4 The SEC may require information from any adviser and subpoena records if needed.

This is not a severe statute. There is relatively little regulation of the nature of services undertaken or methods of performing them and none with respect to the advisers' financial standing or their competence. Some of the state laws are more exacting. However, the general prohibitions against unethical practices, abuse of trust, or concealment of material facts will amply support SEC procedures against unethical or unsound practices, and suspension or revocation of an adviser's registration is an effective sanction even if deliberate fraud cannot be proved. The law thus provides effective moral discipline. It is perhaps unfortunate that the tenets of a free society make it awkward to examine advisers' competence; since neither appropriate investment objectives nor methods of attaining them can be defined exactly, the law avoids setting proficiency tests. There may some day be voluntary professional organizations whose self-imposed membership tests will fill this gap.

Securities investor protection act of 1970   This act is intended to head off brokerage-house bankruptcies and to insure investors against certain losses when bankruptcies occur. It sets up the Securities Investor Protection Corporation, a quasi-public body, to administer an industry-financed insurance system and to liquidate insolvent securities firms. It also strengthens the SEC's control over broker- and dealer-firm finances and paperwork.

This new act was passed after serious financial and operating difficulties had engulfed the securities industry during the 1967–1970 period and demonstrated the inadequacy of existing safeguards. Unexpected surges in trading volume had overtaxed the record-keeping and certificate-handling facilities of many brokers and dealers, and subsequent sharp declines in stock and bond prices caused large operating and capital losses in poorly managed or undercapitalized companies. In 1969 and 1970, more than 100 brokerage firms went bankrupt or staved off liquidation only through mergers with stronger houses. Private rescue efforts cost the securities industry an estimated $130 million and severely strained the resources of still-solvent firms. Investors lost indefinitely large sums through brokerage-house failures or prolonged delays in stock deliveries and cash payments. Public mistrust of securities firms began to spread, stirring concern that "runs" might develop on securities and cash still held in customer accounts. In this atmosphere, Congress passed the first new investor protection law in 30 years, which has six main provisions.

1   To manage the investor protection system, the Securities Investor Protection Corporation is set up with a reserve fund financed by assessing brokers $\frac{1}{2}$ per cent of their commission revenues until $150 million has been accumulated.

2 The SIPC is empowered to borrow up to $1 billion from the U.S. Treasury if additional funds are needed to pay insurance claims.

3 Each separately owned account in a brokerage house is insured by the corporation against unreturned securities and cash to a maximum value of $50,000, in which cash cannot exceed $20,000.

4 The SIPC is required to consult closely with the stock exchanges and NASD "to detect approaching financial difficulties" in securities firms. The SEC is responsible for supervising the corporation and is given broad powers to intervene in the public interest.

5 While the SIPC is not a government agency, it is publicly controlled. Of its seven directors, five are appointed by the President—two from outside the securities business—and one each by the Treasury and the Federal Reserve System.

6 The stock exchanges and NASD are responsible for detecting financial troubles in their member firms and for reporting these immediately to the SIPC. If the SIPC finds the broker failing to meet its obligations to its customers, the corporation applies to a federal court to appoint a trustee to take over, and perhaps liquidate, the troubled firm. The trustee must promptly notify customers to file claims for cash and securities owed them. The trustee must settle all claims as quickly as possible.

Although the new investor protection system closely resembles other systems which have protected bank and savings and loan account holders for many years, investors may still lose substantial amounts if their brokers fail. The SIPC does not insure against security-value declines that occur after bankruptcy, and court legalities and the poor condition of records in bankrupt firms may delay the settlement of claims for many months.[4]

THE SEC BETWEEN 1968 AND 1973

During these years, the SEC greatly strengthened its grip on the securities industry. Back-office troubles and spreading bankruptcies reduced public confidence in self-regulation, and the effectiveness of disclosure alone as the tool of government regulation was increasingly disputed. The Commission encouraged Congress to pass new laws, issued new regulations on the strength of its existing authority, and exercised persuasive influence over the stock exchanges, the NASD, and the accounting profession. Important reforms aimed at protecting individual investors include the following.

1 Stricter safekeeping and regular audit of customer cash and securities held by broker-dealers. New regulations restrict brokers in the use of customers'

---

[4] In mid-1972, investors in the 41 firms then undergoing SIPC liquidation appeared far from satisfied with the handling of their claims. See "Little Guy's Friend?" *Wall Street Journal*, May 12, 1972, p. 1.

cash and securities. A broker must now use such assets only in ways "related to servicing his customers"—financing clients' margin transactions, for example—not to financing the broker's own business or underwriting activities. Brokers also must "physically examine and count" on a quarterly basis all securities held for their customers, account for missing securities, and buy in securities "not . . . reduced to posession or control" within specified periods.

2   *More stringent regulation of brokerage-house finances.* Under new rules, a broker whose debt-to-capital ratio exceeds the limit must immediately notify the Commission and all self-regulatory agencies, and submit monthly operational and financial reports to the SEC as long as difficulties continue. Brokerage firms may now count as capital only a portion of those assets which cannot quickly be converted to cash, and most brokerage capital comes under a new rule providing that it cannot be pulled out if withdrawal would cut capital below required minimum percentages of the broker's debts. During 1972, the SEC proposed that all stock exchange members and over-the-counter houses be required to maintain a minimum 1-to-15 ratio of net, or liquid, capital to aggregate indebtedness (1 to 20 was the prevailing ratio), minimum net capital of $25,000 ($50,000 if they wrote options), and at least 30 per cent of their capital in equity form.

3   *Penalties for firms that fall behind on record keeping or in delivering securities sold by them or their customers.* Any broker whose "books and records are not current" is required to send the Commission "immediate telegraphic notice . . . with a follow-up written report within 48 hours showing corrective steps taken."

4   *New standards of fairness for announcing corporate news and trading on "inside information."* To date, restrictions have been established mainly on a case-by-case basis because of both legal and conceptual difficulties in precisely defining who is an "insider" or what information is "material" to investors' needs.

5   *Rules prohibiting brokers and dealers from quoting bid and ask prices for securities on which they lack proper financial information.* This regulation is aimed particularly against trading in so-called shell corporations which are doing little business and have few or no assets to back their outstanding stock.

6   *Stricter rules for reporting corporate earnings.* These rules would apply particularly in companies where convertible securities, acquisitions, nonconsolidated subsidiaries, nonrecurring income or losses, or bizarre capital structures could be used to confuse or fool investors.

7   *Requirements for corporations making takeover bids for other companies.* They must make the same disclosures as those required in proxy contests.

Institutional investor study report, 1971   This study, requested by Congress in 1969, reflected the lawmakers' concern over the growing power of institutional investors in the securities market and over investor-owned companies. In general, the report found that financial institutions had not undermined stock market stability nor misused their stock ownership in other companies. Specific recommendations included the following.

1 All institutional investors, including banks, investment advisers, certain foundations, endowments, and employee funds, should be required to disclose their activities in securities markets. Extensive reports are now required only of investment companies and large insurance companies.

2 Fixed minimum commissions on large transactions should be eliminated, in order to reduce economic pressures on banks and investment companies to become exchange members. Savings on stock transactions of mutual funds would be passed on to the public through lower purchase commissions.

3 "Offshore funds"—foreign mutual funds that invest in United States securities—should be subjected to SEC regulation.

4 Hedge funds—large trading partnerships that sell short, buy on margin, and make or trade in puts and calls—should be required to register with the SEC. The report found that such funds represent potentially serious conflicts of interest because frequently their managing partners are also the major advisers of large investment companies.

Early in 1973 Congress had not yet acted on legislative recommendations contained in the report. The New York Stock Exchange, however, had meanwhile been persuaded by the SEC to accept negotiated fees on transactions exceeding $300,000, with indications that this minimum would be reduced as low as $100,000 by 1974.

Pending issues in investor protection Other issues involving the safety or fair treatment of investors were still unresolved as 1973 began. The SEC continued deliberations on the extent to which stock exchange membership should be opened to broker-dealer affiliates of mutual funds, insurance companies, and other large institutional investors, and how this change might affect small-investor transactions, stock exchange commissions, and the earning power of brokerage firms. Fixed commission rates drew increasing criticism on the ground that they included payment for investment advice and other services that many investors did not need or could buy elsewhere. Feeling also persisted that the rapid increase in small-lot commissions was driving out the individual investor and depriving the stock markets of needed liquidity. Both the SEC and the New York Stock Exchange had declared themselves in favor of closer ties among the various securities markets and a centralized system for announcing quotations, transactions, and securities prices. Some experts proposed a single, nationwide trading market.

Amid continuing debate over old issues, the SEC moved aggressively in such new directions as imposing tighter rules for exchange-trading of stock options, publicizing a daily list of companies in danger of bankruptcy, requiring publicly held companies to disclose their accounting and tax policies in more detail, and permitting corporations to make public forecasts of their sales and earnings to guide investors.[5] The Commission also announced its intention of asking Congress to narrow the exemption from SEC registration and reporting requirements of the securities of companies regulated by other federal commissions.[6] Another proposed bill would give the SEC and other federal agencies authority to set standards for stock transfers, together with wide powers over transfer agents, clearing corporations, and depositories. The Commission also instructed the NASD and the stock exchanges to set up new "suitability" standards to guide brokers in recommending stocks to their customers; factors to be explicitly considered included the individual's ability to take financial risk, his goals, and his "experience and sophistication in securities transactions." (In response, the NASD early in 1973 proposed new rules requiring securities firms to make sure that customers were financially able to buy the speculative "hot issues" of companies going public.) Finally, in August 1972, the SEC reorganized itself into five divisions, concerned respectively with market regulation, enforcement, investment company regulation, corporate regulation, and corporate finance. The wide scope of these activities suggested that the SEC was strongly resolved to enlarge its role in the nation's securities markets and economy.

QUESTIONS AND PROBLEMS

1 Is it a proper function of government to deny promoters the right to sell stock in a new corporation because the "inside" group is to receive half the stock in return for a patent? Would it make any difference if the state corporation commissioner thought the patent would not work? Suppose the stock was hard to sell and selling costs took 40 per cent of the proceeds?

2 How would you check on the reputation of a firm whose salesman wants you to sell your IBM stock and buy promotional shares which he is offering in a new computer software company?

3 What is a better business bureau?

[5] Companies would not be *required* to report such projections unless they had shown their forecasts to financial analysts or other private interests.

[6] Immediately at issue was the exemption from SEC regulation of commercial paper maturing in less than 9 months. According to an SEC staff study, this exemption permitted the officers of Penn Central Transportation Company to raise money from investors without disclosing the company's worsening financial plight. It also appeared likely that the SEC might soon challenge the effectiveness of securities regulation by other federal bodies, such as the Interstate Commerce Commission, whose historic role has emphasized rate-setting and operating problems rather than financial markets and investor protection. See "SEC Seeks to Tighten Registration Rules to Prevent Cases like Penn Central Crisis," *Wall Street Journal*, Aug. 8, 1972, p. 7.

4 How do stock exchanges protect the public from frauds? How can they compel their member firms to obey their rules?

5 What are blue-sky laws? What sort of law does your state have? (Note: Look it up in the *Corporation Manual.*)

6 Do you favor detailed regulation of procedures in the securities business? Read "Public Regulation of the Securities Markets," by George S. Stigler, in the April 1964 issue of *The Journal of Business*, or a summary of the same article in *Barron's* for April 27, 1964.

7 Do you believe that groups or corporations intent on buying large holdings or control in other corporations should be compelled to disclose their plans before proceeding? The SEC advocated this in 1967, and Congress enacted part of its proposal in July 1968. But see another viewpoint in "Salute to Raiders" in *Barron's*, Oct. 23, 1967.

8 Should all the types of securities now exempt from the Securities Act of 1933 continue to be exempt? See the article "SEC Seeks to Tighten Registration Rules to Prevent Cases like Penn Central Crisis," *Wall Street Journal*, August 8, 1972, p. 7.

9 Obtain and examine several prospectuses. Are they too long and dry to serve their purpose? Should a two-page "opinion of quality and value" by an investment advisory service be appended to each? Are such opinions generally available? (Note: A group of state commissioners in 1967 considered such a statement as a state blue-sky requirement.)

10 Should partners in securities firms be permitted to be corporation directors? If so, should the firm trade in the stock or advise its clients with respect to it? See the SEC's *Special Study of Securities Markets*, Washington, 1963, Part 1, pp. 428–440.

11 Should a director who is well acquainted with the true value of his company's stock be discouraged from buying it when it is too low and selling it when it is too high? Would it be legal for the company to do this, to stabilize the market at a "proper" level?

12 In July 1972, the NASD proposed to prohibit its members from offering "tax-sheltered" securities (oil- and gas-drilling programs, real estate syndications, and cattle-feeding operations) to any but wealthy investors. (Eligible buyers would need a 50 per cent tax bracket and net worth of at least $50,000.) Is such a regulation reasonable and nondiscriminatory? Is it defensible as a self-policing act by a private industry?

13 Would you expect the NASD to interest itself in stock exchange transactions? What does it do? Do stock exchange member firms belong to the NASD?

14 What does the SEC do in connection with bankruptcy reorganizations? Why would it have to "fight for more severe and realistic" reorganization plans? Would the once-burned old securityholders want to set up another top-heavy corporation?

15 Does the Trust Indenture Act of 1939 apply to all bond indentures now outstanding? Would it apply to railroad bonds? Should it?

16 What bad experiences with investment companies led to the Investment Company Act of 1940? Does the act adequately guard against recurrences of these bad experiences?

17 What are the principal features of the Investment Advisers Act of 1940? What else should it do?

18 Review the furor in the financial press in August–September–October 1968 about "inside information" and the Texas Gulf Sulphur and Merrill Lynch cases. Does it make any sense? What should a corporate treasurer do with a well-informed investment counselor who controls millions in investable funds and who wishes to call and become better acquainted with the treasurer's company? What if the caller is a 50-share investor?

REFERENCES

Bellemore, Douglas H., and John C. Ritchie, Jr.: *Investments*, 3d ed., South-Western Publishing Company, Incorporated, Cincinnati, 1969, Chaps. 15, 16.

Commerce Clearing House, Inc.: *Blue Sky Law Reporter* and *Federal Securities Law Reporter*, New York (both loose-leaf).

Graham, Benjamin, David L. Dodd, and C. Sidney Cottle: *Security Analysis*, 4th ed., McGraw-Hill Book Company, New York, 1962, Chap. 51.

Institute of Chartered Financial Analysis: C. F. A. *Readings in Financial Analysis*, 2d ed., Richard D. Irwin, Inc., Homewood, Ill., 1970, Part 5.

Leffler, George L., and Loring C. Farwell: *The Stock Market*, The Ronald Press Company, New York, 1963, Chap. 28.

Loss, Louis: *Securities Regulation*, 2d ed., Little, Brown and Company, Boston, 1969.

Robbins, Sidney M.: *The Securities Markets: Operations and Issues*, The Free Press of Glencoe, Inc., New York, 1966.

Securities and Exchange Commission: annual reports.

Securities and Exchange Commission: *Special Study of Securities Markets*, Washington, 1963, especially Part 4, Chap. XI, or Part 5, Chap. XI.

Securities and Exchange Commission: *Study of Unsafe and Unsound Practices of Brokers and Dealers*, Washington, 1971.

United States Corporation Company: *Corporation Manual*, New York, annual.

part 4
Investment Analysis

An investor needs techniques and standards to help him measure the quality and the value of the securities in which he is interested. The process of measuring quality and value is known as investment analysis.

Investment analysis requires first an understanding of the characteristics and trends which are important in any investment situation, and of the accounting devices which portray these characteristics and trends. Chapter 13 deals with the important characteristics and trends and Chapter 14 with the accounting devices.

Next, investment analysis must utilize its measurement criteria in the light of the individual peculiarities of particular types of securities. To illustrate the process, Chapters 15 through 20 study the features and records of five broad classes of securities: the heavily regulated transportation and utility industries; the relatively free industrials; the partially regulated financial enterprises—notably banks and insurance firms; and finally, public securities—the nearly 600 billion dollars of federal, state, and local government bonds available to American investors. These six chapters illustrate the vital differences between specific classes of securities and show how investment analysis utilizes various criteria and methods in approaching different industries and issuers.

Chapter 20, which studies the characteristics, markets, and prices (yields) of federal, state, and local securities, is especially important. These securities differ markedly, and the investors who use them need to know them well. Likewise, investor-citizens have every reason to know their features from the standpoint of the issuing government, for public economy and the welfare of the securities markets are both affected by public financing.

AN APPROACH TO
INVESTMENT ANALYSIS

Investment analysis means the detailed study of the characteristics, quality, prospects, and value of a particular security. It usually also means a comparative study, for such attributes as quality and value are too abstract to be interpreted clearly except in comparison with other somewhat similar securities. Good investment analysis thus becomes a task of estimating and comparing, involving a review of one or more industries, firms, and individual securities in each case.

Investors generally undertake the analysis of a security after casual inquiry has indicated that it is suitable for purchase or that it should be sold from their portfolios. This is a practical approach, for it means that the investigator knows what he is looking for; he wants a security with particular characteristics of safety, price stability, growth, or other features, and the investigation can be pointed to test for the desired features. Every analytical study will also be a general "fishing expedition" designed to uncover unsuspected attributes in the securities studied, if any exist.

Any investment analysis is a forward-looking inquiry. The main issues to be resolved deal with the earnings and payments the investment can make in the future, the probable future behavior of its price, and the degree of certainty that attaches to these forecasts. Only the future is important, but investors differ widely in the planning periods over which they attempt to peer ahead. This length of view or "horizon," as it is called, significantly affects the relative weights an investor will attach to different factors in his analysis; he will logically emphasize those influences he expects to prove decisive in the interval for which he is committing his capital.

Investment analysis is not a process exclusively devoted to the study of high-grade securities. Good analytical work is of course done by most institutional buyers of bonds, to make sure that their bonds are suitable and that they choose the best available for their purposes, price considered; but even more extensive analysis is done by stock buyers, especially on speculative issues. After all, the need for analysis is greatest in speculative issues, where success may be very profitable and error very expensive.

PROCEDURE IN INVESTMENT ANALYSIS

Because the objectives sought by investors vary greatly and because the types of investments are so distinctive in nature, it is not possible to suggest a few easy ratios which will provide a measure of value for all securities. However, it does seem feasible to suggest a five-part outline for investment analysis which may help the investor to organize the information ordinarily available on corporate securities. The five parts are as follows:

First, the analysis will set forth the basic indications of value which are almost universally used for the quick appraisal of a security. These will be such things as earnings per share, price-earnings ratios, yields, growth rates, overall coverage of interest requirements, and recent price ranges, with the exact items depending, of course, on whether the security being tested is a common stock, a preferred stock, or a bond. These basic indications give a preliminary measure of the quality of a security and of the highness or reasonableness of its price. Since the purpose of the analysis is the anticipation of future values, any tendency of these basic indicators to trend up or down will be especially important.

Second, the analysis will study the industry represented by the subject security, to determine its immediate and long-run characteristics. Third, the analysis must review the firm which issues the security, to determine its strength, position, and future prospects. Fourth, the security itself must be studied, to obtain all pertinent data on its legal rights, market position, and financial strength. Finally, the analysis must reach summary conclusions on the probable future trends of earnings, payments, quality, price-earnings ratios, yield, and normal price.

The detailed items most commonly considered in making an analysis such as this are presented in outline form on the accompanying pages. Obviously, the outline should be adapted to fit the individual case, since industries are not all alike—banks, for example, do not have the same characteristics as computer software companies—but the adaptation will not be difficult. The analyst will need to be reasonably familiar with the key features of each industry which he studies, however, for lack of such background information could lead to grievous errors.

In presenting an outline for investment analysis, this chapter does not intend to suggest that each individual investor should start with primary statistical data and do his own analytical work, ignoring the mass of interpretive studies published by the financial services and brokers. To do so would be wasteful and foolish. But much that is done by these agencies is incomplete, and more than a little of it reaches hasty conclusions. The investor who has his own outline of procedure in mind can borrow facts from many sources, supplement them with calculations of his own, and test his own final conclusions against those of the experts.

Outline for investment analysis

I Basic (preliminary) indications

Common stocks

A Earnings per share: current, recent, average
B Dividends
C P-E ratio, yield
D Growth rate
E Rating, reputation
F Market price record
G Capital structure, book value

Preferred stocks

A Rating, reputation
B Yield
C Market price record
D Call price, cumulation, conversion
E Dividend coverage
F Asset coverage

Bonds

A Rating, reputation
B Yield
C Market price record
D Call price, conversion
E Interest coverage
F Security

II Industry analysis

A Permanence of the industry
B Growth of the industry
C Stability of sales and earnings
D Competitive conditions
E Labor relations
F Governmental attitudes
G Immediate outlook for sales and earnings

III Analysis of the firm

A Size, leadership, dominance
B Growth of earnings, sales
C Product line, diversification
D Product development and research
E Brands, patents, goodwill, established position
F Modernity, efficiency, integration
G Return on equity
H Profit margins, costs, overhead
I Sales outlook
J Stability of sales and earnings
K Assets and operating facilities
L Working capital position and cash flow
M Capital structure
N Earnings estimates

O Dividend estimates
P Management
Q Stockholder position

IV The individual security

A Its legal rights
B Its market position
1 Number of holders
2 Popularity of type
3 Eligibility
4 Additional issue or secondary offerings
5 Market history
C Financial position in capital structure, improvement or weakening

V Conclusions

A Future earnings
B Future payments
C Quality and characteristics
D Future price

THE BASIC INDICATIONS

Little explanation of the "basic indications" of investment value is now needed, in view of what has been said in previous chapters. These items are clearly the ones most commonly quoted in investment studies and whose trends are most eagerly noted. Indeed, the entire analysis is little more than an extension and verification of them.

Because of the common use of these basic factors, it is seldom necessary for the investor to compute them himself. Earnings, dividends paid, market price ranges, capital structures, and the like are commonly tabulated in reference manuals and leaflets such as the *Standard Stock Report* on the B. F. Goodrich Company, which is reproduced in Charts 13-1 and 13-2.[1] All the investor needs to do is to note the figures shown and their trend in order to have preliminary indication of the values he must test.

The investor who stops collecting information at this point must either make a crude guess as to the future of his securities from the evidence of the past, or he must trust the verdict of others who may have looked farther. This latter is not an unsound procedure; one who has not the time or the experience to study his own

---

[1] Other highly convenient sources were reviewed in Chap. 11. For this purpose, the following are useful and readily available: (a) *Standard Stock Reports*, (b) *Moody's Handbook of Common Stocks*, (c) *Value Line Investment Survey*, and (d) *Stock Factographs Manual*.

investments may reasonably follow the suggestions made in Chapters 4 and 11 for dependence upon others. But if the investor decides to make additional studies himself, he usually finds it necessary to undertake detailed surveys of the industry, the firm, and the security itself, before he reaches his final conclusions.

INDUSTRY FEATURES ARE ALWAYS IMPORTANT

The detailed work in the analysis of any corporate security logically begins with the industry. Most industries have important unique characteristics which affect the values of their securities, and the analyst must review these carefully. In fact, industry features are so important that much of the space in investment books— including this one—is given over to describing them. For detailed investment-oriented analyses of many major industries, the *S & P Industry Surveys* are an excellent source.

There are at least seven industry features which investment analysts are likely to consider in appraising a stock or a bond. They are:

A Permanence of the industry   Some lines of business are subject to displacement or loss as a result of technological development, change in demand, or change in the law. Examples in the past generation would include streetcar companies, makers of steam locomotives, and grocery and dry-goods wholesalers. Since industries on the downgrade are likely to be depressed, it seems best to avoid them in most cases. On the other hand, an industry for which there is no foreseeable substitute, such as meat packing or steel production, is at least exempt from early obliteration. Although a tendency toward obsolescence can hardly be an advantage, alert managements can frequently redirect a company's resources into new lines—for example, Textron became a major diversified manufacturing company when the woolen textiles business slowed—so the obsolescence of good companies is less frequent than the obsolescence of products. Investors who read the financial periodicals regularly are usually aware of trends toward obsolescence, but studies of industry sales and profit statistics, plus articles on the uses for products and possible substitutes for them, are readily available when definite information is desired.

B Growth of the industry   It has long been known that an industry which is growing vigorously has three advantages over less dynamic ones: First, there is little occasion for cutthroat competitive tactics, and profits are usually satisfactory. Second, there is opportunity for stockholders to add profitably to their investments from time to time. Third, there is opportunity for early arrivals in a growing industry to develop specialty products, trade names, and customer connections against a day when competitive advantage may be needed. A growing industry is one which enjoys better-than-average gains in dollar sales volume, in

Chart 13-1 *Standard listed stock report, title side.*

GR¹ # Goodrich (B. F.) 1028

Stock —	Price Jun. 26'72	Dividend	Yield
COMMON..........................	24¼	²$1.00	²4.1%

RECOMMENDATION: Potentials of this important rubber fabricator are bright, reflecting broadening foreign operations, favorable long-term prospects for both tire and chemical-plastic lines, and benefits from an asset redeployment program which is closing a number of unprofitable operations. The earnings gains of 1971 should continue into 1972 and beyond, and the shares offer attraction for intermediate- and long-range recovery.

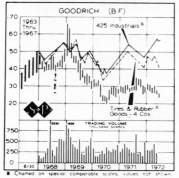

GOODRICH (B F)

Charted on special comparable scales, values not shown.

SALES (Million $)

Quarter:	1972	1971	1970	1969	1968
March.....	347	⁵280	304	296	275
June........		344	313	316	301
Sept.		333	300	303	290
Dec.		⁵280	⁵217	314	306

Sales from continuing operations for 1971 rose 9.1% from those of 1970. Margins benefited from a more profitable tire mix, price increases, and absence of strikes, all of which outweighed weakness in some chemical and industrial rubber prices and reduced defense business. Pretax income advanced 57%. After taxes at 44.8% against 47.9%, and minority interest, net from continuing operations increased 74%. Following smaller losses from discontinued operations, net income was 2.6 times the year-earlier level. Results exclude a special charge equal to $1.94 a share in 1971 and $0.24 special credit in 1970.

For the quarter ended March 31, 1972, sales from continuing operations rose 24%, year to year. Net income was up 79%. Results for the 1971 interim were restated to reflect the equity method of accounting.

³COMMON SHARE EARNINGS ($)

Quarter:	1972	1971	1970	1969	1968
March.....	0.61	⁵0.34	0.55	0.68	0.73
June........		0.72	0.18	0.80	⁴1.23
Sept.		0.60	0.34	0.61	0.60
Dec.		⁵0.40	ᵈ0.28	0.66	0.49

PROSPECTS

Near Term—Sales from continuing operations for 1972 should increase moderately from the 1971 level (the $1.24 billion reported for 1971 will be restated downward as more units are closed). The gain would reflect heavier demand for original equipment and replacement tires, recent price increases on replacement tires and chemicals, a richer product mix, and improving demand for plastics and chemicals. Aerospace business should remain soft.

Margins should benefit from the increased volume, the higher prices, and a better product mix for tires, although higher labor and raw materials costs will be partially offsetting. Aided further by probable benefits from the investment tax credit, earnings for 1972 should post a worthwhile gain from the $2.06 a share (before $1.94 special charges) of 1971. Dividends should continue at a minimum of $0.25 quarterly.

Long Term—Although subject to cyclical influences, sales and earnings should expand over the longer term, aided by product and market diversification.

RECENT DEVELOPMENTS

Effective June 1, 1972 the company increased by 1½% to 2½% the prices for certain passenger, truck, farm, and industrial tires and tubes for the replacement market.

Goodrich recently increased the price of polyvinyl chloride vinyl dispersion resins 1 cent a pound, and all plasticized polyvinyl chloride compounds ½ cent a pound.

The assets of Goodrich's footwear division will be sold in whole or in part.

DIVIDEND DATA

At December 31, 1971 $190,415,000 of retained earnings was unrestricted as to dividends. Payments:

Amt. of Divd. $	Date Decl.	Ex-divd. Date	Stock of Record	Payment Date
0.25...	Jul. 20	Sep. 3	Sep. 10	Sep. 30'71
0.25...	Nov. 16	Nov. 29	Dec. 3	Dec. 31'71
0.25...	Feb. 15	Mar. 6	Mar. 10	Mar. 31'72
0.25...	May 16	May 26	Jun. 2	Jun. 30'72

¹Listed N.Y.S.E.; also traded Boston, Cincinnati, Detroit, Midwest, Phila.-Balt.-Wash., Pitts., and Pacific Coast S.Es. ²Indicated rate. ³Adj. for 3-for-2 split in July 1968. ⁴Incl. $0.19 non-recurr. inc. ⁵Sales excl. discontinued operations & earns. incl. equity in profits/losses of affiliates for 12 mos. Dec. 1970 & 9 mos. Dec. & 3 mos. Mar. 1971. ᵈDeficit.

STANDARD N.Y.S.E. STOCK REPORTS   **STANDARD & POOR'S CORP.**

Published at Ephrata, Pa. Editorial & Executive Offices, 345 Hudson St., New York, N.Y. 10014

Vol. 39, No. 127   Friday, June 30, 1972   Sec. 11

Chart 13-2 *Standard listed stock report, reverse side.*

1028 **GOODRICH (B. F.) COMPANY (THE)**

[1]INCOME STATISTICS (Million $) AND PER SHARE ($) DATA

Year Ended Dec. 31	Net Sales	% Oper. Inc. of Sales	Oper. Inc.	Deprec. & Amort.	Net Bef. Taxes	[2]Net Inc.	[3]Common Share ($) Data: [2]Earns.	*Cash Generated	Divs. Paid	Price Range	Price-Earns. Ratios HI LO
1972--	-----	---	----	----	----	----	---	---	0.50	31⅝ -23⅝	-----
1971--	1,236.7	12.4	153.5	[5]58.46	63.81	29.83	2.06	6.75	1.00	35 -25⅝	17–12
1970--	1,133.8	11.6	131.4	[5]54.96	40.57	11.51	0.79	5.26	1.54	34 -19¾	43–25
1969--	1,229.1	11.6	142.8	48.92	70.57	39.92	2.75	7.04	1.72	66 -28½	24–10
1968--	1,172.1	12.0	141.0	45.76	81.73	44.12	3.05	6.21	1.66	51½ -38¼	17–13
1967--	1,006.2	10.2	102.3	44.33	52.31	29.47	2.14	5.36	1.60	50 -37⅝	23–18
1966--	1,039.1	12.6	131.3	41.72	88.57	48.60	3.53	6.55	1.53⅓	46½ -36	13–10
1965--	980.1	11.0	107.9	35.95	73.56	40.65	2.95	5.57	1.46⅔	45 -34⅝	15–12
1964--	872.4	10.2	88.9	32.88	56.59	33.97	2.47	4.87	1.46⅔	42¼ -32⅝	17–13
1963--	828.8	9.7	80.5	31.64	49.51	27.05	1.97	4.27	1.46⅔	37¾ -28¼	19–14
1962--	812.0	9.6	77.9	27.95	50.03	26.33	1.91	4.10	1.46⅔	48¼ -24¼	25–13

[1]PERTINENT BALANCE SHEET STATISTICS (Million $)

Dec. 31	Gross Prop.	[4]Capital Expend.	Cash Items	Inventories	Receivables	Current Assets	Current Liabs.	Net Workg. Cap.	Cur. Ratio Assets to Liabs.	Long Term Debt	[3]($) Book Val. Com. Sh.
1971--	1,100.4	75.47	43.1	348.2	285.2	684.0	404.9	279.1	1.7–1	291.27	40.15
1970--	1,116.1	97.48	51.0	320.2	270.5	644.3	310.8	333.5	2.1–1	357.29	40.99
1969--	1,086.1	137.79	38.7	312.6	263.3	618.2	362.3	255.9	1.7–1	255.70	40.78
1968--	961.3	122.98	42.9	281.8	241.2	565.9	308.7	257.2	1.8–1	188.71	40.01
1967--	736.6	92.34	36.3	234.6	208.5	479.4	235.3	244.1	2.0–1	103.41	38.46
1966--	653.3	89.29	37.0	242.3	199.8	479.1	195.7	283.4	2.4–1	104.55	38.67
1965--	570.9	59.75	39.2	214.3	178.4	431.8	127.4	304.4	3.4–1	107.65	36.43
1964--	501.8	40.90	45.6	200.3	142.2	388.1	114.5	273.6	3.4–1	87.57	34.67
1963--	476.3	50.29	26.1	185.6	149.2	360.8	98.0	262.9	3.7–1	95.36	33.83
1962--	454.7	52.30	40.0	178.4	146.8	365.2	93.3	271.9	3.9–1	97.21	33.25

[1]Consol.; incl. Ameripol, Inc. aft. 1967. [2]Incl. equity in earns. of affiliates aft. 1969; bef. spec. chgs. equal to $1.94 a sh. in 1971, $0.15 in 1969 & spec. crs. of $0.24 a sh. in 1970 & $0.41 in 1967. [3]Adj. for 3-for-2 split in 1968. [4]Incl. investments & acqs. [5]Incl. deprec. on discontinued opers.
*As computed by Standard & Poor's.

Fundamental Position

Goodrich, one of the Big Four rubber fabricators, derived 54% of 1971 operating revenues from tires and related products; 22% from chemicals, plastic materials and synthetic rubbers; and 24% from all other activities.

General Motors is the largest original equipment outlet for tires, but a portion of the requirements of Ford and Chrysler also is supplied. Replacement sales are handled through thousands of independent dealers, by the sale of private brand tires to oil companies and a large mass merchandiser, and through approximately 475 company-owned or operated retail stores, which also sell a wide variety of non-tire items. Daily tire capacity at six plants is estimated at 90,000 units. Tire capacity has been consistently expanded in recent years, with the current emphasis being placed on radials.

Through its chemical division, the company is one of the largest factors in polyvinyl chloride resins, and also produces such products as latex and other synthetic rubbers, polymer chemicals, water-soluble polymers, acrylic film, caustic soda, and chlorine.

Other products include tire cord and industrial fabrics, adhesives, building products, sheet rubber, vinyl upholstery, furniture cushioning, mattresses, and pillows.

There are five factories in Canada, and subsidiaries or associates operate in over 20 other countries. Initial production of crude rubber began during 1963 from rubber trees planted in 1955. About 15,000 acres of rubber plantation in Liberia are owned.

Resumed in 1939, dividends averaged 70% of earnings in the five years through 1971.

Employees: 55,806. Shareholders: 34,685.

Finances

In June, 1972 Goodrich announced plans to raise about $100 million in the public market, probably through a combination debt and equity offering. Proceeds will be used to reduce short-term debt.

Capital expenditures in 1970 and 1971 included $24,715,000 expended for the acquisition of N.V. Rubberfabriek Vredestein, a Dutch tire company. Expenditures for 1972 are budgeted to exceed the $75,474,000 of 1971, with most of the emphasis on expanding radial capacity.

Operations outside the United States and Canada accounted for $213 million of assets at December 31, 1971. For 1971, these operations accounted for $5,491,000 of consolidated net income.

Following recent studies of operations, several manufacturing operations have been closed in 1971 and thus far in 1972. This asset redeployment program produced an extraordinary charge to 1971 net income of $28,094,000, or $1.94 a share.

CAPITALIZATION

LONG TERM DEBT: $291,266,000.
MINORITY INTEREST: $17,380,000.
COMMON STOCK: 14,471,853 shs. ($5 par); some 16% owned by Northwest Industries.
OPTIONS: To purchase 201,937 shs. at $22.94 to $48.15.

Incorporated in N.Y. in 1912. **Office**—500 S. Main St., Akron, Ohio 44318. **Pres**—H. B. Warner. **Secy**—C. R. Couts. **VP-Treas**—F. X. Reilly. **Dirs**—O. P. Thomas (Chrmn), G. Alexander, G. Edwards, B. Gross, J. W. Keemer, A. Kelly, R. S. Laing, B. T. Leithead, D. L. Luke, III, T. B. Nantz, H. C. Nolen, H. B. Warner, J. L. Weinberg. **Transfer Agent**—Bankers Trust Co., NYC. **Registrar**—Morgan Guaranty Trust Co., NYC.

Information has been obtained from sources believed to be reliable, but its accuracy and completeness, and that of the opinions based thereon, are not guaranteed. Printed in U. S. A physical volume of products, and in earnings; it probably is developing new products or new uses for its products or both; and, if it is to continue as a growth industry, it should not be approaching either a saturation point for sales or an end to its innovations. Information about growing industries and their products can be obtained in all the usual sources—financial services, periodical articles, brokers' literature and government and trade association statistics.

C Stability of sales and earnings Although it is not imperative that every industry show as steady sales volume as the electric power companies, it must be conceded that the extreme irregularity shown during the past 20 years by railway equipment makers or copper-mining companies, for example, makes it difficult for stocks in these industries to promise stability in earnings, dividends, or stock prices, though their average earning capacity may be good. Such concerns attempt to avoid fixed charges and to reduce expenses in dull periods, but the maintenance of even moderate dividend stability is a difficult problem. The investor who contemplates commitments in any industry whose behavior and outlook are not familiar to him will do well to study the history of sales, prices, profits, and dividends in the industry and to compare past situations with the present one, before he makes his decision. Data may be found in the financial services, in periodical articles, and in government reports.

D Competitive conditions Some industries, such as retailing, are inherently competitive. Others, such as the manufacture of simple electrical components, may be entered with little capital and may quickly become crowded with competitors whenever profits rise. Still others, such as the cement makers in the years 1966–1968, become overbuilt and engage in cutthroat practices. Although it is not possible to foretell accurately the progress of competitive conditions into the distant future, investors do well to examine the conditions of supply and demand, price leadership, and competitive tactics in industries they are considering. A complete lack of effective competition would probably betoken a dangerously unstable condition, but a stable marketing and pricing situation permitting reasonable profit margins is defintely to be sought. Competition from without as well as within the industry merits consideration—the cotton-goods industry, for example, is keenly affected by the competition of synthetic fibers.

E Labor relations An industry which is effectively dominated by aggressive unions, as the coal-mining and ocean-shipping industries are, is often a relatively insecure place for investors' money. This is particularly true if other industries or foreign interests can compete in the field, even though the government is currently attempting, by subvention or otherwise, to assist American-owned enterprise. The best industries from the investor standpoint are those in which (1) unionism is weak and seems likely to remain so, (2) labor costs represent only a small portion of the costs of operation, (3) labor has a tradition of reasonable attitudes, or (4) mechanization provides a feasible alternative.

F Governmental attitudes Industries in which there is a pronounced trend toward government participation or extensive regulation should be approached with caution. In the prosperous years since World War II, the government has seemed reasonably friendly toward business, but the troubles of the electric power industry in the thirties, under the twin afflictions of the public power mania and the Public Utility Holding Company Act of 1935, should stand as a warning to investors. In recent years, frequent antitrust proceedings have served notice that political factors still bulk large among investment hazards. Another aspect of governmental intervention is of major import to investors: A number of industries, such as air transport, sugar production, and fluid milk distribution, are organized around government subsidies or marketing restrictions. Removal or alteration of the government's policies would cause drastic changes in the industries.

G Immediate outlook for sales and earnings Even if business and competitive conditions appear completely sound in the long run, it is not desirable to overlook the market hazards of investment in industries which are facing sales or earnings difficulties in the immediate future. Such difficulties may spring from excess inventories, temporary demand peculiarities, labor troubles, or other sources, but in any case they may cause declines in the prices of the affected securities. If sales and earnings prospects are bright, however, there is a corresponding strong chance for price advances.

INVESTMENT FACTORS IN THE INDIVIDUAL FIRM

Even though an industry operates under favorable conditions, the promise of an investment in it will still depend heavily on the position of the firm. An unstable or poorly managed firm often does poorly under excellent conditions, even as a strong firm sometimes does well in a faltering industry. The following factors most often measure the strength and promise in an individual firm.

A Size, leadership, dominance Unless they have palpably "gone to seed," the larger firms in an industry are likely to afford the best-quality opportunities for security investments. Such firms will have diversification of lines, production facilities, and sales outlets, as well as great resources. As examples, General Motors, International Business Machines, General Electric, Goodyear Tire and Rubber, and Exxon might be mentioned. If a large firm has price, design, and research leadership, and if it is maintaining its reputation and strength, there is reason to regard it as a sound and conservative choice. Smaller firms, even promising ones, are likely to be a little more speculative in nature, though for the same reason they may have more dynamic possibilities.

B Growth The firm whose recent history and current experience emphasize growth is usually a good one to invest in. There is nearly always a reason for growth—good management, good products, good service to customers—and the securityholders are likely to be beneficiaries. As outstanding examples, attention is called to the growth of Sears Roebuck, Xerox Corporation, and American Home Products during the past 20 years. Effective growth will usually mean both sales growth and earnings growth, it will show no signs of slowing down, and it will equal or exceed the growth trends of competitors and of industry in general.

C Product line diversification Needless to say, a firm finds great advantage in a well-balanced line of products which can be made together and sold together efficiently. An adequately broad line which can be made in the same plant, stored together, identified as related products, and sold to the same customers by the same sales force should be a strong basis for earnings. The firm may also be better off from the investor's point of view if it makes diversified lines of products, in diversified locations, from varied types of raw materials, intended for customers in various lines of business, who live in different parts of the country. Under such conditions, the loss of a single contract or the deterioration of a single market will not be a completely devastating blow. However, it must be conceded that many firms making a few items for a very few customers—for example, automobile parts manufacturers supplying only three or four automobile makers—have had long and stable relations with these customers.

D Product development and research Most of the successful corporations in recent decades have devoted great attention to inventing and developing their products. Such firms as Proctor & Gamble, Minnesota Mining, IBM, and Eastman Kodak have offered a constant stream of new and improved products. These serve new and profitable markets and provide much of the earnings growth for which these companies are famous. Obviously, many of the new products and processes developed by corporations come from the research laboratories operated by the companies. Investors have every reason to scrutinize the research and development outlays made by their companies and their record of performance, for this is one of the vital areas of company progress.

E Brands, patents, goodwill, established position These intangibles are truly among the principal earning assets of American investors. Such manufacturers' labels as General Electric and Zenith command respect and obtain sales; the tremendous patent positions of RCA and du Pont produce revenue and product leadership; such brand names as Simmons and Jello and Firestone carry an auto-

matic competitive advantage; and the tremendous earning power associated with
Sears, Roebuck's customer following is justly impressive. Intangible assets are far
more difficult for competitors to reproduce than tangible ones are, and for that
reason they are strong bulwarks for investors' hopes.

F Modernity, efficiency, integration The profit margins in modern industrial
enterprises average only about 6 per cent of the sales. This leaves little room for
complacency; labor costs and taxes rise inexorably, and competitors try constantly to reduce their costs and selling prices. Consequently, a concern remains profitable and grows only if its plants are efficient and its methods modern. The successful steel company is the one which shifts to oxygen furnaces and continuous
casting at exactly the right time, and the successful auto tire maker builds new
automated plants as soon as demand and technology make them possible. Iron
mines in Labrador and rubber plantations in Liberia may also provide reliable and
economical sources of raw material. Since the investor's chances of success rest
upon a thin profit margin which in turn depends largely on low costs achieved by
modern facilities and efficiency, possibly aided by the advantages of integration,
investors must be constantly aware of their companies' progress in this important
competitive arena.

G Return on equity A company's profitability and growth potential can be
measured in various ways, but the most comprehensive yardstick available to the
analyst is the ratio of after-tax common share earnings to book value per share.
This figure expresses the percentage of common stock equity that is returned in
profit each year, either to be paid out in dividends or reinvested to compound
future earnings. A company's rate of return on equity imposes a ceiling on the rate
at which its future earnings can grow[2] or on the generosity of its dividend payments. Companies that demonstrate consistently high rates of year-to-year earnings growth, such as Sears Roebuck, Proctor & Gamble, American Home Products, and IBM, are characterized by returns on equity in the 12 to 20 per cent
range. So are consistently generous dividend payers like General Motors and
Exxon.

H Profit margins, costs, overhead Profit margins and such specifics as labor
costs, fuel costs, property taxes, and selling costs are important on a per unit basis
and as a percentage of sales, and their trends up or down are doubly important.
Although a high profit margin is prima facie a demonstration of efficiency and

---

[2] For example, if a company earns $1 on a $10 per share book value, and if all earnings are reinvested,
then a continuing return on equity of 10 per cent will enable earnings per share to grow by 10 per cent annually. If this year's $1 of earnings is plowed back, next year's earnings will amount to $1.10, 10 per cent of
the $11 now backing each common share. Retaining these earnings will produce earnings of $1.21 in the
third year, and so on.

competitive effectiveness, it may merely reflect a high degree of integration and a heavy capital investment per unit of sales; yet even in this case, it demonstrates financial strength and an ability to withstand competitive pressure. Inflexible overhead costs, such as office salaries, rentals, and property taxes, are a disadvantage. Profit margins and principal costs for the major companies in most industries are shown in time trends and compared in Standard & Poor's *Industry Surveys*, *Studley-Shupert Industry Basic Studies*, and other sources. In some instances a study of past profit margins and expense ratios will provide estimates of a firm's "break-even" volume or of the profit margin available with a given volume of sales.[3]

I Sales outlook There is no more vital determinant of a firm's future prosperity than its sales outlook. Investors usually believe, and with some justification, that a firm which can make sales will somehow control its costs and operate profitably. Consequently, they devise many ways of estimating future sales, both in the near term and for the distant future. For example, long-term average future sales are often estimated by projecting past sales trends, possibly with adjustments made to allow for commodity price-level changes; or estimates may be made as percentages of national income, or per capita in the territory served, or as a share in an industry total which has been projected. For shorter-term estimates, percentages over or under those of the previous year are often used. When price levels have been unsettled, it is often desirable to gauge sales trends by some measure of unit volume, such as barrels of petroleum products sold, or number of automobiles sold, or store sales deflated for price changes.

J Stability of sales and earnings Because fluctuations in sales and earnings often cause sharp fluctuations in the prices of a firm's securities, it is important to check the record to see if such occurrences are common either in the industry or in the particular firm. The possession or lack of certain contracts, sales outlets, or special incomes may make enormous differences in these matters. For example, the New York Central Railroad had rather erratic results from its railroad operations in the years 1946–1967, but it had very reliable rental and dividend income of over $25 million per year, which helped considerably. Information on all these matters can be had from the usual sources.

---

[3] The "break-even point" is a much-discussed figure in industries with high fixed costs and fluctuating sales volume, such as railroading and steel production. It refers to the volume of sales necessary to cover all expenses including taxes, and thus to avoid a loss. It is difficult to compute because unit selling prices and the unit prices of cost items are unstable, being affected by the same economic forces which influence sales volume; and, for that matter, overhead costs are not totally fixed nor are variable ones totally variable. But, despite the difficulties, break-even point estimates are a fascinating topic. The same techniques used to compute the break-even point may also be used to compute the probable size of the profit or loss at any given rate of output.

K   Assets and operating facilities   Where fixed assets such as buildings, mines, machinery, and equipment are very important to the corporation, the investor would usually like assurance that they are adequate, modern, adaptable, and reasonably well located with reference to supplies, labor, and markets. The appraisal of fixed assets from these viewpoints is not usually easy, for neither time of construction nor cost is positive evidence of value. Financial services and periodical articles frequently express opinions which may or may not be fully reliable. It is a familiar axiom of finance that a well-integrated concern with ample raw material and fixed-asset resources is strongly fortified in hard times, for it is able to operate with a minimum of cash payments to outsiders, thus conserving its liquid resources. Contrariwise, a concern which buys its supplies and leases the premises it occupies may feel the pressure on its cash resources when business is bad.

L   Working capital position and cash flow   These are important indicators of a firm's capacity to pay dividends and to maintain its competitive efficiency. Working capital is usually measured as the excess of cash, short-term cash investments, receivables, and inventory over the total of accounts payable, short-term bank loans, and taxes payable. A firm is said to be in a sound working capital position if it has enough resources to buy the inventory it needs and to extend its customers the credit they need, without ever being embarrassed for cash or forced into abnormal indebtedness itself. To remain in a sound working capital position, a firm must not only conduct its ordinary business with discretion, but must also be prepared to finance all impending bond and mortgage maturities, expansion and modernization plans, and seasonal requirements without strain. A poor working capital position is not necessarily a harbinger of trouble when business is good, but it is very difficult to correct under adverse conditions. A sound working capital position is therefore essential before the securities of a firm can be called good in quality. Investors usually investigate a firm's working capital position by studying its most recent balance sheet in conjunction with past balance sheets; the adequacy and reliability of its earnings and other cash sources; and the impending cash needs for expansion, debt repayment, and other uses. A number of calculations comparing liquid assets with short-term liabilities and cash receipts with cash outgo are commonly used in studying working capital position; these will be discussed in the next chapter.

M   Capital structure   The term *capital structure* refers to the proportions of a corporation's resources furnished by the various groups of its creditors and stockholders.[4] Thus Textron, Inc., at the beginning of 1972 reported that its net re-

---

[4] The orthodox definition of capital structure refers to the proportioning of long-term debt, preferred stock, and common stock, leaving current debt out of the calculation. The authors believe their suggested calculation to be more significant.

sources came 29 per cent from short-term creditors, 16 per cent from long-term lenders, and 55 per cent from common stockholders. A sound capital structure involves at least three requirements. (1) Debt and preferred stock are sufficiently limited so that the corporation can, in most years, earn enough to discharge its obligations to them. (2) Impending maturities of both long- and short-term debt are of manageable size and composition. (3) The company can at all reasonable times sell new securities to meet its permanent financing needs. A capital structure characterized by excessive debt or by noncallable bonds and preferred stocks with onerous privileges is not good for common stockholders, nor for other security-holders if the firm needs to undertake new financing or refunding. As many companies also learned during the tight-money era of 1969–1970, short-term debt is more dangerous than long-term debt because it must continually be renewed under unforeseeable conditions. A capital structure including a large percentage of common stock equity—in other words, a low-leverage situation—might well suggest that all the securities are good quality. The nature of a firm's capital structure may reasonably vary with the type of the firm and the industry—stable earnings, well-established position, and large size will justify a larger percentage of debt and preferred stock than a new or small firm should have.

N Earnings estimates Estimates of future earnings are made in many ways. Crude estimates may be made by projecting the trend of past per share earnings, possibly with allowances for changes in price levels or sales volume. More accurate estimates are possible by making estimates of future sales and deducting projected percentages for various costs and taxes. If earnings before income taxes bear a reasonably constant ratio to sales, this may be a simple basis for estimate. If near-term earnings rather than average future earnings are to be estimated, known factors, such as inventory gains or losses or other temporary phenomena, must be allowed for, and estimates based on increases or decreases in the previous year's income and expenses may be most significant.

O Dividend estimates Long-range dividend estimates for common stocks are usually made with reference to estimated earnings. Inspection of past policies will indicate whether any typical percentage of earnings is normally distributed and whether regular or irregular distributions are likely. Probable cash receipts from operations (cash flow) and estimated cash needs will be vital here. Working capital position, expansion needs, needs for debt retirement, and the expressed ideas of the management will all assist in making the estimates. Dividend estimates are very important to the investor; the rate of payments to be made in the future will be one of the important factors controlling the market price of the stock. For the near term, any increase or decrease in the dividend rate will be significant because it is almost certain to cause a sharp change in the price of the stock.

P   Management   A management which is able, vigorous, and possessed of good commercial and financial connections is of great advantage to the firm. Such managements inspire cooperation and confidence, obtain internal efficiency, and also secure advantageous purchase, sales, and credit terms for the firm. Incompetent and indifferent managements are an obvious disadvantage, as are those racked by dissent. Over the longer range, one-man organizations are also of doubtful attractiveness because of the obvious hazard if the key man is lost. It is difficult for an investor to appraise a corporate management from published reports. The list of directors may be examined to note their other corporate connections, and the occasional public relations–inspired biographical letters "about our executives" may be read, but these are of limited value. More reliable impressions can often be obtained by personal observation of company employees and representatives—their energy and initiative, powers of decision, freedom from red tape and bureaucratic thinking, etc. Mostly, however, the investor must judge management by its ability to make profits.

Q   Stockholder position   A corporation is usually in a better financial position if its stock is widely held, if its stockholders are familiar with it from long experience, and if its important stockholders include some groups of financial experience and power. If the stock is held by investment companies, endowment funds, and other prestigious institutions, its reputation and market strength are enhanced, although active trading by institutions in a stock will make its price unstable, and wholesale selling of a stock out of institutions' portfolios will depress the price severely. A wide distribution of stock facilitates new financing among the stockholders and promotes price stability, especially if the stockholders know the company well. Financial experience and power among the stockholders mean that competent groups will watch the company's progress, possibly contribute to the management, and sponsor the company in transactions with financial institutions. The best evidence of wide distribution of stock will be in the published data on the number of stockholders and the number of holdings of various-sized blocks. Important stockholding groups may be identified if they are represented on the board of directors or if large holders have been named for other reasons.

THE SECURITY INVESTIGATION

The portion of an investment analysis which deals with the position of the individual security, as distinct from the study of the industry and the firm, has usually to do with three elements: its legal rights, its financial strength, and its market position. The legal position of a security is determined by its statutory, (bond) indenture, and charter rights—such matters as mortgage security, call prices, voting rights, etc. These have been reviewed in earlier chapters, so the reader will have no difficulty in listing the ones which will be most pertinent in considering any particular stock or bond.

The financial position of an issue has chiefly to do with its place in the capital structure and the improvement or weakening of that place as time goes on. The best evidence of improving financial position for a bond would be a steadily increasing earnings coverage for its interest and asset coverage for its principal. The best evidence for a stock would be that an increasing percentage of operating earnings remained as "earnings for common" after all senior claims and that the common stock equity represented an ever-increasing percentage of the balance sheet total.

The market position deals mainly with factors previously considered in studying the markets for stocks and bonds—the number of holders, the volume of trading in the issue, whether dealers and brokers sponsor the issue, where it is traded, whether it is seasoned and well known to the public, the popularity of such issues with the public, eligibility (of bonds) for institutional purchase, possibility of new offerings or secondary distributions, and the market price history of the issue. The problem here is to determine whether the stock or bond being studied will be considered by enough potential buyers and sellers so that its merit will be properly reflected in its price, and also to determine whether the market is broad enough to absorb any probable selling or buying without radical price fluctuations. Clearly, it would be unprofitable to buy a security for price appreciation if the issue had no broad market and if several large blocks were known to be awaiting sale at the earliest opportunity; nor would one be willing to buy a stock on a normal price-earnings basis if it were evident from recent price ranges that the price frequently fluctuated far below a normal range. One of the more objective items to be noted with reference to a security's market position is the history of its price-earnings ratios and yields: If a stock has consistently sold at a higher-than-average price-earnings ratio or if its price-earnings ratio (in terms of year-by-year prices and earnings) is trending upward, some presumption of a strong market position may be entertained. If a stock or bond customarily sells on a low-yield basis or has been rising in price with a consequent declining yield tendency, the same presumption of strong market position may be deduced. Finally, the investor must consider the probable price variations of the security, whatever its long-term merits, and decide whether he will feel comfortable holding it. The past price record and the beta measure discussed in Chapter 10 offer some guidance here.

REACHING CONCLUSIONS

Supplied with the plethora of facts and estimates as thus outlined, an investment analyst would be able to judge the quality, characteristics, and future of the securities before him as well as any man could hope to do. The specific function of these "conclusions" is to make a final summary of future earnings, dividends, investment features, quality, price-earning ratios, and yields and to translate these into probable future market values. The analyst could not hope to be right all of the time, for the unforeseeable facts of new discoveries, political events, wars, and human imponderables would often confound his estimates, but he should be right more often than not, and proper diversification would then care for his errors. Many of the techniques which may help in drawing wise conclusions have already been discussed, and others will suggest themselves in individual cases. However, the task is fundamentally one of exercising an informed judgment.

Security analysts continue to develop new analytical and decision-making techniques which rely on electronic data-processing equipment. Information and judgments on the points discussed in this chapter can be stored on computer tapes or memory discs and then retrieved, sorted out, and summarized as desired. Computer tapes containing such information as capital structures, earnings and dividend records, securities price ranges, financial ratios, and even subjective judgments on important features of companies' affairs can be used in conjunction with current prices to perform such feats as sorting out securities which seem to be most attractively priced, or to offer maximum yield and growth with least risk, or to provide the characteristics needed in a balanced portfolio. Computer tapes containing basic information on many hundreds of securities can now be purchased from research agencies or investment advisory firms, thus permitting analysts to concentrate their attention on the investment characteristics and combinations which they wish to find. The scope and variety possible with computer-based techniques make them an all-but-indispensable aspect of modern-day security analysis.

QUESTIONS AND PROBLEMS

1 Why is investment analysis usually made a comparative study? Could you not determine whether General Motors Acceptance Corporation debentures were satisfactory just by studying them?

2 Would investment analyses be needed on United States government bonds? On American Telephone bonds?

3 Would the Outline for Investment Analysis presented in this chapter cover the information needed to study the stock of the Morrison-Knudsen Company, a contracting firm which builds dams, highways, bridges, and heavy industrial plants in many countries? Is anything missing?

4 As a practical matter, should middle-class professional men, such as professors and lawyers, make their own investment analyses, or should they rely on others?

5 Does the *Standard Stock Report* on B. F. Goodrich stress the right things, for a condensed report? What vital things are omitted, if any?

6 Investigate the rapidly growing radio and TV manufacturing industry, and decide whether Admiral Corporation has reaped the alleged benefits of industry growth.

7 What faith do you have in a fruit and vegetable canner such as Del Monte Corporation in this day of frozen foods, rapid transportation of fresh products, and improvement of paper-packaged dehydrated foods? How would you check on these hazards?

8 Make an investment analysis of B. F. Goodrich common stock, and compare it with Goodyear Tire and Rubber. Do you detect any signs of growth advantages in the Goodrich record?

9 If you had all the necessary data with which to work, how would you go about estimating Goodrich's probable sales for the next 2 or 3 years?

10 How would you estimate the Goodrich earnings for the same period? The probable dividend rate? Can Goodrich continue to build plants at recent rates, increase inventories and receivables as needed, pay installments on the bonded debt, and still continue the dividend?

11 How would a reduction in its product prices, with no changes in its principal costs, affect a concern's break-even point?

12 Why are investors concerned about the proportion of a concern's expenses which consists of "inflexible overhead" costs?

13 Define working capital. Why is it so important? Would it be as important a factor to an established, low-leverage concern as to a new, high-leverage competitor in the same industry? Explain.

14 How would you identify a sound capital structure? An unsound one? Would a high-leverage structure necessarily be a risky one?

15 Summarize the principal market factors you would want to know if you were considering long-term investment in the stock of Continental Can Company.

16 Will careful investment analysis eliminate errors? If not, why should you bother with it?

17 Why are computers an almost indispensable adjunct of modern-day security analysis?

18 Using the Outline for Investment Analysis given in this chapter, compare the investment merits at present market prices of U.S. Steel and Inland Steel; of International Business Machines and Control Data Corporation.

REFERENCES

Amling, Frederick: *Investments*, 2d ed., Prentice-Hall, Inc., Englewood Cliffs, N.J., 1970, Chap. 10.

Badger, Ralph E., and Paul B. Coffman: *Investment Analysis*, McGraw-Hill Book Company, New York, 1967, Chap. 23.

Badger, Ralph E., Harold W. Torgerson, and Harry G. Guthmann: *Investment Principles and Practices*, 6th ed., Prentice-Hall, Inc., Englewood Cliffs, N.J., 1969, Chaps. 5, 7.

Bellemore, Douglas H., and John C. Ritchie, Jr.: *Investments*, 3d ed., South-Western Publishing Company, Incorporated, Cincinnati, 1969, Chap. 16.

Graham, Benjamin, David L. Dodd, and C. Sidney Cottle: *Security Analysis*, 4th ed., McGraw-Hill Book Company, New York, 1962, Part 1.

Hayes, Douglas A.: *Investments: Analysis and Management*, 2d ed., The Macmillan Company, New York, 1966, Chaps. 13, 14.

Institute of Chartered Financial Analysts: *C. F. A. Readings in Financial Analysis*, 2d ed., Richard D. Irwin, Inc., Homewood, Ill., 1970, Part 3.

Latané, Henry A., and Donald L. Tuttle: *Security Analysis and Portfolio Management*, The Ronald Press Company, New York, 1970, Chaps. 10–12, 16.

Lerner, Eugene M.: *Readings in Financial Analysis and Investment Management*, Richard D. Irwin, Inc., Homewood, Ill., 1963, Secs. 3–5.

MAKING USE OF
FINANCIAL REPORTS

Most investors are familiar with the balance sheets and income statements which are published annually or at more frequent intervals by nearly every important business corporation. These statements are the source of data for the most basic of investment calculations, such as those of earnings per share or the current ratio, and they also figure importantly in much of the more detailed work of investment analysis. They contain so much of the fundamental information on working capital position, capital structure, sales, expenses, and earnings that no investor can afford to ignore them; yet they are technical enough to require an understanding of accounting assumptions and techniques for their proper interpretation.

It is clearly beyond the scope of the present volume to discuss the art of accounting. An attempt has been made in an earlier chapter to define the difference between a consolidated and a corporate statement. Assuming that this distinction is already clear to the reader, the functions of the present chapter must be reduced to three: First, it seems desirable to review a number of accounting practices which investors must understand in order to interpret financial statements correctly. Second, a brief study of the most important financial ratios used in investment analysis will be in order. Third, a survey of the five most important elements in investment evaluation and suggestions for measuring them will be presented.

ACCOUNTING PRACTICES WHICH AFFECT INVESTORS

Many of the errors made by investors in their attempts to interpret financial statements can be credited to the failure of the investors to understand the ordinary principles of accounting, such as those which underlie depreciation estimates or inventory valuation. This is not a problem for accountants, or even for writers of texts on investments; those who wish to catch the nuances in financial statements must go to an appropriate authority and learn how. A second source of investors' errors appears to be lack of alertness or laziness, as reflected in failure to realize the exact implications of statement titles, footnotes, and accompanying "schedules" of supplementary data. These are carefully presented in prospectuses and company annual reports, but are commonly omitted or condensed in most reference sources and other published accounts. A third source of investors' errors centers on the fact that accounting practices and definitions are far from uniform. Despite valiant efforts by the SEC, various public utility regulatory agencies, and leading accounting associations, there are important differences in accounting techniques which may cause uncertainty even among experts. At the risk of adding to the confusion, it seems desirable to note 17 different instances in which investors are likely to misunderstand financial statements.

1 Nonconsolidated subsidiaries and investments American corporations often send their stockholders "consolidated" financial statements which include the detailed incomes, expenses, assets, and liabilities of domestic subsidiaries in types of business similar to the parent company's, but which do not include the detailed accounts of foreign subsidiaries, domestic subsidiaries in unrelated activities (such as a "captive" finance company), or affiliated concerns in which ownership is partial or does not imply control. In such cases the consolidated income statement may include in a single figure the parent company's entire equity in the subsidiary's undistributed earnings and the consolidated balance sheet may show an investment in the subsidiary at the subsidiary's full book value; this would cause the net income and net worth figures to be fully consolidated. (Conglomerates owning insurance companies often pick up the latter's portfolio gains in consolidated income statements even when these subsidiaries do not conventionally include such gains in their reported income.) But alternatively, the consolidated statements may include only dividends received and investment cost in respect to the nonconsolidated subsidiaries or affiliates; this leaves the consolidated net income and net worth possibly larger or smaller than true consolidated totals. In 1972 the leading accounting association advocated the full consolidation of earnings and net worth at least of both domestic and foreign subsidiaries. It also ruled that companies should include in their reported income their proportionate share of the net gains or losses of unconsolidated subsidiaries, joint ventures, or other corporations in which they held 20 per cent or more of the outstanding stock. However, these rules admit of various exceptions, particularly with respect to foreign properties. Investors must therefore still inquire into the completeness of the earnings and net worth figures furnished to them, for very important fractions of these items may not be included in the "consolidated" statements. Footnotes to the financial statements and explanatory paragraphs in the text of the annual report or prospectus will usually disclose the needed information.

2 Foreign subsidiaries and branches Foreign subsidiaries and branches operate in foreign nations, using foreign currencies which are not always readily convertible into dollars, and are subject to foreign tax laws. Earnings in foreign countries are often subject to foreign dividend taxes if repatriated, to American corporate income taxes if received here, and to foreign exchange losses if moved. Are unrepatriated foreign earnings really earnings and are foreign current assets really current? Should American income taxes and foreign dividend taxes which would be levied if foreign earnings were repatriated be deducted before consolidating foreign earnings which are not being repatriated? Some concerns do this; most do not. On another point—the most common accounting technique in consolidating foreign subsidiaries is to evaluate foreign earnings and foreign net current assets at current quoted rates of exchange, but to show foreign fixed assets at the dollar values they represented at the time of construction, less regular depreciation allowances. This doubtless is a good system, but it has the novel result of forcing the consolidated net income and net worth up or down as foreign exchange fluctuations change the carrying value of the foreign subsidiaries' current assets. If the impact on net income is substantial, the result is both nonrecurring and misleading. It will normally be explained in statement footnotes. Many American corporations do not consolidate foreign subsidiaries' operations, though most of them do so.

3 Depreciation Reported earnings may change radically if companies adopt different depreciation methods, assume different lives for depreciable assets, or anticipate different salvage or resale values. These differences may also sharply affect earnings comparisons between seemingly similar enterprises.

Two tax-incentive measures have long encouraged distortions in depreciation charges and income tax expenses. First, the Revenue Act of 1954 permitted corporations to use tax depreciation formulas which charge off large amounts in the initial years of an asset's life and progressively decreasing amounts in later years. Second, new tax depreciation "guidelines," adopted in 1962, permitted the use of shorter assumed asset lives and allowed supplemental depreciation charges to bring prior years' reserves up to newly permissible levels. These two devices may be or not used, and if used, the depreciation charges used in the earnings statements sent to stockholders need not be the same as those used in the tax computations. Two problems for the investor emerge here: (a) whether the depreciation charges being deducted in stockholder statements are realistic and normal, and (b) whether the tax expenses as shown in the stockholder statements are normal or temporarily distorted. Three possibilities exist: (1) The companies may use rapid depreciation methods for both tax and stockholder accounting, along with the reduced tax expenses; this would result in temporary reductions in both taxes and indicated net income. In later years, depreciation charges would decline and taxes would rise about half as much, causing an increase in indicated net income, unless new depreciable assets introduced additional rapid depreciation. This accounting method has been used to some degree by the more conservative industrial companies. (2) Alternatively, the company may use accelerated depreciation for tax purposes but on its stockholder reports use as expenses normal depreciation plus actual taxes plus a supplemental bookkeeping tax expense charge equal to the tax saving occasioned by the accelerated depreciation. The supplemental tax expense charge would be credited to a reserve for future taxes, which would in turn be charged with a portion of the abnormally large taxes which could result if depreciation charges decline in the future. This system, which is used by most public utilities and industrial companies and is endorsed by the American Institute of Certified Public Accountants, is designed to "normalize" earnings as reported to stockholders despite the irregular impact of taxes. (3) Finally, the railroads and steel companies use a third approach, which involves reporting on stockholders statements simply normal depreciation charges and actual taxes based on earnings after deduction of accelerated depreciation charges. This method enables companies to enlarge their reported net earnings, since both depreciation charges and tax expense are reduced below normal levels; and continuing large investment outlays, such as the steel companies were making in the early 1970s, may shield them from the increasing taxes that would otherwise fall upon them. Lengthening the depreciation *period* on fixed assets also will reduce depreciation charges and produce higher reported earnings. In 1969, the financially hard-pressed airlines bettered their results by stretching out depreciation on their jet aircraft from 11 to 12 or 14 years.

4 The investment credit A modernization-incentive measure in effect during 1972 provides that 7 per cent of the cost of eligible new machinery may be credited against the year's tax. Most corporations regard this tax credit as a simple reduction of the year's tax expenses, and thus allow it to "flow through" to net income. However, a strong minority of conservative corporations regard the tax credit as an offset to the cost of the asset, to be spread over the life of the asset as a reduction in the cost of using it. The difference in earnings as reported to stockholders could be very important, for 7 per cent of investment in eligible new equipment could be a large figure in a year when a new plant is completed. And in most corporations, major plant completions occur irregularly, thus distorting yearly earnings reports when the flow-through system is used.

5 Pension-fund expenses Companies can increase their reported earnings by deducting less from present revenues to meet future pension costs. This is ordinarily done, as United States Steel and Boeing Company did in 1969, by making new and more favorable actuarial assumptions. There is nothing illegitimate about improving actuarial assumptions if facts justify the move and if it does not result in underfunded pension liabilities which impair future earnings by causing higher pension-fund charges in future years. However, the tendency for companies to discover improved actuarial assumptions in years of financial difficulty rather than in good years suggests that investors should ponder such changes with healthy skepticism. While the American Institute of Certified Public Accountants now recommends that all companies pay or accrue at least all current costs every year and that adequate disclosure of accounting methods and pension-fund status be made regularly, the information available to investors in 1971 annual reports was generally far from adequate or even informative. In many companies, pension costs now exceed normal-year dividends to shareholders, and they often dwarf the total earnings reported in poor years. Companies may, of course, persistently underfund their pension obligations for employees' past services, or choose to ignore a growing excess of vested benefits over pension-fund assets, either of which results in an overstatement of present earnings. However, the outside investor can rarely obtain detailed or accurate information on these matters.

6 Installment sales A large percentage of retail installment sales is now made under the "installment method" of tax accounting, which permits the retailer to defer payment of income taxes on his profits until the installments are collected. Since traditional accounting would recognize the merchandising profit as soon as the sale is made, the tax deferral creates the same confusion of alternatives which exists in the case of accelerated depreciation. The American Institute of Certified Public Accountants recommends that a tax charge to expense be made in the period in which the sales revenue is recognized—that is, when the sale is made—thus establishing a reserve for deferred taxes. The investor needs merely to know whether abnormal merchandizing profits or tax items are distorting the reported profit figures and impairing their apparent trends.

7 Tax adjustments Two kinds of income tax adjustments should be noted here. First, reviews of corporate tax returns for prior years frequently result in large additional payments or in recoveries of prior payments. These are sometimes handled through reserve or surplus accounts, but frequently—especially in the case of tax recoveries—the adjustment is made by charging or crediting the current year's tax expense account, thus affecting the reported net profit. Second, corporations sometimes operate at a loss, and under the tax laws the loss may at various times be "carried back" to reduce prior years' profits and obtain an income tax refund or "carried forward" into profitable years to reduce or offset the taxable income of those years. If the loss is carried back and a refund obtained, the refund is usually credited as income in the loss year, and will make the net loss appear gratifyingly small; if the loss is carried forward, it could exempt 1, 2, or 3 future years from income taxation, and make them appear unusually prosperous.

8 Inventory valuation Firms which have a substantial investment in inventory usually are consistent from year to year in their methods of inventory valuation, but the method used may greatly affect the earnings and net worth reported to the stockholders and the net income as measured for tax purposes. There are several systems used in valuing inventories, but two general types of results appear, the traditional First-in First-out (FIFO) valuation and the more recent Last-in First-out (LIFO) valuation. The FIFO system appraises the end-of-period inventory at its recent cost or replacement prices, and assumes that the balance of the period's purchases plus the preceding end-of-period inventory represent the cost of the First-in merchandise which was sold. This seems realistic; it matches the actual cost of the sold merchandise against its selling price to measure profit, and it uses an up-to-the-minute valuation of present inventory for balance sheet purposes. The LIFO system, on the other hand, regards inventory items which are constantly sold and replaced as continuing assets, to be valued at original cost unless finally and permanently closed out. The purchases during a fiscal period are regarded as the cost of goods sold during that period, except for those used to enlarge the inventory. This system tends to match selling prices received against the current cost of replacing the goods, in computing profits. During a period of rising or falling commodity prices, the LIFO system seems to measure profit more accurately, at least with reference to the firm's cash position after maintaining a stable inventory; but over a long period of rising or falling prices, the original cost balance sheet valuations may depart substantially from market values. Either system is legally acceptable in computing taxable incomes; the present wide use of the LIFO system is due to the fact that it lessens tax liability during an inflationary era. An investor needs to know these things in order to judge whether his firm's reported earnings are inflated, deflated, or unaffected by price changes, and whether the current assets position is realistically stated or somewhat distorted.

9 Merger Accounting The great volume of corporate mergers has posed another problem for accountants and investors—how to enter the assets and net worths on the books of the surviving concern so that the combined depreciation charges and net income in the future will be both realistic and consistent with the figures reported in the past. In some cases these two objectives—realism toward the future and consistency with the past—are inconsistent, and the investors may find that the merger has changed both the combined total earnings and the combined net worth even before it makes any change in the physical operations of the companies. Basically, there are two approaches to merger accounting: if two concerns of comparable size are merged, and if both groups of stockholders stay in the business, the combination may be handled as a *pooling of interests*, which means that both sets of asset and net worth accounts will be entered on the combined accounts approximately unchanged; but if the merger is essentially a purchase of one firm by another, accounting rules require it to be recorded as a purchase of assets on the continuing company's books, each asset to be recorded at an assigned purchase price and thereafter depreciated on that basis. If the total price paid exceeds the sum of prices at which the separate assets are recorded, the difference must be entered on the purchaser's books as goodwill and written off as a non-tax-deductible reduction in future earnings over a span of not more than 40 years. Investors must clearly understand the accounting basis on which mergers

are proposed or consummated in order to assess their financial implications and
ultimate benefits.

10   Plant openings and closings   Plant openings and closings are expensive and
account for substantial nonrecurring costs, some of which may be expensed or
capitalized at management's option. Interest on borrowed money and property
taxes on plants in process of construction, the cost of obtaining and moving and
training employees, and the inevitable inefficiencies in the early weeks generally
impair profits when important new plants are opened. Separation pay, losses in
closing out inventory, and losses on equipment make the closing of an obsolete
plant expensive. Since these two things usually occur simultaneously, investors
need to make mental allowance when major changes of this sort occur.

11   Gains or losses on sale of fixed assets   This is sometimes a large item but
generally not. And in income statements, it is sometimes included in the final
periodic net income on which per share figures are based, and sometimes not.
The investor's problem here is to make sure whether nonrecurring incomes or
losses are affecting the per share profit figures upon which he relies, and to what
extent. Occasionally these gains or losses may be to some extent recurrent; for
example, the airlines for many years sold semiobsolescent aircraft to foreign airlines or freight carriers at prices in excess of depreciated book value. This has also
become a source of revenue to appliance leasing companies.

12   Research and development   These costs are very substantial to firms such as
General Electric or United Aircraft or Boeing. To a large extent, they are deductible for tax purposes as expended, but certain major items, such as Boeing's development costs on its jet airliners, may be capitalized on the company books for
amortization as the product is manufactured and sold. If research costs are expensed as incurred, the investor must decide whether current costs are really
building up valuable assets in the patent vault for future use, to an extent greater
than current advantages from prior years' research. If so, the current earnings
are being understated, at least from an investment standpoint. If, on the contrary, research costs are being capitalized, the investor must decide whether they
will really be recovered in future sales and profits.

13   Intangible drilling and development costs   Many kinds of development outlays, such as drilling oil wells or uncovering ore bodies in mines, do not create
tangible salvageable assets and are therefore regarded as deductible expenses for
income tax purposes. But a producing oil well or a useful mine tunnel is an asset
to its owner, and its cost could properly be capitalized rather than expensed on
the company books. In fact, this is the common procedure among oil, mining, and
similar concerns. However, company policies vary; Superior Oil, for example,

charges all of the cost of drilling new oil wells immediately to expense. As long as the company continues to grow, its drilling costs are far greater than depreciation charges on old wells would be; hence it is clear that this practice reduces the reported net income as well as the balance sheet assets and net worth. Similarly, Kennecott Copper charges many mine development outlays to expense. By contrast, in 1972 such companies as Occidental Petroleum Corporation, Texaco, and Coastal States Gas Producing Company were capitalizing all exploration and development costs without regard to the success of the ventures, which permitted them to stretch over many years the costs of unsuccessful operations that most oil firms reported as current expenses. In such cases, the investor's problem is to sort out the influences of accounting policy and evaluate reported earnings as best he can.

14 Percentage depletion Percentage depletion is an optional form of tax deduction allowed as producers use up their underground supplies of oil, natural gas, coal, limestone, and other minerals. The law authorizes such depletion deductions at stated percentages of the market value of the output, not limited by the cost of the property. Since most mineral producers record depletion on their own books as prorata portions of property cost but use percentage depletion to minimize taxes, their income taxes are often small in ratio to reported net earnings. Percentage depletion is politically controversial, and its abolition or modification might seriously impair earnings from many of the best oil and mining properties. Oil and gas producers would be the most sharply affected.

15 Write-off of skeletons It is desirable, and often imperative, for investors to recognize when undisclosed losses are building up in a company from such various causes as unfulfillable sales contracts, insufficiently depreciated assets, losing ventures or departments, or capitalization of fruitless outlays. In such cases, the company sooner or later must acknowledge its mistake and announce a deferred write-off of the bad item, with the result that stockholders' equity, reported earnings, and common share price may all plunge drastically. Recession years, when earnings are likely to be poor in any case, are often utilized by managements to clean their closets of these financial skeletons, an opportunity exploited on a wholesale basis by computer leasing and software companies in 1970–1971. Since root problems of this kind are not disclosed, the investor at best can only *suspect* their presence in a company where he is an outside owner. However, an implausibly high growth rate in reported earnings or a preoccupation on management's part with growth at a neglect of sound operating procedures is often a warning that unreported losses are piling up behind a facade of favorable reports.

16 Contract completions Much large-scale modern business is done under contracts which take many months to complete. Despite the fact that the buyer usually makes progress payments to help finance the job, the producing company must plan its own accounting for handling receipts and outlays prior to completion of the contract. Most such firms do include conservatively estimated portions of contract earnings in their income statements as a job proceeds, but some do not report any contract earnings until the job is complete. It is apparent, then, that a fiscal year or quarter in which several contracts were completed might appear very profitable, and an equally busy one which was lacking in completions might show poor earnings. And if losses instead of profits began to appear likely, the impending losses might be included immediately in full in reported statements, or they might be reported month by month as sustained, or they might be held in suspense until finally proven at the completion of the contracts.

17 Standards of maintenance Maintenance expenditures and similar outlays are in considerable part under management control. They can be made generously and charged to expense when earnings or cash position or cost conditions justify, or they can be skimped. The results can affect reported earnings to a measurable degree, especially in industries such as railroading where maintenance expenditures often amount to as much as one-third of gross revenues.

Other exercises of accounting discretion may affect a company's reported earnings or distort earnings comparisons between companies in the same or different industries. Utility companies, and some airlines, capitalize interest charges on money used to finance facilities not yet in operation, to keep them from reducing reported income. Bookkeeping reserves set up at one date may be used to cushion the effect on earnings when losses are announced later on. Through various accounting maneuvers, nonrecurring gains may find their way into regularly reported income, while nonrecurring losses may be charged directly to retained earnings. The potential list of these variations is very long and grows quite technical, but the examples offered should suffice to show that earnings reported by different companies, or even by the same company at different points in time, may differ widely in quality—and even in existence.

TECHNIQUES IN USING FINANCIAL STATEMENTS

In making use of financial statements, investors resort to many devices and expedients. Obviously, the statements are used for immediate interpretive analysis, to determine such things as earnings per share, current ratio, and bond interest coverage. Second, the statement figures and ratios show highly significant trends when studied over a period of time; most analytical work stresses the *trends* in sales volume, earnings, profit margins, debt ratio, and the like. Third, analysis of financial statements is often comparative; J. C. Penney's sales growth, current ratio, or profit margin can be compared to those of Sears, Roebuck, the Montgomery Ward division of Marcor, Inc., or an industry average. Finally, the financial statement data are often tested by comparison with external or nonfinancial data; for example, sales figures can be divided by appropriate index numbers to obtain an indication of growth in physical volume of sales, or gross revenues on a railroad can be divided by ton-miles moved, to gauge the trend of freight revenues per ton-mile. These varied devices are all used by professional analysts as well as individual investors, and will be illustrated in the publications of all the investment advisory services.

But users of financial data, both self-compiled and furnished by the services, must be alert to avoid comparing unlike things and thus reaching illogical conclusions. As has been noted, differences in accounting methods can produce drastic differences in figures and ratios; these accounting differences are not reconciled or adjusted by most of the financial services in compiling data such as those reported in the *Standard Stock Reports*, for such arbitrary revisions would scarcely be feasible. Further, differences in method of operation between firms would differ so markedly that appropriate standards of working capital adequacy, leverage, operating ratio, and similar measures must vary from industry to industry. Furthermore, companies themselves increasingly operate in several industries and under differing contractual arrangements and with different degrees of vertical integration. As a result, ratio comparisons are not reliable even between companies in the same industry. Clearly, circumstances alter the meanings of statement terms and ratios, and the user must read them with knowledge and with care.

How, then, does one go about using financial statements and ratios? There is probably no one best way; some analysts compile great columns of sums, per share figures, and ratios, and read them in the light of known accounting methods, business methods, and industry characteristics. Historical trends should thus emerge with reasonable clarity, and comparisons with other firms and other industries can be made on the basis of judgment. But an alternative approach is available; the analyst can inspect the situation at hand and make his study by checking out the factors in the situation which seem important to him. He may feel, for example, that he should check the realism of reported earnings and their probable trend; or the cash flow and cash requirements and their dividend implications; or the long-term financial strength of the company in terms of the debt ratio, coverage of fixed charges, lease and pension obligations, ownership of essential raw materials and facilities, and permanence of the industry. In the end there may be little real difference in these two approaches.

By now it has become abundantly clear that the use of financial statements in the 1970s is not a process of inspecting income statements and balance sheets. These statements must be read in relation to other known facts, mostly gleaned from the notes appended to the financial statements and from the texts of annual reports and prospectuses, along with additional items reported by the financial services. These supplementary facts and items are potentially almost too numerous to mention. Suffice it to recall that a preceding section has noted 17 important factors which cause reported earnings figures to deviate from otherwise normal amounts.

FINANCIAL RATIOS

There are a number of commonly used financial ratios and calculations which are both important and significant in many industries. Although all ratios are subject to the weaknesses noted in the preceding section and must be used with discretion, they are widely applicable. They are not the only useful ratios; many others are used to bring out details in various situations, and still others have special applications in specific industries. Also, this list is limited to ratios developed from financial statement data and, therefore, does not include calculations which make use of nonfinancial data such as price indexes, measures of physical volume, or national income figures. These ratios can be conveniently grouped in five categories. The first four are designed to shed light in turn on a company's liquidity, profitability, leverage, and effective utilization of assets; the fifth, to alert investors to possible discrepancies in its financial reporting practices and to the chance that earnings may be overstated. Two supplementary indicators of a company's liquidity position also deserve brief discussion.

A Liquidity ratios These ratios measure a company's ability to meet its cash obligations. A liquid firm is not only free from fears of default but also able to avoid strains and emergencies that might force resort to high-cost money sources or to terms of borrowing injurious to the stockholders' interest. There are four principal liquidity ratios.

1 Current ratio The ratio of total current assets to total current liabilities is used to measure the adequacy of the current assets to meet all early obligations. This is the best known of all the ratios. Traditionally, a 2-to-1 (200 per cent) ratio is said to be the dividing line between adequacy and inadequacy, but this universal rule is not sound; utilities and railroads hardly need a 2-to-1 ratio, but manufacturers and retailers who must carry inventories and receivables usually need a higher one. Firms which do a heavily seasonal business are likely to have high ratios in the dull seasons but low ones in the busy seasons when large operations are being financed on credit. Note that all figures which include inventories may be distorted if LIFO valuations are used.

2 Net current assets This is not a ratio, but the simple excess of current assets over current liabilities, often referred to as net working capital. It measures the amount of current assets provided to the firm by its permanent investors rather than obtained from short-term sources whose continuing availability may be doubtful. Any tendency of net working capital to increase or decrease is very important to investors as an indication of the financial health of the business and of its capacity to pay dividends. In poorly managed or unfavorably situated companies, net working capital shows persistent tendencies to disappear into fixed assets during good times, and into operating losses during bad ones.

3 "Acid test" This is a ratio of the most liquid current assets to the current liabilities, often defined as the ratio of all current assets except inventory to the current liabilities. A ratio of 1 to 1 is said to be usually adequate. The test supplements the current ratio, to indicate whether the business is truly in a liquid condition.

4 Percentage of net current assets to sales This ratio is an attempt to measure the adequacy of the net working capital to handle the existing volume of sales. No typical ratio applicable to all industries can be suggested, but comparison of a present ratio with that of prior years and with that shown by competitors is often illuminating.

B Profitability ratios These measures show how productively the firm's capital is being employed in the stockholders' interest. Five profitability ratios are of special significance to the investor.

1 Return on equity This ratio was discussed at length in Chapter 13. Expressed as the percentage of net profit to net worth, it indicates the company's basic ability to use the stockholders' investment to produce dividends and capital growth. Its reliability is of course subject to the accuracy of both the net profit and net worth figures, which are in turn dependent upon many elements of accounting policy and procedure.

2 Gross profit to sales This comparison is usually expressed as the percentage of gross profit to net sales. The figure is important in merchandising operations as an indicator of competitive pressure and the amount of markup obtainable. It varies more in response to price-level changes when FIFO inventory values are used than when LIFO methods are followed.

3 Operating ratio This very important calculation, computed as the percentage of operating expenses to sales, varies somewhat in customary content from one industry to the next. The general idea is to gauge the percentage of sales revenue absorbed in the wage, salary, material, and general (not income) tax cost of conducting the business. The higher the ratio, the more dangerous is an increase in expenses. A low ratio suggests security and relatively stable earnings. The operating ratio is used more in analysis of securities in service industries—for example, utilities, railroads, and banks—than in merchandising or manufacturing industries.[1]

4   Percentage of operating earnings to sales   This is an important measure of the concern's capacity to retain a percentage of its gross revenue as earnings available for its securityholders. A decline in the ratio suggests a decline in the quality of the earnings, even though their amount does not decline. This ratio is of course the complement of the operating ratio.

5   Percentage of bad debts allowance to sales   The portion of the annual sales which will be lost because the resulting receivables cannot be collected must be estimated and the amount included in the year's operating expenses. This ratio is important in merchandising operations but even more important in the case of banks, finance companies, and other lenders. If the allowance is too small, the earnings will be overstated, and vice versa. However, conclusions must not be reached hastily; a high bad debts allowance may mean poor credit management, or the deliberate assumption of credit risks to gain higher profits through more sales, or simply bad debt allowances in excess of actual losses.

C   Leverage ratios   The following three ratios indicate the extent to which the company is relying on borrowed funds, and the margin of safety with which debt financing is being employed.

1   Total debt to net tangible assets   This is a measure of total current and long-term debt compared with total assets, excluding such intangibles as goodwill, patents, and bond discount. The strength of the firm is obviously greater when the debt ratio is small, though it is always necessary to remember that the book value of assets does not necessarily measure either their market value or earning power.

2   Net worth to net tangible assets   This is the obvious complement to item 1 and a measure of leverage as it affects the stockholders.

3   Earnings available for fixed charges to fixed charges   This crucially important ratio measures the adequacy of operating earnings plus other income to meet bond interest and other fixed charges such as lease rentals. Earnings available for fixed charges should ordinarily be computed before deductions for income taxes. A ratio of 3 to 1 is sometimes said to be satisfactory when earnings are stable, but

---

[1] Depreciation is included in operating expenses when computing the operating ratio of an industrial company.

4 to 1 would seem to be a safer minimum. When income taxes are deducted before arriving at income available for fixed charges, a lower ratio would be tolerable. In industries with unstable earnings, the minimum average ratio must be much higher than 3 to 1.

D   Asset utilization ratios   This family of ratios measures the efficiency with which a company is using its assets to generate sales revenue or other income. Three such ratios are listed here—the reader can easily visualize other possible ones.

1   Asset turnover   This is the ratio of total sales to net assets and is designed to measure the effectiveness of the use of assets by seeing how active they are in producing gross income. This ratio is subject to manifold distortions, including the effect of comparing earlier-year cost valuations of fixed assets with current inflated-dollar sales values.

2   Percentage of net receivables to sales   This ratio is used to gauge the success of collection efforts. A rising ratio of receivables might indicate that collections were slowing down or that bad receivables had accumulated on the books, though it might indicate merely an increasing percentage of credit and installment sales. In recent years the increasing sale of consumer durables on the installment plan caused this ratio to rise in many lines of business. However, many firms are now selling their receivables to finance companies and banks; this greatly complicates the interpretation of the ratio.

3   Percentage of inventory to sales or (better) of inventory to cost of goods sold   This measures the soundness of an inventory investment. If inventory is large in relation to sales, it may be excessive in amount, ill-selected and not effectively salable, or purchased at a too-high price. This ratio is of little use when LIFO inventory values are the only ones available.

E   Verification ratios   Four further ratios are useful in verifying the soundness of the foregoing financial tests and the reliability of the balance sheet and income statement figures on which they are based. If the following ratios depart significantly from those of competing companies or from industry averages, the investor is warned that something may be amiss.

1   Percentage of depreciation plus maintenance to cost of fixed assets   Some industries, notably utilities and railroads, can reduce actual depreciation to small amounts by constant maintenance and replacement. In such cases the total of the two items, both of which are operating expenses, makes a better indication of proper accounting than would either, separately.

2 Percentage of depreciation plus maintenance to sales Because depreciation and maintenance are both related to the amount of use imposed on the assets, it sometimes seems better to compare them with sales than with asset costs. This is especially true of utility and railroad statements. A low ratio suggests under-statement of expenses and overstatement of profits; a high ratio, the opposite.

3 Income tax provision to net profit If a corporation's expense accounting conforms closely to income tax rules, the federal and state income tax provisions at 1972 rates will approximately equal the posttax net profit. However, many legitimate tax savings devices, such as the investment credit, accelerated depre-ciation, and low-taxed dividends received, may hold down the income tax bur-den. Consequently, the cautious investor merely notes the tax percentage and attempts to reconcile it with the reported net income. If the tax provision can be reasonably reconciled with net income on a fair and apparently recurrent basis, the investor has a reason for confidence.

4 Percentage of depreciation to cost of fixed assets The annual depreciation (expense) allowance to spread the cost of fixed assets over the estimated life of the assets is one of the operating expenses. One way for an ineffective manage-ment to make a good impression on stockholders is to increase profits by under-estimating depreciation. This ratio enables the stockholder to compare this year's depreciation rate with the depreciation rates of other years and other concerns.

In addition to the foregoing ratios, the investor should be familiar with two other tools of financial analysis: the cash flow concept, and the sources and ap-plications of funds statement.

Cash flow This is an attempt to provide a supplementary measure of net income and available cash on a per share basis. It is usually made by adding back all de-preciation, depletion, and other noncash expense charges to the reported common stock net income and dividing this total by the number of outstanding common shares. Allegedly, this measures the cash return per common share which is avail-able at management discretion for debt payment, added investment in the busi-ness, and dividends. Certainly the figures show the impressive cash strength of good companies with large fixed assets and low debt ratios. Some writers also state that the cash flow per common share is an important gauge of true earning power, perhaps a better gauge than reported net earnings in a period when de-preciation allowances based on historical costs of assets or on accelerated tax formulas may not accurately measure true depreciation costs.

The cash flow concept is often misused. It is not adequate to test cash position, for it does not gauge the availability of cash from other sources—for example, sale of inventories or collection of receivables—and it does not gauge necessary cash outgo for new construction, equipment, sinking funds, maturities, or added

Table 14-1 *Consolidated statement of changes in financial position: Pfizer Inc. and subsidiary companies*

	Year ended December 31	
	1971	1970
	(All amounts in thousands)	
Funds provided by		
Operations		
Net earnings	$ 90,585	$ 83,292
Depreciation	28,600	26,700
Non-current deferred taxes	(600)	1,300
Working capital provided by operations	118,585	111,292
Sales of common stock under stock option plan	12,197	7,255
Dispositions of property, plant and equipment	4,620	3,828
	135,402	122,375
Funds applied to		
Additions to property, plant and equipment	85,100	54,900
Dividends and distributions	43,161	43,547
Decrease in long-term loans	5,624	6,817
Increase (decrease) in investments, deposits and advances	2,783	(2,081)
Increase (decrease) in deferred charges	4,173	(3,214)
Other changes—net	(701)	2,453
	140,140	102,422
Increase (decrease) in working capital	$ (4,738)	$ 19,953
Changes in working capital		
Current assets—increase (decrease)		
Cash, time deposits and short-term investments	$ 4,086	$ 47,517
Accounts receivable, less allowances	39,850	17,880
Inventories	18,445	37,348
Prepaid expenses and income taxes	(7,254)	8,195
Increase in current assets	55,127	110,940
Current liabilities—increase (decrease)		
Short-term debt	74,751	43,670
Accounts payable	266	10,795
United States and foreign taxes on income	(12,254)	15,744
Other current liabilities	(2,898)	20,778
Increase in current liabilities	59,865	90,987
Increase (decrease) in working capital	$ (4,738)	$ 19,953

Source: Annual Report, 1971.

inventory and receivables. As an improved measure of net earnings, it has limited merit—it would always, for example, make a profitless concern which owned and depreciated large amounts of fixed assets appear to "earn" substantially, even if the large depreciation charges had to be offset by large and unavoidable purchases of new equipment. The cash flow idea is very helpful when soundly used, but in much current literature it is more often misleading than illuminating.

Sources and applications of funds statement This breakdown, required since 1970 in the annual reports of publicly owned companies, explains in detail the changes occurring since the previous year-end balance sheet in cash, cash and short-term securities, or net working capital.[2] Table 14-1 shows the sources and applications of funds statement which appeared in the 1971 annual report of Pfizer, Incorporated. This statement, which defined funds as net working capital, consists of two parts. The upper part lists the particular operating factors and financial changes which have provided or absorbed working capital during the year and the extent to which each has done so. The lower part details the specific changes in current assets and current liabilities which account for the total change reported above in net working capital. For comparative purposes, changes for the preceding year are also shown. Obviously, such a statement enlarges the investor's understanding of what is happening to a company's liquidity position, and why.

STANDARD RATIOS

Investors often like to compare the financial ratios of their companies with average ratios representing large groups of companies in the same industry. Such average or typical ratios are frequently termed standard ratios. Standard ratios are available for investor comparison in Standard & Poor's *Industry Surveys*, in the Special Features sections of the Moody investment manuals, and in a number of other financial services. More detailed ratio studies for particular industries are made by several trade associations, and the Graduate School of Business Administration of Harvard University has made a number of such studies. Dun & Bradstreet, Inc., and the Robert Morris Associates have made extensive ratio studies from the point of view of credit men.

FIVE TEST AREAS

Although data from financial statements are used in many tests and measures made by investors, there are five areas in which elementary tests are so simple

---

[2] The term *funds* is defined by accountants in various ways for various purposes and may legitimately have any of the three meanings cited, depending on a company's judgment as to which is most significant in its particular situation.

and obvious that they require special mention. These areas are (1) the reality of earnings and earning power, (2) the rate of earnings and sales growth, (3) cost and profit percentages, (4) working capital position, and (5) capital structure and leverage. Other important factors of corporate performance and stock valuation were pointed out in Chapter 13, but these five are critical items which most well-informed investors will note each time they check any company's financial statements.

The earnings-per-share figure derived from any corporate income statement can be eminently honest but highly misleading. Before placing too much reliance upon an earnings figure, the investor should determine whether accelerated depreciation was charged against corporate earnings; whether large tax savings stemming from accelerated depreciation were "flowed through" to net earnings; whether pension provisions were charged to expense in reasonable amounts; whether any large tax adjustments affected the expenses; whether nonrecurring gains or losses from sales of assets or large write-offs were included; whether extraordinary costs such as plant openings or closings or product development costs were included; and how much these items distorted the earnings figure. Allowance must also be made for probable or potential change in the number of shares as a result of conversions or the exercise of stock purchase warrants; in making annual reports, companies are required to tell investors what earnings per share would have been had all such outstanding options been exercised.[3] Finally, if there is reason to believe that circumstances within the firm, the industry, or the national economy caused the year's operations to be better or worse than normal, an estimate of normal earning power is probably needed, to be arrived at by averaging the results of several years or simply by making an informed judgment. It seems appropriate to add that between 1965 and 1972, the quality of earnings reported by publicly owned companies probably declined for several reasons, including more liberal accounting procedures, higher debt ratios, a rising proportion of interest charges, and depreciation allowances insufficient to replace fixed assets at inflated prices.

Earnings growth and sales growth are both vital to investment values. Long-term trends are usually gauged by charting the figures and fitting growth trends which can be projected. Shorter-term calculations can be made over 5- or 6-year spans by calculating the compound rate of growth required to raise an earlier figure (say the 1967–1969 average) to the current level. Or the percentage gains or

---

[3] Under present accounting rules, corporations with other securities than common stock outstanding must present two earnings-per-share figures in their public reports: (1) "primary" earnings per share, in which earnings available to common stock are divided by the sum of common shares and "residual" securities; and (2) "fully diluted" earnings per share—the *pro forma* earnings which would have occurred if all convertible senior securities, warrants, etc., outstanding had been converted to common stock. Residual securities are senior or other securities which derive a major portion of their market value from conversion rights or other common stock characteristics; as noted above, they must be counted as common stock in all earnings-per-share computations. See Accounting Principles Board Opinion No. 9, especially par. 33, in *Accounting Principles* listed in references at end of chapter.

declines from each year to the next can be computed, and trends projected from these. In any case, it is essential that the earnings or sales figures for the most recent years be realistic and consistent with the earlier ones, or the growth measures will go far askew.

Cost and profit ratios vary so much from industry to industry and company to company that general rules can scarcely be provided, but it is clear that a decreasing ratio of operating expenses to sales in a power company or an increasing ratio of cash flow to sales in a cement company or a declining ratio of net profit to sales in a department-store chain would be important and perhaps illuminating to an investor. Obviously, these ratios would be most illuminating when their trends over a period of years could be studied, or if they could be compared with similar ratios from competing firms.

Working capital position is important because it affects the company's ability to operate and to grow efficiently, because it measures sensitivity to a possible financial squeeze arising out of tight money or credit rationing, and because it affects dividend policy and the price of the securities. Working capital in the final sense is simply that portion of a company's current assets financed from equity or *long-term* debt sources; thus it comprises the current resources which are exempt from any problem of renewal with the firm's creditors. Investors generally look at a company's current ratio, at the size of the cash and salable short-term investment holdings, and at the bank loans or any other large current liabilities. These can be compared with the similar figures from other years, and with those of competitors. But the real test of working capital position lies in the company's ability to meet its cash needs and pay dividends over the coming months. Can the expected cash flow plus any assured cash from sale of securities and fixed assets cover maturing debt, sinking funds, construction and equipment purchase contracts, necessary increases in inventories and receivables, interest payments, and dividends? Business budgets usually plan these things with care, so that working capital positions will remain under control unless the budget earnings fail to materialize or the securities markets are adverse and money from the sale of securities is not forthcoming. In that case—and the possibility could probably be disclosed by a careful check—the company might need to resort to bank borrowing and might well reduce or omit dividends.

Capital structure and leverage are crucial items in an investor's calculations. A conservative, low-leverage firm is one with a modest ratio of debt to asset values and a modest ratio of fixed charges to available earnings. As such, it will usually have a more than adequate cash flow and it will almost certainly have a powerful credit standing. In earlier decades the basic tests for a strong capital structure were balance sheet ratios—the ratios of common stock net worth to total assets and of total debt to total assets, essentially. Now, however, the widespread use of leased premises and the common practice of making long-term contracts for the purchase and sale of commodities—natural gas, for example—and the great importance of patents and technological capability have introduced additional variables into the investor's calculations. Balance sheet values alone do not reflect the earning potential of a firm's reputation and brand names, its sales and production skills, its favorable contracts, its research organization, its patent position, and its personnel, nor do they gauge the extent of the fixed costs involved in lease rentals and other long-term contracts. These things do affect sales growth and profit margins, however, and require that measures of capital structure and leverage place major emphasis on such items as the ratio of net profit to sales, the ratio of net profit to gross profit on sales, and the ratio of rents and other fixed charges to gross profit on sales. Needless to say, the trends of these ratios over time and their size compared to those of competing firms will be most illuminating.

QUESTIONS AND PROBLEMS

1   The Interstate Commerce and Federal Power Commissions impose uniform systems of accounts upon the railroads and the power and gas companies respectively. Would it be in the investor's interest for the SEC to specify uniform accounting systems for different classes of manufacturing companies?

2   If a firm's current assets contained a large item labeled Miscellaneous Stocks and Bonds, what would you need to know about it in order to assure yourself of the firm's true working capital position?

3   Explain the difference between inventory valuation on a traditional basis and on a LIFO basis. Which would make a company's surplus account the largest after a long period of rising price levels? Which gives the most accurate portrayal of net working capital? Which best measures competitive effectiveness and long-term earning power?

4   Does tax-incentive legislation which causes great confusion over depreciation, tax expense, and the true amount of net income conform to the "full disclosure" objectives of the Securities Act of 1933? Is it necessary that economic stimulants also produce confusion?

5   How would you decide whether Bethlehem Steel's depreciation allowances were adequate? How would you define an adequate allowance?

6   Would it be reasonable to set certain "minimum standards" for statement ratios—for example, the current ratio and the operating ratio—and to say that all concerns falling below the standards were in poor condition and all rising far above were in good state? Explain.

7   Why are financial statement titles and footnotes important? What kind of thing would they show?

8   Explain the different ways of including an 80 per cent–owned subsidiary in a "consolidated" balance sheet or income statement, assuming that other wholly owned subsidiaries are also included. Then look up the annual reports of American Telephone and Telegraph, Chrysler Corporation, and Westinghouse Electric, and see how they do it. Watch the statement titles carefully.

9   Is it reasonable to charge to current expense both current-service and past-service funding payments made to employee pension trusts?

10   Colgate-Palmolive Company does half its business abroad, and its assets must be scattered in many countries. It consolidates its foreign subsidiaries' statements with its own. Could you appraise its working capital position successfully?

11   Why does the current ratio fluctuate with the seasons in many concerns? Would net working capital fluctuate similarly?

12   What is the operating ratio? Would it be significant to subdivide the operating ratio and study the trend of each of the operating expenses separately in relation to sales?

13   In evaluating Westinghouse Electric stock, it would be desirable to have an estimate of average earnings per share over the next several years. Can you outline a method for making such an estimate?

14   Explain how a statement of Sources and Applications of Cash Funds, appearing in an annual report, better delineates a company's cash position than the annual cash flow figure.

15   What is the true value of a company consisting of department A, which earns $1,000,000 per year, plus department B, which loses $1,000,000 per year after $2,000,000 in depreciation charges? What would the company earn after taxes if it closed down department B?

REFERENCES

American Institute of Certified Public Accountants (Accounting Principles Board): *Accounting Principles*, Commerce Clearing House, Inc., New York, annual, September 1.

Badger, Ralph E., and Paul B. Coffman: *Investment Analysis*, McGraw-Hill Book Company, New York, 1967, Chaps. 14, 15.

Bellemore, Douglas H., and John C. Ritchie, Jr.: *Investments*, 3d ed., South-Western Publishing Company, Incorporated, Cincinnati, 1969, Chaps. 17–20.

Briloff, Abraham J.: *Unaccountable Accounting*, Harper & Row, Publishers, Incorporated, New York, 1972.

Cohen, Jerome B., and Edward D. Zinbarg: *Investment Analysis and Portfolio Management*, rev. ed., Richard D. Irwin, Inc., Homewood, Ill., 1973, Chaps. 4, 6–8.

Financial Handbook, rev. ed., The Ronald Press Company, New York, 1968, Sec. 8.

Foulke, Roy A: *Practical Financial Statement Analysis*, 6th ed., McGraw-Hill Book Company, New York, 1968.

Graham, Benjamin, David L. Dodd, and C. Sidney Cottle: *Security Analysis*, 4th ed., McGraw-Hill Book Company, New York, 1962, Part 2.

Graham, Benjamin, and C. McGolrick: *Interpretation of Financial Statements*, 2d ed., Harper & Row, Publishers, Incorporated, New York, 1964.

Hayes, Douglas A.: *Investments: Analysis and Management*, The Macmillan Company, New York, 1966, Chaps. 9, 11.

Institute of Chartered Financial Analysts: *C. F. A. Readings in Financial Analysis*, 2d ed., Richard D. Irwin, Inc., Homewood, Ill., 1970, Part 1.

Paton, William A.: *Corporate Profits: Measurement, Reporting, Distribution, and Taxation*, Richard D. Irwin, Inc., Homewood, Ill., 1965.

Securities and Exchange Commission: *Accounting Series Releases*, Washington. Also, *Regulation S-X*.

Widicus, Wilbur W., and Thomas E. Stitzel: *Personal Investing*, Richard D. Irwin, Inc., Homewood, Ill., 1971, Chap. 5.

Williams, William D.: "A Look Behind Reported Earnings," *Financial Analysts Journal*, January–February, 1967.

The American transportation system is of vast extent and complexity; among industries with tangible output, only manufacturing and electric power exceed it in total investment and annual gross revenues. It includes the nation's airlines, railroads, trucking companies, bus lines, oil pipelines, barge lines, freight forwarders, truck rental companies, and other branches of lesser significance or of a more conglomerate type. The securities of its three largest segments—airlines, railroads, and trucking companies—are of major interest and importance to investors; they comprise the subject matter of this chapter.

The analysis of particular transportation industries and their securities will be more compact and coherent to the reader if the economic and financial features common to all transportation enterprises are first set down and briefly explained. Six such features are important enough to emphasize.

1 *Large long-term investment.* All transportation undertakings require a large investment in powerful, costly, long-lived equipment. By comparison, current asset needs are typically minor. As a result, fixed costs and break-even sales volume are high relative to those of most manufacturing companies. Depreciation flows are ordinarily substantial, and companies' methods of accounting for accelerated tax depreciation and the investment credit may significantly affect the earnings reported to stockholders.

2 *Heavy debt financing.* Long-lived, standardized, readily salable fixed assets, such as passenger airplanes, locomotives, freight cars, and highway trucks, have high collateral values, and in buying them, transportation companies can usually borrow a high percentage of the purchase price. The railroads also have found it easy to mortgage their main and branch lines, terminals, and other real estate. Because borrowing is easy, transportation companies may be overprone to rely on debt for financing equipment and fixed assets, particularly at times when stock prices are unfavorable or when managements are anxious to avoid a dilution of earnings or of earnings growth.

3 *High leverage.* Large, fixed operating costs mean that operating earnings will change more rapidly than sales, while substantial interest charges cause net profits to fluctuate more widely than operating earnings do. Consequently, transportation companies typically combine high degrees of both operating and financial leverage. This in turn leads to marked instability of after-tax earnings, since most transportation businesses are extremely sensitive to ups and downs of the economy.

4 *Dependence on traffic mix.* In most instances, long-haul transportation service is more profitable to provide than short hauls; freight is more profitable to transport than people are; bulk shipments are more profitable than small and diverse lots of merchandise. Some types of business are inherently more dependable than others, either because they are less sensitive to business conditions or because there are no competitors for their patronage. Thus, traffic mix plays a large part in the earning power and stability of individual carrier companies. For example, it largely explains why the western and southern railroads prosper while the eastern roads go bankrupt.

5 *Large labor costs.* Although huge, costly machinery provides the apparatus for modern transportation services, people are needed to guide and maintain this complicated equipment, to operate the related system of ticket offices, terminals, and controls, and to keep the business running smoothly. As a result, wages are the largest single cost element in any transportation enterprise. Most transportation companies are highly unionized, and managements are painfully conscious of labor union power. Since transportation services cannot be stored up in inventories for later resale, a strike threat brings greater anguish to a carrier than to an industrial company. Hence, transportation firms have greater difficulty controlling their labor costs than do most other businesses; wages have an almost chronic tendency to encroach on profit margins.

6 *Regulation.* The rates, and to a considerable degree the services, of all carriers are regulated by one or more agencies of government. Rate regulation arises from an application of the public utility concept which the following chapter will develop in more detail, but the essentials may be stated here. Most carriers enjoy a mixture of monopoly on some routes and competition on others; some customers are at their mercy while others may be able to demand service at ruinously low rates. Since monopoly prices are unfair to the public, and since excessive competition would soon ruin the carriers, government regulation of rates and services has developed as a substitute for the uncertain controls of the free market.

The guiding principle of regulation is to permit a necessary but semimonopolistic industry to earn a fair return on the investment it uses in serving the public. A carrier's investment in useful long-lived and current assets usually comprises its *rate base*, the property value on which it is entitled to earn some *allowed rate of return*. The law specifies that the rate of return must be fair to both carrier and public. The rate set normally allows for bond interest as a cost and attempts to give the stockholders about the same return on book value as they would earn in a low-risk industrial enterprise.

The regulatory notion has worked more effectively with the nearly monopolistic public utilities, where rates can be set on an individual-company basis, than among the carriers where industry-wide—or at least region-wide—rates must prevail. Transportation companies usually compete with rival carriers in both their own and other industries, and owing to competitive forces, there is no guarantee that a given pattern of rates will assure a company the earnings which a regulatory commission intends it to receive. Depending on its relative efficiency, location, traffic mix, and degree of competition, a particular carrier operating at industry-wide or regional rates may achieve profits far above or far below the fair-return level set by a regulatory commission. In general, neither the railroads nor the airlines realize the profit objectives set by their regulatory agencies. Fierce competition within the industry has reduced the profitability of the airlines, and competition with other forms of transportation has held down railroad earnings. By contrast, superior efficiency has enabled the large, stockholder-owned truck lines to earn at rates far above the industry average on which motor freight rates are based.

THE AIRLINE INDUSTRY: A STUDY IN CYCLICAL GROWTH

The airline industry is much smaller in both sales volume and total assets than the railroads or the trucking business, but its growth rate of 10 to 15 per cent per annum, and the spectacular fluctuation of its earnings and stock prices, make the stocks of great interest to many investors. The industry is dominated by 10 large "trunk line" companies which carry passengers, mail, express, and freight, but there are also 2 major air freight lines and a considerable number of smaller airlines and local-service and helicopter lines.

Along with rapid growth and extreme sensitivity to swings in the economy, the airlines are broadly characterized by seven other influences: (1) high labor costs and operating ratios; (2) a continuing race between traffic growth and seat capacity; (3) widely fluctuating seasonal demands; (4) intense competition over major routes; (5) heavy reliance on debt financing; (6) high technological turnover, with a major reequipment cycle every 8 years on the average since 1930; and (7) severe regulation by the federal government. Ups and downs in the air transport business (and its stocks) seem to have resulted as often from regulatory mistakes as from cyclical changes in business or the introduction of excess capacity by the airlines themselves.

From 1961 through 1971, the airlines' domestic passenger traffic grew at an annually compounded rate of 15.6 per cent. This growth occurred despite great irregularities, including declines to .3 per cent in 1970 and 1.9 per cent in 1971. In the same interval, international traffic grew at a 12.9 per cent rate. In 1971, the domestic airlines carried 72.5 per cent of all inter-city passenger miles, excluding those traveled in private autos. The industry's future traffic prospects are exceedingly bright, thanks to the rise in leisure time and living standards and to an increasingly young population that favors air travel.

However, rapid growth failed to bring sustained prosperity to the air carriers. In 1971, the airlines' total net income was only $29 million, far below the record of $428 million set in 1966, though comfortably above the $200 million loss recorded in recession-ridden 1970.

REGULATION AND ALLOWED EARNINGS

The airline industry is subject to twofold regulation by federal government agencies. The Civil Aeronautics Board wields authority over rates, routes, and economic matters, while the Federal Aviation Agency oversees traffic control, airport development, and safety questions.

The CAB grants franchises to the airlines to operate over prescribed routes and to make prescribed stops; lightly traveled routes are generally monopolistic, but important routes between major cities are competitive; for example, three airlines have direct routes between New York and Los Angeles. The CAB makes changes in these franchises occasionally, and the airlines occasionally propose mergers to combine them advantageously. The Board has used its authority to alter the competitive balance among the carriers, usually to strengthen the smaller trunk lines at the expense of the four largest ones—United, American, Eastern, and TWA, which in 1971 carried 69 per cent of the total passenger, freight, and mail business. The CAB has been criticized for bringing about excess competition by certifying new carriers on profitable routes whenever the industry is well along on a traffic upswing.

The CAB has set 12 per cent as the fair return for the major domestic airlines, and proposes to allow slightly more for the smaller lines. The rate base includes normal fixed and current assets and progress payments on aircraft in process of construction, but it excludes the capitalized value of leased aircraft. The Board also prescribes standard load factors on which the airlines must base their petitions for fare increases, a measure intended to prevent growth of excess capacity.[1]

Because both revenues and expenses are unstable, earnings may fluctuate above and below the rate-of-return objective for considerable periods. Historically, airline fare trends have alternated between increases to shore up inadequate earnings and decreases inaugurated by the Board to share rising profits with airline customers. Despite numerous fare changes, the industry achieved a 12 per cent return only once in the years 1957–1971.[2]

AIRLINE EARNINGS: MAJOR INFLUENCES

While airline revenues may swing sharply with changes in traffic volume, fare levels, and traffic mix, the bulk of operating costs is relatively fixed. Regardless of the number of passengers or total revenues, such expenses as crew wages, landing fees, fuel, maintenance, depreciation and interest charges, and insurance vary

---

[1] In 1972, standard load factors were 55 per cent for trunks and 44.4 per cent for local airlines.

[2] Until 1971, however, the fair return was 10.5 per cent.

little. Once the percentage of seats at which an airline can break even has been occupied, its profit margin rises explosively; between 85 and 90 per cent of the additional revenue will be carried forward to pretax income.

The break-even load factor for trunk lines has been about 50 per cent in recent years, and the introduction of jumbo jets with larger capacities but little additional speed is not expected to alter this figure substantially. Airline load factors and earnings are influenced in large degree by (1) the rate at which new equipment comes into use versus the rate of traffic growth; (2) the trend of average revenue per passenger mile flown, reflecting first class–tourist fare mix, discount fare plans, etc.; (3) wage rates and labor force trends; and (4) financing costs. Other influences include (5) number of flights scheduled; (6) use of older, less efficient aircraft; and (7) fare levels.

The airline industry experienced a squeeze on profits in the early 1960s as jet aircraft were introduced. From 1961 through 1966, airline earnings improved dramatically. Traffic growth outstripped additions to capacity, and break-even load factors dropped precipitously because the new jets had about twice the speed and capacity of the older piston-engine planes. From 1967 through 1971, these trends and factors were generally adverse.

REVENUES AND EXPENSES   Airline revenues are comprised of about 90 per cent passenger fares, 6 per cent freight revenue, and the balance in mail, express, and miscellaneous charges. The trend of revenues depends on traffic growth and the yield factors noted earlier, such as fare levels, fare mix, and discount plans.

Operating expenses average almost 90 per cent of normal-year revenue including only about 11 per cent depreciation, so that amounts available for capital expansion, debt repayment, interest, and dividends are not large. Labor costs, which absorb about 45 per cent of revenue, increased at a 6.8 per cent rate from 1965 to 1969 and at a 13.3 per cent rate in 1969–1970. Between 1969 and 1972, the airlines sought to combat rising labor costs by reducing their total employment by 24,000 persons, or about 8 per cent.

Aside from wages, airline costs are largely fixed, a fact which makes the airlines particularly vulnerable to strike threats by a highly unionized labor force. Since the companies can neither stockpile seats during a strike nor sell from inventory afterward, strike losses are unrecoverable. Managements are under strong temptations to avoid strikes, even if this means excessive wage settlements.

Table 15-1 presents the revenues and expenses of the domestic trunk airlines for 1964, 1967, and 1970, and shows major categories by which the companies report their receipts and costs.

CYCLICALITY AND COMPETITION   Nearly two-thirds of all domestic air travel is accounted for by business travelers. Consequently, airline traffic and earnings are extremely sensitive to the business cycle. Management and regulatory practices abet the industry's inherent cyclical tendencies. In periods of strong

Table 15-1 *Revenues and expenses of domestic truck airlines in 3 recent years*

	1964		1967		1970	
	Million $	Per cent	Million $	Per cent	Million $	Per cent
Operating revenues						
Passenger	$2,504.9	89.8	$3,901.5	88.3	$5,632.5	89.8
Express	27.2	1.0	30.8	0.7	31.3	0.5
Freight	141.0	5.0	235.8	5.3	391.0	6.2
Excess baggage	15.2	0.5	6.3	0.2	10.4	0.2
Nontransportation	18.5	0.7	33.4	0.8	54.0	0.9
Other	22.0	0.8	112.4	2.5	15.2	0.2
Total nonmail revenues	2,728.8	97.8	4,320.2	97.8	6,134.4	97.8
U.S. mail	62.1	2.2	99.2	2.2	138.4	2.2
Total operating revenues	$2,790.9	100.0	$4,419.4	100.0	$6,272.8	100.0
Operating expenses						
Flying operations	$ 677.0	27.2	$1,101.5	27.5	$1,831.0	29.3
Maintenance	514.5	20.6	735.4	18.3	973.4	15.6
General service and administration						
Passenger service	214.0	8.6	396.4	9.9	653.8	10.4
Other service and administration	825.8	33.1	1,374.0	34.3	2,125.4	34.0
Total	$1,039.8	41.7	$1,770.4	44.2	$2,779.2	44.4%
Depreciation and amortization	262.7	10.5	402.0	10.0	671.6	10.7
Total operating expense	2,494.0	100.0	4,009.3	100.0	6,256.0	100.0
Operating profit	296.8		410.1		16.7	
Nonoperating income (or loss)	(52.2)		(30.7)		(158.3)	
Total income before tax	244.6		379.4		(141.6)	
Provision for income tax	110.2		145.3		(41.2)	
Net income	$ 134.4		$ 244.5		($100.4)	
Ratio of operating revenue to operating expense		111.9		110.2		100.3

Sources: Standard & Poor's *Industry Surveys* and the Civil Aeronautics Board.

traffic growth, the airline managements increase schedules and services to obtain a larger share of the market. This calls for more equipment and accelerates the purchase of new airplanes, so that capacity begins to expand faster than traffic. The CAB intensifies the contest by awarding new routes. Load factors decline and profit margins start to narrow. In the next recession, traffic diminishes and earnings plummet. The airlines then rush to cut operating costs and to reduce equipment purchases. An extended period of excess capacity and subnormal earnings afflicts the industry until the rate of traffic growth revives and profits again start to expand. The cycle then repeats itself, as it has done several times since 1945.

Since competing airlines usually offer identical equipment and charge the same fares, competition consists largely in manipulating and expanding flight schedules and in increasing passenger-service amenities. Through superior service or more convenient schedules, an airline may be able to build a dominant reputation on many of its inter-city routes. In the past, however, airline managements all too often have acted on the assumption that flooding the market with seats would improve or hold a market share, and this form of competition has led to prolonged losses for all carriers on the routes affected.

AIRLINE ACCOUNTING AND FINANCES

Although the CAB supervises airline accounting and imposes a number of broad uniformities in financial reporting, the accounting practices of individual airlines still vary widely and are responsible for substantial differences in reported earnings. Most such differences are traceable to (1) the different lives assumed for equipment (chiefly airplanes), and (2) handling of the investment tax credit. For stockholder reporting purposes, a 727 plane is depreciated at straight-line rates, but United Airlines depreciates it over a 16-year span to a $100,000 residual value, whereas Eastern uses a 15-year life and 5 per cent residual worth; Braniff, 14 years and 15 per cent; and American, 12 years and 15 per cent. Similar disparities are present in treatment of the investment tax credit, which greatly benefits the rapidly expanding airlines. Continental, Delta, National, and Western report the credit on a conservative basis, amortizing it over the life of the equipment. Other lines generally employ flow-through methods.

FINANCES   Because retained earnings and depreciation have fallen far short of the huge outlays needed to finance new equipment, the airlines have been forced to borrow very large sums. In September 1971, the long-term debt of the nation's 12 major airlines amounted to $5.2 billion against total stockholders' equity of only $3.2 billion. Average net worth equaled only about 30 per cent of total assets. The airlines have tended to avoid equity financing and convertible debt issues. The industry has a number of bond issues available to investors, but its major borrowing has been done through term loans and private placements with financial institutions. Table 15-2 shows the financial structure of the domestic trunk airlines during recent years.

The heavy reliance of the airlines on long-term debt in financing new equipment has led to rapidly rising interest charges. The industry's interest expense in 1971 totaled $246 million, more than 4 times the level of a decade earlier. Most airline bonds are of lower-medium grade, and the large use of debt financing substantially reduces the quality of earnings on most airline common shares.

Table 15.2 *Combined balance sheet of the domestic trunk airlines for 3 selected years*
(In millions of dollars)

	1964	1967	1970
Total assets	$3,420.3	$6,912.0	$9,579.1
Current assets	882.7	1,769.1	1,782.8
Investments and special funds	175.1	697.5	998.3
Operating property and equipment (net)	2,320.9	4,370.5	6,640.6
Deferred charges	38.9	69.6	142.9
Current liabilities	$ 686.8	$1,080.7	$1,652.4
Long-term debt	1,436.1	2,988.6	4,280.5
Deferred credits	321.5	568.6	900.2
Capital stock	180.5	316.0	221.2
Surplus	790.6	1,940.6	2,264.9
Ratios:			
Current assets to current liabilities	1.3–1	1.6–1	1.1–1
Long-term debt to total assets	.42	.43	.45
Long-term debt to equity	1.81	1.32	1.72

AIRLINE STOCKS

Airline stocks must be classed as somewhat speculative but likely to benefit from
growth in a high-return industry. They must be bought with care, however, for
the stock prices fluctuate extensively with variations in the per share earnings and
the market's evaluation of near-term prospects.

Because of high underlying debt ratios, no airline stocks can be considered high
grade. The wide swings in earnings and occasional deficits on most lines have produced extreme fluctuations in price-earnings ratios. Heavy capital expenditures
have dictated conservative dividend policies, and dividend suspensions and re-
sumptions over the years have been common for most of the companies.

The market for airline stocks is highly sensitive to short-term changes in traffic, but resulting price moves are ordinarily erratic, often reversed, and usually
costly to incautious speculators. The big money in airline stocks appears to be
made at intervals of 6 to 10 years, by catching basic trends involving speed-ups of
traffic growth over rising capacity. The great rise in airline earnings between 1963
and 1966 clearly offered investors this kind of opportunity. From a low of 19.62 in
June 1962, Standard & Poor's index of six airline stocks rose to a high of 137.5
in May 1967. After 1966, however, airline capacity began to overtake traffic
gains. The farsighted investor took his profits and ignored airline shares during
the next several years. By July 1970, the S & P airline share index had fallen to
38.39; an increase of nearly 600 per cent in airline stocks had been followed by a
drop of almost 70 per cent.

CARGO CARRIERS AND REGIONAL AIRLINES

To be complete, an examination of the airline industry requires brief mention of two other phases: cargo carriers and the regional airlines. From 1962 through 1971, the domestic cargo business of the trunk airlines grew at a 15.7 per cent annual rate, more rapidly than passenger traffic though from a much smaller base. Cargo contributed 8.1 per cent of airline revenue in 1970 versus 6.5 per cent in 1962. Further rapid growth is predicted for the air freight market over the next decade, since only .2 per cent of all revenue ton-miles of inter-city freight was moved by air during 1970. However, some authorities believe that not more than about 2 per cent of all inter-city freight could be carried economically by air at present rates and costs.

The regional airlines have been generally unprofitable throughout their history, and they depend heavily on federal subsidies for continued operation. There were 14 of them in 1955, but by 1972 a series of mergers had shrunk their number to 7.

Both operating and financial factors militate against profitability for these smaller carriers. Profit margins are characteristically narrow. The average haul for regional airlines during 1971 was 289 miles versus 792 miles for the trunk lines, and load factors ran significantly lower for the regional companies. Because of the heavy burden of fixed and semifixed costs on short-haul business, average fares are higher for regional airlines than for the trunks. Although traffic of the regional companies grew between 1961 and 1971 at a 19 per cent annual rate, conversions to jet aircraft, added debt burdens, and the steady inflation of operating costs brought frequent deficits after 1967. By 1970, several carriers were in danger of default on their obligations. Improved operations during 1971 cut the group deficit to $8.7 million from $27.6 million in 1970, but profits remained elusive.

CAB relief for the regional airlines has assumed the form of additional route grants and enlarged subsidies. The uneconomical service which these lines provide to smaller communities is widely subsidized through mail pay as a public interest policy.

❃ ## RAILROAD SECURITIES

The nation's 72 Class I railroads—those having annual revenues of $5 million or more—offer investors almost every type and quality of security. There are serial bonds, mortgage bonds, debentures, income bonds, preferred stocks, common stocks, guaranteed securities, long maturities, short maturities, high-grade investments, and hazardous speculations.

Although the railroads' share of the nation's transportation has declined, their operations are enormous and vital in scope. The American railroads in 1971 earned transportation revenues amounting to more than $12 billion, employed 544,000 people, and produced nearly 39 per cent of inter-city freight transportation in the country. They represented a capital investment of more than $33 billion and spent during the year nearly $1.2 billion on new equipment and structures. They had 385,000 stockholders, and despite net income after taxes of only $298 million, they paid out more than $1 billion in dividends and interest to their investors.

The railroad business has for many years been classed as "affected with a public interest"; hence it is subject to public regulation on matters of rates, service, and capital structure. Regulatory authority is divided between federal and state commissions, but the Federal Interstate Commerce Commission has established dominance in both policy and procedure. The purpose of regulation is to assure the public of adequate service at reasonable rates and to assist the railroads in obtaining a fair return without the burdens of rebating and rate cutting.

ECONOMIC CHARACTERISTICS OF THE INDUSTRY The railroads are in a hotly competitive arena in which the volume of traffic needed to assure low operating costs can be obtained only by charging moderate rates. Much of the transportation they controlled before 1940 has been lost to younger, more vigorous competitors. Trucks dominate short-haul and package freight. Pipelines share petroleum transportation. Private automobiles and buses have more than 95 per cent of the short-haul passenger business, and airlines have obtained most of the long-haul passenger and mail business.

The railroad business is notably cyclical. Earnings are highly leveraged both by fixed operating costs and by heavy debt structures. Traffic and revenues are highly sensitive to business changes. Thus, earnings and stock prices tend to follow the course of the business cycle, often with exaggerated swings.

Traffic volume is very important to the railroads, for their earnings tend to increase in much greater ratio when volume increases and to decline in greater ratio when volume declines. The reason for this tendency is to be found in the relatively large percentage of fixed and semifixed expenses borne by the railroads. Their costs for maintenance and depreciation of track, bridges, and buildings, their outlays for station and office crews, and their property taxes are heavy items which vary only moderately with changes in traffic volume. An increase in volume therefore adds only a moderate amount to expenses, mostly in the categories connected with train operations, and contributes disproportionately to earnings; a decrease in volume naturally has an opposite result.

Of course, railroads are not all alike. Some are located in or serve rapidly growing territories, where even a declining percentage of total traffic will permit increases in volume. The transcontinental roads connecting California with the East are examples of this. Others, such as the Pocahontas district coal carriers, are located in regions where heavy, bulky, and long-haul freight traffic abounds. Trucks are often unable to handle such business economically, hence the railroads have plenty of profitable business. Still other railroads are located in areas where maintenance, fuel, and other operating costs are relatively light. The investor therefore has ample opportunity to find profitable commitments in the railroad industry. In general, the southern and western railroads have proved profitable, earning 4.83 per cent and 3.52 per cent respectively on their invested properties during 1971. By contrast, the eastern roads, five of which were in bankruptcy,[3] collectively ran a large deficit.

The principal railroad expenditures are those for labor, fuel, supplies and repair materials, and taxes. Although the percentage of gross revenues disbursed on these items varies somewhat from year to year, the first three show no striking long-term trends; labor costs seem to average about 48 per cent, fuel about 4 per cent, and supplies about 11 per cent. Taxes, however, climbed from about 6 per cent in 1929 to about 9 per cent in 1971. In general, it appears that railroad operating costs other than labor and taxes are not threats to the investor's position. Labor costs are important because of the relative importance of the item among railroad expenses. Since 1946 the improved efficiency of the railroads has assisted in absorbing general cost increases, but earnings have remained modest because a combination of public regulation and rate competition from other forms of transportation has kept rate increases from keeping pace with increases in the cost of labor, supplies, and taxes.

RAILROAD RATES

Though shippers, chambers of commerce, cities, and even states are always ready to clamor for lower railroad rates, it is probably fair to say that the regulatory authorities are friendly to the roads. Rates are not adjusted upward so often or so promptly as some rail managements desire, but a casual effort to do the proper thing is evident. The Interstate Commerce Commission is instructed to prescribe rates which will enable carriers to provide "adequate and efficient service." It is unlikely that rates could be set high enough to average 5½ per cent return on the railroads' investment without driving necessary volume to competitors. Consequently, the railroads have had to content themselves with the low rates of return shown in Table 15-3.

The only feasible principle of rate making is to charge what the traffic will bear, making sure that no item is charged less than the out-of-pocket cost of handling it, nor so much that desirable business will be lost. Clearly, high-value items such as clothing, processed foods, and manufactured articles must pay higher freight rates per ton than heavy items like coal, lumber, and building stone. Because handling costs at terminal points are a large percentage of a railroad's total costs, most rates per ton-mile are far lower on a long haul than on a short one. However, trucks and other competitors can compete more effectively on

---

[3] The Penn Central, Reading, Lehigh Valley, Central of New Jersey, and Boston and Maine.

Table 15-3 *Financial performance of class I railroads in 3 selected years*

	Operating revenues (in billions of dollars)	Times fixed charges earned	Net income (in millions of dollars)	Return on net investment (per cent)
1971	$12.79	1.54	$298.0	3.29
1967	10.37	2.28	570.1	3.79
1963	9.56	2.89	651.5	3.12

	Retained earnings	Total depreciation charges (in millions)	Gross capital expenditures (in millions)	Net property (in billions)
1971	—	$807.1	$1,215.9	$28.20
1967	$ 16.8	764.6	1,209.7	27.73
1963	268.5	668.9	1,842.9	25.77

		Funded debt		
	Equipment obligations (in millions)	Other debt (in millions)	Total debt (in millions)	Debt as per cent of total capital
1971	$4,544.0*	$7,037.0*	$11,581.0*	41.6
1967	4,204.4	5,792.9	9,997.3	35.8
1963	2,650.4	6,288.3	8,947.7	33.4

	Cash items (in millions)	Working capital (in millions)	Operating ratio
1971	$1,215.9	$ 634.0	79.3
1967	1,209.7	774.3	79.2
1963	1,842.9	1,275.2	77.9

*Estimated.
Source: Standard & Poor's *Industry Surveys*.

short hauls than on long ones. Railroads therefore often find it necessary to accept lower earnings margins on short hauls than long ones. The ICC's rate formulas and patterns are reasonably uniform for like services on different railroads and over whole groups of states. As a result, well-located railroads with heavy traffic and moderate costs do well in regions where poorly located competitors are hard-pressed to pay expenses. The vested interests of shippers make the *pattern* of railroad rates highly resistant to change—for example, California orange growers are definitely opposed to lower rates from Florida to New York and Chicago unless rates from the Pacific Coast to these areas are correspondingly lowered. Thus, blanket percentage increases or decreases are easier to impose than regional or specific adjustments. Although the general cost of living has risen more than 60 per cent since 1951, the railroads are only collecting about 20 per cent more per freight ton-mile than they did then. This is not enough to permit good earnings, yet higher charges might drive essential business volume to competing forms of transport.

EFFICIENCY

In answer to charges that they are laggard in accepting new ideas, the railroads point to the steady improvement in their services—faster trains, more economical locomotives, door-to-door delivery of freight, larger freight cars, piggyback and containerized freight services, and the widespread use of computers for record keeping, shipment routing, and equipment utilization. They also cite impressive performance gains. Between 1951 and 1970, freight-train speeds increased an average of 20 per cent, and 19 per cent more freight volume was handled with 20 per cent fewer train miles.

Unfortunately, economically sound innovations often meet resistance from vested interests. Local officials demand the continuation of unprofitable branch-track mileage. Labor unions cling to division points which limit a trainman's run to three or four hours, and to work rules based on obsolete functions. Regulatory authorities often obstruct promising new services because of the protests of competitors. Railroad mergers are authorized by law when the ICC finds them to be in the public interest. The roads believe that combined use of maintenance shops, rolling stock, terminals, and track and the elimination of duplicating facilities would save many millions. However, the protests of local authorities, complaints by competing roads, and the ICC's desire to include unprofitable roads in the merged systems, have either delayed mergers or impaired their effectiveness. Of the three mergers authorized since 1967, one—the merger of Atlantic Coast Line and the Seaboard Airline Railroad into Seaboard Coast Line Industries—appears highly successful; the second—the formation of Burlington Northern, Inc., out of Northern Pacific and Great Northern—looks promising; the third and largest—the merger of the Pennsylvania and New York Central into the Penn Central—terminated in bankruptcy within two years' time.

FINANCIAL SITUATION

Most railroads still have fixed and contingent (income bond) charges which absorb so much of their earning power that their stocks are distinctly speculative. There are a few exceptions—the Union Pacific, Norfolk & Western, Santa Fe Industries, and a few others have moderate debt burdens—but most railroad stocks are both cyclical and speculative because heavy prior charges make the net profits unstable.

The railroads finance new rolling stock through equipment trust issues, and capital improvements are paid for out of depreciation allowances and retained earnings. Refunding of maturing bond issues is a main financial concern for the heavily bonded roads; in fact, one of the essential items in analyzing the securities of such roads is a check to see whether any bond issues mature within the next decade. Although maturing issues can usually be refunded or extended if interest payments are reasonably assured, an impending maturity is always a hazard until finally cared for.

A railroad's working capital position can be called satisfactory if the ratio of current assets to current liabilities is 1½ to 1, if the net working capital amounts to 10 per cent or more of annual operating revenues, and if no unusual drains upon working capital are in immediate prospect. A strong working capital position is advantageous for any business, but on the whole it is less imperative for a railroad or a utility than for other forms of business, if fixed charges are comfortably covered by earnings.

In the early 1970s, the railroad industry was clearly running short of capital. Depreciation allowances and retained earnings fell far short of financing the replacement and modernization of facilities needed. The weak financial position of many roads—the industry covered its fixed charges only 1.54 times during 1970— restricted the sale of new equipment issues to finance additional freight cars. Although the total debt was nearly $10 billion, working capital at year-end was only $634 million. Many railroads seemingly had been living off their capital, paying out in dividends funds that should have been retained to replace or improve facilities, and using working capital to buy long-lived equipment or to finance annual losses.

Although the inauguration of AMTRAK in 1971 relieved the railroads of an estimated $500 million annual loss on long-haul passenger business, the overall financial and earning-power position of the industry remained precarious. Even the relatively profitable southern and western roads were continuing to earn returns on their investments far below those of public utility concerns or the long-term averages achieved by most of the trunk airlines. The eastern roads continued to run huge deficits and to swallow massive volumes of working capital—even when run by court-appointed receivers with wide authority to achieve economies. As 1973 began, many observers in government and the financial community were increasingly convinced that government ownership and operation, at probably staggering costs to the nation's taxpayers, was the only practicable solution for the bankrupt eastern roads, and in the long run—very likely—for the industry as a whole.

In the event of nationalization, the holders of railroad bonds might expect to fare satisfactorily in terms of dollar recovery of principal and whatever back-interest payments would be due, although how much purchasing power a continually inflating dollar might leave them by that time would be difficult to predict. By contrast, holders of perferred and common stock, in their capacity of risk bearers, could look forward to little recompense, if any, for their investment in bankrupt roads; the position of equity holders in profitable roads that underwent nationalization would lie unpredictably in the lap of future politics.

INCOMES AND EXPENSES

The freight business now contributes about 90 per cent of operating revenues for the typical railroad and is the main source of earnings for practically all the roads. Long-haul passenger business is now the financial concern of AMTRAK, a quasi-government corporation, although the railroads continue to operate the much-reduced number of passenger trains. Mail and express business has been unprofitable since World War II and is rapidly shrinking in volume.

Many railroads own securities and property investments other than those used in their transportation business. The bankrupt Penn Central has large holdings of real estate and securities. The Union Pacific owns securities, real estate projects, pipelines, and mining ventures, and is one of the country's major producers of crude oil. Other railroads have heavy interests in coal, lumber, and other projects. The income from these sources varies widely in amount, dependability, and prospects of further growth. To aid diversification or to accelerate the development of land and other owned resources, a number of railroads have transformed themselves into holding companies. The more promising of these endeavors include Union Pacific Corporation, Illinois Central Industries, and Kansas City Southern Industries.

The *operating expenses* of a railroad consist of five categories—maintenance of way (roadbed) and structures, maintenance of equipment, transportation, traffic, and miscellaneous. The maintenance items include all labor and materials costs involved in the upkeep of properties, plus depreciation allowances as required. Investors expect maintenance of way to average about 13 per cent of revenues and maintenance of equipment about 18 per cent, though these figures vary between roads and from time to time. The railroads keep these maintenance percentages from rising greatly when business is slack by skimping maintenance at such times. Transportation expense includes train and station labor, train and station supplies, and fuel; this item averaged 40 per cent in the prosperous years from 1967 through 1969. The other two categories of operating expenses are small, aggregating about 7 per cent. Total operating expenses averaged about 80 per cent of operating revenues in the same period. This percentage is known as the *operating ratio*.

Railroad earnings statements subtract the total operating expense from the total operating revenue and label the difference *net railway operating revenue*.

Table 15-4   *Class I railways combined income statements, 1967 and 1971**

	Millions of dollars		Per cent of total operating revenues	
	1967	1971	1967	1971
Freight revenues	$ 9,130	$11,786	88.1	92.2
Passenger revenues	485	380	4.7	3.0
Total railway operating revenues	10,366	12,790	100.0	100.0
Maintenance of way	$ 1,288	$ 1,817	12.4	14.2
Maintenance of equipment	1,868	2,394	18.0	20.3
Transportation expenses	4,186	4,970	40.4	38.9
Total railway operating expenses	8,205	10,231	79.2	80.0
Operating ratio, per cent	79.2	80.0		
Net railway operating revenue	2,162	2,559	20.9	20.0
Federal income tax	$ 66	$ 108	.6	.8
All other taxes	367	405	3.5	3.2
Equipment and facility rents	575	841	5.5	6.6
Net railway operating income	676	606	6.5	4.7
Other income	$ 373	$ 321	3.6	2.5
Available for fixed charges	1,050	928	10.1	7.3
Fixed charges	461	601	4.4	4.7
Times fixed charges earned	2.28	1.54		
Income after fixed charges	589	327	5.7	2.6
Contingent interest charges	$ 35	$ 29	.3	.2
Net income	$554	$298	5.3	2.3

* Condensed statements.
Sources: Moody's Transportation Manual and Standard & Poor's Industry Surveys.

From this sum is next deducted the road's property and income taxes and the net rents (this item may be an addition if the road owns excess equipment which is used by others) paid for the use of rolling stock, terminals, bridges, etc. This determines the *net railway operating income,* the final measure of the earning power of the railroad as a transportation agency.

Since many railroads own securities or businesses apart from their railroad operations, it is next necessary to add in the *other income* and subtract out the *miscellaneous deductions.* The other income item is often very important, sometimes equaling the net railway operating income. This summation of operating income and vested income produces a total which is called *income available for fixed charges.*

Fixed charges include bond interest, amortization of bond discount and expense, and rentals paid for leased trackage and other property. If some of the bonds are income bonds, their interest is usually shown separately under the heading *contingent charges*. When all fixed and contingent charges are deducted from the income available for fixed charges, the remainder is the *net income*.

This summary of railroad income accounting follows the standard ICC form as used by all the railroads, and is illustrated in Table 15-4. [4]

EIGHT IMPORTANT INVESTMENT FACTORS

Every industry has unique features which require examination by its investors. Eight of the factors relating to the railroad industry will be noted here.

An investor who is interested in the securities of a railroad will often start his investigation with a careful scrutiny of the earnings available for fixed charges. He will need to determine their adequacy, their stability, and the trend of growth or decline. A railroad is usually a large business rendering services to a diverse group of customers, so the trend of its earnings should be a reliable guide to its future.

The investor's second area of investigation should deal with operating revenues, operating expenses, and the operating ratio. Net operating revenues are considered of good *quality* if the operating ratio is low; this is especially true if this ratio is low because the transportation expense is low.

A third item is the financial position, as measured by impending bond maturities, the need for additional financing, the current ratio, and net working capital.

Fourth, the amount and quality of other income must be considered. Other income is of high quality if it comes from dependable, long-lasting sources and is not likely to be affected by adverse business conditions. On the other hand, other income drawn from such investments as coal mines, standing timber, and stock-holdings in other railroads has often been intermittent in nature.

Fifth, traffic volume and its future prospects must be studied. A railroad which has heavy annual gross revenues and ton-mileage per mile of track operated should do well, particularly when such high "traffic density" occurs on a link in an important long-haul chain (as, for example, between Chicago and San Francisco). Growth of the area served, in terms of population, industrialization, and general prosperity, is a vital factor which tends to increase total available traffic.

---

[4] A special form of report is submitted annually by some of the recently reorganized railroads which have income bonds outstanding. These roads are required by their bond indentures to set apart certain portions of their remaining income after payment of bond interest, and additional portions after payment of income bond interest, to be used for bond retirements or capital improvements on the railroad. Since these sums are not available for income bond interest or dividends, it is necessary to compile a special form of financial (income) statement to show clearly what earnings may be used for these purposes.

Sixth, the nature of the traffic is important. Noncompetitive business is both more profitable and more dependable than competitive business. Long-haul business, carload-lot business, and items like coal which can be loaded mechanically have lower handling costs and are more profitable than packages or passengers. The railroads north of the Ohio and east of the Mississippi normally have a heavy volume of short-haul, package, and less-than-carload-lot business, which has resulted in burdensomely high operating ratios.

Seventh, operating problems or advantages inherent in the route demand consideration. These include mountain grades, areas subject to flood, availability of fuel, and the obstacles imposed by weather. The Denver and Rio Grande Western has both grade and weather problems in the Colorado mountains. The Southern Pacific finds great fuel economy in the oil-rich territory it serves.

Eighth, the condition of a railroad's property and equipment is a factor in its position. The probable level of maintenance on a railroad can be tested by comparing its maintenance ratios with those of other railroads and by comparing maintenance-of-way expenditures per mile of track with those of other roads. Also, the ages of its locomotives and other rolling stock can be compared with those of other railroads, and the published statistics on bad-order rolling stock awaiting repairs will give indication of the need for maintenance work.

RAILROAD BONDS

Railroads have generally mortgaged their property to secure their bonds, so both the coverage of fixed charges and the protection provided by lien security must be examined. For a rail bond to be of satisfactory quality, fixed charges should be covered, on the average, 4 times over. However, in computing this ratio the investor should add income taxes back to the officially reported earnings available to cover fixed charges. The appraisal of lien security involves examining the indenture terms to make sure that they are acceptable, plus some attempt to gauge the importance of the mortgaged property and its adequacy in amount. This last endeavor must rely on judgment—there is no acknowledged formula.

High-class railroad bonds are as readily accepted for institutional and other conservative investment as utility or industrial bonds. However, the railroad industry still has outstanding many millions of bonds which grade down from almost high class to frankly hazardous. The market prices on the lower-quality bonds are low and unstable, reflecting the possibility of long delay without interest payments and compulsory conversion into income bonds or stock if bankruptcy reorganization should become necessary.

The most highly regarded railroad securities are their equipment obligations, which are discussed in Chapter 6. These are usually issued in sums not to exceed 80 per cent of the value of newly purchased equipment and mature serially over a 10- to 18-year period. The maturities occur somewhat faster than the equipment depreciates, and the equipment itself is vital to the railroad and presumably sala-ble if repossessed. Defaults on equipment obligations practically never occur. Because of these factors, the yields are usually less than on mortgage bonds.

Most of the railroad income bond issues now on the market are the obligations of railroads which underwent bankruptcy reorganizations in the period 1933–1948. In such cases, the interest-bearing debt was usually reduced to an amount on which the interest could be earned in all but very poor years. Unearned interest on income bonds need not be paid, but unpaid amounts usually cumulate to the extent of 3 full years' interest, and both current interest and arrears must be paid to the full extent earned in any year. Fairly heavy sinking funds for debt retire-ment and property improvement are required in many cases, but the sinking-fund requirements are mainly junior to income bond interest, not senior to it. Few of the reorganized railroads have any early bond maturities of significant size. Few railroad income bonds are well enough protected by income and mort-gage lien to be called high grade, but many of them are preceded in rank by rela-tively small fixed-interest claims, hence are practically certain of some income every year.

RAILROAD STOCKS

Over the past decade, railroad stocks have sold at lower price-earnings ratios and have yielded more than industrial stocks of apparently comparable quality. There is reason for this. Even if one is convinced that the railroads have many decades of essential service before them, their limited growth and numerous problems prom-ise the stockholders only modest gains in the better stocks and considerable risk in the others. The small percentage of gross revenue remaining as pretax income highlights the speculative nature of many rail stocks. Because of the leverage that exists in almost every railroad financial structure, the position of the stocks is far more speculative than that of the business as a whole. Obviously, the rail stocks which have the highest investment quality are those like Santa Fe and Chesapeake & Ohio, with their relatively low fixed charges.

✴ THE TRUCKING INDUSTRY: CYCLICAL GROWTH BUT STEADIER PROFITS

This robust young giant now dwarfs both railroads and airlines in annual revenues and after-tax profits. During 1971, Class I and II truck lines—those with annual revenues exceeding $1 million and $300,000 respectively—set new records. They enjoyed sales of $16.7 billion and earned an all-time high of $438 million. They accounted for 54 per cent of the nation's surface freight rev-enues and carried about 22 per cent of its inter-city ton-miles.

Although private truckers, firms which provide their own transportation in owned or leased trucks, far outnumber the truckers for hire, about 55 trucking companies are now publicly owned, with revenues ranging from $30 million to $320 million per year. Because of their high average-year profitability, rapid growth, and opportunities for large further gains, trucking company stocks have been of increasing interest to enterprising investors.

Truck lines have benefited from the geographic dispersion of industry which has increased the demand for short-haul, multi-origin, multi-destination freight movement which the trucks can handle more flexibly and more economically than the railroads. The freight revenues of regulated trucking companies rose from $7.2 billion in 1960 to nearly $17 billion in 1971, and the property investment of Class I and II motor carriers increased in the same interval from $5.8 billion to $13.7 billion.

COSTS AND OPERATING FACTORS

Changes in trucking volume are closely correlated with industrial production, and historically, the tonnage hauled by trucks has been extremely sensitive to business conditions. However, fixed expenses are lower for truck lines than for railroads or airlines, and this fact, combined with effective cost control and conservative financial structures, has prevented unduly wide earnings swings for most companies.

Profit margins are narrow, with operating ratios of Class I and II companies typically between 93 and 96 per cent. Operating economies are limited by regulatory restrictions on vehicle size and weight. Labor costs absorb about 60 cents of each revenue dollar. The industry is strongly unionized, and during the 1960s, the average annual wage increase for trucking employees far exceeded that of most other industries. For this reason, truck lines rely largely on higher rates to maintain profit margins.

Transportation costs typically absorb about 44 per cent of truck-line revenue. This item includes driver wages, fuel, and equipment rentals. Terminal costs account for another 19 per cent, but a rising tendency for this expense is being offset by the use of computers and decentralized terminals. Maintenance costs average about 9 per cent; operating taxes and licenses, about 7 per cent; depreciation, about 4 per cent. Other expenses absorb 10 to 13 per cent of revenue, to leave operating margins of 4 to 7 per cent.

The trucking companies are expected to benefit from the completion of the Federal Interstate Highway System, scheduled for 1975. This development will permit trucks to move more rapidly through congested areas. Progress also is being made with state regulatory authorities to increase the size and load limits on vehicles, which would improve unit capacity and reduce on-road ton-mile costs. Higher charges are also gradually being obtained on small shipments now handled at unremunerative rates. Finally, the larger truck lines are achieving widespread economies by using computers for accounting, billing, payrolls, maintenance programming, management information, shipment tracing, dispatching, and scheduling freight runs.

FINANCIAL POSITION

Current ratios of motor freight companies are typically low, averaging 1.08 to 1 in 1970. The companies maintain no sizable inventories, and ICC regulations require freight bills to be paid in 14 days, bringing a comfortably rapid turnover of receivables. A more meaningful measure of truck-line liquidity is days of cash operating expense carried in current assets. An 18- to 20-day level is considered adequate.

Few trucking companies have marketable debt outstanding, but substantial amounts of equipment are financed through secured loans. Maturities are usually geared to equipment life and to expected cash generation. Most larger companies have revolving credit lines, with borrowing permitted up to a stated percentage of depreciated values. Truck-line analysts pay considerable attention to the ratio of cash throw-off to funded debt, which is the percentage of its total funded debt that a company could pay off in one year if all cash throw-off were used for that purpose. This ratio for Class I and II carriers in 1970 was 47.5 per cent.

The accounting practices of truck lines vary. Companies may report to stockholders in accordance either with generally accepted accounting principles or with ICC procedures. The former treats tax reductions attributable to accelerated tax depreciation or the investment tax credit as a deferred federal income tax liability and charges it to net income. ICC procedures flow the tax reduction through to net income. Differences in current ratios also result, depending on whether tires and tubes are capitalized or expensed. Other differences reflect the proportion of operating property leased instead of owned.

TRUCKING COMPANY STOCKS

Owing to economies of size, extensive route systems, automated terminals, and more sophisticated managements, the large, publicly owned truck lines are more efficient than the industry as a whole. Consequently, they benefit from the fact that ICC rates are based on average industry costs. The major companies have grown, and continue to grow, in considerable degree by absorbing smaller truck lines, which are often marginally operated by founder-owner-managers.

Net income as a percentage of revenue is low, even for highly efficient trucking companies. For the 11 stockholder-owned companies shown in Table 15-5, it was only 3.27 per cent in the record-breaking year 1971. However, capitalizations are modest, and in normal times, revenues amount to about 5 times net worth, resulting in very ample returns on shareholders' equity.

The stocks of leading truck lines are likely to be growth-type issues with pronounced cyclical swings. Dividends are conservative and most companies retain

Table 15-5 *Financial performance of motor freight lines, 1969, 1970, and 1971 (Average per share data, 11 major companies)*

		1969	1970	1971
Sales (in dollars)		$99.00	$96.90	$113.71
Operating income (in dollars)		10.29	8.67	13.91
Profit margin (in per cent)		10.39	8.95	12.24
Depreciation (in dollars)		$ 4.17	$ 4.52	$ 4.57
Taxes (in dollars)		2.41	1.50	4.02
Earnings (in dollars)		2.15	1.27	3.72
Dividends		0.85	0.67	0.74
Earnings as per cent of sales		2.17	1.31	3.27
Dividends as per cent of earnings		39.5	52.8	19.9
Return on book value (per cent)		15.50	9.04	22.56
Price (1941–1943	High	52.52	41.46	76.27
= 10)	Low	34.46	23.28	41.58
Price-earnings	High	24.4	33.0	20.5
ratio	Low	16.0	18.4	11.2
Dividend yield	High	2.47	2.88	1.78
(in per cent)	Low	1.62	1.60	0.97
Working capital (in dollars)		$ 2.95	$ 3.03	$ 3.89
Capital expenditures		9.92	6.86	6.06

Source: Standard & Poor's *Industry Surveys.*

substantial fractions of earnings to provide equity backing for growth and for further borrowings. Earnings per share in most companies have trended rapidly upward and stocks have enjoyed frequent splits. As a class, trucking stocks have outperformed the stock market averages over many years.

OTHER TRANSPORTATION ENTERPRISES

Except for Greyhound Corporation, whose main subsidiary operates a prosperous inter-city bus and parcel service, other transportation enterprises are of limited interest to the American investor. Barge lines, oil and coal slurry pipelines, car rental agencies, and taxi- and limousine-service companies are typically either the captive subsidiaries of larger, more diversified firms, or privately owned, or too small for their securities to be of more than local interest. The huge, heavily capitalized natural gas pipelines are classed as public utilities and will be considered in the next chapter.

Local bus and transit lines are generally speculative. Their costs for labor, fuel, and maintenance absorb a high percentage of operating revenues and are by no means stable. Operating revenues themselves are highly cyclical, and rates are held down by automobile competition and by determined public and political pressure. Most privately owned local transit systems have proved increasingly unprofitable since the coming of the automobile, and a majority of companies have now been taken over by the cities and openly subsidized out of tax revenues.

MARKETS

The stocks of major transportation companies are widely held, and the large stock issues are mostly listed on the New York Stock Exchange, and often on the regional exchanges as well. As a rule, their markets are broad and active.

As has been noted, railroad equipment obligations and well-secured bonds are held by institutions and conservative investors. Less amply secured railroad bonds, rail income bonds, and airline bonds are widely held by individual investors. The equipment obligations, small bond issues, and the guaranteed stocks and bonds of the railroads are traded over the counter. These markets do not appear very active, but because of the considerable number of such issues outstanding, there is always some trading in them.

QUESTIONS AND PROBLEMS

1 Do the large debt structures of airlines today pose the same hazard to the financial system and economy that the high debt ratios of railroads did in 1929? Should a cyclical industry be encouraged to employ that much debt?

2 Which earnings are of better quality: those of Western Air Lines, Inc., or those of Continental? Why?

3 Is a 12 per cent allowed rate of return to the trunk airlines realistic if it is a (a) above that of most other regulated industries, and (b) difficult to realize in the face of political and customer attitudes?

4 During 1971–1972 the average of airline stock prices more than doubled. Why? Does such a rise constitute "growth"? Explain.

5 Why are airline debentures usually rated no better than Ba? Investigate (a) American Airlines sub. conv. deb. 4¼s 1992; (b) Braniff Airways sub. deb. 5⅜s 1986; and (c) United Airlines sub. conv. deb. 4¼s 1992.

6 Are the railroads declining in importance as economic institutions in the United States? Is it clear that railroading as a method of producing transportation is becoming uneconomic, or does the decline of railroading reflect uneconomic disadvantages placed upon it?

7 Is it socially economic or equitable (a) that railroad employees should have a vested interest in the continuation of outmoded methods and unnecessary jobs; (b) that railroads should be denied the privilege of reducing rates between coastal or river ports in order to get additional traffic, because this hurts barge lines or discriminates against other communities without water facilities; (c) that commuters have a vested interest in a service which was once profitable but now fails to pay its way?

8 What is likely to be done to salvage the railroad industry, which is socially and technically economic but which is losing ground financially? What are the investors' chances? Can the conglomerate idea help?

9 Why have railroad maintenance ratios declined since 1953 while transportation ratios have been rising? Which is the more significant ratio?

10 Is a populous and prosperous territory important to a railroad? How do you account for the fact that the Atchison, Topeka & Santa Fe, which connects Chicago and California via New Mexico and Arizona, is prosperous?

11 Look up the "other income" of Burlington Northern, Inc. Would you call it good quality? Is Burlington Northern common stock of investment caliber? What are your criteria?

12 Investigate the Missouri Pacific Income 4¾s of 2020. Are they acceptable as a medium-risk investment? Are they as good quality as the average good industrial stock? Do you think life insurance companies would buy them? Should they? Would these bonds be satisfactory speculations for market profit?

13 The year 1970 produced a sharp decline in railroad earnings. Why?

14 Will it be possible for the railroads to sell new long-term bond issues to refund existing bonds as they mature? If not, can the railroads earn enough to pay them off? What might happen?

15 Do you think the railroad industry is headed for government takeover? Why, or why not?

16 Is net working capital as important to a railroad, airline, or trucking company as to an industrial firm? Explain.

17 How is it possible for trucking companies to show earnings on stockholders' equity of 15 per cent or more when only about 3 cents of each revenue dollar is retained as profit?

18 Why have the truck lines proved more consistently profitable in recent years than airlines when the airlines have enjoyed a more rapid rate of revenue growth?

19 Compare the financial structures of Yellow Freight System and Consolidated Freightways with those of American Airlines and Braniff Airways. Which pair of companies is more conservatively financed? Why? What difference may this make in future years?

20 Why does the ICC basis of rate making for the motor freight industry virtually guarantee that the large, efficient stockholder-owned companies will be profitable and grow rapidly?

21 Do you see any significant difference between the guiding principles under which the ICC and the CAB regulate the trucking and airline industries respectively?

REFERENCES

Badger, Ralph E., and Paul B. Coffman: *Investment Analysis*, McGraw-Hill Book Company, New York, 1967, Chap. 22.

Bellemore, Douglas H., and John C. Ritchie, Jr.: *Investments*, 3d ed., South-Western Publishing Company, Incorporated, Cincinnati, 1969, Chap. 23.

Dougall, Herbert E.: *Investments*, 8th ed., Prentice-Hall, Inc., Englewood Cliffs, N.J., 1968, Chap. 28.

Moody's Transportation Manual, Special Features section, Moody's Investors Service, New York.

Standard & Poor's Corporation: *Industry Surveys*, sections on air transport, railroads, trucking, New York.

The public utilities—telephone, electricity, gas, water, and telegraph companies—probably provide securities investments for more people than any other industry group. The utility business offers a wide assortment of securities, including bonds, preferred stocks, and common stocks, and affords a considerable variety of qualities in each. Needless to say, the utilities in the United States represent a very large aggregate investment. At the beginning of 1973, their total invested capital exceeded 245 billion dollars.

The utility industries which are of greatest interest to investors are typically characterized by rapid growth, monopoly franchises in their service areas, dependable earnings, capital structures employing large percentages of bonds and preferred stocks, and extensive public regulation of operations and earnings. Each of these characteristics has an important bearing on the investment qualities of the securities and must therefore be examined in some detail.

THE UTILITY INDUSTRIES

The various utility industries do not by any means exhibit the same economic characteristics. The three largest, electric power, telephone, and natural gas, have grown with extraordinary speed and the first two appear likely to continue to do so for some time. They do not have serious competition from either similar or substitute products, and consequently their earnings can be made large or small simply by adjusting their rates. Their sales volumes are not acutely affected by economic fluctuations, and their earnings are highly dependable. These are the utility industries in which the greatest investor interest exists and with which this chapter is chiefly concerned.

The electric power business is by far the largest of the utility industries. It is probably also the most depression-resistant, for its sales volume dropped less than 15 per cent and its earnings from operations less than 20 per cent between 1929 and 1933. No recession since 1938 has noticeably affected its sales or earnings. The reasons for this fine record lie in the rapid growth of the industry, which means that a recession causes a slowdown rather than a retrogression in sales volume, and in the fact that most of the industry's revenue comes from residential and commercial use, which is very stable. Some differences appear at times between companies which have varying percentages of rural, urban, and industrial load and between companies which depend on steam power, hydroelectric generation, and purchased power. Steam plants are subject to fuel costs, hydroelectric plants are subject to drought, and purchased power is subject to whatever terms occur in the purchase contract. However, these factors are usually secondary rather than fundamental in importance.

Telephone operations are only a little less stable than electric power. Between 1929 and 1933 the Class A telephone systems showed a decline of nearly 35 per cent in net operating earnings, and an 8 per cent drop was experienced from 1937 to 1938. The shrinkage was somewhat greater in toll business than in local exchange operation, but both suffered. Owing to heavy mechanization of local and long-distance service, the telephone business is probably little more sensitive to increases in labor and materials costs than is the power business. The rise in prices and wage rates from 1968 to 1972 obliged both telephone and power companies to ask for increased rates. The telephone industry has proved itself to be a dependable outlet for investors' funds. It seems to be relatively free of public competition and seldom encounters regulatory hostility or franchise fights. The telephone business in the United States is dominated by the great American Telephone and Telegraph Company system, which handles 90 per cent of the nation's telephone business. The system is conservatively financed and ably managed. The second-largest system, comprising General Telephone & Electronics Corporation and its subsidiaries, does about 5 per cent of the nation's telephone business.

Natural gas companies divide themselves into two types, pipeline operators and retailers. Some companies are both. The pipeline companies buy gas from the oil fields under long-term contracts or produce it themselves, and transport it in pipelines to towns and cities where it is sold to the local gas companies. The local companies send the gas through their city mains to customers' home and business establishments. Both pipeline transmission and retailing of natural gas have developed on a large scale only since World War II. Although the growth rate of natural gas sales has slowed perceptibly in recent years, the industry seems to have established itself solidly and gives promises of steady and profitable performance. However, over the past 20 years federally imposed gas rates have been well below the value of natural gas as a premium fuel. Uneconomically low rates have encouraged gas consumption where coal or fuel oil might have served. They also have discouraged the discovery and sale of new reserves. Thus, long-range problems of gas supply overhang the industry. This, and the highly conjectural possibilities of future competition from electrically powered heating devices, are the chief hazards.

Water service systems are municipally owned in most places, but several major companies and a number of minor ones operate as private enterprises. Generally speaking, the water companies grow about in proportion to the populations in the areas served. Their earning power is extremely stable, and because of this factor, most companies employ a high percentage of senior capital in their financing. The American Water Works Company system, largest of the privately owned water supply organizations, is typical of the operating experience of the industry.

The telegraph business consists of the Western Union Telegraph Company, several property-owning companies whose properties are leased to Western Union, and a scattered few radio and cable companies. Western Union acquired American Telephone and Telegraph Company's "TWX" public teletypewriter exchange system in 1969. The company is an aggressively managed organization whose expansion into such fields as money transmittal, stock ticker and quotation services, private teletype service, data processing and transmission, and microwave communication has scarely managed to compensate for the inroads made by airmail and telephone competition into its message business. A large part of the operating costs of the telegraph business has always been labor cost, and although mechanization is increasingly possible, high labor costs have been unavoidable as the value of labor time has risen. Western Union stock has slipped since 1929 from investment to speculative quality, but the business is still capable of substantial earnings and possibly of some earnings growth.

REGULATION AND FRANCHISES

The public utility industries are all subject to extensive regulatory control by municipal, state, or federal authority. The extent of municipal authority is generally limited to powers expressly delegated by the states, which may be minor or very far-reaching, depending on the policy of the state. The state power over intrastate utilities extends to regulate the area served, the quality of service, the capital structure of the utility, the accounting practices followed, the rate structure, and the general level of rates for the purpose of limiting the utility's earnings. Federal authority is theoretically effective only as it concerns interstate commerce and the use of streams supplying navigable waters. But under federal laws relating to holding companies, interstate transmission of natural gas, and water power, the federal government has been able to extend its influence far beyond the nominal limits of its powers.

A long line of court decisions, beginning shortly after the Civil War and extending down to the present time, outlines the justification for, and the guiding principles of, utility regulation. The monopolistic features of the business plus its importance to the public justify regulation in the public interest. Use of the public streets and the need for eminent-domain powers are added occasion for control. It is commonly said that utility regulation extends only to regulation of *what* is done and does not enter the management province of determining *how* it is done. However, the increasing scope and detail of regulation seem constantly to narrow the field of management authority and increase that of the regulating commissions. Such matters as a decision to build a new generating plant, a plan for refunding a bond issue, or even the accounting treatment of the cost of floating a bond issue are as much subject to commission decision as to the judgment of management.

Most utilities operate in the communities they serve and use the public streets under long-term permits known as franchises. In many instances the franchises are contractual in nature, assuring the utilities of certain privileges and in return obligating them to pay certain taxes, maintain certain standards of service, and accept specified rates of return. Usually the franchises assure a monopoly during their term. Sometimes they contain options permitting the municipality to buy the property at stated times and prices. Franchise policies vary greatly from state to state and from municipality to municipality, but they are important enough so that no utility security should ever be bought without first investigating the company's franchise position. Investment reference manuals and new-issue prospectuses generally review franchise matters.

PUBLIC OWNERSHIP AND PUBLIC COMPETITION

Municipalities have for many years ventured into utility ownership as a means of obtaining certain desired services at low cost. Municipally owned water systems operate in thousands of cities and towns. New York City owns its subway system; San Francisco and many other cities own streetcar and bus systems; Los Angeles, Seattle, Omaha, Chattanooga, and dozens of other cities and towns own electric power systems.[1] Gas, telephone, and telegraph properties, however, are seldom municipally operated.

The federal government in the past 50 years has engaged in a number of water power developments which were too large to be attractive to private enterprise, or which were financially possible only when land reclamation, flood control, and navigation were combined with power operation. These projects included the Tennessee Valley Authority, the Grand Coulee development in Washington, Hoover Dam on the Colorado River, Shasta Dam on the Sacramento River, Bonneville Dam on the Columbia River, and other less ambitious undertakings in the Mississippi basin and on the Atlantic seaboard. Comparatively few of these projects would pay for themselves as power developments, even when completely exempt from taxation and financed with low-cost money provided by the government. However, the sale of power by these ventures at the best prices obtainable is justifiable business, if the venture as a whole is to be undertaken.

Federal policy toward private enterprise in the electric power field has been an unstable one. Prior to 1933 it was customary to sell power generated at federal dams to municipal or private utilities without discrimination; for example, the Los Angeles Department of Water and Power and the Southern California Edison

---

[1] The incentives to municipal ownership are varied, but two are obvious. First, a municipally owned utility pays no federal income tax, a cost which would absorb 10 to 15 per cent of a private company's gross revenue. Second, the publicly owned utility can finance itself by selling tax-exempt bonds; this should save at least 1 or 2 per cent per year in necessary earnings on the investment and permit a 4 to 8 per cent saving in rates. These two items would save the local consumer 14 to 23 per cent in rates at the expense of the federal revenues. In addition, a municipally owned utility could make additional large tax savings if absolved from state and local taxes.

Company obtained power at Hoover Dam on similar terms. Between 1933 and 1941, the federal policy was hostile to private enterprise. Not only were private companies often denied access to federal power, but in many instances federal loans and gifts were made to induce municipalities to construct retail power lines to distribute power in competition with existing private facilities, franchises permitting. Since the start of World War II the federal attitude has been more moderate, but it is probably wise for investors to study the circumstances surrounding proposed public projects before investing in utilities operating nearby.

In the absence of federal intervention the development of municipal utility enterprises has not usually been destructive to honest private investment. Duplication of private facilities by a municipality is not likely if the project must pay for itself. It is better to buy out the private company. Negotiations for municipal purchase of a private plant are often accompanied by some rancor and name calling, but passably equitable results are usually achieved. Investors are of course wise to seek out utilities with sound public relations as well as sound franchise position; thus they may avoid ultimate loss as well as occasional nerve-racking episodes.

RATES AND EARNINGS

From the investor's viewpoint, the most important aspect of utility regulation is the one relating to rates and earnings. In almost all jurisdictions at present, the regulating authority has the right to prescribe or control the rates charged by the utilities. Since the earnings of the utilities depend very closely upon the rates permitted by the regulating authority, the attitude and promptness of the authority become of paramount importance. A utility is legally entitled to "reasonable" earnings under the "due process" clauses of the federal constitution, and the courts will intervene on behalf of one which is unfairly treated, but investors will do well to investigate the reputation of a regulatory commission before investing heavily under its jurisdiction.

The classic objective of rate making is to permit "a fair return on a fair valuation of the property used and useful in the public service." That is, rates are to be set at a level which will allow the utility to earn a fair percentage on its investment after deducting all costs including income taxes. The fair percentage in most jurisdictions is to be earned on the total investment in necessary property—fixed assets, equipment and supplies, accounts receivable, cash, and all other operating essentials[2]—regardless of whether the assets represent stockholders' or borrowed capital. Out of the permitted overall earnings, the stockholders must pay interest

---

[2] In instances where rate of return is allowed on fixed assets only, or on some other partial tabulation of used and useful property, the rate is simply made high enough to allow adequate total earnings. The valuation upon which the fair return is allowed is technically known as the "rate base."

on borrowed funds at whatever rate they have contracted to pay. The rest is profit.

A second objective of rate-making authority is that of allowing earnings sufficient to "maintain the company's credit standing and attract capital." In historic commission and Supreme Court decisions, notably in the Hope Natural Gas case[3] and in the Northern Natural Gas case,[4] this objective has received close attention. These cases have established the idea that an overall fair rate of return on the company's assets can reasonably be established by computing a weighted average of (1) the cost of borrowed money to the company, (2) the dividend rates paid on its preferred stock, and (3) the percentage of earnings needed on the common stock net worth to keep the market price of the stock somewhat above its net worth (recognized book value)[5] most of the time. Thus, if a company's capital structure consisted of 50 per cent debt costing 6 per cent interest, 20 per cent preferred stock paying 7 per cent dividends, and 30 per cent common stock equity whose shares would sell slightly above book value if they earned 12 per cent of book value, the necessary overall average rate of return would be 8.0 per cent. It is clear that the overall rate of return needed under this formula will be affected by the capital structure of the company as well as by the cost of money. In a few instances, conservative companies have been urged by the regulating commissions to use more low-cost borrowed money and less high-cost common stock equity, but this has been a disputed point less frequently since interest rates rose sharply during the late 1960s.

A fair percentage rate of return is theoretically a substitute for the average rate which might be earned with equal risk in competitive industry. It should therefore be set with reference to average interest rates on borrowed money and average profit rates in stable industries. Also, as the preceding paragraph noted, it should be set at a level which will attract necessary equity capital into the utility field. The rise of bond yields to between 7 and 9 per cent during the 1969–1973 period and the utilities' continued need for money for expansion pushed rates of return into the $7\frac{1}{2}$ to 9 per cent area. Still higher returns would be necessary to keep the utilities in good financial health if interest rates remain at high levels as successive issues of old utility bonds, financed at 3 to 4 per cent yields, come due for refunding. To help weaker companies attract investors' money, the state commissions have usually permitted them to earn higher returns than strong concerns operating in safe areas. The Federal Power Commission has long indicated a be-

---

[3] *Federal Power Commission v. Hope Natural Gas Company*, 320 U.S. 591 (1944).

[4] *Northern Natural Gas Co. v. Federal Power Commission*, 1 P.U.R., 3d 310 (1954) or 206 F.2d 690 (1953).

[5] If the price is somewhat above book value, then the company can sell new stock and pay the costs of sale without diluting the existing book value. When the rate base valuation appraises the common stock equity above book value, the higher figure may be used as the market price criterion.

lief that natural gas companies need to earn about one percentage point more than the typical electric power company.

When a fair percentage rate of return has been determined, it is still necessary to establish a valuation (a rate base) for the property employed by the utility. It is generally conceded that this valuation should be a net figure after allowance for depreciation. However, the basic theory for valuation of utility property for rate-making purposes has been much disputed. Some experts hold that the prudently invested historical cost of construction is the proper beginning point; others insist that the cost of reproduction at current prices is more logical; and there are several variations of each approach. The Federal Power Commission, the SEC, and a number of influential state commissions are known to regard the actual historical prudent cost of construction as the proper beginning point. However, many statutes, commissions, and court decisions are slightly evasive, declaring in favor of a "fair" value arrived at after considering all possible methods. Between 1935 and 1950 it seemed that the historical-cost principle would be almost completely adopted, but problems arising out of postwar conditions—depreciation charges inadequate to replace worn-out assets, fixed earnings (based on cost of assets) inadequate to attract capital in an inflationary period, rising costs which repeatedly impaired already inadequate earnings—have led many commissions and courts back to a "fair value" concept in which cost of reproduction also plays a conspicuous part.

Rate making has further complications. Most commissions have insisted on setting rates which *would have been* fair in some "test period" already terminated; a small but growing number are willing to project trends of costs and sales volumes and make rates prospectively. Some permit prompt adjustments to cover major increases in costs as they occur, but others wait for a demonstrated need after costs have risen. Policies and procedures—and the results—are thus highly varied.[6]

It should be emphasized at this point that utility rate adjustments are not made on a month-to-month basis expressly to keep the utilities' earnings always at the same rate. Rather, adjustments are made at infrequent intervals and on a long-range basis, in response to permanent changes in costs or values. For example, a system depending on hydroelectric plants would have to bear the temporary losses which might result from a drought, and it could keep the high profits occurring in a year when water was abundant; but the effects of a permanent change in wage rates would sooner or later be compensated by a change in power rates.

[6] The study of utility rate making is extensive and complex. Interested readers are referred to any good book on utility regulation (for example, M. G. Glaeser, *Public Utilities in American Capitalism*, The Macmillan Company (1957), and to a line of Supreme Court decisions culminating in and cited in *Federal Power Commission v. Hope Natural Gas Company*, 320 U.S. 591 (1944). See also digests of recent rate decisions in *Moody's Public Utility Manual*; also James C. Bonbright, *Principles of Public Utility Rates*, Columbia University Press, New York, 1961.

In contrast to the regional plan used in establishing rate levels for the railroads, the level of utility rates is usually set separately for each utility operating company. A company which serves sparsely settled territory or finds its fuel costs higher by reason of its location is therefore not penalized. It is allowed rates high enough to pay its justifiable costs plus a fair return on its investment. Of course, a poorly managed or inefficient utility would probably not be allowed rates higher than those charged by well-managed neighboring concerns. For this reason, investors commonly compare a given utility's rates with those charged by neighboring companies before buying its stock.

ESTIMATING REASONABLE EARNINGS

The investor who wishes to test the current earnings of a utility for reasonableness and to determine whether future rates will probably permit the same, smaller, or larger earnings can do so by computing the percentage of present earnings (including bond interest) to an estimated rate base valuation. If the overall earnings fall within a "normal" range[7] or close to a normal objective for this and similar companies, they may be assumed stable and dependable; otherwise, increase or decrease may be in order.[8] If the investor prefers to estimate a normal or reasonable earning power for his utility, he may apply a "normal" rate of return to an estimated rate base to obtain an overall earnings figure which should typically be available to cover interest and net profit.

The calculations require the investor to have some knowledge of the rate of return permitted and the rate base valuation established for his utility. These figures may be determined in a rough way by a study of the practices of the commission having jurisdiction, the briefs and decisions in commission and court cases involving the company, and the company's own recent financial history. However, these materials are not readily available to the average investor, and the financial services do not report them in adequate detail. The investor who wishes to make these tests must therefore usually base them on the utility's own financial statements, and interpret the results with caution.

For many years, most large utility systems have been required by regulating commissions to follow fairly standard accounting practices. Asset values are generally based on the actual dollar cost of each item to the company which first "dedicated" it to utility service, less depreciation to date. Consolidated statements

---

[7] The normal range has crept upward as bond yields and other money costs have climbed. Immediately after World War II, a 5 to 6 per cent return was normal for an electric power company. By 1967–1968, the range had risen to 6 to 7 per cent. In 1973, it was 7½ to 9 per cent.

[8] The earnings of any year must be compared with the average value of property in service during the year, not with the value at the end of the year. Because of the rapid rate of utility growth, the difference is often important.

usually follow the same principles, and footnotes explain special situations which require clarification. It is therefore reasonable to make an estimate of a rate base valuation *on the historical-cost principle* from the utility's balance sheets. To the extent that cost of reproduction is allowed as a factor in rate base valuation, the actual rate base is almost certain to be higher than the utility's statement values, for cost-of-reproduction figures have been rising during the inflationary years since World War II; but in most jurisdictions the final rate base will be set much closer to historical- than to reproduction-cost values.

Three further cautionary remarks are in order. First, there are still instances in which utility companies and regulating commissions are in disagreement about the proper original cost of assets or the amount of accumulated depreciation. Thus, some balance sheets may not reflect recognized rate base values. Second, some assets such as "cost of subsidiaries' stocks in excess of related book value" and "discount on sale of securities" will not be recognized as good rate base assets, and capital donated to the utility by customers to pay for extensions of service lines required for the customers' convenience would not be allowed to earn a return. Third, a utility's statement may include an investment in an unprofitable unit such as a local transit company; this investment would not be added to an electric power rate base and compensated out of power revenues. It would, in practice, be a separate unit.

As an example of an estimate to test earning power, the case of the New England Electric System may be considered. This company and its subsidiaries sell electricity in all New England states except Maine. Rate base valuations are mostly on a historical-cost basis.

Table 16-1 shows a condensed version of the New England Electric System's 1971 balance sheet. According to this statement, the company valued its assets at $1,210,456,000 after deductions for depreciation. But there are three items on the balance sheet which probably are deducted in establishing a historical-cost rate base, and two others which may be doubtful. First, the $2,009,000 of selling costs on common shares is not a useful asset; it probably is regarded as a contra-net worth item. Second, there is $2,332,000 on the liabilities side of the balance sheet labeled Contributions in Aid of Construction. Since this money was provided by outsiders to reduce the company's risk in making certain service extensions, the assets purchased with it are probably not included in the company's rate base. Third, the $23,227,000 of Accumulated Deferred Federal Income Taxes is in a similar position; although the case is debatable, the money has been collected from the utility's customers, and its temporary use by the utility probably should not enlarge the rate base. Fourth, the miscellaneous Investments item of $49,004,000 is not standard utility property; two-thirds of it consists of the company's share in an experimental, jointly owned, atomic-powered generating plant, and the balance covers certain other nonutility ventures. Finally, there is $105,805,000 of Construction Work in Progress. This large investment is not yet

Table 16-1 *New England electric system and subsidiaries consolidated balance sheet at December 31, 1971* (000 omitted)*

Assets:

Property, plant, and equipment at cost:

Electric plant (Note B)	$1,114,507
Gas plant	107,252
Construction work in progress	105,805
Total	$1,327,564
Less reserves for depreciation	273,335
	$1,054,229

Current assets:

Cash	20,031
Accounts receivable less reserves	59,010
Materials and supplies at average cost	17,636
Prepaid expenses and temporary deposits	2,465
Total current assets	99,142
Investments, at cost, in atomic electric companies ($33,290), nonutility property, and other investments	49,004
Commissions and expense on common shares	2,009
Deferred charges	6,072
	$1,210,456

Liabilities:

Common shares, par value $1 per share	$ 15,663
Paid-in surplus	213,185
Capital surplus	1,822
Consolidated earned surplus	89,554
	$ 320,224

Shares of subsidiaries held by the public:

Preferred stocks (see accompanying statement) & premiums	$ 138,232
Common stocks, premiums, and surplus	854
	$ 139,086
Long-term debt of system and subsidiaries	$ 522,689
Total capitalization	$ 981,999

Current liabilities:

Long-term debt due within one year	$ 8,000
Notes payable	149,805
Accounts payable	12,349
Accrued taxes (Note F)	9,985
Accrued interest, payrolls, and other expenses	7,478
Other current liabilities	2,416
Total current liabilities	$ 190,033
Unamortized premiums (less expenses) on long-term debt	1,139
Other reserve and deferred credits	1,878
Contributions in aid of construction	2,332
Accumulated deferred federal income taxes (Note F)	23,227
Accumulated deferred investment tax credits (Note F)	9,848
	$1,210,456

* This balance sheet has been condensed and rearranged for textbook purposes. It omits details and explanatory notes carried in the System's 1971 *Annual Report*, from which it is taken.

in service and is not entitled to be compensated out of customers' rates. However, an interest allowance of 5 to 7 per cent per annum is added to the rate base value of the asset items (the accounting credit goes to the interest-cost account), making the net effect the same as though the investment had a modest earning power. Since many utility balance sheets do not separate assets under construction from those already in service, it seems best to calculate as though all were in service; this will overstate earning power by only a modest amount.

If the first three items, totaling $27,568,000, are removed from the balance sheet of $1,210,456,000, a remainder of $1,182,888,000 is found. Since it seems likely that the miscellaneous investments and the properties in process of construction will contribute in some way to company earnings, they may be left in the total, and the $1,182,888,000 thus becomes a crude original cost base upon which earning power may be estimated.

Under 1971 conditions, New England Electric System was probably entitled to earn between 6½ and 7½ per cent on its rate base, or roughly between $76,888,000 and $88,717,000 on its $1,182,888,000. This would represent total earning power available to service the bank loans and all securities outstanding at year-end 1971 after deducting all other expenses and taxes. (Actual 1971 earnings on this basis were $71,553,000; but these were earned on average, not year-end, assets.) Examination of the System's position at year-end 1971 indicated that interest charges were then running at about $34,000,000 per annum and that preferred dividends and minority interest claims were about $8,900,000. These amounts total $42,900,000. If this sum is subtracted from the estimated totals of $76,888,000 to $88,717,000 of permissible operating earnings, there will remain $33,988,000 to $45,817,000 for the 15,663,000 common shares outstanding at year-end. This would mean annual earnings of $2.17 to $2.93 per common share, with the exact figure depending on the rate of return obtained. (Remember, these figures are slightly overstated because they assume full earnings on a plant not yet in service.)

New England Electric System's reported per share earnings in 1971 were $2.10. This indicates an overall rate of return slightly below the minimum of the equitable range.[9] In addition, New England Electric is a high-leverage system with a large percentage of its resources provided by debt, much of which still reflects the low interest rates of former years. This factor allows net earnings of slightly more than 10 per cent on the $20.44 book value of the common stock and permitted it to sell in mid-1972 at $23 to $25 per share. In view of the risk on a high-leverage stock, this price is minimal. It does not meet the terms of the rate-of-return arithmetic outlined in the Hope Natural Gas case, and considerations of

---

[9] This assumes that the System's income-statement accounting for such items as rapid depreciation, deferred taxes, investment credit, pensions, and business promotion costs is both realistic and accepted by the regulating commissions. Some deviation occurs, but income-statement accounting is increasingly regulated into conformity.

both equity and long-range financial health point up the company's need for stronger earnings. However, New England Electric received several rate increases late in 1971, and earnings per share would have been at least 10 cents higher had not President Nixon's price freeze delayed the effective date of the improved revenues.

The investor who uses this method of testing a company's normal earning power must realize that his balance sheet computations attempt to establish the rate base as of the exact date of the balance sheet. Application of a fair percentage rate to this computed rate base will produce an earnings figure which is normal only for the assets held and the securities outstanding at the date of the balance sheet. Deduction of amounts required as of that date for interest charges, preferred dividends, and minority claims will indicate the total normal earning power for the common shares outstanding. However, if the company maintains a fairly constant proportioning of bonds, preferred stock, and common stock equity as it grows, this sort of estimate may give a fairly durable indication of its position.

It must also be conceded that the process here suggested is an extremely crude one, a rough-and-ready method of estimating. It attempts only a historical-cost valuation, which may be quite inadequate. Second, in a utility system it lumps together different subsidiary companies which may be rendering different types of service under different regulatory jurisdictions. Third, it includes the "investments," which in a utility are most likely to consist of securities in partially owned affiliated companies, in some cases not even in the utility business, as part of the estimated rate base; this is excusable only if the item is small. Yet an estimate of this type is worth making; if, for example, an investor in 1972 discovered that a stock he was considering had attractive earnings per share only because the company was earning more than 8½ per cent on its apparent rate base, he would have been warned to proceed with caution.

UTILITY CAPITAL STRUCTURES

Because of the high degree of stability inherent in utility earnings, it has become customary to use large amounts of senior capital in utility financing. A typical capital structure might consist of 50 per cent debt, 15 per cent preferred stock, and 35 per cent common stock equity. Even less conservative structures are used, though regulating commissions usually advocate a debt maximum not much over 60 per cent and a common stock equity not much under 25 per cent.

Some managements attempt to introduce the maximum feasible leverage into their capital structures, in order to maximize earnings on the common stockholders' investment. Suppose that a 50-25-25 structure can be financed on the average with 5½ per cent bonds and 6 per cent preferred stock. If a 7½ per cent rate of return were permitted, $7.50 would be earned annually on every $100 of company investment. Of every $100 invested, $50 would be provided by the bond-holders at an interest cost of $2.75, and $25 by preferred stockholders at a dividend outlay of $1.50; the other $3.25 of earnings would remain for the common stockholders as a 13 per cent net profit on their $25 investment. Earnings of this magnitude would ordinarily permit the payment of a $2.25 annual dividend on every $25 of common stock investment.[10] It is true that the common stockholders must bear the risk and absorb any losses which occur, but the generous returns which accrue to this kind of risk bearing make it undeservedly popular among investors.

Table 16-2 indicates the proportioning of debt and stock interests in several important utility systems as shown in their consolidated balance sheets dated December 31, 1971. In most instances, the proportions of debt, preferred, and common stock equity appear to be about what the utilities' ultimate plans contemplate.

Some students of finance believe that it is safe for a growing and monopolistic utility to use a 60-15-25 capital structure, because little chance of damaging financial reverses seems to exist. However, railroads, streetcar companies, and manu-

[10] A common share representing a prudently invested $25, on which the per share earnings averaged $3.25 and which paid a $2.25 dividend, would normally sell between $32.50 and $45.

Table 16-2 *Consolidated capital structures of representative utility systems, December 31, 1971*

	Percentage of resources represented by		
System	Bonds plus current debt	Preferred stocks and minority interests	Common stock equity
American Electric Power	59	8	33
American Natural Gas	62	0	38
American Telephone and Telegraph	45	3	52
Boston Edison	54	11	35
Columbia Gas System	55	0	45
Commonwealth Edison	60	7	33
Consolidated Edison of New York	52	15	33
Detroit Edison	55	12	33
Oklahoma Gas and Electric	53	10	37
Pacific Lighting	48	12	40
Southern California Edison	53	11	36
Texas Eastern Transmission	65	7	28
Texas Utilities	50	12	38
Transcontinental Gas Pipe Line	67	10	23

factured gas companies once regarded their positions as financially impregnable, and many of them used high-leverage capital structures just as some growing utilities do now. The result was financial confusion and, in many cases, bankruptcy when growth ceased and competing industries forced limitation of rates. It would seem that many utilities are disregarding the lesson of history in planning their capital structures.

Because sales and cost stability and growth rates differ, it is not proper to set down universal rules to define a sound consolidated capital structure for a growing utility. If a rough-and-ready rule is required, the following seems reasonable: Determine first the total net good assets after deducting depreciation reserves and all questionable (non-rate-base) assets. Second, determine a typical or average earning power after allowing for income taxes but before deducting for interest. The structure meets accepted standards (1) if total current and bonded debt is less than 55 per cent of asset value and if interest charges are covered 3 times over after tax allowances; and (2) if debts plus preferred stocks plus minority interests do not exceed 70 per cent of the net assets and do not absorb over 55 per cent of the posttax earnings.

The foregoing implies that a common stock equity have a 30 per cent interest in net good assets and a 45 per cent equity in average earnings is acceptable in quality, if no other weaknesses appear. An equity of this grade is doubtless fortified against early obliteration in a depression or a cost inflation, but it cannot be said to be immune to a long-term market revolution such as the railroads encountered between 1920 and 1960. A really high-quality utility common stock should have a 40 per cent or better equity in net good assets and at least a 50 per cent equity in posttax earnings. Such a stock could bear the loss which a lowered rate of return would impose, regardless of whether the lower return stemmed from economic change or from adverse regulatory policy.

OPERATING REVENUES AND EXPENSES

Monopoly position, dependable sales, and persistent growth relieve the utilities of many of the problems which beset ordinary competitive businesses. Another factor, that of constantly increasing technical efficiency, has held down or lowered operating costs for many years. Aside from harassment of a political or regulatory nature, therefore, the utility industries have had relatively few serious operating problems. Sharply rising price levels have been the most burdensome; these have at times caused increases in labor, fuel, and materials costs at a speed which mounting efficiency plus occasional rate increases by slow-acting commissions could not always match. Tax increases have imposed heavy burdens. Finally, occasional impairment of earnings due to drought affects companies dependent on hydroelectric installations.

The utilities which were affected first in the price inflation of 1946–1958 were the telephone companies, whose relatively heavy labor and materials costs increased sharply. Natural gas companies felt the cost increases a little later, especially as their costly expansion programs developed. The electric power companies during this period had unusual advantages in cost-saving technological developments and in increased sales per customer, which shielded them from part, but not all, of the impact of inflation. Construction costs soared for all utilities, and as the percentage of new, high-cost plants on the books increased, depreciation charges rose. The long rise in interest rates after 1946 increased long-term borrowing costs and tended to raise the fair return on capital. From 1959 through 1965, price levels and interest rates rose only gradually, and utilities' needs for rate relief diminished substantially. But the return of inflation and rising money costs after 1965 confronted the utilities with a new era of rate problems and strained customer relations. By 1972, it was clear that electric, gas, and telephone companies were again locked in a cycle of the 1946–1958 type, now intensified by environmentalist complaints, power brownouts, and natural gas shortages.

WORKING CAPITAL POSITION

Except when important construction or refunding programs are under way, the utilities are not likely to possess large amounts of working capital. Current assets amounting to 10 per cent of total assets would usually be sufficient, and of these, two-thirds might well be offset by current liabilities. Steady and dependable earnings make small amounts of net working capital and a low current ratio tolerable.

Because most of their assets are permanently employed in fixed capital, the utilities are not likely to employ serial bonds, serial bank loans, or any large bank loans at all except those incurred temporarily to finance construction outlays, pending more permanent financing by sale of securities.

DIVIDEND POLICIES

Steady and dependable earnings make it possible for a utility to pay regular dividends which amount to a fairly high percentage of average earnings, possibly 75 per cent or more. This is the common practice, except for a few companies urgently in need of small amounts of additional capital which can be drawn from earnings, and a few whose managements have unique ideas about dividend policies.

The precedents for the industry are set by such conspicuous concerns as the American Telephone and Telegraph Company, whose quarterly payments were unchanged from 1922 to 1959 and whose uninterrupted dividend record goes back to 1881. Other leading utilities have similar long records of uninterrupted payments, including Boston Edison Company since 1897, Consolidated Edison Company of New York since 1893, Commonwealth Edison Company (Chicago) since 1890, and Pacific Lighting Corporation (California) since 1909. These are outstanding rather than average records, of course, but they illustrate the capacity of the industry as well as the precedents which are now generally recognized to be appropriate.

Generous regular dividends are usually popular with stockholders. They are good business for companies whose growth is so rapid that large sums must be raised by selling new stock. The stockholder who gets a satisfactory dividend is usually willing to buy new stock when the company needs extra money; the company can get back its dividend money and more too if it needs it, and at low cost. Utility managements are well aware of these facts, and generous dividend policies are coupled in most companies with occasional common stock sales to stockholders on a "rights" basis.

Frequent opportunities to buy additional stock on a rights basis, or to sell the rights, provide utility stockholders an important source of extra income. Suppose a utility offers its common stockholders the privilege of buying 1 new share for every 15 held, every 2 years. If the offering is made at book value, and if the new stock is worth 20 per cent or more above book value, as is usually the case, each set of rights will be worth at least 1.1 per cent of the value of the stockholder's total investment. In other words, such rights could add about .55 per cent per annum to the yield of the stock without diluting the book value or earning power of the stock in any way. This is a conservative estimate; the American Telephone rights averaged more than 1 per cent per year on the value of Telephone stock in the 1946–1962 period.

FINANCING POLICIES

Despite some loss of financial strength since 1965–1966, the electric power, telephone, and natural gas retailing companies are still in reasonably sound condition. Heavy sales of new high-yielding bonds to finance surging construction programs have reduced the average interest coverage on utility bonds from about 5 times in 1960 to only about 3 times in the early 1970s,[11] but most utility bonds remain of investment grade, suitable for institutions and trust funds. Consequently, a large percentage of utility bonds in recent years has been sold to institutional buyers and conservative accounts. Because of a larger supply, new utility bonds

---

[11] The reader may understand this by noting that $200 of operating earnings will cover interest charges on a $1,000 bond 5 times if the bond pays 4 per cent, but only 3 times if the bond pays 6⅔ per cent. In the 30 months ended at mid-1972, a total of 53 utility bond issues were downgraded by one of the two leading bond-rating agencies.

typically yield somewhat more than industrial bonds of the same quality. New-issue yields ranged between 7 and 9 per cent from 1969 through 1972. Since 1966, rising yields have made utility bonds increasingly attractive to individual investors. Over many years, the American Telephone and Telegraph Company has sold very large issues of convertible debentures to its stockholders, a number of other utilities have sold convertible debentures through investment bankers under terms designed to induce conversion and thus indirectly provide more net worth, and the gas pipeline companies have sold large quantities of medium-grade bonds on a generous yield basis to the general public.

Preferred stocks sold by these utilities in recent years have also been of generally good quality. They have gone into both institutional and personal holdings, largely as investments for liberal income. Owing to their greater business and market risks, utility preferred shares have traditionally yielded one-half to one percentage point more than bonds of the same companies. However, preferred stocks have a special advantage for corporations with surplus funds to invest, since dividends received by one corporation from another pay federal income tax at a maximum rate of only about 7½ per cent. Beginning in the early 1960s, strong corporate buying drove the prices of utility preferreds upward until the best grades yielded little more than did top-quality corporate bonds. At such low yields, the utility preferred stocks merit little attention from individual investors (unless they are convertible), since good bonds offer greater safety with little sacrifice of yield.

Most new common stock financing by utility companies is obtained by offering new common stock on rights to existing stockholders, who seem to favor the use of rights wherever possible. When large sums are needed and it appears that large stock offerings would be hard to sell, convertible bonds or preferred stocks are used. In strong stock markets, companies may sell their shares outright to investment bankers for resale to the general public. Rapidly growing utilities favor this method because it distributes their shares more widely and makes additional stock financing easier; numerous stockholders also represent good public relations and political strength.

Since 1969, sales of common stock by utilities have increased in frequency and size. Two circumstances have accounted for this trend. First, rapidly growing construction programs have outrun the companies' cash flows and forced them to rely on external financing. Second, the inflationary increase in operating costs has slowed the growth of retained earnings, and many companies can no longer support substantial sales of new bonds and preferred stock without first selling more common stock. This is particlarly true where bond-interest coverage ratios have declined dangerously enough to imperil the utility's bond ratings. Large new-share sales, slower earnings growth, and fewer dividend increases have served to depress the price of public utility common stocks, and in 1971–1972, utility issues sold at far lower earnings multiples and at far higher yields than industrial shares of equivalent quality.

Most good utilities have large numbers of common stockholders, especially small stockholders. Large numbers of investors are attracted by earnings stability, generous dividends, and steady if unspectacular growth. Utility stocks are commonly used in portfolios in which regular cash dividends must be maximized. They have also been regarded as "defensive" stock investments, havens for investors who fear that depression may shortly impair the attractiveness of industrial stocks but who do not wish to accept the modest income and lack of growth which characterize bonds. Clearly, however, the rise of bond yields to the 7 per cent plus zone after 1968 reduced the relative appeal of utility shares to income-minded investors.

GROWTH IN UTILITY STOCKS

Many investors appear to regard utility stocks as stable, income-producing issues, unattractive for long-term growth. Yet, during the less inflationary eras since 1950, particularly in 1955 through 1965, the common shares of most utility companies enjoyed a substantial and almost steady rise in annual net earnings. The earnings growth in utility shares has come largely from three sources. First, reinvested earnings have increased the rate base per share and thus the earnings per share. Second, the regulating commissions have permitted gradual increases in the utilities' rates of return, and this has resulted in increased earnings per share. Finally, the new stock sold during the period has mostly been sold above the book value of the existing stock and has thus served to further increase the rate base and earning power of existing shares.

Obviously, the earnings growth per share has been greater in expanding companies located in rapidly growing areas. Also, investors in growing utilities receive a very important capital gains advantage; since these stocks usually sell well above book value, there is an almost automatic market price bonus to the investor in every dollar of reinvested earnings or of new stock subscription money which his company can use.

The investor can find a wide range of dividend yields and expected growth rates among utility common stocks. Such "growth" utilities as Florida Power & Light, Texas Utilities Company, and Houston Lighting & Power have benefited from rapid population and industry gains in their service areas and/or liberal regulatory climates. These companies have increased their net earnings per share at average annual rates of 7 per cent or more over the past two decades. Such stocks have often sold at more than 20 times earnings, yielded less than 3 per cent, and offered strong attraction to growth-minded investors. By contrast, such "income" utilities as Union Electric Company, Columbia Gas, and General Public Utilities Corporation have experienced somewhat slower rates of earnings growth and have occasionally sold as low as 10 times earnings and yielded 7 to 8 per cent in current dividends.

MARKETS AND MARKET BEHAVIOR

Most of the more important utility stocks and bonds are listed on the stock exchanges. Smaller issues are traded over the counter. Bonds and preferred stocks of good quality are usually very stable in price, fluctuating only with money-rate conditions and other general factors which affect all good-grade, low-yield securities.

The medium-grade preferreds and the common stocks of utility companies seem to behave on the markets just about as industrial stocks do, though their fluctuations are a little less extreme, probably because of the relative stability of their earnings and dividends. Under ordinary conditions, utility and industrial stocks fluctuate together, following the primary and secondary swings of the market to about the same degree and at about the same time. However, there are two points of difference, especially as respects common shares: First, utility stocks are not so sharply affected by permanent changes in the price levels as are some industrials, for price-level changes do not directly alter their rate base values and consequent long-term earning power, whereas industrial stocks may be sharply affected. Second, the utilities are a homogeneous-enough group so that either favorable or adverse circumstances might cause their stock prices as a group to deviate from the market pattern. This was especially manifested in the period 1933–1941 when they were under political attack, in the winter of 1957–1958 when they were extremely popular as "defensive" stocks in a period of economic recession, and from 1966 to 1972 when widespread inflation fears and competition with soaring bond yield severely depressed their prices.

Because most utility common stocks pay higher percentages of their earnings in dividends than the average industrial stock does, they usually yield a little more than industrials of similar quality. For the same reason, they will sometimes command slightly higher price-earnings ratios.

TESTING UTILITY SECURITIES

The plan of analysis outlined in Chapter 13 is definitely appropriate for utility securities. Because utility accounting is reasonably well standardized and because utilities of similar types are much alike in their methods of operation, analysis by means of financial ratios is more than usually significant.

In studying utility securities, there are 10 topics which analysts invariably check. Most of them have already been mentioned, but some repetition in summary may perhaps be justified.

1 A reasonably stable and prosperous territory is desirable, in which volume can grow enough to keep the present plant occupied and to permit addition of new and more efficient plants from time to time.

2 If the utility's sales volume is from mixed services, a maximum percentage of electric power, telephone, natural gas, or water sales is preferable; manufactured gas or transportation service is less desirable. Residential, commercial, farm, and industrial loads are stable and profitable in descending order, hence preferable in that order.

3 Public competition is to be avoided. Neighboring federal power projects, local municipal ownership enthusiasm, unsound franchise situations, and bad public relations are warnings to the investor.

4 The attitudes and policies of regulatory commissions are important, particularly on matters dealing with rate base and fair return, holding company structures, and dividend policy.

5 The company's rates should be compared with those of similarly situated companies, to make sure that inefficiency does not make high rates necessary in order to earn a profit.

6 The company's reasonable rate base and normal earning power should be checked. A noninflationary climate should result in a return on equity of about 10 per cent. For each percentage point of expected price inflation, a good utility stock should offer an additional percentage point of return on equity. With 4 per cent price inflation, a utility stock earning less than 14 per cent on equity would be unattractive to the investor concerned with real, as opposed to current-dollar, return from his investment.

7 The capital structure and earnings coverage should be tested, to make sure that debt is not excessive and that the common stock has a reasonable equity in assets and earnings.

8 The operating ratio and other cost ratios should be checked. Operating ratios for most utilities have risen in late years as a result of increases in the cost of labor and supplies. The earnings of some utilities have consequently tended to deteriorate in quality, though increased volume and occasional rate increases have maintained their per share amounts.

9 The growth rate should be checked. A growing utility whose stock generally sells above book value can provide a valuable advantage to its stockholders.

10 In the case of power companies, it is important to note the proportions of hydroelectric and steam generation, the modernness of the installations, and the dependability of hydroelectric power, if any.

THE GAS PIPELINES—A SPECIAL CASE

The past generation has seen spectacular growth in the gas pipelines. These new utilities have sold securities to the general public and introduced certain unique features into their financing. Since the pipelines have assured value only as long as their gas supply lasts, it has become customary to establish sinking funds designed to retire bond issues and even preferred stock issues over a 20- or 25-year life span. Initially, most pipelines were financed with a high debt ratio in the 60 to 80 per cent range, in the expectation that sinking-fund operation would soon reduce the debts. However, the pipeline business has grown quite rapidly, and proportionate new financing for expansion purposes has kept the debt ratios higher than was originally intended. Despite this, pipeline finances are thus far in good shape: pipeline franchises have been kept on a regulated monopoly basis, with franchises granted only when a gas supply and a sales outlet were assured; the gas purchase and sales contracts have worked out well; and the regulatory commissions have allowed satisfactory rates of return plus realistically rapid depreciation write-offs to be recovered in rates.

For many reasons, the mortgage bonds and many of the debentures of the pipeline companies seem quite dependable. The common stocks remain speculative. Earnings are highly leveraged, and the industry's future growth is uncertain. Twenty years of rapid expansion have left few untapped markets. In existing service areas, population and the number of households will continue to rise, but atomic power and mine-mouth generating plants are reducing the cost of electricity, and gas heating faces increasing competition from this aggressive rival. To utilize their pipelines for off-season transmission and thus to improve efficiency, the companies have developed underground and liquefied storage facilities near major consuming markets. But increasingly they have also sought to diversify their revenue sources into nonpipeline activities—oil and gas production, fertilizers, and chemicals—where regulation is less of a problem and growth seems assured. At the beginning of 1973, long-range problems of gas supply clouded the future of the pipeline companies.

QUESTIONS AND PROBLEMS

1 Does the "cost plus" nature of utility regulation penalize and discourage efficiency in this industry? Does it deny stockholders of better-managed companies a share in the benefits of savings from lower-cost operation and construction?

2 Investigate the diary of recent rate cases as shown in the Special Features section of *Moody's Public Utility Manual*. Do you discern a trend toward any one of the rate base methods? Are the permitted rates of return trending up or down?

3 If a utility's capital structure consists 50 per cent of 7 per cent bonds, 20 per cent of 8 per cent preferred, and 30 per cent of common stock equity, what overall rate of return will be needed to assure a return on common equity of 12 per cent?

4 If the natural gas pipelines have contracts to buy gas at regulated prices and contracts to sell it to retail distributors at regulated prices, do they need much net worth in order to be sound financially?

5 What tangible advantage would it be to existing stockholders if a utility sold 100 per cent more shares (new stock) to new stockholders at a price 50 per cent higher than the book value of its existing common stock?

6 Why are federal hydroelectric projects dangerous to investors in neighboring power companies? Can you imagine why the private power companies fought so vigorously in 1949 to keep the federal government from building its first steam generating plant in connection with its TVA development?

7 Explain the concept of a "fair return on a fair valuation." How has the doctrine of the Hope Natural Gas case affected the "fair return" idea?

8 What difference does it make, in 1973 after a substantial inflation in the price level has occurred, whether historical prudent cost or cost of reproduction is used in evaluating a utility for rate-making purposes?

9 Will utility common stockholders get any important advantage out of utility growth if new stock is sold to underwriters instead of to the stockholders on a rights basis?

10 At December 31, 1973, the Hotwire Electric Company has $4,000,000 of current assets and $46,000,000 of net fixed assets after deducting depreciation reserves. The assets appear to be properly valued. The company owes $2,000,000 in outstanding accounts and $20,000,000 in 5½ per cent bonds, and has outstanding $14,000,000 in 6 per cent preferred, and 1,000,000 shares of common stock. In 1973 the common stock earned $1.65 per share and paid $1.10 in dividends. Can these rates of earning and payment be continued?

11 Is this common stock good grade? What would it sell for on the market?

12 Should investors' financial advantages derived from utility growth be regarded as a part of the rate of return obtained by the utility?

13 Look up the last balance sheet of the Pacific Gas and Electric Company and determine what rate of return would be necessary in order to permit the common stock to earn $3.25 per share on an original-cost rate base. What would be a reasonable per share earnings figure? What does the company actually earn? Is Pacific Gas common a good stock?

14 Try the techniques of question 13 on the consolidated balance sheet of American Telephone and Telegraph, with $5 per share as the earnings objective. Is Telephone on a historical-cost rate base?

15 Since good rate base and rate-of-return data are hard to come by, would it not be just as well to compute an average percentage of actual earnings per share to book values in past years and estimate current earning power by applying this average percentage to present book value?

16 Why is working capital position not of outstanding importance in utility security analysis?

17 Investigate the utilities listed in Table 16-2 to determine whether they follow the policy of paying 75 per cent or more of their earnings in dividends. Is this a sensible policy?

18 Do the stable earnings and dividends of the utilities exempt their stocks from market fluctuations? What are "defensive" stocks?

19 Is it sensible for a community to depend on a private utility if public ownership is feasible?

20 When a utility receives tax deferrals under the federal incentive plans described in Chapter 14, how does this affect its regulated income and its rate base? (See data on commission decisions in *Moody's Public Utility Manual*, Special Features section.)

21 In April 1964, the Federal Power Commission reversed a previous policy and held that utilities under its jurisdiction could recover in rates (a) depreciation allowances based on actual wear and obsolescence, and (b) income taxes paid currently in cash, but not accelerated depreciation or provisions for deferred taxes. How does this affect companies now obtaining lower taxes under the 1954 "accelerated depreciation" law and the 1962 "guidelines"? Is this ruling consistent with the government's 1954 and 1962 plans for tax incentives to stimulate capital outlays by business firms?

22 Should utility firms be permitted to form holding companies, as several railroads have done, to diversify into other businesses that offer their stockholders a chance for larger profits? Should this opportunity be allowed utilities in declining industry-branches, such as manufactured gas or local transit systems?

REFERENCES

Badger, Ralph E., and Paul B. Coffman: *Investment Analysis*, McGraw-Hill Book Company, New York, 1967, Chaps. 20, 21.

Bellemore, Douglas H., and John C. Ritchie, Jr.: *Investments*, 3d ed., South-Western Publishing Company, Incorporated, Cincinnati, 1969, Chap. 22.

Dougall, Herbert E.: *Investments*, 8th ed., Prentice-Hall, Inc., Englewood Cliffs, N.J., 1968, Chap. 27.

Farris, Martin T., and Roy J. Sampson: *Public Utilities*, Houghton Mifflin Company, Boston, 1972.

Graham, Benjamin, David L. Dodd, and C. Sidney Cottle: *Security Analysis*, 4th ed., McGraw-Hill Book Company, New York, 1962, Chaps. 20, 21, 42, 43.

Hayes, Douglas A.: *Investments: Analysis and Management*, The Macmillan Company, New York, 1966, Chap. 17.

Moody's Public Utility Manual, Special Features section, Moody's Investors Service, New York.

Standard & Poor's Corporation, *Standard Industry Surveys*, sections on electric, gas, and telephone utilities, New York.

INDUSTRIAL SECURITIES

In securities market parlance the term "industrial" applies to almost any manufacturing, extractive, or merchandising concern. Railroads, public utilities, and financial institutions are not industrials, but steel companies, motor companies, meat packers, oil companies, shoe manufacturers, department stores, retail drug chains, and a host of others all belong in the industrial category. Obviously, such a diverse group of industries will not be alike or even similar in their investment characteristics. This limits the field for fruitful generalization, so most of this chapter will be devoted to analyzing, along the lines suggested in Chapter 13, the dominant investment features of four particular industries: steel, oil, drugs, and office equipment. A few final paragraphs will deal with the special analytical problems raised by highly diversified or "conglomerate" companies. By reviewing such representative cases, the reader should acquire some feeling for the nature and behavior of the economic forces underlying, and in some degree peculiar to, each industry's structure of profitability, fluctuation, and growth.[1]

From the investor's point of view, the outstanding features of the industrial category are general freedom from government regulation and the prevalence of competition. These features lead immediately to the great emphasis upon sales and selling, intangible assets, managerial alertness, cost control, and other variables with which this chapter is mostly concerned. Industrials are typically involved in a rough-and-tumble, competitive scramble in which weakness may be disastrous, but in which strength and skill may be richly rewarded. The securities of strong industrial concerns are unquestionably of investment grade, but those of some of the weaker concerns can hardly even qualify as intelligent speculations. This competitive scramble is a never-ending affair; although the great entrenched concerns may maintain a relatively stable position in it, many of the weaker ones are alternately very prosperous and drably unprofitable as their operations proceed. Consequently, the per share earnings of individual industrial stocks often rise or fall in marked degree as their business affairs appear to surge or falter.

Because stock buyers are reluctant to buy stocks whose earnings are declining or whose dividends seem to be in danger, most stocks drop sharply in price under such circumstances. Similarly, enough buyers will usually believe in, or hope for,

---

[1] A convenient, well-recognized source of further information on specific industries is Standard & Poor's *Industry Surveys*, reviewed in Chapter 11.

the continuation of a higher earnings level, to cause a stock's price to rise sharply when higher earnings are reported. Even when the corporations reporting lower or higher earnings also indicate that the causes are transient—for example, lower earnings could be caused by break-in costs in new plants or by an inventory glut and price weakness in the industry—the stock-buying public is often skeptical of such explanations and allows the stock prices to react sharply to the earnings figures. Obviously, an earnings change which proves transient will not affect the value of the stock in the long run, but the 1965–1972 records of such stocks as Chrysler, Anaconda Company, Control Data, Levitz Furniture, Motorola, and Fairchild Camera testify to the volatility of both earnings and prices in this area.

THE PRICE-LEVEL FACTOR

The prices charged and paid in an unregulated, competitive, cost-conscious industry have a general tendency to follow the average trends of commodity prices. This is not a universal rule, and certainly there is no dependable proportionality between the prices in an individual industry and the level of all commodity prices, but the tendency is marked enough to be important to investors. If prices rise, an industry's inventories and fixed assets theoretically tend to appreciate in proportion to the increase in replacement costs, and normal profit percentages should produce a corresponding increase in dollar earnings. Price declines would of course induce a contrary effect. Actual tendencies for individual stock prices, earnings, and dividends to follow commodity price changes were noted in Chapter 4.

Industrial securities thus seem to offer the investor a rather promising opportunity to hedge his income and property values against changes in the general price level. This is particularly true if the investor avails himself of the diversification possible through participation in a number of the different industries in the industrial category. Any single industry might be an exception to the general rule, to the discomfiture of its investors. After all, price-level changes are often accompanied by working capital problems, changes in operating costs, changes in consumer demands, changes in competitive pressure, and disturbed securities markets, any of which may upset the most logical investment calculations; but a diversified position should assure its holder of reasonably typical results. It should be emphasized, however, that periods of *on-going* rapid price-level inflation, such as 1969–1970, produce serious liquidity and working capital problems for most companies; these phases are typically accompanied by falling stock prices. Industrial stocks have outgained the general price level since 1945 by a wide margin, but most of their progress has occurred in intervals of relative price stability.

It is not to be expected that industrial bonds, preferred stocks, and common stocks will all be affected in similar fashion by price-level changes. Like all senior securities, industrial bonds and preferreds have limited claims to income and assets, whereas common stockholders occupy a residual position. Price-level increases which cause the corporate earnings to consist of a larger number of less valuable dollars will make the senior securities' income more secure while debasing its buying power. This might actually be an advantage to a medium- or speculative-grade bond or preferred, for an increase in quality might cause its price to rise, but the holder of a good bond or preferred would suffer a decline in the buying power of his income with no compensating capital gain. Common stockholders in a company which had senior securities outstanding would presumably have disproportionately larger per share earnings as a result of price-level inflation. Deflation would present all these tendencies in reverse.

❧ THE STEEL INDUSTRY

The steel industry, with its 24-billion-dollar assets, is a mature giant. While indispensable to the nation's economy and defense, it is relatively slow-growing, highly cyclical in sales and profitability, and vigorously competitive. Large overhead and high labor costs are prominent features, and its price structure is subject to frequent close scrutiny by the federal government. Because of their wide market swings, the common stocks of steel companies have traditionally been classed as speculations or, at best, medium-grade holdings. However, some steel companies, such as United States Steel Corporation, Bethlehem, and Inland Steel, offer investors one or more issues of unquestionably high-grade bonds.

Steel company earning patterns are typical of a mature industry. In years of normal business, slow demand growth, together with excess productive capacity and growing imports of foreign steel, often prevents prices from rising in step with costs. Strong, welfare-minded unions have pushed employment costs up rapidly, contributing to an almost steady decline in earnings during the 1966–1971 period. The industry also may suffer in some degree from waning vigor of management; its rapid-growth era is past, and steel company executives often appear to treat their tasks as custodial rather than innovative.

PERMANENCE AND MATURITY

The myriad of shapes, plates, rails, pipes, tubing, wire products, sheets, and strips fashioned by the nation's steel mills find their way into every nook and corner of the American economy. Steel plays a permanent and indispensable part in durable consumer goods, in the manufacture of machinery, equipment, and military weapons, and in all phases of the construction industry. While aluminum, other metals, and a growing variety of plastics provide substitutes in some applications, the strength, hardness, and durability of steel make it irreplaceable in most uses for either peace or war.

The steel industry as a whole comprises seven distinct classes of companies. First come the major, integrated producers, who participate in all phases of steel-making, often possess their own supplies of coal, ore, and other raw materials, and offer their customers a wide range of steel products. This category includes such well-known firms as United States Steel—the nation's largest steel company —Bethlehem, Armco, Inland, Republic, National, Jones & Laughlin, and several others. The second category comprises the smaller integrated producers of which Kaiser and McLouth are representative. The third division consists of the stainless steel producers—Allegheny Ludlum and Cyclops. Fourth come the specialty steel companies—Bliss & Laughlin, Copperweld, and Lukens. The fifth class are the ore producers, led by Cleveland Cliffs Iron Company and Hanna Mining. The sixth grouping, merchant blast-furnace operators, includes a number of relatively small firms, and the seventh, the refractories group, is dominated by one large company, General Refractories, which makes lining materials for most of the nation's steel furnaces.

Some 90 per cent of the industry's finished steel shipments consists of carbon or "tonnage" steel, the domain of the major companies. Alloy steels make up 8 per cent of shipments and are shared by large and small companies. Stainless steel comprises 1 per cent and is manufactured largely by medium- and small-sized concerns. One per cent of the industry's final output falls in a scattering of miscellaneous steel products that defy classification.

Most authorities foresee only a 2 to 3 per cent yearly growth in steel demand, and experience shows that this will be punctuated by continuing cyclical swings. The industry's profits rose in the early 1960s with good volume growth, effective cost control, and substantial benefit from earlier capital expenditures. Industry-wide net income reached a peak of more than $1 billion in 1966, but fell to $532 millions in 1970 and recovered only to $540 millions in 1971, owing partially to the severe demand fluctuations which surrounded labor-contract bargaining. The domestic industry has not been a net exporter of steel since 1959, and steel imports have played a part in the shrinking profits of the American steel companies. After imports reached a 1971 level of 18.3 million tons, equivalent to more than 20 per cent of total domestic output, the federal government reacted strongly, and in May 1972, import quota agreements were signed with the European Economic Community, Japan, and the United Kingdom.

SALES, COSTS, AND EARNINGS

Steel industry sales are both cyclical and subject to considerable price instability, while costs since 1966 have proved difficult to control, largely as a result of overcapacity in the domestic industry itself. The steel business is an example of what economists call "oligopolistic competition," meaning that a few large producers dominate most markets. Since excess capacity is the industry's normal state, steel firms are under frequent temptation to cut prices in hope of enlarging their share of the market, a tactic which enables the individual company to increase its profit by spreading overhead costs over a larger volume of unit sales. However, competing firms retaliate, and this leads to general unofficial price cutting in which companies agree privately to sell steel to customers at quotations well below list prices. In consequence, profits fall throughout the industry.

The demand for steel is cyclical and depends heavily on industrial spending for new plants and equipment, construction volume, and automobile and appliance output. Demand is especially strong in years when a breakdown in union contract negotiations may lead to a steel strike, but such "stockpiling" sales usually are borrowed from the demands of future sales quarters.

The steel industry's cost breakdown for 1971 is representative of recent years. Employment costs (wages, pensions, other benefits, and welfare) absorbed 39 per cent of gross revenues; materials, fuel, and supplies accounted for 48 per cent; depreciation comprised about 5 per cent, taxes 3 per cent, interest and dividends about 2 per cent each, and retained earnings 1 per cent. About 15 per cent of employment costs comprise fringe benefits. Between 1967 and 1971, employment costs in steel companies rose an average of 32 per cent, while physical output per man hour increased only 5 per cent. Labor costs vary from company to company, depending on degree of integration and type of product; companies which produce their own ore and raw materials incur higher proportionate labor expense.

The cost of raw materials, principally iron ore and coal or coke, is of major importance in determining a steel producer's competitive position. As a whole, the American steel industry benefits from large domestic reserves of iron ore (from the Mesabi and other Lake Superior ranges), high-grade metallurgical coal (from Pennsylvania and West Virginia mines), a widespread abundance of limestone (used as flux in making steel), and a prolific supply of steel scrap (chiefly from junked automobiles and appliances). However, domestic ore supplies are declining; the Lake Superior district now provides only about one-half the steel industry's iron ore requirements, as against three-fourths a decade ago; this change reflects both the depletion of better domestic reserves and the discovery of high-grade foreign sources. One-third of the American industry's ore supply is now imported, largely from Canada and Venezuela.

Steel scrap, which constitutes 47 per cent of the average furnace charge in steelmaking, exerts a volatile influence on steel companies' operating costs. From 1966 to 1972, scrap prices varied between $20 and $50 per ton. The price of scrap fluctuates closely with the percentage of steelmaking capacity in use.

Transportation costs are an important influence on steel company profits because it requires $2\frac{1}{2}$ tons of raw materials to make a ton of ingot steel. Companies located close to high-grade supplies of ore or coking coal enjoy appreciable economies on raw-material procurement costs. Other material costs in steelmaking include chemical reagents and alloying elements such as manganese, chrome, silicon, nickel, molybdenum, tungsten, and tin.

Despite massive outlays for new facilities and processing methods, the steel industry from 1966 through 1971 failed to preserve its profit margins against rapidly rising costs of labor, materials, and purchased services. As Table 17-1 suggests, total tonnage sales were static between 1965 and 1972, and industry-wide sales margins fell from 6.1 per cent in 1964 to 5.9 per cent in 1965–1966 and to 2.8 per cent in 1971. Because of normal overcapacity, prices could probably not have kept pace with rising costs in any case, but as matters developed, both government pressures and competition from imported steel abetted market forces in maintaining steel prices at only marginally profitable levels.

The steel industry as a whole requires operation at about 70 per cent of capacity to break even on its high fixed costs. A rate of about 90 per cent is considered to be most profitable, since this level of activity permits enough shutdown time for adequate maintenance of the costly facilities.

Steelmaking technology has made noteworthy progress in the past two decades, although in the 1950s and 1960s, European and Japanese steelmakers exploited new processes and equipment more aggressively than did American companies. Oxygen and electric furnaces have greatly reduced both the time and the labor needed to make a ton of steel, and continuous casting of slabs, billets, and blooms has lowered both the space and the investment required for steel plants.

Although steel profits were low and declining in most years between 1966

Table 17-1   *Steel industry performance, between 1962 and 1971, selected data*

Year	Output (millions of tons)	Profit margin (in per cent)	Earnings as per cent of sales	Average price-earnings ratio on common shares	Return on book value of equity	Earnings per common share*
1962	70.5	14.7	4.07	19.15	5.24	$3.22
1965	92.7	16.7	5.99	10.96	8.72	6.02
1968	91.9	14.0	5.52	9.12	7.84	5.99
1969	93.9	12.3	4.49	10.20	6.88	5.34
1970	90.7	9.7	2.95	12.55	4.47	3.40
1971	87.0	10.2	2.83	11.82	4.35	3.33

Source: Standard & Poor's *Industry Surveys.*
*Based on Standard & Poor's index of steel company stocks.

and 1972, the industry's outlays of more than 15 billion dollars during these years have improved efficiency and laid the basis for substantial earnings improvement if sufficient volume can be generated and if control of labor costs can be regained. In 1972, more than 53 per cent of all American steel was made in basic oxygen furnaces and 17 per cent by the still newer electric process.

Government attitudes play an important part in the industry's profitability, and the economy's return to relative price stability would give the steel companies welcome relief from both federal interference and wage-cost pressures. (The industry showed substantial profitability in 1963 through 1966 when union wage gains were held about equal to increases in labor productivity.) However, steel prices affect costs in most other industries, and the steel companies are regarded as prime movers in the "cost-push" type of price-level inflation. This has made them a conspicuous target for government threats and exhortations aimed at holding down prices after costs have already advanced.

FINANCES AND STOCK VALUES

Because of cyclical sales and large overhead costs, the better-grade steel companies make only moderate use of long-term debt. In 1972, the ratio of funded debt to book value of total capital was only 29 per cent for United States Steel, 31 per cent for Inland Steel, and 34 per cent for Bliss & Laughlin. Dividends have typically been generous in years of large earnings, with most companies increasing regular rates during boom periods instead of paying extras; this practice has led to frequent dividend cuts during intervals of earnings adversity. Between 1962 and 1971, earnings made no sustained advance, and price-level inflation devoured millions in working capital and depreciation allowances, forcing companies to retain a larger fraction of earnings than before; in this interval, total dividend payments by steel companies fell 20 per cent. Since, as Table 17-1 reveals, the average price-earnings ratio on steel stocks dropped from more than 19 times to less than 12, it is clear that steel company stockholders fared very poorly during the increasingly inflationary decade of the 1960s.

As already noted, no steel stocks can be considered high grade, but the basic earning power and long-run values of the different companies vary considerably with at least five fundamental factors: (1) integration of operations, (2) control of raw materials, (3) location of plants, (4) product diversification, and (5) modernity of plants and facilities. Integrated operations foster operating economies and permit a company to profit from all phases of steel manufacture and processing. The integrated companies have shown superior earnings stability over business cycles of the past 30 years. Control of raw materials assures a company of steady supplies and controlled costs of steelmaking ingredients. In this respect, United States Steel Corporation enjoys great advantages through ownership of large iron ore reserves, coal mines, and limestone deposits. The best-located plants are those with ready access to raw materials, low-cost water transportation, and large steel-consuming markets. Large sheet-steel manufacturing capacity in the Chicago area, close to Detroit's automobile plants, has contributed substantially to the stability of sales and earnings for the Inland and National steel companies. Diversification reduces a company's dependence on the fluctuating demands for a narrow range of steel products and often provides access to rapidly growing markets for new types of steel or fabricated steel goods. Some steelmakers derive important earnings benefit from nonsteel lines; for example, U.S. Steel's Universal Atlas Division is the world's largest cement producer, and Allegheny Ludlum Industries owns a one-half interest in the world's largest titanium company. Finally, modern plants and steelmaking processes provide major cost economies through savings on labor, fuel, and scrap losses. Much of the improved performance of Bethlehem Steel Corporation during the 1970–1972 period was due to completion of the company's new Burns Harbor, Indiana, plant.

Like other competitive industries, the steel industry in normal times consists of marginal and infra-marginal producers. The marginal producers are likely to operate profitably only in periods of great prosperity when vigorous demand provides them with a seller's market; only then can they recoup their high production costs by operating close to capacity and charging boom-level prices for their product. Infra-marginal companies, with more stable customer demand and/or inherently lower operating costs, will show some earnings under conditions of all but the deepest depression; their earnings will rise less sensationally in boom periods, but their dividends will increase, and their stocks will avoid the extreme price swings that afflict the stocks of marginal companies.

❋ THE PETROLEUM INDUSTRY

The nation's giant and prosperous petroleum industry includes companies ranging from the 20-billion-dollar Exxon Corporation down to firms that own a few oil wells or engage in small-scale oil wildcatting. The large companies' securities are regarded as sound in quality and are widely held by investment companies, pension funds, and trustees. The smaller oil and gas companies are usually of interest as speculative ventures. The industry provides indispensable products, enjoys satisfactory demand growth, possesses adequate reserves, and, despite some fluctuations, has been profitable throughout most of its history.

TYPES OF OPERATIONS

Oil companies are commonly classified as oil-producing companies, refining-marketing companies, landowning and oil-royalty companies, and integrated companies, depending on the functions which dominate their operations. Companies like Amerada Petroleum and Superior Oil are predominantly concerned with oil discovery and production. Ashland Oil and Standard Oil Company of Ohio are known as refining and marketing companies. Landowning and oil-royalty companies are concerns such as Southland Royalty Company, whose principal income consists of oil royalties received from other companies which produce oil on Southland's properties. Finally, the integrated companies are diversified concerns, typically large ones, which produce, transport, refine, and market a wide range of oil products. Ordinarily, the integrated companies do not produce as much oil as they refine and market, for hundreds of small producers also have oil to sell, and the big companies are the natural buyers. The largest integrated companies also have major investments in pipelines, ocean-going tankers, oil-storage facilities, and trucks, which not only transport their own products but earn substantial common-carrier revenues as well. Most of these companies also own important and profitable operations in petrochemicals, and several are at least experimentally concerned with nuclear energy and fuels. Major oil companies control about 70 per cent of domestic natural gas reserves, which they supply to gas pipelines and other users. Financial data for major divisions of the petroleum industry during two recent years are presented in Table 17-2.

The big American oil companies also hold very large investments in foreign oil production, especially in the Middle East, North Africa, Venezuela, and Canada, and in refining and marketing operations in Western Europe and other free-world population centers. Oil-production costs are typically lower abroad than in the United States, and foreign oil demands are growing at approximately twice the domestic rate. Although the host countries in which oil is produced have usually insisted on a gradually larger share of production revenues, foreign oil production has generally been very profitable where large, accessible reserves could be exploited. Clearly, however, an investor assumes some hazard in owning oil property subject to the sovereign authority of foreign, and typically less developed, countries.

DEMAND AND PRICING INFLUENCES

For several decades, a close relation between economic growth and energy consumption has produced a persistent rise in the demand for petroleum products. This trend promises to continue. In 1972, oil provided 44 per cent of this nation's energy sources, and natural gas provided 32 per cent. Over longer periods, inexorable demand growth has permitted the prices of petroleum products to rise at least in step with the cost of finding, producing, and refining the crude oil. The United States is now depending increasingly on foreign oil supplies, and imports, which in 1972 comprised 28 per cent of domestic consumption, are expected to reach 58 per cent by 1985.[2] Rising prices for foreign crude oil should strengthen the prices of domestic output and improve marketing and profit margins for domestic companies. Higher prices also appear needed to stimulate exploration and reserve development in the United States, particularly in view of oil's essential part in the nation's defense.

Over shorter periods, which have ranged from a few months to a decade, oil prices and oil company profits fluctuate moderately with the relation between end-product demands and the industry's margins of capacity. Gasoline prices, particularly, have weakened in times of recession and when competition has become severe from so-called independent marketers. Oil-industry operations are divided into four phases: (1) production (which includes exploration), (2) refining, (3) marketing, and (4) transportation. A company's profit from each phase is affected by different influences, and how profitably a company operates over extended time intervals depends greatly on the mix of its activities. Integrated companies whose dependence on any single phase of activity is minimal generally earn the steadiest profits.

A company's ability to produce oil depends on the success of its exploratory program. Here large-scale operators who can spread their risks over many drillings and areas have a clear advantage. Only 1 out of 9 exploratory wells can be expected to find oil or gas, and only 1 out of 35 proves the existence of a major field. The cost of drilling wells is rising rapidly as companies must go to greater depths to find oil or engage in costly offshore work; these factors have increasingly concentrated domestic exploration in the hands of large companies. International companies have the advantage of exploring areas where new discoveries are individually much larger than in the United States. The possession of large crude-oil reserves also gives an integrated company freedom to buy oil from independent firms when prices are cheap, and to draw on its own production when crude prices are higher, thus minimizing its crude-oil costs from period to period.

Oil-refining companies need a proper balance between refining capacity and demand, and optimal use of refining capacity is between 80 and 85 per cent. A good balance between demand and capacity strengthens product prices and diminishes price wars by reducing the supply of product to private-brand and unbranded marketers. Refining capacity was generally in excess supply from 1967 through 1971, and profit margins were low in those years for both refiners and marketers.

Product mix is also a troublesome issue for refiners. Petroleum products include gasoline, heating oils, lubricants, and a variety of other items, all joint products of the refining process. The proportions of the joint products can be varied,

---

[2] The United States, with only 7 per cent of free-world oil reserves, accounts for one-third of total world consumption.

but only at some expense; and the need for variation often becomes apparent only after a poor motoring season or a warm winter, or when some other disturbance has created a glut or a shortage in certain products. Sharp temporary increases or decreases in specific companies' earnings are often occasioned by these factors.

Marketing has been the lowest-margined sector of the oil business in recent years because of keen competition and overcrowding. In 1972, a number of companies were withdrawing from uneconomical marketing areas—those in which they held low market shares, those afflicted with chronic price cutting by independent marketers, or those involving unduly long lines of distribution. Since marketing provides the easiest entry to the industry, lower profits here, on the average, seem inevitable.

Oil transportation is dominated by the large international companies which hold most of the world's 300 million deadweight tons of oil-tanker shipping under direct ownership or long-term charter. This influence operates against newcomers in the petroleum business and strengthens the position of established firms. Domestically, the large integrated companies add to their profits through extensive ownership of pipelines and oil-storage facilities.

Table 17-2 *Petroleum industry performance, 1965 and 1971, selected data, by major industry divisions (Composite per share data, based on Standard & Poor's group stock price indexes)*

	Integrated international companies		Crude-oil producers		Integrated domestic companies	
	1965	*1971*	*1965*	*1971*	*1965*	*1971*
Sales	$83.83	$142.7	$39.63	$120.5	$82.16	$123.9
Operating income	17.47	31.08	22.82	42.34	16.53	23.97
Profit margin	20.84	21.78	57.58	35.14	20.12	19.35
Depreciation	6.02	9.04	11.53	16.40	8.10	11.41
Taxes	4.35	12.82	3.99	9.50	1.66	3.90
Earnings after taxes	8.81	12.31	7.87	11.47	6.66	7.60
Dividends	4.73	6.27	4.19	4.64	2.87	3.89
Earnings as a per cent of sales	10.51	8.63	19.86	9.52	8.11	6.13
Payout ratios	53.69	50.93	53.24	40.45	43.09	51.18
Average price	135.4	127.7	197.2	291.6	93.71	103.3
Average price-earnings ratio	15.37	10.37	25.10	25.42	14.06	13.66
Average dividend yield	3.50	4.98	2.15	1.62	3.08	3.78
Return on book value	11.36	11.67	9.30	N.A.	10.39	8.99
Working capital	17.17	21.02	15.36	16.76	15.96	17.36
Capital expenditures	11.48	18.01	10.46	21.56	12.57	17.30

Source: Standard & Poor's *Industry Surveys.*

OIL COMPANY ACCOUNTING

Oil company accounting practices vary widely enough that reported net earnings may be halved or doubled. There are three main areas in which accounting policy may make an important difference in reported figures: (1) geological-geophysical surveys in the search for oil, (2) lease acquisition costs, and (3) drilling costs. As these expenditures are made, the accounting charges may go either to expense accounts or to asset accounts; if they go to asset accounts, the accounts may be charged off to expense quickly or over a long period of time. It is clear that an oil company's earnings may vary greatly, depending on (1) its amount of exploration, leasing, and drilling activity, and (2) the method by which costs are accounted for. An extensive oil-finding program is very likely to reduce reported current profits even if successful, whereas a smaller program, even if unsuccessful, would permit a company to report larger earnings. Furthermore, the longer the actual charging of outlays against revenues can be postponed, the larger earnings a company will be able to report in periods immediately ahead.

In 1972, a number of companies, including Occidental Petroleum, Texaco, and Texas Oil and Gas Corporation, were switching to a new controversial "full cost" method of accounting for oil and gas exploration expenses. This method capitalizes all exploration and development costs without regard to the success of any individual venture; thus a company can stretch over many years the costs of unsuccessful operations that most companies report as current expenses. Obviously, the "quality" of earnings reported by concerns using this method is substantially lower than the profits of companies which immediately write off much or all of the expense of unsuccessful endeavors.[3]

OIL COMPANY TAXES

Oil companies are subject to the usual domestic taxes, of which property taxes, payroll taxes, and income taxes doubtless bear most heavily. Excise or sales taxes such as the familiar per gallon gasoline tax ostensibly fall upon the retail customer but doubtless serve as a handicap vis-a-vis competing fuels. The petroleum in-

---

[3] Historically, the most vital area of oil company accounting has been the handling of drilling costs. Most companies charge all costs on unsuccessful oil wells immediately to expense. The major difference has been in the area of "intangible" drilling costs on successful wells. Intangible drilling costs are the 75 to 80 per cent of drilling costs which are expended in the process of drilling the hole, as contrasted with the 20 to 25 per cent which goes into well pipe, derrick, pumps, and other recoverable facilities. Most companies capitalize both intangible and tangible drilling costs on a successful well and write them off over the life of the well. However, the more conservative companies regard a nonsalvageable hole in the ground as no asset and charge all intangible drilling costs immediately to expense, leaving only the smaller tangible costs to be capitalized and depreciated over time. Obviously, a major drilling program by a company following this second method might almost preclude any reported earnings, and a *growing* company following this procedure might for years show very limited assets and a small net worth because the most valuable assets—the oil wells—would be on the books at a fraction of their value.

dustry also occasionally encounters a discriminatory levy known as a severance tax—a tax on the production of crude oil which approximates a capital levy on its underground resources.

But this industry enjoys two peculiar provisions of federal income tax law which together reduce the income tax payments of growing oil-producing companies to relatively small amounts. First, all intangible drilling costs—expense-type outlays for labor, drilling muds, expendible tools, drill bits, etc., which comprise 75 to 80 per cent of total drilling costs—may be deducted for tax purposes in the year expended. In a growing company, and in view of the high cost of present-day drilling, this provides a very substantial tax deduction. Practically all companies take advantage of it, even though they capitalize intangible drilling costs on their own books. Second, the law provides that a depletion allowance of either 22 per cent of the wellhead value of oil and gas produced on each property, or 50 per cent of predepletion taxable profit on the property, whichever is smaller, may also be taken as a tax deduction. This may be taken as long as production continues, even though the cumulated deductions far exceed the cost of the property. Until 1971, the depletion allowance of 27½ per cent was a continual target of political attack. In 1972, many legislators from non-oil-producing states were seeking further reduction or even abolition of the percentage depletion allowance for oil companies, but a spreading awareness that domestic reserves are limited and that search for new oil sources must be encouraged will probably safeguard the 22 per cent rate.

PUBLIC REGULATION

Important phases of the oil industry are regulated by the state and federal governments. Since the industry has been prone to overproduction, and since overproduction would break prices, certain state proration boards and regulatory boards undertake to limit the monthly output of each producer. Texas, the leading oil-producing state, sets limits which may fall as low as one-third of capacity. This naturally hurts oil companies which depend on the restricted wells for output and earnings, but it does help to keep prices up. However, high prices in the United States are immediately attractive to American companies owning low-cost Venezuelan and Near Eastern oil. Oil imports are limited under quotas set by the federal government, to the continual annoyance of both Venezuela and the Arab states as well as the American international companies. However, the rising domestic energy shortage has led to a considerable relaxation of import quotas. At the same time, the level of "allowable" domestic well production has been raised by Texas and other oil-producing states. Thus, reasonably stable markets and prices have been maintained.

Federal regulation of the natural gas industry also is being relaxed. Interstate sales of natural gas came under regulation by the Federal Power Commission in

1956, and in the interest of consuming areas, rates were held substantially below the prices that would have prevailed in a free market. By 1970–1971, petroleum company commitments of gas reserves to interstate commerce had declined sharply and new gas discoveries also had fallen off. In 1972, the Commission liberalized prices for gas originating in newly discovered or extended fields, and it seemed likely that prices for all gas would soon be liberalized.

Aside from the perennial issue of the percentage depletion allowance, the oil industry's chief government problems revolve around the question of allowable oil-import levels and rising agitation by environmentalist organizations. During 1972 the latter groups blocked the starting of the proposed trans-Alaskan pipeline, and their demand for banning sale of all but nonleaded gasolines would require the oil companies to spend hundreds of millions of dollars to convert their refineries to this new and expensive product.

FOREIGN SOURCES AND RESERVES

The concessions obtained by the large, international American oil companies in the Middle East and Venezuela several decades ago have proved highly profitable; the oil has been discovered and produced at low cost and reserves are vast and long-lasting. In recent years, however, both Venezuela and the Arab states (including those in North Africa where large additional reserves were found later) have insisted upon a larger split of oil-production revenues plus a gradual transition to partial or total ownership of the oil concessions themselves. Although serious disputes and outright expropriations of American-company properties are always possible and have occasionally occurred (as in Cuba and Iraq) the transition toward larger revenue sharing and joint ownership of concessions appears on the whole to be proceeding smoothly. Although the foreign governments hold a whip hand legally and politically, they are hardly in position to operate a petroleum industry without the technical assistance, capital investment, and machinery supplied by more developed countries; this factor almost certainly will forestall widespread nationalization for many years. Meanwhile, it is likely that the producing nations themselves will use part of their growing oil revenues to acquire interests in refining, marketing, and transportation enterprises in the importing countries. Such large investments by members of the Organization of Petroleum Exporting Countries would lessen the likelihood either of nationalization moves or of embargoes on oil supplies to consuming areas.

The supply of oil is potentially very large. Although so-called proven domestic reserves are projected to last only another 10 to 12 years, secondary recovery methods will reclaim much additional oil from old, abandoned fields. Known free-world supplies will provide for 35 years' usage at present rates, and large new reserves are being discovered and developed in recently explored areas such as Alaska, the North Sea, and offshore Indonesia. In addition, domestic oil-shale deposits in Colorado, Wyoming, Utah, and other Western states are estimated to contain more than one trillion barrels of petroleum hydrocarbons, double the world's currently known reserves. The hydrogenation of enormous coal deposits, potentially equal to a century's consumption or more, offers another possible source of future oil and gas. At present these expedients are neither necessary nor economical, but it seems logical to assume that if they are needed, suitable technologies will be promptly forthcoming.

FINANCES AND CAPITAL STRUCTURE

The larger, older oil companies have relatively modest long-term debt positions. This is true of such firms as Exxon Corporation, Texaco, Inc., Standard Oil Company of California, Mobil Oil, Gulf Oil, and Standard Oil Company of Indiana. The newer and smaller companies rely more heavily on borrowed capital, but in recent years the stronger ones, such as Quaker State, Texas Oil and Gas, and United Refining, have increased their earnings more rapidly than the major companies. However, even these companies typically borrow no more than 35 to 40 per cent of their capital funds, and internally generated sums ordinarily cover 60 to 65 per cent of their capital expenditures. The oil industry is capital-intensive rather than labor-intensive, and large outlays are required to accommodate rapid expansion. In 1972, the industry was generating about 70 per cent of its capital needs, down from 87 per cent in 1963 but still sufficient for the financially stronger companies to meet the costs of both physical expansion and price-level inflation without serious deterioration in debt-to-equity ratios.

Since the equity positions of leading oil companies are strong and their cash flows adequate, dividends are typically generous and have risen over the years in step with earnings. As noted in the beginning of this section, the major oil companies are widely favored as vehicles for long-term investment.

❖ THE DRUG INDUSTRY

Drug manufacturing is one of America's fastest-growing and most profitable industries, and long-term investors in the leading drug stocks have reaped large rewards over the past two decades. The industry has benefited from the rising proportion of personal income spent on health care and from the spread of health insurance programs sponsored by government, industry, and private companies. Drug makers must continually finance large research outlays, and sustained high profits depend crucially on a continuing flow of innovations and discoveries. But once earnings are achieved, the 17-year protection period provided by United States patent laws effectively shelters them unless superior competing products are discovered. Extensive branding and customer goodwill provide further market protection to the sales and earnings of individual companies. Competition in the drug industry is generally on the basis of product reputation and advertising, rather than on the profit-devouring score of price cutting.

Drug company sales and earnings have shown relative immunity to swings of the business cycle, although they may vary noticeably with changing levels of illness. The expiration of important patents or unfavorable publicity concerning particular drug products may adversely affect the earnings and stock prices of individual companies, and important new discoveries are likely to produce opposite results. Longer-range changes in industry profits as a whole are linked to the pace of new drug discoveries; in the early 1970s, this rate was conspicuously less than it had been in the early 1960s, accounting for a somewhat slower rate of industry earnings growth. However, American drug companies are expanding into faster-growing markets overseas, and several are diversifying into other promising products, such as cosmetics and disposable hospital supplies. Overall sales and earnings for leading companies have been rising between 6 and 7 per cent annually.

ETHICAL DRUGS

The drug industry contains two major divisions: ethical drugs, which are sold by prescription, and proprietary drugs, which are nonprescription medicines used for treating relatively minor illnesses. Some major drug companies, such as Bristol-Myers, American Home Products, and Sterling Drug, Inc., have strong representation in both fields.

The 10 largest companies account for about 52 per cent of all domestic sales of ethical drugs, and no one firm dominates the market. About three-fourths of all sales are made to retailers and wholesalers, the rest going chiefly to hospitals and other institutions. Research outlays, directed toward new drugs and the refinement and improvement of existing drugs, average 10 per cent or more of sales. Only 1 out of every 8,000 chemicals tested results in a marketable new drug product, a factor which strongly favors major companies with their large-scale research and stronger finances.

Aside from the slower discovery of revolutionary new drugs, the ethical drug industry's chief problems in recent years have arisen out of growing government regulation. The 1962 Kefauver-Harris amendment to the Drug Act of 1938 requires drug producers to prove the effectiveness as well as the safety of their products. The Federal Drug Administration (FDA) now tests drugs and rates them as "ineffective," "probably effective," and "effective." Newspaper publicity, usually based on FDA announcements, affects sales of specific drug products with increasing frequency.

A second issue disturbing the industry's composure has been agitation by various legislators and consumer groups for a law requiring companies to sell prescription drugs under generic rather than brand names. This would not only result in lower drug prices but would largely destroy the "segmented" markets built up by the careful advertising of brand names. Drug companies spend substantial sums on representatives who directly contact physicians and others to promote prescription writing by brand names, and thus far about two-thirds of ethical drug sales remain on a brand-name basis.

PROPRIETARY DRUGS

Proprietary drugs include analgesics, antacids, vitamins, cough and cold products, laxatives, burn remedies, sleeping aids, and calming agents. They are sold over the counter in drug stores, supermarkets, department stores, and other consumer outlets. Sales are growing steadily at between 6 and 7 per cent annually, and profits of leading companies are substantial and strongly resistant to cyclical declines.

Since competing products are often made from the same chemical ingredients, brand-name promotion is highly important. The proprietary drug makers spend heavily on television, newspaper, and magazine advertising. However, regulatory agencies are becoming increasingly strict about product claims, and brand-name sales of more or less uniform products such as aspirin appear vulnerable to the agitation for generic-name sales which has already beset the industry's ethical-drug branch.

FINANCES AND DIVERSIFICATION

The finances of leading drug companies are strong, with well-maintained working capital positions and relatively little funded debt. Most outlays, including continuing large expenditures for research and development, are comfortably financed from depreciation flows and retained earnings.

The drug companies earn extraordinarily high returns on their book equities, averaging about 21 per cent during the three years shown in Table 17-3. The 10 companies summarized in the table have paid out slightly more than 50 per cent of their earnings as dividends. However, the stocks typically sell at price-earnings ratios of 25 or more, reflecting investors' confident expectations of further rapid earnings growth. As a result, the dividend yields of these companies were low, averaging not much more than 2 per cent.

Diversification within and outside the drug industry enhances both growth and quality of earning power for most leading manufacturers. Of the 10 largest companies, 8 have important representation in both ethical and proprietary drug lines. American Home Products, Warner-Lambert, and Smith, Kline and French have large interests in cosmetics, and American Home Products also makes Chef Boy-ar-dee Spaghetti, Aerowax, and other profitable food and household products.

Table 17-3 *Performance of the drug industry from 1963 to 1970, selected years (composite per share data, based on Standard & Poor's group stock price indexes)*

	1963	1967	1970
Sales	$34.87	$44.27	$53.86
Operating income	6.29	9.14	11.50
Profit margin	18.04	20.65	21.35
Depreciation	.66	.98	1.18
Taxes	2.80	3.80	4.81
Profits after tax	2.96	4.39	5.55
Dividends	1.68	2.49	2.84
Earnings as a per cent of sales	8.49	9.92	10.30
Payout ratio	56.76	56.72	51.17
Average price	66.44	119.29	144.65
Average price-earnings ratio	23.12	26.79	26.06
Average dividend yield	2.48	2.12	2.00
Book value	15.84	18.55	24.83
Return on book value	18.69	23.67	22.35
Working capital	9.55	14.73	16.03
Capital expenditures	1.06	2.37	3.05

Source: Standard & Poor's *Industry Surveys.* Data shown are based on the following drug companies: American Home Products, Bristol-Myers, Eli Lilly, Merck, Pfizer, Richardson-Merrell, Schering-Plough, Searle, Sterling Drug, and Warner-Lambert. 1941–1943 = 10.

Greater regulation appears to favor the large, established companies. These firms can defend their interests more effectively before regulatory bodies and in the courts, and can also contend with the mass of paperwork and red tape which is beginning to swamp the industry.

THE OFFICE EQUIPMENT INDUSTRY

The prosperous and highly diverse office equipment industry comprises three major segments. Two of these, electronic data-processing equipment and copying and duplicating devices, are highly favored by growth-minded investors and symbolized respectively by the awesome records of International Business Machines and Xerox Corporation. The third category, general office equipment, is really a catchall which includes such highly diverse items as cash registers, accounting machines, business forms, adding machines, calculators, typewriters, dictating machines, office furniture, postage and mailing equipment, bank equipment and security systems, staples and stapling equipment. Although popular thinking continues to identify office equipment companies with particular products—for example, Diebold with bank safes, Dictaphone with dictating machines, and Addressograph-Multigraph with duplicating equipment—the investor must remember that all companies are more or less diversified. A superficial association of company names with single products and historical beginnings is almost invariably misleading.

The industry's general progress seems well assured by rising demand, aggressive research and development, and forward-looking, energetic management. The steadily expanding demand for office equipment reflects such durable economic trends as automation, the information and "paperwork" explosions, rising wage and salary costs, the increasing proportion of white-collar workers, and the growing importance of communication and control in business, industry, and government. Further developments in computers, copiers, and other existing means of processing, reproducing, and storing information promise continuing large returns to well-entrenched companies, while such new developments as copier-duplicating equipment, facsimile transmission, and industrial process controls offer high rewards to successful innovators. Most office equipment firms spend large sums on research and development. The industry also benefits from the government's military and space programs, rapid developments in the graphic arts, and rising expenditures on education. However, overall rapid growth and prosperity also conceal wide disparities in individual company fortunes, and consistently strong earners, such as Moore Corporation and Burroughs, mingle with inconsistent performers like Anken Industries and SCM Corporation.

ELECTRONIC DATA-PROCESSING EQUIPMENT

The various kinds of electronic data-processing (EDP) equipment account for three-fourths of the office equipment industry's revenues. Sales of EDP and software *services* are rising by 25 per cent annually, time-sharing services are increasing by 20 per cent per year, and mainframe and other computer hardware sales show 15 per cent annual growth. The principal markets for computers and related services and equipment include service bureaus; educational institutions; medical and health centers; federal, state, and local governments; banking; finance and insurance companies; retail establishments; and manufacturing firms. Replacement sales have been high since the industry's early years because the greater speed and versatility of each new generation of computers have improved the performance-to-price ratio about tenfold.

Although the digital computer field is dominated by IBM, each of several competing companies specializes in particular customers and equipment types. IBM has 75 per cent of the large computer market and about 80 per cent of all sales made to the insurance, chemical, manufacturing, and petroleum industries. Honeywell, Incorporated, is strong in medium-sized computers and sells largely to the electrical machinery, transportation, and printing and publishing businesses and to state and local governments. The Univac Division of Sperry Rand Corporation specializes in small computers and in sales to the federal government and the communications industry. Digital Equipment is the leader in the minicomputer market, which is growing by 20 per cent annually. Burrough Corporation dominates sales of computers and related equipment to the aggressively automating banking industry.

The computer business also includes the production and sale of peripheral equipment: tapes and disc drives, storage equipment, key-punch devices, terminals, and the like. Independent manufacturers of these items include Telex Corporation, Memorex Corporation, Potter Instruments, and Ampex. These firms have always had to share the peripherals market with the large makers of mainframe computers, but in 1972 they faced even heavier competition as a result of IBM's decision to compete more vigorously in peripheral items. As a result, prices and profit margins of the independent companies declined sharply.

Software (programming) services are marketed by numerous independent small firms as well as by the mainframe manufacturers. The field is crowded, easy to enter, and thus typically low-profit-margined.

The leasing of computers to business and other users developed during the 1960s into a major industry. Several companies, including Leasco Data Processing, Booth Computer, and ITEL Corporation, reported substantial and rapidly rising revenues for several years, largely from computer leases made at lower rates than those charged by mainframe manufacturers. However, the introduction of IBM's 370 computer series made many of the leased systems obsolete, the 1969–1970 recession cut revenue growth back sharply, and expiration of the 7 per cent investment credit (which had been "flowed through" to current earnings) sharply reduced reported profits. Already precipitous declines in the erstwhile "glamor" stocks of these companies accelerated sharply in 1970–1971 when it developed that some of them had employed questionable accounting methods to obtain the profits reported in their years of ostensibly rapid growth.[4] Like software services and peripheral equipment making, the computer leasing industry is relatively easy to enter, fiercely competitive, and only marginally profitable for most participants if full costing is applied against revenues.

COPYING AND DUPLICATING DEVICES

Copiers are distinguished from duplicators in that they produce a copy directly from original material without preparation of the mat or stencil required in duplicating. Also, they are more costly to manufacture than duplicators, involve a more advanced technology, and are usually leased, whereas duplicators are sold.

Since copiers are much newer than duplicating devices, they comprise the more

[4] In several instances, computer leasing companies "improved" reported earnings by reducing (for purposes of investor reporting) the depreciation charged on leased equipment. Usually, estimated depreciable lives were lengthened and salvage- or resale-value estimates were increased.

profitable market for successful firms. The 600,000 copier machines in use during 1971 brought $2 billion in revenues to their lessors as against only $300 million in 1962. The copier business, growing by 10 to 15 per cent annually, is dominated by Xerox Corporation, which has retained 75 per cent of the copier market despite intensifying competition.

Most copiers operate by reproducing an original document on sensitized paper. Xerox enjoys its strong position by controlling key patents on an electrostatic process which permits copying on plain paper. Other makers of electrostatic copying machines, such as Litton Industries, Pitney-Bowes, and Sperry Rand, pay licensing fees to Xerox. Between 1960 and 1967, several firms introduced copiers using other reproduction methods, but most of them withdrew from the field after suffering large financial losses.

Copier company profits depend strongly upon machine usage, and this factor showed increasing sensitivity to business conditions during the 1969–1970 recession. The "heavy usage" market, involving 5,000 copies or more monthly per machine, is the most profitable to enter but also the most costly; in 1972, Xerox virtually monopolized this market. However, competitors and new developments continue to threaten the leader's position. In 1972, Addressograph-Multigraph, the leading company in duplicators, was renewing its long-time effort to win a substantial part of the copier market, as were several Japanese firms. The 1970 decision by IBM to enter the copier field also posed an ultimate threat to Xerox's supremacy. Heavy research and development outlays in several other firms were aimed at developing color copiers or combined computer-copier technologies which would at least partially obsolete the Xerox process.

GENERAL OFFICE EQUIPMENT

The residual category of *general* office equipment includes a wide range of record-keeping, dictating, and mailing equipment, postage meters, adding and calculating machines, typewriters, business forms, and several revolutionary new products. The outlook in this wide field is generally favorable because of the immense increase in paperwork, the rising proportion of white-collar workers, and the widespread drive for cost-saving automation of office and sales procedures. Office equipment is becoming more closely linked to data processing, and systems approaches are being applied to many types of office operations. Product innovation and development are important to success in all branches of office equipment, and for many products, competition from imports is a significant factor in sales and profits.

The most promising fields in general office equipment are found in such innovative items as automatic addressing machines, scientific calculators, systems for communicating data between computers, and point-of-sale electronic terminals. The terminals loom as a particularly rapid growth area, since these devices are candidates for replacing many of the nation's 3.3 million cash registers. The Friden division of Singer Company holds a commanding lead in this market. Other competitors include Pitney-Bowes, National Cash Register, Litton Industries, General Instrument, and Addressograph-Multigraph.

Slower-growing branches of general office equipment include typewriters, office calculators, and office furniture. The last is cyclical and, with many small-scale, low-profit-margin manufacturers, highly competitive.

MAJOR FACTORS IN PROFITABILITY AND GROWTH

The preceding discussion has noted some of the industry's salient characteristics. A complete list would include (1) rapid changes in the state of the arts; (2) vulnerability of products and services to new developments; (3) the necessity of large outlays for research and development; (4) the frequent advantage conferred by major breakthroughs, particularly when accompanied by patent protection; (5) the effect of large rental revenues in stabilizing earnings; (6) the financial strains associated with rapid growth; and (7) in older lines, such as office furniture, cyclical demand patterns and destructive price competition. An office equipment maker's success depends primarily on the dominance of high-profit items in its sales mix, a condition which reflects its participation in markets that are growing rapidly enough to ease competitive pressures and allow ample profit margins. This in turn calls for frequent large outlays on new-product development and on capital investment which carries the potential for either very large profits or near-ruinous losses. It also calls for an ability in management to spot new demand trends and technological possibilities and to gain an early position in rapidly growing markets. An example was the alertness of leading business-forms companies in shifting from the production of salesbooks to continous forms for EDP output as computer usage grew.

Despite the industry's rapid growth, all but the strongest companies carry a substantial business risk for the investor. A broadly based product line, demonstrated capability in research and engineering, vigorous marketing, and access to adequate financial resources appear indispensable to a company's stability and long-term growth. Smaller firms, heavily dependent on single products or vulnerable technologies, may sustain large losses from shifts in demand or the discovery of new processes. The lack of a broad product line also handicaps sales efforts. One of IBM's great advantages has been the ability to sell the customer a total package of hardware, systems know-how, and related office equipment.

Adequate financing is an industry-wide problem, afflicting successful and unsuccessful firms alike. Rapid growth combined with widespread leasing of equipment has subjected many office equipment companies to serious financial strains. The development of new products and entry into new markets call for large capital expenditures which are recovered only gradually in years ahead;

these deferred recovery outlays are greatly increased if the new equipment is leased instead of being sold outright. As return flows of cash from older "generations" of equipment build up, new cycles of product development and marketing devour them voraciously. Chronic cash shortages have forced most office equipment makers to retain a large proportion of net earnings and to pay conservative dividends to stockholders. Even then, internal sources of capital have been inadequate, and office equipment companies have been obliged to rely heavily on the external debt and equity markets. To an increasing degree, some companies are financing their rental equipment through sale-and-leaseback arrangements or through the sale of lease paper to financial institutions.

SOURCES OF EARNINGS VARIATIONS

The investor in office equipment securities must be prepared to understand why earnings of these companies may vary sharply from year to year. Major sources of variation include (1) stage and outcome of new-product developments, (2) behavior of operating costs, (3) changes in the sales-lease mix, (4) impact of the business cycle, and (5) the vagaries of company accounting.

Outlays for new-product or service developments affect both the size and timing of a company's earnings. Even when innovations are highly successful, considerable time must elapse between investment in a new venture and the return flow of sales and profits. Unforeseen delays in either design or manufacture of the new products will cause earnings to fall noticeably short of a company's announced goals.

Labor is the largest component of operating costs for office equipment companies, followed in order by materials, taxes, depreciation, research, advertising, and interest. With the nation committed to virtually full employment, wage rates and labor costs are rising rapidly. In some sectors of the office equipment industry, notably computers, demand has grown so strongly that manufacturers have had little trouble passing higher wage costs on to customers through higher prices. For much of the industry, however, rising labor costs have kept profit margins in continual jeopardy; this has led to great emphasis on automation and cost control.

A company's mix of leases versus outright sales affects both its reported earnings and its cash flow. Equipment rentals, as a rule, magnify a company's profits over the life of the leased equipment, but the financing burden will be larger because the company's return flow of cash from its investment is deferred. Outright sales produce larger reported earnings and larger cash flows in the current period.

The effect of business fluctuations varies for the different industry branches. For office furniture, typewriters, and other durable items in which replacement demand is dominant and customer purchases are postponable, revenues and earnings swing noticeably with the curve of business activity. Growth lines, including computers and copiers, have enjoyed large backlogs of unfilled orders and thus have enabled stronger companies in these fields to increase sales and profits even during recessions.

Considerations of space permit only the general warning that the reader should always check the accounting basis on which an office equipment company reports its earnings. Major sources of variation include amortization of development expenses, depreciation schedules on rented equipment, and inclusion or exclusion of foreign sales and profits. Marketing, engineering, and other development expenses for rented systems are often capitalized and then charged off over a 3- to 5-year period; this avoids penalizing reported earnings during the development period. Depreciation charges on leased equipment will be reduced if the company increases its estimate of useful lifetime or residual value, and reported earnings will consequently rise. With computer leasing companies in particular, the investor must read financial reports carefully in order to determine whether a substantial rise in earnings is due solely to operating gains or at least partly to a change in the basis of charging off capitalized costs.[5] Finally, it should be clear that companies which consolidate foreign sales and earnings will typically show greater "visible" growth than those that exclude the unremitted portion of earnings abroad.

STOCKS AND FINANCES

Table 17-4 illustrates the salient financial and common stock characteristics of the leading office equipment companies. Rapid growth of sales, earnings, book values, and dividends are combined with high profit margins and large returns on equity. Although dividend payouts are substantial and increasing, high price-earnings ratios for common shares—as with the drug stocks—produce very low dividend yields. However, Table 17-4 reveals that working capital has risen much less rapidly than other indexes of growth, including capital expenditures; thus, even amidst prosperity, the companies experience financial strain.

Funded debt ratios for leading office equipment makers in 1972 ranged from 9 per cent of book value equity for IBM to 79 per cent of equity for National Cash Register. The average debt-to-equity ratio for nine major companies was 43 per cent.

Despite rapid overall industry growth, only a few companies have maintained consistently high profitability and year-to-year growth for common share earnings: these have included IBM, Xerox, Burroughs, and Moore Corporation. However, casualties have been numerous, particularly in the computer and copier

---

[5] Major computer makers differ considerably in reporting depreciation charges to their stockholders, although all use accelerated methods for federal income tax purposes. IBM reports most conservatively, spreading sum-of-the-years'-digits depreciation over a 4-year life. By contrast, Control Data, the least conservative, employs straight-line depreciation over 5- and 6-year lives.

Table 17-4 *Performance of the office equipment industry in 3 selected years, 1962 through 1970 (Composite per share data, based on Standard & Poor's group stock price indexes)*

	1962	*1966*	*1970*
Sales	$98.51	$177.31	$ 318.06
Operating income	27.54	57.86	102.31
Profit margin	27.96	32.63	32.17
Depreciation	10.05	22.38	40.59
Taxes	9.38	17.48	30.45
Profits after tax	8.85	17.93	31.05
Dividends	3.32	7.33	15.17
Earnings as a per cent of sales	8.98	10.11	9.76
Payout ratio	37.51	40.88	48.86
Average price	428.82	642.63	1,098.50
Average price-earnings ratio	48.46	35.84	35.38
Average dividend yield	0.84	1.15	1.48
Book value	57.35	111.81	213.73
Return on book value	15.43	16.04	14.53
Working capital	31.12	37.57	79.34
Capital expenditures	13.68	51.59	76.11

Source: Standard & Poor's *Industry Surveys.* Data shown are based on the following companies: Addressograph-Multigraph, Burroughs, Control Data, IBM, National Cash Register, Pitney-Bowes, SCM Corporation, and Xerox. 1941–1943 = 10

fields: General Electric, for example, lost more than $200 million before selling the major interest in its computer division to Honeywell in 1970; and RCA Corporation took a quarter-billion-dollar write-off after selling its computer manufacturing operation to Sperry Rand in 1971.

Government intervention thus far has been a serious threat only to IBM. Federal pressures were at least partially responsible for IBM's decision, made in 1970, to "unbundle" its former charges for a total package of computer services into separate sales of hardware and software. Late in 1972 the Department of Justice announced inauguration of antitrust proceedings aimed at IBM's eventual breakup into several competing companies. At the time, however, neither company officials nor stock buyers appeared seriously disturbed by this momentous, but almost certainly distant possibility.

DIVERSIFIED OR CONGLOMERATE COMPANIES

Three lessons stemming from review of the four preceding industries would appear to be (1) the difficulty of trying to set precise limits on what an industry includes; (2) a recognition of the wide variety of product combinations, market opportunities, and earning power positions present in companies included under an industry definition; and (3) the importance of carefully studying and evaluating each company after looking at the industry as a whole. These problems confront the investor in appraising so-called one-industry firms. Obviously, his task becomes greatly magnified when his interest shifts to diversified companies or conglomerates, as they are sometimes labeled. This designation covers such well-known enterprises as FMC Corporation, Litton Industries, Textron, Incorporated, International Telephone and Telegraph, and Bangor Punta—firms operating in a number of unrelated industries[6] and prepared to enter entirely new businesses tomorrow if profit prospects are sufficiently enticing.

Diversified companies represent a relatively new dimension in both corporate management and investment analysis. Their intent is to combine the diversity and flexibility of the investment company with the operating responsibilities of the traditional multidivisional firm, such as General Motors or General Electric. But objectives and policies, rather than structure and organization, are what really distinguish the diversified company from earlier forms of enterprise.[7] The new "free form" company is founded on an expectation of change and a willingness to change. Diversification across traditional industry lines is sought both as a hedge against the risks of change and as an assurance of capitalizing on the opportunities that change brings about. The company's management operates on the assumption that stagnation and slow decay can be avoided only by sticking to growing products in growing industries. The highly diversified company looks upon its products and divisions as a portfolio of profit-making activities, to be pruned and added to with the passage of time. To replace products of diminishing profitability and growth, new lines at earlier stages of the product cycle must continually be added, either by acquisition or through internal development. In the process, the company seeks to diversify its risks, offsetting cyclical products with stable consumer lines, defense business with civilian goods, and so on.

Thus far, the new pattern has shown only scattered and doubtful success. Conglomerate stocks as a group climbed rapidly in price from 1966 through 1968, but collapsed disastrously during the 1969–1970 recession and bear market. Only a few companies, such as Textron and International Telephone, were able to maintain some per-share earnings growth during 1970–1971, and the latter firm drew heavily upon the unrealized capital gains of an insurance subsidiary to create this effect.

Many of the spectacular year-to-year rises in earnings per share which con-

---

[6] Textron, Inc., for example, makes Bell helicopters, Gorham silverware, Eaton papers, Homelite chain saws, Polaris snowmobiles, Scheaffer pens, Speidel watchbands, and Talon Fastners. Besides these defense and consumer items, the firm owns a large group of companies making industrial and metal products.

[7] Some earlier suggestions of conglomerate enterprises were found in W. R. Grace & Company and Olin Mathieson Chemical Corporation (now Olin Corporation). However, these firms operated their subsidiaries as permanent properties and refrained from opportunistic purchase and sale of their divisions. The new "free form" conglomerates have come into existence only since about 1960.

glomerate companies reported during the 1960s did not result from increasing profitability of operations but were the product of financial and accounting legerdemain. Many companies greatly increased their debt to impart larger leverage to common share profits. Next year's earnings rise was often "bought" by using the conglomerate's high-multiple stock to acquire the lower-multiple shares of new subsidiaries engaged in nongrowing, cyclical lines of business.[8] Illusions of earnings growth were further fostered by indiscrimately "pooling" the unsustainably high, boom-time profits of the new subsidiaries with those of the parent companies.[9] Beginning in 1969, these bootstrap earnings devices became less available; the laws permitting tax-free exchanges of securities in acquisitions were tightened, and new accounting rules narrowed companies' freedom to choose between "pooling of interests" and "purchase" accounting in mergers. After their profits and stock prices collapsed in 1969–1970, many conglomerates began selling off their ill-fitting (and often unmanageable) acquisitions.

Obviously, the long-run investment worth of a conglomerate company depends not only on the stability and complementarity of its various divisions, but also on an unusual degree of competence and versatility in management. To operate in many diverse businesses, managers must be authorities on literally dozens of different industries—on their prospects, operations, problems, and people. They must be good judges of markets and timing. And to coordinate diverse and often far-flung activities, they must be experienced, untiring, skilled, and versatile beyond the measure of ordinary executives. Clearly, not every company that aspires to diversify can assemble a management with these qualifications.

CAPITAL STRUCTURES AND MARKET PRICES

The capital structures of conglomerate companies vary but are generally complicated, and they often include both large debt obligations and several issues of convertible preferreds and warrants, originally issued to acquire other companies.

---

[8] Suppose, for example, that company A has one share of stock earning $1 but selling for $40 because of high promise or past growth. Company B, a cyclical firm with an indifferent record, has one share earning $3 and selling for $30. If A exchanges one new share for the share of B, the two shares of A (the surviving company) will each report earnings of $2 per share if *pro forma* comparisons are avoided, as they generally were in the 1966–1968 period. Will A continue to sell for only 40 times earnings, showing "growth" like this?

[9] Pooling of interests violates the principle that the total value of consideration given in a business combination be accounted for in recording a purchase transaction. Aside from misuses of pooling, conglomerates also jacked up earnings by using warrants and low-dividend convertible preferred stocks to acquire other companies' stock. Until 1969, they were not required to show in their annual statements what dilution of common share earnings would take place if all warrants and conversion options were exercised. Since 1969, all companies have been required to report earnings per share on both a "primary" (present number of common shares) and a "fully diluted" basis. Since 1971, large diversified companies have had to report to the SEC their sales and earnings for each line of business accounting for 10 per cent or more of total sales, profits, or losses. This information is made available to security analysts, brokers, and the public upon request. However, companies are left free to define "lines of business" as they see fit, and so-called segmented reporting had not, through 1972, proved notably illuminating.

Litton Industries and LTV Corporation present capitalizations that virtually defy analysis. In many companies the convertible senior securities frequently offer higher yields and larger appreciation possibilities than does the common stock.

In 1971–1972, investors were pricing conglomerate shares about in line with stocks of other cyclical companies.

QUESTIONS AND PROBLEMS

1   Explain what is meant by an "industrial." Are industrials as homogeneous a group as utilities?

2   Explain how working capital problems, changes in operating costs, changes in consumer demands, and changes in competitive pressure may operate to prevent an industrial's earnings and dividends from following price-level changes closely.

3   How could medium-grade industrial preferreds profit from a price-level inflation? Could they profit from a deflation also?

4   Investigate and comment on the sales outlook for Scovill Manufacturing Company, Eaton Corporation, American Home Products, and McDonnell Douglas. Which has the best immediate prospects? The best long-run prospects? Why?

5   Would the break-even point be relatively high for a company with high fixed costs as compared with one having chiefly variable costs?

6   What features characterize industries in which competition is the most severe?

7   Explain how the amount of exploration work done by an oil company can affect its reported profit for the year. Would this be true of the research work done by General Electric or RCA Corporation, or of a big sales promotion campaign by a cigarette maker?

8   Other things being equal, which is the most conservative investment: stock of a department-store chain which owns its own buildings, or that of a chain which leases its buildings? Would this conclusion hold good of an integrated producing-refining-marketing oil company, as compared with one which buys, refines, and markets? Could there be a disadvantage in integration, in that it compels a top management to try to understand too many things?

9   Why do bond buyers prefer concerns with substantial fixed assets?

10   What kind of capital structure should be employed by a fruit and vegetable canner who must build up a huge inventory during the canning season and sell it all out during the next few months? Do Green Giant, Stokely-Van Camp, and Libby, McNeill & Libby do as you think best?

11   Do you regard IBM common stock as a sound investment at the present price? Why, or why not? If earnings continue to grow at the rate of the past 10 years, how many years will elapse before earnings reach 10 per cent of the present price? What long-term risks confront this company that might jeopardize its future growth?

12   What was the nature of dividend controls under President Nixon's Phase 2 program of price and wage controls during 1971–1972? Were such controls then necessarily adverse to investor interests? Would a long period of years under such controls be salutary?

13   Look up the income sources of the following concerns and identify their points of strength: General Mills, Colgate-Palmolive Company, Phelps Dodge, Perkin-Elmer Corporation, Bristol-Myers Company, Singer Company.

14 Review the factors that led to dividend cuts in 1962 by United States Steel and Bethlehem Steel. Why was Inland Steel able to maintain its dividend?

15 Which has the best prospects for earnings growth: one of the great international oil companies, or a company whose operations are mostly domestic?

16 Chart 2-1 in Chapter 2 suggests that corporate income taxes are mostly shifted to consumers. If this is true, who benefits from the tax deductibility of percentage depletion and intangible drilling costs? Would enlarging these allowances stimulate exploration activity?

17 What would you consider a fair multiple of earnings to pay for the common stock of Texas Instruments? Justify your figure.

18 Identify the earnings sources of the following diversified companies: International Telephone and Telegraph, Bangor Punta Corporation, Indian Head, Inc., and Doric Corporation. Do you see these combinations as "synergistic"—that is, the diverse parts being worth more under one corporate umbrella than as separate companies? Explain.

REFERENCES

Amling, Frederick: *Investments*, 2d ed., Prentice-Hall, Inc., Englewood Cliffs, N.J., 1970, Chaps. 11–17.

Bellemore, Douglas H., and John C. Ritchie, Jr.: *Investments*, 3d ed., South-Western Publishing Company, Incorporated, Cincinnati, 1969, Chap. 21.

Latané, Henry A., and Donald L. Tuttle: *Security Analysis and Portfolio Management*, The Ronald Press Company, New York, 1970, Chaps. 15, 17.

Merrill Lynch, Pierce, Fenner & Smith, Inc.: *Security and Industry Survey*, quarterly.

Standard & Poor's Corporation: *Standard Industry Surveys*, loose-leaf, continuous, New York.

Value Line Investment Survey, loose-leaf, Arnold Bernhard & Co., Inc., New York, continuous.

Vaughn, Donald E.: *Survey of Investments*, Holt, Rinehart and Winston, Inc., New York, 1967, Chap. 13.

FINANCIAL SECURITIES: BANK AND SAVINGS AND LOAN SHARES

Financial securities include the stocks and bonds of commercial banks, stock-holder-owned savings and loan associations and insurance companies, personal and commercial finance companies, and a few miscellaneous categories such as the publicly owned brokerage firms. As a class, financial securities have certain common characteristics of asset-liability structure and profit and loss mechanics. They obtain funds for lending or investment from clients for whom they perform a specialized service. Their profits depend largely upon three factors. The first is the margin or spread between the return on the funds they lend or invest and their cost of obtaining these funds. The second is the operating cost they incur in performing the service owed their clients and in otherwise running the business. The third is the rate at which the volume of the funds attracted to the company through deposits, premium collections, etc., is growing, since this factor, along with the profit margin, determines the rate at which total profits will rise from year to year. As with other industries, profit growth largely determines the extent to which new ownership capital can be added to the company out of retained earnings or through sales of new stock at prices advantageous to existing stock-holders. This latter factor is important because most financial institutions operate with high degrees of financial leverage; each dollar of owners' investment supports several dollars of funds borrowed from depositors, insureds, and others. However, as the business grows, the owners' equity must grow proportionately to maintain a cushion against possible losses. Financial institutions also must preserve varying degrees of liquidity in their asset structures; this need is most pressing for commercial banks, whose deposits are demand liabilities, and least important for life insurance companies, whose inflows and outflows of cash are usually stable and predictable.

In considerable degree, two trends are beginning to blur the long-standing distinctions among different kinds of financial institutions. First, banks, insurance companies, finance companies, and brokerage firms are actively diversifying into other lines of business, usually by forming holding companies which first acquire the stock of the original institution and then purchase or form subsidiary corporations to operate in the new fields. Life insurance companies, for example, are acquiring mutual funds, entering the casualty insurance business, and becoming active in real estate development. Second, conglomerate enterprises are acquiring financial institutions, particularly fire and casualty insurance companies whose large investment portfolios have often accumulated substantial profits which the conglomerates can realize by selling off the profitable securities. These multiple sources of income and expense are making it more difficult for investors to analyze and appraise the securities of financial institutions, since the source of earnings reported is often no longer clearly attributable to one industry or one single economic factor. In some instances, earnings must be traced through a virtual labyrinth of holding company—subsidiary relations, each facet of which is subject to the vagaries and complexities of special accounting rules and judgment.

The present chapter will consider the securities of the two main kinds of deposit-type financial institutions which may be owned by stockholders; these are commercial banks and savings and loan associations. Chapter 19 will deal with the securities of insurance firms and finance companies, and very briefly with those of brokerage houses.

❋ BANK SECURITIES

The stockholders of the 13,800 American commercial banks have more than 43 billion dollars invested in the net worth accounts of the banks, and the buyers of bank debt securities have invested some 6 billion dollars more. The stocks of well-managed banks have always been regarded as secure and stable income producers. The business is one in which both incomes and expenses are fairly steady, making reasonable earnings possible for most institutions in most years and enabling good banks to maintain steady dividend payments. Banks did not issue capital notes and debentures until the 1960s, but these securities are generally of high grade and have proved readily acceptable to conservative investors.

Since the middle 1960s many banks have diversified rapidly into financial undertakings not traditionally part of banking, and, to a limited extent, into nonfinancial enterprises. The chief vehicle for such changes has been the organization of one-bank holding companies whose stock is accepted by the bank's shareholders in exchange for its common stock. Under the holding company umbrella thus provided, the bank enters other businesses through holding company subsidiaries or affiliates which operate small-business investment corporations, real estate investment trusts, data-processing centers, and the like. Although these sideline businesses already play a considerable part in the earnings of many bank holding companies, they conform to no common pattern susceptible of general investment analysis. Accordingly, this section will confine itself to examining the banking business proper, which still comprises the major investment and largest earnings source of most diversified one-bank holding company systems.

THE BUSINESS

American banks range in size from small local institutions with a very few stockholders to the huge metropolitan and branch banks with many thousands of stockholders. Though the larger banks presumably have the advantage of greater diversification in sources of income, it is not possible to say that either is preferable as an investment. Innumerable small local institutions have proved their worth for many years. However, the opportunity for investment in the small banks is available only infrequently to most people, whereas the larger banks' stocks are always purchasable as desired. This chapter will therefore deal chiefly with large banks.

Banks are business concerns whose main activities consist of managing customers' deposit accounts and of lending or investing money. They trade on the spread between what money costs them to obtain and what they can get from loans or investments. Thus the three most important factors in the financial success of individual banks and of the banking industry as a whole are (1) the volume of bank earning assets, (2) the rate at which earning assets are growing, and (3) the spread between the cost of funds and the return therefrom.

About 92 per cent of a typical bank's resources consists of customer cash deposits which the bank agrees to return on demand or on short notice. The bank is permitted to use the money while it remains on deposit; in return, the bank provides checking service and other bank facilities free or at low cost and pays interest on time and savings deposits. The bank's principal problem is to earn enough by lending or investing to pay expenses and make a fair profit on its own net worth. It must avoid all risk of serious loss and maintain adequate cash resources to meet all withdrawal and legal requirements. As a separate function, banks operate incidental services such as collection and exchange departments, safe deposit facilities, and a variety of trust activities.

The management of a bank's resources is influenced by regulatory requirements, by the bank's need for liquidity and safety, by the bank's customers' demands for loan service, by banking custom, and by the preferences of the bank's top managers. In general, regulatory requirements plus operating requirements will keep about 15 per cent of a bank's assets in cash. Between 10 and 20 per cent more will be in highly liquid *secondary reserve* items, mostly short-term government securities; these can provide cash for seasonal or other major withdrawals and for urgent increases in loans. That leaves 65 to 75 per cent of the resources for other uses; of these, 35 to 55 per cent will normally be in loans— short-term business loans, term business loans, mortgages, personal loans— leaving perhaps 10 to 40 per cent to be distributed mostly among medium-term government bonds, state and municipal bonds, and a limited amount of corporation bonds.

Secondary reserves need to be short-term items of very high quality, easily salable without loss and largely due from out-of-town debtors, not the bank's own customers. Short-term government obligations, open market commercial paper, and bank acceptances are useful for this purpose—but these items often yield a relatively poor interest income; in early 1972, for example, it was only between 3 and 4 per cent. Secure short-term investments of this type are also much sought after by corporations and individuals with temporary holdings of cash—tax accumulations, for example—and good yields on them are likely only when a booming economy and a restrictive Federal Reserve policy create a cash stringency, as in 1969–1970. The banks would earn more if their secondary reserves could be kept in long-term bonds or in loans, but long-term bonds can go down in price when money is scarce, and local customers cannot be pressed too hard under such conditions. Short-term items are therefore necessary.

Between 60 and 65 per cent of the gross earnings of the average bank consists of interest on its loans. The types of loans vary from bank to bank, and the percentage of resources employed in loans varies also, but the item is always important. The interest rates earned on loans are much higher than those earned on other bank investments, and even after administrative costs and losses, the loan accounts are usually much more profitable than bond holdings.

The medium- and long-term government and municipal bonds held by banks serve mainly as additional reserves and as secure sources of income, but most large banks do a securities merchandising business in such bonds also, using the bank's investment account as a substantial and convenient merchandise inventory. Many large banks participate in the underwriting of new issues of municipal bonds and retail them through their bond departments.

Corporation bonds are of minor importance as bank investments, and bank real estate and facilities usually amount to less than 1 per cent of total resources.

Table 18-1 presents a comparative summary of commercial bank resources and liabilities from 1959 to 1971. Significant trends shown by the table include (1) a substantial decline in the percentage of government securities to total assets, (2) a sharp increase in all categories of loans, (3) a steady growth in capital accounts, and (4) notable gains in state and municipal bond holdings and in time deposits. Since 1959, bank holdings of longer-term government securities have been sharply reduced in favor of higher-yielding loans and tax-exempt municipals. Time deposits growth has been caused by higher interest rates paid on such deposits. The capital accounts have grown a little more slowly than the total assets of the banks, indicating a fall in the margin of safety, and the ratio of capital accounts to assets at risk (all assets except cash and government securities) has declined, reflecting the relative decline in government securities and increase in loans. Note, however, that the table's footnote states that a large, unused loan-loss reserve has been deducted from the assets and therefore is not counted as part of the capital accounts.

The increase in the loan ratio, as shown in Table 18-1, plus the rise in interest rates since 1959 would naturally increase bank revenues. Between 1959 and 1971, bank operating revenues rose 276 per cent, expenses rose 373 per cent, and earnings before income taxes and securities gains and losses gained 97 per cent. The operating and income ratios in Table 18-2 make clear the persistent rise in banks' interest expense and their difficulty, despite automation and other expense-cutting devices, in holding down operating expense.

LEVERAGE

Table 18-2 indicates that in 1971, banks' gross revenues from all sources amounted to only 6.03 per cent of total resources, and final net income only .87 per cent. Clearly, bankers do not earn their profits by employing their own funds. They earn them by employing the much larger amounts of other people's money which are left on deposit with them. The capacity of a bank to earn a good return on its net worth (capital funds) depends in large part on its ability to attract and hold large deposits which can be lent or invested.

Under present conditions, a bank whose capital funds constitute more than

Table 18-1 *Combined condition statement of all insured commercial banks end of year (In millions of dollars)*

	1959	1966	1971
Assets:			
Cash and cash items	$ 49,211	$ 68,652	$ 95,535
U.S. securities	46,164	55,904	75,705
State and municipal bonds	16,754	40,832	77,790
Other securities	3,438	7,550	3,644
Business loans, etc.	60,702	116,364	175,685
Real estate loans	28,031	54,100	76,448
Personal loans	24,134	47,992	69,433
Bank premises, fixtures, other real estate	2,901	5,620	10,837
Other assets	2,033	5,933	8,484
Total (minus loss reserves)	$243,423*	$402,946*	$593,561*
Liabilities:			
Demand deposits	$151,538	$191,737	$246,168
Time and savings deposits	67,473	161,103	258,368
Other liabilities	5,180	18,413	44,054
Capital accounts	19,232	31,693	44,971
Total	$243,423	$402,946	$593,561*
Percentages at end of year:			
Loan to total assets	45.5%	54.2%	54.0%
Capital accounts to total assets	7.9	7.9	7.5
Capital accounts to assets at risk	14.2	11.4	10.1

* Asset and capital totals are after deduction of loan-loss reserves of $2,172 millions in 1959, $4,337 millions in 1966, and $6,264 millions in 1971.

Table 18-2 *Selected operating and income ratios of all insured commercial banks (In per cent)*

	1959	1966	1971
Operating revenues to total assets	4.07%	5.04%	6.03%
Operating expenses except interest and income taxes to total assets	1.94	2.07	2.66
Interest expense to total assets	.70	1.69	2.26
Net operating earnings (pretax) to total assets	1.43	1.28	1.11
Net income to total assets	.63	.69	.87
Net income to capital accounts	7.94	8.70	11.68
Interest rate earned on U.S. securities	2.80	4.13	5.67
Interest rate earned on loans	5.75	6.32	7.31
Interest cost on time and savings deposits	2.36	4.04	4.78
Salaries and wages to operating revenue	26.30	24.00	23.08
Operating expenses to operating revenue	64.78	76.64	73.29
Interest cost to operating revenue	16.34	32.09	37.39

Source: Annual reports of the Federal Deposit Insurance Corporation.

10 per cent of total resources may not earn a fair return, and one whose capital funds amount to less than 5 per cent of total resources may not have enough capital, for losses or even temporary shrinkages in the value of investments could impair its position very quickly. At the end of 1971, the average American bank had capital funds (including contingency reserves) amounting to about 7.5 per cent of total resources. However, bank capital funds are being increased steadily out of retained earnings augmented by accelerating sales of debentures and capital notes. The ratio of capital funds to total assets will doubtless rise in any year in which inflationary expansion of bank assets does not occur.

The nature of a bank's assets also influences the amount of capital needed. If the resources were all in government bonds and cash, it might be argued that 2 or 3 per cent would be enough capital. On the other hand, a bank whose assets are predominantly employed in loans should have a high percentage of capital, to absorb any possible losses. Analysts usually consider this risk factor in relation to capital funds by computing the percentage of capital funds to *assets at risk*. It is assumed that cash and government bonds are risk-free. Therefore, the ratio becomes the percentage of capital funds to assets other than cash and government obligations. Table 18-1 indicates that the combined ratio for all insured commercial banks in 1971 was only 10.1 per cent, down sharply from the levels of 1959 and 1966.

Though the most important effects of the capital position of a bank are those concerned with earnings and degree of risk, the dividend rate and market price of the stock may also be affected. If the capital is inadquate, the directors will be very likely to limit dividends in an effort to increase the capital out of earnings. They may also plan to offer additional stock for sale, which may depress the market because of the dilution of per share earnings which would follow.

GROWTH OF DEPOSITS

Since a bank's earning power depends on its ability to obtain and hold deposits, the investor must consider this phase of its operation. Even when a bank is short of capital, it must usually compete actively for new business, for a stagnant institution is not likely to retain the business it has. In general, the growth of deposits depends on the growth and prosperity of the community served, on the type of customers and industries the bank ordinarily serves, and on the competitive success of the bank. Banks in rapidly developing communities and those whose principal service is to rapidly growing industries typically achieve rapid deposit growth. A bank's ability to give customers the services and accommodations they desire is a major factor in attracting and holding their deposits. The great Bank America Corporation, in California, grew much faster than some of its competitors during the period 1937–1959 by convincing depositors that it would provide any type of banking services they needed whenever the need arose.

There is considerable question whether time and savings deposits are altogether profitable for the banks. The interest cost on these deposits is almost as high as the average yield on the banks' government securities; the additional cost of operating the accounts and investing the funds must approach 1 per cent per annum; and the deposits themselves are highly sensitive to the yields on competing short-term, open market securities. During 1969–1970, the Federal Reserve System held ceilings on large-denomination certificates of deposit (CDs) far below yields available on treasury bills and commercial paper. CDs outstanding at large commercial banks fell 50 per cent, and the banks were forced to borrow Eurodollars from their overseas branches, to rely on sales of commercial paper by their one-bank holding companies, to sell government and municipal securities at substantial losses, and in many instances to ration loans to their customers. Of course, the banks count on keeping most time deposit funds in loans and tax-exempt bonds; this may make the funds mildly profitable most of the time.

Finally, it should be noted that deposit growth for all banks, and thus the growth of their earning assets, is closely related to general economic conditions. During a boom or a wartime expansion, the banks are able to accept customers' notes and newly printed government bonds as assets in return for newly created deposits credited to these borrowers on their books. In periods of business deflation or government fiscal surplus, the borrowers obtain title to existing bank deposits and pay off their notes or bonds by canceling the deposits against them. This familiar banking process affects very greatly the total deposit supply of the nation and the total volume of earning assets which the banks hold.

GROWTH OF LOANS

The importance of loans to the banks is attested by the fact that in 1971 the average income on loan funds was 7.31 per cent, while government securities holdings earned only 5.67 per cent. Banks make business loans, mortgage loans, and personal loans; the last two types bring particularly high yields and have grown swiftly, as Table 18-1 emphasizes.

In order to grow rapidly, a bank must be willing to take necessary risks and adapt its procedures to the borrowers' needs. Such a bank expects to take occasional losses, but the large revenue from its loans provides a generous reserve to absorb the losses. By contrast, banks that limit their loans to routine and ultrasecure cases must content themselves with moderate earnings as the price of their security.

Risks in lending increase as banks seek additional loans or higher returns by lending either to more doubtful kinds of customers or for longer periods of time. Traditionally, bank loans to businessmen have been for short-term purposes and for self-liquidating transactions. Since about 1960, however, many banks have become large makers of term loans; this type of business loan may be made on either a secured or an unsecured basis, typically runs from 3 to 7 years, and is repaid in regular installments which include both interest and a portion of principal. Funds for term lending have been sought from longer-term sources, particularly time deposits and, more recently, bank debenture capital. However, the trend toward term loans is clearly a step toward larger risks and lower liquidity in bank loan portfolios.

The loan opportunities which come to a bank depend upon its location and clientele. Investors need to study these factors carefully and to make certain that a bank's loan opportunities are adequate. One of the major reasons for the bank mergers of the past 20 years has been the banks' desire to diversify their business sources by merging with institutions serving different types of customers, in order to be assured of ample loan opportunities in the future.

LIQUIDITY

A bank is said to be in a liquid condition when it has ample holdings of cash and secondary reserves. Such reserves are important because a liquid bank can readily provide funds for withdrawals, and it also can provide funds for additional loans or bond investment if these opportunities are present and attractive. Other things being equal, an investor should always prefer a liquid bank over a nonliquid one.

Traditionally, bank liquidity has been measured in two ways: by the ratio of cash and government bonds to total assets, and by the ratio of cash plus government bonds maturing in 5 years or less to total assets. The second of these calculations cannot always be made, since the banks do not all publish maturity data on their bonds, but it is usually possible to get some fragments of information about them. Many banks state the average time to maturity of all their government obligations. This provides a measure of relative liquidity.

Many bankers today dispute the relevance of traditional liquidity measures. They prefer to emphasize what is called *liability management.* This means that banks obtain loan business or make attractive investments first and worry about getting the funds afterward; they respond to monetary pressures less by liquidating assets than by offering higher interest rates on time deposits, selling commercial paper through their one-bank holding companies, or borrowing Eurodollars from their foreign branches. Banks that stress liability management clearly incur greater risks with the intention of obtaining higher returns.

CURRENT OPERATIONS

As in other forms of business, investors in banks are keenly interested in the trend of gross income, the trend of expenses, and the ratio of expenses to gross income.

The importance of deposit volume and loan volume has already been noted. The other major factor helping to determine gross earnings is the rate of interest earned. This factor is largely determined by business conditions, competition, and Federal Reserve policy insofar as secondary reserve items and loans to big business are concerned. These competitive rates are subject to considerable fluctuation. The yield on long-term bonds and on mortgage, small-business, and personal loans is more stable, for various reasons, and tends to lend relative stability to the gross revenues of the smaller banks. A factor adding some stability to the larger banks' receipts is the volume of fee earnings from trust departments and miscellaneous services, which may amount to as much as 15 to 25 per cent of total gross revenues.

About 25 per cent of the average bank's gross revenues is paid to employees in salaries or pensions. Another 20 to 40 per cent is paid as interest on deposits, 3 per cent goes for property taxes, and 10 to 15 per cent goes to cover cost of materials, services, rent, depreciation, and miscellaneous items. The total of these items for all insured banks averaged 81.5 per cent in 1971 as compared with 74.6 per cent in 1966 and 61.4 per cent in 1952. This ratio of operating expenses to gross revenue is called the *operating ratio.* A low operating ratio is regarded as a point of strength, for it indicates that a sizable percentage decrease in gross revenue or increases in expenses could be absorbed without incurring a deficit.

In general, it appears that big banks which specialize in large-business accounts have lower operating ratios than the branch banks or small banks which handle smaller accounts. However, the big-business banks do not necessarily make more money. The small-account banks will generally get higher interest rates on loans and a larger gross revenue per dollar handled, and can therefore earn a good profit after meeting their higher expense ratios.

Table 18-3 *Bank America Corporation consolidated statement of earnings*

	Year ended December 31,	
	1971	1970
Operating Income		
Interest and fees on loans	$ 970,318,000	$1,009,460,000
Interest and dividends on:		
United States Government securities	121,689,000	95,575,000
State, county and municipal securities	110,183,000	108,283,000
Other securities	35,243,000	25,207,000
Interest on funds sold	43,699,000	56,603,000
Service charges on deposit accounts	40,563,000	41,151,000
Trust Department income	28,422,000	24,927,000
Other operating income	170,689,000	131,227,000
Total	$1,520,806,000	$1,492,433,000
Operating Expenses		
Salaries	$ 278,217,000	$ 249,898,000
Pension, profit sharing, and other employee benefits	42,524,000	38,617,000
Interest on deposits	643,084,000	705,399,000
Interest on borrowed money	59,642,000	53,583,000
Net occupancy expenses—bank premises	51,765,000	45,889,000
Equipment—rentals, depreciation, maintenance	23,662,000	20,941,000
Other operating expenses	128,939,000	107,704,000
Loan loss provision	35,465,000	28,035,000
Total	$1,263,298,000	$1,250,066,000
Income before income taxes and securities transactions	$ 257,508,000	$ 242,367,000
Applicable income taxes	79,106,000	75,880,000
Income before Securities Transactions	$ 178,402,000	$ 166,487,000
Net profit on securities transactions after related income tax effect (1971—$5,490,000; 1970—$604,000)	4,685,000	569,000
Net Income	$ 183,087,000	$ 167,056,000
Earnings per share:		
Income before Securities Transactions	$5.18	$4.84
Net Income	$5.32	$4.86

REPORTING OF BANK INCOME:
NET OPERATING EARNINGS AND NET INCOME

Most bank income statements resemble the statements in Table 18-3 in recognizing two kinds of earnings figures: *income before securities transactions* and *net*

income. Income before securities transactions consists of the regular, recurrent operating revenues (interest, fees, etc.) minus the regular recurring expenses (salaries, interest paid, property taxes, supplies, etc.) and a loan-loss provision which ordinarily reflects the bank's average level of loan losses over the previous 5 years.[1] The final net income figure simply adds the net profit or loss on securities (after adjustment for tax effects) to the income before securities transactions.

Bankers emphasize income before securities transactions as the important figure for stockholder attention because gains and losses on securities often fluctuate violently from year to year and make final net profit figures erratic. Yet it is clear that exclusive reliance only on the "recurring" earnings figures is not sound, for, over a period of years, securities profits contribute substantially to a bank's financial performance.

Investors need to be familiar with the concepts of valuation reserves and contingency reserves as these are used in bank statements. Both are illustrated in Table 18-4. Valuation reserves are, in theory, offsets to asset accounts to reflect deterioration which has already taken place. Contingency reserves are segregated portions of the bank's net worth which will be reduced to offset certain losses if and when the losses take place.

Nearly all banks have an important "valuation" reserve, labeled *reserve for loan losses* or some similar term. The reserve exists because the federal income tax law permits the banks to deduct annually from taxable incomes a provision for very large possible future loan losses. Because of the tax deduction, the loss reserve is increased by about twice as much as the *net* amount deducted from earnings. When loans go bad, the loan account and the loss reserve are reduced; if something is recovered on a bad loan, the loan account and the reserve are equally restored. Over the past 20 years most banks have been able to provide loss reserves far in excess of actual losses; as a result, these valuation reserves are really the equivalent of additional bank capital.

Gains and losses on banks' portfolio investments, real estate, and other special transactions are erratic in timing and frequently large; they may cause the banks' undivided profits accounts to fluctuate sharply. To avoid this, most banks have established a special account called *reserve for contingencies*. This reserve may be credited with the securities profits and other special gains, and charged with the losses; the adjustment of other special account values not involving current earnings is sometimes made to this account also. Under present regulations, the reserve for contingencies appears on the condition statement as part of the bank's capital accounts. Table 18-4 illustrates this.

[1] Bank-accounting methods, in effect since 1969, require banks to charge against income a portion of their actual loan losses. Previously, all charge-offs were against special reserves for loan losses and did not affect earnings per share figures. Accounting regulations now require a minimum charge to operating expenses, usually computed by using a 5-year average ratio of net charge-offs to total loans. The rule results in distributing the effect on earnings of sharp changes in loan losses over several years (since these will alter the 5-year ratio), but the banks are no longer able to prevent large increases in loan losses (such as those experienced in 1970) from filtering through to reported net earnings.

Table 18-4 *Bank America Corporation consolidated statement of condition*

	December 31, 1971	December 31, 1970
Resources		
Cash and due from banks	$ 7,201,348,000	$ 5,405,771,000
United States Government securities	$ 2,807,632,000	$ 2,309,358,000
State, county and municipal securities	2,890,810,000	2,488,846,000
Other securities	996,889,000	946,131,000
Total Securities	$ 6,695,331,000	$ 5,744,335,000
Loans	17,016,039,000	15,951,414,000
Funds sold	1,340,099,000	741,414,000
Customers' liability for acceptances	573,686,000	876,694,000
Bank premises and equipment	457,391,000	431,371,000
Other resources	702,012,000	600,890,000
Total Resources	$33,985,906,000	$29,751,889,000

			December 31, 1971	December 31, 1970
Liabilities				
Capital Funds:				
Capital Notes, 6¼% due 1978			$ 75,845,000	$ —
Common Stock, par value $6.25			$ 215,308,000	$ 215,031,000
	1971	1970		
Shares authorized	50,000,000	50,000,000		
Shares outstanding	34,449,247	34,405,053		
Surplus			693,194,000	641,451,000
Undivided profits			352,551,000	315,996,000
Reserve for contingencies			90,119,000	74,123,000
Equity capital			$ 1,351,172,000	$ 1,246,601,000
Total Capital Funds			$ 1,427,017,000	$ 1,246,601,000
Reserve for possible loan losses			276,102,000	276,001,000
Demand deposits			$ 9,706,174,000	$ 9,245,499,000
Savings and time deposits			19,367,127,000	16,397,716,000
Total Deposits			$29,073,301,000	$25,643,215,000
Funds borrowed			1,795,678,000	1,002,733,000
Liability on acceptances			579,899,000	882,863,000
Other liabilities			833,909,000	700,476,000
Total Liabilities			$33,985,906,000	$29,751,889,000

BANK CAPITAL ACCOUNTS

In most cases bank capital is still supplied by a single class of common stock. However, since 1960 a number of banks have sold preferred stock or capital notes when deposit growth made added outside capital necessary.

Banks have traditionally maintained three net worth accounts, labeled capital stock, surplus, and undivided profits. The capital stock and surplus accounts are regarded as permanent capital, whereas the undivided profits item is available for dividend purposes. Under the present rules of the banking authorities, a bank's reserve for contingencies is also classed as a net worth account, and securities analysts typically include it in computations and ratios involving bank capital. In the opinion of the authors, the reserve for loan losses should also be regarded as bank capital. It is not available for dividends, but it can absorb any possible losses and can serve as protection for depositors, which is all the capital stock and surplus accounts can do. Regulations require that the amount of unused loan-loss reserves be disclosed in bank annual reports either as a deduction from the loan accounts or as an entry on the liabilities side of the condition statement.

Debt securities issued by banks totaled about 6 billion dollars at the end of 1972, consisting principally of straight capital notes or debentures; about one-fifth of these securities were convertible into common stock, and maturities at time of issue ranged from 7 to 30 years. Capital debt for banks and bank holding companies in 1972 amounted to only about 10 per cent of total capital funds, but the proportion of debt funds was increasing rapidly. In 1964 and 1965, Federal Reserve authorities indicated their belief that debt capital up to one-third of total capital was acceptable for banks. Bank debentures and capital notes are of course junior to deposits as bank obligations.

Several incentives have encouraged the banks to use debt securities in their capital structures. The long period of prosperity since 1945 has reduced bankers' worries about future depression and deflation and encouraged them to seek for bank stockholders the same sort of capital leverage which the stockholders of utilities and other stable industries have long enjoyed. The tax-deductible interest on debt funds operates to reduce the banks' overall capital cost, and funds provided through capital notes and debentures are not subject to reserve requirements or interest-rate ceilings as are certificates of deposit, proceeds of commercial paper sold through holding companies, or Eurodollar borrowings from foreign branches: these latter advantages, plus the distant maturities of the capital debt, assure the banks of retaining the funds through tight-money periods in years ahead. Finally, the rapid growth of deposits has obliged the banks to raise more capital at times when advantageous prices could not be obtained for new stock.

Banks have made little use of preferred stock, probably because interest payments on capital notes or debentures enjoy a large tax advantage over preferred-stock dividend payments. At the end of 1971, insured banks in the United States had only 117 million dollars in preferred stock outstanding.

DIVIDENDS

Bank dividend policies incline toward stability and regularity. The large banks usually pay on a regular quarterly basis, with extra payments or increases in the regular rate when circumstances warrant. Payouts of 40 to 50 per cent of net profits before securities transactions have been typical in recent years, because rapid deposit growth has compelled most banks to retain a rising proportion of earnings to preserve satisfactory ratios of capital funds to deposits.

The generally conservative nature of bank dividend policies and the stable nature of the business readily lead to continuity of dividend payments. It is not unusual for banks to have unbroken dividend records extending back for many decades.

INFLATION AND THE BANKS

The steady inflation of the nation's money supply since 1941 has proportionately enlarged the banks' volume of deposits and earning assets. Between 1960 and 1972, time deposits grew fourfold, accelerating the expansion of earnings assets; loan volume and interest rates rose markedly, and bank earnings more than doubled. Reinvested earnings plus some sale of new stock and increasing sales of capital notes kept capital accounts up to an adequate level.

Thus far, bank stocks generally have proved a satisfactory inflation hedge for their holders, with earnings outrunning the price level and dividends roughly keeping pace. However, ratios of capital to deposits and of bank liquidity have fallen in the process, and some of the favorable performance of bank earnings since 1965 appears to have been achieved at the expense of protective margins. It seems probable that further inflation at 1967–1971 rates would oblige banks to seek more capital to balance their growing deposits. At any event, a further expansion of loans and high-yielding investments by running down their lower-earning liquid assets now appears unfeasible, and this factor could well hold earnings growth well below rates of the past decade.

GOVERNMENT REGULATION

Although statutory authority to regulate the banking business is scattered in irregular fashion among a number of state and federal agencies, a fairly consistent pattern of regulation has emerged. Regulatory activities may be classified into three groups. First, banks are regulated as public service enterprises authorized to undertake traditional banking activities only. Such related activities as the handling of trusts, escrows, and municipal bond sales, the preparation of payrolls for business firms, and the mailing of dividend checks for corporations are permitted, but unrelated functions—for example, the billing and collection of a power company's accounts for a fee—would not be allowed. Second, banks are subjected to rules and supervision designed to assure the public of their solvency. New banks or branches are limited to avoid undue costs and competitive pressures; interest payments to depositors must not exceed prescribed maximum rates; and minimum capital standards are imposed. Bond holdings are restricted as to quality; loans must be diversified and good in quality; stock investments are virtually forbidden; all assets are reviewed by bank examiners; and deposit insurance is made virtually mandatory. Third, the banks are subjected to credit controls imposed for the good of the general public. They are compelled to hold varying portions of their deposits in cash reserve accounts, and their loans are often limited by law or regulatory pressure.

The general effect of these restrictions is not excessively burdensome. Limitations on competitive pressure are helpful, quality restrictions on loans and investments are desirable, and any effective Federal Reserve limitations on total lending power are likely to be compensated by higher interest rates on available funds. Some earnings are lost as a result of personal and securities credit restrictions, but profitable banking is unquestionably possible. The regulations do not limit either earnings or dividends, except to discourage reckless lending and operations with inadequate capital.

BANK HOLDING COMPANIES

As already noted, most large banks have transformed themselves into one-bank holding companies. In addition, in 1971 there were 153 multi-bank holding companies which controlled $134 billion of deposits, equal to 24.9 per cent of the nation's total. Large multi-bank holding company systems may provide geographic diversification for obtaining deposits and loans and can often supply specialized services which the separate banks could not offer.

Holding companies may control banks only to the extent permitted by state banking laws; some states forbid their banks to join interstate holding company systems, some limit holding company groups to certain geographic areas, and some forbid holding companies entirely. Until 1970, federal laws prevented holding company systems which included two or more banks from owning subsidiaries engaged in most lines of nonbanking activity. The 1970 amendment to the Bank Holding Company Act of 1956 placed one- and multi-bank holding companies on a common footing with respect to nonbanking activities, and today both types of holding companies may own nonbanking subsidiaries where not prevented by state laws or federal banking rules.

Securities dealers usually regard bank holding company stocks as the equivalent of bank stocks, and the same markets and information sources serve for both. Yields and price-earnings ratios appear similar for the two categories.

PRICE AND MARKETS

Bank stocks are highly regarded by conservative investors and are favorite investments for fire insurance companies, trust funds, and endowments. Although many major bank holding companies list their shares, most bank stocks are traded over the counter. Bank stock prices seem generally comparable with those of high-grade, medium-growth industrials; their price-earnings ratios are similar and their yields average only slightly lower. Most bank debentures and capital notes are rated Aaa or Aa and sell at yields close to those available on high-grade public utility bonds.

SOURCES OF INFORMATION

All the usual sources of information provide data about bank stocks. In addition, dealers in bank stocks compile excellent comparative statistical sheets which enable a reader to appraise relative values and choose among the advantages offered in various banks. Table 18-5 suggests the nature of some of these dealers' compilations. The outstanding statistical compilations are the *Keefe Bank Stock Manual* and *Comparative Analysis of Major Banks and Bank Holding Companies*, published annually by Keefe, Bruyette & Woods, Inc. Other useful studies include *Commercial Bank Stocks*, published annually by the First Boston Corporation; *Bank Stock Quarterly*, published by M. A. Schapiro & Co., Inc.; and the Banks section of Standard & Poor's *Industry Surveys*.

SAVINGS AND LOAN ASSOCIATIONS

Only about 700 of the nation's 5,700 savings and loan associations are stockholder-owner companies, but the industry's 20-fold growth in savings volume during the years 1946–1971 and its continuing favorable outlook have attracted the attention of numerous investors. The most widely owned association stocks are those of holding companies, organized since 1958 and usually operating in California where mortgage foreclosure proceedings are faster than in other states. The leading holding companies include First Charter Financial, the nation's largest savings and loan holding company with 24 offices in California, and Financial Federation, with a 26-branch-office network.

The profitability of savings and loan operations depends largely upon four factors. (1) The rate of new construction, particularly in residential housing, measures the strength of demand for mortgage loans of which the associations are the largest supplier. (2) The rate of savings inflows affects both the volume and cost of funds available for loan by the associations; strong inflows enable the industry to avoid both costly dividend rates to attract savings accounts and still more costly charges on borrowings from the Federal Home Loan banks.

Table 18-5 *Per share data, selected bank stocks*

Per share values and ratios	Chase Manhattan, New York	Conill Corporation, Chicago	First National Bank of Dallas	First Pennsylvania Corporation, Philadelphia	Bank America Corporation, California
Price, 3/31/72	58	49	68	45	40½
Price range, 1971-1972	37–62	29–45	29–59	19–38	24–36
Indicated dividend rate 3/31/72	$2.00	$1.84	$1.60	$1.16	$1.10
Indicated yield 3/31/72	3.4%	3.8%	2.4%	2.6%	2.7%
EPS growth rate, 1967–1971	7.7%	10.0%	15.0%	14.9%	8.2%
Dividend growth rate, 1967–1971	8.0%	8.6%	10.5%	10.1%	6.0%
Increase in deposits 1967–1971	29%	56%	53%	58%	52%
Income before securities transactions, 1971	$4.63	$4.07	$4.11	$2.77	$2.59
Average income before securities transactions 1969–1971	$4.13	$3.66	$3.51	$2.47	$2.40
Price-earnings ratio, average income before securities transactions	12.5	12.0	16.5	16.2	15.6
Ratios: 1971 or year-end 1971					
Earned on capital	11.1%	10.8%	12.8%	14.6%	12.0%
Earned on assets	.60%	.69%	.79%	.83%	.52%
Expenses/operating income	82.2%	77.5%	71.5%	81.4%	80.7%
Capital/assets	8.2%	7.0%	7.4%	8.0%	5.0%
Loan/assets	58.4%	56.8%	48.5%	59.4%	50.1%
Capital and reserves/ deposits	9.9%	8.4%	8.0%	12.0%	5.9%
Capital and reserves/ gross loans	15.8%	12.4%	12.8%	14.3%	10.0%
Loan-loss provision/income before securities transactions	2.5%	3.0%	1.0%	2.3%	2.3%
Number of domestic bank offices 12/31/71	170	1	1	78	997
Consecutive years dividends paid	124	36	97	144	39

(3) The level of mortgage loan rates and (4) the cost of savings determine the gross spread at which the associations can make loans. In early 1972, the prime mortgage lending rate in California was 7¼ to 7½ per cent, while savings had an average cost of about 5½ per cent; this spread appeared clearly profitable. The four factors just cited may vary considerably over different sections of the country, so that association stocks may not always follow uniform price trends.   A fifth factor, occasionally important, is the trend of mortgage foreclosures and the volume of foreclosed property in association hands.

Savings and loan associations must compete for funds with other savings outlets, including marketable debt securities, and they must keep their interest rates competitive with those paid by other small-scale, short-term liquid investments which are available to savers. Since 1966, the Federal Home Loan Bank Board has regulated the maximum rates which associations can offer on different classes of account- and certificate-savings. While these regulatory ceilings are intended to prevent the associations from impairing their capital by paying uneconomically high rates to attract funds, they adversely affected the industry's growth during the 1967–1970 period. Ceilings on share-account dividends fell substantially below yields on high-grade bonds and short-term marketable securities, and the associations suffered heavy withdrawals of funds by depositors who reinvested in better-yielding marketable instruments, a process called *disintermediation*. The savings associations have the privilege of emergency borrowing from the Federal Home Loan Bank System, which serves the industry as a central bank. In 1970 the industry's indebtedness to the Federal Home Loan banks equaled 10 per cent of its total liabilities. Since these borrowings cost an average of 7 per cent or more, association profits were severely strained and prices of their stocks declined sharply. Heavy savings inflows during 1971 and 1972 were partly used to pay off these emergency FHLB loans, and most associations showed substantial profit gains in those years.

Savings and loan associations enjoy appreciable tax advantages through tax-free transfers of earnings into reserves. These transfers may be based on either 3 per cent of the net increase in loans during the year or on a certain percentage of income remaining after expenses and interest payments have been deducted.[2] Under the second alternative, which most associations use, the remaining income is taxed at regular corporate rates. Profits applied tax-free to reserves are not available for either cash dividends or liquidating disbursements to stockholders until income tax is paid, and computations of stockholder equity in either individual associations or savings and loan holding companies must be adjusted to reflect this requirement.

---

[2] Under present tax laws, the percentage of income after expenses which an association may transfer into reserves free of income tax is scheduled to drop from 49 per cent in 1973 to 40 per cent in 1980. Subject to the annual limitations noted in the text, such tax-deductible transfers may accumulate until an association's sum of surplus, undivided profits, and general reserves equals 12 per cent of its savings accounts.

OUTLOOK FOR SAVINGS AND LOAN STOCKS

In 1972, a number of factors brightened the longer-range outlook for savings and loan company stocks and for holding company systems in particular. The disintermediation difficulties of the late 1960s had been erased by record inflows of new savings during 1971–1972, and associations could comfortably afford to pay interest rates that compared favorably with those of competing outlets. In 1971, the Federal Home Loan Bank Board expanded the lending territory of associations to a 100-mile radius from any branch or agency located within the same state, and branching was made easier. Lending regulations were liberalized; associations were authorized to participate more heavily in mobile home financing and to lend up to 95 per cent of market or appraised value (whichever was lower) on privately insured conventional mortgages. The Emergency Home Finance Act of 1970 also created a secondary market for conventional mortgages and authorized forward commitments of up to 24 months for purchase of loans made to finance new multifamily properties. Finally, the Federal Home Loan Bank System in 1972 gave strong support to the new proposal for variable-rate mortgages. These would considerably ease the savings and loan industry's disintermediation problem in future periods of tight money by keeping the interest rates paid by borrowers in closer alignment with the associations' cost of funds.

The President's Commission on Financial Structure and Regulation in 1971 recommended that savings and loan associations, along with mutual savings banks, be permitted to make mortgage loans on all types of residential and nonresidential properties without statutory or regulatory restriction, and that they be allowed to make construction loans in the same manner as commercial banks. It also recommended that they have limited authority to make direct investments in real estate, to make consumer loans, to purchase equity securities, and to provide checking-account and credit-card services to individuals and non-business organizations. A final recommendation that savings and loan associations be allowed to raise money by issuing subordinated debentures and capital notes was approved by the Federal Home Loan Bank Board late in 1972; the new instruments will rank below saver deposits and certificates in the event of liquidation, but they will provide an additional capital cushion to support future expansion of savings and loan mortgage lending.

DIVIDENDS

Since the rapid expansion of savings and loan associations requires substantially all earnings, taxed and untaxed, to meet reserve requirements, most stockholder-owned associations pay only stock dividends. Most holding companies were unable to pay cash dividends between 1966 and 1972, but some stock dividends were paid.

The financial strains associated with the industry's rapid growth is encouraging associations to convert from the mutual to the stock form to make capital easier to raise. For most associations, surplus, undivided profits, and general reserves remain well below the 12 per cent ceiling allowed under the tax law. Late in 1972 the Federal Home Loan Bank Board lifted a 9-year suspension on conversions of federally chartered associations from mutual to stock ownership; new rules would permit the savings and loan associations to make initial stock issues to share-account holders in proportion to their "deposits," and to sell additional stock to the public as more capital was needed. It appeared that if mutual associations (and probably mutual savings banks as well) were to "go public," billions of dollars in new stock would be handed over to their account holders.

SOURCES OF INFORMATION

Stockholder-owned savings and loan shares are covered in Standard & Poor's *Industry Surveys* and in S & P's various series of *Stock Reports*. A wealth of general background on the industry is available annually in the *Savings and Loan Fact Book*, published by the United States Savings and Loan League, and in the annual reports of the Federal Home Loan Bank Board.

QUESTIONS AND PROBLEMS

1 Why would a branch banking system have a high operating ratio? How could it be profitable?

2 Would the net asset value (book value) of a bank stock be of any importance to investors? Explain.

3 If a bank has a very high capital ratio and a price-level inflation causes its assets to double without requiring it to obtain additional capital, what will happen to its earnings per share?

4 If a bank with $95 million of deposits and $5 million of capital funds sold 20 per cent more shares for $1 million, what would happen to its earnings per share? To the value of its stock?

5 Are bank stocks a plausible inflation hedge? Why, or why not?

6 Which offers the most promise at present, investment in the stock of the big New York banks or of those in outlying cities? Why?

7 Explain why a bank's deposits grow when the surrounding community is prosperous.

8 Which would need the largest secondary reserves, a bank in a copper-mining community or one in a diversified city such as St. Louis? Why?

9 Are bank stocks suitable "defensive" holdings for investors who fear possible business recession? Explain.

10 Is the traditional definition of assets at risk sensible today? Are 1- to 5-year municipals as risky for a bank as long-term government securities?

11 Are bank stocks suitable investments for growth?

12   Criticize the following statement: Interest rates are going up and the increase should be good for bank stocks.

13   Examine the operating expenses per dollar of total assets as shown in Tables 18-1 through 18-4, and determine how much interest a bank can afford to pay on time deposits if a 5 per cent cash reserve must be held and the balance can be lent out at 7½ per cent or invested in tax-exempt bonds at 5 per cent.

14   Do rising interest rates benefit savings and loan shares? Why, or why not?

15   Are variable-rate mortgage loans a practical way to protect savings and loan associations from disintermediation? Will borrowers accept variable-rate mortgages when mortgage rates are low?

16   List and discuss the principal attractions of savings and loan stocks as long-term investments.

17   Are the capital notes of major banks as sound a type of debt security as high-grade industrial or utility bonds? What about the capital notes of savings and loan associations, assuming they will be authorized? The notes of savings and loan holding companies?

REFERENCES

Badger, Ralph E., and Paul B. Coffman: *Investment Analysis*, McGraw-Hill Book Company, New York, 1967, Chap. 16.

Badger, Ralph E., Harold W. Trogerson, and Harry G. Guthmann: *Investment Principles and Practices*, 6th ed., Prentice-Hall, Inc., Englewood Cliffs, N.J., 1969, Chap. 13.

Bellemore, Douglas H., and John C. Ritchie, Jr.: *Investments*, 3d ed., South-Western Publishing Company, Incorporated, Cincinnati, 1969, Chap. 24.

Dougall, Herbert E.: *Investments*, 8th ed., Prentice-Hall, Inc., Englewood Cliffs, N.J., 1968, Chap. 28.

Federal Deposit Insurance Corporation: *Annual Report*, Washington.

Moody's Financials Manual, Special Features section, articles on banking, Moody's Investors Service, New York.

Standard & Poor's Corporation: *Industry Surveys*, section on banking and savings & loan operations, New York.

U.S. Comptroller of the Currency: *Annual Report*, Washington.

FINANCIAL SECURITIES: INSURANCE, FINANCE, AND BROKERAGE COMPANIES

The nondeposit type of financial intermediaries of interest to investors includes insurance companies (both property and liability firms and life insurors), commercial (sales) and personal finance companies, and in recent years at least 15 investor-owned brokerage houses. The publicly traded shares of these enterprises had a market value in mid-1972 of slightly more than 20 billion dollars.

Property and liability insurors and personal finance companies are almost always owned by private stockholders, but the other businesses among those mentioned are largely in other hands. The nation's life insurance industry is dominated by the 154 large mutual companies, which are technically owned by their policyholders but actually controlled by self-perpetuating boards of directors. The largest sales finance companies are captive subsidiaries of giant industrial firms. Finally, most brokerage companies are still privately held, although the industry's urgent need for more capital to back its liabilities to customers and to finance modern back-office facilities has induced a rising number of investment houses to "go public" since 1968.

INSURANCE COMPANY STOCKS

Insurance companies in the United States fall into three classes: property-liability companies, life insurance companies, and multiple-line companies whose business divides about equally between the first two types. The multiple-line class includes Aetna Life, American General Insurance, Connecticut General, CNA Financial, Travelers, and several other major companies. However, the property-liability and life insurance businesses are economically very different, and the insurance industry can be conveniently analyzed through these two categories if the reader bears in mind that multiple-line companies do both kinds of business. Furthermore, property-liability companies often have small life insurance subsidiaries, and vice versa, so that most companies have some interests in each branch of the insurance industry.

Like other financial institutions, insurance firms have been transforming themselves into holding companies. Among benefits they have sought have been (1) greater freedom to diversify and to acquire other companies, (2) use of debt financing through holding-company bond issues, and (3) occasional accounting or tax advantages. Since 1968, insurance holding companies have expanded rapidly into such new fields as real estate and mortgage management, variable annuities, mutual funds, computer services, title insurance, and real estate development and financing.

THE PROPERTY-LIABILITY STOCKS

The stocks of property-liability insurance companies are generally regarded as conservative investments, suitable as long-run holdings for endowed institutions, trustees, and small investors. Most of the companies issue only common stocks, though a very few preferreds exist. It is often said that a property or liability insurance company is really a mixture of closed-end investment company and insurance carrier. The stockholders invest their funds in the capital and surplus of the insurance company, which in turn invests the money in good income-producing stocks and bonds. These holdings constitute a guarantee fund on which the company may draw if its insurance business sustains unexpected losses, but their principal function is to contribute interest, dividends, and an occasional capital gain to the company's earnings. The insurance underwriting activities also contribute to earnings; the underwriting departments usually expect their expenses and insured losses to absorb 95 to 100 per cent of the premiums paid in by policyholders, thus leaving up to 5 per cent for profit to the company. In addition, the practice of collecting premiums in advance gives the insurance companies custody of large amounts of policyholders' money at all times; this money is mostly invested in bonds, thus adding to the companies' interest income. The typical company in normal years obtains about 70 per cent of its net earnings from its investments and the other 30 per cent from insurance profits.

The insurance business is vigorously competitive, and regulatory control of rates has been exercised as often to keep them up as to bring them down, since the solvency of the companies is a matter of great importance. Federal intervention in the regulatory field is legally possible, but Congress has thus far left the task to the 50 states. Their regulation includes the control of rates, examinations to assure solvency, and supervision of policy forms to assure soundness and fairness.

The volume of insurance underwriting varies with the nation's population, the level of business activity, and the fluctuation of commodity prices. Business booms usually mean more business firms, more new homes and automobiles, bigger business inventories, higher insurable values because of higher prices, and a population able to pay for the insurance it needs. Recessions or deflationary price movements would produce opposite tendencies, slowing the growth of insurance volume and possibly, as in the 1929–1932 debacle, causing total volume to decline.

TYPES OF BUSINESS

Table 19-1 shows the percentage breakdown of property-liability premiums written in the United States during 1970. Some companies specialize heavily in closely related lines, such as automobile liability and physical damage or fire and home multiple-peril insurance. Other underwriters are highly diversified. Investors can usually regard diversified lines favorably because they add stability to premium income and economize by means of combined operations through the same sales offices and agencies.

There also are *reinsurance* companies, which agree to share the risks on policies written by other companies. Insurance companies do not like to carry policies of large size, so they contract in advance with other companies to share the premiums and the losses on large risks. These reinsurance arrangements are often made by direct-writing companies among themselves, but there are a number of companies which do nothing but a reinsurance business. On the whole, it appears that reinsurance companies have a more unstable record, as to both volume of business and earnings, than the direct-writing companies, but the average experience of well-managed concerns is very satisfactory.

It is easy for the insurance-stock investor to select a company whose operations are diversified or highly specialized, as he chooses. Wide diversification offers the probability of stable earnings experience, but investment in specialized companies gives a close student of loss trends an opportunity to select stocks whose earnings appear likely to improve.

Table 19-1 *Per cent distribution of net premiums written by U.S. property-liability insurance companies, 1970*

Category	Per cent of total
Automobile, bodily injury liability	18.3
Automobile, physical damage	14.6
Automobile, property damage liability	8.0
Straight fire	8.3
Homeowners multiple peril	8.7
Extended coverage	2.4
Workmens compensation	11.1
Miscellaneous bodily injury	6.1
Inland marine	3.2
All other	19.3
Total	100.0

Source: Standard & Poor's *Industry Surveys.*

INVESTMENT POLICY

State regulations usually require a property-liability company to maintain some minimum portion of its investments in cash or high-grade bonds, but leave the companies free to allocate the major part of their investments as they see fit. In general, the fire and casualty companies have confined their investments to stocks and bonds. Some of them own their home office buildings and a few make mortgage loans, but investments of this type are neither common nor extensive.

In planning the investment of their funds, the companies must keep three fundamental facts in mind: First, between one-third and two-thirds of their resources consist of premiums collected in advance and held available to pay future losses and expenses. Such funds must be kept safe. The companies therefore plan their investments so that cash on hand plus premiums in course of collection plus holdings of high-class bonds will equal all probable obligations. Second, about 10 to 15 per cent of resources will always consist of premiums in course of collection and cash balances actively used in the business. These are regarded as safe assets. Third, incoming cash premiums will usually be more than enough to pay all current expenses and losses, so all resources except the modest amount of cash and receivables can be kept continuously invested. Typical investment policy therefore requires (1) maintenance of a maximum invested position, employing all funds not needed in cash and receivables; (2) investing policyholders' and creditors' money only in bonds; and (3) investing the stockholders' equity in bonds, preferred stocks, or common stocks. Usually only a portion of the stockholders' equity will be invested in stocks. This portion can be relatively large without sacrifice of safety if the stockholders' equity represents a large percentage of the company's assets.

Table 19-2 indicates the large investment made by property-liability insurance companies in common stocks and non-treasury bonds, chiefly tax-exempts and corporates. However, the proportions in which these investments are held vary widely from company to company. Historically, insurance company investment policy has aimed at steady income and value stability rather than capital appreciation. More recently, however, stock selections have also emphasized capital gains, particularly since a number of property-liability firms have been acquired by growth-minded conglomerates.[1]

---

[1] As, for example, the acquisition of Hartford Fire Insurance Company by International Telephone. The unrealized portfolio profits of a property-liability insurance subsidiary may provide the conglomerate parent with a convenient "mine" of net income, to be drawn upon in years of otherwise deficient earnings. Enough of the subsidiary's profitable investments are sold off for the profit taken into the holding company's account to bring reported net income for the year to the desired level. The undesirability of this practice from the insurance company's standpoint should be evident, since it can easily lead to the untimely sale of rapidly appreciating investments, unnecessary income tax payments, etc.

Table 19-2 *Percentage distribution of assets in stockholder-owned property-liability and insurance companies, as of December 31*

Asset	1969	1970
U.S. government bonds	8.1	7.5
Other bonds	37.4	39.2
Common stock	34.4	32.1
Preferred stock	2.6	2.9
Other	17.5	18.3

Source: Standard & Poor's *Industry Surveys.*

UNDERWRITING POLICY

Underwriting policy has many aspects, but the investor needs to be keenly interested in two—the amount of insurance written and the degree of selectivity attempted. A large volume of insurance is advantageous because the policyholders' premium money can earn interest for the company, because large volume is economical from a clerical standpoint, and because total underwriting profits may be larger on larger volume. It is disadvantageous in that the possibility of disastrous losses is cumulated with increased volume, and the company's investments must therefore be kept to a greater degree in stable but low-yielding bonds. An average company writes net premiums amounting to about 45 per cent of its total assets annually and has a stockholders' equity equal to about 55 per cent of its total assets, but these ratios vary from company to company.

Insurance companies usually attempt to control their losses by accepting good risks and rejecting poor ones. However, excessive caution would be poor business, for it would alienate both insureds and selling agents. Good loss control therefore becomes a long-run problem of developing a relatively low-risk clientele. Some companies have been able to do this to an outstanding degree—St. Paul Companies and Chubb Corporation, for example—while others have had to accept less desirable business. From the standpoint of investment in insurance stocks, these successful companies are always attractive. However, their success is well known and is reflected in relatively high prices for their stocks.

UNDERWRITING RATIOS

Investment analysts measure the profitableness of fire or casualty underwriting operations by the use of the loss ratio, the expense ratio, the loss-and-expense ratio, and the underwriting profit margin.

The loss ratio is the ratio of losses incurred to premiums earned. The losses incurred are those which occur during the fiscal period in question. The premiums earned are the portions of premiums previously and currently collected which apply to the months of the fiscal period being studied. (The premiums currently being collected apply mostly to future fiscal periods.) The loss ratio as here defined shows the percentage of losses to the corresponding premiums earned.

The expense ratio is the ratio of selling and operating expenses to new premiums collected. More than three-fourths of a fire or casualty insurance company's expenses consist of advertising, sales commissions, premium taxes, and other items related to the acquisition of new business. It is consequently reasonable to relate expenses to new premiums collected rather than to premiums earned.

The loss-and-expense ratio is the total of the separately computed loss and expense ratios. It seems reasonable to state, for example, that if losses absorb 60 per cent of premiums earned and expenses take 36 per cent of premiums written, losses and expenses combined are tending to amount to 96 per cent of premium revenues.

The underwriting margin is the percentage of a company's premium earnings which is remaining as underwriting profit. It is computed by subtracting the loss-and-expense ratio from 100 per cent. It is obvious that each of these four ratios is of high importance to investors. Not only is it important to know the size of each ratio in the most recent year; any recent trends up or down, and the reasons for the changes, may be of great investment significance. Company annual reports do not always include the needed details, but much more information, including the loss experience on different types of insurance, can be found in the reference manuals.

Table 19-3 indicates that the years 1962–1970 produced heavy loss ratios for the property-liability companies. (Fire and automobile underwriting, particularly,

Table 19-3 *Premium volume and underwriting ratios, all stockholder-owned property-liability insurance companies, selected years, 1962–1972.*

Year	Premiums written	Premiums earned	Loss ratio	Expense ratio	Combined ratio
1962	11,207	10,898	63.6	35.3	98.9
1965	13,855	13,379	69.2	32.7	101.9
1967	16,343	15,853	67.2	31.7	98.9
1969	19,970	19,108	70.3	30.3	100.6
1970	22,430	21,448	69.7	29.6	99.3
1971	24,824	23,789	66.7	29.1	95.8
1972	27,100	—	65.5	29.0	94.5

The 1972 figures are estimates.
Source: Standard & Poor's *Industry Surveys.*

incurred frequent large losses.) The companies endeavored to correct these difficulties through rate increases and improved risk selection, and 1971 appeared to
show substantially better results. Expense ratios have been kept under good control and have declined continuously throughout the period shown.

FINANCIAL STATEMENTS

Since the computation of earnings per share and net asset value per share becomes
rather complicated when insurance companies are holding companies controlling
other insurance companies and when the insurance business extends to both
property and liability lines, the analysis of insurance stocks is usually done by
experts. However, some of the fundamentals in the process should be understood
by all investors. Table 19-4 is based on the 1971 annual statement of the St. Paul
Fire and Marine Insurance Company, the property-liability subsidiary of St. Paul
Companies. This company does a diversified underwriting business, with about
40 per cent in fire, mutiple-peril, and marine lines, and about 30 per cent each
in automobile and casualty underwriting.

Table 19-4   *St. Paul Fire and Marine Insurance Company and subsidiaries: Consolidated
statement of income, 1971* (In thousands)*

	Statutory basis	*Additions or (deductions)*	*Adjusted basis*
Underwriting income:			
Net premiums written	$475,739		$475,739
Increase in unearned premiums	24,950		24,950
Net premiums earned	450,789		450,789
Losses and loss expense incurred	280,839		280,839
Underwriting expenses incurred	140,322	$(6,236)	134,085
Total losses and expenses	421,161	(6,236)	414,925
Underwriting income	29,628	6,236	35,864
Net investment income	29,056		29,056
Total underwriting and investment income	58,684		64,920
Other expenses	3,672	(28)	3,643
Income before income taxes	55,012	6,264	61,277
Federal and foreign income taxes	15,012	3,000	18,012
Net income	$ 40,000	$ 3,264	$ 43,264

* Statement is condensed and simplified for textbook purposes. Totals are imperfect because
of rounding.

The 1971 earnings statement shows the company's earnings computed on two accustomed bases: *statutory net income*, which is reported to state regulatory authorities and used to determine the company's income tax liability on its underwriting operations; and *adjusted net income*, which is computed in accordance with generally accepted accounting principles on a profitability basis roughly comparable with that used for industrial concerns. The middle column in the table shows the dollar-amount adjustments made to conform statutory income with accepted accounting principles.

Both income calculations begin by computing premiums earned as the difference between premiums written and the increase in unearned (prepaid) premiums remaining on the books. Premiums earned thus becomes the basic item of underwriting income. From this premiums-earned figure are next deducted the losses and operating expenses incurred during the year, to obtain the *statutory* underwriting profit (or loss) for the year. However, the computation is not a very logical one, for it charges all the expenses incurred in obtaining a large amount of new business (note the large increase in unearned premiums during the year) to the operations of 1971, whereas the premium income resulting from this business will be spread over the entire period covered by the policies. The result is that the statutory underwriting profit sometimes appears as a loss in a year when the company has obtained a large amount of attractive new business, because of the heavy acquisition costs charged to current expenses. Likewise, a very bad loss year might show a statutory underwriting profit if new business declined greatly so that sales commissions and other acquisition costs were lower for the year.

Neither investors nor company managements accept the view that this *statutory* underwriting income correctly represents underwriting earnings for the year. They are aware, for example, that St. Paul Fire and Marine Insurance during the year prepaid the acquisition costs on $24,950,000 of new business which contributed nothing to the year's premium income. To adjust the statutory underwriting income to a more realistic figure, a percentage of these costs should be deferred (with the purpose of adding them into future expenses proportionally as the related premiums come into earnings). Company accountants usually make a correction by adding back up to 30 per cent of the *increase* in unearned premiums to the statutory underwriting profit. St. Paul Fire and Marine has done so, first subtracting $6,236,000 (about 25 per cent of the increase in unearned premiums) from the year's underwriting expenses, with the result that adjusted underwriting income is increased by this amount to $35,864,000.

To adjusted underwriting income the St. Paul statement next adds the investment department's net income of $29,056,000; this consists of interest, dividend, and rental income (net after investment department expenses). The next item comprises other expenses of a miscellaneous nature, with a minor adjustment of $28,000 shown in column (2). This gives the company's income before income taxes. Finally, income taxes are subtracted from both statutory

and adjusted income, the deduction from adjusted income being enlarged by a
$3,000,000 allowance for future income tax on estimated profits added to the
unearned premium reserve. These steps result in total net income for the company of $40,000,000 on a statutory basis and $43,264,000 on an adjusted one.[2]
Obviously, the adjustments made have added $3,264,000 to the company's
adjusted net income.

Two other comments on the company's 1971 earnings performance are
necessary. First, the company realized a capital loss of $467,000 on investments
actually sold during the year, but these were included on the parent company's
Statement of Consolidated Shareholders' Equity, shown in Table 19-5. Since
capital gains, both realized and unrealized, fluctuate widely from year to year,
investment analysts generally agree that they should be excluded from the adjusted earnings calculation. Second, the company enjoyed a substantial *unrealized*
appreciation in the market value of its stock and bond portfolio. This gain is
reported in the section entitled Unrealized Appreciation of Investments, at the
bottom of the shareholders' equity statement in Table 19-5. Like earnings retained from investment income, sustained capital gains will increase the book
value of the company's common shares; this growth of equity will permit a larger

---

[2] This amounted to about 86.5 per cent of the $50,004,000 net income reported by the parent company to
its stockholders.

Table 19-5 *Statement of consolidated shareholders' equity, St. Paul Companies, Inc., and
subsidiaries, December 31, 1971* (In thousands)*

Common stock	$ 31,454
Additional paid-in capital	12,991
Retained earnings:	
Beginning of year	209,784
Net income	50,004
Realized gain (loss) on sale of investments	(467)
Cash dividends to shareholders	(12,582)
End of year	246,739
Unrealized appreciation of investments:	
Beginning of year	87,979
Increase in unrealized appreciation for year	32,218
Change in mandatory securities valuation reserve	(1,303)
End of year	118,644
Total shareholders' equity	$409,828

*Statement is condensed and simplified for textbook purposes. Totals are imperfect because
of rounding.

volume of underwriting activity (and earnings) without diluting the position of existing shareholders. Moreover, it should be noted that realized capital gains and losses do not always reflect the success of a company's investment program. A successful investor may simply hold the issues that are giving him rapid long-term growth and sell off the minority of investments that prove disappointing. Thus his realized transactions may show a balance of losses, although his overall investment results are highly rewarding.

Insurance companies also publish balance sheets which present assets, liabilities, and shareholders' equity on both the statutory and the adjusted basis. A condensed version of the 1971 balance sheet of St. Paul Fire and Marine is presented in Table 19-6. Three of the adjustments deserve special comment. The first consists of the addition to the company's adjusted assets of $63,200,000 of Prepaid Insurance Acquisition Expense. This represents the acquisition cost

Table 19-6 *St. Paul Fire and Marine Insurance Company and subsidiaries consolidated balance sheet, December 31, 1971* (In thousands)*

	Statutory basis	Additions or (deductions)	Adjusted basis
Assets:			
Bonds	$358,701		$358,701
Preferred stocks	13,385		13,385
Common stocks	382,660		382,660
Cash	6,797		6,797
Receivables	76,094	$ 6,702	82,796
Prepaid insurance acquisition expense		63,200	63,200
Other admitted assets	15,141		15,141
Other adjustments		5,593	5,593
Total	$852,778	$75,495	$928,273
Liabilities:			
Unearned premiums	$223,431		$223,431
Loss and expense reserves	318,174		318,174
Accrued expense and taxes	27,745		27,745
Deferred income tax—prepaid expense		$31,060	31,060
Deferred income tax—unrealized appreciation		34,564	34,564
Reinsurance reserve	11,413		11,413
Other liabilities	27,516	(11,180)	16,336
Total liabilities	608,279	54,444	662,723
Shareholders' equity	244,499	21,051	265,551
Total	$852,778	$75,495	$928,273

* Statement is condensed and simplified for textbook purposes. Totals are imperfect because of rounding.

already met on the $223,431,000 of unearned premiums shown on the liabilities side; in effect, therefore, this Prepaid Insurance Acquisition Expense is being subtracted from unearned premiums and added to the adjusted stockholders' equity. Second, the management recognizes that the company will owe income tax on profits that will eventually flow from unearned premiums and from realization of the appreciation on the company's investment portfolio. Two liability-side adjustments, Deferred Income Tax—Prepaid Expense, and Deferred Income Tax—Unrealized Appreciation, in effect subtract this estimated future tax obligation from the adjusted stockholders' equity. Third and finally, the algebraic sum of these adjustments and other miscellaneous ones is added to the company's statutory unassigned surplus to produce an adjusted unassigned surplus figure which is the final item before the adjusted *total* stockholders' equity.

Although it is not shown on the accompanying tables, the common stock of the parent St. Paul Companies at year-end 1971 had a net asset value per share of $39.09. This is always an important figure to insurance stock investors, for it measures the maximum amount which normally should be invested in stocks, as well as the basic sum of earning assets which will remain in the investment account even if the volume of insurance underwriting declines drastically.

The foregoing examples should convince the reader that all per share earnings and net asset value figures for insurance stocks are inevitably estimates, even when reported by the companies themselves. It will always be important to know whether such figures are statutory or adjusted, and if adjusted, what adjustment methods were used. Also, since many important insurance companies are holding companies, it is essential to know whether the per share figures are based on consolidated statements. Finally, it is not to be expected that all security analysts, in making their calculations of earnings per share and net assets per share, will arrive at the same figures. They will use varying methods and assumptions and get close, but not identical, results.

One further word of caution is perhaps necessary. The item, Losses Incurred . . . , which appears on the income statement, Table 19-4, and Loss Claims Pending, which appears on the complete balance sheet, are necessarily estimates. If these estimates subsequently prove erroneous, any intervening financial statements also will be wrong. A number of companies have made large-scale underestimates in recent years and have had to make subsequent drastic adjustments. A prospective investor is therefore well advised to inquire about the adequacy of his company's loss reserves.

CORPORATE INCOME TAXES

Property-liability insurance companies enjoy one tax advantage: their taxable income from operations is based on their statutory underwriting profits, not on the more accurate (and ordinarily larger) adjusted underwriting profits. Except for the relatively minor sums paid on investment capital gains, insurance companies' taxable corporate incomes are roughly measured by the following formula: Taxable income equals premiums earned minus losses incurred minus expenses paid plus taxable interest earned plus approximately 15 per cent of dividends received. Consideration of this formula will indicate that a steady growth of premium sales would minimize taxation and that a decline would increase it. Statutory underwriting profits and taxable interest income are fully taxed, whereas only about 15 per cent of dividend income is included in the tax base.

Corporate income taxes are usually not included in the expenses used to compute the expense ratio, nor are they included in the customary computations of underwriting profits per share or investment income per share. They are deducted separately after these computations are made, as shown in Table 19-4.

EARNINGS EXPERIENCE

For property-liability insurance companies, the 1961–1971 decade presented sharp contrasts in investment and underwriting profitabilities. Along with the volume of premiums written, net investment income more than doubled during this interval, although heavy common stock holdings depressed portfolio values during times of market weakness. Underwriting operations were generally unprofitable, owing to (1) inflation-fostered increases in claims costs, (2) rapid growth in the number of automobile casualties, (3) an unusual run of major hurricane losses, plus increasing property destruction resulting from crime and racial and civil disorders. Until 1971, loss claims outran rate increases, particularly in fire and automobile lines.

The stockholder-owned companies also lost an increasing proportion of business to competing mutual and other direct-writing companies during these years. These companies were able to operate with expense ratios of 25 to 30 per cent instead of the 30 to 40 per cent typical under the traditional agency system. Since these direct-writing competitors were recording profits at prevailing premium rates, insurance commissioners were loath to authorize premium increases; and the stock companies hesitated to charge more than their competitors. They tried to avoid high-loss business and to reduce costs by reducing agents' commissions, by selling composite "packages" of different kinds of insurance, and by mechanizing and economizing paperwork and administrative procedures. As Table 19-3 shows, they reduced their expense ratios materially over the decade.

PERFORMANCE RECORD AND DIVIDEND POLICY

The total performance of an insurance stock can roughly be gauged by summing two elements—dividend distributions and the increase in net asset value per share—and dividing by the initial net asset value to obtain a percentage figure.[3]

---

[3] Average gain in liquidating value plus dividends paid as percentage of average initial liquidating value.

However, insurance companies have long held to a curious tradition that under-writing profits are a public trust, to be retained to strengthen the finances of the company, and that their dividends must therefore be paid only out of interest and dividend income. Most companies keep their dividend disbursements well below their investment incomes. Only in the long run do stockholders benefit from underwriting profits, when these profits have been invested in income-producing securities which add to the company's investment income.

The investment income of property-liability insurors is sure and steady, and the tradition justifies dividends from it even when underwriting losses are experienced, unless the losses are very severe. As a result, insurance company dividends have been incomparably dependable; most of the leading companies have unbroken dividend records extending back 50 to 100 years. In the 1960–1970 decade, dividends averaged 47 per cent of net investment income before taxes. Most companies have limited their dividends in some degree to build up net worth to support additional underwriting business. The aim of building up net worth has in many cases been achieved with the help of capital gains on stock investments.

STOCK PRICES

Insurance stocks fluctuate in value along with the general level of stock prices and to about the same extent as other stocks of similar quality. They also reflect at any time the conditions and prospects of the insurance business. On the whole, price-earnings ratios for property-liability insurance stocks seem a little lower than those on industrial stocks of comparable quality. Yields are also somewhat lower, reflecting the conservative dividend policies of the industry. Most insur-ance stocks sell below net asset value most of the time, usually ranging between 60 and 100 per cent of it, but some sell well above it at times. Naturally, the bet-ter-grade and more profitable stocks sell for a higher percentage of asset value than the weaker issues. Table 19-7 presents an illustration of price relationships in property-liability insurance stocks.

LIFE INSURANCE STOCKS

More than half the life insurance in force in the United States, and some two-thirds of all life insurance company assets, are in the hands of mutual companies. Although the stock companies do a considerable amount of business on a limited-profit participating basis, they write enough policies on a fixed-premium basis to make their stocks a matter of comparatively high interest to investors. Three stock companies—Aetna Life, Travelers, and Connecticut General—are among the 10 largest life insurance companies in the United States, and 23 stock compa-

Table 19-7 *Price relationships in property-liability insurance stocks, 1971*

Company	Stock price range 1971	Consolidated net asset value, 12/31/71	Adjusted underwriting profit	Net investment income	Other income*	Income tax	Net earned per share	Net capital gains	Dividends paid, 1971	Net investment income	Net income
							Consolidated earnings per share, 1971				*Average annual growth, 1966–1971 (per cent)*
Chubb Corporation	47–33	$27.59	$1.77	$1.78	$.44	$0.88	$3.11	$0.12	$1.07	10.2	18.9
Continental Corporation	48–33	46.18	1.15	3.12	.33	1.11	3.49	1.26	1.86	6.2	7.9
Government Employees Insurance	45–25	8.02	0.63	1.16	—	0.30	1.49	–.05	0.65	22.0	14.5
Hartford Steam Boiler Inspection	49–33	40.41	4.78	2.44	.31	2.54	4.99	–.07	1.44	11.4	14.9
St. Paul Companies	75–53	41.98	2.78	2.77	.79	1.42	4.92	–.04	1.16	9.4	16.3
U.S. Fidelity & Guaranty	52–37	34.37	1.33	2.55	.23	0.90	3.21	–.03	2.20	9.9	9.3

* Net income of noninsurance subsidiaries or adjusted net of life insurance subsidiaries.

nies rank among the 50 largest companies. There are more than 1,600 smaller life insurance companies, many of them owned by public stockholders.

The life insurance companies sell individual and group life insurance, annuities, and some accident and health insurance. The bulk of this business is in life insurance, which is typically characterized by long-term contracts under which the insured pays periodic premiums until a stipulated date or his earlier death, is credited with a contractual rate of interest on his accumulating equity, and can count on a death benefit, a lump sum, or an annuity in ultimate settlement. The premiums charged assume a definite mortality rate among the insureds, a rate of interest to be earned by the company on the insureds' money, and an allowance for expenses.

The past three decades have been very favorable to life insurance companies. Mortality losses have been declining; insureds live longer, pay more premiums, and defer their death claims longer than the actuaries had anticipated. Furthermore, interest rates have been rising, and the companies are earning more than the rates promised to policyholders. Even expenses have not risen unduly, despite a major increase in income taxes in 1958. Finally, the volume of insurance sales has been large and these advantages have been pyramided upon relatively small stockholder net worths.

As in the case of fire and casualty companies, a growing volume of business requires that initial selling and recording costs be paid by the companies before the offsetting premium income is received. Consequently, company net income figures are understated when volume increases, because of immediate expensing of first-year costs which will be recovered in premiums in future years; and company net worths are understated because these expense advances are certain to be recovered but have been charged against new worth. Until 1971 most security analysts believed that a reasonable allowance for such company investment per $1,000 of life insurance business in force was $15 for ordinary business and $5 for group business. (These were *average* figures; the investment in whole life is different from endowment or term.) Consequently, analysts added these amounts per $1,000 of insurance in force to a company's capital accounts to compute an "adjusted net worth." They also added such amounts per $1,000 of *increase in insurance in force* to the company's reported net income in computing "adjusted net income."[4] Since 1971 the American Institute of Certified Public Accountants and the SEC have permitted life companies to use "Generally Accepted Accounting Principles" and spread the initial expenses of writing a policy over a period of years. The "adjusted" earnings reported by companies under the new guidelines appeared in 1972 to average nearly 30 per cent more than would have been reported on a statutory basis.

---

[4] These adjustments typically added 15 to 30 per cent to the companies' reported earnings and slightly larger percentages to their net worths.

The enthusiastic advocates of life insurance stocks point out that the volume of insurance in force is growing at 8 per cent per year and that mortality experience should continue to improve. Even if interest rates cease to rise, the business should thus continue to profit and to grow. Consequently, the enthusiasts class the stocks as growth stocks and accept them at very high price-earnings ratios. Low dividends are explained as necessary in order to maintain net worths at 5 to 8 per cent of the rapidly growing total assets. All these arguments appear to have validity when applied to carefully chosen life insurance stocks.

However, it should be noted that life insurance companies differ in their abilities (1) to obtain insureds whose mortality rates will be low, (2) to keep down operating expenses, (3) to achieve success with their investments, (4) to avoid policy types and clauses which incur losses, (5) to develop attractive and salable policies, and (6) to sell an increasing volume of insurance without incurring heavy costs. In other words, success in this business is not automatic. It requires good management, good merchandise, a good name, and possibly some good luck. Successful investors will need to know something of the intricate analytical criteria upon which operating efficiency is judged.

One threat to the life companies has been inflation, which impairs both the protective and savings features of dollar sum insurance. Against rising risks that the public might turn away from traditional life insurance policies, the companies, both stock and mutual, have begun adding equity-based contracts to their offerings. In 1972, some 280 life companies had affiliated mutual funds; 110 offered variable annuities, and several had proposed to sell variable life insurance once the regulatory jurisdiction was clear.[5] In addition, a rapidly rising portion of insured pension plan reserves was being invested in common stocks. At year-end 1971, the life companies held a total of nearly 17 billion dollars in common stocks, 4 times the amount owned 10 years earlier.

Equity-backed pension plans, mutual funds, variable annuities, and variable life insurance are new fields that present the life companies with major opportunities for diversification and faster growth. Some of the growth, however, would almost certainly be borrowed from their dollar sum insurance business. A switch by insurance buyers to mutual funds or equity-backed policies would also affect prices and yields in the nation's securities markets, strengthening the demand for common stocks and reducing the markets for bonds and mortgages.

---

[5] In January 1973, the SEC ruled that variable life insurance contracts are securities. Like mutual-fund shares and variable annuities, they must be registered and are legally offerable to buyers by prospectus only. Offering companies must make extensive disclosure and limit their sales pitches. However, the Commission exempted companies offering variable life policies from the Investment Company Act of 1940, which limits sales charges. State authorities regulate the commissions charged by life insurors, but the terms are more liberal than the federal law allows mutual-fund salesmen. In February 1973, a group of mutual funds petitioned the federal courts to overturn the ruling, arguing that it would give variable life insurance an unfair selling advantage over the funds.

Several stockholder-owned life or "mixed" insurance companies, notably Travelers Corporation, have sold bonds in recent years, and in 1972 the first mutual concern, New England Mutual Life Insurance Company, marketed 50 million dollars in 7⅜ per cent debentures. Although long-term debt financing by life insurance companies is still rare, their bonds are rated investment-grade and have sold readily at yields comparable to similarly rated utility offerings.

Table 19-8 presents earnings and market-price data on five selected life insurance companies. Table 19-9 performs a similar office for five large multiple-line companies.

THE MARKET

The stocks of small and medium-sized insurance companies trade over the counter; most large insurance holding companies are now listed. The larger companies have many stockholders, and trading in their stocks is moderately active. Because of their quality and dependable market, insurance stocks have a high rating as bank collateral. Since the markets for most life company shares are too narrow for the easy purchase or sale of large blocks, institutional investors thus far have shown only limited interest in them.

SPECIAL SOURCES OF INFORMATION

In addition to the leading securities information services, data on insurance stocks can be obtained from specialized sources. For reference manuals, the leading publications are the annual Best's Insurance Reports, which appear in two volumes, *Property/Liability Edition* and *Life/Health Edition*. This publisher also offers an extensive financial analysis of more than 125 leading stock insurance companies in the publications *Best's Insurance Securities Research Services*; *Best's Executive Data Service*, which examines the premium and loss experience of 1,100 carriers; and *Best's Market Guide*, which tabulates the securities holdings of insurance companies. In addition, the firm offers *Best's Review*, a monthly journal on the insurance industry, and a weekly entitled *Best's Insurance News Digest*.

Investors will also find important use for the elaborate statistical comparisons of insurance stocks which dealers and brokers prepare. These show for each company the size of the company; amount of business done; type of investments held; amount of each type of insurance written; and on a per share basis, the net asset value, detailed earnings record, dividend rate, and stock price. On both property-liability and life insurance stocks, for example, outstanding compilations are made by Legg, Mason and Company. Standard & Poor's *Industry Surveys* also provides useful coverage of both insurance industry segments.

Table 19-8 *Price relationships in life insurance stocks*

	Franklin Life	Jefferson Pilot	South-western Life	U.S. Life Corp.	California-Western States Life
Total assets in millions, 1971	$1,314	$1,528	$1,162	$1,129	$459
Net worth per share per statement	9.69	22.30	11.02	17.63	13.37
Value of insurance in force per formula	3.95	6.84	7.88	8.22	6.75
Adjusted net worth per share, 1971	13.64	29.14	18.90	25.85	20.12
Earnings per share, per statement, 1971	1.15	2.16	1.42	2.52	1.15
Adjustment for increase in force	.43	1.02	.51	.56	.12
Adjusted earnings per share, 1971	1.58	3.18	1.93	3.08	1.27
Average annual gain in insurance in force, 1966–1971	4.8%	8.2%	7.0%	—	7.0%
Annual dividend rate, 1971	.50	.86	.77	.50	.40
Price range, 1971	23–14	50–27	37–27	50–34	16–7

Table 19-9 *Price relationships in stocks of multiple-line insurance companies*

	Aetna Life & Casualty	American General	CNA Financial	Trans-America	Travelers Corp.
Total assets in millions, 1971	$10,865	$2,178	$3,769	$3,935	$7,617
Adjusted net worth per share	50.36	18.94	18.95	11.24	35.43
Adjusted earnings per share:					
Life insurance	2.21	1.00	.47	.51	1.16
Property-liability insurance	2.50	.48	1.15	.41	1.34
Other*	.37	.21	.29	.21	.18
Consolidated	5.08	1.69	1.91	.86	2.68
Net capital gains	—.03	—.01	.19	.05	0.00
Annual dividend rate, 1971	1.55	.50	.50	.53	.80
Average growth rates, 1966–1971, per share:					
Life insurance earnings	—1.0%	8.0%	0.0%	0.2%	2.0%
Property-liability earnings	15.0%	—14.5%	9.2%	—	10.1%
Consolidated net income	7.7%	0.5%	9.5%	—3.1%	5.8%

*Net income of holding company and noninsurance subsidiaries.

FINANCE COMPANY STOCKS

Finance companies include commercial finance companies, which lend to business firms, and personal finance companies, which lend to individuals. Both types of companies utilize equity capital and long-term borrowed funds to meet the minimum volume of loan demands expected from their customers, and rely upon commercial paper issues, bank borrowings, and other short-term sources to meet seasonal or cyclical peaks. Spreads between the rates at which these companies can lend and borrow funds are highly important to their earnings, and the greater their dependence on short-term money sources, the less stable their profits are likely to be.

The major commercial finance companies—C.I.T. Financial, Heller International, and Talcott National—are widely diversified in both financial and non-financial activities. Lending outlets include automobile sales financing, industrial loans, factoring, leasing, and business credit. These companies are highly dependent on short-term debt, but they also possess great flexibility in the charges they can make for credit. Thus the demand for credit exercises greater influence on their earnings than interest rates do. Their profits fluctuate with the business cycle and with manufacturing companies' needs for additional working capital. Much of their lending is secured by the pledging of inventories and receivables.

Closely akin to the commercial finance companies are the large, captive finance-company subsidiaries of such giant industrial firms as General Motors, General Electric, and Sears, Roebuck. These firms—General Motors Acceptance Corporation (GMAC), General Electric Credit Corporation, and Sears Roebuck Acceptance Corporation—do not sell stock to the public but market frequent, multimillion-dollar issues of long-term, interest-paying notes; these are typically A-rated and offer yields comparable with high-grade industrial bonds.

PERSONAL FINANCE COMPANIES

Cash loans to individuals dominate the business of personal finance companies, which receive keen competiton from banks and credit unions. Profit margins are extremely sensitive to the cost of short-term funds because loan volume is fairly steady and interest rates charged to customers are relatively inflexible and ordinarily subject to regulatory ceilings under state laws. Interest costs are the second largest expense for these concerns, and the large-scale advance in commercial paper rates during 1969–1970 dropped profits for most companies.

The outlook of the personal finance companies in 1972 appeared somewhat mixed. Favorable influences included the public's growing tendency to spend on services, continuing moderate loss rates despite the increase in average loan maturity from 17.5 to 33.9 months since 1951, and a continuing rise in the average size of loan made. Among adverse factors were the rising use of credit-card financing by consumers and the likelihood of future monetary and interest-rate instability.

Among personal finance companies, Household Finance Corporation and Beneficial Corporation are more heavily financed from long-term sources and have shown steadier earning power than Family Finance and American Investment Company, which rely chiefly on short-term financing. All finance companies, both personal and commercial, have usually sold at higher yields than the average industrial stock.

BROKERAGE STOCKS

Some 15 brokerage firms, all New York Stock Exchange members, have sold stock to the public since 1968. The outlook for these shares seems generally good, since the issuers are among the larger, better-diversified members of an industry in which size and varied income sources are increasingly important. The commission business of the larger New York Exchange members was unprofitable in 1970 and, except for firms specializing in institutional business, only moderately profitable on the average in 1971. However, these companies enjoy lucrative earnings from customers' credit balances, margin-account interest, underwriting fees, private placements, advisory services, block positioning, commodity trading, and their role as securities dealers.

QUESTION AND PROBLEMS

1 Why do property-liability insurance companies invest heavily in tax-exempt bonds? In stocks? What are the factors controlling the extent of investment in stocks?

2 Would you prefer to invest in a fire insurance company which writes a small percentage of premiums to capital, or one which does a large amount of insurance business? Are there any tax disadvantages to operating as "an investment company which does a little insurance underwriting on the side"?

3 If you wished to predict the probable net earnings per share of a property-liability company over the next few years, could you make an estimate using the trend of premiums earned per share, the trend of loss-and-expense ratios, the trend of investment earnings per share, and a computed tax rate? Explain the technique.

4 Explain the difference between statutory underwriting income and adjusted underwriting income. Which is larger in a year when premiums written decline below those of previous years?

5 Why do some analysts argue that "liquidating value" of a fire insurance stock should be computed by adding an equity of about 17½ per cent of unearned premium income and subtracting 25 per cent of unrealized security profits from net worth as shown in the balance sheet? Is this realistic if the purpose is to gauge net worth as a factor in future operations?

6   Is a property-liability company's insurance operation unprofitable if the loss ratio is 63 per cent and the expense ratio 38 per cent? What action would you take if you managed such a company?

7   If the direct-writing process is lower in cost than the traditional agency system, why do the major property-liability insurors not change over? Will they remain at a cost disadvantage indefinitely?

8   Explain the process by which a property-liability insuror's statutory underwriting income is adjusted. What adjustments in the company's balance sheet are thereby implied? What analogous adjustments are made in the income statements and balance sheets of life insurance firms? Why?

9   Can the stock life insurance companies expect to enjoy both rapid volume growth and a wide margin of profit indefinitely? Consider the mortality tables, interest-rate basis, and expense loading which regulatory authorities will demand in fixed-premium (guaranteed cost) policies.

10   Does the life annuity business have the inherent profit advantages which characterize life insurance underwriting? What about accident and health?

11   Is the value of a life company's "insurance in force" analogous to the "equity in unearned premium reserve" used in fire insurance analysis?

12   Compare the growth rate of earnings and net worth for Franklin Life, Lincoln National, and Southwestern Life with American Home Products, Texas Utilities, and Bank America Corporation. What conclusion do you reach about the comparative attractiveness of life insurance issues and representative nontechnological growth stocks in other industries?

13   Should a property-liability insurance company's statement of stockholder net worth include the value of unrealized securities profits? Would a "lower of cost or market" valuation of securities held be more conservative and less beguiling to investors?

14   Is it more advantageous for a personal finance company to borrow heavily at long term than for a commercial finance company to do so? Why, or why not?

15   What factors dominate brokerage-house earnings? Are the stocks of brokerage firms in general likely to make good long-term investments?

REFERENCES

Badger, Ralph E., and Paul B. Coffman: *Investment Analysis*, McGraw-Hill Book Company, New York, 1967, Chap. 18.

Badger, Ralph C., Harold W. Torgerson, and Harry G. Guthmann: *Investment Principles and Practices*, 6th ed., Prentice-Hall, Englewood Cliffs, N.J., 1969, Chap. 14.

Bellmore, Douglas H., and John C. Ritchie, Jr.: *Investments*, 3d ed., South-Western Publishing Company, Incorporated, Cincinnati, 1969, Chap. 25.

Best, A. M., Company: *Best's Insurance Reports* (two volumes: Life/Health and Property/Liability), annual; *Best's Insurance Securities Research Service*, *Best's Executive Data Service*, both loose-leaf, Morristown, N.J.

Dougall, Herbert E.: *Investments*, 8th ed., Prentice-Hall, Inc., Englewood Cliffs, N.J., 1968, Chap. 30.

Griffith, Reynolds: *The Valuation of Life Insurance Stocks*, Financial Publications, Inc., Denton, Tex., 1967.

Hayes, Douglas A.: *Investments: Analysis and Management*, The Macmillan Company, New York, 1966, Chap. 21.

Standard & Poor's Corporation: *Industry Surveys*, sections on insurance company stocks, finance, and personal loans, New York.

**PUBLIC
SECURITIES**

The classification *public securities* includes the certificated debt of the United States Treasury and of the various federal government agencies which borrow on their own account, together with the sum total of debt-type obligations sold by the 50 states and their almost innumerable political subdivisions. Although these securities span an enormous range of issuers, types, terms, maturities, and marketability and yield characteristics, they are generally the domain of conservative investors. For the most part, the obligations of American governments —national, state, and local—can be considered to be of high quality and largely free of the credit risk. The Treasury's marketable obligations are also substantially exempt from the market risk, and this is reasonably true of the larger issues of state and local government securities. On the other hand, since all government securities are debt-type obligations, all are strongly affected by the price-level risk, and the longer-term marketable issues are also heavily subject to the money-rate risk. Along with other marketable debts, American government securities have experienced a large rise in yields during the inflationary years since 1965, and the continuing popularity with investors of the longer-dated issues seems certain to hinge upon the nation's ability to slow down the shrinkage of the dollar's buying power.

From the standpoint of both investor appeal and market behavior, the public securities market divides most naturally into a United States government securities sector in which the interest paid is subject to federal income tax, and a state and municipal obligations category in which interest is generally tax-exempt. This chapter, following the customary division, begins with federal government obligations.

UNITED STATES GOVERNMENT SECURITIES

The total interest-bearing debt of the United States government in June 1972 stood at approximately 427 billion dollars. Not all of the government's debt was available for private investment, since government-operated agencies and trust funds such as the social security reserves and deposit insurance funds owned about 111 billion dollars and the Federal Reserve banks held nearly 72 billion dollars more, but the remaining 244 billion dollars still comprised a tidy sum.

Government securities are owned by large numbers of investors. At year-end 1971, these securities constituted 12 per cent of banks' earning assets, a substantial part of the liquidity reserves of financial and nonfinancial corporations, and at face value, nearly 80 billion dollars of individual wealth.

INVESTMENT STANDING OF GOVERNMENT SECURITIES

United States government securities are generally reputed to be about as certain of payment as any obligation known on this troubled planet. They are included without question on all lists of securities permitted as investments for banks, trust funds, and insurance reserves, and they yield as little as any securities of comparable maturity and tax position.

It is said that the two prime tests of quality in a sovereign government's obligations are its ability to pay and its willingness to pay. The ability of the federal government to pay its expenses plus the interest and principal on its debts does not seem open to serious question, and its full taxing and borrowing powers stand behind the Treasury's obligations. The government also controls the banking system and in particular the Federal Reserve banks: whenever payments and borrowings from private investors fail to meet the Treasury's needs, bank credit and currency expansion can always provide any reasonably required sums.

The general willingness of the American electorate to pay the public debt also seems firm: there is no bitterness against office holders or former public officials which might cause a desire to default. High taxes are willingly accepted by the American people, and political leaders are fully aware of the importance of government bonds to the country's financial life. The trend of federal finances and the federal debt over the years since 1929 is presented in Table 20-1.

Although the government's credit stability and close liaison with the banking system appear to guarantee that its obligations will be paid, the never-ending procession of federal deficits and perpetually rising debt confronts investors with two other possibilities: first, that continuing credit inflation may sharply raise the price level and conversely cheapen the dollars in which government and all other bondholders are paid; and second, that there may possibly be occasions when the public welfare will require some restriction of bondholders' rights. For example, it might some day be necessary to forbid banks to sell their government bonds for a time, or to deny individuals the privilege of cashing their savings bonds, as part of a program of inflation control. This would be no more drastic than the government's repudiation in 1933 of its promise to pay its outstanding bonds in gold coin of stipulated weight and fineness.

On balance, however, it seems fair to say that government securities offer the investor an unexcelled financial reserve resource, readily cashable or marketable, and eligible for every kind of trust or bank investment. Price-level inflation, as it continues, will affect all other dollar obligations similarly. And in 1972 any restriction of bondholders' rights seemed remote and unlikely.

TYPES OF FEDERAL OBLIGATIONS

The federal credit is at present involved in assuring payment of four groups of obligations: the public debt of the United States Treasury, federal agency securities, government-sponsored agency securities, and the participation certificates issued by federal agencies. Of these four, the public debt is the largest and most important. In mid-1972 it included $257 billion of marketable public debt, so called because the securities may be sold by one private citizen to another; $79 billion of nonmarketable debt, such as savings bonds; and $90 billion of special bonds sold to government agencies, such as the social security and veterans life insurance trust funds.

The second type of federal obligation, the bonds of the nonguaranteed federal agency, is the debt of a federally controlled agency whose credit is not guaranteed by the United States, but which is likely to be supported because the federal government's supervisory authority implies the capacity to prevent defaults. Bonds in this category include those of the Government National Mortgage Association, the Export-Import Bank, and Tennessee Valley Authority. The total volume of this debt in mid-1972 aggregated $11.3 billion.

The third and most rapidly growing sector of federal credit consists of the debt of government-sponsored "privatized" agencies, including the Federal Home Loan banks, Federal National Mortgage Association, Federal Land banks, Federal Intermediate Credit banks, and Bank for Cooperatives. Most of these institutions are former federal agencies, now technically converted to private ownership but still borrowing under the federal umbrella and virtually certain to be supplied with funds by Congress should defaults ever threaten. This debt, nonexistent as a category before 1968, totaled $40.4 billion in mid-1972.

Despite the overwhelming likelihood that both federal agency and government-sponsored agency obligations would never be permitted to default, these taxable, nonguaranteed bonds yield a slightly higher rate than can be had on direct or fully guaranteed obligations. All these securities usually qualify as legal investments for savings banks and trust funds in most states.

The fourth category of federal securities comprises the participation certificates (PCs) of the Export-Import Bank and the Government National Mortgage Association (GNMA). The bulk of the PCs outstanding consists of GNMA "pass through" instruments whereby investors receive monthly payments of principal and interest from pools of government-guaranteed mortgages, whether payments are collected or not. Private lenders pool mortgages of the Federal Housing Ad-

Table 20-1   *Trend of federal finances, 1929–1972 fiscal years ended June 30*

Year	Revenues, billions	Expenditures, billions	Total interest-bearing debt, billions	Revenues as a per cent of national income
1929	$ 4.03	$ 3.85	$ 16.64	4.6
1933	2.08	4.33	22.16	5.1
1937	4.98	7.76	40.47	7.2
1941	7.23	13.39	54.75	7.8
1945	44.48	98.42	256.77	24.5
1950	36.50	39.62	255.21	16.9
1955	60.39	64.57	271.74	18.3
1960	77.76	76.54	283.24	19.1
1970	193.74	194.46	370.3	24.2
1971	188.39	210.32	397.5	22.1
1972	208.60	230.51	426.7	23.1

Sources: Adapted from *Treasury Bulletin* and *Federal Reserve Bulletin.* Revenues and expenditures figures of 1950 and prior years are older series slightly different in composition from subsequent data. Debt figures do not include matured securities not yet presented for payment, averaging about 4 billion in recent years.

ministration and the Veterans Administration and sell the securities against them, and "Ginnie Mae" (GNMA) guarantees the securities with the full faith and credit of the United States. Interest is not exempt from federal income, estate, or gift taxes, but the fact that it is paid monthly makes the yield slightly higher than on similarly priced bonds. Mortgage-backed pass-through securities were available during 1972 in denominations as low as $25,000.

MARKETABLE TREASURY ISSUES

The $257 billion of marketable treasury obligations outstanding at mid-1972 included $49 billion of treasury bonds, $113 billion of treasury notes, and $95 billion of treasury bills. No treasury certificates of indebtedness were outstanding at the time.

The treasury bonds consisted of 22 issues maturing between 1972 and 1998 which were originally issued for terms running from 10 to 40 years. Interest rates range from 2½ to 7 per cent, reflecting the different rates which the Treasury had to pay at various times in order to sell its bonds at par. Most issues were available in either coupon or registered form. Minimum denominations available in the various issues were either $500 or $1,000, and maximums went as high as $1,000,000. Of the 22 issues, 17 were acceptable at par value by the government in payment of taxes levied upon the estate of a deceased owner. All issues were fully subject to federal income tax. Since all these features affect the usefulness of the bonds to their owners, they also affect the prices of the bonds. It is important, therefore, for an investor interested in treasury bonds to compare the details of the issues and obtain the ones which best suit his purposes, price considered.

Treasury notes are obligations whose term exceeds 1 year but does not exceed 7 years. Interest rates on notes issued between 1967 and 1972 ranged from $4\frac{1}{2}$ to $8\frac{1}{8}$ per cent. The coupon form is generally used, and the minimum denomination is ordinarily $1,000. No restrictions are placed on ownership, transferability, or use as collateral, and no federal tax exemptions or special tax privileges are granted.

Treasury certificates of indebtedness are short-term obligations, usually of 1-year term in coupon form, noncallable, unlimited as to ownership, transferable, fully usable as collateral, and subject to all federal taxes. None were outstanding in 1972, and none had been issued by the Treasury since 1966.

Treasury bills are short-term obligations, mostly maturing either 13 or 26 weeks after issuance, but also including 1-year issues and occasional issues scheduled to mature on federal tax payment dates not more than a year away. The 13- and 26-week issues are offered for subscription each week. Bills do not bear running interest; they mature at face value and are sold initially at a discount below face value. It is the Treasury's practice to invite subscribers to indicate the maximum amount they are willing to pay for new bills at a weekly auction. Anyone may subscribe; bids are forwarded by banks and brokers to the Federal Reserve banks, and the Treasury then allots bills to the highest-bidding subscribers at their own bid prices down to the lowest bid price it finds itself compelled to accept in order to raise the necessary money. Since 1969, bills have not been available in denominations of less than $10,000 (a limit set to discourage small savers from withdrawing savings and loan accounts to buy bills when bill yields were higher than yields on share accounts.) Bills are salable, pledgeable, and fully subject to federal taxes. In 1967–1972, the interest yield on 13-week bills ranged between 3 and 8 per cent.

TERMS AND FEATURES

Instead of the contractual bond indenture which is customary in the issuance of corporation bonds, the usual public obligation follows the terms indicated in the statute authorizing the bonds, with the addition of such details as the statute may leave to the discretion of the supervising officer. The actual terms and features of each issue are summarized in the official announcement offering the bonds. No corporate trustee is used, as the enforcement of the terms of the issue is the obligation of regular public officials, and all payments are made through Federal Reserve banks or Treasury offices.

Significant terms and features which may characterize federal obligations include the following:

1 Maturity and call dates Federal obligations run for terms ranging from 60 days to 50 years. Several of the longer issues are callable at par in their last 1 to 5 years; such issues are cited as though they had two maturity dates, as, for example, the Treasury 4¼s of 1987–1992, but the earlier date merely indicates the date the bonds become callable at par; the later date is the maturity date. Most issues are noncallable. Call price is always par plus accrued interest, without premium. Savings bonds and a few other issues will be paid off in cash on demand or upon short notice, at the request of the holder.

2 Denomination and form Denominations vary from $500 to $1,000,000, with most long-term bonds available in units ranging from $1,000 to $100,000. Most issues are available in either coupon or fully registered form, with either one exchangeable for the other, but variations exist. Savings bonds are available only in registered form.

3 Eligibility to own Marketable government securities may be owned by anyone. Savings bonds are variously restricted as to ownership and the amounts a single holder may acquire within a year's time.

4 Transferability and collateral value All the so-called marketable issues are transferable from one holder to another and, consequently, are useful as collateral for loans. Savings bonds are transferable only upon the death of the holder and in a limited number of other specified situations, hence are not useful as collateral.

5 Acceptability for taxes Seventeen large issues of marketable bonds are acceptable at par and accrued interest in payment of estate taxes levied at the owner's death. However, tenders for estate taxes have reduced the outstanding volume of these bonds in recent years, and federal law now bars the issuance of new bonds with the estate tax privilege.

6 Taxability All federal bonds are free of state and local property and income taxes, but fully subject to federal income tax. No bonds have any exemption from federal or state estate and inheritance taxes.

NONMARKETABLE FEDERAL ISSUES

Nonmarketable (i.e., nonsalable) federal obligations in public hands at mid-1972 included $56.5 billion of United States savings bonds and $19.8 billion in other obligations, mostly notes or certificates issued to foreign governments or central banks in exchange for unwanted dollars. United States savings bonds consisted of $46.7 billion of Series E and $8.8 billion of Series H bonds.

United States savings bonds are unique in that they are medium-term (5 years, 10 months to 10 years) obligations which may be cashed in before maturity at the option of the holder. The yield on the investment is reduced if the bonds are not held for their full term, but the complete arrangement provides a yield commensurate with the term of holding plus perfect liquidity. The various series of savings bonds have been designed to appeal to different investors, and from time to time the proffered features have been changed to conform to market conditions. Outstanding savings bonds are therefore not all alike; two series of bonds and one of notes are outstanding and eight different versions of Series E (different in length of term, yield, and redemption values) have been sold from 1942 through 1972.[1]

The popular Series E savings bonds have always been intended principally for sale to individuals. They are continuously offered for sale by post offices, banks, other financial agencies, and through payroll deduction plans in denominations ranging from $25 to $1,000 maturity value.[2] The bonds do not pay running interest; they are sold at 75 per cent of face value, and their cash value rises annually by a progressively increasing amount until maturity is reached. The Series E bonds sold in 1972 were promised a full-term average rate of 5.5 per cent; they mature at 102.98 per cent of face value in 5 years and 10 months. Earlier Series E bonds receive still higher rates during their later years, a change made in 1970 and designed to bring their full-period yields to 5.5 per cent when they are held to maturity. All Series E bonds have the privilege of at least one 10-year extension at maturity, or they may be converted at accrued value into Series H bonds at any time.

Rising interest rates and difficult borrowing problems have prompted the Treasury to make important concessions to the holders of older Series E bonds. First, to encourage holders to retain their unmatured older bonds instead of cashing them in, the Treasury in 1959, 1965, 1968, 1969, and 1970 raised the yield rates on such bonds. Second, the Treasury announced that maturing bonds need

---

[1] In 1952, 1957, 1959, 1965, 1968, 1969, and 1970, certain features such as the term to maturity, the yield rate, the schedule of redemption values, the annual per person purchase limits, and the extended-maturity options were changed. The changes were not all retroactive, so outstanding bonds are not all alike.

[2] A $10,000 denomination bond is sold, but only through payroll savings plans.

not be cashed (in which case the interest accumulation would be subject to ordinary income taxes) but instead may be retained without change to earn a new 10-year term of compound interest. The option to cash in the total accumulation at any time remains available. Third, older bonds dated in the 1940s, which were previously permitted to start a second decade of interest earnings, were allowed a third interest cycle when the second cycle ended.

Series E bonds are issued in registered form only and may be issued in the name of one individual, in the names of two individuals either of whom is entitled to payment, or in the name of one individual but payable in case of his death (P.O.D.) to a second named individual. Certain categories of personal fiduciaries, associations, partnerships, and corporations may also own the bonds. Transfers are not permitted except to an heir in case of the death of the owner(s) and in a limited few other cases; hence the bonds cannot be resold or used as collateral. Since 1970, an individual owner has been able to purchase up to $5,000 face value of Series E bonds in any one year. This limit applies per person; co-owners may each buy a full quota.

Interest earned on savings bonds is subject to federal income tax as ordinary income, not as capital gain, but it may be reported either as it accrues or when it is collected. Interest earned on Series E bonds is not collected until received in cash; extensions of Series E bonds or conversions into Series H bonds defer taxability.

The Series E bonds have three unique tax advantages which deserve special emphasis. First, an investor may cash them and take the interest income for tax purposes (or report the accumulated accrued interest and shift thereafter to an accrual basis) in any year when lack of income or deductible losses reduce his tax bracket or make his year tax-free. Second, investors more than 49 years old may expect to carry their bonds into postretirement years when their incomes will be low and their exemptions greater, thus reducing the tax depletion of the interest earnings. Third, investors holding Series E bonds may at any time convert them at accumulated cash value into Series H bonds. No income tax is payable on the accumulated Series E interest until the Series H bond is finally paid in cash. Meanwhile, the Series H bonds pay cash interest on their full face value.[3]

Series H bonds resemble Series E bonds except that they are sold at face value, pay interest semiannually by check, and mature in 10 years. Their average yield rate as established in 1970 is 5.5 per cent for the full 10-year term. They are issued

---

[3] Another kind of tax advantage may accrue to parents who wish to build an education fund for their child. They may buy E bonds registered in the child's name. After the first year, they file a federal income tax return for the child, reporting the current interest on the bond. No income tax is owed if the child's income is less than $900 per year. In later years, no tax return for the child is required unless his income exceeds $600. When funds are needed for college expenses, the bonds can be cashed in with no income tax to be paid on the accumulated interest.

in denominations of $500, $1,000, and $5,000, and each investor is limited to an annual purchase of $5,000. The names in which bonds may be issued and the transfer limitations are the same as for Series E. Series H bonds are always cashable at par any time after 6 months from issue date. The interest payments on this bond are not uniform in amount; in order to provide an incentive to the holder to retain his bond, the interest payments average 5.12 per cent during the first 5 years and 6 per cent for the remaining 5 years to maturity. Like Series E bonds, Series H bonds issued before August 1970 have been adjusted to the new yield rates; the increase will show up in checks during the second 5 years, as well as during any extended holding periods.

"Freedom Shares," United States savings notes sold to E-bond purchasers in the 1967–1970 period, have been discontinued, but holders have been granted a 10-year extension beyond their original 4½-year maturity. Like extended savings bonds, Freedom Shares will pay a flat 5½ per cent during their extension period.

From the mid-1950s until 1970, the yields on savings bonds were generally below those offered by savings accounts and money-market instruments, and from 1964 through 1970, investor cash-ins of savings bonds annually exceeded new sales. In 1972, however, the 5.5 per cent yield on savings bonds noticeably exceeded the 5.3 per cent average yield available from savings and loan share accounts, the 5.1 per cent expected from the average mutual savings bank, and the 4½ to 5 per cent offered by short-term savings-type deposits in commercial banks.

The government has made every effort to keep the legal technicalities which affect the ownership of savings bonds at a minimum. For example, a savings bond issued to two persons as coowners (John Doe or Mary Doe) may be cashed before maturity or collected at maturity by either, and the interest checks are cashable by either. On the death of one coowner no transfer is required; the survivor has full authority. At the survivor's death the bond is a part of his estate. In the case of bonds issued to an individual but payable at his death to a named beneficiary, the bonds will be cashed or transferred to the name of the beneficiary after the owner's death without waiting for probate orders or other legal details, if the beneficiary obtains possession of the bond and delivers it, with proper proof of the owner's death, to the transfer office. These procedures can be very useful to investors who wish to make some of their funds available to their heirs without the delay and expense of probate.

OWNERSHIP OF TREASURY OBLIGATIONS

The government's direct obligations are widely scattered among all sorts of owners. In mid-1972 the commercial banks held 14 per cent of them, the reserve banks 17 per cent, individuals 18 per cent, insurance companies 1 per cent, state and local government agencies 5 per cent, federally controlled trust funds 26 per cent, corporations 2 per cent, foreigner interests 12 per cent, and other holders 5 per cent.[4]

The uses made of government securities by their institutional holders become apparent in the maturity classifications of the holdings. Because of the great size of the government securities market and its freedom from price fluctuations other than those caused by changes in interest rates, its short-term securities can be safely used for temporary employment of funds, and longer-term ones can be used for funds which are held for long-term investment, even if the money is to be switched to long-term corporates or mortgages as these become available. Savings banks, state and municipal pension funds, and government-administered trust funds have used a high proportion of long-term treasury bonds in their investment portfolios, maximum yields being their main consideration. Banks, business corporations, and foreign investors, all of which emphasize liquidity, hold large quantities of bills and notes. Corporations make particularly heavy use of treasury bills for temporary storage of working capital and as a device for accumulating income tax reserves; the latter use has become so important that the Treasury sometimes sells special issues of bills designed to mature on tax payment dates.

ECONOMIC POSITION OF GOVERNMENT SECURITIES

Despite their safety, liquidity, and widespread popularity with investors, government securities raise four kinds of problems for the American economy. (1) The enormous growth of the total federal debt, including especially the obligations of government-sponsored agencies, increasingly threatens to monopolize the nation's capital markets and crowd out other meritorious and necessary types of financing. (2) The continuing management of this large debt calls for great skill on the part of Treasury and Federal Reserve officials who share this responsibility. (3) The continual shortening of the average maturity of this huge debt increases the difficulty of controlling excess liquidity and inflationary threats in the economy. (4) Finally, the prices of longer-term government obligations have become extremely unstable as the economy fluctuates between tight-money episodes imposed by attempts to control inflationary booms and easy-money interludes arising from still more frantic efforts to arrest alternating tendencies toward recession.

In recent years, the Treasury's direct debt has grown much less rapidly than the "unofficial" debt which the government has incurred through various avenues of "back-door" financing, notably the privatized agencies. Table 20-2 illustrates the scope of this problem. It shows that from mid-year, 1965, through year-end,

---

[4] Statistics on ownership of government securities may be found regularly in the *Federal Reserve Bulletin* and in the *Treasury Bulletin*.

Table 20-2   *Grand totals of federal and agency debt, 1965 through 1971 (In millions)*

Fiscal Years	Public debt securities	Federal agency issues*	Privatized agencies†	Grand total
1965	$317,274	$ 9,335	$ 8,309	$334,918
1966	319,907	13,377	10,436	343,720
1967	326,221	18,455	9,937	354,613
1968	347,578	24,399	10,873	382,850
1969	353,720	14,249‡	25,031‡	393,000
1970	389,158	12,510	35,742	437,410
1971	389,130	12,163	37,086	447,379
1971 Dec	424,131	11,044	39,840	475,015

*Includes debt of the Government National Mortgage Association, Export-Import Bank, and Tennessee Valley Authority, and for fiscal years 1965 through 1968, also the Federal National Mortgage Association, Bank for Cooperatives, and Federal Intermediate Credit Banks.

†Includes debt of the Federal Home Loan banks and Federal Land Banks, and for fiscal years beginning 1969, the Federal National Mortgage Association, Federal Intermediate Credit Banks, and Bank for Cooperatives.

‡Reflects switch of the three last-named agencies from federal to privatized status.

1971, the direct public debt increased by 34 per cent while the debt of privatized government agencies swelled by 379 per cent. The government also incurred additional potential debt through a widening range of guarantees for private debt securities, such as the one accorded Lockheed Corporation and the government-guaranteed Penn Central trustee certificates whose issuance began in January 1971.

Nearly all government and government-sponsored agencies appear to be expansion-minded, and if they can employ money they will borrow it. In 1972, it was estimated that federal and federally assisted borrowing would account for half the nation's total credit demands during the year. In increasing degree, borrowers whom market forces might otherwise oblige to curtail their requests are demanding the sponsorship or guarantees of the federal government to ensure their ability to borrow in competition with private enterprise. A number of agencies already utilize government backing to assist borrowing by the housing industry. A bill pending in Congress in 1972 would create a Federal Financing Bank; presumably this institution would not only consolidate the borrowing efforts of existing government agencies, but would also extend the protective umbrella of government-assisted borrowing to state and local governments, minority business enterprises, bankrupt railroads and defense contractors, and other necessitous borrowers with political influence. In these circumstances, it seemed probable that unless government-backed borrowings were more carefully disciplined than they had been through 1972, serious capital shortages might develop for corporations and other nonsponsored users of borrowed funds.

Growth of the public debt also imposes mammoth tasks of management upon Treasury officials. Treasury financing is so enormous in scope that it impinges heavily on the monetary system, on the general level of interest rates, and on the availability of loan funds to private borrowers. Careful calculations as to the amount and nature of the new treasury securities offerings which the market can absorb, and the cooperation of the Federal Reserve System in making sure that temporary financing through banks and government bond dealers can be had, are virtual necessities in connection with a bond sale.

In order to market medium- and long-term securities with a minimum of money-market disruption, the Treasury has developed three definite techniques:

1   Medium- and long-term offerings for cash are avoided or limited when state, municipal, corporate, and mortgage borrowers are pressing on the supply of funds, except when national economic policy is agreeable to a tightening of money rates, or when it seems possible to sell a refunding issue directly to the holders of a maturing issue.

2   Holders of maturing securities are frequently permitted to exchange their holdings on a moderately favorable basis for new securities. Often they are offered a choice of two or three new securities, some of which may be "reopenings" (additional amounts) of securities already outstanding. Because these "rights" (exchanges) have a slight value advantage and are known in advance, holders or purchasers of the old securities usually exchange them and disruption of normal loan channels is not excessive.

3   In order to prevent maturities, the Treasury engages in "advance refundings." Holders of outstanding issues within 10 years of maturity are occasionally invited to exchange them on attractive terms for other issues having more distant maturity dates.

Efforts to lengthen out the Treasury's debt have proved uniformly unsuccessful over the past two decades. In mid-1972, the average maturity of marketable United States Treasury securities was only 3 years and 3 months. This suggested that much of the debt was so close to maturity that it could not be depreciated significantly in price by a Federal Reserve tight-money policy, and that it would probably supply a dangerous degree of liquidity in any inflationary boom. However, since 1965–1966, when long-term yields rose sharply, the Treasury has been forced to do practically all its borrowing on a short- or medium-term basis. Legislation dating from 1917 and 1918 prohibited the Treasury from placing a coupon of more than $4\frac{1}{4}$ per cent on any obligation of more than 5 years' maturity (since 1967, more than 7 years). This obsolete limitation was partially lifted in

March 1971 when Congress granted the Treasury authority to issue up to $10 billion in bonds without regard to the 4¼ per cent ceiling. By late 1972, more than $7 billion of bonds with coupons in the 6 to 7 per cent range had been sold by the Treasury under its new authority, but the government's long-range ability and willingness to lessen the liquidity of its publicly held debt remained open to question.

Although the Treasury's immediate interests would doubtless be served by the maintenance of stable interest rates and consequent stable bond prices, the general public interest requires Treasury cooperation with the Federal Reserve System in a program of monetary control. Since 1951 the money supply and Treasury refunding programs have ostensibly been coordinated to restrain inflationary booms and stimulate the economy in recessions, and since 1960 an attempt to hold down long-term interest rates while maintaining short-term rates at a medium-high level has been added. (The latter objective is a balance-of-payments palliative to encourage the temporary investment of foreign-owned funds here.) These monetary control programs, plus natural economic forces, have produced unprecedented fluctuations in the price of treasury bonds during these years. For example, the Treasury 3⅛s of 1990 were marketed at par in recessionary 1958, sold at 84 during the tight-money period in 1959, rose again to 96 during the 1960 recession, fell as low as 74 during the 1966–1967 credit squeeze, rose to 87 during 1968, fell to 59 in mid-1970, and rose as high as 80 during 1971–1972. Monetary control programs are of course relatively harmless to the holders of short-term securities. Investors can therefore obtain absolute certainty, high marketability, and great liquidity in short-term governments, plus yields which ranged as high as 8 per cent in 1970. On long-term securities, the same high certainty and marketability prevail, but price changes as great as 30 per cent are possible.

It would of course be impossible for government bonds to move in response to money-supply and interest-rate changes without similar fluctuations in other bond yields and prices. After all, if government bond yields declined because of increased money supplies, people would sell governments and buy high-grade corporates until the two yields were again in a normal relation. Similarly, yields on treasury bills and other short-term papers are related. Table 20-3 illustrates these tendencies.

MARKET FOR GOVERNMENT SECURITIES

Though treasury bonds are listed on the New York Stock Exchange, the principal market for all transferable government securities is over the counter. About two dozen large-scale dealers, including the bond departments of several banks, are usually ready to buy or sell any issue of federal bills, certificates, notes, or bonds. Several of these dealers act regularly as brokers or dealers in transactions involv-

Table 20-3 *Percentage yields of fully taxable government securities compared with private obligations (Average annual yields)*

Year	Bills, 3 months*	Bonds and notes, 3 to 5 years	Bonds, over 10 years	High-grade corporate bonds	Finance company paper, 3 to 6 months
1965	3.95	4.22	4.21	4.49	4.27
1966	4.88	5.16	4.66	5.13	5.42
1967	4.32	5.07	4.85	5.51	4.89
1968	5.34	5.59	5.25	6.18	5.69
1969	6.68	6.85	6.10	7.03	7.16
1970	6.46	7.37	6.59	8.04	7.23
1971	4.35	5.77	5.74	7.39	4.91

* New issue rate.
Source: Federal Reserve Bulletin.

ing the Reserve System and are known to cooperate in implementing Reserve System policies. In addition to the large-scale dealers, many of the large banks of the country make dealers' markets in selected issues.

Dealers' markets on government securities are remarkably close; for example, bids and offers on substantial sums in treasury bonds are usually separated by only one-fourth to one-half of one percentage point, and on treasury notes this spread is often only one-eighth or less. On small quantities, the spread is approximately doubled. On treasury bills, which are used for temporary investment of cash by large businesses, local tax collectors, and financial institutions, transactions in multiples of 1 million dollars are frequent and very low in cost. The dealers' market is not available exclusively on large transactions, either; small banks, trust funds, and substantial individual investors can often obtain the inside market price by going directly to the dealers. However, it is more convenient for most individuals to transact their government bond business through their banks or regular brokerage connections; in such cases the brokerage commission is usually ¼ of 1 per cent of the par value of the bonds. Most personal market transactions in government securities are in units of $5,000 to $10,000 or more, because small investors who might deal in lesser sums usually prefer the nonmarketable savings bonds.

As has been previously noted, treasury bonds, notes, and certificates are quoted in percentages of par value, with fractional percentages expressed in thirty-seconds. For convenience in writing, the unit percentage is placed before, and the number of thirty-seconds after, a decimal point; thus, 101.5 means 101⁵⁄₃₂, and 101.29 means $101^{29}\!/_{32}$. Treasury bills are quoted in terms of yields; for example, 6.23 per cent bid, 6.01 per cent asked. A three-month bill yielding an annual rate of 6 per cent would sell at approximately $985.22 per $1,000 of maturity value.

�֍ STATE AND MUNICIPAL BONDS

Approximately 175 billion dollars worth of state and municipal bonds were held by American investors in 1972. Although this sum represents only about 20 per cent of the total volume of all bonds in investors' hands, it is of great importance to those who emphasize a combination of safety and tax avoidance. Most state and municipal bonds are high grade, and the interest they pay is exempt from federal income tax.

Since 1965, most of these bonds have been issued in $5,000 denominations, or in multiples thereof, which have succeeded the older, conventional $1,000 unit. "Tax-exempts" are usually issued in bearer form. For the sake of brevity, bond dealers often refer to all types of state and municipal bonds collectively as "municipals."

TAX-EXEMPT INTEREST: THE OUTSTANDING FEATURE

The principal appeal of state and municipal bonds lies in the already noted fact that their interest is not includable by a taxpayer as gross income in his federal income tax return. The exemption rests upon specific provisions of present federal tax statutes, plus the assumption that the sovereignty of the states would make unconstitutional any federal tax which burdened the borrowing operations of either the states or their subordinate units. However, there is no clear constitutional provision to this effect, and many people argue that federal taxes could be levied upon state bond interest just as readily as upon state salaries. Also, many people argue that interest paid on assessment bonds which finance sewers or pavements serving private property, or on revenue bonds which finance a municipal power plant, can hardly be called a cost of government. In any event, the tax law is still definite; state and municipal interest payments are exempt from federal income taxes.

The states are of course free to tax the interest paid by their own bonds, by those of other states, and by municipal obligations of all states when the bonds are held by taxpayers within their jurisdictions. The states which use income taxes generally tax the interest on out-of-state municipals, but the home-state bonds are usually exempt if owned by individuals and often when owned by banks or corporations. Investors are thus induced to favor bonds originating in their home states.[5]

Tax-exempt bonds have great attraction for high-bracket individuals, private trust funds, and fully taxable corporations, for obvious reasons. Ownership figures in the 1966 annual report of the Secretary of the Treasury indicate that in 1966, individuals, partnerships, and personal trusts held 38 per cent of those outstanding, commercial banks held 40 per cent, and insurance companies 14 per cent. Since high-bracket investors obtain greater advantage from the tax-free feature than others can, they customarily bid the bonds up to a yield basis which is unattractive to a low-income investor.

The great importance attached to the tax-exemption feature leads many dealers in municipal bonds to publish *tables of tax-free yield equivalents*, which are intended to point out the small amount of tax-free interest necessary to equal the posttax remainder from any taxable income. Such tables (see Table 20-4 for an example) usually assume that the highest tax bracket into which an investor's income reaches is the one which is applicable in determining investment policy. Thus Table 20-4 indicates that for a man with $50,000 of taxable income whose highest bracket rate is 62 per cent, a 3.04 per cent tax-free yield is as good as an 8 per cent taxable yield. This is weighty reasoning which probably deserves consideration by many people who know nothing of municipal bonds, but it must also be remembered that other forms of investment also have their advantages — superior liquidity, price-level protection, possibility of lightly taxed capital gains, etc.

[5] For a brief review of the tax status of all public bonds, see *Moody's Municipal and Government Manual*, Special Features section.

Table 20-4 *Excerpts from table of tax-free yield equivalents*

Individual tax		Gross yield of taxable securities, in percent					
Taxable income	Bracket tax rate in 1971, %	4.00	5.00	6.00	7.00	8.00	9.00
		Equivalent yield of tax-exempt securities, in percent					
$ 2,000	19	3.24	4.05	4.86	5.67	6.48	7.29
6,000	24	3.04	3.80	4.56	5.32	6.08	6.84
10,000	27	2.92	3.65	4.38	5.11	5.84	6.57
20,000	38	2.48	3.10	3.72	4.34	4.96	5.58
50,000	62	1.52	1.90	2.28	2.66	3.04	3.42
100,000	70	1.20	1.50	1.80	2.10	2.40	2.70
Corporation	48	2.08	2.60	3.12	3.64	4.16	4.68

Two further comments concerning state and municipal bonds need to be made. First, these bonds are fully subject to all applicable federal and state taxes on estates, inheritances, and gifts; and capital gains on them are taxable. Second, there are many long-term, low-coupon municipals which sell at a discount, hence have satisfactory yields to maturity composed partly of cash interest and partly of appreciation of principal. In nearly all such cases, only the cash interest is tax-exempt; when the profit on the principal is finally realized by sale or collection of the bond, it is a capital gain, subject to both state and federal income taxes at the low capital gains rates. If a municipal bond is purchased at a premium above par, no tax-reducing capital loss can be realized if the bond is held to maturity and collected at par; in this case the premium is assumed to be amortized against the cash interest to net a yield below the coupon interest rate.

TYPES OF BONDS

State and municipal public bodies in the United States derive their powers from the sovereign authority of the states, through the provisions of the state constitutions, state statutes, and state-granted municipal charters. The powers of each state and its municipalities are unique to that state and need not be closely parallel to those found in other states. It is therefore necessary for an investor in state or municipal bonds to examine the powers and limitations of the borrower as well as the nature of the promises made on the bond if he is to understand his investment. To facilitate this task, it seems necessary to classify the bonds into four general types and the borrowers into five.

State and municipal bonds may be roughly classified as (1) full faith and credit bonds, (2) revenue bonds, (3) assessment bonds, and (4) hybrids between these three groups. It is important to remember that although bonds within the groups will be similar in many respects, there will also be great differences in both the legal and financial positions of different issues.

Full faith and credit bonds, which are also referred to as general obligations or as fully tax-supported obligations, are those whose payment is unconditionally promised by a governmental unit which has the power to levy taxes. The majority of state, county, city, town, and school district obligations are of this sort, though the types of taxes which these units may use vary considerably. In general, fully tax-supported public obligations are highly regarded and command the highest prices and lowest yields in the public bond group.

Revenue bonds are bonds issued by publicly owned business agencies such as water departments, electric power departments, toll bridge authorities, and the like, on which payment is promised only from the earnings of the business. Most revenue bonds are the obligations of monopoly utilities serving growing demands, their record has been good, and the bonds in general have been highly regarded. In scattered instances, revenue bonds based on transit systems, irrigation water systems, and other unstable enterprises have fallen into default, but the weaknesses were usually due to earnings instability, not to the legal nature of the bonds.

Assessment bonds are bonds issued to finance improvements such as pavements or sewers and payable from the proceeds of specific assessments levied upon each lot or field in the benefited area. The assessment district in its simplest form has no taxing power; it may collect from each lot only its proportionate share of the original total assessment necessary to finance the improvement.[6] Assessment bonds are reliable investments when the assessed property is highly valuable compared with the size of the assessments; but many defaults occurred during the period 1930–1935 in districts in which heavy assessments had been levied on vacant lots or other low-value property.

Hybrid types of bonds are found in instances where revenue bonds are guaranteed as to payment by the state or municipality which owns the borrowing department, or when some other such combination of money sources exists. One peculiar hybrid between a full faith and credit bond and a revenue bond should be particularly noted: A number of borrowers, including state agencies in Alabama, Pennsylvania, and Washington, have sold bonds on which payment is pledged only from specified taxes, such as gasoline taxes or liquor excises; there is no unconditional promise to pay.

THE DEBTORS

The five types of debtors to be distinguished are (1) the states; (2) municipalities with broad powers, such as counties, cities, and towns; (3) districts with limited powers, such as school districts, road districts, and similar taxing agencies; (4) assessment districts; and (5) departments and authorities.

The American states have long been regarded as high-class credit risks. They have effective revenue sources available in sales taxes, gasoline taxes, motor vehicle taxes, income taxes, inheritance taxes, and general property taxes. Their usual expenditures for highways, institutions, aid to schools, and general government have been less burdensome than the national government's welfare and defense outlays or the municipalities' local services, with the result that state budgets have been comfortably balanced and state debts kept small. However, the states are now contributing to school and other local costs and to welfare programs on a large scale. These outlays press increasingly on their revenue sources, and they have already lowered the credit standing of such states as New York and Vermont.

Cities, towns, and counties are heavily dependent on the general property tax

[6] These bonds are also called revenue bonds in some jurisdictions. In this usage the term *revenue bond* is applied to any bond whose payment is made contingent on the adequacy of specific earnings or levies.

for revenue, though business license taxes, sales taxes, and even income taxes are used. Expenditures include police and fire protection, health, schools, sanitation, and an increasing list of regulatory and service functions, plus, in the case of the counties, extensive pension, relief, and welfare work. These costs are substantial and appear to be more burdensome on the available revenue sources than those financed by the states. Also, the service on existing city and county debt is often heavier than that borne by the states.

In general, cities, towns, and counties with large middle- and upper-class populations must be classed as good credit risks. However, a number of so-called central cities, notably New York, are losing their more productive citizens and some business firms through suburban migration, while they gain numerous low-income families that require expensive outlays for schools, police, and welfare services. These municipalities are doubtful credit risks, as the downgrading of their securities by the rating agencies has indicated.

Districts with limited powers, such as school districts, road districts, park districts, and drainage districts, are usually completely dependent on the general property tax. The tax rate they may impose is sometimes restricted by law, and the rate's effectiveness is often limited by the capacity of the taxpayers. In districts where public expenditures are reasonably limited, where debt service is not too burdensome, where property is valuable, and where taxpayers have substantial and diversified income sources, the bonds are likely to be good. Under opposite conditions, defaults are possible.

During 1972, cities, counties, and districts were cheered by congressional passage of the Revenue-Sharing Act. This will make a portion of each year's federal revenue receipts available to local governments, in effect shifting part of their financial burdens to the federal taxpayers and relieving to some degree their overdependence on local property taxes. Revenue sharing should strengthen the overall position of local governments and improve the standing of their bonds, although it may prove unavailing in the long run unless their spending also is brought under effective control.

Assessment districts are usually organized to finance a single public improvement like a paving or street-lighting project. As such, they will usually not have offices or officers; all business is transacted by city or county officials, subject to state statutes which outline all procedures in detail. Each lot in an assessment district is obligated to make regular annual payments into a fund from which interest and maturing bonds are paid. Failure to pay obligates the supervising city or county officials to take steps to foreclose the "improvement lien" and sell the lot to recover the sums due, but this process is often delayed, especially if many lot owners fail to pay. Defaults by lot owners naturally cause the district to fall behind on its interest and principal.

States, cities, and counties frequently have "departments" which operate water systems, electric power systems, or other publicly owned business ventures. The municipality usually provides some equity capital, and revenue bonds serve as the funded debt. Since the municipal venture is free of almost all taxes and can usually be assured a monopoly, it has every chance to succeed. Sometimes a publicly owned business venture is operated by a specially created "authority" whose powers are detailed by its own statute. The Port of New York Authority, created jointly by the states of New York and New Jersey, and the California Toll Bridge Authority, created by the state of California, are examples of such agencies. The department or authority may be compared to a business corporation: It must try to earn enough to pay its debts, and if it fails to do so, the stockholder (the state or municipal owner) must decide whether to provide the money or to permit the bondholders to seek a remedy in the courts. The record of revenue bonds in general is good, and their use is increasing rapidly. They are usually a little lower in price or higher in yield than general obligations of the same municipality.

BOND FEATURES

State and municipal bonds are issued pursuant to the constitutional, statutory, and charter powers which govern the borrowers. In most instances, bond statutes are so complete that they practically outline the terms of the bonds, and when a few administrative details are furnished in the official announcement, no further description is needed. Trust indentures and trustees are seldom used, as officials designated by law carry out the procedures outlined in the bond statutes.

Some of the legal features which affect the investment standing of public bonds, and which are commonly prescribed by bond statues, are:

1 Maturities Both straight and serial maturities are common, with the latter commonly used to finance pavements, school buildings, and other depreciating assets. Maturities may range from 1 to 40 or 50 years. About 5 per cent of outstanding debt at any time consists of temporary financing, notes which mature in 3 to 18 months.

2 Sinking funds Large-scale borrowers such as New York City often find straight maturity bonds easier to sell than serials, but provide for debt amortization through sinking funds which purchase or call prescribed amounts of outstanding bonds annually.

3 Call prices Increasing numbers of bond statutes now provide call prices for both sinking-fund and general retirement purposes. Older public bonds are largely noncallable.

4 Pledged revenues Except for revenue bonds, the great majority of public bonds are debentures which have no lien or preferential rights to any specific property or revenues.

5 Debt limits Statutes which prevent the incurrence of public debt in excess of stated percentages of assessed property value or some other reasonable limit are important to bondholders. Debt limit statutes are sometimes evaded by creation of additional overlapping tax districts or by use of revenue bonds which are not included in the calculations.

6 Tax limits Tax limitation laws which prevent the levying of general property taxes in excess of a stipulated rate are helpful if they bar extravagant spending without preventing debt service. Most tax limit laws apply only to levies designed for current spending and permit unlimited extra taxes for debt service only. This is an important feature.

7 Tax collection system A tax collection system which is equitable and efficient, and which is fortified by appropriate penalties on delinquents, is important. It is desirable that taxes for debt service be included in the same levy as those used for ordinary public expenditures, as tax collectors are sometimes indifferent about collecting bondholders' money if funds for current expenditures are separately collected. Furthermore, the law should require that tax money collected for debt service be segregated immediately in separate bond funds.

8 Tax delinquencies The statutes should provide for prompt and complete tax sales of defaulting property and should require that tax collectors be diligent in selling delinquent property in order to collect back taxes and restore the property to a tax-paying basis for the future.

DEFAULT EXPERIENCE

During the depression of the 1930s an estimated 3,000 public debtors, including counties, cities, towns, taxing districts, and assessment districts, committed various kinds of debt defaults exceeding 2 billion dollars. Most of these were of short duration and soon repaid, so total ultimate losses to investors were relatively small. However, in some cases bondholders had to accept new bonds with longer maturities, lower interest rates, and even reduced principal sums.[7]

[7] The State of Arkansas in 1933 attempted to force its creditors to exchange their outstanding 4½ to 6 per cent bonds for new 3 per cent ones by the simple expedient of authorizing interest payments on the 3s and refusing to pay on the others. Since private citizens may not sue a sovereign state without its consent, the bondholders were without a legal redress, but the threats and protests of investors and bond dealers were instrumental in causing Arkansas to rescind its action. See *Moody's Governments Manual* for 1934 and 1935 for a summary of this affair.

State laws always prescribe the legal remedies which unpaid bondholders may take against cities, school districts, and other subordinate political bodies which default on their bonds. Generally, however, the adjustment of serious public bond defaults is slow, awkward, and unsatisfactory in most states. The holders of small amounts of bonds can hardly afford to go to court to press their claims; unless a protective committee comes forward, the small bondholder waits helplessly for something to happen. Investors in public bonds are well advised to avoid bonds in which serious defaults seem even remotely possible. In cases in which the debtor carries on regular governmental services, such as fire departments, schools, health services, and the like, expenditures for these purposes are often given precedence over debt payments when the money supply is limited, even if this means that the bondholders get nothing.

Defaults are most likely on assessment bonds or revenue bond issues. These defaults are likely to be only partial, however, and available funds will be distributed as the law directs, pending the final outcome of the situation.

GUIDES TO BOND QUALITY

As with the federal debt, tax-supported state and municipal bonds can best be tested by inquiring as to the debtor's willingness and ability to pay.

Willingness to pay is indicated by the debtor's record and by the observed attitudes of officials and lay people. Most American states and municipalities are willing to pay their obligations and will bear taxes adequate for the purpose. Exceptions are likely to occur only (1) where bitterness over local government waste or corruption leads to tax strikes, refusals to pay assessments, etc.; (2) where taxpayers and communities are hopelessly overburdened; or (3) where penalties for nonpayment are too light or where assessed property is not worth the charges. Willingness to pay thus appears to be closely associated with ability to pay without inconvenience.

The ability of a public debtor to pay its debts is dependent upon the financial capacity of its citizens to carry the burden placed upon them. In gauging the situation, it is necessary to note both the financial position of the debtor unit and the total burdens imposed on the taxpayers by state, county, city, school district, and possibly several other overlapping road, park, sanitary, and special improvement districts. When important bond issues are offered for sale, the underwriters usually employ Dun & Bradstreet or some equally experienced firm to make a survey of the overlapping tax and improvement districts, in order to measure the aggregate debt and tax burden to be borne by the area.

Ability to pay may be gauged by studying the following eight factors, and by comparing the debtor in question with like debtors:

1   The debt burden: Is the aggregate tax-supported and assessment debt rea-

sonable *(a)* in ratio to property valuation, *(b)* on a per capita basis, and *(c)* in ratio to the aggregate earning power of the community?

2 The tax burden: Are the taxes reasonable in ratio to property valuation, on a per capita basis, and in ratio to aggregate incomes?

3 Tax delinquencies: Are taxes and assessments *(a)* paid on time, and *(b)* finally paid in full?

4 Condition of the budget: Is the community budget balanced? Are floating debts accumulated by use of tax anticipation warrants?

5 Is the trend of expenditures reasonable?

6 Is the trend of the public debt reasonable?

7 Is the community financially well-to-do, stable, and diversified as to property holdings and income sources?

8 Does the population contain a substantial percentage of native-born, educated, income-tax-paying, propertied citizens?

Statistics and analytical reports covering these points can be found in the financial services or can be supplied by municipal bond dealers. Since the bare statistics are not too meaningful, it is customary to compare the figures of any municipality with those of others of the same size and type; if the figures appear relatively good and the trends are satisfactory, the risk should be acceptable. It is best to compare only municipalities of the same size and type; larger cities and more populous counties, for example, usually have higher expense and debt ratios and can bear them if their affairs are not trending adversely. Vigilance is necessary in statistical analysis to make sure that all figures are representative and comparable—that overlapping debts and taxes are all included, that property values are stated at actual rather than fractional assessed valuations, that allowance is made for self-supporting debt such as municipal water supply bonds, etc.

In the analysis of a revenue bond which has no supplementary tax support or municipal guarantee, the main issue is the earning power of the business project. This would be studied in a fashion similar to that used in corporate situations, anticipating sales, costs, earnings, and expansion needs, and contrasting the available earnings with the amounts required to service the bonds. Matters dealing with such items as additional debt, depreciation accounting, annual audits, adequate insurance, rate levels, disposition of excess earnings, and remedies available to bondholders in case of default could be very important to revenue bondholders.

The larger municipal bond issues are rated by Moody's and Standard & Poor's on the same letter-grade basis (triple-A, double-A, etc.) as corporate bonds. These quality ratings strongly affect the interest costs an issuer must pay. Since local governments have recently been subject to increasing financial strains, they have become more sensitive to the ratings applied by the rating services and more inclined to criticize them as arbitrary or based on insufficient investigation. In early 1973, it seemed likely that several large cities, including New York, would ask Congress for a new law regulating the methods by which the financial services may rate municipal obligations.

LEGALITY

Because the state statutes governing the authorization and issuance of municipal bonds are usually explicit and technical, it appears necessary to use extreme care in creating a new issue if questions as to its legality are to be avoided. This leads bond buyers to place great stress on the "legal opinion" of a law firm experienced in such matters. A few recognized law firms in each state make a specialty of advising municipalities and securities underwriters on the creation of bonds, and each bond is usually delivered to its purchaser with a copy of the law firm's "legal opinion" of its validity attached. In many instances a bond is difficult to sell unless accompanied by this testimonial.

MARKETS, PRICES, YIELDS

New issues of state and municipal bonds are purchased in the usual manner by underwriting syndicates and dealers who specialize in these issues. Large banks also participate in the underwriting of general obligation bonds. New issues are sold at retail by both securities dealers and banks, and both maintain dealer markets to purchase and resell bonds which private holders wish to sell. Although prices in the secondary market are steady, changing chiefly in response to basic interest-rate and market-supply factors, and dealer spreads are reasonable, the secondary market is only moderately active. Most bonds disappear into permanent holdings and are infrequently traded.

About 1 securities firm in 20 maintains an active municipal bond department, but any securities firm or bank can do business on an over-the-counter basis with the active municipal bond dealers. Some of these dealers are known to specialize in certain types of municipal bonds and to make markets in them regularly, but most dealers buy and sell a wide range of issues as opportunity offers, without attempting to maintain an inventory in specific issues at all times. The most active dealers print daily or weekly *offering sheets* which list both the new and secondary offerings which they have for sale, and scores of dealers advertise each day in a publication called *The Blue List of Current Municipal Offerings*. The *Blue List* advertisements indicate on a single line the name of the bond, the coupon rate, the maturity date, the yield to maturity, the type of bond, the number of bonds offered, and the name of the offering dealer; hundreds of new and old issues and hundreds of millions in amount are listed every day, enabling dealers and brokers to locate available offerings on a nationwide basis.

State and municipal bonds are usually quoted on a yield-to-maturity basis (e.g., 4.10 per cent bid, offered at 4.05 per cent), though quotations in terms of percentages and eighths are commonly used in pricing certain large issues of non-serial revenue bonds. Most transactions between dealers or brokers and their customers are on a "principal" basis, the firm selling to or buying from its customer, with no commission involved; on this basis the "spread" between what a customer would get for municipal bonds and what he would pay for them would normally range between $\frac{1}{2}$ and 2 per cent of the sum involved, the exact amount depending on the size of the transaction, the marketability of the bonds, the quality of the bonds, and the relationships of the parties.

The prices and yields of tax-exempt bonds as a class are dominated by four factors: (1) the yields available on competing securities, particularly high-class taxable bonds; (2) the number of tax-exempt bonds available; (3) investors' feeling of assurance that these bonds will remain tax-exempt; and (4) the strength of individual and institutional demands for these bonds. Different classes of investors buy different maturities of tax-exempts. Commercial banks prefer short and intermediate maturities; when loan demand is deficient and easy monetary policies are piling up excess reserves, they may absorb more than 70 per cent of all new municipals marketed. Casualty insurance companies and trustees also buy the intermediate maturities. Wealthy individuals buy most long maturities, although common stocks compete strongly with tax-exempts for their favor. The strength of individual demands for tax-exempt bonds depends heavily upon two factors: (1) the severity of high-bracket tax rates, which determines the relative attractiveness of tax-exempt securities; and (2) the number of high-bracket incomes, which measures the need for tax-exempt investments.

The influence of all these factors can be seen in Chart 20-1. During World War II the federal tax rates were greatly increased, at a time when war prosperity was lifting many individuals' incomes into high tax brackets. This caused an increase in the demand for municipals just when municipalities had ceased to borrow because their construction activities were suspended by the war. Municipals therefore rose sharply in price and declined in yield. After the war the number of high incomes decreased, competing corporate stock and bond yields rose, and both states and municipalities sold new tax-exempt bonds in great quantities. Accordingly, municipals dropped in price and their yields rose. In late 1947 a spectacular drop in the prices of municipals occurred because it became apparent that the Revenue Act of 1948, then in preparation in Congress, would permit married couples to split their income in separate tax returns; this would give each spouse a separate set of tax brackets, keep the (combined) income from reaching into the high tax brackets, and thus make tax-exempt municipal bonds less necessary. The sharp increase in the price of municipals in 1950 reflected the expected increase in income tax rates at that time, and their relative price weakness in the period 1957–1958 (note that tax-exempt municipal yields then exceeded government bond yields) can be attributed to market flooding because of the

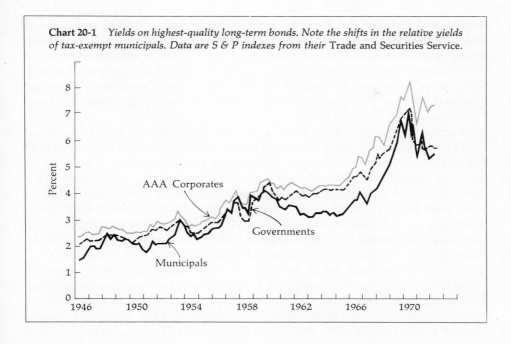

Chart 20-1 *Yields on highest-quality long-term bonds. Note the shifts in the relative yields of tax-exempt municipals. Data are S & P indexes from their* Trade and Securities Service.

very great volume of municipals then being sold. In 1959–1962, municipals again rose in price and declined in yield, this time because of demand inspired by the growth of time deposits in banks and by income tax increases on life insurance companies and mutual savings institutions. From 1962 to 1967, high-grade municipals yielded about one-fourth less than the best-grade corporate bonds, reflecting their large tax saving. Two factors accounted for the violent rise in municipal yields during 1969 and 1970: the virtual cessation of bank purchases, owing to the Federal Reserve's squeeze on bank reserves, and widespread fears that Congress would end the tax-exempt privilege. As these fears subsided, and as monetary policy turned easy during 1971, municipal yields again fell well below those available on corporates.

SPECIAL CLASSES OF TAX-EXEMPTS

Three forms of tax-exempt issues deserve special mention. The first are known as PHAs or New Housing Act bonds. The Federal Housing Act of 1949 authorizes the Federal Public Housing Administration to enter into contracts with state or municipal agencies which desire to build low-rent public housing projects for occupancy by low-income citizens. Under these contracts the federal government agrees to pay annual cash subsidies equal to the entire sums needed to pay the interest and principal on the serial revenue bonds which finance the projects. These bonds are technically state or municipal revenue bonds, hence have the tax-exempt status of municipals. But since the federal subsidy is earmarked for bond service, they have the unimpeachable quality of federal obligations. Although these bonds are offered at irregular intervals, they usually total several hundred million dollars per year and therefore supply an especially large volume of long-term bonds.

A second conspicuous type of municipal is the highway revenue bond, otherwise known as the "turnpike" bond. At least 20 states sold these bonds and built toll highways in the 1950s; some are still adding to their systems. In general, the turnpike bonds have been regarded as good rather than highest in quality, but their tax-exempt yields, which in 1972 ranged between 5.0 and 8.0 per cent, have made them attractive to many investors. The turnpike bonds are usually "term" bonds (i.e., all maturing at one date) of very long maturity with a provision for using available earnings to retire bonds through a sinking fund. This avoids defaults in poor earnings years and also adds to the marketability of the bonds.

A third development, which became prominent during the 1960s, is the so-called industrial aid bond. These bonds have been sold by municipalities in about 40 states to finance new industrial plants for lease to business firms which agree to establish operations and payrolls in the community. The bonds are usually revenue bonds, to be serviced only out of the lease rentals earned by the property, but the low interest rates paid on tax-exempt bonds permit the lease rentals to be minimal. A great volume of industrial aid bonds in 1967 and early 1968, averaging close to $100,000,000 per month, caused the Congress to amend the income tax laws to classify industrial aid bond issues over $5,000,000 in amount and sold after January 1, 1969, as industrial bonds and not tax-exempt municipals. The tax-exempt bonds sold prior to the cutoff date remain tax-exempt. Apparently most of them are proving to be sound investments.

OUTLOOK FOR MUNICIPAL BONDS: 1972

Looking ahead, the municipal bond market in 1972 appeared to confront two main problems: (1) a prospective shortage of investors, and (2) adjustment to growing pressures for national tax reform. Each of these difficulties threatened a future rise in the relative level of municipal bond yields, and each suggested a growing limitation of their historic tax-exempt status.

During the 1960s, state and local debt doubled, but municipal bonds found a receptive market, thanks to a massive switch of bank assets from United States government bonds into tax-exempts. Clearly, this one-time change could not be repeated in the 1970s. Growing demands for business loans and the increasing availability of leasing and other tax-sheltered outlets made it doubtful that the banks would or could support the municipal market as strongly as before. Nor were enough individual investors in high tax brackets likely to be found to purchase at reasonable yields the 31 billion dollars of net new state and local bonds expected annually by 1980. To sell all the bonds slated for marketing in years ahead, it seemed probable that cities and states would have to turn, partially at least, to high-yielding taxable bonds to tap other investors such as pension funds and life insurance companies. Congressmen were already discussing new legislation to provide offsetting subsidies from the Treasury to local governments which would sell bonds whose interest was subject to federal income tax.

Tax-reform efforts also appeared likely to diminish the appeal of tax-exempt securities, if only by increasing investors' uncertainty over how long the tax-exempt privilege would survive and in what possible form. The abortive drive in Congress during 1969 to do away with tax exemption had depressed municipal bond prices and raised their yields to record levels. Fresh attacks seemed likely to renew these tendencies.

SOURCES OF INFORMATION

Quotations on government securities are found on the usual newspaper financial pages, in financial periodicals, and on dealers' offering sheets. Brief descriptions of all issues are contained in the regular reference services and on circulars and offering sheets distributed by dealers. In choosing issues for specific purposes, for example, with reference to liquidity for estate tax purposes, it is sometimes desirable to obtain the details about the issue by studying the official announcements at the time of offering. These can be had by request to any Federal Reserve bank, by reference to announcements in financial periodicals dated at the time of issuance, and from the files of dealers or banks.

Investors interested in savings bonds will find a summary of all matters pertaining to ownership, transfer, payment, and redemption in the Treasury Department's pamphlet *Regulations Governing United States Savings Bonds (Department Circular* 530, 9th revision amended, May 1966) with the supplements thereto. Two other pamphlets, *Department Circulars* 653 and 905, each in its current revision, explain the investment details, yield, and redemption mathematics for Series E and Series H bonds, respectively. Additional pamphlets on such specialized topics as the legal intricacies of ownership and tax matters are occasionally available.

For municipal bonds, the information available to the nonprofessional investor is rather sketchy and difficult to understand, compared with the extensive literature on corporate securities. Investors depend on *Moody's Municipal and Government Manual* for useful summaries of available information, though data on overlapping districts are often incomplete. This service also assigns "quality ratings" to the larger issues. Comprehensive prospectuses can be had in only a few instances, and annual reports analogous to corporate reports simply do not exist.

An understanding of the available financial data is also difficult for the amateur, for it requires a knowledge of the statutes of each state with respect to municipal bodies and their taxes, debts, and procedures.

Most nonprofessional investors accept the advice of an expert whom they trust, or rely upon conspicuous large borrowers whose standings are easily ascertained, or confine themselves to local issues whose legal features and economic circumstances they know at first hand. The experts have access to detailed analytical services covering borrowers and issues of significant size, and also providing special reports on the smaller issues.

Important general information for municipal bond buyers is found in several periodicals, including *The Money Manager* and *National Municipal Review*, and in other investment sources. An excellent bibliography on state and municipal finance is contained in the annual *Municipal Year Book*. Extensive statistical data will be found in the Census Bureau's annual reports *Governmental Debts in the United States*, *Financial Statistics of Cities*, and *Financial Statistics of States*, and in other census reports; in the *Annual Report* of the Secretary of the Treasury; in the *Statistical Abstract of the United States*; in the *Municipal Year Book*; and in the statistical section of *Moody's Municipal and Government Manual*.

QUESTIONS AND PROBLEMS

1   Is it conceivable that the present willingness of the American people to bear taxes for the support of the public debt might be replaced by a desire to default? Consider any political and economic trends which might lead in that direction.

2   Do you agree it is likely that government bondholders will be repaid in cheaper dollars? That they may have to submit to ex post facto modification of their rights because of a paramount public interest?

3   Are savings bonds regarded as "direct" federal debt? Define federal agency securities, nonmarketable debt, treasury bills.

4   Explain this sentence: The Treasury 3¼s of 1978–83 were quoted yesterday at 75.12 to 75.16, while last week's issue of bills was 5.40 to 5.25.

5   How do long-term treasury bond issues differ? What features would an individual investor probably seek?

6   Why are large commercial firms and local tax collectors important in the government securities markets? How do they use governments?

7   If you directed a $10,000,000 savings and loan association which had $9,000,000 in installment mortgages, $200,000 in a working bank balance, and $800,000 to be kept in government bonds as a seldom-used secondary reserve, what kinds of governments would you choose?

8   Is there enough difference in yield between governments and good corporate bonds to justify investment in corporates by small investors? Consider the risk, time to maturity, commission costs, taxes, legal ownership factors, price stability, and liquidity.

9   What type of government security would you recommend to an elderly couple with $250,000 net worth who wish to provide liquid resources for $25,000 of state inheritance

taxes and $25,000 of federal estate taxes, but who want to obtain the maximum income meanwhile. Assume that the Treasury 4¼s of 1987–92 are selling at 80. If you choose marketable bonds, would you use low-coupon or high-coupon bonds?

10 Would an individual who pays income taxes have the same total posttax earnings if he bought Series E bonds, held them for 5 years and 10 months, and then cashed them, as he would have if he bought Series H bonds and placed all his interest receipts (after taxes) in a savings bank at 5.5 per cent?

11 Inspect Chart 20-1 and determine who benefits most from the federal tax exemption on municipals, the borrowing municipalities or the bondholders. If the municipalities could not sell tax-exempt bonds, could they borrow at the same interest rates paid by corporate borrowers with the same quality rating?

12 Look up and classify the bonds of the following debtors as to type and quality: **(a)** Mobile, Alabama; **(b)** Louisiana; **(c)** Imperial Irrigation District, California; **(d)** Los Angeles Department of Water and Power; **(e)** Delaware; **(f)** St. Louis, Missouri. Use *Moody's Municipal and Government Manual.*

13 Should managed open-end investment companies be permitted to invest in tax-exempt bonds and function as "mere conduits" in distributing tax-exempt interest to their share-holders?

14 What are the principal revenues and disbursements of your state? Are they increasing faster than the income of the average person?

15 Would a rapidly growing municipality be as good a credit risk as a well-established and slowly growing one? (Consider the amount of new municipal construction required, the amount of private real estate debt in a new community, and the stability of personal and business income.)

16 Why would state laws prescribe serial maturities or sinking-fund bonds for the financing of pavements and school buildings?

17 If you hold an A-rated 15-year municipal paying 5½ per cent and selling at par, and if A-rated corporates are paying about 7 per cent, how much will your bond decline in price if it is made fully taxable?

18 What are the most important measures of a municipality's ability to pay tax-supported bonds? How could you tell the meaning of a statement that the total tax-supported debt in your city is 8 per cent of the property valuation?

19 Could your state make money by buying up entire new issues of high-yielding local bonds with the proceeds of large-scale state issues?

20 For an investor whose top federal tax bracket is 38 per cent and whose state bracket is 5 per cent, which offers the most: **(a)** a home-state 4 per cent 20-year municipal at 4.60 per cent, or **(b)** a similar bond on another state at 5 per cent?

21 Does your state have a statutory interest-rate ceiling on state and local bonds? What is it? Does it apply uniformly to all classes of bonds and all types of issuers? What would be the effect on borrowing by your state and local governments, agencies, and revenue-producing services if municipal bond yields in general rose above 7 per cent?

22 After New York City's general obligation bonds were downgraded by the rating agencies, the city comptroller complained that this was the arbitrary act of a few men. Do you agree? Does a city that borrows long-term funds to meet current deficits deserve a high bond rating?

484 INVESTMENT
ANALYSIS

REFERENCES

Badger, Ralph E., and Paul B. Coffman: *Investment Analysis*, McGraw-Hill Book Company, New York, 1967, Chap. 24.

Bellemore, Douglas H., and John C. Ritchie, Jr.: *Investments*, 3d ed., South-Western Publishing Company, Incorporated, Cincinnati, 1969, Chaps. 27, 28.

Dougall, Herbert E.: *Investments*, 8th ed., Prentice-Hall, Inc., Englewood Cliffs, N.J., 1968, Chaps. 5, 6.

Financial Handbook, rev. ed., The Ronald Press Company, New York, 1968 Sec. 11.

First Boston Corporation: *Handbook of Securities of the United States Government and Federal Agencies*, New York, biennial.

Hayes, Douglas A.: *Investments: Analysis and Management*, The Macmillan Company, New York, 1966, Chaps. 22, 23, 24.

Investment Bankers Association of America: *Fundamentals of Municipal Bonds*, 3d ed., Washington, 1963.

Joint Economic Committee: *A Study of the Dealer Market for Federal Government Securities*, Washington, 1960.

Moody's Municipal and Government Manual, sections on United States government securities; Special Features section, articles on tax-exempt bonds. Moody's Investors Service, New York.

Rabinowitz, Alan: *Municipal Bond Finance and Administration*, John Wiley & Sons, Inc., New York, 1969.

Robinson, Roland I.: *Postwar Market for State and Local Government Securities*, National Bureau of Economic Research, Princeton University Press, Princeton, N.J., 1960.

Scott, Ira O.: *Government Securities Market*, McGraw-Hill Book Company, New York, 1965.

Treasury-Federal Reserve Study of the Government Securities Market, Washington, 1959–1960.

part 5

Other Investments

Part 5 is designed to integrate a quick review of miscellaneous investments into a book which deals mostly with stocks and bonds. The presentations in these chapters are sometimes brief, but they cover the essentials on six widely used groups of investments. Chapter 21 deals with investment companies and personal trusts, Chapter 22 with savings-type accounts and money market instruments, Chapter 23 with social security and employer pension plans, Chapter 24 with life insurance and annuities, Chapter 25 with real estate and mortgages, and Chapter 26 with foreign securities and property.

Each of these six investment areas has grown enormously during the past two decades, each has become vastly more complex, and each has clear-cut characteristics which affect the building of a balanced investment program. Investors need facts and opinions about them. Furthermore, these areas are currently subject to rapid innovation, expanding public regulation, and new tax developments. These chapters attempt to supply an up-to-date perspective.

INVESTMENT COMPANIES
AND TRUSTS

Investment companies are variously known as investment companies, investment funds, and investment trusts. They offer the investing public some 850 securities representing more than 250 different issuers having nearly 11 million shareholders and total assets of 63.5 billion dollars at year-end 1971.[1]

The basic function of an investment company is to offer an investor the security of diversification plus some degree of management supervision in a single investment. It does this by selling its own securities to the public and investing the proceeds in a diversified list of stocks and bonds. Subsequently these investment holdings may be sold and replaced by others as circumstances warrant. The objectives of the investment company, its method of operation, the types of investment it will make, and the degree of risk it will assume are all matters for decision by the individual company. The investor chooses the investment company and the type of security in it which meet his needs and his tastes but delegates the burden of studying business corporations, industry trends, and market conditions to the management of his company.

It is clear that an investment company will have certain operating expenses to pay and that these expenses must necessarily be interposed between the investor and the underlying securities which are the source of his income. This means that an investment company security is a wise choice only if the diversification and management advantages which it offers are worth the added cost. The added annual costs typically amount to .2 to .5 per cent of the principal sums managed by the more economical companies;[2] and in addition, the "loading charge" which must be paid as an entrance fee can in some instances run as high as 9 per cent of the investor's principal.

Investment companies in the United States are a relatively recent development, most of them having been founded since the early twenties. The idea is allegedly borrowed from the British, who have operated investment companies extensively but, on the whole, conservatively for many years. The American investment company movement did not have a conservative early history; much of its early experience was gained during the boom of 1927–1929 and the depression

---

[1] For later data, see annual issues of Wiesenberger's *Investment Companies*.

[2] See Table 21-2.

which followed and is replete with error, fraud, and losses.[3] This era of confusion may be said to have closed with 1940, for in that year the Investment Company Act imposed upon the whole industry the high standards which the best companies had developed through experience.[4] It cannot be said that investment companies are now immune to losses due to management error, but it is fair to say that they are in nearly all cases operated openly, honestly, and in the interests of their securityholders.

FORM OF ORGANIZATION

Investment companies are usually either corporations or Massachusetts trusts. Directors or trustees may be elected, or a board of trustees may be self-perpetuating, as in the case of some of the older Massachusetts trusts. Directors or trustees establish the company's policies within the scope of the charter or trust indenture, supervise the investment portfolio, and choose the investment advisers and company managers. Although the Investment Company Act prohibits any single investment banking firm from furnishing a majority of the directors for an investment company, many companies are regarded as closely allied to investment firms: for example, Tri-Continental Corporation is identified with J. & W. Seligman & Co., Lehman Corporation with Lehman Brothers Co., and Century Shares Trust with Brown Brothers Harriman & Co. Investment counsel firms whose chief function is the sale of research service to investment companies, and securities distributors whose main function is the selling of investment company shares to the public, are identified as dominant in the affairs of other investment companies. For example, the Calvin Bullock organization sponsors eight companies with total assets at year-end 1971 of 875 million dollars. Other investment companies, such as Adams Express Company and the funds in the Massachusetts Financial Services group and the Wellington Group of mutual funds, are regarded as independent of brokerage-company or investment banker control, though they of course have directors who are in the securities business.

Though final decisions on investment policy and the purchase or sale of individual investments will be the province of directors or trustees, an investment company must either maintain or employ a research organization of considerable scope to provide information and advice. This work is done by investment company employees in a substantial number of cases, but in many instances it is done on a contract basis by investment counsel firms. In a number of such instances the investment counsel firms organized the investment companies, with the marketing of their services as a chief objective. A third method of providing adequate

[3] See Securities and Exchange Commission, *Report on Investment Funds and Investment Companies*, Washington, 1939–40.

[4] The act is reviewed in Chap. 12.

research and advice is that of maintaining a research agency jointly with others. The Tri-Continental group of five investment companies finds this convenient.

When investment counsel is contracted for and all investments are kept in securities, there is little occasion for an investment company to maintain an employee organization. Consequently, the entire management of an investment company is often contracted for, except for policy matters on which instructions can be issued to the contracting firm by directors or officers. Even the securities owned by an investment company are usually in the safekeeping of a bank, trust company, or an investment house. These devices help to keep down the company's expenses.

TYPES OF INVESTMENT COMPANIES

In a basic sense there are only two types of investment companies in America today, the closed-end type and the open-end type. Of these, the open-end type is the more important, representing 92 per cent of all investment company resources in 1971.

A closed-end investment company is an ordinary business concern whose operations are similar to those of any business corporation. It is unusual only because its corporate business consists largely of investing its funds in the securities of other corporations and managing these investment holdings for income and profit. The stockholders and bondholders in a closed-end company are perfectly free to sell their holdings on the securities markets for whatever they will bring or to buy more from others if they are so minded. However, they have no right to ask the investment company to redeem their shares or to sell them more. The company functions as an ordinary business corporation, earning what it can from dividend receipts and market profits and paying dividends when it can. If its operations are extraordinarily successful or promising, the market price of its stock may rise above the net asset value per share of its investment holdings. If it does not do well, the market price is certain to drop below the net asset value. Most closed-end investment companies are corporations, but the group includes a number of Massachusetts trusts, such as Amoskeag Company and Boston Personal Property Trust, and at least one joint stock company, the Adams Express Company.

An open-end investment company is one which continuously offers new shares for sale and which stands always ready to redeem existing shares in cash at the request of any shareholder. Meanwhile, the resources in the possession of the company are invested in securities, and periodic dividends are paid to shareholders as earnings warrant. Although shareholders are free to sell their stock to others or to buy more from others, it is clear that market prices can never deviate far from the sale and redemption prices set by the company. Most open-end companies sell new shares at net asset value (total market value of asset holdings minus liabilities divided by number of outstanding shares) plus a "loading" or marketing fee, and redeem shares approximately at net asset value.[5] This keeps any possible resale price between these two limits. Open-end companies are usually either Massachusetts trusts or corporations. In recent years the trade literature has referred to the open-end companies mostly as *mutual funds*.

Since the open-end shares must constantly be sold on a nationwide basis, most companies have sales "distributors" to carry on this task. The distributor is usually an established securities firm or a selling firm organized for the purpose, which has an exclusive franchise to buy all new shares issued by the investment company. The distributor organizes a selling group of securities brokers and dealers to retail the shares or, alternatively, organizes his own retail firm. The retailing firms may then get new shares from the distributor at a concession from the public offering price for sale to their customers. The public offering price per share must usually be high enough (1) to add a sum equal to the net asset value of existing shares to the company's resources, (2) to pay the clerical costs of recording the new share, (3) to pay the distributor, and (4) to pay the selling group member. Most open-end companies make the public offering price 106 to 109 per cent of net asset value[6] for investments under $10,000, a figure which compares reasonably with the cost of marketing common stocks in ordinary corporations. However, many mutual funds are changing into "no load" funds which make neither a selling markup nor a surrender charge. These funds are operated by investment advisers who sell only on application to their own organizations, and who are compensated only by the annual management fee paid by the fund.

There is a small-scale over-the-counter resale market in the shares of some of the larger open-end funds through which an investor might be able to sell to a dealer at a price slightly higher than net asset value. Since open-end shares are usually transferable much like other stock, the dealer could then resell the shares. However, the Investment Company Act and NASD rules forbid any broker or dealer to retail open-end shares below the regular offering price established by the fund's distributor. For this reason the resale market is not widely publicized or extensive.

CAPITAL STRUCTURE AND LEVERAGE

Investment company shares can be given a speculative quality akin to leverage in at least three ways. First, the investment company itself might be financed on a leverage basis by sale of bonds and preferred stock as well as common. Second, the investment company might invest in the common stocks of high-leverage

---

[5] Values for sales purposes will be computed at least twice daily, and for redemption purposes at least once daily, in order to keep abreast of changing stock market prices. The value of any open-end share thus changes daily in proportion to the changing values of the investments held by the company.

[6] Funds investing chiefly in bonds often sell at 104 or 105 per cent of net asset value.

corporations. Third, the investment company might invest its capital in speculative ventures or in dramatic growth situations where volatile stock prices constitute both risk and opportunity. Various investment companies do each of these things.

Most mutual funds are forbidden by statute or their bylaws to sell senior securities; only the closed-end companies make important use of leverage through their own capital structures. Not all closed-end companies have senior securities outstanding — in fact, over half of them have not — but those which have provide both conservative and speculative investment opportunity. Few bonds are available, but preferred stocks are more numerous and range from good-quality issues to slimly covered speculations. There are also a few convertible preferreds. The common stocks of the closed-end companies must therefore range from debt-free ownership in the nonleverage companies to moderate-leverage and high-leverage situations.

INVESTMENT AND OPERATING POLICY

An investment company must make three decisions with respect to its investment policy. First, it must decide whether it is to be strictly a diversified investment company, or whether it wishes to invest substantial sums in "special situations" where it may have an important voice in the management. The open-end investment companies are mostly diversified, meaning that as a rule they neither place more than 5 per cent of their assets in any one stock or bond, nor own over 10 per cent of the stock of any corporation. However, some of the closed-end companies occasionally buy large or controlling interests, develop the corporations involved, and either hold the investments indefinitely or sell entire commitments when opportunity offers. Often a portion of an investment company's resources is invested in special situations and the balance is kept in a diversified portfolio.

Second, the investment company must decide whether to operate as a balanced fund, a bond fund, a preferred stock fund, a general common stock fund, or a specialized industry fund. A *balanced fund* is one which undertakes to maintain a portfolio of securities of all types, including always the proportion of bonds and stocks which a well-balanced individual portfolio would have at the time. The proportioning naturally changes as conditions change. The balanced fund is the most completely managed diversified investment available, since the management decides on both portfolio tactics and choice of securities. Balanced funds constitute the second largest category of investment companies. *Bond or preferred stock funds* are those committed to investment largely or exclusively in these types of securities. On the whole, they have not been outstandingly popular, though they make it possible through diversification for medium-grade securities to afford the investor a fair degree of safety. The *general common stock funds* constitute the largest group of investment companies. The investor in a common stock fund regards it as a diversified and managed common stock investment; other elements in his portfolio can be provided by other investments. Of course, a general common stock fund may on occasion retire from the stock market and hold large amounts of cash or government bonds, but its major functions are investment and speculation in common stocks, and it will be "out of the market" only until attractive common stock opportunities become available. An interesting variation in common stock funds is provided by *specialized industry funds*, in which the investment is confined to a single industry and the management's function is limited to choosing the stocks in which the available resources are to be kept. The investor in a specialized industry fund procures a prorata interest in a group of selected steel stocks or oil stocks or utility stocks or whatever industry he chooses. Within the industry chosen by himself he obtains diversification and professional selection.

The third decision of investment policy involves a choice of objectives. Shall the company spend heavily on study and research, in the hope of earning market profits, or shall it invest conservatively, operate economically, and offers its shareholders a stable dividend income? If it chooses to try for market profits, shall the effort be made in good-grade stocks, or will it be better to use risky ones and depend on diversification for security? In seeking market profits, is the policy to be one of selecting promising growth stocks and holding them until they develop, or is it to be one of attempting to "beat the market" by a constant process of buying low and selling high? Although investment company policies are not always consistent on these points, it will be possible to determine where the emphasis lies by studying their portfolios and their records.

Since about 1960, increasing numbers of investment companies have been emphasizing quick profit performance rather than long-term investing, and some of them appear to be succeeding. However, this kind of operation requires large-scale trading in speculative and volatile stocks, often those of lesser-known concerns, and leads to a decline in portfolio quality. Large-scale trading by investment companies has another unfortunate aspect—it imposes sudden large bids or offers upon the market for specific stocks and causes unwarranted fluctuations in the stock prices.

The Investment Company Act of 1940 requires that each investment company state its general investment and operating policies clearly and thereafter change only after shareholder approval. These statements may be found in the prospectuses of the open-end companies, and the financial services summarize them in their descriptions of all companies. The investor may therefore select an investment company whose policies conform to his needs and tastes.

SPECIAL SERVICES AND DEVICES

The open-end investment companies have made great efforts to couple their share offerings with special services and devices which may be convenient or economical for their investors. These include tax-saving devices, opportunities for group

or installment purchases at a reduced loading charge, small-scale installment purchase plans, and various trust or agency services. Several of these require brief
mention.

1 Converting in open-end groups A novel opportunity for diversified speculation is afforded by certain groups of open-end companies. An investor entering
one of these groups has a choice of specialized investment companies, perhaps including one which owns only bonds, one owning only preferreds, one owning
very high-grade common stocks, one owning very volatile common stocks, or one
each in several specialized industries, such as steel, oil, or utilities. After he makes
his initial choice, he is permitted to surrender the shares he holds in exchange for
shares in one of the other specialized companies, if he wishes. There is usually
some cost to this shift, although it is often nominal. This privilege affords a small
investor opportunity to readjust his portfolio as his needs or ideas change, with
the constant advantage of diversification and professional selection at very
modest cost.

2 Large-scale purchases It is reasonable and customary that the loading charge
on large-scale purchases by investors should be reduced substantially, thus
making the shares available at a lower price. The reduction in loading is greater
on larger amounts, starting with investments of $5,000 to $10,000, and may
amount to as much as two-thirds on a $100,000 transaction and even more on
larger sums. This makes mutual funds reasonable investment management devices for endowed institutions, pension funds, and other organizations as well
as for individuals. Large investors may get into the lower-charge brackets by
"bunching" all their purchases over a period of time, which may in some cases
be as long as 13 months, by submitting a "letter of intent" to invest the necessary
amount. Purchases may then be made whenever desired, at the per share prices
prevailing on the date of purchase, but the lower loading charge percentage will
apply to all. Individual fund holdings of $1 million are no longer rare, and sales
of funds in $250,000 blocks are not uncommon. In 1969 about 52 per cent of all
new money going into funds ranged in units of $25,000 and up.

3 Installment plans Many of the open-end investment companies' shares may
now be purchased on installment sales plans under which an investor may make
periodic or even irregular small investments in the company over a span of years.
The investor's "account" is usually placed in trust with a well-known bank, to
which he remits his payments. Each payment is invested in trust shares when
received, at net asset value plus a loading charge of about 9 per cent. In some
cases the loading charge is disproportionately concentrated in the first year (the
"front-end load" plan), absorbing as much as 50 per cent of the first year's invest-

ment, although the 1970 amendment to the Investment Act imposes strict conditions on the selling company: it must agree that the entire transaction can be rescinded in the first 45 days and that, over the first 18 months, the shareholder can get a refund of his payments except for a 15 per cent commission. The investment company usually sells fractional shares to installment accounts, so that the net funds are always fully invested. Dividends on the shares held may be added to the new payments to buy additional shares. Sometimes, for a small additional cost, the investor may buy life insurance covering the period of his investment contract, to assure that his saving program will be completed even in the event of premature death. If the investor wishes to drop his program or withdraw his paid-for shares before completion of the contract, he may in some cases do so without penalty, though the front-end load plans might result in loss in this case.

These plans are attractive to many people. The loading cost is high but the advantages of dollar-cost averaging may offset the loading costs in part. Coupling the program with insurance may also suit many investor's needs. However, the formality of an installment contract is in most cases unnecessary, for the open-end companies are willing to sell new shares in very small quantities at any time without any prearranged plan.

4 Installment liquidation   The growing use of open-end shares as retirement resources has prompted a number of open-end funds to arrange systematic liquidation plans under which an owner's holdings are liquidated on a pre-arranged schedule and the proceeds remitted to him in cash each month or quarter.

5 Reinvested dividends   Various plans exist under which all dividends or all capital gains distributions may be automatically reinvested in new fund shares. These reinvestments are sometimes made at a concession below the regular public offering price.

6 Other devices   Some funds make arrangements under which an individual's installment purchase account may be transferred to a nominated heir in the event of the owner's death. At least one company has an elaborate pattern of trust arrangements under which an owner's holdings constitute a revocable trust which may receive a variety of instructions. A number of funds operate trusts which accumulate shares purchased by self-employed individuals as retirement savings under the Keogh law. One fund sells its shares accompanied by a contract under which an affiliated life insurance company pledges itself to receive the proceeds from the liquidation of the trust shares as the purchase price of a life annuity at guaranteed rates when and if the owner requests it. (Quite possibly the growth of the variable annuity will induce other developments in this area. See Chapter 24.)

INVESTMENT COMPANIES AND INCOME TAXES

An investment company operating as a corporation, joint stock company, or Massachusetts trust is basically subject to the same income taxes which any business corporation would pay, and its dividends are taxable to its stockholders just as any corporate dividends would be. However, the income tax laws for some years have provided special tax advantages for "regulated investment companies" which follow prescribed diversification and dividend procedures. The distinction may be important for investors attempting to limit their tax burdens.

An investment company being taxed as an ordinary corporation has two general types of taxable income. The first, which may be called *taxable investment income*, consists of 100 per cent of taxable interest received plus (approximately) 15 per cent of dividends received, minus all operating expenses and general taxes. This is taxable at the regular corporate rate, which in 1972 was 48 per cent. The second type, *capital gains*, consists of profits realized on sale of investments. Net short-term capital gains (those on assets owned less than 6 months) are taxable at 48 per cent and net long-term capital gains at 30 per cent. When an investment company in this tax category pays dividends to its shareholders, the dividends are usually also taxable income to the shareholders.

An investment company may at its own request cease to be taxed as an ordinary corporation and instead become a *regulated investment company* for tax purposes, if it (1) obtains at least 90 per cent of its gross income from interest, dividends, and securities profits, with less than 30 per cent from short-term profits; (2) maintains a substantial degree of diversification, as defined in the law; (3) is not a holding company; and (4) pays out in dividends at least 90 per cent of its net investment income. A regulated investment company pays no income tax on any of its income or capital gains which it distributes to its shareholders in dividends. On the undistributed portion it pays the regular corporation rates. The shareholders of a regulated investment company must be notified as to whether their dividend receipts originate in investment income plus short-term capital gains or in long-term capital gains. The shareholders must record the former as ordinary taxable dividend income, but the latter they may count as their own personal long-term capital gains, to be taxed at the favorable capital gains rates.

If a regulated investment company elects not to distribute its capital gains in dividends but instead pays the 30 per cent capital gains tax and retains the net posttax capital gain, the investment company shareholders are subjected to a complicated but proper income tax calculation. First, the shareholder must include *his proportionate share* of the investment company's retained pretax capital gain on his own tax return as his own personal capital gain. Second, he must take credit for his proportionate share of the investment company's capital gains tax payment as a payment on his own personal income. Third, he must add his pro-

portionate share of the company's *net posttax retained capital gain* (70 per cent
of the actual market profit), on which his capital gains tax has now been paid,
to the recorded cost of his own investment company shares. This last addition is
designed to prevent the capital gain being taxed a second time, if he sells his investment company shares.

The whole plan of taxation of regulated investment companies is based on the
so-called *conduit theory*, which regards the regulated company as a mere organized conduit between the investment company shareholders and the diversified
underlying investments which they own. The investment company presumably
does not conduct a business and is therefore not a taxpaying entity. Its transactions and obligations should therefore be attributed pro rata to its shareholders.

An investment company which can meet the requirements for "regulated" tax
status can make important tax savings for itself and its shareholders, especially
if it has many shareholders in low personal tax brackets. Nearly all the open-end
companies and most of the diversified closed-end ones are now regulated.

RECENT DEVELOPMENTS

The rapid growth of the investment company idea has frequently stimulated innovations in the business. Since 1960 at least three new forms of investment company and several new types of sponsors have appeared. Some of these new developments may prove to be unimportant, but they should receive brief notice.

First, eight sponsor groups are now offering open-end funds which invest exclusively in tax-exempt state and municipal bonds. These funds are unmanaged
trusts which distribute tax-exempt interest to their shareholders and offer redemption on demand at asset value. They carry a one-time sales charge of about $3\frac{1}{2}$
to $4\frac{1}{2}$ per cent. An annual fee of less than $1 per $1,000 bond usually is charged
for supervision of the bond portfolio and for the custodial services of the trustee.
A total of 123 series of tax-exempt bond funds with an aggregate value of $1.6
billion has been sold since 1961, and this type of fund appears to be increasingly
popular with both large and small investors.

Second, some 33 "Centennial-type" mutual funds were organized between
1960 and 1967 to exchange their shares on a market-value basis for large blocks of
appreciated stock held by private investors. Unless a new law is passed by Congress, these tax-free exchange funds are of only historical interest except to the investors who hold the $1 billion of their shares already outstanding. No tax liabil-
ity was incurred by the exchanges; the investor's original cost was transferred to
his fund shares and stands as the fund's cost for tax purposes. The investor thus
gained a diversified and liquid position. These funds all made their exchanges at
the time of initial organization and dealt only in relatively large blocks of stock.

Third, there are now seven "dual-type" closed-end funds, mostly listed on the
New York Stock Exchange, all of which began business in 1967. These funds are
large, averaging over 50 million dollars in assets, and are all capitalized at equal

amounts of (approximately) 6 per cent cumulative participating preferred stock and common stock. The charters vary in their details, but in general they provide that *all* net investment income is to be paid regularly to the preferred shares, but that after 10 to 15 years the fund is to be liquidated, the preferred is to be retired at par plus unpaid cumulative dividends if any, and the common is to receive the balance of the assets. These funds are really a device for doubling both the dividend return to the preferred shareholder and the capital growth return to the common shareholder, since each of these investors has double his own invested sum at work for him. If market price-earnings ratios remain as they were in 1967 and if corporate per share earnings growth continues at an average 4 per cent rate, the preferreds should get a little more than their basic cumulative dividends and the common shares should obtain *capital gains* of at least 8 per cent per annum compounded when the funds are liquidated. Obviously, the managements will attempt to choose investments whose value growth will exceed the 4 per cent earnings growth of the market averages. One note of warning: These are closed-end shares, and their prices may sell above or below their net asset values. Since the dual fund common shares are long-term non-dividend investments, they may be especially vulnerable in weak markets.

The enormous growth of the mutual-fund idea naturally attracts new competitors to it. Since 1968, three different groups of competitors have moved to enter the field, and in the process they may introduce some new features and some new types of funds as well. First, more than 90 life insurance companies have established mutual funds or purchased the sponsors of established funds. Fund shares are being sold by life insurance agents either as separate investments or in conjunction with life insurance contracts, largely as a means of hedging the price-level risk. Ultimately, this could be a momentous development affecting the whole concept of life insurance and reacting drastically on the stock market, the bond market, and the mortgage market. Second, the large commercial banks have become interested in establishing no-load mutual funds which would be operated by their trust departments. The First National City Bank of New York actually began operating such a fund, but suspended it in 1971 when the Supreme Court ruled that the Banking Act of 1933 forbids such activities by banks. However, an amendment to the Banking Act or a modified mutual fund which could be operated under present law seems equally possible. Third, nonsecurities firms have entered the mutual-fund field, notably Sears, Roebuck, which in 1969 followed up successful ventures in the insurance and savings and loan businesses with the establishment of its Allstate Fund.

FINANCIAL REPORTS

Investment companies usually furnish thorough and informative financial reports to their shareholders. The year-end annual reports are supplemented by quarterly interim reports, and ample data can usually be had in the financial reporting services if desired. The reports to shareholders generally contain a balance sheet, an income statement, a list of securities held, and various analytical summaries classifying the company's securities, analyzing its surplus account, explaining its position with respect to unrealized profits and losses, and discussing its objectives and its investment record.

Although conventional financial statements are not ideal for displaying investment company performance, they are normally used with elaborate explanatory footnotes and supplementary schedules. A typical example is found in Tri-Continental Corporation's annual report, which contains formal statements but organizes the essentials in a statistical table from which Table 21-1 has been adapted. Tri-Continental Corporation is a very large closed-end investment company.

Table 21-1 sets forth a number of items which should be noted. First, it values the assets at market value rather than at cost. The net asset value per common share thus becomes realistic and significant. Second, it emphasizes the impact on asset values which the exercise of the outstanding stock purchase warrants would have. Third, it points out the enormous unrealized gains of nearly 313 million dollars in the investment portfolio; if these gains were realized by sale of the securities, either the company or the shareholders would have to pay between 50 and 75 million dollars in capital gains taxes. Fourth, it calls attention to the measurement of *net investment income*. This is a conventional measure which consists of the normal recurrent dividend, interest and miscellaneous income minus normal operating expenses. The normal operating expenses include management expenses, investment research costs, and ordinary taxes. However, gains or losses from securities transactions and brokerage fees and taxes connected with securities transactions are not usually included, for they are not regarded as regularly recurring incomes and expenses.

The net investment income per share is the figure usually tabulated in pocket manuals and other compilations in which per share earnings are shown. This may often be a deceptively small figure, for it obviously does not include an investment company's realized or unrealized securities profits, nor does it in any way recognize the value of the undistributed earnings of the corporations whose stocks are owned, yet it does include the expenses involved in selecting and watching the securities on which profits are expected.

Table 21-1 and most similar statements point up a tax problem which bothers many investment company managements. The unrealized profits on securities purchased early in the postwar period are very large. Like all others, these securities should be sold if their prices become too high or if money is needed for other opportunities—yet each sale would realize a large capital gain which must either be distributed as a taxable dividend to the recipient or retained as a taxable profit in the investment company. Either outcome is especially unfair to a new shareholder in an open-end investment company who has just paid net asset value plus

Table 21-1 *Tri-Continental Corporation financial summary for year and year-end 1971*

Assets:

Total assets at market value	$738,622,184.00
Amounts owed	25,988,389.00
Investment assets	712,633,795.00
Preferred stock at par value	37,637,000.00
Assets for common stock	674,996,795.00
Assets per common share	35.54
Assets per common share assuming exercise of warrants	34.71

Taxable long-term gains:

Total gains realized	$ 27,871,585.00
Gains realized per common share	1.47
Unrealized gain, end of year	312,913,833.00

Income:

Total dividend and other income	$ 18,251,191.00
Expenses and taxes	1,806,859.00
Net investment income	16,444,332.00
Preferred stock dividends	1,881,850.00
Net investment income on common stock	14,562,482.00
Net investment income per share	.77

Distributions per common share:

Dividends paid from income	$ .77
Capital gains distribution	1.21
Number common shares	18,991,627.00

Notes: (1) Preferred is $2.50 cumulative, $50 par. (2) Outstanding warrants entitle the holders to subscribe to 575,951 common shares at any time at $7.20 per share. (3) Corporation is a regulated investment company and distributes all income and gains, hence pays no federal income tax. (4) No provision has been made for possible tax if unrealized gains are realized. (5) Assets per common share include a $1.52 capital gain distribution pending at Dec. 31, 1971.

a loading charge for his shares, and any shareholder is reluctant to have his net asset value depleted by taxes. Consequently, investment company managements are reluctant to "manage" their resources as effectively as they might if tax depletion were not a factor.

OPERATING RESULTS

The efficiency of management in investment companies is commonly measured in two ways: by test of the statement of income and by a long-term measure of *performance*. Neither is a perfect check, because neither allows for the degree of security which has been afforded by conservative handling of the assets. Income

statement analysis has the further defect of failing to allow for deliberate choice
of low-dividend or nondividend stocks which appear likely to rise in price or for
high research expenses in a search for profit opportunities.

In the statement of income, the three essential figures are the total income, the
total operating expenses, and the net investment income. The ability of management to keep the gross and net income high and the expenses low is a measure of
efficiency. All of these items may properly be shown as percentages of the average
value of assets held, though the percentages must be expected to vary from year to
year because of fluctuations in the market value of the assets. Expenses are also
shown as percentages of total income. Table 21-2 shows percentages compiled
from 1971 company reports and year-end market prices.

An *index of performance* is a percentage measure of total gain or loss in an
investment fund between two dates. For example, if a fund had a net asset value
per share of $10 at the beginning of a year, paid a $1 dividend during the year,
and ended the year with a net asset value of $11, it is clear that the performance
gain for the year was $2, or 20 per cent of the initial $10 value. An index of performance might cover only a single year, or it might be measured over a long
period, such as 10 years. The purpose of an index of performance is to measure
the actual total success of an investment company management, whether that

Table 21-2   *Investment company cost and income factors, year and year-end 1966—data in
per cent of net asset value, year-end 1971*

Company	Total cost to acquire shares	Gross income, 1971	Operating expenses, 1971	Net investment income, 1971	Unrealized appreciation in portfolio
Adams Express	85.4	3.3	.45	2.9	21
Carriers and General	80.1	3.2	.99	2.2	60
Dominick Fund	78.3	2.4	.48	1.9	24
Lehman Corporation	91.6	1.9	.29	1.6	51
Tri-Continental	87.9	2.5	.28	2.2	46
Affiliated Fund	107.5	4.8	.37	4.4	0
Broad Street Investing	108.5	3.0	.29	2.7	35
Massachusetts Investors Growth	108.5	1.9	.34	1.6	42
Massachusetts Investors Trust	108.5	3.8	.23	3.6	34
T. Rowe Price Growth Fund	100.0	1.5	.51	1.0	25
Wellington Fund	108.5	4.1	.44	3.7	0
Moody's 125 Industrials		3.0		3.0	

success is achieved in obtaining large dividend income or market profits. The index will also enable stockholders to compare the results of different investment companies, if the comparison covers a long enough period for accidental variations to be averaged out and if due allowance is made for differences in safety. To be most significant, a long-period measure of performance must begin and end at dates when the stock market is neither very high nor very low, for investment company assets invariably reflect general market trends, and a measure of performance which merely records part of a market cycle will be misleading.

Different analysts compute indexes of performance in slightly different ways, though the general theory remains the same. The simplest method, that illustrated in the preceding paragraph, is applicable to investment company common shares only. This method measures the total gain per share for the period by adding up dividends paid plus increase in net asset value per share (or decrease if a shrinkage has occurred) plus the value of rights or stock dividends paid, and expresses this total gain as a percentage of the net asset value on the beginning date.

If it is desired to measure the performance of the *total assets* of an investment company instead of just the net asset value of the common stock, the calculations become complicated because of changes in capital structure of the companies. The technical differences in methods used make it necessary for the reader to consider the method followed in order to understand the figures.

Table 21-3 shows the year-by-year performance records of a number of investment companies over an 8-year span. The hypothetical performance of an imaginary fund having no expenses, holding no cash or bonds, and invested continuously in the stocks comprising Moody's price index of 125 industrial stocks is shown for comparison. No attempt has been made in this table to cumulate these annual figures into an 8-year total; perhaps a measure of average performance for these years could best be attempted here by computing a geometric average of the annual performance percentages for each company. The general impression gained by inspection of Table 21-3 and more detailed similar records is that the managements of investment companies can provide diversification and a fair degree of investment supervision, but that they find it difficult in normal years to select superior securities, pay their operating expenses, and still surpass the expense-free "performance" of a collection of good-grade stocks such as those included in Moody's index.

Performance comparisons have been criticized on the ground that they are rarely adjusted for risks. This criticism applies particularly to comparisons on a year-to-year or other short-term basis. In rising stock markets, the least conservative funds tend to score the largest percentage gains, but in major market declines they typically suffer the largest losses. A recognition of this point has led to suggestions by both industry representatives and SEC spokesmen that funds should report risks taken as well as gains achieved. One way to do this would be to ac-

Table 21-3 *Performance of investment company common shares: percentage gains and losses in the years 1964 through 1971*

Company	1964	1965	1966	1967	1968	1969	1970	1971
Adams Express	16	13	— 6	27	19	—12	7	11
Carriers and General	18	4	—13	21	11	— 4	12	14
Dominick Fund	11	21	0	33	3	— 6	—11	12
Lehman Corporation	14	19	— 3	28	6	— 2	— 7	27
Tri-Continental	13	11	— 6	25	10	1	0	22
Affiliated Fund	17	12	— 6	24	18	—14	2	9
Broad Street Investing	16	10	— 8	18	15	— 4	5	20
Massachusetts Investors Growth	10	25	2	29	2	0	6	23
Massachusetts Investors Trust	16	10	— 8	20	10	— 5	1	9
T. Rowe Price Growth Fund	12	26	— 1	27	8	3	— 8	32
Wellington Fund	11	5	— 7	8	8	— 8	6	9
23 large growth funds	14	32	— 1	42	10	—11	— 7	24
142 maximum gain funds	12	36	— 3	56	22	—17	—15	24
38 growth-and-income funds	15	18	— 6	26	15	—11	0	14
32 income funds	14	14	— 7	24	21	—15	6	15
22 balanced funds	12	10	— 6	19	14	—11	3	14
Moody's 125 Industrials	18	14	—14	29	9	— 6	4	15

These performance figures reflect dividend distributions and charges in net asset value, but acquisition costs are not included in initial cost figures. Data adapted in part from Wiesenberger's *Investment Companies.*

company each fund's performance measure with the beta coefficient of its securities portfolio, perhaps combining the two into a single *risk-adjusted* measure of performance. Aside from the theoretical shortcomings of beta as a measure of risk, the idea seems both plausible and fair as a basis for comparing fund performance.

DIVIDENDS AND YIELDS

Because of the income tax advantages inherent in the practice, most investment companies consistently distribute both net investment income and net realized capital gains to their shareholders. As Table 21-2 shows, the net investment income is likely to average a little less than the yield on the market indexes, but capital gains distributions[7] may make up the difference. If an investor pays more than net asset value for his stock his yield will be correspondingly less, but if he

---

[7] NASD rules require that capital gains distributions not be confused with regular dividends paid out of net investment income, and a different term is used.

buys for less than net asset value his yield will be greater. Because of the regularity of interest and dividend income in a diversified portfolio, the net investment income in most investment companies is reasonably stable, but the yield rate as a percentage of market price will vary as the market price level varies.

In order to permit investors to accumulate larger holdings conveniently, many open-end investment companies offer their shareholders the option of reinvesting their dividends in additional shares in the company. In the case of capital gains distributions, the reinvestment is often permitted at a price equal to net asset value, without payment of the customary loading charge. This is a valuable privilege, since it is equal to the privilege of making a diversified stock investment with much less than normal brokerage expense.

The stocks of the larger closed-end companies are traded on the stock exchanges, and the smaller ones usually have good over-the-counter markets. Strange as it may seem, the closed-end company shares often sell below net asset value, sometimes by as much as 25 to 30 per cent. The discounts on stocks with poor records tend to be larger than the others, but all seem to fluctuate irregularly as can be seen in Table 21-4. Discounts are usually larger in weak markets than in bullish ones. Because of the discounts, a closed-end stock can usually be purchased at a price on which the dividend yield will be considerably more than can be had on an open-end share of similar quality. In fact, the discount is often large enough so that the investor's yield on dividends out of net investment income is as great as the company's gross dividend and interest yield on the value of its holdings. In other words, the discount endows the management costs. The market prices of closed-end common stocks fluctuate in sympathy with the general market.

Table 21-4 *Discounts on closed-end common stocks at December 31, selected years (In per cent from net asset value)*

Company	1958	1962	1967	1969	1971
Adams Express	4	4	6	6P	12
Carriers and General	3	7	21	14	10
Dominick Fund	20	5	5	2	24
Lehman Corporation	11P	4P	16P	14P	7
Leverage Fund			19	15	1
Niagara Share	16	3	11	12P	15
Petroleum Corporation	6	5	3	4P	6
Scudder Duo-Vest			15	19	14
Tri-Continental	17	15	16	2	9

P indicates premium, net discount.
Leverage Fund and Scudder Duo-Vest are dual-type funds.

1969 THROUGH 1972: PERIOD OF DIGESTION

Two particular problems beset the investment companies during the 1969–1972 period, largely as a consequence of the too-aggressive investment and marketing practices which some mutual funds had pursued during the 1967–1968 bull stock market. To an increasing degree, investors appeared to question both the investment abilities of professional fund managers and the justification for the large sales loads charged by the funds. Both forms of discontent surfaced during the first half of 1972. For the first time in history, the mutual-fund industry suffered a 6-month excess of fund-share redemptions over new-share sales. The difference, amounting to 882 million dollars, appeared to consist largely of redemptions from fundholders attempting to get even for purchases made a few years earlier. Meanwhile, intensifying competition among investment companies sharply accelerated the number of funds converting from a load to a no-load sales basis. By mid-1972, more than 23 per cent of all mutual funds were being operated as no-load companies.

For mutual funds particularly, these problems raised issues to ponder. If investment companies were to become identified with speculation rather than investment, then their outlook would indeed change for the worse, since long experience demonstrated that speculators, in contrast to investors, typically suffer long-run loss and disappointment. During the late 1960s, investment companies as a whole had gathered an increasingly speculative aura and reputation. "Go-go" funds had emerged with "gunslinger" managers who made spectacular gains in rising markets and equally large losses in declining ones. The turnover of securities in mutual-fund portfolios had accelerated from an annual rate of around 16 per cent before 1965 to nearly 50 per cent in 1969. Many stockbrokers had tended to "push" mutual-fund shares in the manner of speculative stocks. Whether these practices would return in future bull markets, with still more serious public disillusionment and bitterness toward the funds, remained to be seen. Ultimately, it seemed, the question would have to be faced either privately by the industry's own forces of self-regulation or publicly by the SEC and Congress.

Reduced sales loads posed a more direct challenge to the industry, though almost certainly a less serious one. During 1972, the SEC recommended new legislation which would free brokers to set their own commissions for mutual-fund sales, and thus force sales loads down through competition. Early in 1973 the Justice Department filed an antitrust suit against the National Association of Securities Dealers and 15 leading brokerage firms and mutual funds, contesting the legality of the long-standing requirement that investors buy or sell all mutual-fund shares through the funds themselves; this suit aimed at developing a new central market in which investors could trade mutual-fund shares with one another. However, the long experience of both the closed-end companies and several older no-load funds demonstrated that investment companies did not require added revenue from sales commissions to operate efficiently. Thus it appeared that, under pressure of competition, sales loads among mutual funds would tend to disappear unless they were justified either (1) by superior service to investors on the load funds' part, or (2) by the fact that, as with life insurance, the salesman's role was indispensable to effective merchandising. The long-standing failure of the closed-end companies to hold their market share against the mutual funds tended to support claims that heavily compensated selling services were essential to industry growth, although the recent surge in no-load funds could be cited in rebuttal. At year-end 1972, the no-load funds still controlled only about 13 per cent of all mutual-fund assets.

Meanwhile, other factors brightened the outlook for investment companies. A continuing rise in stock exchange commissions for small investors had narrowed the gap between the costs of common stock investment and mutual-fund ownership. The Investment Company Act amendment of 1970 contained no provisions likely to impair the industry's growth or financial health. Attacks by do-gooder groups on the investment freedom of fund managers had come to naught, and the few funds that had organized to invest heavily in such causes as consumer protection, civil rights, and a clean environment had failed to find strong followings, a result suggesting that even socially conscious investors find profits indispensable. Finally, during 1972 Congress held hearings on a new, individual retirement benefits bill which, if passed, would obviously bring immense new business to the investment companies. This legislation would allow tax deductions for individuals setting up their own pension plans and for those contributing to corporate pension plans. It would also liberalize the so-called Keogh plans for the self-employed.

CONCLUSIONS

It is clear that investment company shares are varied in nature and function. They probably have a place in most portfolios and perhaps should constitute the principal common stock holdings of many small investors, but an inappropriate selection will obviously limit the usefulness of even these investments. A proper choice must consider (1) the investment objectives desired, (2) the amount of risk which may be borne, (3) whether specialization is desirable, (4) the need for a conversion opportunity, (5) the dividend policy, (6) the performance record, and (7) the price. Since consideration of all these factors requires a mastery of the subject far beyond the scope of most investors, it is probable that investment company opportunities are not fully utilized.

Nevertheless, the investment company idea has grown momentously. It has appealed to both institutional investors and individuals, and the present attractive variety of investment features will be enlarged as innovations continue.

Many pronounced opinions about investment companies are held by individual investors and by securities dealers, most of which are founded on individual

tastes as well as factual background. Some of the more important of these are as
follows:

1   Open-end shares are preferable to closed-end shares because *(a)* the sales
loading pays for full explanations by salesmen and in the sales literature; *(b)*
the sales loading is not much greater than brokerage commissions, plus odd-lot
differentials on a diversified portfolio, would cost the average investor; *(c)* the
assurance of a redemption price based on net asset value is an important safeguard to a small investor; *(d)* convenient special features are available to serve
many investment needs; and *(e)* the opportunity to dollar-average by buying
small quantities periodically or on an installment contract is profitable.

2   Closed-end shares are preferable to open-end ones because *(a)* the shares
may often be bought far below net asset value, hence their dividends and market
gains based on their own assets may be large compared to the investor's purchase
price; *(b)* the brokerage charge of 2 or 3 per cent does not deplete the investor's
principal as much as an 8 per cent loading; *(c)* brokerage charges are low enough
to make speculative buying and selling possible; and *(d)* market price fluctuations
make trading profits possible.

3   Balanced funds are preferable to common stock funds because *(a)* they provide a balanced assortment of securities, not just stocks; and *(b)* they contain
bonds and preferred stocks, hence are relatively safe and stable in price.

4   Common stock funds are preferable to balanced funds because *(a)* they
earn more; *(b)* management costs and loading fees pay for management service on
common stock money, where it is needed, not on bonds and savings account
money, where it is not needed; and *(c)* bonds and savings accounts can be kept
separate, hence available in emergencies without the necessity of surrendering
any stocks (the stock portion of a balanced fund share) at a possible loss.

5   A very large investment fund is preferable to a small one, because *(a)* it can
be more widely diversified; *(b)* it can afford the research costs necessary to sound
portfolio management; and *(c)* its cash operations with respect to sale and redemption of shares (in an open-end fund) are likely to be more stable, hence to
permit a more stable investment policy than would be possible in a small fund.

6   A small fund is preferable, because it can make investment shifts, selling
one holding and buying another, without a large impact on the market price of
the stocks, whereas large-volume trades by large funds drive the market down as
they sell or up as they buy.

7   A no-load fund is preferable to a load fund because *(a)* it involves no
acquisition cost; *(b)* the investment record of no-load funds *at least* equals that of
load funds; and *(c)* as wide a range of fund types and objectives is available
among no-loads as can be found among load funds.

8   A load fund is preferable to a no-load because *(a)* the load pays for selling
services which better acquaint the investor with the fund's features and his own
purpose in investing; *(b)* a load fund's managers have stronger incentives and try

harder; and *(c)* load funds typically offer superior services, such as in-group conversions, at no additional charge.

Information about investment companies is easy to obtain. Perhaps the most comprehensive source is the annual issue of *Investment Companies*, published by Arthur Wiesenberger & Company, and available in most libraries and securities houses. This book is replete with information and statistics about investment companies in general and all the important American management companies individually. A second important source is Arthur Lipper Corporation, also of New York City, which also publishes comprehensive statistics on the mutual-fund industry and its component companies. For mutual-fund ratings that are judgments rather than just rankings, *Forbes* and *Fundscope* magazines are the best sources usually available to individual investors. S & P's *Industry Surveys* contains a survey of the business and comparative data on leading closed-end investment companies. Several other investment periodicals, notably *Barron's*, cover this field frequently and are especially faithful in studying incomes, expenses, and performance records at quarterly or semiannual intervals. The investment reference manuals cover investment companies as thoroughly as they do other types of investments.

The interest of the securities business as it relates to investment companies is heavily concentrated in the open-end companies. The sales loading on these shares is great enough to finance a vigorous sales effort supported by advertising and quantities of sales literature, and the real merit of most of the shares supplies any other needed incentive to the trade. The closed-end companies, on the other hand, usually have little market sponsorship. The stocks of the larger closed-end companies, such as Adams Express, Lehman Corporation, and Tri-Continental Corporation, are listed on the stock exchanges; those of the smaller companies are traded over the counter.

❁ ADDENDA

Although there are many types of collective investments available in the American markets, there are a few whose histories or structure seem particularly appropriate to consider here. Space limitations permit only a few words of definition and comment on each, but at least the opportunities these items afford can be noted.

SMALL-BUSINESS INVESTMENT COMPANIES (SBICs)

Although the small-business investment companies are properly finance companies rather than investment companies, they are to an extent comparable to closed-end special-situation companies. The SBICs are private corporations licensed by the Federal Small Business Administration to make loans or stock investments in small American business firms. The SBICs may borrow from the federal government, or under a new law passed in 1972, the Small Business Administration may guarantee their debentures. Their investment losses are deductible from ordinary taxable income, and they may elect to be taxed as regulated investment companies. In addition, SBIC stockholders may deduct any capital loss sustained on SBIC stock in full from ordinary taxable income.

The federal law authorizing the SBICs was passed in 1958 and the first companies began business in 1960. About 700 charters have been issued, most of them in the first 4 years of the program, but of 577 SBICs licensed to do business in 1967, only about 300 remained in 1972; the others have become straight venture-capital firms, ordinary operating companies, or subsidiaries of other concerns. Only about 50 SBICs sold shares to the public; the others are privately owned lending ventures or affiliates of banks or other lending institutions. The SBICs invest principally in long-term, speculative development-type loans which are convertible into stock. Thus far, as was expected, the loans have resulted in a fair quota of losses, a few spectacular gains, and many holdings which are as yet neither proven successes nor failures. Like all closed-end investment company shares, the publicly owned SBIC stocks are free to fluctuate in price independently of the asset values behind them, and their price fluctuations have been violent. The larger SBICs are reviewed in the financial services and their stocks are traded over the counter.

FACE-AMOUNT CERTIFICATES

Face-amount certificates are savings contracts under which an investor makes a lump-sum payment or agrees to make periodic cash payments over a period of years, and is entitled to collect a lump sum representing his payments plus accumulated compound interest at the end of the contract term. If he terminates his contract before it is complete or fails to make the agreed payments on schedule, his interest earnings are reduced. Obviously, these contracts can be made more attractive by coupling borrowing privileges or group life insurance contracts with them. Face-amount certificates must be registered with the SEC and can be sold only by face-amount certificate companies registered under the Investment Company Act of 1940.

HEDGE FUNDS

A hedge fund is an investment partnership which in principle seeks to balance its risks by "hedging" long positions in some stocks with short sales of others. However, most hedge funds "trade the market" aggressively, concentrating their investments in a few stocks, buying and selling at comparatively short intervals, dealing heavily in puts and calls, and borrowing maximum amounts on margin from brokers, banks, and other lenders. This type of fund became popular during the late 1960s, and in 1969 some 300 of them were operating with a total invested capital of about 2 billion dollars.

Only a dozen or so hedge funds are available to the investing public. The great majority consist of private partnerships which have fewer than 100 partners, do not solicit investors at large, and thus avoid both registration with the SEC and most of the Commission's regulatory sway. The private funds typically demand initial investments of $100,000 or more from each limited-partner investor in the fund. The managers are usually compensated with 20 per cent of the market profits they make. The managers of public hedge funds receive a percentage of the net asset value of the fund similar to the fees paid the managements of conventional mutual funds. In addition, most public funds carry a loading charge of between 7 and 9 per cent.

In practice, hedge funds are largely vehicles by which well-to-do persons engage professional portfolio managers to speculate for them. Overall, these funds have achieved unimpressive records. A number made above-average profits during the stock market rise of 1967–1968, but during the market decline of 1969–1970, relatively few sold short on a sufficient scale, and most of them sustained losses of 50 per cent or more on highly leveraged long positions.[8]

During 1969, several aspects of hedge-fund operation excited the suspicions of the SEC, particularly the conflicts of interest latent in the participation of more than 200 brokerage-house officials and salesmen in hedge-fund partnerships. Other questions arose with respect to the amounts and sources of money borrowed by the funds, their methods of operation, and their effect upon stock market prices. The Commission collected considerable information from the funds through questionnaire surveys, and in 1971 appealed to Congress for additional legislation to bring hedge funds under effective regulation. But in mid-1973, Congress had still failed to act.

OIL-DRILLING PARTICIPATION FUNDS

These relative newcomers to the family of quasi funds offer high-tax-bracket investors the chance to participate in a diversified "pool" of speculative oil-well drilling ventures together with substantial tax shelters for both money outlays and financial returns. Funds are sold in the form of "participation units," with a fixed price per unit. For example, while most units are priced in the $5,000 to $10,000 area, they range from $1,500 to $25,000. The size of the total funds themselves varies from a few million dollars to 100 million dollars or more. Besides the original unit price, some programs require investors to put up more money to

---

[8] A study of 28 hedge funds, published in the May 1971 issue of *Fortune* magazine, reported that only 1 fund made a profit in 1969–1970, while 21 of them suffered losses of 50 per cent or more.

develop any producing properties found, although this sum is usually limited to 20 per cent of the original fund investment.

The investor's benefits from a drilling fund consist heavily of income tax savings. Ordinarily, about 75 per cent of the investment in an oil or gas project is deductible from taxable income as a write-off of intangible drilling costs, i.e., outlays essential to drilling a well—roads, wages, drilling muds, and so on—but having no salvage value. If a fund has its total capitalization invested in different oil projects, the holder of a fund unit can ultimately deduct about $750 from his taxable income for each $1,000 of drilling units owned. This tax saving operates to reduce his net cost of the fund. For example, an investor in the 70 per cent tax bracket would realize a tax saving of .70 $\times$ $750, or $525, leaving a net cost per unit of $475.

Besides the favorable tax treatment from writing off the intangible drilling expenses, the investor will derive large tax benefits from depletion allowances and equipment depreciation if the well is successful. The depletion allowance is 22½ per cent of gross income (not to exceed 50 per cent of net profit), and thus a substantial proportion of the income from producing wells is tax-free. Depreciation write-offs of pumps, derricks, tanks, casings, and other equipment further increase the tax-free return of cash.

The production income from successful wells is considered a return of capital until the net investment is recovered. Once this investment is recouped, the individual may still receive a long flow of tax-favored income over the life of the well. Most drilling funds employ accounting firms to prepare combined drilling-production tax reports which the investor can simply attach to his federal income tax return, thus eliminating any bookkeeping worries on his part.

Although drilling participations offer investors the chance of exceptionally high returns, the potential for loss is also very great. Some 14 out of every 15 wildcat wells drilled in the United States result in dry holes, and only 40 to 50 per cent of all development-well drilling proves successful. Clearly, such risks should be borne only by high-tax-bracket investors with large financial reserves. The prospectuses of most reputable participation funds have long stated that investors should be in at least the 50 per cent tax bracket. In mid-1972 the NASD approved new rules prohibiting the offer of drilling units to investors with tax brackets below 50 per cent or net wealth below $100,000. Oil-drilling participation funds are registered not under the Investment Company Act but under the Securities Act of 1933, which is less exacting. In mid-1972, the SEC asked Congress for new legislation which would subject oil-drilling funds to the Investment Company Act.

Orange-grove funds and funds for the feeding or breeding of cattle are further variants of the investment company principle. In these undertakings, the investor's legal status is usually that of a limited partner. Various tax advantages may benefit the high-bracket investor, but the funds themselves are inherently hazardous; most of those organized in recent years appear to have lost substantial sums for their investors.

A few mutual funds have been organized to trade in commodities, but none has proved permanently successful. At the opposite extreme, at least one fund has been organized to facilitate small-unit investments in pools of marketable government securities.

TRUSTS

A trust is a legal device under which property is administered by one who is not the owner, acting under written instructions or court order, for the benefit of one or more beneficiaries designated in the trust instructions.[9] As such, the trust is not a collective investment in which one buys shares. It is a managerial device established to supervise investments and distribute the proceeds according to the maker's instructions. Because the property laws in all states permit the creation of trusts and require diligent performance by trustees, and because trusts have definite tax advantages, the trust idea is popular and growing.

The individual who furnishes the property and gives the trustee his instructions is the maker, donor, grantor, or trustor of the trust. The person or persons who are to receive income or principal from the trust are termed beneficiaries. The person having possession and control of the property is the trustee; the trustee may be an individual, a group of individuals, or a corporation. A trust may be established very simply; the trustor simply executes a declaration of trust or a will in which he sets forth his instructions to the trustee, and provides for delivery of the property. The trustor may instruct the trustee as to the nature of the investments to be used, the identity of the beneficiaries and the benefits to be given them, and the discretion which the trustee may exercise in dealing with emergencies. The trust may be made revocable at the option of the trustor, or once effective, it may be irrevocable; and the trustor may direct that he or others shall or shall not have the right to change the instructions to the trustee at a future date. The trustor may deliver the property to the trustee when the trust is planned, or he may leave it by his will, or he may have life insurance proceeds paid to the trustee.

Trusts do not die with their makers. Indeed, one of their common functions is to administer property and care for two or three generations of beneficiaries. Although trusts for other than charitable purposes are not permitted to continue indefinitely, it is usually possible to maintain them for "the longer of designated lives now in being plus 21 years," or some equally extended period. An individual

---

[9] This definition emphasizes one form of trust. However, trusts are also used to hold title to corporate property pledged to secure bond issues; to hold the title and possession of securities and money deposited in escrows; to hold decedents' estates pending their final distribution; to manage bankruptcy estates; and for many other purposes. The operation and management of corporate pension and profit-sharing trusts are discussed in detail in Chapter 23.

may, for example, establish a trust which will care for his wife's needs and his own, thereafter care for his children as long as they live, and finally be distributed to his grandchildren. Income or principal or both may be paid out at such times or under such conditions as the trustor stipulates.

Because of the hazards incident to illness and mortality, long-lasting trusts are usually placed in the care of self-perpetuating boards or of corporations. Endowed hospitals, schools, and charitable foundations are often "owned" by boards of trustees who elect new members to fill vacancies. (Other such institutions are organized as nonprofit corporations with self-perpetuating boards of directors.) Many trusts created to administer personal or family resources are operated by the trust departments of banks or trust companies. However, many family trusts are administered by members of the family, or by a board consisting of members of the family plus the family attorney, or by a member of the family plus a bank trust department. Trusts established while the trustor is living (living trusts) may be organized and conducted very simply as private contractual arrangements; but those established by will or court order (court trusts) must in many cases continue indefinitely under judicial scrutiny, making periodic reports to the court about such matters as investments, disbursements, and the measures taken to carry out the instructions of the trustor.

A trustee is legally obligated to exercise reasonable diligence and competence in administering any trust, and failure to do so will render him personally liable. This applies to individuals, boards of trustees, and corporate trustees. However, if the trustee follows the trust instructions and controlling laws with reasonable diligence and competence, he is not liable for losses sustained.

Although careful and specific trust instructions may be important to the trustor in assuring that his desires are carried out, it is often useful to grant considerable discretionary authority to the trustee in order to permit him to cope with changing circumstances. The needs of the beneficiaries may change, economic circumstances may require a flexible investment policy, or the whole purpose of the trust may become obsolete.

The amount of money being administered in trusts is very large. The commercial banks of the United States were administering approximately $262 billion of trust property at year-end 1972, and this total was growing at 6 per cent per year. Substantial additional sums are held in trust by life insurance companies, nonbank trust companies, individual trustees, and numerous boards of trustees who handle family trusts or institutional endowments. The grand total compares impressively with the 1972 total assets of $237 billion in life insurance companies and $230 billion in savings and loan associations.

The great flexibility of the trust arrangement would make it possible, if there were no laws to prevent, for trustors to immobilize property for long periods and for purposes which might become absurd or obsolete. Consequently, many statutes have been passed to regulate the nature, functions, and duration of trusts and to deny validity to trusts which do not comply with the law. Among the types of statutes commonly passed by the states are those limiting the duration of trusts, discouraging or forbidding trusts which do not pay out income to beneficiaries, forbidding trusts created for the sole benefit of the trustor, and forbidding trusts from which the beneficiary may withdraw principal as well as income at his discretion at any time. Because the state statutes vary, it is necessary for trustors to be sure of the law under which their trusts are established. When trustor, trustee, and beneficiary may all reside in different states, the possibilities of confusion are evident.

The supervision of trusts held by banks and trust companies is basically a matter of state law. However, any bank which is a member of the Federal Reserve System must also obtain the consent of designated federal authorities before undertaking a trust business. The consent is routine when the bank appears to be large enough, sound enough, and competent to carry on this type of business, and if there appears to be a need for its services. The bank is required to keep each trust's assets separate from all others and from its own, to keep a separate set of records for each trust, to manage the trust assets diligently and lawfully, to refrain from selling to or buying from the trust, and to execute the trustor's instructions faithfully.

The investments in which a trust's assets may be placed are always a matter of concern. If the trustor chooses to stipulate the investment policies to be followed, the trustee must follow instructions. If the trustor grants "full and complete discretion" to the trustee, reasonable policies followed by the trustee are usually acceptable in law. If the trust instrument makes no statement about investments, the trustee is bound to follow the statutes or ruling court decisions of the state whose laws govern the trust. Of the 50 states, 45, including Massachusetts, Michigan, Illinois, California, and New York, observe in varying degrees what is known as the "prudent man" rule; that is, they allow an uninstructed trustee considerable discretionary authority to purchase investments of any type, including common stocks, which an ordinarily prudent man would find suitable in the case at hand. The rest of the states are "legal list" states; that is, they tend to hold that uninstructed trust funds must be rigorously preserved, hence must be conservatively invested in very secure bonds and mortgages of the types prescribed for savings banks. In any case the trustee is obligated, within the scope of his authority, to obtain suitable yield and diversification.

Because reasonable diversification in small trusts is difficult to obtain, all 50 states now have passed special statutes authorizing banks to combine the funds of small trusts into diversified investment pools. These pools are known as common trust funds; they are operated in a fashion similar to open-end investment companies, except that the only investors in them are the trusts handled by the bank. A bank may operate several common trust funds, possibly one invested entirely in stocks, another entirely in mortgages, and a third holding an assortment of securities; this would permit any trust to have the safety of diversification in a type of security suitable to the needs of the trust. No special charge for either establishment or administration of the common trust fund is made by the bank; it is compensated by the regular fees paid by the trusts. Common trust funds are still new, having been practically unknown in the 1930s, but in 1970 nearly 1,700 such funds were in operation, administering more than 10 billion dollars in assets owned by 412,000 separate individual trusts.

Trust investments are generally handled with great stress upon preservation of principal, and the assets are normally all of good quality. However, the rising emphasis is on price-level protection and capital growth and the great appreciation of many common stock holdings have caused the common stock portions of trust funds to increase as percentages of the whole. On a market-value basis, the personal trust investments held by insured commercial banks in 1970 consisted of about 68 per cent common stock, 20 per cent bonds, 6 per cent real estate and mortgages, and the balance miscellaneous. Common trust funds were slightly more conservative, including 56 per cent in common stocks and 31 per cent in bonds.

The asset distributions noted in these surveys suggest that most long-term private trusts probably obtain gross incomes amounting to between 4 and 5.5 per cent, with the norm about 4.5 per cent. (This does not include capital gains on stocks.) From this must be deducted the trustee's fees and taxes. In a full management trust in which the trustee bears the responsibility of selection of diversified investments, safe deposit, accounting, tax reporting, and some discretionary supervision of beneficiaries' needs, the trustee's fee will fall between .30 per cent and .75 per cent of the principal per annum, with a minimum of $150 per year. If the trustee's functions include management of real estate, supervision of businesses, or other extensive activity, the cost will be greater; if the investments are to consist permanently of government bonds or investment funds chosen by the trustor, or if the trustee is otherwise relieved of work and responsibility, the cost will be less. The trustee's fee would not be greater if he were instructed to keep the entire fund or some stipulated part of it in good stocks, with the objective of maximizing income and capital gains.

There are no serious tax disadvantages in the use of trusts. General property taxes, when applicable, are assessed to the trustee and charged to the trust at the same rates as if assessed to an individual. The income of a revocable trust, or one in which the trustor has control or is the beneficiary, is taxable to the trustor; otherwise, distributed income is taxable to the beneficiaries and undistributed income is taxable to the trust as though it were a person. When the trustor dies, any property in a trust in which he had control or an interest is taxed as a part of his estate; but if he creates an irrevocable and completely independent trust during his lifetime, the property will escape probate costs and death taxes when he dies but may be subject to an immediate gift tax. Nevertheless, a trust may have great cost and tax advantages; property placed in trust during the trustor's lifetime does not pass through probate at his death; and a trust, once established, may care for successive generations of beneficiaries without further probates or death taxes, if the trust is properly independent of the beneficiaries' control.[10]

The usefulness of trust services is probably little understood by most investors. For an annual fee very little larger than that charged for investment counsel alone, the trustor obtains professional investment management, safe deposit, and accounting services. He may place his trusteed property beyond the reach of his own or his heirs' mistakes, where creditors and importuning relatives cannot get it. He may instruct the trustee as to the normal distribution of benefits and also give him further discretionary authority to assist beneficiaries in unusual situations. All this may simplify and reduce probate and death tax costs. Finally, these advantages are available to large and small investors. Bank trust departments actively solicit trusts of $50,000 and up, and they will take them as small as $20,000 or $25,000, especially if the bank has a common trust fund which may be used as the means of investment. The charges imposed on a very small trust are proportionately somewhat greater than those on a large one, but they are seldom so high as to be prohibitive.

QUESTIONS AND PROBLEMS

1   What are the basic purposes of an investment company? Are they worth the cost?
2   Would you recommend a balanced fund or a diversified stock fund plus an independent holding of bonds for a general portfolio? Which would provide emergency liquidity to best advantage?
3   Would you prefer open-end or closed-end companies for your own investment? Would you choose differently for a widowed aunt who knows little of business?
4   Should the law set maximum portfolio turnover rates for mutual funds? Should funds be required to hold their stocks for certain periods before selling them?
5   Does the preferred stock of an investment company which owns mostly common stock really have a senior position, or is it just common stock in quality without the customary common stock advantages?
6   Is net investment income per share in an investment company comparable with net income per share in an ordinary business? Is this an appropriate "earnings" figure for pocket manuals to display?
7   Are the tax privileges given to regulated investment companies fair to other taxpayers and other forms of business? Should these privileges be extended to funds whose principal objective is market profits? Are they?
8   Over what minimum period should investment company performance be measured for purposes of comparison? Why this choice of period?

---

[10] The cost of probating and settling an estate consisting of securities, including attorneys' and executors' fees but not including taxes, might typically amount to 10 per cent on $10,000, 6 per cent on $50,000, or 4 per cent on $100,000. Death taxes are considered in Chap. 27.

9 Could a corporation afford to invest its pension funds in a large open-end fund? In several large open-end funds?

10 How do you explain the fact that, on average, the no-load funds have performed at least as well in recent years as the load funds? What does the investor purportedly pay for in a loading charge?

11 Do you expect the dual funds to perform well for their investors?

12 Will life insurance companies simply add mutual funds to their line of merchandise, or will they integrate saving in stocks with life insurance and life annuity protection? Will they attract enough additional demand into stocks to have an impact on stock price levels? Could this trend possibly affect interest rates on bonds and mortgages?

13 Because investment companies are professionally managed, would not speculators in bull markets be better off buying closed-end company shares or no-load mutual-fund shares than trying to select specific company stocks?

14 How would you go about choosing an investment company stock for your own use? Plan a definite procedure, considering the decisions you would have to make and the sources of information you would probably use.

15 What sort of "free competition" and "full disclosure" rules would promote economical operation and minimal loading charges by mutual funds? Does the life insurance business have government rules limiting operating expenses and selling commissions?

16 Should banks be allowed to establish mutual funds either separately or cooperatively? If a big bank operated a mutual fund, should its smaller correspondent banks be permitted to sell shares in it? Would SEC regulation be needed?

17 The Treasury is said to favor a proposal which would impose estate taxes on a family trust every time one beneficiary died and another succeeded him. Would this be feasible and equitable?

18 If a grandfather wishes to leave $300,000 to provide a life income for his son and two daughters and for ultimate distribution to his grandchildren, would you approve a testamentory trust which makes the three the trustees and stipulated investment of 25 per cent each in government bonds, one large open-end fund, one large closed-end fund, and the common stock of one dual fund?

19 If a trust is instructed to pay a life income to one beneficiary and its principal ultimately to a remainderman, should the trustee invest heavily in low-income growth stocks? Who ought to get capital gains and small stock dividends?

20 Many trustees are instructed to make payments from principal when the trustee believes that any beneficiary requires certain types of emergency assistance. Is this a proper obligation for a bank trustee?

REFERENCES

American Institute for Economic Research: *Investment Trusts and Funds from the Investor's Point of View*, Great Barrington, Mass., occasional.

Badger, Ralph E., and Paul B. Coffman: *Investment Analysis*, McGraw-Hill Book Company, New York, 1967, Chap. 19.

Bellemore, Douglas H., and John C. Ritchie, Jr.: *Investments*, 3d ed., South-Western Publishing Company, Incorporated, Cincinnati, 1969, Chap. 26.

Bogert, George C.: *Law of Trusts*, 4th ed., West Publishing Company (Hornbook series), St. Paul, Minn., 1963.

Cohen, Jerome B., and Edward D. Zinbarg: *Investment Analysis and Portfolio Management*, rev. ed., Richard D. Irwin, Inc., Homewood, Ill., 1973, Chap. 16.

Investment Company Institute: *Mutual Fund Fact Book*, New York, annual.

Sauvain, Harry: *Investment Management*, 3d ed., Prentice-Hall, Inc., Englewood Cliffs, N.J., 1967, Chap. 20.

Securities and Exchange Commission: *Special Study of Securities Markets* Washington, 1963, Part 4, Chap. XI. Also, *Public Policy Implications of Investment Company Growth*, 1966.

Stephenson, Gilbert T.: *Estates and Trusts*, 4th ed., Appleton-Century-Crofts, Inc., New York, 1965.

Study of Mutual Funds, Report of the Committee on Interstate and Foreign Commerce, HR 2274, 87th Congress, 2d session, 1962.

Weisenberger, Arthur G.: *Investment Companies*, New York, annual.

Widicus, Wilbur W., Jr., and Thomas E. Stitzel: *Personal Investing*, Richard D. Irwin, Inc., Homewood, Ill., 1971, Chapter 10.

In the past generation the American economy has made increasing use of high-quality short-term investments. Individuals and business firms alike have been prosperous, and a prosperous community can afford the luxury of a comfortable supply of liquid resources, even if at most times they earn a little less than long-term securities. Furthermore, the very large sums which business firms must now accumulate for tax payments, dividends, bond interest, debt installments, and business capital outlays should be profitably employed in short-term investments until they are needed. These situations create a demand for many billions of short-term investments.

On the supply side it has become evident that government agencies, banks, finance companies, and other major financial institutions can safely borrow and use large amounts of savers' temporary funds, depending on collections or new loans from other savers to provide the money to meet the maturities as they occur. Some of these money-using agencies, notably the banks and savings and loan associations, borrow by using modernized forms of their traditional time deposit and savings account techniques. Others, such as the federal government agencies and the sales finance companies, borrow from large-scale investors through the sale of instruments which are effectively short-term securities.

As the importance of the short-term investments has grown, the institutions borrowing such funds and the dealers who market such obligations have developed fast and efficient methods for selling the obligations and paying them off when due. In some cases, efficient secondary markets also permit resale of the obligations if the holders cannot wait for maturity. Because these processes are safe and easy, big business firms now tend to budget their cash requirements and lend out their surplus cash on almost a daily basis. This is a considerable task in a far-flung major corporation, for it requires almost daily assembling and dispatch of cash at a central place, but it is a profitable operation when interest rates are normal or high.

All the short-term investments to be discussed in this chapter are available for investment by individuals, though some are usually sold only in rather large amounts. Business firms are not eligible to own certain types of deposit accounts, but all the money-market instruments are available to them. The term money-market instrument (or money-market investment) is loosely applied to all types of short-term high-quality obligations which are transacted in substantial amounts on an impersonal basis to effect temporary employment of funds.

Table 22-1 illustrates the rapid growth of savings-type accounts since 1950. The money-market investments have grown similarly, and both types are so economical and so liquid that investment of a bank's surplus cash for as short a period as one day and business or personal funds for as short a period as one week is feasible. Most money-market investments mature in a time range between 30

Table 22-1 *Savings funds in selected institutions, December 31, 1920–1971 (In billions of dollars*

Year	Deposits in mutual savings banks	Time and savings deposits in commercial banks	Unpledged shares and deposits in savings and loan associations	Credit unions, shares and deposits
1920	$ 4.8	$ 10.5	$ 1.7	
1925	7.3	16.3	3.8	
1930	9.4	19.0	6.3	
1935	9.8	13.2	4.3	$ .1
1940	10.6	15.4	4.3	.2
1945	15.3	30.2	7.4	.4
1950	20.0	36.5	14.0	.9
1955	28.1	49.7	32.2	2.4
1960	36.3	73.1	62.1	5.0
1965	52.4	147.1	110.3	9.3
1970	72.0	230.6	146.4	15.5
1971	81.9	271.8	174.5	18.3

Sources: United States Savings and Loan League, *Saving and Loan Fact Book; Federal Reserve Bulletin*; and Credit Union National Association, *Credit Union Yearbook.*

days and 6 months, but almost any desired maturity date can be had, and most of the items are salable if the money is needed unexpectedly.

Since surplus cash can be invested as received and recovered when needed, business firms and local government agencies and individuals all now operate with relatively smaller demand deposit balances than they formerly maintained. In effect, short-term investments are a near-money supply, providing economic liquidity and unquestionably having an effect on interest rates and aggregate demand. As long as they exist in great quantity in an effective market, they permit a relatively limited supply of demand deposits and currency to circulate with extremely high velocity. Since the Federal Reserve System's procedures for credit control involve mostly control of the availability of demand deposits, the presence of a large volume of liquid short-term investments tends to make their operations tricky and difficult. However, no plans to extend quantitative regulatory devices to this market have been proposed as yet.

Investors considering short-term investments need to compare them with reference to eight basic criteria. Paramount among these, of course, are (1) safety
and (2) net yield. The others are (3) denominations and practicable amounts, (4)
taxability, (5) suitability of maturity, (6) possible sale or withdrawal without
loss, (7) convenience to buy and collect, and (8) ownership form.

❋   ## SAVINGS-TYPE ACCOUNTS

The accounts to be considered in this section are the interest- or
dividend-paying investments regularly available in commercial banks, mutual
savings banks, and savings and loan associations. These have a varied nomenclature—they may be called deposits, certificates, accounts, or some other term,
and their earnings may be dubbed either interest or dividends—but they are
nearly all short-term items, payable in dollars, substantially safe, and highly
liquid.

Because these savings-type accounts can be handled personally at a teller's
window in transactions of any desired size, they have long been the province of
the small investor. They provide him the opportunity for small investments, the
convenience of an emergency financial reserve, a persuasive credit reference,
and a ready introduction to a loan source when he desires to purchase real estate
or an automobile. And his savings institution probably also operates safe deposit
vaults, sells money orders, transacts business in savings bonds, and cashes checks,
and hence is highly convenient to him.

However, the great growth of the short-term markets in recent years has led
the commercial banks and the larger savings and loan associations to compete
actively for larger-scale business accounts as well. This has brought these savings
institutions into direct competition with the money-market borrowers, and has
resulted in some adaptation of the traditional savings-account forms as well as
some sharp fluctuation in the interest rates paid on accounts.

Competition with other money-market borrowers and particularly between
banks and savings and loan associations tends to affect the interest rates paid
and also the flow of funds to lending institutions and through them to their borrowers. Consequently, when tight-money conditions in 1966 caused intense competition, the principal regulatory authorities involved—the Federal Reserve officials, the Home Loan Bank Board, and the deposit-insurance agencies—asked
Congress for power to establish interest-rate ceilings on each type of institution,
with further power to discriminate between accounts by size and time duration
and by geographic location of the institution. This regulatory power lapsed in
1968 but has been indefinitely extended. It makes possible the allocation of savings to institutions and users by regulatory fiat, and helps to relieve the institutions of the discipline of competitive pressure. When it is recalled that all three of

these institutions—commercial banks, mutual savings banks, and savings and loan associations—are already freed of considerable competition because new institutions and branches are permitted only where they will not bring severe pressure upon existing ones, the regulatory philosophy becomes clear.

All the institutions under discussion are regulated to a considerable degree as respects types of investments, accounting methods, loss reserves, net worth, and similar matters. The regulatory authorities conduct occasional examinations to test their solvency and the adequacy of their business practices, and unquestionably do try to correct unsatisfactory situations. However, the examination reports are not made public; the better institutions are discouraged from advertising the statistics which demonstrate their excellence; and the investors in the better-managed and more profitable institutions—even in the "mutually owned" ones—are not permitted to know they have chosen wisely.

INTEREST-PAYING DEPOSITS IN COMMERCIAL BANKS

In mid-1972, interest-paying bank deposits in commercial banks had grown to more than 290 billion dollars and represented more than one-third of the more liquid holdings of American investors. As Table 22-1 shows, interest-paying bank deposits grew at a spectacular rate after 1960. This growth was caused in large part by a sharp increase in the interest rates paid by the banks.

The nature and yield of interest-paying deposit accounts are greatly affected by regulations imposed by the Federal Reserve System on all member banks, by the Federal Deposit Insurance Corporation (FDIC) on insured nonmember banks, and by state banking authorities. The Federal Reserve regulations are contained in Regulation Q, which divides all interest-paying deposits in commercial banks into three categories: (1) passbook or certificate *savings* accounts, which are available only to individuals, individuals in joint accounts, and nonprofit organizations; (2) *open-account time deposits*, which are passbook or automatically renewed certificate accounts available to all depositors; and (3) *time certificates of deposit*, which are interest-bearing promissory notes with a definite maturity date, also available to everyone. Savings accounts must stipulate that the depositor may be required to give 30 days' notice of an intended withdrawal, though the bank may (and nearly always does) make payment without advance notice. Open-account time deposits and time certificates of deposit must stipulate that the funds may not be withdrawn prior to an agreed maturity date or, alternatively, without 30 days' advance notice to the bank, and the bank may not elect to pay in advance.[1] During 1971–1972 maximum interest rates which the Federal Reserve members could pay were limited to 4½ per cent on savings accounts and

---

[1] These classifications and rules are obeyed, but advertising nomenclature varies. For example, the 5½ Savings Certificates widely offered to individuals in 1972 are technically time certificates of deposit.

to a range of 4½ to 5¾ per cent on certain classes of open-account time deposits and certificates. The commercial banks in a few states were limited to even lower maximums, because Federal Reserve member banks may not pay more than state rules permit state banks to pay.

The rates of interest offered by banks on savings and time deposits are often below the maximums permitted by banking regulations. However, competition is a factor here. During 1972, most banks were offering the ceiling rate of 4½ per cent on savings accounts but most new deposits were being received in the form of open-account deposits or time certificates of deposit which paid higher rates. Surprisingly, the ordinary savings account totals were slowly rising despite the availability of higher earnings on the other types of accounts. On the whole, interest calculations seem more satisfactory on time certificates than on savings deposits; the interest on a certificate runs from its initial date to maturity, when it may be renewed or automatically extended, whereas savings accounts frequently receive interest only on the minimum balance in the account at any time during a calendar quarter.

The interest rates paid by commercial banks on ordinary passbook savings accounts seem generally competitive with yields on United States savings bonds, but below most money-market yields. This is probably because many savers elect the convenience and familiarity of bank savings accounts and disregard the alternatives. However, time certificates of deposit appear to serve a more competitive market; over the years their yields have closely approximated those available on bankers' acceptances and nonguaranteed federal agency notes. Table 22-2 illustrates the yields on various deposit accounts at selected dates.

All forms of bank accounts must be regarded as satisfactorily safe. The high quality of most banks' assets is verified by bank examinations, and accounts are protected by FDIC insurance up to $20,000 per account.[2] This amount of insurance is ample to cover most savings accounts, but in recent years the time certificates of deposit purchased by large investors often run into hundreds of thousands of dollars. It is well to remember that deposits of this size are solely the

---

[2] National banks are examined by the Comptroller of the Currency; member state banks, by the Federal Reserve System; insured banks which are not in the Reserve System, by the FDIC; and all state banks are subject to state banking authorities. The FDIC insures 97 per cent of American commercial banks; the insured banks have over 99 per cent of the interest-bearing deposits in all commercial banks. In the event of weakness in an insured bank, the FDIC will endeavor to prevent insolvency by arranging a merger or providing financial aid. If this is not feasible, the insured deposits will be made available at once in a solvent bank or a new one, and the FDIC and the uninsured claimants will share equitably in the assets of the failed bank. Finally, it should be noted that the banking laws in a number of states require the segregation of the assets belonging to the savings and time deposit department away from those of the commercial department, in a state bank; and since the loan and investment regulations in such cases are often more stringent on the savings and time deposit funds than on the commercial department funds, the assets are sometimes better grade.

For deposit insurance purposes, all deposits in the same bank owned by one person constitute one account. Joint accounts, partnership accounts, etc., are usually classed as separate accounts.

Table 22-2 *Ratio of interest paid to average account balances, 1935–1971*

Year	Commercial bank time and savings deposits	Mutual savings bank deposits	Savings and loan accounts	Long-term U.S. bonds
1935	2.6	2.7	3.1	2.7
1940	1.3	2.0	3.3	2.2
1945	.9	1.7	2.5	2.4
1950	.9	2.0	2.5	2.3
1955	1.4	2.7	2.9	2.8
1960	2.6	3.5	3.8	4.0
1965	3.7	4.1	4.2	4.2
1970	4.9	5.0	5.0	6.6
1971	4.8	5.1	5.3	5.7

Source: United States Savings and Loan League, *Savings and Loan Fact Book.*

responsibility of the bank unless the investor purchases commercial deposit insurance.

Bank deposits may be made in almost any amount desired by the investor. Savings accounts can be opened with an initial deposit of five or ten dollars, and added to or drawn down at will. Time deposits or time certificates of deposit require a minimum investment of $500 or $1,000 at most banks; this money can be withdrawn only at maturity or after 30 days' notice. Time certificates of deposit may run for any chosen number of days up to 1 year or longer, or may be made automatically self-renewing every quarter until further notice. Many of the larger certificates of deposit are made negotiable; in fact, as will be noted later, there is an active over-the-counter market in New York for such certificates in $500,000 or larger denominations.

The convenience of bank deposits is a strong argument in their favor. Deposits or withdrawals can be made in person or by mail at conveniently located banking offices and at convenient hours. No fees, commissions, or taxes are involved in making transactions. Related banking services, such as loans, safety deposit, money orders, and checking accounts, are available in the same institution. The possession of a substantial savings or time deposit is an item always reported by a bank to a credit-investigating agency; therefore, it improves the depositor's credit standing. Finally, bank deposits can usually be made under a variety of legal titles—by an individual, by a number of individuals but payable to any of them, by a partnership, by a corporation, by a trustee for another, and by individuals in joint accounts. The joint account is one whose balance is payable to any of the participants while all are alive but which is very simply transferred to the survivor or survivors upon the death of one, without necessarily being subject to the delay and expense of probate proceedings. The state laws and precedents in each state govern the types of accounts which the banks may accept, but they are usually carefully planned for the convenience of depositors. Investors are well advised to consult with the bank's account expert before selecting the legal form in which they will record their deposits.

Interest earned on bank deposits is subject to all federal and state income taxes. The deposits themselves are subject to such general property taxes as may be levied upon them, but it is the practice in most states to exempt them or to tax them very lightly. However, the property tax liability should be investigated; even a light tax on principal can make great inroads upon the limited income received. Bank deposits enjoy no exemption of any kind from federal or state estate, gift, or inheritance taxes.

In summary, it may be said that savings or time deposits in commercial banks are very satisfactory investments from the standpoints of liquidity, safety, and convenience. Their earning power is modest and they have no tax advantages, hence the investment of large sums for long periods of time in this way seems relatively unprofitable. Yet, as a means of accumulation, as a device for employing short-term funds, and as an investment for moderate amounts of emergency reserves, bank deposits offer definite advantages.

MUTUAL SAVINGS BANKS

Mutual savings banks are state-chartered deposit institutions whose function is to administer small and medium-sized savings deposits with safety and reasonable profit. These institutions have no stockholders or stock capital; they are controlled by elected or self-perpetuating boards of trustees and, in time, accumulate a surplus or corporate net worth by retaining a small portion of their earnings for the purpose. Semiannual or quarterly "dividend" payments based on the bank's earnings are declared by the directors and paid on the various classes of deposit accounts. Mutual savings deposits are an important form of investment. At December 31, 1971, their deposits totaled nearly $90 billion and the average regular account (excluding school savings, Christmas clubs, etc.) amounted to $3,639. Mutual savings banks are operating in 18 states, but their greatest development has occurred in the northeast section of the country, in New York, Pennsylvania, and the New England states.

The laws of the various states control the types of accounts which their mutual savings banks may offer and the forms of legal ownership in which the accounts may be carried. In general the accounts are similar to savings accounts in commercial banks, with the further stipulation in several of the states that the accounts may not exceed prescribed sums, although New York in 1971 removed its $25,000 limit on single-name accounts. The purpose of the deposit limitations is to prevent the accumulation of large accounts which might embarrass the bank by large withdrawals.

Mutual savings bank deposits have an enviable record for liquidity. Although the deposit agreement obligates the customer to give the bank 30 to 90 days' notice of an intended withdrawal, the banks are accustomed to pay on demand. They have been able to do so even during depressions. This has required very careful management at times, for the need to maximize earnings has required that the earning assets be principally long-term bonds and mortgage loans. Liquidity has been managed by maintaining small amounts of cash and secondary reserves, spacing the maturities of bonds and mortgages to provide a regular cash inflow, using amortizing mortgages, and cultivating a reputation for strength which avoids "scare" withdrawals. The banks have in recent years also developed co-operative rediscount agencies to which they may sell mortgages or bonds. A few have secured borrowing facilities by joining the Federal Home Loan Bank System. At December 31, 1971, the combined assets of all mutual savings banks consisted of approximately 2 per cent cash items, 6 per cent government and United States agency securities, 69 per cent mortgages, 9 per cent corporate and other bonds, and 14 per cent other loans, securities, and investments. Generally, mutual savings banks are permitted to hold small amounts of common and preferred stock. In 12 states they may make consumer loans. In six states they may accept demand deposits.

The safety record of the mutual savings banks has always been excellent. The banks are heavily concentrated in a part of the country which is financially stable, thus reducing their loan losses, but much of the credit for safety must be given to the rigid investment restrictions under which most of them operate. The states which charter savings banks usually limit their loans and investments to conservative and high-grade items and require effective diversification. For example, Massachusetts as recently as 1948 authorized only first mortgage loans on real estate located within 50 miles of the bank; other mortages guaranteed by a federal agency; bonds issued or guaranteed by the United States, the state of Massachusetts, and certain other states; certain types of municipal bonds; certain types of railroad and utility bonds; bank stocks; and short-term loans on high-grade collateral security. In Massachusetts and in other states, elaborate criteria respecting the size and financial condition of the issuer are prescribed to govern the selection of bonds, and in many states the banking commissioner prepares a list of bonds from which all savings bank bond investments must be chosen.[3] Under such close restriction, it is not surprising that the mutual savings banks have remained strong; neither is it surprising that their earnings have been mod-

[3] These laws and lists identify the bonds which are generally described as "legal for savings banks" or are referred to simply as "legals." Because the savings bank demand itself is heavy, and because other institutions, trustees, and persons rely on the legal list as a badge of excellence, such bonds usually sell on a relatively low-yield basis.

est. The Massachusetts laws and those of other leading mutual savings bank states have been relaxed since 1948 to permit wider discretion in the choice of mortgages and the use of limited amounts of "nonlegal" bonds and stocks. The President's Commission on Financial Structure and Regulation recommended late in 1971 a significant broadening of investment powers for mutual savings banks, including more unrestricted types of mortgage lending, construction loans, limited direct investments in real estate, consumer lending, and more common stock investment, as well as the right to sell subordinated debentures. In the past, however, the banks have been very slow to avail themselves of less-secure investments and less-traditional services, even when the laws permit them. For example, 79 per cent of their funds are invested in mortgages; of these, nearly half are government-insured.

Only 327 of the nation's 490 mutual savings banks were insured in the FDIC at December 30, 1971, but these banks held 87 per cent of all mutual savings deposits. All but one of the other savings banks were insured by state deposit-insurance funds. All mutual savings banks as a group had surplus and reserve accounts approximating 7.1 per cent of their total assets and 7.5 per cent of assets at risk; this compared with commercial bank capital accounts of 7.5 and 10.1 per cent, respectively. The mutual savings banks are also comfortably large; as a group they averaged 183 million dollars in assets against 46.5 million dollars for commercial banks. Although the investor may not carelessly assume that every institution has all the advantages of sound assets, strong deposit insurance, large surplus, and the strength commonly associated with size, it appears that most mutual savings banks do have them.

The average rate of dividends paid on deposit accounts in FDIC-insured mutual savings banks is shown in Table 22-2. The figures in the table indicate that dividend payments on deposits approximated 5.1 per cent for 1971. However, lower rates were paid on special deposits which obtain a restricted rate and deposits which lost dividend privileges because of withdrawal or other activity during the dividend period. Rates offered by savings banks in New York State in late 1972 ranged from 5 per cent on passbook accounts up to 6 per cent on longer time deposits.

During 1971 the average savings bank obtained a total income of about 6.13 per cent on its average assets. Roughly 15 per cent of this was paid out in operating expenses, 76 per cent was allocated to interest, and the balance went into loss reserves and surplus.

Because of their function as cooperative savings institutions, mutual savings banks pay relatively modest income and property taxes. However, the dividends which they pay to their depositors are fully taxable income, and the principal is subject to any state or local taxes which may be laid upon savings deposits. The deposits are fully vulnerable to estate and inheritance taxation.

Mutual savings banks offer many of the same convenience services which commercial banks make available to their depositors. They operate safe deposit vaults, sell money orders, cash checks, furnish data to credit agencies, and transact business in government savings bonds. A number of them also sell life insurance, either in conjunction with savings accounts or independently, at a cost slightly lower than that of ordinary insurance companies because the savings banks make no costly effort to *sell* insurance. They merely take orders for it when an applicant wishes to buy. Some banks are authorized to sell mutual-fund shares on the same basis. However, the President's Commission on Financial Structure and Regulation has proposed a sweeping expansion of savings bank services which would include checking-account and credit-card operations, with Federal Reserve System membership made compulsory for mutual savings banks. They would then, in effect, be commercial banks with a major emphasis on savings deposits.

Investors are justified in regarding deposits in a typical mutual savings bank as liquid, safe, mildly profitable, and reasonably convenient. All these qualities may vary with the individual bank, however; so the investor should himself investigate such matters as the quality of the assets, size of the surplus, management, earning power, dividend policy, deposit insurance, types of deposits and legal form, and convenience services. If the bank is typical, a deposit in it may have a very useful place in the investor's portfolio.

SAVINGS AND LOAN ACCOUNTS

Savings and loan associations[4] are institutions which receive investors' savings and invest the money principally in long-term residence mortgage loans. About 79 per cent of savings and loan assets are held in mutual associations in which the savings funds technically are invested in "membership shares"; the remaining 21 per cent are held in stockholder-owned associations where the public's money is received as creditors' deposits. There is really not much difference between these from the investor's viewpoint. Operating methods are much the same and the interest-dividends received by investors are treated as interest under income tax law.

Since 1945 the savings and loan associations have shown remarkable growth, as Table 22-1 indicates. The number of savings accounts has grown from less than 7 million to more than 50 million, and the assets of the associations have increased by nearly 2300 per cent. An official estimate placed the size of the average savings and loan account at $3,427 in 1971.

[4] Savings and loan associations are known in certain areas as building and loan associations, cooperative banks, or homestead associations. Many of these institutions now use the name "savings association" to emphasize their fund-attracting service.

Savings and loan associations are incorporated by the federal government and by each of the states. At December 31, 1971, there were 2,049 institutions holding federal charters and 5,544 holding state charters. In each instance the appropriate public authority stipulates the terms upon which investors' funds may be received, the types of investments which may be made by the association, and other essential operating procedures. Savings and loan associations, like all important savings institutions, are examined periodically by the incorporating and insuring authorities, to verify their solvency and general observance of legal requirements. Because it is impossible to review the rules of all the states in a short space, descriptions here must stress practices common to most associations though not necessarily followed in all of them.

The savings and loan associations receive money on two types of account plans, the passbook account and the certificate account. Passbook accounts are more flexible but pay lower dividends. Any amount can be added to or withdrawn from a passbook account at any time, and dividends are paid quarterly, semiannually, or at other intervals set by the association. Different classes of accounts may pay considerably different rates. Certificates are issued in fixed amounts with fixed maturities, and all may earn a higher rate than is paid on passbook accounts; rates rise with larger denominations and longer maturities.

Savings and loan yields to investors in recent years have averaged about the same as those of long-term government bonds and about $\frac{1}{2}$ per cent more than the average paid on savings by commercial banks. The ceiling rates prescribed by the regulatory authorities in 1972 ranged from 5 per cent on regular passbook savings up to $7\frac{1}{2}$ per cent on certificates of $100,000 or more with 1- to 10-year maturities. Many associations, however, do not pay the ceiling rates and there is variation among them as to the types of accounts used and the rates paid on them.

There are few restrictions on the ownership of accounts in federal associations. The original federal charter form (Charter K) states:

> Share accounts may be purchased and held absolutely by, or in trust for, any person, including an individual, male, female, adult, or minor, single or married, a partnership, association, and corporation. The receipt or acquitance of any member, including a minor person or a married woman, who holds a share account shall be a valid and sufficient release and discharge of the association for any payment to such person on any share account. Two or more persons may hold share accounts jointly in any manner permitted by law.

One of the useful account forms is the so-called *trustee account,* in which the individual owner of an account constitutes himself a "tentative trustee" for another who is designated to receive the account at his death. The owner operates the account as his exclusive property during his lifetime, but at his death the designated beneficiary may obtain immediate title to the account, without need for probate orders, by presenting the passbook, proof of the former owner's death, and a release from the inheritance tax authorities.[5]

Savings and loan associations are permitted under federal regulations to make loans to members on the security of their accounts, to make first mortgage loans not exceeding $45,000 in amount on residential properties located within 100 miles of the association's office, to buy government, state, and municipal bonds, and to invest in Federal Home Loan bank securities. In order to permit some latitude, federal associations are permitted to make a limited volume of loans on nonresidential property and to buy "participations" in the loans of other associations which have attractive loan opportunities in their communities. An association may make FHA-insured and veterans' (GI Bill) loans, as well as the higher-yielding uninsured types. The latter may equal 95 per cent of the appraised value or purchase price of residential property (whichever is less), provided that the loan is covered by private mortgage insurance; loans must be repaid in monthly installments over not more than 30 years or, if not amortized, must pay interest at least semiannually and mature within 5 years or less. Certain additional types of loans or investments may be made when authorized by the Federal Home Loan Bank Board.

About 90 per cent of savings and loan mortgage loans are made on residential properties, including apartments. The balance includes loans on commercial property, land being developed, and churches. Relatively small amounts are lent on consumer-type loans and mobile homes. About 86 per cent of all mortgage money is lent on a conventional basis, not covered by FHA and VA insurance. Most loans are amortizing loans and many are retired ahead of schedule; repayments of principal average about 12 per cent per year.

There has been some suggestion that savings and loan associations would be more profitable and more useful to their communities if their investment and lending powers were broadened to permit them to buy bonds, make personal and installment loans, and perhaps make a variety of other loans. A few states permit their state-chartered associations much greater freedom than the federal associations have. There are arguments pro and con, but some added flexibility would seem to be desirable. As indicated in Chapter 18, the President's Commission on Financial Structure and Regulation in 1971 recommended major expansion of both the lending and money-raising powers of associations.

Savings and loan associations usually try to maximize earnings by keeping most of their funds invested in mortgage loans. About 85 per cent of assets were so employed at year-end 1971. The balance consisted of 8.7 per cent in cash and government bonds; 1 per cent in foreclosed real estate; 1 per cent in Federal Home Loan bank stock; and a total of 4.5 per cent in nonmortgage loans, state and

[5] This practice grew up informally in some of the mutual savings banks, particularly in New York, where careful court interpretation has given it standing. See re *Matter of Totten*, 179 N.Y. 112.

municipal bonds, office buildings and fixtures, and miscellaneous assets. Liabilities consisted of 84.6 per cent savings accounts, 9 per cent borrowings and miscellaneous accruals, and 6.4 per cent in net worth accounts, which are generally labeled *reserves*.

Liquidity is sought by savings and loan associations in five different ways. First, they must maintain a small reserve in cash or government bonds, as has been noted.[6] Second, they undertake to obtain a constant inflow of new funds in both old and new accounts. Third, they lend chiefly on amortizing loans, which assures a steady stream of incoming payments. Fourth, they are privileged to borrow moderately from commercial lenders and to sell mortgages. Finally, they have the right to ask their Federal Home Loan banks for loans on mortgage collateral in amounts not exceeding 50 per cent of their savings accounts.[7] These sources of funds seem to be adequate to maintain liquidity at practically all times in well-managed associations which have earned the confidence of their investors, although the withdrawals are surprisingly heavy, averaging 33 to 36 per cent of savings balances each year.

Savings and loan accounts are ordinarily withdrawable upon demand, this being both association and Home Loan Bank policy. However, the terms of the accounts permit an association to demand 30 days' notice of intended withdrawals, and federal law authorizes the association to limit total withdrawals to specified fractions of its cash receipts, if it cannot meet all requests. Deferment of withdrawals under this provision does not constitute default or insolvency; it was used in the depression years to protect the associations from excessive losses in forced liquidation. However, the American public has long since become accustomed to immediate "cashability" for savings-share accounts, and any widespread tendency for associations to invoke such waiting periods would probably prove disastrous to the further growth of their "deposits."

The ultimate safety of a savings and loan account is compounded of two factors, the strength of the association itself and the assurance provided by account insurance in the Federal Savings and Loan Insurance Corporation. There is good reason to expect the average association to be strong. Amortizing home mortgages are highly dependable investments, especially when federally insured. Examinations by regulatory bodies should find and correct weaknesses in associa-

[6] Home Loan bank members are required to maintain any ratio between 4 and 8 per cent which the Home Loan Bank Board prescribes.

[7] The 11 Federal Home Loan banks are federal chartered and supervised institutions similar in many respects to the Federal Reserve banks. Mortgage-lending institutions may become "members" of a Home Loan bank by buying small amounts of stock in it. The Home Loan banks obtain additional funds to lend to their members by receiving deposits from members and by selling their bonds to the public. Members may use Home Loan bank funds both to help satisfy heavy demands for mortgage loans in their communities and to maintain their own liquidity, although excessive dependence on Home Loan bank funds is discouraged. At the end of 1971, only 81 per cent of savings and loan associations were members, but these members held 98 per cent of all savings and loan resources.

tion practices, and statistics indicate that the average association at the end of 1971 had an adequate bulwark of reserves and surplus amounting to 6.4 per cent of total assets. In the relatively few cases of insolvency which occur, the investor in insured associations is fully protected up to $20,000; and 77 per cent of associations holding 97 per cent of all accounts are insured.

The earnings of savings and loan associations are substantial. Their gross earnings in 1971 averaged close to 6.85 per cent on average assets, and expenses totaled about 1.15 per cent. The remaining 5.7 per cent would permit generous dividends on share accounts except for one thing. The very rapid growth of the associations, which averaged 9½ per cent per year in the decade 1961–1971, requires a proportionate growth in the associations' reserves which must be accumulated out of earnings. Thus a rate of growth which betokens success could also be a factor which restricts dividends.

Finally, it should be noted that some savings and loan associations are very large and some are very small. Some operate numerous branches, and some are restricted to one office. Some solicit large corporate accounts on a short-term basis, and some prefer smaller personal accounts. The average size of the nation's 5,544 associations in 1971 was about $37.2 million; 94 associations exceeded $300 million in assets, while the 706 smallest ones were below $1 million.

In summary, it may be said that savings and loan accounts meet proper safety standards and provide average yields for short-term investments. The amounts involved are flexible and may serve either small savers or major corporations. The income and principal sums are fully taxable. The money is instantly available when needed, though quarterly interest dates or certificate maturity dates may need to be respected to avoid loss of income. The convenience of window service or transactions by mail is very high and there is no transaction cost. Ownership and title features of the accounts are adequate, there are often special provisions for limited family access to funds tied up in probate, and the trustee accounts may be very useful.

OTHER SAVINGS DEPOSITARIES

Two other forms of savings depositaries, credit unions and industrial or Morris Plan banks, should be noted briefly. Credit unions are state or federal chartered associations, usually composed of employees in a single business organization. The credit union sells "shares" to its members and sometimes receives interest-bearing deposits also. The funds are used to make relatively short-term installment loans to members to finance automobiles, furniture, home purchases, or personal emergencies; if available funds exceed the loan demand, they may be invested in savings banks, savings and loan associations, high-class bonds, or loans to other credit unions; if loan demands exceed available funds, the union may borrow reasonable sums. Withdrawal procedures are similar to those of savings and loan associations, but the dividend period is ordinarily one full year. By act of Congress, the National Credit Union Administration was established to insure savings in credit unions and to provide federal supervision and examination of their operations. This program, which insures accounts to $20,000, resembles the other two federal depositor insurance programs. However, credit unions lack the service of any central banking institution. State-chartered unions which are not federally insured are supervised by state authorities.

The solvency record of credit unions is good, though their dividend records are far from uniform. At the end of 1971 there were more than 23,400 active credit unions in the United States, having 24 million members and total assets of $21 billion.[8] Loans outstanding amounted to $16 billion. Despite the heavy use of consumer credit during the past generation, most credit unions have had difficulty in keeping their funds fully occupied. A few large credit unions were in operation, but about half were reported to have total assets under $200,000.

Investors in credit unions receive dividends ranging from 2½ to 6 per cent per annum, 5 to 6 per cent being the common range. The attractiveness of a credit union as an investment, apart from its social and convenience aspects, seems to vary with the policies and circumstances of each individual case. The Credit Union National Association maintains a mutual life insurance company whose coverage is available to both savers and borrowers through most local credit unions.

Industrial banks are privately owned, state-chartered finance companies whose business is to make personal, collateral, automobile, and commercial loans, mostly on an installment payment basis. These institutions are permitted to receive limited amounts of savings or time deposits, typically not more than 10 times their own capital accounts, for use in their business. These deposits are repayable after an agreed period of notice, or at a definite maturity date, with interest at a contractual rate which is commonly 4 to 6 per cent. The industrial banks are eligible for deposit insurance and membership in the Federal Reserve System, but most of them have not used the privileges. In general, their safety record is good.

❋   MONEY-MARKET INVESTMENTS

The growing market for impersonal short-term investments for personal, business, and local government funds centers around the eight groups of investments listed in Table 22-3. It should be noted that these are groups of investments rather than single types—there are, for example, several types of tax-exempt notes in the market and several different federal agencies issuing their

[8] *Credit Union Yearbook,* 1972.

separate notes—and the list is not entirely complete. It does not, for example, recognize the large-scale temporary accounts which some of the larger savings and loan associations receive from business firms.

This is by no means a small market. The outstanding volume figures in Table 22-3 total an estimated $186 billion, and they do not include many billions of short-term treasury obligations other than bills, municipal and corporate bonds nearing maturity, or the temporary savings and loan accounts previously mentioned. Most of the items listed in Table 22-3 turn over, on the average, three or four times yearly as they mature; the trading volume in bills is especially large. Dealer transactions in bills alone exceeded $2 billion daily during 1972.

Investors obtain money-market investments in a variety of ways. Bank certificates of deposit can be obtained directly from the issuing banks. Treasury bills can be had by subscription at the weekly bill offerings conducted by the Federal Reserve banks, finance company notes can be had directly from the company or from one of its agent banks, and tax-exempt or federal agency notes can be bought when offered by securities underwriters. However, immediate purchases are often desirable in this market, as are opportunities to sell. The bond departments of most of the very large banks and a number of securities houses which stress short-term investments maintain extensive inventories of such investments and buy and sell freely.

As might be expected, elaborate management techniques have grown up in this market. Transactions are arranged by telephone, and money transfers are made by telephone or wire. Treasury and federal agency securities, tax-exempt notes, commercial paper, bankers' acceptances, and securities sold under repurchase agreements are often placed in the custody of a New York bank and "delivered" from one owner to the other within the bank's trust department; this eliminates transportation and insurance costs and enables the custodian bank to collect the funds and remit to the owner at the maturity date. Treasury securities can be delivered to any Federal Reserve bank and reissued within the hour at any other Federal Reserve bank for a transaction cost of $3.

One of the profitable facets of short-term investment management involves playing the pattern of rates. Short-term rates are very volatile. The 90-day bill rate, for example, may easily move by 10 per cent of itself in a few days' time because of seasonal or other forces. Thus there is greater security and convenience for investors requiring high liquidity in paper which is within 60 or even 30 days of maturity, and such paper often sells to yield one-tenth to one-third less than its 90- to 180-day counterparts. This affords investors whose needs for cash are less imminent a profitable opportunity to sell holdings which are nearing maturity and to reinvest in longer maturities. Large-scale investors do this in great volume.

Investors who use the money-market investments reviewed in this section and summarized in Table 22-3 will usually be influenced in their choices by the factors noted in the left-hand column of the table, notably purchase availability, rate of

Table 22-3 *Features of principal money-market investments for business funds*

Feature	Treasury bills	Repurchase agreements	Federal agency notes
When available	Daily	Daily	Daily
Probable rate of income	Market rate	Slightly above bill rate	About one-twentieth more than bill rate
Denominations	$10,000 up		$10,000 up
Normal minimum investment	$100,000 up	$1,000,000 or more	$50,000 up
Length of term to maturity	New issues 91 days, 182 days, 1 year	Most under 30 days but 60–90 possible	1 year or less
Resale market	Dealer spread 1 to 10¢ per $100	By agreement	Net prices, spreads 4 to 25¢ per $100
How quoted	Yield percentage		Prices net in 32ds plus accrued interest
Interest payment	None. Sells at discount from face	Included in repurchase price	Face plus interest paid at maturity
How purchased	From dealers or banks or weekly auction	Negotiated with dealer or bank	From dealers on offerings or secondary
How paid at maturity	Federal funds at any reserve bank	Federal funds	Federal funds at any reserve bank
Ownership form	Bearer	Named payee	Bearer or registered
Volume outstanding, mid-1972	$98 billion	Estimated $4–$5 billion	$10 billion

Table 22-3 *Factors of principal money-market investments (Continued)*

Tax-exempt notes	Directly placed finance company paper	Commercial paper	Bankers' acceptances	Bank certificates of deposit
New offerings or as on hand	Daily	As offered or when on hand	As available	Daily
About two-thirds of bill rate	About one-tenth more than bill rate	About one-tenth more than bill rate	About one-tenth more than bill rate	Close to bill rate
$5,000 up	$25,000 up	$100,000	Odd amounts, $25,000 to $1,000,000	$5,000 up
$10,000 up	$25,000 up	$100,000 up	$25,000 up	$5,000 up
3 to 14 months	3 days to 9 months as agreed	One to six months	3 weeks to 6 months	30 days to 1 year. Mature any chosen date
Varies, average 4 to 25¢ per $100	Dealer or company or bank might buy	Dealer or bank might buy	Dealers. Spread about 2 to 10¢ per $100	Dealer market for $500,000 up
Yield percentages	Discount basis from face	Discount basis from face	Discount basis from face	Yield basis to nearest basis point
Usually by coupon	None. Sells at discount from face	None. Sells at discount from face	None. Sells at discount from face	Face plus interest paid maturity
From dealers or banks	From issuer or through dealers or bank agencies	From dealers	From dealers	From issuer
Mostly clearinghouse funds in New York or Chicago	Federal funds in city agreed upon	Federal funds in New York or Chicago	New York clearinghouse	Federal funds
Bearer	Named payee	Bearer	Bearer	Named payee
$10 billion	$19 billion	$12 billion	$7 billion	Estimated $25 billion

yield, normal amount invested, term to maturity, taxability, and salability. Safety may reasonably be assumed in all of these. Since these investments all fluctuate subject to market conditions, the all-important item of yield may vary enough to divert the choice from day to day. The tax factor may be highly significant if tax-exempt notes of suitable maturity are readily available. If pinpointed maturity dates are important, directly placed finance company paper or bank certificates of deposit should be considered. And of course treasury bills can meet practically every need where sums of $100,000 up are involved. The investor must simply understand his needs and the alternatives before him and make his choices. If he needs to sell his money-market investments prior to maturity, he can readily do so, especially if his holding is large; Table 22-3 indicates that the cost might amount to 1 to 25 days' interest (1 cent per $100 would be one day's interest at a yield rate of 3.65 per cent) depending upon the type of paper, the amount to be sold, the nearness to maturity, relationships of the parties, and market conditions.

Treasury bills   are issued every Thursday to the winning bidders in auctions which are conducted every Monday. Written bids are received at Federal Reserve banks from banks, dealers, corporations, and individuals. Bids must state the price which the bidder will pay, but on amounts up to $200,000 the bid may be the "average accepted bid price." The Treasury accepts the best bids, each at its own price, until the necessary total is reached. All maturities occur on Thursday, and all payments for new bills and repayments for old ones are made simultaneously in federal funds. Dealers and major banks also buy and sell bills over the counter; the spread between bid and ask will range from 1 to 10 cents per $100 (about 1 to 10 days' interest), depending on the dealer's inventory position, the term to maturity, and the size of the transaction. Small additional costs for custody services or shipping may be encountered, an extra charge of $5 to $10 will be made on dealer transactions below $50,000, and a stockbroker or nondealer bank may add another fee if their services are employed as negotiators. Treasury bills are exempt from state and local income and property taxation, but are subject to all federal taxes.

Repurchase agreements   are contracts under which a government bond dealer or a bank sells securities (usually treasury bills) to a bank, a corporation, or a person and simultaneously contracts to repurchase them later at a price which includes interest to the repurchase date. The repurchase date is usually fixed but is sometimes left open until one of the parties asks to terminate the arrangement. The amounts involved usually are $1 million or more, except that transactions between correspondent banks may be much smaller. The transaction is usually looked upon as a loan by the purchaser to the repurchaser; the securities in question are usually in the custody of a New York bank under an arrangement which permits the seller-repurchaser to withdraw securities which it wishes to sell and to substitute similar ones. The arrangement is thus a convenient device for financing a government bond dealer's inventories, with the "sold" securities really serving as collateral for a loan transaction. This is also a convenient way for one bank to borrow from another without encountering statutory loan limits, and for dealers in commercial paper and bankers' acceptances to finance their inventories.

Federal agency notes   include short-term obligations of the Federal Land banks, Federal Home Loan banks, Federal National Mortgage Association, Banks for Cooperatives, Federal Intermediate Credit banks, Federal National Mortgage Association, Export-Import Bank of Washington, Government National Mortgage Association, and other government-affiliated borrowers. These "agencies" are corporations owned or controlled by the government, but their debts are not usually guaranteed by the government. Nevertheless, their securities are regarded as moral obligations of the government and are highly rated. These securities can be bought occasionally as new issues, but government bond dealers and banks make over-the-counter markets in them regularly. These dealers and banks quote net prices with a spread between bid and ask of about 4 to 25 cents per $100, depending on time to maturity, and the other usual factors. Since the spread will equal from 4 to 25 days' interest, transactions other than an initial purchase would not normally be profitable. These notes are payable at maturity in federal funds at any Federal Reserve bank. Interest is subject to federal income tax, but no state or local income or property tax applies.

Tax-exempt notes   are state and municipal obligations with maturities of a year or less. They may be federal– or state housing act–guaranteed notes of top quality, tax-anticipation borrowings by cities or counties, or almost anything. They may be superb or medium grade in quality, and the issues may be large or small. The issues of really marketable size — $5,000,000 and up — are offered by bank or dealer underwriters at yield rates which will usually fall between 60 per cent and 80 per cent of the prevailing bill rate. The yield will depend on the quality and size of the issue, the time to maturity, the location of the issuer, and the issue's Moody credit rating. The larger issues of these tax-exempt notes usually have a dealer secondary market, normally on a net basis with spread between bid and ask similar to that prevailing on federal agency notes. The notes themselves are commonly left in the custody of a New York bank, and deliveries of sold notes are made by transfer of custody receipts. The notes are usually in bearer form with interest coupons. Payment is made at designated banks in clearinghouse funds. Interest on these notes is exempt from federal income taxes; the state and local tax position varies.

Directly placed finance company paper   consists of unsecured notes sold directly or through agents by the largest finance companies. Denominations range from

$25,000 to $1,000,000 and maturities can be negotiated to any exact date desired between 2 days and 9 months. The finance companies maintain their own liquidity by constant sale of new paper and use of large open lines of credit at banks. The paper is generally sold at a discount from face value and is payable at maturity in federal funds in New York, Chicago, or a city chosen by the investor. There is no organized resale market in such paper but the companies will, if practicable, repurchase paper prior to maturity to accommodate a holder. The yields offered on this paper vary with the length of time to maturity; they are announced regularly by the companies, are available to all comers, and generally run about one-tenth above the treasury-bill rate on similar maturities.

Commercial paper   consists of unsecured notes sold by large business firms and some finance companies through commercial paper dealers. Denominations range from $50,000 up, and original maturities of an issue may be 30 days to 6 months. This paper is generally sold on a net basis at a discount from face value and is payable at face in federal funds in New York or Chicago. There is no organized resale market, but the selling dealer may repurchase paper if practicable as a service to a customer. Yields to investors are about the same as on directly placed paper. More than 600 large United States firms borrow in this market. The National Credit Office, Inc., a division of Dun & Bradstreet, supplies a credit report and a "rating" (Prime, Desirable, or Average) on each issue of commercial paper, and many issues are also rated by Standard & Poor's Corporation in grades running from A-1 to A-3. From the middle thirties until 1970, there were no losses and only one or two delayed payments on Prime or Desirable paper. The spectacular default by Penn Central Corporation on more than 50 million dollars worth of commercial paper in mid-1970 shook buyers' confidence for several months and obliged the rating agencies to scrutinize issuers more carefully, but by mid-1971 the market appeared to have recovered fully from this first shock in a generation.

Bankers' acceptances   are commercial drafts payable at a designated later date, drawn by a creditor upon a bank and "accepted" (i.e., signed) by the bank. Acceptance of a draft makes it the equivalent of the bank's promissory note. The draft is generally due at face value between 1 and 6 months after acceptance, payable in clearinghouse funds at the accepting bank or its New York correspondent. Since the draft is usually drawn by a firm which sells merchandise to a customer of the accepting bank, and since the accepting bank is merely providing the acceptance service for its customer, the drawer of the draft owns it and often sells it to an acceptance dealer. Acceptance dealers thus obtain inventories of acceptances of various and usually odd denominations, maturing at various times and at various banks. Acceptances are usually regarded as high-class items and they normally yield about one-tenth more than treasury bills. They are salable to dealers at a relatively small price concession. Because of the accounting and administrative routine involved, acceptances are most attractive to medium-sized banks and to the accepting bank itself.

Bank certificates of deposit (CDs)   are offered in various forms and denominations and maturities, at yields which ordinarily run slightly above the bill rate. They are issued at face value and redeemed at maturity in federal funds by the issuing bank. Their term may be as short as 30 days or as long as a year, and maturity on any date desired can usually be had. Government bond dealers make a secondary market at very low transaction cost in CDs of $500,000 or larger. Smaller CDs are usually salable only at greater cost, for the issuing bank cannot legally redeem them before maturity. Interest payable by the banks on CDs is regulated by the Federal Reserve Board's Regulation Q, and in periods of monetary restraint, the Board may intentionally set the "Q ceilings" at uncompetitively low levels to make CDs unattractive to investors and thus to hinder the banks in raising lendable funds by this method.

QUESTIONS AND PROBLEMS

1   How could state or local governments make use of short-term investments? Do they actually do so?

2   Would it be practicable for a 100-million-dollar savings and loan association which had heavy loan demands to advertise for large corporation accounts? Is this ever done?

3   Would the savings and loan associations be any more useful to their lending areas if their lending powers were broadened? Would they be less safe? More profitable?

4   Would it be desirable to require deposit institutions to make a quarterly statement available to depositors upon request, indicating (**a**) the percentage of net worth to total assets; (**b**) the types of bonds, loans, and other assets held; (**c**) the percentages of loans more than 90 days in arrears; and (**d**) the percentage of assets invested in foreclosed real estate and other undesirable items? Should this be accompanied by an income statement indicating whether interest or dividend payments on accounts were being comfortably earned?

5   Is it correct to say that savings and loan associations "borrow short and lend long"? Is this generally a sound financial practice? If it is not, how do the associations usually avoid trouble? Can they always avoid trouble from this practice?

6   What should an electric power company do with the large sums accumulated day by day and disbursed in 1 million- to 10-million-dollar sums at irregular intervals 15 or 20 times yearly to pay interest, taxes, and dividends?

7   If the power company had a 1-million-dollar property tax bill to pay in San Francisco on Wednesday, April 5, could it accumulate the money in directly placed finance company paper maturing in New York on that day? Would there be any real loss in having the paper mature on Tuesday?

8   Would it be feasible for this power company to accumulate treasury bills as cash became available (perhaps in sums ranging from $100,000 to $500,000 per day) and sell them when money was needed?

9   Investigate the "federal funds" market as utilized by the commercial banks.

10 Are any of the forms of deposit accounts exempt from property taxes? From income taxes? From death taxes?

11 Should the corporate taxes levied on savings institutions tax the earnings which they distribute? (Compare ordinary corporations, mutual funds, life insurance.) What about undistributed earnings?

12 Do you think that a savings and loan association should keep a 25 per cent cash and government bond reserve, with the idea of remaining liquid? Why?

13 Compare the savings and loan "trustee account" with the P.O.D. arrangement on a government savings bond. Are they essentially the same?

14 What is a credit union? Is it in any way similar to an industrial bank? To a savings and loan association?

15 Do money-market instruments ever yield more than government and corporate bonds? When, and under what circumstances?

REFERENCES

Credit Union National Association: *Credit Union Yearbook*, Madison, Wis., annual.

Federal Reserve Bank of Cleveland: *Money Market Instruments*, occasionally revised.

Federal Reserve Bulletin.

Federal Reserve Chart Book.

Financial Handbook, rev. ed., The Ronald Press Company, New York, 1968, Sec. 1.

Kendall, Leon T.: *The Savings and Loan Business*, Prentice-Hall, Inc., Englewood Cliffs, N.J., 1962.

Morgan Guaranty Trust Company: *Money Market Investments*, New York, occasionally revised.

National Association of Mutual Savings Banks: *National Fact Book of Mutual Savings Banks*, New York, annual.

U.S. Department of Health, Education, and Welfare: *Federal Credit Union Handbook*, Washington, 1956. See also *Report of Operations*, Federal Credit Unions, annual.

United States Savings and Loan League: *Savings and Loan Fact Book*, Chicago, annual.

Social security, employee pension rights, and life insurance play a dominant part in the lifetime financial plans of most individuals and families. These elements provide the foundation on which an investor typically builds and arranges his other assets, and they significantly affect the margin of funds which he may safely devote to the purchase of securities or real estate. As economic factors, these institutions also exert major influence upon the nation's savings and investment patterns, tax burden, capital markets, and level and structure of security prices. They are important to investors both as materials of investment and as investment-market forces. This chapter deals at some length with social security and employer-sponsored pension plans; the next chapter covers life insurance and insurance-related annuities. The scope and growth of pension plans and social security coverage since 1945 are summarized in Table 23-1.

SOCIAL SECURITY

Social security benefits extend in some measure to more than 140 million Americans, and more than 110 million of them have been in the program long enough to qualify for benefits at retirement. In 1972, nearly 29 million persons were already drawing social security checks. The average retired worker at the end of 1972 was receiving a monthly check for $160, and the average retired couple $268. The maximum benefit that could be claimed by a worker retiring at age 65 was scheduled to rise rapidly: from $259 for a worker retiring in 1972 to $313 for one retiring in 1978, with 50 per cent extra to his wife in each instance. The capital value of a life annuity at age 65 is close to 170 times its monthly payment, so the investment significance of this pension expectation is obvious.

For eligible workers below retirement age, the social security program offers other important benefits of a contingent nature. Workers or their dependents may receive monthly cash benefits if a breadwinner dies or becomes disabled. These benefits are especially important to families with children under 18, wives or widows aged 60 and more, or dependent husbands or parents aged 62 or older. Government rules and regulations determining these benefits and their size are too lengthy and complex for discussion here, but they deserve thoughtful study and thorough familiarity by anyone whose dependents fall in any of these classes.

The social security program is operated by the federal government on a trust-fund basis. Contributions are raised through payroll taxes imposed equally on employed persons and their employers, and on self-employed workers at a rate about two percentage points higher than the rate paid by employees alone. About 85 per cent of the resulting tax revenues go into the Federal Old-Age and Survivors Insurance Trust Fund and the Federal Disability Insurance Trust Fund. The money is used to pay the benefits and administrative expenses of the retirement, survivors, and disability insurance programs and cannot be used for other pur-

Table 23-1 *Number of persons covered by major pension and retirement programs in the United States, 1945 through 1970 (In thousands)*

			Government-administered plans				
	Private plans		*Railroad*	*Federal civilian*	*State and local*		*Social*
Year	*Insured*	*Noninsured*	*retirement*	*employees*	*employees*	*Total*	*security*
1945	1,470	5,240	1,842	2,928	1,976	13,456	39,418
1950	2,755	7,500	1,745	1,856	2,854	16,710	42,171
1955	4,105	12,290	1,574	2,262	3,877	24,108	60,674
1960	5,475	17,540	1,246	2,557	5,090	31,908	67,517
1965	7,040	21,060	1,176	2,893	6,685	38,854	78,489
1970	10,980	24,100	1,055	3,327	8,450	47,912	87,545

Source: Institute of Life Insurance, *Life Insurance Fact Book*, 1972.

poses. The remaining 15 per cent collected is used to finance the medicare program and is placed in two other government trust funds out of which hospital insurance and other benefits and administrative costs of the federal government's medical insurance program are partially met.

Federal Old-Age, Survivors, and Disability Insurance (OASDI) taxes paid during 1971 amounted to $38.3 billion, including $18.5 billion collected from employers, $18.0 billion received from employees, and $1.8 billion contributed by self-employed workers. Total payments made by the OASDI program during 1971 amounted to $37.2 billion.

The tax receipts not needed for current benefit payments or expenses under the social security programs are invested by their respective trust funds in interest-bearing United States government securities, most of them nonmarketable treasury obligations of long maturity. Combined assets of the OASDI trust funds at year-end 1971 totaled $40.4 billion.

NATURE OF SOCIAL SECURITY BENEFITS

Nominally, retirement and other benefits under the social security program must be regarded as dollar items subject to purchasing-power deterioration as the cost of living continues to rise. Furthermore, they are not contractual, and some individuals might receive smaller benefits if Congress should revise the benefit formula.[1] On the other hand, both long experience and political realities suggest that Congress is likely to increase the benefit payments as the nation's standard of living rises and will almost certainly raise them as substantial increases in living costs occur. Reductions in benefits are most unlikely, though some groups may be more favored than others as revisions are made. For practical purposes, then, social security expectations can be counted as a major asset which enjoys an element of price-level protection and even the possibility of sharing in the long-run increase in the nation's living standard.

On the other hand, these mounting benefits in later years seem certain to involve sharply rising costs to the worker who is still some years distant from retirement. Both the social security tax rate and the amount of a worker's income which is subject to the tax have risen steeply in recent years. When Congress passed a 20 per cent rise in social security pensions over President Nixon's veto in 1972, the bill also provided that, beginning in 1974, social security taxes would be levied on the first $12,000 of a worker's annual pay; his tax rate would rise to 6.05 per cent in 1978. Thus in 1978 the man or woman earning $12,000 or more per year will pay $726 in social security taxes, and this large increase over the maximum 1972 tax of $468 will be matched by an identical increase to be paid on each such worker by his employer.

The recent tendency in social security taxation has been to increase the taxable base of workers' earnings rather than the tax rate itself. Beneath this new trend lies a major shift in the payroll-tax burden from lower-wage workers to people earning above-average incomes. Most of the added cost for higher pensions in years ahead is expected to be paid for by higher-salaried workers and their employers, and by middle-and upper-income self-employed persons.

CRITICISMS OF SOCIAL SECURITY

The social security program in recent years has been criticized from at least four standpoints, each of which raises significant questions for people in particular age brackets. First, without formal statement of intention, the government seems to be changing the program from one providing for minimum retirement needs toward one aimed at meeting all the economic needs of retired persons. Second, the benefits probably due younger workers under social security appear to fall far below those which tax-sheltered private annuities or retirement plans could plausibly finance with the same money. Third, if population growth declines, as begins to appear likely, the economy would have considerable difficulty financing the benefits already promised to those who will retire early in the next century.

---

[1] There is some danger, in the authors' opinion, that social security benefits of well-to-do retired persons might be reduced or eliminated if a socialistic or equalitarian-minded Congress should come to power at some future date.

Fourth, prolonged criticism has been directed at provisions of the law which deny, in whole or in part, social security benefits already earned if a retired person takes a job yielding him worthwhile added income. Some comment seems needed to place each criticism in useful perspective.

The original idea of social security was to provide workers with "a basic floor of protection" to which, if they were enterprising, they could add through their own efforts. The original law called for a 1 per cent tax rate to be paid by both employer and employee on the employee's first $3,000 of annual earnings. Although inflation has clearly justified some upward revision of these figures, the rise in the maximum tax from $30 per year in the 1930s to at least $726 in 1978 has clearly outstripped the declining dollar by a wide margin. Obviously, both taxes and promised benefits are moving in the direction of benefits that would meet all the needs of the elderly. Some advocates of still further expansion of social security benefits believe that these payments should ultimately be made large enough to replace private pension plans, personal savings, life insurance, and private investments. Aside from the obvious result of weakening people's incentives to provide for their own retirement, the continuing enlargement of benefits is open to three serious objections. First, it is questionable how much additional social security tax the public will accept, particularly since many families now pay more in social security deductions than they do in federal income tax. Second, the portion of the growing cost burden that is shifted to employers will largely be passed along to the public in the form of higher prices. Third, private insurance and savings will be substantially reduced, and this will result in a shortage of investment funds for private industry and, almost certainly, in rising levels of unemployment.

The second objection that younger workers will contribute more than they can hope to receive in benefits must also be taken seriously, particularly by those whose careers are still largely or wholly in the future. At 1971 rates, the maximum contributions by a person then 18 years old came to $19,270 over a working life of 46 years. His employers also would contribute $19,270 during this period. In return for this $38,540 contribution, he would draw maximum social security retirement benefits of $80,888, including those for his wife or widow, if he lived to age 79 (which is more than 7 years longer than his 71.9-year life expectancy under the actuarial tables used by the Internal Revenue Service). This total, however, ignores the interest which the young person's money could earn if not taxed away by social security. If interest is calculated at 5½ per cent (much less than high-grade bonds were yielding in 1971–1972), the 18-year-old's contributions alone would compound to $85,724. Since his employers would contribute a similar amount, the total contribution, privately invested, would come to $171,448. With this sum the worker could buy a private annuity that would pay him $17,316 per year, or $224,242 over the life expectancy assumed by the social security system. It thus appears that, financially speaking, social security is no bargain, although the argument remains that the law does force large numbers of improvident people to save for their old age. In these instances, perhaps, the relative inefficiency and high cost of government pensions are justified. For people willing and able to save, the merit of social security is at least disputable. It would seem only fair to offer thrifty and enterprising citizens the opportunity to elect competing private pension systems for investment of their own funds plus matching employer contributions. However, social security has become both a vested bureaucracy and a political football, and the chances of enacting any such commonsense reform in public pension arrangements appear nonexistent.

The third criticism of social security amounts to a charge that the system is underfunded, given already-promised benefits and present trends toward slower population growth. If the American population stabilizes in coming decades, then by about the year 2010, when workers who began their careers between 1965 and 1970 begin to retire, an increasingly serious disproportion will develop between retired people and those of working age. Some forecasts contend that between the years 2000 and 2025, the aged population will increase three times as fast as the productive one. Under these conditions, it has been estimated that between 15 and 20 per cent of total taxable payrolls would be needed to meet social security benefits at present levels, adjusted only for future price-level changes.[2] Although these projections involve a large degree of forecast and sheer guesswork, they must be taken seriously, particularly by young people on the threshold of their careers. It seems doubtful that the young and middle-aged population of the years 2000 and onward will submit to taxation of the degree which would be necessary, given a stable population, to fulfill the social security benefits already promised those who will then be retiring. If they do not, social security may prove much less beneficial to a person retiring in 2015 or 2020 than one safely under the wire in 1975 or 1985.

The fourth major criticism of social security is that the law does not allow a pensioner less than 72 years old to earn more than $2,100 annually in wages or salary without forfeiting part or all of his social security benefits. Those who advocate removing such limits argue—the authors think, correctly—that government pensions, like private ones, have been earned and paid for by their recipients during their working years. Thus the question of their undertaking other employment has no bearing on their right to receive back funds contributed and earmarked to provide them with retirement income. It is further pointed out that social security annuitants who receive other types of additional income—private pensions, insurance annuities, or investment income, which are often quite large—are not penalized on their social security checks. Finally, it is emphasized that older persons often need the added income a job will provide,

---

[2] See "Social Security's Hidden Hazards," by Robert J. Myers, chief actuary of the Social Security Administration from 1947 to 1970, *Wall Street Journal*, July 28, 1972, p. 8.

either to meet unusual commitments or to offset continually rising living costs for which the government itself is largely to blame.

Although each foregoing criticism is significant, the problems raised are clearly beyond an investor's personal control. Consequently, he must accept social security as it exists and as it is likely to evolve over the years during which it will affect his financial future. On the whole, its benefits appear to take more definite shape and promise greater reliability for those whose retirement is years, rather than decades, away. However, it is usually true, as Chapter 2 noted, that distant benefits must be discounted more heavily than those soon to be enjoyed. Wise investors will keep this point in mind whether considering social security benefits, company pension rights, or the unpredictable outcome of very long-range investments in real estate or securities. The most important point to remember about social security may well be that the program was originally established to provide a minimum base of retirement income to which the individual could then add through his own thrift, enterprise, and luck. Although recent expansions of social security benefits suggest a program tending toward meeting fully the financial needs of all retirees, it seems doubtful whether even the vast wealth of this country can move considerably further in that direction. It appears probable that in years ahead, public hostility to rising taxes, together with other urgent needs for government spending, may leave relatively less than has been available during the 1960s and early 1970s for larger old-age pensions. Almost certainly, social security payments can be expected to keep abreast of price-level inflation, but that may prove to be the limit of their further growth. Under these circumstances, investors aiming at care-free old age must clearly look to other sources of retirement income.

PENSION PLANS

Pension plans are employer-sponsored programs that aim at providing qualified retired employees with a periodic cash income for life. They are important to investors for three reasons. First, most investors are themselves numbered among the 50 million Americans covered by major private and public pension and retirement plans; as already noted, these promised benefits play an important, and often dominant, role in the lifetime financial planning of established persons; and the selection of an employer or field of work which will provide generous retirement benefits is also an important consideration for young persons starting their careers. Second, pension funds and the closely related profit-sharing funds and insured pension plans exercise great influence upon the nation's securities markets and the prices of investments. Finally, pension commitments comprise a rapidly growing and increasingly burdensome cost item to investor-owned companies; in many corporations, promised benefits are badly underfunded, and they appear capable of making substantial inroads on future net profits and stockholders' equity.

Business and public-employee pension plans vary enormously, as might be expected. Not only do the promised annuities differ in size but the computational methods, the years of service required to obtain an annuity, the benefits obtained by an employee who quits his job or dies before retiring, and other matters make a concise analysis difficult. In general, it is fair to state that these pension plans frequently deprive an employee who changes jobs or who dies early, though this is not universal. Most of the plans base the promised annuity in part on years of service. About one-third are drawn so that rising standards of living and rising price levels are reflected in the promised benefits and two-thirds are not; but constant revision of pension programs seems to increase the promised benefits in the latter group fast enough to compensate for price-level inflation at least. Because each plan is a law unto itself, it is not possible to characterize them as dollar-type, as price-level protected, or even as assured assets; but they are important enough to require analysis and recognition in any investment and insurance program.

While more than 13 million Americans are in government-administered plans designed for federal civilian employees, state and local government employees, and railroad workers, private pension-plan participants are nearly three times as numerous. In mid-1972, private pension plans covered an estimated 35 million employees, held $153 billion in assets, and were paying out some $9 billion a year to more than 5 million beneficiaries. Most private pension plans are small-scale undertakings, but a majority of workers participate in a relatively few large plans. The American Telephone and Telegraph Company's pension fund in 1972 had assets of more than $9 billion, surpassing in size all but six of the nation's large industrial corporations; the General Motors pension plan, with assets of $3.15 billion, had more assets than all but 78 American private companies.

Business pension plans are tax-subsidized by laws which make employer payments into them tax-deductible and the earnings of the plans' own investments tax-exempt. To be tax-exempt, however, plans must meet certain Treasury-imposed requirements, and contributions made by employers and employees (if they contribute) must be deposited in a trust or with an insurance company under a carefully spelled-out contract. Pension-plan terms are frequently set by labor agreements, and the United States Labor Department shares regulatory power over the plans with the Internal Revenue Service.

Pension plans are set up because they benefit both employers and employees and because the nation's taxpayers subsidize them with tax exemption. The tax advantage to the employer on his contributions and on the plan's earnings enable him to buy a much larger benefit for his employees per dollar outlay than he could achieve by direct payments. Employers often adopt pension plans to reduce labor turnover, to hold experienced employees, and to strengthen employee job incentives, though it is also obvious that plans are often forced on employers by union demands or by the action of business competitors who establish plans for their employees. For employees, pension plans permit the accumulation of retirement capital on a scale not otherwise possible, an advantage that applies especially to high-salaried managers, and still more to stockholder-officers; through pensions the latter can accumulate part of the earnings on their capital free of tax; otherwise, these earnings would be taxed twice—once as earnings to the corporation and again as dividend payments to themselves.

TAX ADVANTAGES AND QUALIFIED PLANS

In addition to tax-free contributions and earnings accumulation, qualified pension plans offer other tax benefits to eligible employees. If an employee dies, the first $5,000 of death benefits paid from the fund are received by his beneficiary free of income tax. To the extent that they are attributable to company contributions, death benefits paid to a named beneficiary (excluding an employee's executor) are not includable in his gross estate for federal estate tax purposes. Finally, when an employee with a vested interest in a qualified plan irrevocably designates a beneficiary to receive payments at his death, he need not pay gift tax on the sums which represent his employer's contribution.

To obtain these tax advantages, however, a plan must be "qualified," i.e., approved by meeting specific standards imposed by the Treasury Department. These standards are not unreasonable, and any honestly conceived pension plan should have little difficulty in qualifying. The two principal requirements are that benefit allocations must follow a definite formula, and that they must apply impartially to all members of the plan. Pension plans may not discriminate in favor of highly paid employees, but they may and often do postpone eligibility for benefits long enough to eliminate transients and short-term workers. However, the inclusion of high-turnover employees may profit those with longer service, since benefits forfeited by transients will increase the pension accounts of those who stay on. Again, however, if too many forfeitures wind up in the accounts of highly paid employees, a plan may be disqualified.

TYPES OF FUNDED PLANS

Funded employee plans capable of providing retirement benefits belong to three basic types. (1) Under *profit-sharing plans*, the employer contributes out of annual profits to a trust for investment and accumulation, the benefits of which will eventually be distributed under prescribed conditions to employees or their beneficiaries. (2) *Stock bonus plans* are qualified plans under which the employer's contributions are made in stock; contributions are not necessarily geared to profits. (3) *Pension plans* undertake to provide through systematic contributions for definitely determinable benefits to employees and their beneficiaries.

Pension plans differ from profit-sharing plans by promising a definite scale of benefits and thus imposing a largely unavoidable charge on operations. A company's older employees are inclined to favor a pension plan because of the more precisely calculable benefits. Profit-sharing plans are less burdensome to an employer, and younger employees often regard them favorably as a financial reserve upon which they can draw in emergencies. The tax code permits any percentage of profits to be contributed to a plan, but the employer cannot deduct from his taxable income a contribution larger than 15 per cent of all compensation paid to participants during the year. Profit-sharing plans may be of the "current-distribution" type under which cash payments are made as soon as shares can be determined. For permanent employees, these plans are usually a poor substitute for the longer-range benefits and tax advantages of a *deferred* profit-sharing plan. It is possible for employers to combine profit-sharing and pension elements in a single qualified plan.

Pension plans are more flexible than the other types. They permit immediate retirement of older employees with benefits based upon employment prior to the plan's adoption. Pension plans usually include life insurance protection for employees during their years of employment. Finally, pension plans may be contributory as well as noncontributory. A contributory plan may enlarge an employee's opportunity for tax-free accumulation of capital.

TYPES OF PENSION PLANS

All pension plans, whether contributory or noncontributory, are of either the insured, pay-as-you-go, or trusteed type. Insured plans require the employer to pay contributions to an insurance company for the purchase of either group or individual annuities for member employees. Pay-as-you go plans have no funding arrangement, but meet benefit payments out of the employer's current revenues. Trusteed (or self-administered) plans provide for contributions to a trust in amounts which, together with trust-fund earnings, will provide the employee with benefits promised under the plan. The trustee is ordinarily a bank or trust company, which holds and invests the contributions and pays benefits according to terms of the trust and the plan provisions. Some trusteed plans are deferred profit-sharing plans which provide for income at retirement.

Insured pension plans in 1971 had 11.5 million enrolled members, held reserves of $46.4 billion, and received contributions during the year of nearly $5 billion. Group annuities, of which there are several kinds, involve setting up a single fund for all employees in the pension group. As an employee retires, money is withdrawn to buy him an annuity. In 1971, 6.8 million persons were covered by this type of insured plan. About 2 million others were covered by deferred group annuity plans under which a paid-up annuity is purchased annually for each employee; the sum of these benefits is paid as monthly income upon his retirement. Other plans in effect used whole life or endowment policies keyed to retirement, which also provided life insurance protection during the working lives of participants.

Legislation in most states allows insurance companies to maintain separate investment accounts for particular pension plans or groups of plans. Considerable latitude is allowed for equity investment of insured pension funds, and pension-plan variable annuities are now legal in well over half the states. At the end of 1971, life insurance companies held $7.1 billion of pension reserves in separate accounts.

Insured pension plans, though less numerous than trusteed ones, possess certain clear-cut advantages, especially for employers and employees in smaller concerns or associations. The most conspicuous advantages are (1) the investment experience of the insurance companies, (2) the guaranteed interest rate earned by contributions, (3) a minimum of administrative work, and (4) the effective shifting of the investment risk to the insurance company. While trusteed plans have received wide criticism from 1970 through 1972, legislators, labor unions, and the general public apparently have found nothing worth condemning in the insured plans.

TRUSTEED PENSION PLANS

Trusteed pension plans are the oldest and most widespread type. At the end of 1971, they covered more than 24 million persons, held nearly $100 billion in assets, disbursed pension payments of $5.5 billion, and received contributions of $10 billion, with employers paying most of this amount.

The duties of a pension trustee are similar to those in ordinary trusts. His most important task is to invest the amounts received from the employer and to accumulate income. In establishing a pension or profit-sharing trust, the employer usually sets forth in the trust instrument the trustee's powers and duties with respect to investment. Where the trust agreement is silent, the trustee must invest the funds according to the laws of the state in which the trust is being administered.

The trustee is usually a corporation and ordinarily a bank or trust company. However, trustees also may be individuals who make final decisions, with the bank or trust company acting merely as custodian of the pension-fund assets. Since bank fees for trust services are substantial and the performance records of their investment managers sometimes disappointing, a number of large pension funds have company or "in-house" trustees. The pension funds of Bethlehem

Steel, National Distillers, and Atlantic Richfield are managed wholly or partially by company trustees.

Administrative decisions on a trusteed pension plan usually are made by an advisory or pension committee consisting of three to five members, comprising a mixture of directors, officers, and employee representatives of the company. This committee decides specific cases involving such matters as an employee's eligibility for plan membership, the benefits attaching to an early retirement, and approval of beneficiary designations; it maintains the records and accounts of the plan and instructs the trustees to make payment to eligible recipients.

PENSION-PLAN BENEFITS

Both employees and job applicants need thorough knowledge of a company's pension plan. Significant features include (1) eligibility to participate, (2) benefit formula used, (3) retirement age, (4) supplementary benefits, and (5) vesting. A brief discussion of each feature follows.

Eligibility   In the majority of pension plans, new employees either become members of noncontributory plans when they achieve full-time status or of contributory plans when they agree to contribute. Some plans, however, require a specified age or length of service, or both, before an employee is eligible to participate.

Benefit formulas   Formulas for retirement benefits typically reflect the economic conditions of the industry as well as the needs of the employees covered. Benefit formulas may be based upon (1) whatever annuity an employee's accumulated pension-account money will buy (a "money-purchase" benefit); (2) a flat benefit, the same for all eligible employees;[3] (3) a flat percentage of compensation; (4) a percentage of compensation times years of service;[4] or (5) the use of a variable annuity.[5] All plans take social security payments into account in setting benefit levels. A few older plans still adjust company benefits downward as social security payments increase, though few recently adopted plans do this.

[3] This sort of benefit has been widely negotiated by the United Auto Workers union. Depending on the company concerned, the plans provide retirement benefits ranging from $4 to $10 per month for each year of service.

[4] An increasing number of companies base an employee's retirement benefits on his average salary during his best 5 years rather than on his career average. Consolidated Freightways, for example, uses this sort of calculation.

[5] The Treasury Department has ruled that equity-based annuity plans can satisfy the requirement of the tax regulations that a qualified pension plan provide for the payment of a definitely determinable benefit. Plans that increase or decrease benefits with the moves of a recognized cost of living index also can be approved by the Internal Revenue Service.

Retirement age Most plans provide for normal retirement at age 65, but some
have no age requirement and others specify as high as 70 and as low as 55 years
of age. Other age-service combinations are common, such as 10 years' service
plus age 60, or 20 years' service at age 55. Some plans provide for employees'
early retirement on an immediate, reduced lifetime benefit computed on the basis
of the company's normal retirement formula.

Supplementary benefits Pension plans may provide medical benefits for retirees,
life insurance for employees, or options for partial withdrawal of pension-fund
accumulations during employment. Severance benefits for dismissed employees
are often paid out of pension-fund reserves. Disability benefits, when provided,
generally bear some relation to the amount of normal pension accruals up to the
time of an employee's disability; some plans pay an additional benefit until the
employee becomes eligible for social security. Clearly, these supplementary benefits have potential value to an employee or a prospective worker.

Vesting Vesting gives qualified employees the right to their pensions, or a part
of them, even if they leave the company or are discharged before reaching retirement age. Vesting may be immediate, i.e., from the beginning of pension-plan
membership; it may take place ratably over the period of membership; or it may
be based on service, age, or both. Some plans vest no rights at all until an employee retires, dies, or becomes disabled.

From the employee's standpoint, the shortest vesting period is best. This is not
necessarily true from the employer's standpoint. However, strong criticism of
present pension plans has come from workers who have been laid off after long
service and left without pension benefits. President Nixon in 1972 suggested a
"rule of 50" federal standard which would require that pensions become at least
half-vested when an employee's age and the number of years he has been in a
pension plan add up to 50. The amount vested would then increase annually
until the pension became fully vested 5 years later.

Allied to, but distinct from, vesting is the problem of pension "portability,"
which involves the transfer of assets from one pension plan to another. Portability poses more difficult problems than vesting, since one pension plan may be
fully funded; another, only 30 per cent.

Since 1960, pension plans have shown a strong trend toward earlier retirement, wider coverage, earlier vesting, and much-expanded benefits. These
changes have rapidly increased the pension-cost burden to sponsoring companies.
The fact that pension costs in 1972 were rising at an annual rate of about 20 per
cent obviously helped account for the aggressive investment policies which many
pension funds and their trustees have felt called upon to adopt.

PENSION COSTS

An investor who thinks of himself as an employee will almost certainly look with satisfaction upon large pension benefits in his own employer's plan. As a stockholder in another company, however, he is likely to be concerned by the obvious and growing size of pension costs. Clearly, the dominant factor in what pensions cost a company is the scale of benefits promised times the number of employees eligible to receive them. Companies recognize this and sometimes attempt to reduce their required contributions by setting an upper limit to the amount of benefits regardless of salary.[6] Companies may also seek to reduce their pension costs by trying to limit pension-plan eligibility to permanent employees. Probation periods of up to 5 years may be approved by the Internal Revenue Service if they do not appear to be biased in favor of officers and other highly paid employees. A minimum age of 30 may be required, but higher age limits may disqualify a plan. Plans also may cover only salaried workers in companies where hourly employees have high turnover—the Internal Revenue Service has ruled that employee classification for pension purposes is not discriminatory per se.

Many companies allow their employees some measure of pension credit for service given prior to a pension plan's adoption. This results in a large unfunded obligation for "past-service" costs, and may add substantially to the annual contributions required to fund pensions fully by the time employees retire. The income tax law limits the portion of past-service costs that can be deducted annually from gross income to 10 per cent of unfunded past-service costs, although an employer may contribute more on a non-tax-free basis.

Once the benefits under a pension plan have been fixed, the prospective cost is further determined by two sorts of assumptions. (1) *Mortality assumptions* deal with the number of employees likely to die before reaching retirement age, how long retirees will probably live, and related problems such as the volume of expected severance payments, dismissal benefits, and partial or total vesting of benefits by departing employees. Mortality assumptions are made by professional actuaries from insurance mortality tables, company records, projections of current personnel statistics, etc. (2) *Earnings* or *interest assumptions* concern the rate at which contributions invested in the pension fund will multiply through interest or dividend earnings and through capital gains realized on the investments. Earnings are very important to a pension fund because even a small increase in the yield of trust investments can make a substantial difference in the employer's cost, the size of benefits provided employees, or both. Over 40 years' time, for example, an increase in investment yield of one percentage point can either de-

---

[6] This is sometimes necessary in order to qualify a plan.

crease pension costs by 20 per cent or raise benefits by 25 per cent. In recent years, corporations have tended to maintain their pension outlays while enlarging their scale of benefits by improving both their actuarial and their earnings assumptions.

PENSION-FUND INVESTMENT POLICIES

The investment policies of pension funds are affected by company attitudes, the trust laws of 50 states, the investment philosophies of different trustees, and the size of the trusts concerned. The pension trust agreement can empower the advisory committee to direct the trustee how to invest trust funds, or it can give the trustee full discretion with respect to investments. Large pension funds often "split" the investment responsibility among two or more trustees, requiring them to compete with one another, and basing the additional funds each trustee receives in a coming period upon his investment performance in the previous period.

Some companies restrict or ban certain types of investments by their trustees. The Columbia Broadcasting System, for example, prohibits investment in its own stock and limits the percentage of its pension funds that may be invested in common stocks. American Tobacco's pension plan prohibits investments in stocks of the company's competitors. Texaco, Incorporated, uses the "split funding" principle: part of the company's contribution is placed with trustees for investment in stocks, and part, including all employee contributions, is placed with insurance companies. However, the general trend has been toward granting sole investment responsibility to the trustee, and thus sole accountability for the choice of investments. Ordinarily, a company meets at length with its trustees to define carefully their objectives, responsibilities, and allowable risks.

Federal tax laws place few restrictions on pension-fund investments, but state laws may prohibit certain selections. A few states restrict trustees to a "legal list" of investments and then subject them to a rule of prudence in making selections from that list. Most states follow the less restrictive "prudent man" rule and permit a trustee to make "any investment which a man of prudence, discretion, and intelligence would select in managing his own affairs, considering safety of principal and production of income." This is the rule of New York State, in which trustees hold a large percentage of the nation's total noninsured pension-fund accounts.

Originally, pension funds assumed conservative rates of interest-earnings, but the large growth of benefits in recent years (often the result of union bargaining agreements) has increased pension-cost burdens substantially and encouraged many employers to demand higher trust-fund earnings. Most pension plans are still relatively young and will continue to build up reserves for many years before annual benefits begin to exceed employer contributions. For these plans, the present problem is not to obtain the cash to pay benefits, but to invest—at the maximum yield consistent with safety—the cash continually pouring in from contributions. Some plans and trustees are still content to use dollar-cost averaging, although this is often combined with a market-timing device to improve performance; for example, investment may be postponed in any quarter in which a leading market average has dropped 5 per cent or more. Increasingly, however, trustees are "managing" both the stock and bond portions of pension-fund portfolios, adjusting their size and composition noticeably in step with price trends in the securities markets.

Chart 23-1 indicates that between 1960 and 1971, pension funds reduced the percentage of corporate bonds in their portfolios from 40 per cent to 21 per cent, and the percentage of government securities from 7 per cent to only 2 per cent. In the same period, common stocks rose from 43 to 68 per cent of total portfolio holdings. Except for mortgages and real estate, other types of investments play minor parts in pension trust portfolios.

Government securities are always rated as "legal" trust-fund investments; however, their returns are lower than those offered by corporate bonds, and pension funds now use treasury issues mainly to provide liquidity. Pension trusts hold 10 times as many corporate bonds as they do governments. Private place-

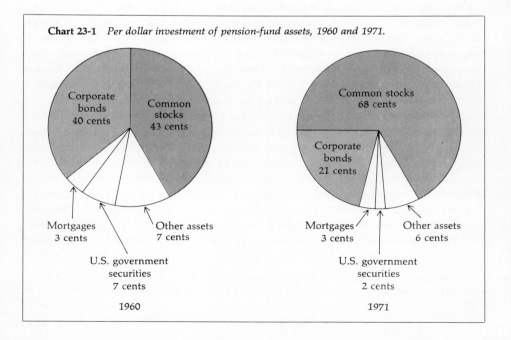

Chart 23-1 *Per dollar investment of pension-fund assets, 1960 and 1971.*

Corporate bonds 40 cents

Common stocks 43 cents

Mortgages 3 cents

Other assets 7 cents

U.S. government securities 7 cents

1960

Common stocks 68 cents

Corporate bonds 21 cents

Mortgages 3 cents

Other assets 6 cents

U.S. government securities 2 cents

1971

ments, which offer still higher yields, also are bought heavily where marketability is not required. Pension funds buy convertible bonds, but preferred stocks are of little benefit to the nontaxable trusts. The funds also hold minor amounts of Federal Housing, Veterans Administration, and conventional mortgages, and in 1972–1973, Government National Mortgage Association "pass through" participation certificates and GNMA bonds were increasingly popular pension-fund investments. Large commercial and industrial mortgages also are held, many from the 1969–1970 tight-money period; these typically give the pension trust a generous yield plus some share in the borrower's profits or gross receipts. Real estate, real estate investment-trust shares, purchases and leasebacks of buildings, and equipment leases are occasionally found among pension-fund assets, and a few funds supply venture capital to new firms.

The fact that common stocks comprise two-thirds of total pension trust holdings raises at least four questions concerning the future stability of both pension funds and stock prices. First, stocks, unlike bonds, are not actuarially predictable in their yields over short or even relatively long periods. Second, the management of billions of dollars in pension funds by the trust departments of a few large banks has produced an unhealthy and perhaps dangerous concentration of stock market power.[7] Third, the tendency for pension trustees to buy and sell at more frequent intervals, to trade the short swings of the stock market, and to "gang up" in buying and selling the same stocks, has almost certainly reduced the stability and liquidity of the market. Finally, billions of pension reserves might be wiped out by some future stock market crash, or a prolonged failure of stock prices to rise could produce a wholesale underfunding of pension trusts. Nevertheless, even the conservatively run government retirement plans now permit considerable common stock investment; since 1966, the New York State teachers' retirement system has invested up to 20 per cent of its assets in equities.

Most pension funds still seek reasonable diversification for both stock and bond components, although the view is spreading among trust investors that *overdiversification* leads to mediocre performance. Some states—notably Indiana, New Hampshire, and Tennessee—have statutory diversification requirements for trust funds, but ordinarily the degree of diversification and the choice of diversified securities are left to the discretion of the pension fund or its trustees.

The need to diversify can pose difficult problems for the pension trusts of companies with a dozen to a few hundred employees, and banks in various parts of the country have established qualified investment trusts—pools of commingled

---

[7] A 1972 survey of 3,407 bank trust departments showed that more than one-third of all pension money was held by just 3 large banks; three-quarters of it, in 22 banks. See *The Money Manager*, Nov. 6, 1972, p. 19.

funds—to invest these trust monies advantageously. Participating pension and profit-sharing trusts purchase units of the pooled funds on a basis similar to investment-trust shares; funds may be operated as equity, fixed-income, or balanced funds. Many small pension plans also obtain diversification and professional management by investing directly in mutual-fund shares. The purchase commissions charged trust funds are lower than those charged individual investors, since unit sales are typically much larger.

PENSION-FUND REGULATION

Pension funds have been described as the largest pool of unregulated capital in the United States. Except in "legal list" states, the investment practices of committees and trustees are under few restrictions. Actuarial assumptions and funding estimates are almost totally at the discretion of sponsoring companies. Pension plans are not required to be audited or insured against loss. Both pension and profit-sharing plans are exempt from coverage under the Securities Act of 1933 unless they are voluntary plans which involve an investment in the employer's firm of more money than the employer puts into the fund. The Investment Company Act of 1940 also largely exempts pension plans from SEC regulation. The Internal Revenue Service has laid down certain requirements in order for employer contributions to qualify for tax exemption, and periodic fiscal reports must be filed with the Department of Labor; but no single government agency has overall supervision of pension systems or is empowered to make certain that workers will receive what they expect to get when they retire.

Meanwhile, the rapid increase in benefits, the trend toward earlier retirement, and the heavy dependence of pension plans on corporate profits and an advancing stock market have prompted many observers to ask whether the plans in general are being soundly funded and whether money will be available to meet the huge volume of pension commitments now accumulated. Since pension claims are, in effect, a "prior charge" against stockholders' earnings and equity, the position of pension funds is also a matter of growing concern to investors.

During 1971 and 1972, the financial news and developing controversies made investors conscious of at least three problems connected with pension-fund operation. First, the generally vague reporting which companies made on the obligations and status of their pension funds cast increasing doubt on both the adequacy of pension funding and the validity of currently reported corporate earnings. Second, growing evidence suggested that pension underfunding was both widespread and serious. Third, occasional revelations of self-dealing and other abuses between companies or company officials and their pension trusts pointed to the need for stricter fiduciary standards in pension-fund administration.

Pension-fund reporting Although the assets of trusteed pension funds exceed 100 billion dollars, few corporations say much about them to their stockholders. This is true despite the facts that pension costs are rising much faster than earnings or dividends, that pension-fund assets are growing more rapidly than company assets or stockholders' equity, and that companies' annual pension-fund contributions and the return on fund assets are important determinants of company profits. Stockholders usually receive some information concerning a company's pension fund but rarely enough figures and facts to determine where the company stands with respect to its total pension obligation or what pension-fund earnings rate or actuarial assumptions are being used.

The American Institute of Certified Public Accountants requires companies to charge their pension costs in certain ways, but compels very little real disclosure. Companies must charge pension costs against reported income each year whether funds are actually transferred to a pension trustee or not. Plans that operate on a pay-as-you-go basis must charge costs against earnings as employees earn their pension rights, whatever the timing of actual payments. Finally, corporations are not allowed to use previous overpayments to a pension fund, or capital gains on securities held by the fund, as a substitute for current charges; overpayments and capital gains must be spread over at least a 10-year period. These rule may prevent some deceptive pension-cost bookkeeping aimed at manipulating reported earnings, but they do nothing to assure stockholders, employees, or creditors that a company's pension charges are adequate or that its pension liabilities are being soundly funded.

Some companies, including Polaroid, Continental Corporation, and Litton, made no mention at all of pensions in their 1971 annual reports. Others dismissed pension obligations with a brief footnote. Bunker Ramo, Charter New York, Gulf and Western, and Mead Corporation reported current pension costs but avoided year-to-year comparisons and said nothing about the overall status of their pension funds. About half the major companies in one survey, including Eastman Kodak, du Pont, International Telephone, and Minnesota Mining, mentioned their amortization period for past-service costs but omitted the more significant figure of past-service liability. Gulf and Western admitted in its 1971 annual report that vested benefits fell nearly 48 million dollars short of being covered by fund assets, but the company failed to report the size of either liabilities or assets. Only a few companies, such as General Electric and Pitney-Bowes, reported the interest- (or earnings-) rate assumptions on which their pension plans were based.[8] Clearly, the usual fragmentary details on pension costs and liabilities do not enable investors to make meaningful projections of the degree to which

---

[8] General Electric assumes a 6 per cent future-income rate, which provides for systematic recognition of a portion of the unrealized appreciation in the fund's common stock portfolio. Pitney-Bowes assumes a 5½ per cent annual rate.

future pension-fund obligations may effect a company's earnings or stockholders' net worth.[9]

Underfunding   Under present laws, pension-plan sponsors are not required to maintain assets sufficient to pay the claims of vested workers if plans are terminated. Terminations can result from the failure of a business or the merger of a sponsoring company. Even if a firm's present funding reserves appear adequate, future pensions may still not be assured. A market decline may permanently reduce the value of pension-fund assets. Or a company's earning power may shrink, limit the future contributions the employer can make, and leave the fund unable to meet its obligations.

Several large companies admitted in their 1971 annual reports that vested employee benefits exceeded their pension-fund assets. For example, General Motors' $3.15 billion of assets fell $700 million short of accrued pension liabilities, while American Telephone had more than $9 billion in assets but was $119 million short of complete funding. Almost certainly more serious than those confessed shortages were a much larger number of unrevealed ones.

To safeguard current earnings, many corporations seem anxious to "discover" new interest-earning and actuarial assumptions that justify reductions in pension-fund contributions. United States Steel decreased its 1971 pension costs to $62.1 million from $104.8 million in 1970 by revising upward its assumed rate of return on pension-fund assets. Even with this revision, however, the company's pension costs for 1971 were $1.93 per share, 13 cents more than the annual dividend paid stockholders. Total employee benefits paid by the company, including insurance, social security taxes, union welfare and retirement payments, and savings plans, amounted to 2.3 times total profit. The heavy burden of pensions and other benefits in steel companies suggests the dangers that beset mature industries with strong unions and high wage costs.

Most employees appear to believe that their pension rights are guaranteed, and they are not aware of possibilities that their benefits might be reduced or even terminated. All funded private pension plans, however, contain provisions for termination if the company goes out of business; funds are then distributed, in order of preference among the various beneficiaries, as far as they will go. From 1968 through 1971, pension-plan terminations rose sharply as expanding conglomerate companies absorbed or liquidated acquired firms, and many long-service employees lost their supposedly accumulated benefits. In 1963 when

---

[9] United States Steel Corporation's detailed accounting of its pension and other welfare costs in its 1971 annual report was a refreshing exception to the hazy information most corporations provided. Besides a long pension footnote, the U.S. Steel Report tabulated 2-year comparisons of benefit costs and their allocations, and contained three tables on the trusteed pension fund, including a breakdown of the portfolio by types of investments.

Studebaker stopped automobile production and its pension plan was terminated, some 4,500 workers under 60 years of age with fully vested pension rights had to settle for only 15 per cent of their earned benefits.[10]

The insufficient funding of many pension plans and the losses suffered by workers in terminated plans produced widespread demands during 1972 for legislation to require full funding of pension obligations, together with a federal insurance scheme for covering loss to employees caused by premature plan terminations. It appeared likely that such legislation would soon be enacted, with the result that pension costs to most companies might rise even more steeply in years ahead, with consequent pressures on earnings and dividend payments.

Self-dealing and abuses   Present laws impose few specific requirements of fiduciary responsibility for safeguarding pension-fund assets. Some plans administered by company officials have habitually invested a large share of assets in company stock, and others have made questionable loans to the sponsoring company or to its subsidiaries and affiliates. In other instances, excessive administration costs have been paid to bank-trustees in which company officers have held large interests. Such policies may imperil the safety of pension funds, and they clearly result in higher costs and loss of earning opportunities for the fund, both of which are detrimental to the interests of employees and the general body of stockholders alike.

As 1973 began, Congress was urged to enact various reforms in the noninsured pension system. Strongly supported changes included (1) improved vesting standards; (2) fuller and prompter funding; (3) insurance to cover benefits in terminated plans not fully funded; (4) fiduciary standards for trustees, including a limitation on pension-fund investment in a sponsoring company's stock; (5) an independent agency to regulate pension funds; (6) a nationwide system of voluntary pension portability; and (7) a more complete disclosure of pension rights to employees and of pension-fund financial condition to stockholders and public authorities. Probabilities appeared strong that most of these changes would be enacted into law during the following 2 years.

GOVERNMENT-ADMINISTERED PENSION PLANS

Aside from social security, the federal government also administers a number of retirement plans for federal civilian employees and the Railroad Retirement System. The civilian retirement plans cover employees of the civil service, Federal

---

[10] Average age of this group was 51; average service with the company was 21 years. When the plan was terminated, the $25 million in assets were divided as far as they would go. Full pensions went to 3,600 workers already retired or over age 60. Another 4,000 employees between 40 and 60 received 15 per cent of what they had coming to them. The remaining 2,900 workers under age 40 got nothing. Some pension actuaries contend there was nothing wrong with the Studebaker pension plan. The problem, they say, was with the company itself, which failed from competitive reasons before enough money could be pumped into the fund.

Reserve, Tennessee Valley Authority, and other government branches; in 1970, these plans paid total retirement benefits of $2.8 billion to 970,000 retired workers or their survivors, had accumulated assets of $23.9 billion, and received employer-employee contributions of $3.9 billion. The Railroad Retirement System, established in 1935, covers about 600,000 workers, paid about $1.7 billion in benefits during 1970, and is the only federally administered social insurance system covering a single private industry.

Almost all state and local governments have retirement plans, designed to cover teachers, policemen, firemen, and other employees of states, counties, and cities. In 1970, these plans held total assets of more than $50 billion, paid benefits of $3.1 billion to 1,272,000 retired workers, and had total contributions of $7.1 billion. Most state and local employees are also covered by social security.

The financial integrity of the social security, federal civil service, and railroad retirement programs appears beyond question; Congress establishes the benefit rates, prescribes the desired contributions, and implies coverage of any shortages out of the presumably bottomless federal treasury. All federal pension funds invest exclusively in government obligations. Most of the state and local civil service pension plans similarly prescribe benefits and contributions, but in many cases there is a less obvious willingness on the part of the taxpayers to underwrite shortages. The pension funds are managed by boards or trustees whose investments are generally limited to a legally prescribed list of items. In recent years, in an understandable effort to obtain capital gains on some investments, some of these state and local funds have been authorized to make major investments in common stocks and real estate.

KEOGH PLAN PENSIONS

Under provisions of the Keogh Act,[11] a self-employed person may pay not more than 10 per cent of his earnings and not more than $2,500 per year into a special trust which will provide him with a life annuity at retirement age. Payments into this trust are deductible from taxable income and its compounded earnings are tax-exempt. However, the postretirement annuity will be taxable, just as employer-financed pensions are. Plans may be operated as pools or as members of an association or group, but a self-employed beneficiary must include in his plan all full-time employees with more than 3 years' service; he must contribute the same percentage of their salaries as he does of his own.

Keogh plans must be approved in advance by the Treasury to qualify for favorable tax treatment. Once established, they cannot be changed without permission. Contributions to plans and earnings thereon cannot be withdrawn, borrowed upon, or assigned; they are "locked up" until the beneficiary reaches

---

[11] Self-employed Individuals Tax Retirement Act of 1962, as amended.

age 59½ or more, dies, or becomes truly disabled. Because the Keogh Act is complex and its plans are complicated to implement, an investor is wise to seek legal assistance before starting a plan.

Keogh Act investments may take one of five forms. (1) Annuity contracts, fixed or variable, may be purchased from life insurance companies. (2) Funds may be placed with a corporate trustee (normally a bank) with the individual exercising partial or full discretion over investment selections. (3) Mutual funds may be purchased and held by the trustee, or (4) face-amount certificates may be used.[12] Finally, special United States Retirement Plan Bonds are available.[13] More than 200 mutual funds offer Keogh plans and most life insurance companies sell Keogh-approved annuities.

QUESTIONS AND PROBLEMS

1 Should an investor consider his prospective social security pension a dollar sum item, subject to the purchasing-power risk? Explain.
2 Since social security benefits have been steadily enlarged during the past generation, is it plausible for a young worker today to rely on his future social security pension to meet most of his retirement needs?
3 Does social security appear to be a bargain for middle- and upper-income salary earners? Cite figures to support your answer.
4 What is meant in saying that the social security system is underfunded? Can this be true, if the federal taxing power fully backs all promises of social security pensions?
5 Do insured pension plans offer sounder prospects than trusteed plans? Why? Which type of plan would be likely to appear less costly to a large employer? Why?
6 Do stockholders' interests in pension plans tend to harmonize or collide with those of employees?
7 Explain the difference between a pension plan's "mortality" and "earnings" assumptions. What has been the recent tendency of employer-corporations with respect to these assumptions? Why?
8 What features characterized the evolution of pension-fund investment policies in the years 1955 through 1972? Do you consider these tendencies to have been wholesome?
9 Most trusteed pension funds today are based principally on common stock investment. Is this actuarially sound? What issues are raised here?
10 Do pension funds need greater regulation? If so, in what areas?
11 Does pension-fund disclosure appear sufficient to meet the needs of all interested parties? Why, or why not?

[12] Face-amount certificates are described in Chapter 21.

[13] For self-employed pension plans, these bonds are sold at par in denominations of $50, $100, $500, and $1,000, and in 1972 provided an investment yield of 5 per cent per year compounded semiannually. They may be registered only in the name of natural persons in single ownership or beneficiary form and must be registered in the name of the self-employed person or employee for whom they are bought. Bonds will be reissued if lost, stolen, or destroyed.

12 Should Keogh Act plans be made available to all savers? Consider specifically persons already covered by public or private pension plans but desirous of increasing their tax-sheltered savings for old age?

13 What type of common stocks would you consider appropriate for the trusteed pension fund of a large manufacturing company?

14 Do you think limits should be placed on the yields and price-earnings ratios at which common stocks should be purchased for pension-fund investment?

15 At the yields available in early 1973, would you consider common stocks or high-grade bonds more attractive for pension-fund purchases? In what proportions would you divide your buying between stocks and bonds if you were manager of a large trusteed pension fund? Justify your allocation.

REFERENCES

Badger, Ralph E., Harold W. Torgerson, and Harry G. Guthmann: *Investment Principles and Practices*, 6th ed., Prentice-Hall, Inc., Englewood Cliffs, N.J., 1969, Chap. 20.

Bowen, William G., and others: *The Princeton Symposium on the American System of Social Insurance*, McGraw-Hill Book Company, New York, 1967.

Collier Books: *Social Security and Medicare Simplified*, New York, 1970.

Holzman, Robert S.: *Guide to Pension and Profit Sharing Plans*, Farnsworth Publishing Company, New York, 1969.

Metzger, Bert L.: *Investment Practices, Performance, and Management of Profit Sharing Trust Funds*, Profit Sharing Research Foundation, Evanston, Ill., 1969.

Murray, Roger F.: *Economic Aspects of Pensions*, Columbia University Press, New York, 1968.

Myers, Robert J.: *Social Insurance and Allied Government Programs*, Richard D. Irwin, Inc., Homewood, Ill., 1965.

Prentice-Hall, Inc.: *Pension and Profit Sharing Report* and *Social Security Tax Service*, both loose-leaf, Englewood Cliffs, N.J.

Schottland, Charles I.: *The Social Security Program in the United States*, 2d ed., Appleton-Century-Crofts, Inc., New York, 1970.

Thomas, Conrad W.: "Sure as Death and Taxes," *Barron's*, Aug. 28, 1972, pp. 3 ff.

U.S. Social Security Administration: *Social Security Handbook* (revised occasionally), and *Your Social Security* (revised frequently), Washington.

Life insurance policies provide the cornerstone of most family financial programs and have extensive business uses as well. Private annuity plans offered by insurance companies play an important part in the retirement programs of millions of Americans. The extent of American use of insurance and insurance-related annuities is illustrated by the fact that in 1971, life insurance companies held nearly $180 billion of policyholders' funds earmarked for these purposes. Life insurance in force totaled more than $1.5 trillion and provided average protection of $25,700 for 86 per cent of the families that owned one or more life policies. Annuities and life income contracts payable from insurance proceeds numbered nearly 10 million. All these figures are growing at rates of between 4 and 7 per cent per year.

These statistics demonstrate the great importance of life insurance and annuities among types of investments. Of course, insurance is seldom purchased solely for investment reasons—in fact, the mortality costs and operating expenses incident to life insurance would usually make the investment unprofitable if the life protection feature were not needed—but as an investment combined with protection, the insurance device is unique for safety, profitableness, and convenience. It therefore occupies an important place in most carefully planned investment programs.

FUNCTIONS OF LIFE INSURANCE AND ANNUITIES

Investors include insurance in their investment plans in order to accomplish a variety of objectives. These objectives are not equally important to all investors, but the following eight need to be considered in connection with almost every investment program.

1 **Immediate estate** Perhaps the most widely recognized function of life insurance is to provide an "immediate estate" to the family of a breadwinner who dies before he has had opportunity to accumulate a competent sum for its support. The amount needed to raise a family, provide for emergencies, and afford security to a widow or other dependents is so great that most families find it hard to finance adequate insurance for this purpose, especially while the family and the breadwinner are young. This problem is so important that the average family should make solution of it a cornerstone of its investment program. In solving

the problem consideration should be given to the adequacy of existing resources, possible social security benefits, probable assistance from relatives, and ultimate inheritances.

2 Annuities for beneficiaries One of the major functions of life insurance is to provide annuities for beneficiaries. Nearly all life insurance policies give the beneficiary the option of taking a long-term or remainder-of-life annuity instead of a lump-sum settlement; they also permit the insured to designate this as the mode of settlement. Many modern family policies provide a temporary annuity (generally a "family income" until children are grown) in addition to a permanent settlement.

3 Savings Life insurance is one of the greatest savings systems employed by American families. In a previous chapter it was noted that the typical life insurance policy is designed as a combination of decreasing insurance protection plus increasing savings account, which together equal the face amount of the policy. The policyholder's premium payments are used in part to build up the savings account in his policy, and as the savings account increases, the amount of insurance protection which he buys constantly decreases. Although the ever-increasing savings element earns only $2\frac{1}{2}$ to 4 per cent in most companies, it is kept in safe investments, may be used as collateral if the policyholder needs to borrow against it, may be obtained by "cashing in" the policy if that becomes desirable, and may be exchanged for a retirement income if the policyholder ultimately requests it.

4 Cash resource Most "ordinary" life insurance policies—that is, those sold in units of $1,000 and up, in private rather than employee group contracts—contain clauses outlining the terms under which a policyholder may borrow from the company, using his policy as security. The loan may usually amount to almost the entire "reserve" or savings account in the policy, is compulsory on the company, carries a stipulated rate of interest usually between 5 and 6 per cent, and has no definite maturity date. Thousands of businessmen took advantage of low-cost policy loans on their life insurance during the credit squeezes of the late 1960s. A life insurance policy may also be assigned to a bank or other creditor as collateral, but the convenience of direct borrowing from the company is very great. Surrendering a policy for cash is an equally simple process.

5 Disability income Few American families are insured against the contingency of long-term disablement of the breadwinner. This is an economic disaster comparable to his early death, but insurance companies have had unfortunate experiences with policies designed to meet the need, and most of them do not now offer adequate contracts. However, some life insurance companies add clauses to insurance policies under which a totally and (apparently) permanently disabled insured may receive an income for life. Assurance of $50 per month under one of these clauses will usually cost the insured $20 to $50 per year, depending mostly upon his age. Some casualty insurance companies also offer disability income policies which partly or wholly meet this need.

6 Retirement income This is a rapidly increasing function. Many holders of life insurance are now converting their insurance policies into life annuities when they retire, and nearly 8 million employed persons will receive life annuities through employer pension plans maintained in life insurance companies. Most privately purchased life insurance policies give the insured the option to surrender his policy and receive in return a life annuity equal in value to the cash value of the policy. Some insurance policies are written with this ultimate object in mind. In any case, policyholders who do this are accorded the privileges and choices stipulated in their policies. The annuities may run for the duration of either one or two lives, and they may be guaranteed to pay the annuitants or their heirs either for a minimum period of time or up to a minimum sum. A decision to take an annuity does not have to be made by a policyholder until he is ready for the payments to begin, so the hazard of an early choice which later proves inappropriate does not exist.

7 Clean-up fund In addition to life insurance earmarked for long-term objectives, families often have use for insurance policies which will pay expenses of last illness, funeral costs, and adjustment costs incident to death. These usually need not be large and may be omitted entirely in cases where the family resources seem adequate to care for possible requirements.

8 Business insurance There are many business situations in which life insurance can contribute convenience and peace of mind. Three typical situations may be noted. In closed corporations or partnerships, it is often desirable that the other participants be able to buy out the interest of a deceased member, rather than to admit an heir or a new purchaser into the firm. This can be done if each participant owns insurance on the lives of the others, so that the remaining members are provided with cash when any one of them dies. Second, a business debtor may carry insurance designed to help liquidate his debts in case of his death. Third, any individual whose estate will encounter heavy taxes at his death may find life insurance a convenient means of providing the funds.

PROTECTION AND SAVING

All life insurance policies are basically combinations of insurance protection and savings account, and the most basic distinction between forms of policies relates to the proportions in which the protection and savings elements are combined.

In a low-priced policy all, or nearly all, of the premiums collected must be used to pay the insured's share of operating expenses and the death claims on the members of his group who die; consequently, little of his premium money remains to go into a savings fund, and the amount of insurance protection for which he is charged remains high, close to the face amount of his policy. On a high-priced policy the premium payment would be large enough to pay the expense and mortality levies and also make a substantial contribution to the reserve or savings fund. In subsequent years the policy would be credited with interest on its reserve fund in addition to the premium paid in and would be charged for insurance protection on only the difference between the face of the policy and the amount of the reserve fund. Thus the remainder to be added to the reserve fund would probably be even larger in succeeding years.

This may be illustrated by the figures in Tables 24-1 and 24-2, which compare the results of a moderate-cost whole life policy with those of a relatively high-cost 20-pay life contract. The figures are hypothetical, but they are based on a modern mortality table and on average expense rates and interest earnings.

The tables bring out sharply the fact that the investor who accumulates savings in an insurance policy reduces the complementary life insurance protection feature as his policy reserves grow. If his policies are suited to his needs, this is a proper development, for life insurance protection is less needed as the insured lives to earn and save. Also, most insureds are willing to buy less insurance protection as they get older, for mortality rates rise rapidly at older ages. But the insured who wishes to supplement his savings with insurance protection must realize that in most standard policies he buys less pure protection year by year and that this tendency is most pronounced in the highest-priced policies.

LIFE INSURANCE POLICY FORMS

Insurance companies are constantly alert to devise life insurance policies which meet popular needs or tastes, and as a result most of the contracts now offered for sale have special features which do not fit into simple classifications. However, the basic plans can usually be grouped into four types—term insurance, ordinary life, limited-pay life, and endowment insurance.

Term insurance is very low-priced insurance under which the company's obligation is limited to paying the beneficiary if the insured dies within a stated period of years, usually 1, 5, 10, or 20. Since mortality rates at ages under 50 are not great, term insurance covering such ages can be afforded by almost anyone. The reserves and cash values on such policies are negligible. Many term policies carry clauses permitting the insured to "convert" his term policy into a higher-priced permanent form without having to pass a second health examination at the time of conversion. Term insurance is suitable for temporary business protection and for supplementary insurance while children are young or before any

Table 24-1 *Illustration of protection and savings obtained in a whole life policy bought at age 25*

	First year	Tenth year	Twentieth year
Premium paid in	$ 13.60	$ 13.60	$ 13.60
Interest on reserves at 3½ per cent.	.36	3.51	8.07
Total	$ 13.96	17.11	21.67
Share of expenses	$ 3.25	$ 3.25	$ 3.25
Share of mortality cost	1.93	2.20	3.93
Added to reserves	8.78	11.66	14.49
Total	$ 13.96	$ 17.11	$ 21.67
Face of policy	$1,000.00	$1,000.00	$1,000.00
Accumulated reserves to date	8.78	101.85	234.76
Insurance protection this year	991.22	898.15	765.24
Mortality rate per $1,000 this year	1.95	2.45	5.13

Table 24-2 *Illustration of protection and savings obtained in a 20-pay life policy bought at age 25*

	First year	Tenth year	Twentieth year
Premium paid in	$ 22.51	$ 22.51	$ 22.51
Interest on reserves at 3½ per cent	.57	5.95	14.10
Total	$ 23.08	$ 28.46	$ 36.61
Share of expenses	$ 6.27	$ 6.27	$ 6.27
Share of mortality cost	1.92	2.02	3.01
Added to reserves	14.89	20.17	27.33
Total	$ 23.08	$ 28.46	$ 36.61
Face of policy	$1,000.00	$1,000.00	$1,000.00
Accumulated reserves to date	14.89	174.32	414.06
Insurance protection this year	987.11	825.68	585.94
Mortality rate per $1,000 this year	1.95	2.45	5.13

significant savings have been made. Convertible term is especially useful for families whose budgets will bear no savings program at the moment but who need immediate protection and an option on permanent insurance in the future.

People who prefer to do their saving independently of insurance companies frequently buy 20-year term insurance and drop portions of it as their accumulated savings convince them that the insurance is no longer needed. Others who carry term insurance as supplementary insurance or to "pay off the home mortgage" follow the same practice of decreasing the amount as the need diminishes.

Whole life or "ordinary" life insurance is an arrangement under which the company agrees to pay the face of the policy at the insured's death in return for a stipulated premium payable as long as the insured lives. In view of higher mortality rates in the later years, it is obvious that the premium must be high enough to accumulate a reasonable reserve in the earlier years; this reserve provides the usual loan value, cash value, and annuity option features, as well as interest earnings. Ordinary life is the lowest-priced form of permanent insurance. It is suitable for most business insurance uses and for family insurance where emphasis is on low-premium outlay, long-continued insurance protection, and a limited savings accumulation.

Limited-pay life insurance is a form under which the company agrees to pay the beneficiary when the insured dies, but the insured's premium payments are to be made only for the limited number of years stipulated in the policy, or until his earlier death. The premium-paying term may extend for 20 years, 30 years, until the insured reaches age 60, or some other limited period. The policy must therefore accumulate a large reserve during the premium-paying period, so that subsequent mortality costs will be small and interest earnings large; this calls for a fairly high premium rate. Limited-pay life policies which call for only 20 or 30 annual payments are therefore important savings vehicles and excellent investments for families whose budgets can carry substantial savings and whose circumstances justify a rapidly diminishing insurance protection feature; but they are not suitable for families not yet able to afford rapid saving, whose budgets can carry only inadequate amounts of high-premium insurance.

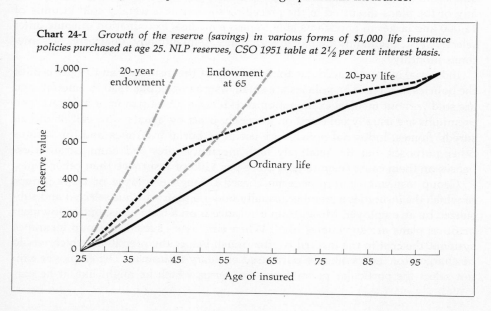

Chart 24-1 *Growth of the reserve (savings) in various forms of $1,000 life insurance policies purchased at age 25. NLP reserves, CSO 1951 table at 2½ per cent interest basis.*

Endowment insurance is a form of contract under which the company agrees to pay the beneficiary if the insured dies during the contract period and to pay the insured if he survives to the end of the period. Endowment contracts are mostly written for 20- and 30-year periods and for periods ending when the insured reaches age 60 or 65. A 20-year endowment period naturally calls for a high premium and very rapid reserve accumulation, for the reserve must equal the face of the policy when the 20-year period is complete. A 40-year endowment maturing at age 65, on the other hand, is a relatively modest program which accumulates its reserve slowly but finally matures the full face value at retirement age. Short-period endowments obviously emphasize rapid saving and quickly diminish their insurance protection; longer-term ones combine a slow savings program with a slow reduction of the complementary insurance feature.

Chart 24-1 illustrates the amount of reserve or savings accumulation in policies written on a typical modern mortality table. Since the policy in each case has a $1,000 face value, the amount of insurance protection furnished by a policy at any time is measured by the distance from the curve, which shows the amount of the reserve, to the $1,000 line at the top of the chart.

ORDINARY, INDUSTRIAL, AND GROUP INSURANCE

Life insurance in private companies is available on three different systems. Ordinary insurance, which accounts for 52 per cent of the amount of insurance in force and about 30 per cent of all policies, is written by practically all companies on any of the plans discussed in the preceding section. It is usually sold in units of $1,000 and larger to applicants able to pass a medical examination or some other selective test. Premiums are payable annually, semiannually, quarterly, or sometimes monthly.

Industrial insurance accounts for 3 per cent of the insurance and 19 per cent of the policies in force. The policies are small, averaging about $520 in amount, and are sold without medical examination or extensive investigation of any sort, and premiums are usually collected on a weekly basis by agents who call at the insureds' homes. Industrial policies are useful as burial insurance and for various other purposes, but the relatively high mortality rates and administrative expenses on them cause them to cost more per $100 of insurance than other types.

Group insurance is insurance purchased through employee or other groups of which the insured is a member, usually under a plan which is selected and subsidized by an employer. Most group insurance is on a term basis, but endowment or other plans are sometimes used. When employers subsidize group insurance systems, the cost to the insured is often much below the premiums which would be charged for independently purchased ordinary insurance. The employee cannot select the particular policy form and terms which he might like, if he participates in a group system, but its economy to him will usually justify arranging his other insurance and savings so that the group policy will "fit in" soundly. Group insurance has grown enormously since 1945, both in life insurance and health insurance forms.

A relatively new variant of group insurance, known as credit insurance, has also grown enormously since 1945. This form of life insurance indemnifies a creditor to the amount of his claim if the debtor dies, and thus relieves the debtor's estate of the debt. The coverage has been especially popular as mortgage repayment insurance for home buyers but is also used in connection with other installment debt. Most credit insurance, though not all, is purchased as group term insurance under a master policy arranged by a lending institution. It may be noted that the purchase of mortgage insurance to cover the unpaid balance on an amortizing real estate mortgage makes a combination akin to an endowment life insurance policy—the diminishing insurance feature covers the diminishing unpaid debt, and the purchaser's increasing equity in the real estate constitutes the reserve (savings) element in the arrangement and, ultimately, the completed endowment.

POLICY TERMS AND FEATURES

An insurance policy is a contract under which the company and the insured agree on a long list of obligations and privileges. While the basic features of insurance policies are standard, there is no such uniformity about the details, and many of the details are of great importance to individual insureds. The fact that these details are technical makes it nonetheless imperative for the prospective purchaser to study them; unless he carefully plans his insurance purchases, he is unlikely to obtain the maximum advantages available in his own particular case.

Among the decisions to be made is to choose between participating and nonparticipating insurance. On a participating policy the insured is charged a premium somewhat higher than the company expects to need. Against this premium are charged a fair share of operating expenses, mortality costs, the necessary addition to the policy reserve, and perhaps some small contribution to the company surplus; the balance can then be returned to the policyholder as a dividend. On a nonparticipating policy the company quotes a definite premium rate, out of which all costs and reserves must be met; the excess, if any, is profit to the company. In general, the premiums on participating policies are much higher than on nonparticipating ones, but the long-run costs are often a little lower. About 61 per cent of life insurance in American companies is on a participating basis. Insureds who choose nonparticipating insurance usually do so because the initial premium costs are lower or because they prefer policies whose net costs are fixed and guaranteed. An occasional insured may choose nonparticipat-

ing insurance because he believes that the companies' future mortality or investment experience will be adverse and that participating policies will therefore
fare badly. The insureds who choose participating policies probably do so because they hope for lower long-run costs, chiefly as a result of improving national mortality rates. Representative premium rates for nonparticipating policies
are shown in Table 24-3.

Table 24-3 *Nonparticipating premium rates per $1,000 for various policy forms, ordinary
department*

	Age at issue		
Policy	25	35	45
10-year term	$ 4.45	$ 5.67	$10.03
Ordinary life	13.60	18.96	27.78
20-pay life	22.51	29.02	37.91
Life paid up at 65	15.11	22.56	37.91
20-year endowment	42.26	43.66	47.48
30-year endowment	25.24	27.74	32.86
Endowment at 65	18.15	27.74	47.48

Most insureds must also decide whether they wish double indemnity and disability waiver of premium clauses in their policies. The double indemnity clause
is a simple addition of accidental death insurance to the basic policy, which results in doubling the death benefit if the insured dies as a result of accident. The
disability waiver clause is more vital to sound family insurance, as a rule; under
it the company agrees to waive all premiums and keep the policy in force in case
of the total and (apparently) permanent disability of the insured. This clause does
not provide a disability income for the insured, but it is very helpful as a guarantee of uninterrupted insurance and savings accumulation, especially when attached to an endowment or similar policy.

Life insurance policies which build up any significant reserve or savings element must make provision for the insured's rights to his savings. Each policy
must therefore clearly state its cash value during each year of the policy term
and the arrangements under which this cash value may be obtained, if the insured
so desires, through a policy loan or surrender of the contract. Most policies also
permit the insured to surrender his policy in return for a full-paid term insurance
policy of equal amount or a full-paid whole life policy of lesser amount, in either
case equal in value to the cash value of his present policy. Finally, and most important, many policies permit an insured to surrender his policy at a date to be
selected by himself, in return for any one of several forms of retirement annuity

or for a series of installment payments. All these options are granted to an insured by express stipulation in his policy, and the sums and privileges granted vary from company to company and policy to policy.

If the proceeds of an insurance policy become payable to the beneficiary by reason of the death of the insured, most policies provide various options as to payment. The insured may select the method of payment in advance, but if he does not, the choice will fall to the beneficiary. Payment may be by lump sum, in cash; it may be made in installments, with interest on the deferred sums increasing the total sum to be paid; or any one of several forms of life annuity may be provided to the beneficiary; or the proceeds may simply be left on deposit with the company to earn interest until withdrawn by the beneficiary. The rates of interest to be allowed by the company, the amounts and types of annuities available, and other features of these beneficiary options are established in each policy.

A great many other important clauses are to be found in insurance policies. Some limit the company's liability if the insured travels by air, engages in hazardous occupations, resides in prohibited areas, serves in the armed forces, or commits suicide. Others limit the company's right to contest the validity of the policy. Other policies may give the insured special privileges that will allow him to convert his policy to some other form if he so desires. Still other policies give the insured various options with respect to policy dividends—he may take them in cash, or in additional insurance, or as an interest-bearing savings account with the insurance company that issued his policy.

EFFICIENCY AND NET COST

A life insurance policy is a sound investment if it provides exactly the features the policyholder needs, is accompanied by efficient administrative and advisory service, and is low in cost. Each of these elements is important. Most insurance policies are the obligations of strong and honest companies, but the insured who does not choose a policy suited to his circumstances does not get his money's worth. Again, life insurance is a complex and technical matter; the average insured will get a better investment in a company whose selling agents are expert and conscientious advisers and in which such matters as policy loans, policy conversions, advice on beneficiary clauses, and service on death claims are handled promptly and sympathetically.

Finally, the cost of an insurance policy is important, since it is usually an investment of major size, on which a small percentage difference can amount to an important sum. It is difficult to measure the cost of insurance fairly, since desirable policy features and good service add to the cost of apparently similar policies. However, two methods are available by which insurance buyers can obtain some idea of the relative economy of similar policies in different companies.

These are (1) the traditional *net cost* (or 20-year net surrender value) method, and (2) the new *interest-adjusted* method developed during 1970 by the insurance industry's Joint Special Committee on Life Insurance Costs.

Net cost is computed by the formula: Net cost equals 20 years' premiums minus 20 years' dividends minus cash value at end of 20 years. This formula simply measures the out-of-pocket cost to the policyholder if he buys insurance, pays the premiums and takes back the dividends for 20 years, and then surrenders the policy for its cash value. The computation can be made either on a historical basis, using the actual histories of policies written 20 years ago, or on a current basis, using present premium rates, dividend rates, and promised cash values. In either instance the company's probable future performance is being gauged by its past or present record.

The traditional net cost method has been criticized for ignoring both the time factor and the interest-earning power of the money sums involved. The interest-adjusted method attempts to overcome these shortcomings. First, the *net* premium payment for each year is calculated by subtracting the expected dividend from the gross annual premium. (Since premiums are paid at the beginning of the policy year and dividends at the end, each dividend payment except the last is deducted from the premium due when the dividend is paid.) Next, the year-by-year net payments are accumulated for 20 years at an interest rate representative of what the insurance buyer might count on obtaining in a personal investment of similar security and stability—4 per cent has been the rate usually assumed. From the resulting sum, the expected dividend for the twentieth year is deducted. The amount thus computed equals the sum an individual would have accumulated at the end of 20 years if he had invested his net premiums at 4 per cent interest. (For nonparticipating policies, the gross annual premium is simply accumulated for 20 years at 4 per cent.) Finally, the cash value of the policy is subtracted from the accumulated net payments. The result represents the net *interest-adjusted* cost to the policyholder during the 20-year period.

Both cost-comparison methods are useful to insurance buyers. The interest-adjusted method gives truer cost comparisons, but the calculations are laborious and difficult to explain, and sufficient data for making them are not ordinarily shown in the rate handbooks available to the general public. As a screening device and guide to further inquiry, net cost comparisons are quick, easily made from available data, and easy to understand.

The reader who undertakes comparisons of different life policies must bear three points in mind. First, the smaller average insurance protection costs on high-priced policies will inevitably make their calculated costs less than those on low-priced ones. This does not prove that high-priced policies are more economical than low-priced ones; it simply shows that cost comparisons are valid only between similar policies issued at the same age, so that the amounts of reserves held and insurance protection furnished are substantially similar. Second, similar insurance in different companies can be expected to show sharply different costs because companies make different assumptions about interest earnings on policy reserves and cash values and show different records of dividends to policyholders. Third, net cost comparisons will produce larger differences than interest-adjusted methods because the failure to discount costs and benefits for passage of time will enlarge the year-to-year amounts used in calculating the net costs.

Table 24-4 illustrates each of the foregoing points. First, the higher-priced policies (20-pay life and the endowment policies) show far lower 20-year net costs than do the cheaper whole life policies. Only in the single case of company C does any policy in a column to the left of another show a lower cost than a higher-priced policy to its right. Second, although all companies shown are strong, respectable, sizable concerns, the net cost comparison suggests that the Purchaser of a $10,000 whole life policy may save $657.60 over 20 years' time if

Table 24-4 *Total 20-year cost per $1,000 of insurance in eight reputable companies (Policies issued at age 35 and surrendered after 20 years, current basis)*

Company	Net cost	Whole life Interest-adjusted cost*	20-pay life (net cost)	Endowment at age 65 (net cost)
A	$43.38†	$ 91.01	$148,07†	$229.87†
B	32.05†	85.36	78.80†	92.38†
C	12.24†	122.69	109.65†	101.78†
D	0.40†	118.94	85.40†	103.60†
E	3.92	112.08	100.49†	124.58†
F	4.02	120.48	99.47†	109.80†
G	11.41‡	130.17‡	24.80†‡	112.41†
H	22.38‡	121.91‡	28.37†‡	216.54†

*From American Institute for Economic Research, *Life Insurance from the Buyer's Point of View*. Interest rate used is 3½ per cent.

†Excess of cash value over cost.

‡Nonparticipating policies.

Source: Data from *Life Rates and Data,* 1972.

he insures with company A rather than company H, if present policy dividend rates remain unchanged. (Of course, better policy features or service in company H might make the higher cost worthwhile, but this must be proved.) Actually, the strongest and most accommodating companies seem often to be the lowest-cost companies as well. Third, the tendency of net cost calculations to widen policy cost comparisons can be noted by contrasting the range of costs shown in the first two columns of Table 24-4. Under interest-adjusted methods, the dif-

ference per $1,000 insurance cost between companies A and H shrinks from
$65.76 to $30.90. The reader should also note that policy cost rankings under the
two methods vary considerably. Although net cost calculations may suggest that
some policies not only are "costless" but actually pay the insured a net return
over 20 years, the interest-adjusted method reveals that when alternative uses of
an insured's money are considered, all policies involve substantial charges for
their service of protection. Finally, Table 24-4 includes data on two companies
selling nonparticipating policies. Their costs are guaranteed, not subject to dividend change.

There are differences in efficiency among insurance companies which affect
their cost results greatly. A company whose underwriting department avoids
bad risks will have lower mortality costs to charge against its policies; a company
with a skillful investment department will earn more interest and suffer fewer
losses; and a well-administered company can keep its operating expenses down.
These factors will affect the policy dividends and net costs on participating policies. Company progress along each of these lines can be studied by the investor
who is willing to make the effort.

BENEFICIARY MATTERS

Most life insurance policies direct the company to make payment to a specific
beneficiary or beneficiaries upon the death of the insured. This is a sound procedure, for direct payment will make the funds immediately available without
subjecting them to the delay and expense of probate, which would be unavoidable if the insurance was payable to the insured's estate. The beneficiary may be
a trustee who will administer the funds as directed by the insured.

Insurance payable to any natural person should also be payable to a contingent beneficiary in case the first-named beneficiary does not survive the insured.
In fact, the problem is doubly complicated; in most instances in which a common
accident or simultaneous illness might result in the first beneficiary's dying
shortly after the insured, it would be better to have the insurance go to the contingent beneficiary rather than into the first beneficiary's estate. Companies have
various ways of solving this problem; some permit a clause designating the first
beneficiary "if living 30 days after my death, otherwise to the contingent beneficiary"; others suggest payments in installments to the first beneficiary if living
on the installment dates, otherwise to the contingent beneficiary.

An earlier section noted that most policies provide several "settlement options," or methods of payment, under which a beneficiary might receive a life
annuity, a cash sum, a series of payments, or a withdrawable savings account.
The insured usually may either choose the method in advance or leave the choice
to the beneficiary when the time comes. The insured who doubts his beneficiary's

business acumen will often make the choice in advance; in fact, he may even arrange for the insurance company or a trust company to hold the proceeds in trust, doling out an annuity or periodic sums to the beneficiary but refusing to honor garnishments or other legal process by the beneficiary's creditors.

Life insurance policies usually declare either that the insured retains the right to change the beneficiary or that he does not do so. The insured who retains the right to change the beneficiary retains complete ownership of the policy, hence may cash it in or borrow on it at will. Since it is wholly his, its cash value is also subject to attachment by his creditors. If the insured does not retain the right to change the beneficiary, he will need the beneficiary's consent if he wishes to cash the policy or borrow on it; and since he does not own it outright, his creditors cannot get it. The beneficiary has no effective rights prior to the insured's death.

ANNUITIES

A life annuity is a periodic payment which continues for the duration of the beneficiary's life. It is really life insurance in reverse—insurance against living too long—for its purpose is to make it possible for the annuitant to consume his entire principal plus the interest earnings on it, without risking the embarrassment of outliving his funds. Life insurance companies sell annuitants a monthly income for life at a price which varies with age and sex. Annuities are usually quoted by naming the monthly income which may be purchased for $1,000 in cash. For example, a leading company in 1972 offered a man aged 65 a life annuity of $8 per month for every $1,000 invested.

Obviously, an ordinary life annuity will be a great bargain for a long-lived annuitant and a source of loss to a short-lived one, for the insurance company

Table 24-5 *Monthly annuity purchasable for $1,000 principal amount (annuities obtained as insurance proceeds are usually 2 to 10 per cent greater)*

Sex and age of annuitant	Ordinary life annuity	Life annuity, 10 years certain	Refund annuity, $1,000	Joint annuity, equal ages	20 years of life contingency
Male at 50	$5.40	$5.25	$5.03	$4.53	$5.51
Female at 50	4.94	4.87	4.68		5.51
Male at 60	6.78	6.62	6.31	5.48	5.51
Female at 60	6.11	6.00	5.72		5.51
Male at 65	7.87	7.40	7.03	6.19	5.51
Female at 65	6.98	6.78	6.77		5.51
Male at 70	9.32	8.25	7.98	7.12	5.51
Female at 70	8.13	7.57	7.57		5.51

must charge each annuitant enough to finance an average period of payments. The possibility that a $1,000 investment might produce only two or three $8 monthly annuity payments before death terminates the bargain causes an ordinary annuity to appear too speculative to many annuity buyers; they therefore ask the company to guarantee monthly payments to the annuitant or his heirs for a minimum period of 5 to 10 years (this is called an annuity certain) or until a stipulated total sum has been paid (this is a refund annuity), with further payments contingent on the life of the annuitant. Since the company's average number of payments to an annuitant group is increased when an annuity certain or a minimum refund is promised in the contract, the monthly annuity per $1,000 invested is somewhat smaller than it would be on an ordinary basis. Table 24-5 shows typical rates for different forms.

Many elderly couples find a joint life annuity attractive. This form of annuity pays as long as either of the annuitant couple lives, though the payment is often reduced in amount after the first death. The cost of the annuity is based upon the two ages.

Annuities may be bought for cash, obtained in return for the cash surrender values of life insurance policies, or taken by the beneficiary of a life policy under the settlement option provided in the policy. As a rule, it is economical to acquire an annuity through a life insurance policy, for the rates made available through such policies are frequently better than cash purchase rates. The great popularity of the annuity idea since 1930 has led most life insurance companies to offer "retirement annuity" insurance policies for sale. These are generally available in units of "$10 per month" of 10 years' certain life income at age 60 or 65, coupled with $1,000 to $2,000 per unit of death benefit if the insured dies before the annuity period begins. Retirement annuity policies are virtually endowment insurance policies, with the endowment proceeds automatically appropriated to buy a life annuity. In 1972, a leading insurance company quoted annual premiums on a $10-per-month retirement income contract on a man (income to begin at 65, policy in amount of $10,000 or more) at $26.25 at age 25, $40.93 at age 35, or $69.28 at age 45.

Table 24-5 indicates that annuities bought at medium ages pay less per $1,000 of principal than the interest yield available on good bonds. This leads many people to conclude that annuities are not a satisfactory investment. However, it must be remembered that life annuities are dollar-type investments of very high quality and that their fundamental protection is against living more years than one expects to. For an investor of moderate means who believes that part of his property should be kept in investments of this quality and type, and who is willing to consume part of his principal in later years, an annuity investment is ideal; it assures him of a substantial and safe dollar revenue as long as he lives and permits him to retain his common stocks and real estate intact for price-level protection and maximum income.

VARIABLE ANNUITIES

Since 1950, variable annuities have gained acceptance in the insurance field, slowly at first, more rapidly since the middle 1960s. Proponents of the variable annuity idea believe that persistent inflation is likely to characterize the American scene in the next few decades, and that common stocks can provide a desirable basis for retirement annuities. Under a variable annuity policy, the insured's premiums buy "shares" in a common stock fund. When the individual retires, his annuity will consist of shares in the fund to be converted into cash month by month as each payment is due. Actuarial tables can be used to determine retirement benefits in the stock fund just as readily as in dollars, and the annuity is thus truly a common stock investment.

The precise details of variable annuity contracts may differ considerably and consequently deserve careful study by prospective purchasers. A few plans base their annuity payments on a cost of living index rather than on common stock prices. With one type of variable annuity, income payments are fixed and guaranteed once they begin, although their initial size depends upon the value of the investment fund. With another type, the income payments themselves vary with the current value of the investments on which the annuity is based. Many variable annuity plans provide for a combination of fixed and variable incomes under one contract. Like regular annuities, variable annuities may be payable as (1) life annuities only, (2) life annuities with 10, 15, or 20 years' payment certain, or (3) refund annuities which, if the annuitant dies, will return to a named beneficiary some computed difference between the paid-in principal and the total payments received prior to the annuitant's death. Or, by agreeing to accept a smaller payment, the purchaser can have payments last for his wife's lifetime as well as his own.

In early 1972, more than 900,000 Americans were covered by life insurance company variable annuities, and 500,000 of these persons came under life insurance group plans with equity-based variable annuity benefits. However, legal difficulties still restrain the growth of variable annuities to some degree. The insurance laws of a few states do not yet authorize the sale of variable annuities to individual purchasers. Supreme Court decisions, rendered in 1959 and 1967, have held that a variable annuity is a security as well as an insurance contract. Therefore, variable annuities must be registered with the SEC unless the insurance company's own investment fund is registered under the 1940 Investment Company Act. As with mutual-fund shares, the buyer of a variable annuity must receive a copy of the issuer's prospectus.

Variable annuities may be acquired either through single-payment purchases or through annual or flexible purchasing contracts. Single-payment purchases are usually restricted to minimum amounts ranging from $3,000 to $5,000, while under flexible and annual purchase-payment contracts, the minimum monthly purchase payment is typically $10 and the minimum purchase period runs from 5 to 7 years.

The cost of buying variable annuities is substantial for two reasons. First, the insurance company must make relatively large deductions from purchase payments to meet its selling and administrative expenses. Second, variable annuity sales are often subject to a premium tax, imposed by states and municipalities, which ranges from .5 per cent to 3 per cent. On single-payment purchases, the insurance company will typically deduct from 4 to 7 per cent of the gross amount paid, depending on the size of the purchase. Under flexible or annual purchase contracts, deductions from purchase payments in the first contract year may range as high as 14 per cent of each payment (some 16 per cent of the amount invested), consisting of about 9½ per cent for sales expense and the balance for administrative costs. In the second and later years, the maximum deduction ordinarily falls to about 8¼ per cent of each payment (9 per cent of the amount invested), divided between about 4½ per cent for sales expense and 3¾ per cent for administration. However, under the Investment Company Act of 1940 (as amended), installment purchasers have the right to cancel their contracts during a 45-day period of grace and receive back their funds.

Stockbrokers and mutual-fund salesmen will usually contend that an investor has a better chance to make his money grow in stocks or mutual funds than in a variable annuity accumulation fund. They cite as disadvantages (1) the large purchase deductions, (2) premium taxes, (3) the conservatism of variable-annuity portfolio managers, and (4) the inflexibility of being "stuck" with the investment policy of one insurance company. Securities salesmen are likely to urge their customers to compare variable annuities with mutual-fund withdrawal plans, another systematic way to use capital for retirement income. They also often recommend that an investor consider turning his capital over to the generally conservative variable-annuity managers only upon retirement, thereby avoiding guaranty costs during his working career.

Against these objections, insurance salesmen correctly point out that variable annuities provide the buyer with a guaranteed life income and that variable annuity accumulation plans enjoy valuable tax-shelter advantages. Under present tax law, an investor who accumulates his annuity fund through a series of installments pays no taxes on dividends or capital gains during the annuity's accumulation period. Once he begins drawing payments from the annuity, he must pay ordinary income tax rates on anything beyond his return of capital, but this can be expected to occur after he has retired and is in a lower income tax bracket.

This tax-shelter feature of variable annuities appears uniquely advantageous for investors in medium tax brackets and warrants their careful consideration. However, the management costs and loads on this type of insurance differ considerably, so a buyer should shop carefully. Prospective purchasers should also, of course, compare alternative investments to determine how much they will be paying for the lifetime guaranty of income.

VARIABLE LIFE INSURANCE

A new equity-backed contract to be offered by several insurance companies in late 1973 or early 1974 is variable life insurance. The reserves behind this type of policy will be invested mainly or wholly in common stocks. A minimum policy face value will be guaranteed, but it may increase if the market value of the securities rises. The cash value of the policy—the amount available for a loan or upon surrender—will be tied directly to the performance of the stock fund. The scale of premiums for variable life policies will run higher than for ordinary life because the investor will be expected to pay something extra for the added attraction of a possibly increasing return. In 1972, a leading insurance company estimated that a man who pays $200 a year, starting at age 35, for an ordinary life policy might pay $220 a year for a variable policy that guarantees him a $10,000 minimum benefit.

In approving variable life insurance for sale early in 1973, the SEC ruled that it is a security and thus subject to federal registration and disclosure requirements. The purchaser of a variable life policy must receive a detailed, carefully worded prospectus, as he would in buying mutual-fund shares. However, the SEC exempted variable life insurance sales from the Investment Company Act which limits the sales charge a mutual fund can impose on periodic purchase plans to 9 per cent. Sales fees on variable life policies will be regulated by the insurance laws of the 50 states, which ordinarily allow commissions of up to 50 per cent of first-year premiums.

TAX POSITION OF INSURANCE AND ANNUITIES

In general, the tax laws deal gently with life insurance and annuity investments. Practically no general property taxes are levied on them. Some of the states levy an excise tax of 1 to 3 per cent on premiums collected by insurance companies, thus confiscating a portion of the money their citizens attempt to invest through insurance, but this is not a recurring levy on the same money. Some increase in federal income taxes on life insurance companies was enacted in 1959, but the total burden is still modest, averaging less than 12 per cent on the companies' interest earnings.

Income taxes are not levied on any payments, whether lump sums, installments, or annuities, which may be paid to beneficiaries by reason of the death of the insured; these payments are not income for tax purposes. Dividends paid to the insured on his life insurance policies are not taxable income, either; they are reductions of the premium costs of his policy. However, if the insured surrenders a policy for cash, or receives the proceeds of a matured endowment policy, he has taxable income to the extent that the cash received exceeds the total premium cost of the policy. Life annuity payments received by the insured, either in exchange for a surrendered life policy or bought for cash, are regarded as current taxable income to the extent that the annual payments exceed the total premium cost of the policy divided by the insured's years of life expectancy when the payments begin.[1] If the insured chose installment payments not subject to a life contingency, such as 120 monthly payments of agreed amount, the total cost of the policy would be prorated over the 120 payments, and any excess would be monthly taxable income. The taxable portions of any of these payments may obtain still further tax relief as portions of the "retirement income" of persons over 65 years of age.

All life insurance proceeds payable upon the death of an insured are included in his estate for federal estate tax purposes, regardless of whether the payments are made to designated beneficiaries or to the estate, if the insurance was owned or controlled by the insured. Because there is often some uncertainty whether death taxes should be paid by the general assets of the estate, thus leaving the insurance proceeds intact to the designated beneficiaries, or whether the taxes should be prorated among all heirs and beneficiaries, the point should be covered in every will. The state inheritance tax laws are inclined to exempt fairly substantial amounts of insurance payable to each beneficiary, in addition to the standard exemption allowed to the same beneficiary on general inheritances from the estate.

It should perhaps be noted that although family insurance and annuity plans must be made with the tax laws in mind, there is no assurance that the tax laws will remain the same for long periods. Changes made in the federal tax law revision in 1954 required extensive modification of many investments and insurance plans.

GOVERNMENT INSURANCE

The United States government has made available to each veteran of World Wars I and II and certain other armed forces personnel a minimum of $1,000 and a maximum of $10,000 of government-sponsored life insurance. This insurance is

---

[1] Thus, if a man aged 68 has an expectation of life of 10 years, and if he surrenders an insurance policy on which his total net premium outlay has been $8,000 in return for a life annuity of $876.30, he would be assumed to receive $800 of principal plus $76.30 of taxable income annually, *regardless of how long he lives*. The expectation of life figure is actuarially computed if the annuity is joint on two lives or on a period certain or a refund basis. An employee whose annuity is mostly paid for by an employer may in certain cases regard his annuity as wholly a return of his capital until he gets all of his own contribution back; thereafter, his whole annuity is taxable income.

the obligation of the government and all operating expenses are borne by the government, thus saving the policyholders the 5 to 15 per cent of their premiums ordinarily absorbed in operating expenses and taxes. Furthermore, gains to policyholders resulting from cashing these policies or collecting endowments for sums in excess of cost are not subject to income taxes.

United States Government Life Insurance (World War I) and National Service Life Insurance (World War II and up to 1951) policies are participating contracts, written basically in the form of renewable 5-year term insurance policies but convertible at the option of the insured into standard permanent policies such as ordinary life, 20-pay life, endowment at 65, and others. If the insured continues his original term insurance, the premium rate increases with his age at each 5-year renewal date. United States Government Life and National Service Life policies provide the usual settlement options to beneficiaries, including a life income option which is especially attractive. The policies also provide for disability waiver of premiums, and for the addition of a very valuable disability income clause to the policy upon payment of an extra premium.

Legislation passed in 1965 provided $10,000 of automatic group life coverage for those on active duty in the armed services. Coverage was increased to $15,000 in 1971, and members of the Reserve Officers' Training Corps and military reserve units and students at United States service academies were made eligible for this insurance. This Servicemen's Group Life Insurance program is supervised by the Veteran Administration, but legal reserve life insurance companies underwrite the policies. Premiums for the term life insurance policies are deducted from the serviceman's pay while he is on actice service, and insurance continues without premium payment for 4 months after his separation from service. The serviceman may convert his policy to regular individual whole life insurance in any commercial life company participating in the program without presenting evidence of insurability.

HOW MUCH INSURANCE IS NEEDED

Clearly, this is a question which cannot receive a definite answer. Business needs, employers' pension plans, family responsibilities, amount of wealth already available, and a variety of other factors enter into individuals' decisions on this matter. Insurance underwriters sometimes say that the average middle-class family should invest 10 per cent of its income in life insurance and that the face value of policies carried should amount to 3 to 6 times the family's annual income. But these are not accurate measures; they disregard the family's special needs, its accumulated savings, and the nature of the policies contemplated. The actual amounts of insurance carried by American families are less than half these suggested sums.

Perhaps the best approach to the "how much" question could be made by tabulating the family's present "estate" and its future savings expectations as a lifetime savings program is pursued. Then the differences between the accumulated estate totals at various times and the amounts necessary for family security in the event of death can be studied, and insurance in suitable amounts and forms can be considered. This is a technical and difficult task which frequently involves the planning of family wills, trusts, and estate tax matters as well as simpler decisions on disposition of business enterprises, whether the family savings are to be invested in insurance, and the adequacy of the family budget. Insurance men refer to this task of analyzing insurance needs as "insurance programming." Insurance companies often maintain experts in this field who are available for consultation when investors' problems prove too complicated for the selling agents.

SOURCES OF INFORMATION

The best source of life insurance advice and information for the average investor is a thoroughly competent life insurance agent. It costs no more to buy insurance through a competent man than from an uninformed insurance peddler, and it may well cost much less.

For the investor who wishes to study the theory and practice of life insurance, there are innumerable textbooks and monographs in every good library, and the United States Superintendent of Documents has several informative pamphlets for sale. The most accessible descriptions of policy terms, premium rates, financial practices, net costs, and similar matters will be found in the *National Underwriter Life Reports*, an annual reference volume published by the National Underwriter Company, and in *Best's Flitcraft Compend*, published yearly by A.M. Best Company. These manuals are available in most large libraries.

INVESTMENTS OF LIFE INSURANCE COMPANIES

Life insurance companies are obligated to pay death claims, annuities, surrender values, and policy loan request to their creditors in dollars. The liabilities of the companies to their policyholders, including special reserves and dividend funds, totaled more than $204 billion at year-end 1971; to meet these obligations they had assets valued at about $222 billion. However, the companies were not having to liquidate assets to meet their obligations; during 1971 their receipts from premium collections and interest were $54.2 billion, whereas only $39.3 billion were disbursed in expenses and payments to policyholders and beneficiaries. Even during the worst years of the depression, back in 1931–1933, the insurance companies as a group collected enough premiums and interest to meet all the calls upon them, including those for policy loans.

The small excess of assets over liabilities, amounting to about 8 per cent, indicates that life insurance companies should invest chiefly in conservative dollar sum investments, for they cannot afford investment losses of any great size. On the other hand, liquidity in the short-term sense does not seem to be required of any large percentage of the assets. The companies have therefore aimed their investment policies mainly at security and maximum income, which they have found in long-term bonds and mortgage loans. A considerable degree of liquidity has been obtained by inclusion of serial bonds, sinking-fund bonds, salable government bonds, and installment mortgages in the holdings; and, of course, the careful spacing of the maturities of long-term bonds provides a periodic recovery of cash in large amounts.

Because of the low interest rates between 1934 and 1957, life insurance companies have been experimenting with stock and real estate holdings for many years. At the end of 1971 the companies held stocks valued at $20.6 billion, or about 9.3 per cent of their total assets. More than four-fifths of this investment was in common stocks, the major portion of them held in separate accounts as backing for variable annuities and as equity funding for insured pension plans. Aside from these separate accounts, most companies keep the total amount of their common stock and real estate investments well below the amount of company net worth; policyholders' interests thus are more than covered by the holdings of cash, receivables, mortgages, and senior securities.

Table 24-6 *Distribution of assets, United States life insurance companies (In billions of dollars)*

End of year	U.S. govern- ment bonds	State, muni- cipal, and foreign bonds	Cor- porate bonds	Mort- gages	Stocks	Real estate	Policy loans	Other assets	Total*
1920	$ .8	$ .4	$ 2.0	$ 2.4	$ .1	$ .2	$ .9	$ .5	$ 7.3
1925	.6	.7	3.0	4.8	.1	.3	1.5	.6	11.5
1930	.3	1.2	4.9	7.6	.5	.5	2.8	1.0	18.9
1935	2.9	1.9	5.3	5.4	.6	2.0	3.5	1.7	23.2
1940	5.8	2.7	8.6	6.0	.6	2.1	3.1	2.0	30.8
1945	20.6	2.0	10.0	6.6	1.0	.9	2.0	1.7	44.8
1950	13.5	2.6	23.3	16.1	2.1	1.4	2.4	2.6	64.0
1955	8.6	3.1	36.1	29.4	3.6	2.6	3.3	3.7	90.4
1960	6.4	5.0	47.1	41.8	5.0	3.7	5.2	5.3	119.6
1965	5.1	6.3	58.7	60.0	9.1	4.7	7.7	7.2	158.9
1970	11.0	3.2	73.1	74.4	15.4	6.3	16.1	7.8	207.3
1971	11.0	3.2	79.2	75.5	20.6	6.9	17.1	8.6	222.1

* Totals may not agree with total of individual items because of rounding.
Source: Institute of Life Insurance, *Life Insurance Fact Books,* 1971 and earlier.

The total real estate investments of life insurance companies in 1971 accounted for $6.9 billion, only about 3.1 per cent of company resources. The real estate consisted of home office buildings, which are held for use plus rental income; large-scale rental housing projects, which are operated for rental income; corporation-occupied business or industrial buildings, which are purchased and leased back to the occupying firms for long periods at rentals sufficient to amortize the purchase costs and yield a satisfactory income; and real estate acquired by foreclosure of loans. The greatest increase in real estate ownership is occurring in the third of these categories; the fourth has been declining. Foreclosed real estate amounting to almost $12 billion was held by the companies in 1936; in recent years it has been unimportant.

The average interest rate earned by American life insurance companies on their invested funds rose to 5.44 per cent in 1971 (5.52 per cent if equity-ladened special accounts are excluded). This was reduced to a net rate of about 4.60 after payment of federal income taxes, but even this constituted the best net earning rate since the early 1930s. The companies averaged 5.07 per cent in the twenties and 4.1 per cent in the thirties, but low general interest rates plus large holdings of low-yielding United States government bonds combined to reduce the figure to low levels in the forties. In 1947 only 2.88 per cent was earned. Since that time as Table 24-6 shows, a great increase of higher-yielding mortgages and corporate securities has helped to increase earnings. However, the companies are holding firmly to the idea that safety of principal is more important than rate of return, and the increase therefore reflects the availability of better yields, not a relaxation of standards.

QUESTIONS AND PROBLEMS

1 Review the major functions which life insurance performs. Is it proper to call a life-insurance policy an investment?

2 Explain how a policy may act as a cash resource. Is it sound family practice to use a policy loan instead of bank borrowing to finance emergencies?

3 Why does an insured person who buys a 20-year endowment policy buy less "insurance protection" than one who buys an ordinary life policy? Does he pay for less?

4 Why does one need less insurance as he grows older? Do insurance policies provide less "protection" as the insured grows older? Explain.

5 What kind of insurance would you recommend for a young man without savings or financial resources, who is aged 25 and about to marry? Would a variable annuity be suitable?

6 What kind of insurance would you suggest for a professional man aged 45, who has a substantial income and wishes to insure the balance of his earning power up to retirement age at 65?

7 Would you prefer participating or nonparticipating insurance for yourself? Why?

8 Distinguish between a disability waiver clause and a disability income clause.

9   What is a contingent beneficiary? Why would one be named? How is this done?
10   Explain the calculation of net cost. Should insurance buyers study this factor before buying policies? How would you go about it?
11   Do you think that the idea of using a life annuity as a dollar sum investment and keeping all the rest on one's savings in stocks and real estate is a sound one for a retired person? Where is the weak spot?
12   Discuss the advice: Buy term life insurance only and invest the difference in a good mutual fund.
13   How would you go about answering the question of "how much life insurance" for yourself?
14   What would a decline in interest earnings do to life insurance net costs? Should the companies be encouraged to venture further into stock and real estate investments?
15   Would you approve of a corporation pension plan which operates entirely on a variable annuity basis?
16   Assuming variable life insurance is approved for sale, how would you propose that a married professional man, aged 30 with two children, divide $100,000 worth of life coverage between variable and dollar sum insurance. Why?

REFERENCES

American Institute for Economic Research: *Life Insurance from the Buyer's Point of View*, and *Annuities from the Buyer's Point of View*, Great Barrington, Mass., revised occasionally.
Athearn, James L., *Risk and Insurance*, 2d ed., Appleton-Century-Crofts, Inc., New York, 1969, Part 1 and Chaps. 7, 9, 10.
Best, A.M., Company: *Best's Flitcraft Compend*, Morristown, N.J., annual.
Dougall, Herbert E.: *Investments*, 8th ed., Prentice-Hall, Inc., Englewood Cliffs, N.J., 1968, Chaps. 2, 23.
Gregg, Davis W. (ed.): *Life and Health Insurance Handbook*, Richard D. Irwin, Inc., Homewood, Ill., 1959, Part 1.
Huebner, S.S., and Kenneth Black, Jr.: *Life Insurance*, 8th ed., Appleton-Century-Crofts, Inc., New York, 1972.
Institute of Life Insurance: *Life Insurance Fact Book*, New York, annual.
McGill, Dan M.: *Life Insurance*, rev. ed., Richard D. Irwin, Inc., Homewood, Ill., 1967.
Mehr, Robert I., and Emerson Cammack: *Principles of Insurance*, 5th ed., Richard D. Irwin, Inc., Homewood, Ill., 1972, Chaps. 1, 2, 20.
National Underwriter Company: *National Underwriter Life Reports*, Cincinnati, annual.
Williams, C. Arthur, Jr., and Richard M. Heins: *Risk Management and Insurance*, 2d ed., McGraw-Hill Book Company, New York, 1971, Part 1 and Chap. 19.

REAL ESTATE AND
MORTGAGE INVESTMENTS

Real estate holdings bulk large among the investments of American citizens and are widely distributed among a great many people. Census Bureau estimates show that in 1960 approximately 65 per cent of American families owned either homes or farms, as compared with an estimated 76 per cent owning checking or savings accounts and 14 per cent owning corporation stocks or bonds. As a rule, the home or farm owned by an American family is its largest single investment and is of consequent high importance.

This pronounced affinity of investors for real estate is the result of a number of causes. Among them are the social esteem which conventionally attaches to real estate ownership; the feeling of independence and security which the possession of real estate engenders; the easy credit which makes the control of properties convenient for many people; the widespread conviction that real estate ownership is profitable; the belief that real estate is a safe investment, perhaps capable of a little fluctuation, but dependably indestructible; the belief that real estate is an effective hedge against prive-level inflation; and the firm belief of many people that they "understand" real estate, hence will not blunder in buying and managing it. Although the attractions which this recital includes may in some cases be more imaginary than real, they are sufficient to stimulate an ever-increasing number of Americans to buy real property. It is probable that real estate ownership is at present more widely disseminated than it has been for many decades.

By far the most common form of real estate investment is homeownership: a 1970 survey by the Bureau of the Census indicates that 63 per cent of nonfarm American families own their homes.[1] Family farms constitute a second common form of real estate investment; 83 per cent of these are owned in whole or part by occupying farmers,[2] and the other 17 per cent are mostly the properties of individual investors who rent them to tenants. The third common form of real estate investment is urban residential rentals, including single-family houses, flats, and apartment houses; this is a field in which both small investors and major corporations have holdings. Finally, the general field of business real estate, including both commercial and industrial property, attracts many small investors as well as very large ones.

[1] *Statistical Abstract of the United States.*

[2] Ibid.

Mortgage lending is also a form of investment which many people have found attractive. The demand for mortgage money has always been high in this country, for properties are frequently bought and sold and there has always been a large amount of new construction as the nation's wealth and population have grown. Prior to 1933, institutional lenders supplied a large, but only slowly growing, portion of the demand for mortgage money; subsequent to that date, they have greatly increased their relative importance, though individual lenders continue to compete. Individual holdings of farm and nonfarm residential mortgages totaled close to 26 billion dollars in 1972, and this figure does not include their very substantial investments in mortgages on nonresidential urban property.

REAL ESTATE VALUES

In general, it appears that reasonably well-chosen investments in improved real estate have many similarities to reasonably well-chosen industrial stock commitments. Individual commitments intelligently or luckily chosen may make great gains, and others stupidly or unluckily chosen may deteriorate rapidly in earning power and value. The great majority of properties fluctuate in value and in earning power as business conditions fluctuate and, perhaps, not much out of proportion to the changing values of good industrial stocks. Improved real property seems to be a fair price-level hedge, just as industrial stocks are; no single piece may be expected to epitomize the average, but the general tendency is for real estate prices to reflect the buying power of the dollar.

Improved real properties fall mainly in the "sunk capital" category; that is, their location, nature, and purpose are definitely fixed, and their value depends largely on what their services will be worth during the next few decades. Although regional or neighborhood changes may add value, they are even more likely to detract, and the investor must therefore make every effort to foresee the long-term future of any property in which he contemplates investing his money. If the population of a town or city grows, real property in its business district and in its most desirable residential areas normally will be in demand, will earn more, and will sell higher, though it is possible that growth may result in the development of new shopping and residential areas to the disadvantage of the old. In general, community development and style factors have their greatest effects on industrial, commercial, and multiple-residence properties in ways which are directly comparable to the competitive and obsolescence factors which constantly threaten business corporations. Small residential properties and farms seem a little less affected by changing demand and style factors, but even here the investor must be concerned with the problem of future earning power.

In a growing and inflationary economy, real estate investments have two profit-making advantages of great importance. First, both an expanding population and increasing buying power impose demands on the supply of land and buildings. Rising demand for land tends inevitably to increase its earning power, and growing demand for the use of buildings assures profitable use of the existing supply. Second, price-level inflation tends to increase the amounts which people can afford to pay for either land or buildings and to raise the cost of competing new buildings; it therefore tends to increase the earning power of both lands and buildings, at least in terms of dollars. Investors in real estate thus may profit in both real buying power and in dollar terms in a period of real growth and inflation.

One important element which tends to add security to an investment in improved real property must be recalled at this point. It was noted in Chapter 2 that most real estate improvements are of the wasting asset type, which means that the investor-owner progressively recovers his capital through the property's gross earnings, in addition to obtaining whatever net income is earned. Since the operating expense on the average real property is relatively low, the owner is almost certain to recover some of his capital (as a depreciation allowance) and perhaps some net gain out of the annual rents, even if the property is poorly designed or located. The value of the property should reflect the present value of all probable future cash recoveries and earnings, plus any speculative potential which exists. In contrast to this situation, an investment in the stock of a poorly designed and located industrial corporation would probably pay the investor nothing, for depreciation allowances and occasional small earnings would doubtless be needed to modernize the business in order to prevent poor results from becoming poorer still. In this case only the speculative potential would contribute to market value.

MEASURING THE EARNINGS

It is not feasible, in a short chapter like this, to undertake discussion of the earnings and cost factors which investors encounter on farms, apartment houses, commercial buildings, or industrial property. The situations are hopelessly diverse, both between the groups and within the groups. Consequently, the examples and most of the discussion will be based upon the single-family dwelling, which is the most widely owned form of real property investment.

The most common issue confronting the investor in real property is one involving the soundness of a proposed price—will an investment at this figure pay? The answer may be a difficult one or a very obvious one, if the investor foresees impending price-level changes, population movements, style shifts, or other factors which will affect the property. However, the more usual situation calls for a review of the probable average incomes and expenses on the property and a comparison of its earning power with the proposed price. It is not unreasonable to assume that a property which can earn a fair rate of return on its cost, under assumed normal rental conditions, after providing for all reasonable expenses, taxes, and depreciation, is a sound investment. Estimates based on assumed normal conditions in the next 5 to 10 years usually give an indication of these amounts.

In applying this doctrine, it will first be necessary to estimate, by comparison or otherwise, what the normal annual rental value of the property for the next few years will be. Neither boom nor depression estimates should be used; a normal or average figure is needed. From this projected annual income must next be deducted (1) expenses of operation, such as heat, water, and janitor service, if furnished to tenants; (2) taxes; (3) depreciation; (4) maintenance; and (5) insurance. Each of these items should be a normal or average estimate based on experience with the given property or others like it. After these items are subtracted from the rental income, the remainder will represent the net earning power of the property. This net earning power expressed as a percentage of the price will provide a measure of the soundness of the investment. The average annual net earning power should be a least 5 per cent. The earnings of the property minus the interest payable on any mortgage debt will of course measure the owner's profit on his invested equity.

These calculations may be illustrated by an example. Assume that a reasonably new single-family dwelling valued at $30,000 (building $24,000 and land $6,000) is held as an investment, for rental to others, and that a $15,000 mortgage debt at 7 per cent is owed upon it. Assume further that an average rental rate of $325 per month is expected and that a normal vacancy loss of 1 month per year is anticipated. If the tenant is to care for lawn and utilities services, with estimated property taxes of $600, depreciation allowance of $480, average maintenance cost of $600, and insurance premiums of $75 to be borne by the owner, the income statement for the average year in the next few years might well resemble the following.

Annual income statement		
Gross income, 11 months at $325		$3,575
Less expenses:		
Operating expenses	0	
Taxes: 2 per cent on value	$600	
Depreciation: 2 per cent on building	480	
Maintenance: 2 per cent on value	600	
Insurance, ¼ per cent on value	75	$1,755
Earning power of property		$1,820
Less interest on $15,000 mortgage		1,050
Net profit on $15,000 owner's equity		$ 770

The anticipated average income statement indicates that the $30,000 property in question would earn about $1,820 annually, or 6.07 per cent, which will in turn allow a return of 5.1 per cent on the owner's $15,000 equity. The earning power of the dwelling will doubtless decline in the distant future, but by that time the owner will have recovered part of his investment through the annual depreciation allowances, and less net earning power will be needed to justify the remaining capital investment.

An analysis similar to the foregoing is commonly used to justify a familiar rule of thumb in testing the soundness of investment in residential property. It has been noted that an average net earning power of at least 5 per cent is needed to justify the hazards of residential property investment (and, as the above illustration suggests, a still greater return will be needed if mortgage interest rates are substantially above 5 per cent). To the 5 per cent return may be added "typical" costs of 2 per cent annually for taxes, 1.6 per cent (based on the whole investment) for depreciation, 2.0 per cent for maintenance, and .25 per cent for insurance, making a total of 10.85 per cent of value which must be recovered annually in gross rental income if the investment is to be satisfactorily profitable. Conservative investors then add another 1 per cent for vacancy and credit loss, bringing the total to 11.85 per cent per annum. This is practically 1 per cent per month. The rule of thumb therefore states that a single-family property is profitable if its gross earning power approximates 1 per cent of its value per month and, conversely, that it is a sound investment at a price of 100 times its normal monthly rental value.

This rule-of-thumb process is interesting and useful to an investor, but it must be critically qualified. In the first place, it depends on estimates of normal or average rents and expenses, not temporary current ones, and thus must not be applied casually to current rents and prices. Second, the percentage amounts allowed for expenses and depreciation should be based on careful studies of the particular property, not on percentage generalities. In fact, close students of the subject insist that expense and depreciation factors vary so much that single-family residences of various types in various locations can be proved to be promising investments at figures ranging all the way from 70 to 130 times their normal monthly rental values. Third, the degree to which the owner is able to supervise the property and to hold down maintenance costs by doing small tasks himself may make a great difference on profitability.

A home investment which is owner occupied is usually much more profitable than a similar property held for rental to others. In the first place, no vacancy or credit loss need ordinarily be expected. Second, an owner who is handy with tools and paintbrush, and whose family is normally careful with family-owned property, can hold maintenance costs to a minimum. Third, the earnings realized from one's equity in his home, which take the form of rent-free occupancy of the premises, are not subject to income tax. Finally, homeownership may have other tax advantages. For those who itemize deductions, taxes paid and mortgage interest paid are deductible in computing taxable income for income tax purposes. Also some states exempt a limited amount of the value of an owner-occupied home from general property taxation.

In the case of residential property over 25 years old, maintenance and depreciation rates sometimes need to be larger in proportion to current values than is the case on new dwellings, and the investment risk is often greater. Consequently, it is sometimes said that while single-family dwellings under 25 years old may sell for 100 to 130 times monthly rental value, those over 25 years will bring only 70 to 100 times monthly rental value. Each figure assumes, of course, that no drastic deterioration of the property or its neighborhood is impending, and as before, each must be regarded as a generality which reflects only general tendencies.

Apartment houses, flats, commercial real estate, farms, and other types of properties may be examined as to earning power by means of the methods just described. These properties vary so much in gross and net earning power, however, that it is not possible to generalize on normal relationships between gross rental income and value. For example, an apartment house which furnishes heat, water, janitor service, and other facilities might readily require an annual gross revenue of 20 per cent of value in order to net a 6 per cent return to its owner; but a neighboring flat providing fewer services might need only 15 per cent. In general, investors expect somewhat higher rates of net return on other forms of urban property than are obtained on investments in single-family dwellings.

None of the analysis of this section takes any account of either economic growth or inflation. The examples may therefore be deemed conservative.

APPRAISAL METHODS

There are many methods of appraising real property. Some are applicable to one type of property, some to another. Often different methods are used on the same appraisal for the sake of verification, or combinations of methods are used.

The appraisal methods most commonly used may be grouped into four general types: (1) those based on comparison of the given property with other properties on which values have recently been established by sale, (2) those based on capitalization of near-term gross or net income, (3) those based on the discounted present value of a series of estimated earnings and capital recoveries over a long term of years, and (4) those based on cost of replacement less depreciation. The first two approaches are used chiefly by individuals and dealers who do not wish to undertake elaborate calculations; they are easy ways to approximate results. The third approach is commonly used in appraising existing office buildings, apartment houses, and similar properties, when the appraiser has access to experience data and engineering estimates which will enable him to forecast probable incomes and expenses over a long period. The fourth approach is one very widely employed by lenders on all kinds of improved property but notably, for present purposes, on dwellings.

Appraisals based on cost of replacement usually follow a process which is well worth a review by the investor. The appraiser usually begins by assigning a per square foot or per cubic foot basic value to the building, based upon the type and size of the structure. These basic values are very carefully estimated on the basis of building costs in the locality. The basic per unit valuation is then multiplied by the number of square feet or cubic feet, to arrive at a basic cost appraisal. Next, the basic cost appraisal is increased or decreased by specific sums as the appraiser identifies good or deficient fireplaces, bathrooms, kitchen installations, hardwood floors, basement, garage, driveways, and the like. When the building replacement cost estimate is complete, it is then reduced by a percentage representing estimated depreciation; this is based on the age of the building, plus observed deterioration and maintenance factors. To this appraisal of the building is next added the estimated current value of the lot, to obtain a total value applicable to a normal dwelling in a normal neighborhood. However, there are several other factors which might justify arbitrary increases or decreases in the appraisal. Among them are (1) the suitability of the floor plan of the dwelling; (2) the suitability of the external appearance of the building; (3) the appropriateness of the building to the neighborhood, as respects size, quality, and style; (4) the apparent prosperity and durability of the immediate neighborhood; (5) the deed restrictions and zoning ordinances which affect the neighborhood; (6) the convenience of shopping districts, schools, employment opportunities, traffic arteries, and public transportation; and (7) the trends of community growth. This entire appraisal process is based fundamentally on cost of construction and is therefore most accurate on relatively new properties, in relatively new areas, and in situations in which the building is clearly suited to its location and function.

THE IMPORTANCE OF FINANCE

As is true of all investment prices, the prices paid for real estate fluctuate with the supply of properties offered for sale and the demand for them. Real properties are relatively durable, and the total existing supply is capable of augmentation or reduction only at relatively slow rates; consequently, any situation which affects either the buying demand or the normal volume of selling offers is likely to have a noticeable effect on selling prices. One of the most conspicuous factors which influence buying demand or selling offers is the mortgage credit situation.

Prior to 1934 the mortgage loans made in the United States tended to follow a pattern calling for a first mortgage not exceeding 60 or 65 per cent in value, plus a second mortgage for 10 to 20 per cent if the borrower needed it. The first mortgage usually required partial amortization, though not always, and matured typically in 3 to 10 years. The second mortgage would run for 2 to 5 years, with

some amortization. Interest rates were usually high, especially on second mortgages, and loans totaling 80 per cent of appraised value or more were difficult
to obtain. High percentage loans were hazardous to both lender and borrower,
because the maturities were very difficult to refund if they occurred during periods of depression. Furthermore, values were unstable because, during depressions, defaults on lump-sum maturities caused foreclosures and forced sales
drove property values down.

Analysis of this situation during the years 1930–1934 led to four important
conclusions. First, loans amounting to 80 per cent of property value or more, if
consistently available, would widen the real estate market at all times by allowing
more people to participate in it and would tend to stabilize values. Second, a
single long-term loan of 80 to 90 per cent of value, repayable in equal monthly
installments, without a lump-sum maturity at any time, would seldom be defaulted. People who cannot manage a lump-sum maturity are often able to make
regular small payments, and if they cannot, there are usually others who will buy
the embarrassed owner's equity for a small sum and assume the payments. Third,
market stabilization plus more secure financing terms will justify lenders in accepting lower interest rates; this will make housing more economical and still
further improve the market for properties. Fourth, an option to the borrower to
repay his loan at a faster rate than required in the contract will enable him to
strengthen both his own and his creditor's position.

These conclusions have played a large part in both federal and state legislation
on housing finance since 1933. The federal savings and loan program, the home
mortgage guarantee provisions of the Servicemen's Readjustment Act of 1944
(the GI Bill), the FHA mortgage insurance program,[3] and amendments to the
banking laws have all favored the high-percentage, long-term, amortizing type
of mortgage. State banking and savings-loan legislation has done likewise. Because this type of mortgage loan has been very popular with borrowers, competition has forced institutions and individual lenders to use it to a major extent
on dwellings and to a very considerable extent on multiple-housing and business-
property loans as well.

The loans made on single dwellings, as an example of this type of financing,
are likely to allow a period ranging up to 30 or even 35 years for repayment.
Nominal interest rates, including mortgage insurance premiums, have varied
greatly since 1960. From a range of 5¼ per cent (on veterans' loans) to 6½ per
cent early in the decade, they moved as high as 8½ per cent on FHA and VA
loans and 9 per cent on some conventional loans during 1970. In periods of tight
money, effective rates were higher than nominal ones, since insurance companies

---

[3] The FHA plan is a mortgage insurance arrangement paid for by the borrower, under which the federal
authorities guarantee to the lender that, if foreclosure of an insured loan becomes necessary, they will take
title to the foreclosed property and reimburse the lender for the defaulted principal and interest. Lenders are
therefore usually willing to make high-percentage loans even in hard times, if the FHA will insure them.

and other final lenders would purchase mortgages only at discounts from their face value; in mid-1973, discounts on 25-year mortgages ran from 1 per cent on the higher-yielding conventional mortgages to 8 per cent on government-insured or -guaranteed loans which carried a 7 per cent rate. The amount of loan available has ranged downward from 100 per cent on some veterans' loans to 80 per cent on FHA-insured mortgages of the less-favored types, or to about 60 per cent on certain noninsured loans. The sums required to meet property tax and fire insurance costs, as well as interest and principal amortization, are collected monthly by the lender. The ease of this method of financing is indicated by the fact that the total monthly payment required to pay principal and interest on a 25-year amortizing loan at 7½ per cent would be $7.39 per $1,000 of the original loan. That is, a $24,000 loan could be paid off in 25 years for $177.36 per month. To this would be added about $70 per month for taxes and insurance, and the borrower would have to provide for maintenance also, but the total would amount to little more than a normal rent. Of course, a $30,000 property which would support an 80 per cent FHA loan might require a $6,000 down payment, or it might possibly be necessary for the seller to accept a second mortgage.[4] On the other hand, a very credit-worthy buyer might obtain a 95 per cent conventional loan, made possible by Mortgage Guarantee Insurance Corporation and other private companies that will insure the final 20 per cent of a high-grade residential loan; the $1,500 the buyer would then pay down on a $30,000 property would be less than the starting equity required of an FHA-insured borrower.

Thus far, the modern amortizing mortgage has performed very well. The borrowers who have needed to sell have been able to find buyers ready and willing to buy their equities and take over the payments. But there has been no time between 1933 and 1972, except for a brief period in 1937–1938, when consumer incomes have declined importantly or when costs of construction have fallen. Not only has consumer buying power in dollars gone steadily upward during this period, but general prices and construction costs have mounted greatly. Property owners have found that their ability to pay and the market values of their mortgaged homes have both risen, thus making their debts easy to service. Furthermore, there has been no period since 1935 when lenders were unwilling or unable to make mortgage loans. It is implicit in present-day mortgage practices that real estate values shall not be impaired by nonavailability of mortgage loans at any time, for serious declines in property values would cause thousands of properties now mortgaged under high-percentage long-term loans to be worth

---

[4] Under Section 203 of the Federal Housing Act, which represents about 80 per cent of all FHA-insured mortgages, the minimum down payment on a new home in 1972 was 3 per cent of the first $15,000 of appraised property value, 10 per cent of the property value between $15,000 and $25,000, and 20 per cent of the value over $25,000. Mortgages could carry maturities of up to 35 years, and the maximum loan allowable for a one-family property was $33,000. In 1971, down payments averaged 8 per cent of total purchase price on FHA homes, 26 per cent on conventionally financed houses.

less than the indebtedness upon them. Government agencies will doubtless be called upon to assist mortgage lenders if ever a serious shortage of mortgage money occurs.

The test, if any, of modern mortgage financing and the property values dependent upon it lies in the future. The long-lived boom of the 1960s produced several million new mortgage loans, made at high percentages of appraised value during a time of price-level inflation, to prosperity-thrilled purchasers whose income sources had not yet stood the test of time. Whether the alleged merits of amortized mortgages will meet the test of the 1970s will depend on the stability of general economic conditions. Favorable influences include a rapid rate of building-cost inflation which quickly raises the owner's equity in an existing home. However, experience of the past decade has demonstrated that residential properties may become overbuilt in particular cities, or homeowners in mass may abandon heavily mortgaged dwellings in towns that lose a major industry; in these instances, which can be counted on to continue, mortgage lenders or the federal government will be left to absorb large losses.

One interesting aspect of mortgage financing must still be noted. If an owner obtains a generous amortizing loan—a high percentage to value, repayable at long term, carrying a low interest rate—he may sell his equity subject to the loan, and the purchaser thereafter has the advantage of the easy terms. This situation now exists in many cases, especially where borrowers have obtained $5\frac{1}{4}$ per cent or lower long-term veterans' loans. A property financed on such a generous basis offers a subsequent purchaser who buys it the excellent terms originally given to the veteran and is for this reason worth more than an identical property not so financed.

TITLES AND TITLE INSURANCE

Investors who buy real property or lend on mortgage security are acutely concerned to obtain a good title or a good lien. To be satisfactory, a title or a lien must not be jeopardized by vague claims of the heirs of former owners, or uncertainty about the release of old mortgages, or the possibility that repairmen may establish mechanics' liens upon the property. There are many such misfortunes which might befall unwary investors or lenders. All states have attempted to assist purchasers and lenders by enacting "recording statutes" which provide that deeds and liens are effective in order of recording in official recorders' offices, but proper evidence may later prove that official records are incorrect and therefore invalid. Also, there are a number of court and tax offices in which other records affecting the title to property may be found.

Investors who buy property or lend upon it have for many years had the titles investigated by attorneys or title specialists, who reported the situation as shown in the official records and expressed opinions as to the acceptability of the titles.

This is still the practice in rural communities and other areas in which real estate activity is not great and in which property histories are well known. However, in major cities the title-investigating companies are now willing to write policies of title insurance, guaranteeing to indemnify the owner or lender if a title weakness, existing at the date of the search but not then discovered, ultimately causes loss. It must be admitted that the title companies pay few losses, but their vigilance in searching out weaknesses is probably a major reason for their good record. Because title insurance is not costly, it is a precaution which few investors should omit.

In many urban areas investors' titles and liens are protected during transactions by a process known as *escrow*. Under this system a buyer and a seller (or borrower and lender, or both simultaneously) designate a bank trust officer or some similar trustee as their escrow agent. The buyer delivers to the escrow agent his money and note and mortgage, the lender delivers his money, and the seller delivers the deed to his property; the escrow agent makes sure that all payments and documents are in order, has the title searched, records the deed and new mortgage instantly as soon as the title is confirmed, and is finally able to deliver a valid title to the buyer, a valid mortgage to the lender, and the money to the seller. There is thus no chance of recording imperfect mortgages or deeds or of delivering money against imperfect titles or instruments.

MORTGAGES, TRUST DEEDS, CONTRACT SALES

The owner of real property frequently wishes to pledge it as security for a loan. In most states private owners pledge their property by means of a mortgage, which is an instrument establishing the mortgage holder's right to have the property sold and the proceeds applied on the debt, if the secured debt is not paid according to its terms. The mortgage must be written, signed by the property owner, and recorded in the official records, if it is to give the mortgage holder prior rights ahead of other possible creditors of the property owner. When the mortgage debt has been repaid, the mortgage is no longer valid, but an appropriate mortgage release signed by the lender should be recorded in order to clear the official records.

A properly drawn and recorded mortgage will establish the holder's rights against the property to the full extent of the borrower's title. However, any existing rights of other claimants to the title, and the rights of old mortgages not yet released, cannot be dispossessed by a new mortgage; the new mortgage has a lien only on the maker's rights, which may themselves be junior to old claims. Taxes and special assessments levied on the property have a claim which is prior in lien to any mortgage or title claim; they must be paid by someone, or the entire rights to the property, free and clear of all mortgage claims, may be sold to satisfy the tax bill. It is clear, therefore, that a title search and possibly a policy of title insurance will be essential before a mortgage loan is made.

Once a mortgage has been properly recorded, the holder of the note and mortgage may sell them to another. The purchaser should obtain and record a written assignment of note and mortgage from the original lender; thereafter he may collect payments due on the note, and when it is repaid, he may execute an effective mortgage release. The debtor under a mortgage may usually also sell his equity in the property. In this case the purchaser will pay an agreed price for the debtor's equity and should obtain and record a deed to the property; thereafter, as the new owner, he must meet the payments due on the mortgage note to avoid loss of the property through foreclosure. The transfer of the owner's equity does not affect the rights of the mortgagee against the property.

If a mortgage-secured debt is unpaid, the creditor must usually sue the debtor in court, obtain a judgment, and then ask the judge to order the sheriff to sell the mortgaged property at auction to satisfy the debt. After the sale the laws of most states permit the debtor to remain in possession for 9 to 18 months, on the theory that he may within this time be able to pay the debt and recover his property. At the end of this period he must either pay up or yield possession to the purchaser at the foreclosure sale. The entire procedure is somewhat cumbersome and expensive, and because of the postsale delay, few good bids are made at the sale; consequently, the unpaid creditor usually has to buy in the property himself in order to obtain an ultimate fair recovery on his investment.

The trust deed is a substitute for a mortgage, which is used by corporations to secure bond issues and by personal borrowers in a few states. Under this arrangement the borrower deeds his property in trust to a trust company, with instructions to sell the property for the benefit of the creditor if the note is defaulted but to deed it back to the borrower or to his assignee if the note is properly paid off. The legal rights and procedures under the trust deed are much the same as though a mortgage were used, except that no foreclosure suit is necessary and no postsale delay period is usually required.

A contract sale exists when the owner of a property and a prospective purchaser enter into a contract under which the purchaser agrees to make certain payments, usually in installments, and the owner agrees to deliver a valid deed when the payments have been completed. The purchaser usually obtains possession at once. The contract, when properly written and signed, may be recorded in the official records; it will then establish the purchaser's rights ahead of any subsequent deed, mortgage, or other instrument which the seller may execute. Failure of the purchaser to complete the payments will enable the seller to nullify the bargain and recover possession; failure of the seller to produce a valid deed can be rectified by court action. Either the purchaser or the seller under a contract of sale may sell his rights during the transaction without disturbing either the rights or the obligations of the other party. For example, a contract purchaser may assign his rights to a new purchaser, who may then take possession, complete the payments, and receive the deed. If it is the contract seller who sells out, his successor receives a deed subject to the contract, may thereafter collect the remaining payments as they come due, and is finally obligated to deliver a valid deed when the payments are complete.

These procedures and documents are very incompletely described here, but the descriptions will serve to preface several remarks which may be important to investors. First, it is evident that the procedures involved in handling deeds, mortgages, contracts, and other instruments are technical and somewhat confusing, but vital. Large sums are involved, and it is desirable to avoid trouble by employing experts to see that all steps taken are sound and correct. Second, title and title insurance matters are a little difficult to control adequately when mortgages are bought and sold and when contract sales are employed. These matters should be thoroughly understood as they operate under local law. Third, the cumbersomeness of foreclosure proceedings is sufficient notice that real estate loans should not be made except on security which is so good that it will not be allowed to come to foreclosure and except to borrowers who are so strong that they are unlikely ever to default. Fourth, a contract purchase should as a rule be made only from a financial institution which is rather certain to be alive, competent, and willing to complete its bargain after several years have elapsed. In buying on the installment plan from individuals, it is safer to obtain a deed and give back an installment note secured by a mortgage. Then, if appropriate receipts for payments have been preserved, it is a simple matter to prove the satisfaction of the mortgage if an issue arises.

GOVERNMENT REGULATION AND COMPETITION

Investors have learned in the last 30 years that among the very major factors determining the profitableness and soundness of their investments are the policies pursued by state and federal governments. Taxes, regulation, subsidies, and public competition are important but unpredictable economic forces. They are forces whose importance in the real property field is steadily increasing. Taxes on property are now so heavy that they are always a factor in appraisals and in decisions to build or not to build. Income taxes are also a factor in keeping many individuals out of the traditionally low-yielding rental housing field.

The most disturbing concept in the rental housing field is that of rent regulation. In 1942, as a part of the wartime attempt at inflation control by direct regulation, the federal government undertook to "freeze" the level of rents on residential properties. Certain state and local authorities enacted parallel legislation. After the war most price-control and wage-control programs were promptly abandoned, but federal rent controls were retained until 1952 and some state and local measures still continue. When it became obvious, long after the war, that new rental units would not be constructed to rent at unprofitable "controlled" rates, the controls were dropped on new properties but retained on existing ones. The whole program was continued so long that the propriety of denying landlords any participation in the price-level expansion of the period, and even of a fair return on their original investments at a time when their properties were in great demand, almost became a part of the national mores. Even the fairness of discriminating between the landlords of "free" and regulated properties at times went unquestioned. The lesson for property owners is that they need never again expect to operate in a completely economic market; when price levels rise or housing shortages again occur, the political authorities have ample precedent for freezing rents at unprofitable levels, if politically powerful groups demand such action. There is, of course, no certainty that this will be done. Federal rent controls were allowed to lapse in 1952 (though New York City continues to exploit landlords even in 1973) and may never be reimposed; but the precedent now stands, and landlords are a minority group.

Subsidies represent another area which affords hazard to investors, for subsidies are subject to drastic changes of many types. They may be increased, decreased, or changed in nature. The federal farm price supports program, for example, subsidizes the earning power of land devoted to certain crops, and probably of farm land in general. Land purchases and farm loans are now based on values which are in turn established by the subsidies, and which would change if the subsidies were changed.

Finally, the risks of public competition must be considered. Before World War II a number of municipally owned, lightly taxed, federally subsidized low-rent housing projects were constructed by city and county housing authorities. These projects were financed by means of tax-free municipal bonds which were virtually guaranteed by the federal government, hence had a low money cost; with low property taxes and a federal subsidy, they have been able to offer apartments at rents far below the essential costs of their privately owned competitors. The Housing Act of 1949 set in motion a plan to construct 810,000 apartments over a term of years on much the same basis, although in 1972 not many more than half the planned units had actually been built. A further housing act, passed in 1968, was intended to provide subsidized homeownership or rental payments for low and moderate-income families by constructing 5 million new housing units under government subsidies and by rehabilitating 1 million existing houses, mostly in the central cities. By 1972, soaring construction costs, rising defaults and foreclosures, and mushrooming scandals involving sales of shoddy houses at exorbitant prices to poor families, had cast growing doubt on the future of this program. However, a precedent for large-scale subsidized public competition with private investors has been firmly established. New momentum for low-cost public housing seems almost certain to develop out of the many proposals, some sound and some grandiose, being made to rebuild the nation's cities. The Department of Housing and Urban Development estimated in 1972 that about 40 per cent of the United States population is eligible for some sort of housing subsidy under the existing laws.

REAL ESTATE SYNDICATES AND REAL ESTATE TRUSTS

Two types of investment companies operating with real properties should be noted. The first of these, the so-called real estate syndicates, began to operate extensively in the middle 1950s. Most of these firms took the legal form of limited partnerships, although some are corporations. The central idea was to sell shares to the general public, buy modest equities in heavily mortgaged properties, escape income taxation by using accelerated depreciation methods, and use the cash flow to pay the mortgage debt. In some cases the cash flow was also sufficient to pay tax-free dividends "out of capital." When the properties were substantially depreciated and the debt interest was reduced so that the income became taxable, the plan called for selling the properties for capital gains and beginning anew. Some of these operations have been quite successful; others have had difficulties of various sorts, and changes in the federal income tax laws, particularly with respect to accelerated depreciation, are making further difficulties. To an increasing degree, real estate syndicates seem to be turning toward real estate development and land speculation in lieu of tax-advantaged property ownership.

The real estate investment trusts were authorized by Congress in 1960 on a plan paralleling the mutual-fund idea. The trusts sell nonredeemable shares to the public and invest the proceeds in real estate or mortgages. Like the mutual funds, they escape corporate income taxes on distributed earnings if they pay out 90 per cent or more of their operating income in dividends and meet certain other standards, including (1) the use of an external management company so the trust does not become an active business entity, and (2) limitation of profits from sale of securities held less than 6 months and real estate held less than 4 years to not more than 30 per cent of total income. Since they are closed-end funds, their shares trade on a supply-and-demand basis and may sell at either a discount from, or premium over, asset worth. Most of them are traded over the counter, but some of the larger ones are listed on national and regional stock exchanges.

Real estate investment trusts (REITs) are of two basic types. *Equity trusts* buy land and buildings for rental income and possible capital gains. *Mortgage investment trusts* make long-term mortgage loans to property purchasers and intermediate- and short-term construction loans to builders and developers. Because the trusts cannot reinvest their earnings for growth, they try to make large profits by relying heavily on borrowed funds; a typical REIT might have a capital structure consisting of 20 per cent equity, 40 per cent long-term debt, and 40 per cent bank loans and commercial paper.

Although the trusts are now a firmly established medium of investment, they appear too risky in general for the average investor. The mortgage trusts prospered during 1969 and 1970, when money was tight; they often were able to lend money to hard-pressed builders and developers at interest rates several percentage points above their own borrowing costs at banks and in the commercial paper market. However, both their profits and their market prices fell sharply during 1971–1972 as interest rates fell and real estate loans became increasingly available from competing traditional lenders. The operations of equity trusts are clearly speculative, and it would seem that investors in them would need an expert knowledge of real estate themselves to evaluate the policies and selections of the trust.

REAL ESTATE INVESTMENT: SUMMARY

Investment in real estate is popular and widely practiced. Most improved real estate has some net cash earning power even in hard times and should therefore have a value stability comparable to that of good-grade stocks. In general, real estate values fluctuate with the general price level, and real estate investments may therefore be used as price-level hedges. Real estate financing is now elaborately organized to make investments easy to finance by means of long-term installment loans. Homeownership is particularly easy to finance and has profit and tax advantages.

Several income tax advantages strengthen the appeal of real estate ownership. First, accelerated depreciation methods may generally be used in writing down investment property (not the investor's home) for income tax purposes. This may greatly reduce income taxes in the early years, enabling the owner to devote the cash flow to debt amortization and also paving the way for ultimate sale at a low-tax capital gain. Second, sales of real estate at a profit may be made under "installment sales" rules, which make the gain taxable only as the proceeds are collected, thus deferring the tax and avoiding possible high brackets in the year of sale. Third, profits on sales of real estate including the investor's home are not taxable to the extent that the sales proceeds are invested in similar property within a few months; in such a case the substitute property assumes the low tax basis of the old.

Disadvantages in real estate investment include the fact that most real estate purchases must be made in large parcels, thus precluding wide diversification. Real estate is not highly salable, nor is it pledgeable at low cost. Heavily mortgaged properties may be lost entirely if misfortune prevents the maintenance of the regular payments. The present unprecedented number of heavily mortgaged properties owned by debtors of doubtful financial strength is a potential danger to the real estate market. Heavy speculation and sharply rising prices in undeveloped land during recent years present another hazard. Government regulation, competition, and subsidy are unreliable factors in the situation. Finally, real estate investments require a somewhat greater degree of management effort and skill than do investments in good-grade securities.

MORTGAGE LOANS

It has been observed that the bulk of mortgage lending on homes and farms is done by institutions and, in the case of farms, government agencies. However, there is still an important volume of individual lending in the home and farm mortgage fields. In the case of apartment-house and small commercial property loans—for example, store building, motels, commercial garages, gasoline stations, vacant lots, and the like—individuals appear to be particularly important as lenders. Most mortgage-lending institutions emphasize security in their loan policies, hence are inclined to prefer loans on more stable and marketable security, such as homes or farms, to those on business properties or vacant lots. The lending institutions are also likely to prefer borrowers who have adequate incomes or other resources, so that their loans are likely to be repaid without trouble; this leaves a considerable amount of borrowing by widows, elderly folk, and overambitious young people to be financed by private lenders.

But not all private lending is confined to cases in which the loans are speculative in nature. In every community there are individuals who choose to invest their savings by making good mortgage loans. Borrowers find these people through their advertisements, through real estate dealers who know them, and through the word-of-mouth contacts of the community. Again, the sellers of real property often take mortgages on the property as part payment for the property. Speculative builders sell new homes on a similar basis. And a very large part of the total volume of individual mortgage lending doubtless consists of transactions within families, which are formalized by the use of lien security.

Second mortgage loans[5] form a somewhat unique phase of the mortgage-lending field. The major lending institutions do not make second loans, but

---

[5] When a real estate owner already indebted on a first mortgage signs a second mortgage, he pledges to his creditor just the rights he has left—namely, the right to repay the first mortgage and continue as owner. If the second mortgagee is unpaid and must force a foreclosure sale, the property is sold *subject to* the first mortgage, on which the buyer must then make the regular payments. If the first mortgage payments are defaulted, a foreclosure sale on its behalf will sell the real estate subject only to unpaid taxes, thus eliminating the second mortgagee's security. Consequently, a second mortgage lender must make sure that the first mortgagee is regularly paid, either by the original debtor or, in an emergency, by the second mortgagee himself.

An owner obligated on a second (or even a third) mortgage or trust deed continues in possession unless dispossessed after a foreclosure sale.

speculative mortgage companies, mortgage dealers, and individuals are often interested in them. Second mortgages come into existence in various ways. Sometimes a borrower who has or can obtain a first mortgage loan on satisfactory terms is compelled to obtain a supplementary second loan on much less attractive terms, to meet his financial needs. Again, the sellers of property often accept in payment the proceeds of the best first mortgage loan the buyer can obtain, plus a cash payment from the buyer's funds, plus a second mortgage for the balance. Speculative homebuilders often mortgage the new home for the maximum amount obtainable on a long-term loan and then sell their equity for a small cash payment plus a second mortgage for the balance. Interest rates on negotiated second mortgage loans during 1972 ran between 8 and 12 per cent. The life of a second mortgage is usually shorter than that of a first lien, often not over 5 years, whether the loan is amortized or not. A second mortgage arising from a sale transaction usually pays one or two percentage points more interest than a first mortgage but is also likely to be of reasonably short maturity. A second mortgage may be a safe investment if the property is adequate in value and if the borrower is able to meet his obligations, but it has the disadvantage, if trouble occurs, of requiring the second mortgagee to make sure that proper payments are made on the first mortgage. Default on the first mortgage would permit the first mortgagee to force the sale of the property for his benefit, possibly to the exclusion of the second mortgagee.

In most large communities, and in many small ones as well, there are dealers who buy and sell both first and second mortgages. Their advertisements appear regularly in the classified sections of the newspapers. Most of these dealers expect to assist amateur investors with the technical details incident to transferring title to the mortgages; many of them guarantee their validity and offer some assurance on their collectibility as well. The prices quoted are similar to those quoted on bonds; in recent years, well-secured first mortgages of moderate size, which might be bought by a trust company for one of its trusts or by an individual seeking safety, have sold on anywhere from a 7 to 10 per cent yield basis. Small ($500 to $5,000) second liens have carried face rates ranging from 8 to 12 per cent. These represent in most cases the balance of a builder's sale price and may sell at a 20 to 35 per cent discount from face value. Even greater discounts are sometimes found in cases in which the security is poor or the payments are not regularly met. There are doubtless wonderful opportunities in these markets for astute investors who are familiar with property law, whose appraisal judgments are keen, and who can evaluate the debtor's willingness and ability to pay. However, a mortgage investor who is compelled to make many foreclosures will probably not find his investments profitable.

In summary, it may be said that mortgages offer the investor who is equipped to handle them a satisfactory outlet for his funds. Well-secured loans to good borrowers are safe and yield considerably more than good bonds. The more speculative types, particularly those bought at a discount, offer some element of price-level protection in the appreciation which will occur in their value if property values rise, and in addition, they offer a chance for a speculative profit if wise selection avoids trouble or losses on them. On the other hand, there are disadvantages in mortgage investments. The principal sums are often large, making adequate diversification impossible to people of limited means; and geographic diversification is truly difficult. Second, most mortgages provide for monthly payments; this makes the bookkeeping a nuisance and returns the lender's capital on a piecemeal basis, so he is very likely to lose some interest on it before he is able to reinvest it. Third, mortgage loans require greater individual effort in making or choosing them soundly, and in watching the security subsequently, than do many other forms of investments. Fourth, the business requires a fund of legal and technical knowledge which is no less formidable than that required for stock investments. Fifth, mortgages are not dependably liquid, for they cannot be readily sold for their true value. They are salable, but only on a negotiated basis, and buyers who will pay fair prices are not always easy to find.

GNMA-BACKED MORTGAGE PARTICIPATION CERTIFICATES

Since 1970, mortgage-backed securities guaranteed by the Government National Mortgage Association have provided large investors with a new and convenient form of mortgage investment that yields a high return and is totally free of the credit risk. These securities are certificates of participation in privately organized pools of 30-year FHA and VA mortgages, all of which must bear the same interest rate. Each certificate is guaranteed as to both principal and interest by the Government National Mortgage Association, and backed by the full faith and credit of the government itself. The large mortgage-lending firms who organize the pools sell the certificates to investors at a yield one-half percentage point below that of the underlying mortgages; the difference goes to the GNMA in return for its guarantee and to the issuer for servicing the mortgages. Each month thereafter, the issuer simply "passes through" to each certificate holder his prorata share of the interest and principal paid by the pooled mortgages. Late or missed payments by mortgagors are made up at once by the GNMA. As noted, the mortgages are written for 30 years, but owing to home sales and refinancing, the average life is expected to be about 12 years. Prepayments by mortgagors also are passed through to certificate holders, making for some fluctuation in the size of their monthly receipts. Interest is fully subject to federal income, estate, and gift taxes.

Like regular mortgages, the "pass through" participation certificates provide a combination of monthly interest and recovery of principal. However, they carry none of the traditional and often laborious burdens of ordinary mortgage investment; they entail no legal expense, administrative work, or worry about late payments and defaults. They enjoy an active, well-organized resale market. In mid-1972, the certificates were yielding about 7 per cent, and since early 1970 more than 4 billion dollars worth had been marketed, largely through brokers, and often in denominations as low as $25,000.

QUESTIONS AND PROBLEMS

1 Which is the most profitable form of equity ownership for a young couple, a home or an assorted stock portfolio? Upon what factors may your answer depend?

2 Explain how the "wasting asset" feature of improved property investment adds security to an investment in it.

3 Review the method of adding taxes, maintenance, insurance, depreciation, and a fair return on the investment, to obtain the gross income percentage at which residence rental values may be capitalized. Is 100 times the monthly rental value a fair appraisal for a new residence in your community? Should it be?

4 Do the banks and savings and loan associations in your community appraise on a replacement-cost basis? What do they regard as a normal relative value of house and lot?

5 What are deed restrictions and zoning ordinances? (These are mentioned but not discussed in the text.)

6 Why are high-percentage, completely amortizing loans regarded as a safeguard against a wave of foreclosures and forced sales?

7 Assuming that most of the properties now mortgaged at high prices and above 80 per cent of value are mortgaged under either FHA or GI loan plans, is it not probable that the federal agencies would hold foreclosed or abandoned properties off the market rather than risk damage to property values as a result of forced sales during depressions? Does this add further hope for stabilized property values hereafter?

8 Who are the principal lenders on real estate mortgages in your vicinity? Do they use amortizing loans? Can a nonveteran obtain an 80 per cent loan on an existing home? On a newly constructed one?

9 Under FHA provisions, a home buyer may obtain a new home valued at $15,000 for 3 to 4 per cent down and on a 35-year payment schedule which initially reduces the debt about .85 per cent per year. Is this sound?

10 Why is a personal search of the official title records not good enough for one who buys or lends upon a $20,000 parcel of city property? What assurance meets the need?

11 What effect does a sale of a parcel of real estate by the mortgage debtor have upon the mortgagee's right to foreclose and dispossess the owner, if the debt is not paid?

12 What effect does the sale of note and mortgage by the original lender to another have on the debtor's obligation?

13 Is there a market in your community through which mortgages are bought and sold? Are mortgages advertised for sale at a discount? Could an investor make money by buying mortgages at a discount?

14 Are second mortgage loans used in your community? Who makes them?

15 If you were a mortgage lender, would you prefer to lend to home buyers at a fixed rate of interest or under an arrangement where the interest rate they paid you would vary with, say, changes in the general level of high-grade bond yields? State the reason for your preference.

16 If you had been a mortgage lender on industrial and commercial property when money was very tight during the 1968–1970 period, which sort of 20-year loan would you have preferred to make: a straight loan at 11 or 12 per cent interest, or a loan at 8 or 9 per cent interest plus, say, 1 per cent of the borrower's gross receipts or 3 per cent of his after-tax profit?

17 Are real estate investment trusts investments or speculations? State the criteria on which you base your answer.

18 Could interest-bearing, "pass through" securities similar to those of the GNMA be issued and sold against pools of conventional home mortgages? What obstacles, if any, do you see to such a development?

19 In October 1972 the FHLB Board chairman, then Preston Martin, proposed a futures market in mortgages as a means of helping lenders and builders to hedge interest-rate risks and thus of stabilizing housing starts. Is the idea practicable? What problems might arise?

REFERENCES

American Institute of Real Estate Appraisers: *The Appraisal of Real Estate*, 4th ed., Lakeside Press, Chicago, 1964.

Badger, Ralph E., Harold W. Torgerson, and Harry G. Guthmann: *Investment Principles and Practices*, 6th ed., Prentice-Hall, Inc., Englewood Cliffs, N.J., 1969, Chap. 15.

Brown, John J.: *The Intelligent Investor's Guide to Real Estate*, Putnam, N.Y., 1964.

Bryant, Willis R.: *Mortgage Lending*, 2d ed., McGraw-Hill Book Company, New York, 1962.

Donaldson, Elvin F., and John K. Pfaul: *Personal Finance*, 5th ed., The Ronald Press Company, New York, 1971, Chap. 7.

Dougall, Herbert E.: *Investments*, 8th ed., Prentice-Hall, Inc., Englewood Cliffs, N.J., 1968, Chap. 11.

Financial Handbook, rev. ed., The Ronald Press Company, New York, 1968, Sec. 26.

Hoagland, Henry E., and Leo D. Stone: *Real Estate Finance*, 5th ed., Richard D. Irwin, Inc., Homewood, Ill., 1972.

Maisel, Sherman J.: *Financing Real Estate*, McGraw-Hill Book Company, New York, 1965.

Pease, Robert H., and Lewis O. Kerwood (eds.): *Mortgage Banking*, 2d ed., McGraw-Hill Book Company, New York, 1965.

Ring, Alfred A., and Nelson L. North: *Real Estate Principles and Practice*, 7th ed., Prentice-Hall, Inc., Englewood Cliffs, N.J., 1972.

FOREIGN SECURITIES
AND PROPERTY

For the past 50 years American investors have paid increasing attention to opportunities outside the boundaries of the United States. Not only has the growing capital supply within this country tended to reduce interest returns here below those obtainable on foreign securities, but American corporations and individual business adventurers have found important outlets for their resources in business projects located abroad. The total value of all privately owned foreign investments was estimated at 13.7 billion dollars in 1945; in 1972 it approached 100 billion dollars.[1] These figures do not include any of the foreign loans made by the United States government or its wholly owned Export-Import Bank.

Foreign investments available to American citizens may be classified into five groups for study purposes. In descending order of present importance, they are (1) foreign branches and subsidiaries of American corporations, (2) securities of foreign corporations, (3) bonds of foreign governments and governmental agencies, (4) individual holdings of foreign real estate or business ventures or loans, and (5) bonds issued by or guaranteed by the International Bank for Reconstruction Development. All these groups showed growth in the period 1945–1972, but the greatest increase occurred in the foreign investments of American corporations.

AMERICAN CORPORATIONS WITH FOREIGN HOLDINGS

Many important American corporations, including such giants as Exxon, International Business Machines, General Electric Company, and Singer Company, have large business investments abroad. Although these holdings and others like them represent a major fraction of American foreign investments, the much more important home properties of these corporations cause the stockholders to place only minor emphasis upon the foreign commitments.

Approximately one-third of the foreign investments of American corporations are in branches and subsidiaries in Canada. These outlays have grown rapidly since 1945, in proportion to the enormous economic growth of Canada. Probably the bulk of them are in extractive industries—petroleum, natural gas, iron ore, and general mining have all developed greatly in Canada—but manufacturing and commercial ventures have also proved attractive. Favorable commercial laws, a sound currency, a common language, and similar business methods make

[1] *Statistical Abstract of the United States,* 1972; *Survey of Current Business,* August 1972.

Canadian operations attractive to firms with established operations in the United States.

Although the largest part of American corporate investments abroad is represented by subsidiaries and branches, there are substantial American-controlled corporations whose properties are almost entirely in foreign countries. Among these may be mentioned the Cerro Corporation (metal mining in Peru), Creole Petroleum (oil production and refining in Venezuela), and Deltec International (banking and meat packing in Latin America and elsewhere). Such concerns are acutely subject to the taxes, property laws, currency problems, and foreign exchange hazards which affect international investments. The owners of their stocks and bonds must be prepared to accept all the ordinary business risks, which occur everywhere, plus many political and economic hazards characteristic of long-term international transactions. Because of the added uncertainties, the price-earnings ratios are likely to be lower and the yields higher than those on strictly American securities of similar quality.

Although American corporations and subsidiaries operating in foreign countries are subject to the various property, excise, income, and dividend taxes imposed by those countries, the United States income tax laws permit deductions for foreign property and excise taxes on consolidated returns, and foreign income and dividend taxes are in most cases allowed as deductions from the United States *taxes* on the same income. Foreign subsidiaries' net income in most instances is not subject to United States income taxes unless repatriated in dividends or unless reported on consolidated returns. Foreign operations by American corporations are thus not handicapped by American tax law, and when the host country's taxes are low they may even enjoy advantages over American domestic operations. However, this tax situation is frequently criticized and may be subject to change.

Information about American corporations engaged chiefly in foreign activities is found in the usual sources, and the securities are traded on the American listed and over-the-counter markets in the usual manner. The legal devices necessary to organize the business properly generally do not affect the investors—for example, Cerro Corporation is an American holding company which controls a number of subsidiaries in various countries. Because the corporation or holding company is American-controlled, American-owned, and financially centered in the United States, the dividends will be payable in American dollars and stock sales and transfers can be managed in familiar ways in American markets.

SECURITIES OF FOREIGN CORPORATIONS

More than half of the 12 billion dollars of foreign-domiciled and foreign-controlled corporate securities owned by Americans are Canadian securities. This is not surprising, in view of the high esteem in which Canada is held by American citizens, and of the similarity of business methods between the two countries. Americans use the Canadian stock exchanges and unlisted markets freely. Canadian securities are marketed in the United States as well as in Canada, and leading Canadian issues are traded on the United States exchanges and unlisted markets. Such corporate names as Canadian Pacific Railway, International Nickel Company of Canada, and British American Oil Company are as familiar in the United States as in Canada. Some of these Canadian concerns pay their interest and dividends (and principal, in the case of bonds) in Canadian dollars only, and the checks must then be sold to exchange dealers by securityholders living in the United States; and some of the corporations declare their payments in Canadian funds but remit the equivalent value in United States dollars to payees living south of the border. In the case of bonds, some bond issues are sold payable in United States dollars.

Interest and dividends paid by Canadian corporations to non-Canadians are subject to a 10 to 15 per cent income tax collected at the source—i.e., withheld by the corporation. This means that the United States investor in a Canadian corporation will receive only 85 to 90 per cent of the payment accrued or declared on his Canadian security, no matter whether payable in Canadian or United States dollars. However, the income tax laws of the United States in most instances permit the deduction of a foreign income tax in full from the domestic tax otherwise payable, so this Canadian tax has no net disadvantage to United States citizens.

The total American investment in foreign-controlled foreign corporations other than Canadian is estimated at a little under 6 billion dollars. These holdings are widely scattered in many countries, and they include such world-renowned enterprises as Volkswagenwerk (the West German auto manufacturer), Olivetti Sp A (the giant Italian office-machine maker), and Shell Transport and Trading Corporation and Royal Dutch Petroleum (British and Dutch owners respectively of the worldwide Royal Dutch Shell group of oil companies). Of particular interest to American investors during recent years have been the South African gold shares, such as American South African Investors and Free State Geduld Mines, Ltd., widely purchased as hedges against inflation and dollar devaluation, and the leading stocks of our southern neighbor, Mexico, especially Tubos de Acero de Mexico, which makes steel pipe and tubing for the government-owned petroleum industry, and Teléfonos de Mexico, S. A., which operates the country's telephone system. Many foreign corporations, such as Farbwerke Hoechst, "the West German du Pont," accommodate American shareholders by depositing their American-held shares in trust in New York, so that American holders may own easily transferable American depository receipts. A few, like Roan Selection Trust, which operates copper mines in Zambia, have established special American shares with a stock transfer office in New York. However, some foreign corporations offer no special accommodations to American shareholders. For example, the American holder of Philip's Lamp, "the Dutch General Electric," must accept foreign "bearer" shares (from which coupons are clipped and mailed abroad to receive dividend payments as these are announced), and also, foreign currency, a foreign market, and foreign transfer methods.

American depositary receipts (ADRs) for foreign stocks (and a few British government bond issues) have become numerous since about 1958, although the device has been known for many years. As previously noted, the American-owned portion of the foreign issue is placed in a trust in an American bank. The bank will issue its depositary receipts to the American stockholders and will maintain a stockholder ledger on these, thus enabling the holders of ADRs to sell or otherwise transfer them as though they were American stocks. Some ADRs are traded on the stock exchanges, but most are handled over the counter. Dividends, rights, annual reports, and other distributions on the basic foreign securities are received by the trustee bank and distributed to the ADR holders; dividends and similar payments will usually be received in foreign money but the bank will exchange this and distribute American dollars. The small cost of this routine service is usually paid by the foreign corporation, though in some cases it is deducted from the ADR holders' dividends. For a small fee, an ADR holder can surrender his ADRs and obtain his foreign shares from the trust, or he can deliver foreign shares and obtain additional ADRs. The ADR device is used with a considerable number of stocks of British, Dutch, West German, Italian, South African, and Japanese companies.

Foreign corporations which sell bonds in the United States practically always sell *dollar bonds*—that is, they borrow dollars and contract to pay principal and interest in dollars. The bonds are standard $1,000 units and a New York bank serves as trustee or paying agent. A number of Canadian, European, Japanese, and other corporations have sold such bonds—Canadian Pacific Railway Perpetual 4s, Copenhagen Telephone 5⅝s of 1978, and Nippon Telephone 5¾s of 1980 are examples.

From the foregoing it may be deduced that there are four possible differences between investment in American companies owning foreign properties and investment in foreign-controlled business concerns. First, the managerial group in the foreign-controlled concern may not be primarily interested in the investment welfare of American securityholders. Second, dividends, interest payments, and other payments may be made in the firm's own national currency, not in dollars, and the American payee may experience some trouble and expense in obtaining dollars. Third, foreign taxes on dividends or interest may intercept some of the income. Fourth, foreign markets and transfer methods may be awkward for Americans.

Information about foreign corporations in which Americans hold securities will be found in the usual American financial sources.

BONDS OF FOREIGN GOVERNMENTS AND AGENCIES

More than half the foreign bonds sold in the United States since 1945 have been the bonds of foreign national governments, states, municipalities, and publicly owned corporations. Over half the total are Canadian, but before 1965 a considerable number of issues from Australia, New Zealand, and Japan appeared, along with a scattering from other countries. A number of prewar bond issues from Latin America and other areas also remain. The outstanding total is probably more than 5 billion dollars.

Foreign public bonds sold in the United States almost always promise payment of principal and interest in dollars. A New York bank is usually designated as the paying agent and administrator of the sinking fund if any. There is no trustee in the usual sense. Sinking funds are common, serial issues are sometimes used, and call provisions are frequently included. Sometimes specific governmental revenues are pledged for debt service; for example, the Republic of Panama once pledged the annual rental paid by the United States for the use of the Canal Zone as security for certain of her dollar bonds.

Historically, foreign public bonds have not performed well for Americans. A tabulation made in 1948 showed that 46 per cent of such bonds were in default, including 77 per cent of those from European countries, 59 per cent of those from Latin America, 56 per cent of those from the Far East and Africa, and 0.2 per cent of those from Canada. However, depression and war were responsible for much of this black showing, and many defaulting debtors have resumed payments or negotiated adjustment plans with their creditors since 1948. Some of these steps have been taken willingly as improved economic conditions and postwar restoration have made them possible. Others have been taken after considerable pressure by the Foreign Bondholders' Protective Council and other creditors' agencies, and because the International Bank for Reconstruction and Development does not consider governments which are indifferent to their present obligations to be good risks for new loans.

There are of course many foreign nations whose governmental units pay their obligations regularly, Canada, Great Britain, France, Norway, Finland, Guatemala, the Dominican Republic, Panama, Uruguay, and Australia, among others, have creditable records. Some units in some of these countries have been in default at times and have even asked their dollar creditors to accept reductions in interest or principal but that has happened among American public debtors as well.

When foreign public debtors default on their dollar bonds, there is usually no court action which American creditors may take. Unless the debtors later become able to pay or wish to rehabilitate their credit by making payments, the bonds remain in default and nothing is done about them. Sometimes well-intentioned

Table 26-1 *Price ranges of selected foreign dollar bonds, 1971*

Issue	High	Low
Antiquoia (Columbia) 3s, 1978*	96	90
Australia 5½s, 1985	85	78
Bolivia 1½–3s, 1993*†	15	8½
Canada 6⅞s, 1988	98	91
Chile 3s, 1993*	50	36
International Bank 8⅛s, 1996	105	102
Japan 5½s, 1980	87	85
Mexico 7s, 1982	91	84
New Zealand 5¾s, 1985	85	78
Norway 5¼s, 1978	86	84
Oslo (Norway) 5¼s, 1978	87	86
Poland 4½s, 1968*†	10	6
Port of London (England) Authority 6½s, 1987–1990	62	35
Quebec (Canada) 9s, 1997	106	100
Rhodesia 6s, 1978–1981	64	20
Uruguay 4⅛s, 1979	100	85

* Adjustment bonds, replacing older defaulted issues.
† Currently in default.
Note that bond prices are affected by a number of factors including quality, coupon rate, time to maturity, and possible arrearages due for payment.

debtors pay interest but default on sinking funds and maturities or make partial payments as the funds become available. Governments which have been compelled to default frequently make adjustment offers to their bondholders under which the old bonds may be exchanged for new ones which pay less interest, call for smaller sinking-fund payments, or have later maturities. Conscientious settlements have been made in this manner by a number of nations, among which Brazil is conspicuous; but the indifference of many debtors until circumstances make payment easy or until part payment opens the door to new credits would seem to justify much of the prevailing cynicism.

Because of the great difference in hazard, the yields available on foreign public bonds vary widely. On a Canadian or Australian national issue, there is little risk, and the yields are comparable to those on high-class domestic bonds; but on doubtful issues, yields of 9 to 12 per cent could be found during 1971–1972, and on default bonds very low prices are often quoted. Table 26-1 shows typical quotations.

Information about foreign public bonds is available in the major financial services, in the financial journals, and in the reports of the Foreign Bondholders' Protective Council and the C. J. Devine Institute of Finance. Investors who wish to invest or speculate in this field should investigate carefully both the debtors' willingness to pay and their ability to pay. The bonds are regularly traded on the stock exchanges and in unlisted markets; hence, quotations will be found in the usual places.

INTERNATIONAL BANK FOR RECONSTRUCTION AND DEVELOPMENT

One of the planned instruments for peace and prosperity in the postwar world was an agency whose intervention could reduce the risks of international lending and investing. The International Bank for Reconstruction and Development is such an agency, whose function is to make or facilitate international loans for productive investment. The Bank was planned at the Bretton Woods Conference in 1944 and began business in 1946. Its stockholders are 117 sovereign nations, which at March 31, 1972, had subscribed $24,340,300,000 of capital and paid in $2,434,030,000; most of the balance will not be paid in but is subject to call if needed. The United States government owns 27 per cent of the stock, Great Britain owns 11 per cent, and others own lesser amounts.

The Bank may lend its own capital funds, it may sell its own debentures to raise additional money, or it may merely guarantee the payment of bonds which eligible borrowers sell to other investors. Eligible borrowers are member governments, states or municipalities within member countries, and private corporations within member countries; but the member national government must guarantee all loans made within its borders. An eligible borrower ordinarily desires a foreign loan either because interest rates are lower than in the home country, or because it needs foreign equipment which it cannot purchase with the home currency because of foreign exchange difficulties. In either case, a loan from the Bank or the sale in a foreign country of the borrower's bonds bearing the Bank's guarantee will solve the problem.

American investors now have opportunity to invest in the dollar debentures of the International Bank: 21 issues maturing from 1973 to 1996, paying 3 to 8⅝ per cent coupon rates and totaling $3.4 billion in amount, were held in the United States in 1972. These debentures are of high quality. The Bank had only $11.22 billion committed to loans in 1972, its borrowings totaled only $6.44 billion, and it has very large uncollected capital subscriptions from the United States and other solvent stockholders which can be used to absorb any losses which may occur. Despite the Bank's somewhat "permissive" lending standards, there will be no risk of investor loss on its debentures until many billions of loans are outstanding, and even then the risk should not be great. In 1972 the debentures were rated Aaa and sold on about the same yield basis as American Telephone bonds.

A similar but unrelated organization, the Inter-American Development Bank, began business in 1960. It is operated by the United States (a 42 per cent stock-

holder) and 22 Latin American countries, to lend in Latin America. In 1971 this
institution had $2.8 billion of subscribed capital and $388 million paid in. It had
borrowed $915 million on 20 bond issues, mostly in the United States, and had
lent or committed most of its funds. Its bonds also are rated Aaa.

CAUSES OF LOSS

Most of the losses which Americans have sustained in foreign investments are
attributable to one or more of eight common situations. These are not listed here
in any order which purports to indicate their importance or frequency, but it is
suggested that the first five deal with willingness to pay and the remaining three
with ability to pay. They are as follows:

1 No recognition of moral obligation There are probably few other countries
in which individuals and governments take as much pride in fulfilling their promises as do those in the United States, Canada, Great Britain, and the Scandinavian
countries. In many countries obligations are recognized by the debtors just as long
as the advantage of a good credit standing outweighs the burden of making payment. A sense of moral obligation to pay debts is most likely to be present among
educated people, people used to commercial transactions, and people who are not
in acute poverty. Investors considering foreign commitments can test for this
moral hazard by examining the nation's record and present political trends, as
well as other pertinent factors. The results will give an indication of the soundness
of corporate investments or direct property ownership as well as the reliability
of public bonds, for a nation which honors its debts is not likely to expropriate
private property without compensation.

2 Jealousy or spite toward Americans There are a number of foreign countries in which Americans are not popular. Regardless of the cause of such attitudes, they certainly contribute to a willingness to default on American claims
and to do things which may injure American property.

3 No immediate need for American cooperation Debt defaults and adverse
legislation toward Americans are much more likely when the nation in question
does not need or cannot get American markets or American credits. Even high-
quality debtors make a more determined effort to pay when nonpayment jeopar-
dizes something urgently desired.

4 Lack of political stability Nations addicted to revolutions or to sharp political upheavals are frequently poor credit risks because their governments cannot
risk either sufficient taxes or sufficient governmental economy to maintain sound

budgets. Furthermore, political turbulence leads to demagoguery and unsound legislation at the expense of foreigners.

5 Misuse of the original funds This hazard applies only to public bonds, but it is an important hazard in that field. Money borrowed and spent unsoundly by an administration which is later removed from power is sometimes not repaid by successor administrations. It is difficult for a new government to feel obligated to pay for the errors or extravagances of predecessors of which it does not approve. On the other hand, revolutionary governments often acknowledge prior debts which were incurred to pay for roads, railways, power systems, and similar good assets.

6 Unsound foreign exchange situation The disturbed state of world trade since 1914 has produced acute foreign exchange problems for many nations. Wars, booms, depressions, internal disturbances, and trade restrictions have caused trade balances to fluctuate widely. Divergent rates of price-level inflation have plunged some countries into chronic deficits on their balance of payments; others, into endless surplus. International lending and capital movements have been sporadic. As a result, international exchange rates have fluctuated greatly, often making dollars very expensive at times when foreign debtors wished to buy them to make payments in the United States. Public debtors have sometimes defaulted on dollar bonds because of the high price of dollars, even when they were able to raise normal sums in their own money. In order to keep the dollar at a reasonable exchange rate, and to be able to pay for normal imports from the United States, national governments frequently impose exchange control systems which limit the number of dollars available to transmit interest, dividend, or debt principal payments into the United States. The situation obviously may turn a sound foreign investment into a poor one. Investors are therefore well advised to consider the strength of a nation's foreign exchange position before investing in its securities or in property located within its borders. The diversification, total value, and price stability of the nation's exports, coupled with the amount of its imports, the size of its external debt, and the trend of its current international capital transactions, are important clues to its exchange position.

7 Unsound internal economy Countries which lack good financial institutions, good laws, or honest government, or which are committed to fanciful economic experimentation, are likely to be stagnant and unproductive. Their political units are poor credit risks because of inability to collect revenues or to control expenses, and earnings from properties and business ventures are less dependable than they should be because of uncertain business conditions.

8 Poorly chosen debtors or properties Even if a national economy is reasonably sound, it is essential that a debtor state or municipality or corporation be financially strong, if its securities are to be good investments. Admittedly, it is more difficult for an investor to appraise the quality of a municipality or a business property in a distant country than if it were near his home, but failure to make the attempt is an invitation to loss.

FOREIGN BONDHOLDERS' PROTECTIVE COUNCIL, INC.

This organization was formed in 1933 as an unofficial but governmentally approved body to represent American investors in negotiations with foreign public debtors. Foreign defaults were rife in 1933, yet the United States government found it politically inexpedient to press the debtors for payment or a plan of adjustment; an unofficial agency could do this with better grace. The Council is financed by private donations and by small charges levied upon the bondholders it serves.

The Council consists of a volunteer committee of leading attorneys, financiers, and statesmen, and a small executive staff. Certain government agencies such as the State Department and SEC cooperate in collecting information. The function of the Council is to approach each defaulting foreign governmental debtor as the representative of the American bondholders, seeking to persuade the debtor to resume payments or to offer an adjustment plan compatible with its ability to pay. If an acceptable solution is reached, the Council endeavors to get the bondholders to accept it; if the debtor proposes an unfair plan, the Council recommends against it and tries to arrange a better one.

The Council has been generally recognized by foreign debtors as the proper American bargaining agency on these matters.

LIMITATIONS ON AMERICAN INVESTMENT ABROAD

"Interest equalization tax" In August 1964, the United States government enacted a "temporary" tax upon American investors who purchase securities from foreigners; its purpose is to reduce the deficit in the American balance of payments by reducing payments for securities. Called the interest equalization tax, it has been extended repeatedly; the last revision provided for tax rates and certain possible exemptions to be established from time to time by the President. The tax rates in 1972 were 11.25 per cent on stocks and from 0.79 to 11.25 per cent on bonds, depending on term to maturity; these rates are supposed to depress the net yields of foreign securities and thus "equalize" them with those available on domestic issues. The tax in 1972 does not apply on *new* Canadian securities, on securities from the less developed countries, or on International Bank bonds.

The tax also does not apply on foreign securities bought from American owners or on certain Canadian stocks which are heavily owned in the United States. It does apply on most outstanding Canadian securities and to numerous attractive securities which would normally be available from European sources and from Australia, New Zealand, South Africa, and Japan.

Since 1967, large deficits in the United States balance of international payments have often placed the dollar among the world's weaker currencies, and between 1970 and mid-1973 devaluations and market depreciation caused the dollar to decline some 20 per cent against the major currencies of Western Europe and Japan. Recurring weakness in the dollar has resulted in large outflows of dollars from this country, many of them originating with American citizens who attempt to convert their funds into stronger currencies. When such "flight from the dollar" occurs, the American investors typically seek to store their newly purchased foreign exchange in the interest-paying obligations of some strong-currency country.

Dollar flight has proved troublesome to such nations as Switzerland and West Germany, since the incoming dollars used to buy the domestic currencies typically wind up in the reserves of these countries' central banks, thereby adding to the money supplies and inflationary pressures. Consequently, strong-currency nations have frequently resorted to exchange controls, prohibition of interest payments on foreign-owned short-term securities and bank deposits, punitive taxes on these investments, or outright prohibition of their purchase by foreigners. To date, American investors have not been prohibited from buying stocks and bonds of these countries, but since October 1972, foreign investors have been allowed to buy Japanese stocks and bonds only to the extent that other foreign investors sell them.

Eurodollar bonds and notes are not legally available to American residents. These securities are sold for, and have principal and interest denominated in, dollars, but they are not registered with the SEC. They are thus intended only for investors of Eurodollars (dollars deposited in commercial banks outside the United States and ordinarily foreign-owned). Eurodollar bond issues often exceed $25 million or more in amount, and they have been used with increasing frequency by foreign subsidiaries of major American corporations. The effective ban on their purchase by American residents is, of course, a balance-of-payments measure intended to reduce the flow of dollars abroad.

Although the high yields and wide price swings characteristic of foreign securities have attracted many small investors, it is probably fair to say that this is a hazardous and hard-to-understand field for one who cannot study it extensively and constantly. Until the world economy is more stable, it will be best for casual investors to limit themselves to American securities. Bonds issued by the International Bank are an exception, of course, as are Canadian securities and property.

SOURCES OF INFORMATION

Information concerning the securities and the economic affairs of foreign nations, municipalities, and corporations can be found in various financial sources. *Moody's Municipal and Government Manual* provides extensive information on the credit records and outstanding dollar securities of foreign governments and their subdivisions. The news bulletins and occasional summary reports of the Foreign Bondholders' Protective Council, Inc., furnish data on public issues, especially on defaults, debt adjustments, and negotiations in progress. Similar material appears in periodic issues of the *Bulletin* of the C. J. Devine Institute of Finance, which also publishes occasional appraisals of the economic position of various countries.

Thumbnail summaries of foreign common stocks are given in Standard & Poor's *International Stock Reports*, published monthly and covering 30 or 40 different companies in each issue. (Perhaps 200 companies will be reported on one or more times during a year.) A two-page summary presents the most recent balance sheet and income statement of each foreign company, shows its dividend and earnings record and other stock data, tells whether ADRs are available, and briefly discusses the company's fundamental position and current outlook. Additional, if less systematic, information on foreign stocks is available in periodical articles and occasional studies by securities dealers.

QUESTIONS AND PROBLEMS

1   Why are the bulk of American foreign investments made by American corporations?
2   Should American corporations with foreign subsidiaries be required to pay American taxes on the foreign subsidiaries' undistributed earnings? On their dividends when received? Should the foreign income taxes be deducted from the American tax on this income?
3   Are American corporations extending their investments abroad at the present time? Are foreign bonds being sold in the United States? Why?
4   Would there be less likelihood of defaults if American-held foreign bonds were payable in foreign money? Would Americans buy the bonds readily under such circumstances? Suppose the foreign borrowers promised to remit to Americans in dollars at current rates of exchange?
5   If a foreign government cannot obtain dollars to pay interest on its dollar bonds, can that government honorably permit its citizens to sell export merchandise in America, use the resulting dollars to buy the defaulted bonds at a low price, repatriate the bonds, and then exchange them for interest-paying bonds in the home currency? Consider all the possibilities here.
6   Investigate the common shares of Unilever N.V. Do you consider them as attractive as those of Proctor & Gamble or Colgate-Palmolive Company? On what factors do you base your judgment?

7 Where would you look up the records of the following foreign governments with American bondholders: Mexico, Yugoslavia, Austria? What do the records of these countries show?

8 Does the plan for the International Bank seem sound? Should American banks and life insurance companies be permitted to hold its bonds? (Note: Most of them are so permitted.)

9 Do ADRs constitute an effective device for making equity capital more mobile between nations? Does their use offend national pride and the public desire for "home rule" in business establishments?

10 Explain the nature of the Foreign Bondholders' Protective Council, Inc.

11 Would you buy the dollar bonds of a foreign government which proposed to use the loan "to maintain a satisfactory standard of living temporarily and to build up our capital resources so a satisfactory standard of living can be maintained permanently"? Suppose the foreign government was expending the bond proceeds on highways, power plants, schools, and hospitals which did not promise a direct contribution to the country's ability to earn foreign exchange?

12 Would Japanese or Australian dollar bonds serve as price-level protection against American inflation? How about bonds payable in yen or Australian dollars? How about Japanese ADRs?

REFERENCES

Badger, Ralph E., Harold W. Torgerson, and Harry G. Guthmann: *Investment Principles and Practices*, 6th ed., Prentice-Hall, Inc., Englewood Cliffs, N.J., 1969, Chap. 18.

Dougall, Herbert E.: *Investments*, 8th ed., Prentice-Hall, Inc., Englewood Cliffs, N.J., 1968, Chap. 10.

Foreign Bondholders' Protective Council, Inc.: *Reports*, Washington, occasional.

Investment Bankers Association of America: *Fundamentals of Investment Banking*, Prentice-Hall, Inc., Englewood Cliffs, N.J., 1949, Chap. 13.

Moody's Municipal and Government Manual, Vol. 2, section on foreign governments, states, and municipalities, Moody's Investors Service, New York.

Standard & Poor's Corporation: *International Stock Reports*, New York, monthly.

Survey of Current Business, "The International Investment Position of the United States," annual (usually in October issue).

part 6
Investment Administration

After an extensive study of investor objectives, corporation securities, securities market techniques, and investments of many types, there still remains a need for a final discussion on investment management. However, investment management often consists in considerable part of tax management, a topic which thus far has received only passing attention.

Consequently, Chapter 27 is devoted to taxes which affect investors' decisions. The emphasis is divided about equally between an analysis of the taxes and comments on what can be done to minimize them.

The final chapter has to do with portfolio management and emphasizes what results can reasonably be expected and the kinds of policies which either individual or institutional investors can most reasonably pursue.

TAXES WHICH AFFECT
INVESTMENT POLICY

Taxes and assessments for the support of public functions are now absorbing more than 30 per cent of the American national income. This terrific burden is collected in diverse ways by the national government, the states, and the municipalities, but the levies are so heavy on both property and incomes that taxpayers have need to adapt their investment policies to the conditions created by the tax laws. The phases of investment policy affected are many and various, but among the important ones will be found (1) liquidity of estate, for the purpose of meeting estate and inheritance levies; (2) desirability of tax-exempt versus higher-yielding taxable investments, in view of high income taxes; (3) relative attractiveness of growth and capital gains instead of cash income, if income is taxed in high brackets; (4) location of residence, safety deposit boxes, family trusts, tangible personal property, and real estate, in view of state property laws and state inheritance tax jurisdictions; and (5) method of holding legal title to family property and incomes, in view of income tax and estate tax burdens. These problems and similar ones are matters for experts when the cases are complicated, but most investors, even those in moderate circumstances, are likely to find that a general understanding of tax planning is advantageous.

Tax problems also bring home to the investor another facet of the increasing complexity of modern life, namely, the necessity for detailed and accurate personal records. The adjusted cost of real estate investments, the actual cash cost of life annuities, the value of inherited property at the time of the previous owner's death, the identification of shares of stock bought at different prices at different times—these and a host of other bits of information may be needed many years after the transactions have faded from memory. Even families with small financial resources need records, for income taxes already reach almost every family, and the taxes of the future will probably require even more detailed reports and calculations.

❋ FEDERAL PERSONAL INCOME TAXES

Because the federal personal income tax is very complicated, very heavy, and steeply progressive, it probably gives rise to more investment problems than any other tax. Federal income taxes are levied upon every citizen or resident who has any significant income.

STRUCTURE OF THE FEDERAL INCOME TAX

The federal income tax is levied annually on the taxpayer's computed taxable income. Taxable income is determined as follows: First, the *adjusted gross income* is found. This sum includes the taxpayer's wages, salary, dividends minus certain exemptions and credits, interest, business profits after business expenses, real estate income after deducting expenses, income from trust funds, certain portions of annuity receipts, and the net balance of profits and losses on sale of investments (i.e., capital gains or losses) as specified by law. It does not include interest on state and municipal bonds, gifts, bequests, social security benefits, most personal insurance benefits, and certain other tax-exempt gains. Second, the *net income* is found. Net income equals the adjusted gross income minus *deductions.* The deductions consist either of an arbitary 15 per cent of adjusted gross income (but not more than $2,000), or of an itemized total of actual "deductions." The itemized total may include interest paid, taxes paid, losses from property destruction, charitable contributions not exceeding 20 (in some cases, 30) per cent of adjusted gross income, medical and dental expenses in excess of 3 per cent of adjusted gross income, and certain other items, all as specified by law. Third, the *taxable income* is found by subtracting from net income a personal exemption of $750 for the taxpayer (or $1,500 if he is over 65 or blind) and an additional $750 for each dependent. Fourth, the tax is determined by applying the current rates to the taxpayer's taxable income. The tax is computed by applying successively higher rates to each "bracket" of taxable income and totaling all these levies. For example, at 1972 rates each taxpayer paid 14 per cent on his first $500 of taxable income, 15 per cent on the next $500, 16 per cent on the next $500, and successively more in higher brackets until a maximum rate of 70 per cent was reached.[1]

The tax rates in effect in 1972 may be illustrated by the accompanying table, which was applicable to the separate income of an individual. Married couples paid rates close to those shown when incomes were small, but rates for couples with very large incomes were as much as 20 per cent less than those in the table. Somewhat lower rates also applied when the taxpayer was an unmarried "head of a household." The Tax Reform Act of 1969 also established a 10 per cent minimum tax on various categories of so-called preferred income, which hitherto had escaped federal taxation altogether, but this is of concern only to the wealthiest class of investors.

---

[1] The rates noted here were effective in 1971 and thereafter. This description is too highly condensed to be thorough and may become out of date the next time the tax law is revised. For up-to-date description and analysis adequate to aid in investment planning, see the tax services by Prentice-Hall, Inc., Commerce Clearing House, Inc., or one of the numerous other annual volumes on the subject.

Federal personal income tax rates for 1972 (Single taxpayer)

On taxable income				Tax is
Over	But not over	This amount	Plus this percentage	Of excess over
$ 0	$ 500	$ 0	14	$ 0
500	1,000	70	15	500
1,000	1,500	145	16	1,000
1,500	2,000	225	17	1,500
2,000	4,000	310	19	2,000
4,000	6,000	690	21	4,000
6,000	8,000	1,110	24	6,000
8,000	10,000	1,590	25	8,000
10,000	12,000	2,090	27	10,000
12,000	14,000	2,630	29	12,000
14,000	16,000	3,210	31	14,000
16,000	18,000	3,830	34	16,000
18,000	20,000	4,510	36	18,000
20,000	22,000	5,230	38	20,000
22,000	26,000	5,990	40	22,000
26,000	32,000	7,590	45	26,000
32,000	38,000	10,290	50	32,000
38,000	44,000	13,290	55	38,000
44,000	50,000	16,590	60	44,000
50,000	60,000	20,190	62	50,000
60,000	70,000	26,390	64	60,000
70,000	80,000	32,790	66	70,000
80,000	90,000	39,390	68	80,000
90,000	100,000	46,190	69	90,000
100,000	No limit	53,090	70	100,000

PROGRESSIVE RATES

It is obvious from the accompanying table that income dollars which are taxed in the higher-rate brackets are severely reduced. Taxpayers therefore find it desirable to escape high brackets by (1) dividing family property and income among members of the family, so that as much of the aggregate income as possible falls in the initial low-rate brackets; (2) utilizing investments whose income is not includible in adjusted gross income and therefore is not taxed; (3) timing the receipts of incomes, and particularly of capital gains and losses, to realize such gains and losses at advantageous times; (4) making full use of deductions; and (5) making full use of capital gains and losses.

In considering some of these measures, investors will have to weigh their income tax advantages against possible gift or estate tax costs and against legal and administrative disadvantages. In doing so, it seems sound in most cases to hold that the income taxes avoided would have been levied in the investor's top bracket, not at his average rate. For example, if a man with a taxable income of $35,000 per year sells $10,000 worth of 7 per cent preferred stock at par and invests the proceeds in 5 per cent state bonds, he will reduce his cash income by $200; but the state bond interest is not taxable, and the elimination of $700 from his taxable income will take that much off his top bracket, which is taxed at 50 per cent. The tax saving at his top-bracket rate will amount to 50 per cent of $700, or $350, and will therefore exceed the loss in gross income.

Top-bracket taxes also affect decisions with respect to the profitableness of risky investments. The individual with a $35,000 taxable income is paying a top rate of 50 per cent. That means that a fairly hazardous stock promising 7 per cent if all goes well can actually yield him only 3.5 per cent. If he can get 5 per cent on a secure tax-free municipal bond, the compensation for risking 100 per cent of his capital is a *reduction* of 1.5 percentage points per year in his retained income! Of course, there are certain other considerations: There is some price-level protection in stock ownership; there may be a chance for a moderately taxed capital gain (under certain conditions the tax on a capital gain is levied at low rates and is limited to 25 per cent for most investors); and the possible capital loss could be partly compensated for by a deduction from taxable income. On the whole, however, it is difficult to see why high-bracket taxpayers are willing to bear business risks except in cases promising substantial capital gains, though it appears that they nevertheless do so.

DIVIDING FAMILY INCOMES

Since the Revenue Act of 1948, the law has given husbands and wives the privilege of combining their incomes and losses advantageously in a joint return. The joint return permits the combining of incomes and deductions and personal exemptions and doubles the size of each income bracket for tax computation purposes.

But there are still substantial income tax advantages for the high-bracket taxpayer who wishes to give property or income to members of his family or to allocate part of it to family-owned business corporations. Some of the devices used are as follows:

1 Gifts of income-producing property to family members will transfer incomes from the top tax brackets of the donor to the presumably lower top tax brackets of the donee. The gifts may be in securities, real estate, partnership

interests in family businesses, or shares in a family corporation; they may be direct transfers, or transfers to trusts with the donee as beneficiary. Moderate-sized gifts in trust to minor children, made by donors other than the parents, with the trust income directed to be spent regularly to provide special advantages for the children, can effectively raise the parents' family income at little tax cost, since the children become the taxpayers on the trust income, with full quotas of personal exemptions and lowest tax brackets. Gifts to accomplish these purposes must transfer the property irrevocably and make it substantially free of sub-sequent control by the donor, and the income must not thereafter be used to meet the legal or moral obligations of the donor. It should also be remembered that these transactions are not all net gain; gift taxes may be encountered, and there may be some disadvantage to the donor in the loss of control over his principal. However, ultimate estate taxes and probate costs may be reduced.

2   As an alternative to gifts of principal sums, donors may give to others the income from property for periods of 10 years or longer; by irrevocably transfer-ring the property to a trust for that purpose, reserving the right to recover the property subsequently. Gifts of income on a shorter or less absolute basis may not remove it from the donor's taxable income.

3   Family partnerships involving services or employment in family corpora-tions may afford means of dividing up large family incomes.

4   Family corporations engaged in business can pay salaries to employed members of the family, which are deductible business expenses to the corpora-tion; if the remaining net income of the business is retained for use in the business, it will be taxed at the corporation tax rates, which may be lower (especially in a small corporation) than the stockholders' personal top brackets. Also, if the business is such as to justify some investments in securities, dividends received by the corporation will be 85 per cent tax-exempt to the corporation. Again, family corporations may under certain circumstances operate pension or annuity plans for the benefit of employees, at a cost which is a tax-deductible expense to the corporation. Family members may share in the benefits as employees.

NONINCLUDIBLE INCOME

There is definite advantage in ownership of income which may be excluded in whole or part from adjusted gross income. If it is not included it will not be taxed, and the entire amount will remain available to the owner. Such income need not be cash income. The services of an owner-occupied home, for example, consti-tute noninclludible investment income. Of course, an investment which is tax-free is not necessarily profitable or suitable for a particular investor. The essential thing is that the investor be familiar with the choices available, so that he may weigh the alternatives for himself. And in view of repeated changes in the tax laws and judicial interpretations thereon, it is desirable to review the situation periodically.

Features of the present laws which permit investors to obtain wholly or partly exempt income include the following:

1 Interest on state and municipal bonds is not includible in adjusted gross income. To a corporation paying a 48 per cent rate or to an individual in a high tax bracket, it may be profitable to buy a tax-free bond with a limited yield rather than a taxable security paying much more. Bond dealers commonly publish tables of "tax-free interest equivalents" which show how much taxable interest a security must pay to individuals in various tax brackets in order to give the holder a net remainder equal to indicated tax-free yields.

2 On corporation bonds bought at a discount, only the cash interest is ordinarily current income;[2] if the market value rises as time passes, the increase will be a capital gain when the bond is sold or collected at maturity. These provisions enable high-bracket taxpayers to report relatively reduced current income and ultimately a capital gain on investments in such bonds.

3 Undistributed corporate profits are not taxable income to the stockholder, and if he ultimately realizes on such gains by selling his stock, he will have a capital gain instead of current income. High-bracket stockholders who do not need large dividends therefore find an advantage in stocks with low dividends, if the situation seems to promise substantial growth in the value of the stock.

4 The services of an owner-occupied home and the value of crops consumed where grown are not included in adjusted gross income. It would thus appear that an individual who owns a home or a garden or an orchard which profitably produces services or crops for his own use has a tax-free income. If his home cost $30,000 and has rental value of $3,000 per year, and if all taxes, insurance, maintenance, and depreciation total $1,500 per year, he has in effect a net income of $1,500 or 5 per cent; but since this is not taxable, it is the equivalent of a much larger net income from securities or rental property.

5 Annuity rights accumulating in an employee pension plan, a tax-sheltered private annuity, goodwill developing in one's own business, increasing value and earning power in real estate owned, and interest earnings on one's life insurance reserves are not taxable income. Some of these may develop into income or capital gains, but the last three may ultimately pass by inheritance without having been depleted by income taxes. High-bracket taxpayers often find it advantageous to put liquid funds into 10-pay life insurance policies, which earn tax-free

---

[2] An exception is the annual amortization of bonds issued in exchange for equity retired by exchange in a merger. Under the Tax Reform Act of 1969, this is treated as ordinary income. For example, the Crane Company 7s of 1994 were allegedly issued at 67, and accrue about $14 per year of noncash ordinary income.

interest on their reserves and provide liquidity both for current purposes and for an ultimate estate.

6 The politically controversial "dividend relief" measure in the Revenue Act of 1954 (as modified in 1964) entitles each taxpayer to $100 per year in corporate dividends free of any federal income tax. This provision encourages all citizens to become stockholders by offering an opportunity to secure a very small amount of tax-free income.

TIMING THE REALIZATION OF GAINS, LOSSES, AND DEDUCTIONS

Because the taxpayer's rate of tax is determined each year by the size of his taxable income, it may be important to take taxable gains in low-income years and to realize major losses and deductions during years when income is greatest. There are many ways of doing this, of which a few may be noted:

1 Since neither a loss nor a profit on the capital value of securities, real estate, or other investments is usually "realized for tax purposes" until the item is sold or becomes utterly worthless, the owner can often choose the year in which he "takes" a profit or loss by choosing the year of sale.

2 When real estate or a business interest is to be sold at a large profit, the gain can be spread over several taxable years by a properly drawn installment sale transaction involving payment in installments. This will prevent the large profit from lifting a small taxpayer into a much higher bracket for the year, and give a large taxpayer greater opportunity to offset at least a part of it with possible losses.

3 For a taxpayer who keeps his books on a cash basis—that is, who records incomes and expenses when received or paid, not when earned or incurred— rental incomes, repair costs, and taxes paid may be to some extent cumulated into desired years.

4 Charitable gifts of substantial size may be made in high-income years. Such items are deductible to the extent of 20 (under certain conditions, 30) per cent of the adjusted gross income. Charitable gifts made in property are valued for deduction purposes at market value at the date of gift, but no gain or loss for gross income purposes is realized in making the gift. It may therefore be advantageous to make the gift in property in which a large unrealized profit exists.

CAPITAL GAINS AND LOSSES

Capital gains and losses are those arising out of transactions in capital assets. Capital assets consist of securities, residence, personal assets generally, and occasional realty holdings. To be classified as a capital asset, an item must be in the nature of an investment, not real estate or equipment used in the taxpayer's business. Profits arising, from the sale of any capital asset are capital gains, but capital losses are not recognized on assets held for personal enjoyment, such as residences or automobiles. Real estate and equipment used in the taxpayer's business and investments in real property extensive enough to constitute a business are not considered capital assets, but gains and losses on them have somewhat similar effects on the owner's tax bill.

The provisions of the present tax laws in regard to capital gains and losses are the result of long experimentation by Congress. It was found by test that long-term holders of investments were reluctant to take profits which would be fully taxed or to take losses which were not deductible for tax purposes. Investment markets would not function normally without a reasonable solution on both points. It also seemed desirable to impose heavier taxes on short-term speculative gains than on longer-term gains; and experience proved that speculative risk bearers would not make commitments unless losses could be reasonably offset against gains. The capital gains section therefore provides for computing *net long-term* gains or losses by adding algebraically all net gains and losses on assets held more than 6 months; and *net short-term* gains or losses are similarly computed on assets held less than 6 months. The tax plan then involves (1) taxing any net short-term gains by adding them to the taxpayer's ordinary income, and (2) taxing long-term gains by either adding half the amount to the taxpayer's ordinary income or taxing them separately at 25 per cent, whichever produces the least tax.[3] A net short-term capital loss may be subtracted from ordinary income to the extent of $1,000 in the year incurred and in each succeeding year, and may be offset in full against any capital gains which occur in the future. However, under the Tax Reform Act of 1969, only half of a net long-term capital loss may be used to offset ordinary income in either a current or a future year.[4] By this change net long-term capital losses have forfeited much of their tax-saving value.

Since these tax rules result in low-rate taxation of capital gains, high-bracket taxpayers frequently search for ways to obtain capital gains instead of ordinary income. Such ways may include (1) investment in promising concerns whose stock may ultimately be sold at a profit; (2) ventures in oil, mining, timber growing, or similar developments; and (3) investments in farms or ranches whose land or stock may be built up to great value without realization of income. Corporation executives may take their compensation in part in stock purchase options of

[3] This rule applies to the first $50,000 of a taxpayer's long-term capital gains. Gains in excess of $50,000 are taxed at a 35 per cent rate.

[4] If there are no offsetting capital gains, only $1,000 of net long-term loss (current or carry-over) may be applied against the current income of any one year. However, $1,000 of net long-term loss offsets only $500 worth of ordinary home.

limited initial value, which may in time enable them to buy the stock at the option price when it has appreciated in value, thus making possible a capital gain.

Taxpayers' experiences with capital gain and loss problems in connection with securities have crystalized in a number of rules for income tax savings, which include the following.

1 Capital assets which rise in value after acquisition should generally be held until the gains become long term. This will reduce the tax rate.

2 Short-term losses should be realized before they go long-term. This will provide a larger offset against ordinary income, if corresponding capital gains are not achieved.

3 If market gains have been realized in any year, they should be offset by realizing losses if appreciable unrealized losses exist in the investor's portfolio. This doctrine assumes that taxes not paid may never need to be paid, hence undertakes to postpone them. This is logical if every loss taken saves taxes in amounts substantially greater than the cost of shifting investments.

4 Assets about to become worthless should be sold before they are finally worthless, to establish the year of loss definitely.

Many investors believe in using "tax switches" to time capital gains and losses to maximum advantage. Such a switch typically involves replacing the sold security with another in the same industry with similar quality and prospects—for example, selling Exxon to establish a timely loss or gain, and purchasing Texaco with the proceeds. Most stockbrokers publish lengthy lists of such suggested trades annually during the tax-selling season in November and December.

The extensive literature on tactics and accounting rules with respect to capital gains and losses includes much practical information which cannot be presented in this volume. However, three fundamental concepts should at least be mentioned. First, every capital asset has a *basis* value, which serves as the owner's cost figure when he sells and must compute a profit or loss. In most cases actual cost plus expenses of acquisition constitute this basis. Sometimes the basis must be adjusted, as in the case of stock which pays a liquidating dividend or real estate upon which additions are built. In the case of a gift, the donor's basis normally becomes the donee's basis. In the case of an inheritance, the new owner's basis is usually the market value at the previous owner's death.[5] Second, any specific asset has its own basis in the investor's hands, if it can be clearly identified; thus, the holder of two U.S. Steel certificates can sell either one and record the gain or

---

[5] Under this rule, which is of long standing, assets which have gained greatly in value in the decedent's hands obtain a new basis at his death, and the capital gain is never taxed. In 1964, Congress rejected a proposal which could have increased the estate tax in such cases, or continued the decedent's cost basis to the heirs.

loss on it without averaging his costs or otherwise involving the other certificate. Third, every gain or loss transaction must be bona fide; a fictitious transaction with a relative, or a sale at a "loss" which is offset by a purchase of the same security within 30 days before or after, and other such devices, are not legitimate or effective for tax purposes.

❖   ## STATE PERSONAL INCOME TAXES

In 1972, personal income taxes were being levied by 43 states at rates which may be described as mildly progressive and not very high. For example, the New York tax, which was typical, allowed certain deductions plus exemptions of $650 per person and imposed a graduated tax which progressed from 2 per cent on the first $1,000 of taxable income to a top rate of 10 per cent on all over $25,000. Long-term capital gains were taxed at half rates. The burden of these rates is further reduced by the fact that state income taxes are deductible in computing taxable income for federal income tax purposes. An individual whose top federal tax bracket is 60 per cent is therefore only out of pocket 40 per cent of the state income taxes which he pays. These facts suggest that state income taxes are as a rule not dominant factors in shaping an individual's investment policy.

Most state income taxes resemble the federal tax in general structure, though inclusions, deductions, and exemptions all differ in detail. The states usually undertake to tax the entire incomes of their residents and also the portions of nonresident's incomes which arise from business activities within the state, but they prevent double taxation by allowing their own residents tax credits on account of taxes paid in other states. A conspicuous difference in income inclusions is the fact that interest on federal obligations is not taxable by a state, while interest on the obligations of other states and their municipalities is usually taxed. An investor who sought bonds which were exempt from both federal and state income taxation might therefore find greatest advantage in the state and municipal bonds issued in his home state.

A few states permit municipalities to levy income taxes. Among these are Ohio and Pennsylvania, where local income taxes preceded statewide ones by many years.

It may be noted that state and local property taxes on intangibles such as stocks, bonds, and mortgages have the same effect on their profitableness to their owners as a tax on their income would have. The methods of assessing and taxing such intangibles are so varied that an inquiry into each individual situation is the only practical approach to an investment policy.

❖ FEDERAL ESTATE TAXES

A federal estate tax is imposed as an excise upon the transfer of the net estate of every decedent who was a citizen or a resident of the United States. The fact that the tax is an excise upon the transfer of property rather than a levy upon the property itself avoids the constitutional prohibition on direct taxation and also enables state and municipal bonds to be included in the tax base. The federal government does not levy property or income taxes on state bonds and similar tax-exempt securities, but it can impose an estate tax on the act of transferring them. For practical purposes, there are no investments exempt from estate taxation.

STRUCTURE OF THE ESTATE TAX

The federal tax is a steeply progressive tax based on the decedent's net estate. It does not affect the majority of families, however, because the net estate is defined as the sum remaining after estate expenses, charitable bequests, the marital deduction, and an exemption of $60,000. The tax is determined as follows:

First, the *gross estate* is computed. This includes the value at date of death or on possible alternative dates of all property owned by the decedent, including his half interest in community property, if any, plus all insurance on his life in which he had some element of ownership, plus his interest in certain types of trusts, plus gifts made "in contemplation of death." Property owned by the decedent is defined to include all property which he held in joint tenancy or tenancy by the entirety with others, except for the portion of such property originally owned or provided by the others. However, real property located outside the United States is excluded from the gross estate.

Second, the *net estate* is found by deducting from the gross estate all funeral expenses, expenses of administration, debts and taxes owned by the decedent, a percentage of any property on which federal estate or gift tax had been paid within 10 years, property left to charity, the marital deduction, and an exemption of $60,000.

Third, the *gross estate tax* is computed by applying the tax rates specified by law to the net estate. From the gross tax, two credits are then deducted: (1) gift taxes previously paid on property included in the gross estate, involving mostly gifts made in contemplation of death, and (2) amounts paid to the states in estate or inheritance taxes, but not in excess of 80 per cent of the "basic estate tax." The gross estate tax minus the two crédits determines the amount actually payable, the *net estate tax*.

The accompanying table indicates the amount of estate tax payable on net estates of various sizes under the rates in force in 1972. Each tax is composed of a total of levies in progressively higher rate brackets. This table indicates selected cases; it is not a complete tabulation of all brackets.

Size of net estate after deductions and $60,000 exemption	Gross estate tax	Maximum rate bracket reached, %	Maximum credit allowable for state taxes
$ 5,000	$ 150	3	$ 0
20,000	1,600	11	0
50,000	7,000	22	80
100,000	20,700	28	560
200,000	50,700	30	2,640
600,000	180,700	35	16,400
1,000,000	325,700	37	36,560
5,000,000	2,468,200	63	398,320
10,000,000	6,088,200	76	1,076,720
20,000,000	13,788,200	77	2,676,400

MARITAL DEDUCTION

Since 1948 the tax laws have provided special rules for the application of estate taxation to transfers of property from the deceased to the surviving spouse. In states having community property laws, the family property accumulated from personal earnings and certain other sources during marriage is regarded as belonging half to one spouse and half to the other. In such cases, only half of this community property is subject to estate or inheritance taxation upon the death of either. To extend this situation equitably to residents of other states, the 1948 Revenue Act provided for a marital deduction which excludes from net taxable estate all the property passing from the deceased to the surviving spouse, up to a maximum of 50 per cent of the adjusted gross estate. Adjusted gross estate is the gross estate minus debts and estate expenses and minus all community property. The practical effect of the marital deduction is to permit any deceased person to leave half of his noncommunity property to his spouse free of federal taxes and, in addition, to apply the $60,000 exemption to the remainder of his estate.

MEETING THE ESTATE TAX PROBLEM

Though the estate tax problem is not severe when estates do not exceed $100,000, it is obvious that the burden on large estates requires careful planning. After all, meeting a $6,088,200 tax out of a $10,000,000 estate would be very difficult unless the estate's investments had been made with that in mind. There are also a number of measures which can reduce the total tax load. The various expedients which investors need to consider in framing their policies include:

1 Total tax load may be reduced through avoiding successive taxes and probate costs on the same money, if the original testator or donor places the property in a trust.[6] The trust may then operate without further estate tax or probate costs for many years, with two or three generations becoming the trust's beneficiaries. Alternatively, the testator may bequeath life tenancies and remainder interests to different people; this also transfers the property but once.

2 Gifts made or irrevocable trusts created during a lifetime, if legally effective, may place substantial amounts of property in the hands of members of a family at relatively small gift tax cost, and thus avoid the high estate tax brackets. This will also reduce the probate costs.

3 Charitable bequests will reduce high-bracket estate tax levies, since they are deductible before computation of tax. Since specific property may be left to charities, it is not necessary to keep the estate liquid to pay such bequests.[7]

4 A proper choice between ownership in joint tenancy, as community property, or as separate property, will be profitable for husband and wife. Estate taxes, gift taxes, state inheritance taxes, and probate costs will all be involved here, as well as the details of law in the state of residence. Joint tenancy will often be useful in estates below $50,000, and separate property is usually preferable in large estates.

5 The estate must always have enough liquid resources, preferably in cash, government bonds, or life insurance, to meet estate expenses and tax liabilities. Certain government bonds are redeemable at par for this purpose, hence are ideal investments for large estates.

6 Business life insurance carried on the lives of partners or stockholders in closely held firms to enable their associates to buy out decedents' shares may be purchased by each participant on the lives of the others. This method of carrying business insurance is advantageous, because if the firm buys the insurance, any death may enlarge the share to be bought out, and if each man carries insurance on his life in favor of the others, his own estate taxes will be increased. There are a number of technical rules in this area; an expert should be consulted.

---

[6] Because the marital deduction provided in the Revenue Act of 1948 may not be used for property which does not become potentially a part of the surviving spouse's estate, this trust device may require two trusts, one effectively "owned" by the survivor and one independent of his control.

[7] The bulk of Henry Ford's fortune was left to the Ford Foundation in this manner. The foundation received nonvoting stock in the Ford Motor Company. The family received the voting stock, retaining control and property sufficient for their needs.

Tax experts generally advise families against making tax avoidance the major factor in planning the disposition of their estates. The tax loopholes have been so carefully plugged by Congress and the courts that complete escape is possible only at the cost of doing bizarre and foolish things with one's property. For example, individuals have given away property to their families and to charity until their own security or the control over their businesses was jeopardized. Worse yet, they have placed property in irrevocable trusts, only to find that subsequent changes in the tax laws eliminated the tax advantages which they had planned. Or they have made other dispositions which were difficult to reverse and then changed their minds about their entire objectives. Instead of making such desperate efforts to avoid all possible taxes, it is usually conceded to be better policy to (1) determine where the control of and the benefits from the property should be at all times, both before and after the death of the owner; (2) plan for gifts, trusts, and a final will to accomplish these things, keeping always in mind that changes in the value of properties, in family relations, or in the tax laws may make it desirable to change the plans while the owner still lives; and (3) review the plans to determine whether minor adjustments may minimize the tax costs. This procedure may cost no more in the long run, and it has obvious advantages.

❋ ## STATE ESTATE AND INHERITANCE TAXES

In 1972 all states except Nevada were imposing taxes upon the transfer of decedents' property. Eleven of these states levied estate taxes based upon the size of the estate, as the federal government does, while the others taxed the heirs' inheritance at rates which usually increased with both the size of the inheritance and the remoteness of relationship between heir and decedent. When the total of the inheritance taxes payable from any estate is less than the available federal estate tax offset, most states add a supplementary tax to absorb the balance. The inclusions and deductions used in determining the taxable estate or inheritance are of course unique in each state law, but there is a general similarity to the federal approach except that (1) only property within the state's jurisdiction is includible, (2) life insurance payable to named beneficiaries is often exempted up to very generous amounts, and (3) property exemptions are much smaller.

At the present time, a state tax on the transfer of decedents' property seems to be able to reach (1) real estate and tangible personal property if located within the taxing state; (2) intangible personal property wherever located, if the decedent is domiciled in the taxing state; (3) intangibles located within the taxing state regardless of the domicile of the owner; and (4) intangibles wherever owned or located, if they must be transferred on the books of a corporation incorporated by the taxing state. Double taxation under item 1 is not likely, and the states do not now impose taxes based on item 4. The greatest hazards of double taxation lie in state laws under which an investor might have domicile in more than one state (item 2) or in which intangibles stored or in trust in a state other than his domicile might be taxed in both (item 3). Double taxation can almost always be avoided by taking proper care, since state laws are not intended to set traps of this kind.

State estate or inheritance taxes commonly exact moderate sums from small estates and fairly large sums from large estates. However, the taxes imposed by the average state on its medium and large estates usually will not greatly exceed the available federal estate tax credit for state taxes paid and will very rarely do so if the beneficiaries are immediate family members (Class A heirs) and if there are several of them. The following table shows the inheritance tax rates effective in Indiana in 1972. These are average and typical; a low-rate state might cut these rates in half, and a high-rate state might add a half more:

Beneficiaries:
    Class A: Husband, wife, lineal ancestor, lineal descendant, adopted or acknowledged child or descendant thereof
    Class B: Brother, sister, or descendant of either, wife or widow of son, or husband of daughter
    Class C: Others
Exemptions:
    Class A: Wife, $15,000; child under 18, $5,000; others, $2,000
    Class B: $500
    Class C: $100
    Life insurance payable to named beneficiaries is entirely exempt.

Tax Rates on Each Inheritance

			Percentage
Successive brackets	*Class A*	*Class B*	*Class C*
First $25,000 less exemption	1	5	7
$25,000 — $50,000	2	5	7
$50,000 — $100,000	3	5	7
$100,000 — $200,000	3	8	10
$200,000 — $300,000	4	10	12
$300,000 — $500,000	5	10	12
$500,000 — $700,000	6	12	15
$700,000 — $1,000,000	7	12	15
$1,000,000 — $1,500,000	8	15	20
Over $1,500,000	10	15	20

If the total state tax payable under these rates is less than the available federal estate tax credit for state taxes, the total Indiana state tax is automatically increased to the amount of the available federal credit.

The investor's principal object in meeting state death taxes is to keep the state taxes down to or below the offset credit allowed on his federal estate tax. If this can be accomplished, the state taxes will cost nothing extra. Useful devices for keeping state taxes down include (1) care in avoiding double state taxation, as previously noted; (2) use of (exempt) life insurance payable to named beneficiaries, especially to Class C or D heirs;[8] use of bequests to many heirs, for example, to wife, children, and grandchildren, to avoid large (high-bracket) bequests to a few individuals; and (4) ownership of real property in other states, which may place this property in lower initial tax brackets in those states instead of in top brackets in the home state. Charitable bequests are in principle deductible in computing state death taxes, but some states do not allow full credit for bequests to charitable agencies outside their own borders.

❉ FEDERAL GIFT TAXES

The federal gift tax is an excise imposed upon the transfer of gifts made by a citizen or resident of the United States. The taxpayer is the donor, not the donee. The tax was enacted in 1932 as a means of taxing transfers made during a donor's lifetime, because such transfers normally escape the estate taxes imposed at his death. The gift tax rates are 75 per cent of the estate tax rates charged in corresponding brackets. No deductions are allowed on account of state gift taxes. Like the estate tax, the gift tax is levied upon the transfer of all kinds of property; tax-exempt securities do not exist.

STRUCTURE OF THE TAX

The gift tax is a progressive tax, imposed annually on the *cumulative total* of taxable gifts made by the donor since June 6, 1932. The amount payable in any year is determined as follows: (1) Apply the present tax rates to the cumulative total of taxable gifts; (2) apply the present tax rates to the cumulative total of taxable gifts up to the end of the preceding year; (3) the difference is the tax for the current year.

The gifts to be taxed include all gratuitous transfers of property, except that the first $3,000 of value transferred to each donee in any year is "excluded" from all calculations. Larger amounts are so excluded for years preceding 1943. Subsequent to the enactment of the Revenue Act of 1948, gifts made by husband and wife to others may be regarded as being made half by each.

Deductions which may be made by the donor from his cumulative total of gifts

---

[8] Most of the states classify heirs into three groups, but several, including Minnesota, Missouri, and Massachusetts, use four classes.

include (1) a single "lifetime" exemption of $30,000, (2) all charitable gifts, and (3) a "marital deduction" equal to half of any gift made by one spouse to the other after April 2, 1948. Gifts to the other by either spouse or portions of his or her half interest in community property are not eligible for the marital deduction.

The gift tax is thus based on the cumulative total of nonexempt gifts minus the deductions. The detailed rules of computation are complex, and the definitions of items to be included, excluded, and deducted are matters for professionals.

GIFT TAX POLICY

Judicious use of gifts may result in a number of tax advantages. The most obvious advantages lie in economies in estate expenses and estate and inheritance taxes. If gifts are made to a number of donees over a period of years, the $3,000 annual exemption to each donee plus the $30,000 lifetime exemption will permit tax-free disposition of a large amount of property. Additional gifts subject to tax will be taxed beginning at the lowest gift tax brackets; yet all sums thus removed from the estate will come off the estate's top bracket. Since the estate will be smaller, its administration costs will also be less. Charitable gifts made while living reduce the donor's income taxes, escape gift taxes, and do not appear in the estate to swell the administrative costs.

It may be noted that complete and irrevocable gifts of property also transfer the subsequent income from donor to donee. Since it is probable that the donee will have a lower top income tax bracket than the donor, a saving of income taxes will subsequently occur.

Gifts are extremely useful between the spouses in equalizing separate property holdings and in creating and dissolving joint tenancies and tenancies by the entirety.

❖ STATE GIFT TAXES

State gift taxes are still in the experimental stage. Only 17 state statutes were in force in 1972 and the statutes themselves were diverse in nature. In general, the state laws have tended to follow the structural plan of the federal gift tax, but with inclusions and exclusions patterned after the state estate or inheritance tax. The rates imposed on taxable gifts are generally related to or identical with those of the estate or inheritance tax and are high enough to merit careful tax planning when large gift transfers are contemplated. State gift taxes may not be offset against federal gift or income taxes; so their impact is usually 100 per cent effective against the taxpayer.

Specific measures for minimizing the state gift taxes are often similar to those employed in dealing with federal gift taxes and state estate or inheritance taxes.

THE TAX EXPERTS

Because tax planning is a complex and extensive field, experts capable of advising on such matters should be consulted by anyone having substantial amounts of income or property. The cost will usually be far less than the amount of unnecessary taxes for which the amateur will become liable.

Income tax advice can be obtained from attorneys, accountants, brokerage-house analysts, investment counselors, and bank trust officers, although it must be remarked that not all who give such advice are competent to do so. However, the simpler income tax problems are widely understood, because so many people are forced to study them. Estate and gift tax planning, and estate planning in general, is a much less widely understood matter. Accountants and attorneys who specialize in estate problems, a few investment counselors, trust officers, and an occasional life insurance agent are the people most likely to be competent.

For the individual who wishes to do his own studying and planning, the income tax field is reasonably well equipped with elementary books and pamphlets, but the estate tax and planning field is, on the whole, lacking in easy and introductory material. A few pamphlets and articles are available, however, and good technical books intended for experts can be found.

QUESTIONS AND PROBLEMS

1 Why do Community Chest and other charitable agencies frequently get their large contributions in the form of stock which has gained greatly in price in recent years?

2 It is equitable that stock or real estate valued at several times the owner's cost should get a new basis when left to an heir? Does this rule tend to "lock in" such property and prevent normal sales?

3 Is there a federal income tax advantage in homeownership if the home is not fully paid for? (Note: Consider the deductions used in determining net income.)

4 If an individual's taxable income is $150,000 per year, how high a yield would a mortgage or a bond have to offer in order to be attractive to him as a 5 per cent municipal bond issue in his home state? Is the situation the same on a stock investment? Would it be worthwhile for this man to select his municipals chiefly from his own state?

5 Should a high-bracket investor confine himself entirely to state and municipal bonds? Why not? Should he take serious business risks in developing new enterprises? Analyze what happens if the $150,000-per-year man buys stock in a speculative oil company and makes $50,000. What if he loses $50,000? Are the possible results offsetting?

6 Do "capital gain or loss" provisions in the tax laws apply to investment companies, banks, insurance companies, and other corporate securityholders?

7 May a wealthy, high-bracket individual obtain any income tax advantage in the process of providing income for a few years for a pair of maiden aunts?

8 Explain the nature of the federal estate tax. What kinds of property are exempt from it? How large an estate would a married couple have to have in order to be subject to the federal estate tax at the first death? At the second death, assuming that all the property then remained in the survivor's estate?

9   What policies of investment selection will minimize personal income taxes?
10   Explain the general nature of state estate and inheritance taxes. Are they important enough to require consideration in estate planning?
11   How much would Indiana tax a $660,000 estate left to the widow of a decedent's son? Would this tax exceed the maximum credit available against the federal estate tax? If the widow has two small sons (grandchildren of the property owner), what would you suggest?
12   Explain the nature of the federal gift tax and the annual and lifetime exemptions.
13   Are there federal or state taxes on charitable gifts? Is there a tax advantage in making such gifts? Explain.
14   How many middle-class investors know enough of income, estate, inheritance, and gift taxes to plan their affairs wisely? How would you suggest that an individual obtain a sound plan for himself?
15   The Treasury for some time has considered a proposal to combine the gift and estate taxes on every individual on a cumulative lifetime basis, to avoid the "two sets of lower brackets" which are now possible. Would this be feasible and equitable?
16   Investigate the government's appraisal for death tax purposes of the estate-tax-privilege bonds described in Chapter 20. Does this present any offset to the nontaxable capital gain an estate achieves when the bonds escalate to par for tax payment?

REFERENCES

American Research Council: *Your Investments*, Rye, N.Y., semiannual.
Bowe, William J.: *Estate Planning and Taxation*, 3d C.L.U. ed., Richard D. Irwin, Inc., Homewood, Ill., 1972.
Casey, William J.: *Estate Planning Desk Book*, 2d ed., Institute for Business Planning, New York, 1968.
Federal Tax Handbook, Prentice-Hall, Inc., Englewood Cliffs, N.J., annual.
Francis, Jack Clark: *Investment Analysis and Management*, McGraw-Hill Book Company, New York, 1972, Chap. 6.
Hoffman, William H., Jr.: *Effective Estate Planning Procedures for Minimizing Taxes*, Prentice-Hall, Inc., Englewood Cliffs, N.J., 1968.
J. K. Lasser Institute: *Tax Protected Investments, Treasury of Tax Saving Ideas*, and other titles, frequently revised; some published by Business Reports, New York.
J. K. Lasser Tax Institute and Ralph Wallace: *How to Save Estate and Gift Taxes*, rev. ed., American Research Council, Rye, N.Y., 1967.
Sauvain, Harry: *Investment Management*, 3d ed., Prentice-Hall, Inc., Englewood Cliffs, N.J., 1967, Chap. 13.
United States Master Tax Guide, Commerce Clearing House, Inc., Chicago, annual.
Widicus, Wilbur W., and Thomas E. Stitzel: *Personal Investing*, Richard D. Irwin, Inc., Homewood, Ill., 1971, Chap. 12.
Wills, Estate, and Trust Service, loose-leaf, Prentice-Hall, Inc., Englewood Cliffs, N.J.
Wormser, Rene A.: *Guide to Estate Planning*, Prentice-Hall, Inc., Englewood Cliffs, N.J., 1958.

This book's first chapter proposed that an investor needs a systematically planned program; it endeavored to outline the principles upon which one can be constructed. The next 26 chapters were devoted to describing many of the types of investments available, the markets in which they are bought and sold, and the factors which determine their value. There remains for this final chapter a discussion of some of the problems involved in establishing investment policies and carrying them out. Since these are to a great extent matters of opinion, it is probable that the authors' own convictions will emerge more strongly in this chapter than they have been permitted to do heretofore, and to the extent that they do, the statements must be regarded as personal advice rather than as presentations of fact.

The suggestions advanced in this chapter are chiefly concerned with equity investment; they deal with strategies appropriate to both individual and institutional investors. However, since this is an introductory book, the discussion is directed primarily to students and others who are aware that they are amateurs in the highly technical business of investing and who are humble enough to accept advice. Competent professionals are obviously informed to an extent which exceeds the pretensions of this book. But this chapter is also intended as a plea to reckless investors, especially young ones. Every investment dealer is acquainted with numerous people who have had no success but who are convinced that "next time" they will make marvelous profits or who simply enjoy the excitement of extensive speculation. Almost without exception the dealers report that the reckless amateurs do not do well, that they all too often conclude their investment operations after the manner of the famous Casey at the bat. Since life is too short to permit many investment strike-outs without the hazard of an aftermath of poverty, it is hoped that the conservative gospel to be here expressed may reach a few of the wayward.

It seems well to preface discussion of these final topics with the comment that an investment program which does not contribute to the happiness, security, and income of its owner is ill-designed. A plan of procedure which keeps the investor distraught and uncertain, which fails to carry assurance of old-age security and other high-priority objectives, or which does not contemplate at least reasonable income or profit, is not soundly conceived. The investor needs to know what his investment objectives are and to have a plan for achieving them which is consonant with his interests, his temperament, and his abilities. These plans are the topic of this final chapter.

PORTFOLIO MANAGEMENT: THE SUBJECT

For three reasons, portfolio management is a difficult subject for the investor to study. First, it is an art, not a science; and its central core of theory is limited in both scope and direct usefulness. Second, despite much recent research, the information needed to choose among contending portfolio policies is lacking. Third, like today's clothing, portfolio management is strongly subject to fads and fashions, and these tend to obscure, and often contradict, sound, time-tested approaches.

As an art, the management of investment portfolios produces results that are not mathematically predictable, or even highly probable. The results depend not only on the investor's intuition and experience, but on his circumstances, objectives, resources, tastes, expectations, and temperament. It is true that this art has a core of central precepts and guiding principles, useful to an investor and deserving of careful study. But the investor's ability to use these theoretical tools effectively depends, as in piano playing or tennis, upon aptitudes and experience which vary almost endlessly from person to person.

The first chapter of this book noted the currently popular theory that investors "optimize" their portfolios by seeking maximum returns for a given level of risk, or by trying to minimize the risks associated with a sought-for level of return. Although this principle is logically sound and mathematically interesting, it amounts to little more than an abstract ideal: to apply it, the portfolio manager must forecast the risks and return he expects from each security he is considering, and then he must decide how the risks on each security behave in relation to the risks on every other security.[1] The goal is to combine securities in the portfolio in such a way that the risks on individual securities offset one another to the maximum degree, thus minimizing risks on the overall portfolio. However, as Chapter 1 explained, there are several kinds of risks, and each must be offset in a different way. The portfolio manager must decide the extent to which he is concerned about market risks, money-rate risks, business risks, and price-level risks, and how much of one risk he is willing to incur to offset another.[2] He also must deal simultaneously with such problems as the liquidity needs, tax position, and possible legality requirements of the specific portfolio. Computer programs have been developed to select portfolios, but they rely heavily on simplifications, such as assuming that risks on securities can be equated with the variability of their

---

[1] This task of estimating the "covariances" of each possible pair of securities being considered for the portfolio is clearly of backbreaking dimensions for the analyst. For 10 different securities, there are 45 such pairs; for 100 securities, 4,950 pairs.

[2] Most investment risks can be offset only by incurring others or by forfeiting substantial opportunity for returns. Chapter 1 noted, for example, that investors in debt securities can avoid the capital-value risk by moving from long-term obligations into short-term ones; this change, however, exposes them to an income risk. Similarly, the business and market risks are generally reducible only by owing securities more heavily exposed to money-rate and price-level risks.

prices, or that all risks except market risks cancel out if enough stocks are included in a portfolio. Even so, the programs are complicated. At best, they can only supply a means of manipulating and combining the judgments and opinions which portfolio managers have already reached concerning specific securities.

A second reason for the unsatisfactory state of portfolio theory is our continuing ignorance of securities market tendencies. The information needed to choose scientifically between rival portfolio policies is largely lacking. Does taking greater risks (however defined) on a portfolio produce greater ultimate returns? Do stocks making the largest price gains in one time period also tend to make the largest gains in the next? How well does a stock's price variability measure the market risk to its buyer? In 1973, securities analysts and academic teachers of investments had devoted nearly a decade of research and statistical study to these questions without producing any conclusive or generally accepted answers.

A final problem for the student of portfolio management arises in the fads and fashions which recurringly beset the subject. The spirit of alchemy still flourishes in Wall Street, and from time to time the investment community becomes fired with enthusiasm for some new formula, hailed as the key to large market profits. Between 1955 and 1972, the fashionable emphasis in investment thinking was successively epitomized by such catchwords and slogans as "growth stocks," "young companies," "computer-managed portfolios," "performance investing," and "the beta revolution." Other abrupt, and sometimes contradictory, changes were visible in the variety of industries and types of securities that rose and fell in popular favor. Obviously, the far-sighted investor will strive, insofar as possible, to insulate his mind from these waves of group-think and mass emotion, conscious that the soaring stock prices they produce are bubbles that burst when least expected.

APPROACHING PORTFOLIO POLICY

Having noted the personal factors, lack of scientific knowledge, and emotional rainbow chasing that surround the subject of portfolio management, it remains for the authors to state their own view of a logical, systematic approach to portfolio policy. In light of the foregoing limitations, it would be both arrogant and dangerous to tell the reader that he should manage his portfolio in any particular way. The sections that follow, therefore, are devoted to exploring a few key issues in portfolio management, to outlining several broad systems of investing which appear both theoretically sound and time-tested, and to noting finally a few administrative details of special importance to individual investors. The emphasis throughout will be upon issues and alternatives, with no attempt to recite any all-embracing theory or list of directives.

Like investment analysis itself, portfolio management logically begins with a forecast of the economic future. Such a forecast is indispensable and cannot be avoided. The portfolio manager can build stable, confident rules for selecting, timing, and diversifying his investments only on a foundation of firm economic expectations. He must hold strong convictions concerning the growth trends, price-level tendencies, cost pressures, profit levels, interest-rate changes, business cycle swings, and other economic forces he will encounter in months and years ahead. Otherwise, he is committed to acting blindly on a day-to-day basis, swept and swayed by the emotional gusts of momentary news. Moreover, the investor who professes to exclude economic assumptions from his thinking on the ground that he is no economic expert implicitly assumes that economic factors will continue in their ongoing pattern: an assumption always questionable, and frequently dangerous, in a rapidly changing society.

A portfolio policy can receive a fair test, and yield its ultimate benefits, only over an extended time interval. Securities markets are notoriously unstable and unpredictable over short periods. Until enough time has passed to average out random and erratic factors, the long-run economic and market forces on which a portfolio policy depends cannot be expected to manifest their steady, underlying influence. For this reason, a portfolio policy must be not only soundly conceived, but also sufficiently believed in by its manager so that he will not abandon it as soon as the going becomes momentarily difficult or discouraging.

Practical portfolio policies differ largely on three counts: (1) *selection*, or the basis on which securities are chosen; (2) *diversification*, or the number and types of securities needed to balance an investor's risks with his sought-for return; and (3) *turnover*, or the frequency with which securities should be bought and sold to improve profits or limit losses. The logic behind these differences will become apparent in the next section, which reviews several specific approaches to portfolio management.

PORTFOLIO POLICIES: SOME EXAMPLES

To have good chances for success, a portfolio policy should rest on sound economic reasoning. It should agree with some major, recurring tendency of securities-market behavior. And it should be expressible in a clear, unambiguous rule of investor action.

Dozens of portfolio schemes have been tried, and many different ones are in use today. However, long experience has convinced the authors that only three approaches to portfolio management fully satisfy the conditions noted here. Because these policies hold the most promise for the average investor, this chapter will review them first and in the most detail. Three less attractive policies will be considered in a subsequent section. The three policies that will be considered first are (1) buying and holding, (2) major-swing trading, and (3) intrinsic-value investing.

Buying and holding   Despite the perennial popularity of devices for timing stock purchases and sales, many successful investors—almost certainly the majority—follow the simple principle of buying and holding sound stocks. One reason for this is that investment selection is inherently easier than stock market timing, and the investor who is content to hold a well-diversified cross-section of good common stocks for many years inevitably capitalizes on the country's underlying growth; thus he is almost certain to earn a substantial return. By contrast, an investor who attempts to outguess the twists and turns of the market undertakes a task at which, experience suggests, he is unlikely to succeed. The reason has been noted: Few men or women have either the judgment or emotional self-control to time securities purchases and sales effectively. The best buying opportunities occur when both logic and emotion suggest that the outlook is darkest, and the most profitable chances to sell arise when prospects appear brightest and optimism is greatest. Few investors have either the mental independence or the nervous stability to buck the opinions and emotions of those around them. However, the long-term investor, by his fundamental approach, is uninterested in the market's shorter swings (except possibly as opportunities to buy attractive stocks or rid his portfolio of unattractive ones), and thus he avoids the emotional cross-currents that buffet and warp the short-term trader's judgment.

A second powerful support for the buy-and-hold portfolio approach is the discovery by "random-walk" analysts that, over most periods of stock market activity, the continuous holding of common stocks has yielded significantly larger returns than various techniques of in-and-out trading. The tests used have consisted of carefully planned simulations in which a computer has bought and sold according to specific trading rules, and the data used have been the historical prices of individual stocks. Whether the tests have involved growth issues, cyclical trading stocks, or stable income-type equities, the buy-and-hold approach has produced larger returns in the overwhelming majority of cases.[3] This suggests that there are no mechanical rules—at least none based on market price sequences—that enable an investor to outguess the market.

On what basis should a buy-and-hold investor select his securities? In the final analysis, this is likely to be a subjective decision, based on the kinds of securities he feels comfortable with. Some investors believe in buying for income: this category might include widows or retired persons, tax-exempt institutions, or investors who believe that the ability to pay dividends is a sounder basis of value than earnings which are not distributed. These investors would argue either that they need current income or that the accumulation and steady reinvestment

---

[3] For the classic summaries of these tests, see Paul H. Cootner, *The Random Character of Stock Prices*, The MIT Press, Cambridge, Mass., 1964, and Eugene F. Fama, "The Behavior of Stock-Market Prices," *The Journal of Business of the University of Chicago*, January 1965.

over the years of relatively generous dividends is a more dependable and time-tested means of capital accumulation than striving for price appreciation.

Other investors prefer stocks capable of giving large capital gains through earnings growth alone, and would prefer not to receive dividends. This group might include wealthy persons with other income sources, institutions with large net cash inflows, and either individuals or institutions who prefer to obtain cash through occasional securities sales rather than through taxable cash dividends.

It is probable, however, that most investors who buy and hold believe in combining dividend accumulation with long-term growth. These investors would argue either for their need for some current income along with longer-range growth or for their belief that portfolios or individual stocks which combine income with growth promise more reliable gains than the pursuit of either growth or income singly.

Although no rules can be laid down for securities selections which must ultimately reflect personal preferences, some comment may be justified on the strengths and weaknesses of each approach. First, the low level of common stock yields since about 1958 suggests that buying for dividends alone is much less rewarding than it was between the middle 1930s and the 1950s. High-grade bonds, which yielded 7 to 9 per cent between 1968 and 1972, would appear better suited to income accumulation than the highest-yielding stocks available during those 5 years. At the bottom of the 1970 bear market, a number of utility stocks were yielding 7 per cent or more, but in the first half of 1970, good bonds were yielding more than 9 per cent. While utility stocks bought in 1970 produced good capital gains for their purchasers as the stock market recovered, it must also be borne in mind that the bonds bought on a 9 per cent basis in 1970 also rose sharply in price as yields in general subsequently fell.

Over much of the past century, dividend accumulation has contributed an average of five percentage points to the common stock investor's annual return as against only about two and a half percentage points for capital growth.[4] Since 1958, however, the dividend return has averaged only about three and a half percentage points as against more than four for capital growth. This change has reflected various influences, ranging from higher income tax rates to a more stable and faster-growing economy than in the 1920s and 1930s. Whether the change will continue in the face of new forces notable in 1973 is a question each investor must finally resolve for himself. The tendency for the government to limit dividend increases as part of an anti-inflation program would appear to militate against basing portfolio policies on dividend-compounding. On the other hand, the possibility exists that economic controls, permanently higher interest rates, spreading hostility to capitalistic enterprise, or a fresh cycle of

---

[4] See Nicholas Molodovsky, "The Many Aspects of Yields," *Financial Analysts Journal* March–April, 1962.

boom-and-bust, could topple stock prices from their recent high multiples of earnings and dividends; in this event, stock yields would again become appreciable, and dividend accumulation might again rival—or even surpass—capital gains as a source of return. Meanwhile, the possibility existed in 1973 that, for the first time since the 1930s, the compound-interest accumulation offered by good bonds might exceed the total investment gain offered by common stocks.

The buy-and-hold investor should time his stock purchases wisely. Dollar-cost averaging, discussed in Chapter 10, is likely to give him at least satisfactory results. If he is both skillful and courageous, he may attempt to accumulate stocks only during bear markets or in other periods of significantly lower-than-average prices. The counterpart of this policy, of course, is to postpone purchases at times when the general market is high or obviously in the grip of speculative forces.

Major-swing trading   Along with the persistent rise in investment values, based on the economy's growth, price-level inflation, and the compounding power of reinvested earnings, come recurring swings in market prices which reflect fluctuations, actual or anticipated, in the nation's business. High-grade bond prices may move 20 per cent or more in a single year in step with major interest-rate changes, while investment-grade common stocks may undergo 50 per cent price changes, and low-grade, cyclical issues still wider ones. In fact as in theory, the investor who can buy and sell in step with these swings may look to much larger market profits than he could expect from a buy-and-hold policy. The strategy of buying stocks in bear markets or recessions, selling them in bull markets or booms, and holding treasury bills or other short-term, liquid securities until stock prices fall again[5] is called major-swing trading. Bond investors often follow a similar strategy, although their timing will be the opposite since bond prices are lowest (and yields highest) near the peak of a business boom, with prices highest (and yields lowest) near the trough of a recession.

While long-term investors concentate on high-grade growth or dividend-paying stocks, major-swing traders find it more profitable to deal in medium- or lower-grade stocks. These stocks belong to companies whose sales are sensitive to business changes or to companies whose highly leveraged financial structures produce wide fluctuations in their earnings. Steels, coppers, railroads, and airlines usually fall in these categories, and it is not extraordinary for such stocks to triple in price, then decline by two-thirds, over a single business or market cycle. Recent writers on investments advise major-swing investors to trade in "high beta" stocks, but the recognition that trading profits are largest in volatile stocks is many decades old.

The ever-recurring fact of the business cycle and the strong tendency of financial markets to move with it give this investment strategy both theoretical validity

---

[5] A sufficiently venturesome investor may, of course, sell stocks short when he thinks prices are ready for a substantial decline.

and practical appeal. The investor's chief problem with this approach lies in timing. Neither business expansions and contractions nor bull and bear markets in stocks and bonds are uniform in duration or amplitude, and the art of forecasting either business or securities price movements is dubious at best. On what signals should an investor decide to buy during a bear market or sell during a bull market? Chapter 10 has outlined the investor's difficulties if he uses the Dow theory for this purpose, and at least equal uncertainties appear to beset all other forecasting devices. An investor who waits until the market averages have confirmed a bull market has usually missed the real bargains; and one who postpones his sales until the averages have confirmed a bear market may already have suffered 75 per cent of the ultimate decline in his portfolio's value. Moreover, the major-swing trader cannot rely on the movement of sales, earnings, interest rates, or other business statistics to time his buying and selling because stock prices move well in advance of business developments, not in response to them. The greatest difficulty, as all experienced traders will testify, comes in effectively timing stock sales. If the investor has strong nerves and normal confidence in the economic future, it is not difficult for him to buy stocks when recessions or other bearish factors have reduced their prices and price multiples to invitingly low levels. It is much more difficult to tell when to take profits in the ensuing bull market and how to avoid the disappointment of either selling out stocks that soon double again in price or overstaying the bull market and selling out only after half one's profits have vanished.

Nevertheless, with time and patience the major-swing approach will ordinarily prove rewarding. The exceptions are likely to arise in periods when price-earnings multiples are trending secularly upward or downward. In the 1950s, for example, price-earnings ratios rose sharply from one market cycle to the next, so that stocks rarely fell back to their low prices of the preceding cycle. In these markets, a buy-and-hold approach surpassed all but the luckiest major-swing trading. This was not true between 1965 and 1972.

Intrinsic-value investment   Chapter 4 outlined an investment method which appears to incorporate stock selection and market timing in a single comprehensive step. This is the practice of buying and selling stocks on the basis of their intrinsic or appraised values, considered in relation to market price. For example, an investor may resolve to buy stocks only when they are selling at 75 per cent or less of their appraised values, and to sell out issues which are selling 40 per cent or more above appraised values.

The difference between appraised value and maximum price to be paid is called the "margin of safety."[6] This margin usually assures three benefits to the investor.

---

[6] For a full and persuasive account of this highly useful principle, see Benjamin Graham, David L. Dodd, and Sidney Cottle, *Security Analysis*, 4th ed., McGraw-Hill Book Company, New York, 1962. Also Benjamin Graham, *The Intelligent Investor*, 4th rev. ed., Harper & Row Publishers, Inc., New York, 1973.

It obliges him to buy stocks only when they are in the lower part of their historic or recent price range; on average, therefore, he is likely to accumulate his stocks at prices well below the average prices which they will sell at in future periods. Second, because he accumulates stocks at conservative prices (and often at attractive yields), he is less likely to be unnerved by further price declines and panicked into selling out at unduly low prices. Third, it lessens the amount of his loss in those situations where a stock fails to come back from a low price because a substantial part of the final decline will probably have taken place before he buys.

The purchasing of individual stocks when they are statistically cheap, and their sale and replacement with more soundly valued issues when they are statistically high, appear to obviate in large degree what to most investors is the greatest single worry: the timing problem. Moreover, this procedure is adaptable to all grades and varieties of stocks; it is only necessary that the investor have some reasonable means of calculating an issue's approximate central value for the current year. With thousands of stocks to choose from, a normally diligent investor ordinarily can expect to find a number of issues in attractive price ranges to replace overvalued ones. On those occasions when the whole market appears overvalued, he can retreat to the shelter of treasury bills or other short-term investments described in Chapter 22. When stocks in general seem undervalued, the investor is privileged to select the greatest bargains.

The authors must confess their personal preference for this approach to investment and portfolio management. Most investors lose money because they buy overvalued issues on a momentary impulse; then when prices start to decline, they see how large their losses may become and they sell out in panic. Intrinsic-value investing has the merit of requiring the investor to make most stock purchases at prices he can live with, thus obviating any compulsion to sell out hastily on small turns in the market.

The chief weakness of intrinsic-value investing parallels that of major-swing trading and arises in eras when price-earnings ratios and dividend yields are undergoing major long-term change. Between the 1946–1949 and 1960-1961 periods, for example, ratios on typical stock averages rose from 6 to 7 times earnings to 14 to 16 times earnings, and dividend yields fell from 7 to 8 per cent to between 3 and 4 per cent. At such times, the "buyer for value" clearly has considerable difficulty adjusting his yardstick to an underlying trend which he may only dimly perceive.

OTHER PORTFOLIO APPROACHES

Three other portfolio policies that were popular in 1972 and 1973 deserve some comment. In general, they appear less plausible in theory or more difficult in application than the three approaches just described.

Relative strength selection The percentage advance in stock prices over any period ranging from a day upward is readily ascertainable. Some investment managers believe that stocks which show the greatest relative strength or weakness in one period will continue to do so in the next. Although it is true that stocks often move in sustained trends, they do not always do so. The random-walk theorists contend that past price action can furnish no profitable clue to future price action, and this view appears well borne out by statistical tests and simulated trading, both based on historical stock-price data. Relative strength in particular stocks may indicate the beginning of prolonged price rises, but it may also reflect erratic fluctuations based on momentary news or emotion. The same is true of relative weakness. Neither theory nor experience supports the relative-strength doctrine of stock selection.

Investing in high beta stocks A popular investment theory is that taking greater risks brings greater rewards. Aside from the prevailing confusion between risk and uncertainty, and between risk and price variability, this theory has some support in both logic and experience. Willing bearers of known risks, such as insurors, ordinarily receive a premium for their risk taking; stocks, which are generally considered riskier than bonds, have traditionally outyielded them; and recent studies have indicated that holders of low-grade bonds receive higher returns across time than holders of high-grade bonds, after all losses are considered.[7] It would seem plausible that over long periods the holders of well-diversified cross-sections of risky stocks might achieve higher average returns than investors in high-grade, predictable issues whose starting prices would reflect their widely recognized appeal; some of the risky stocks would go broke, but a few would probably succeed spectacularly, multiplying many times in value. Recent enthusiasts for this approach advocate buying and holding a large number of high-beta stocks. Broad diversification, they believe, will produce offsetting risks among individual stocks and enable the portfolio to "insure itself."[8] Whatever theoretical merit this policy may possess, its practical appeal appears limited. A volatile-stock portfolio must expect to encounter wide and unnerving swings, and only investors with iron self-control and supreme confidence in their policy seem capable of managing successfully so explosive a combination.

Special situation investment A security which promises unusual gains if certain developments occur is called a special situation. Many investors spend their time trying to discover special situations and base their portfolios on them. For the

---

[7] See W. Braddock Hickman, *Corporate Bond Quality and Investor Experience*, Princeton University Press, Princeton, N.J., 1959.

[8] An able advocate of this view is Charles D. Ellis in *Institutional Investing*, Dow Jones-Irwin, Inc., Homewood, Ill., 1971.

average investor, lacking wide acquaintance in business circles and largely dependent on published information sources, this investment approach appears distinctly unpromising. It is true that special situations always exist and that people close to them are in position to profit from their knowledge. But few professional investors have the time, the information sources or the acumen, to discover many true special situations during an entire working career. For the amateur and part-timer to pin his portfolio hopes on this most demanding of all approaches would seem distinctly foolhardy.

Various other portfolio selection schemes have their followers. The formula plans briefly described in Chapter 10 were popular two and three decades ago. Other schemes proposed from time to time include buying the stocks with highest yields, the lowest price-earnings ratios, the highest price-earnings ratios, the highest reported growth rates, etc. Some investors believe in buying stocks only after they have made new all-time highs or have reached their highest prices in some years, on the theory that such "price breakthroughs" signify overpowering demand for the securities. This list of portfolio selection criteria could be lengthened still more.

Four further points about portfolio selection seem called for. First, none of the foregoing methods can be guaranteed to produce profits. The better policies rest on logical premises supported by past market experience, but there is no assurance that economic and social changes may not alter future market patterns and thus demolish long-standing tendencies. Second, none of the methods described here can be expected to work without close attention, continual study and supervision, and firm self-control on the investor's part. No list of securities can ever be bought and forgotten, and no rule of investment can be worked mechanically and without accompanying perception and judgment. Third, different selection principles can be, and often are, combined advantageously in managing a portfolio. For example, the manager may invest some funds for long-term growth, use some to trade the major swings, and keep back some reserve for special situations. Other combinations may plausibly be assembled. Fourth and finally, most portfolio selection systems leave open many vital issues which the manager must decide through his own experience, judgment, and intuition. Included are such questions as degree of diversification, methods of timing purchases and sales, and the extent to which increased portfolio turnover will be attempted in the hope of improving performance. The next section deals briefly with these issues.

DIVERSIFICATION, TIMING, AND TURNOVER

The extent to which an investor's portfolio is diversified is partly decided by its size and partly by the investor's own choice. Realistically, few rules concerning diversification can be confidently stated. Steeply rising commission costs will prevent a two- or three-thousand dollar portfolio from owning more than a few different securities. Conversely, even with block-trading facilities, a billion-dollar portfolio must spread its purchases among dozens of stocks to acquire them at reasonable cost, and to assure itself, if sales become desirable, the chance to sell without unduly depressing prices.

Most investors, however, are free to diversify as they wish, and there seems to be little agreement on the degree necessary. Recent mathematical studies conclude that a dozen properly selected securities with highly opposite fluctuation sensitivities will sufficiently diversify the largest portfolio if the securities can be bought and sold without unduly affecting market prices. One eminent authority recommends even fewer stocks for the average investor.[9] Among institutions, the trend appears to lie toward holding fewer issues on the theory that above-average performance can be achieved only by concentrating on stocks with superior appreciation possibilities.[10] However, many large pension trusts, investment companies, and property-liability insurance companies hold 100 issues or more in their common stock portfolios.

Timing Effectively timing the purchase and sale of securities is generally considered a more difficult task than selecting them.[11] Stocks may be selected on the basis of their intrinsic value, dividend-paying capacity, good yield, quality, and other more or less calculable criteria; but telling when they have reached the high or low price for a given market move, or when it is time to sell or buy them for maximum profit, lies largely in the realm of intuition and judgment. Experienced traders agree almost unanimously that sales are harder to time than purchases. A stock can be purchased confidently, and usually with ultimate profit, if it is selling well below an objectively calculated value. However, timing sales to capture peak prices or to avoid disastrous price plunges calls again for unusual degrees of intuition and judgment, which most stock traders soon find they lack. The common experience is to take profits in stocks that are rising and then watch the price double again, or to sell out a declining stock at a loss when it is on its exact low and ready for a major price advance.

Most investors who trade in and out of the stock market rely on various combinations of the timing guides already discussed in Chapter 10. These include such well-known devices as the Dow theory, the various doctrines of technical analy-

[9] See G. M. Loeb, *The Battle for Investment Survival*, rev. ed., Simon and Schuster, Inc., New York, 1965.

[10] The tendency of institutional investors to concentrate on such stocks in follow-the-leader style appears to have been responsible, during 1972, for phenomenal price rises in a few dozen heavily favored stocks while the rest of the market remained weak.

[11] This is, of course, a main corollary of the random-walk hypothesis.

sis, and stock-price charting. In recent years, sophisticated investors also have turned to two other devices not discussed in Chapter 10, moving averages and filters.

Moving averages are arithmetic averages of past prices over a fixed number of days, kept up to date by adding each new day's price into the average as it becomes available and dropping the earliest day's price. Enthusiasts for this method use moving averages of various lengths to measure market trends of different duration. For example, a securities analyst may use a 10-day moving average to indicate the short-term trend in a particular stock or in some market index, a 30-day moving average for the intermediate trend, and a 150-day moving average to signify the long-term trend. Under this system of analysis, stocks show strength when their daily price rises above the moving average; weakness, when it falls below. If, using these averages, a stock was selling above its 10- and 150-day moving averages but below the 30-day average, the analyst would probably conclude that its short- and long-term trends were up, but that its intermediate-term trend was down.

Filters (or per cent reversal rules) work on the assumption that stocks usually move in sustained trends that continue over appreciable time intervals and produce substantial price changes, without significant interruption. A familiar filter rule is to buy a stock only after its price has rallied at least 10 per cent from some low price and to hold it until it declines at least 10 per cent from some peak price. Obviously, other filter percentages may be used, and the percentage is usually adjusted to the historic volatility of the stock's price to keep the investor from being "whipsawed" by meaningless, short-term fluctuations.

Although moving averages and filters are often cited in brokerage-house literature, their real usefulness is doubtful. Many researchers, including the authors, have made lengthy computerized tests of both devices, using market data going back to 1926. For most stocks, in most time periods—whether long or short— a simple buy-and-hold technique has yielded larger profits than either moving averages or filters. This has been true of moving averages of all lengths and of filters ranging from 1 per cent to 50 per cent; it has been true even where brokerage commissions and other trading costs were not considered. If costs of buying and selling are included, the buy-and-hold policy shows still greater advantage.

Turnover   The notion that buying and selling securities at more frequent intervals will improve the profits on an investor's portfolio has both a superficial appeal in theory and a tantalizing challenge in practice. Between 1965 and 1972 a majority of investment companies, pension trusts, and other institutional investors sought better portfolio performance through increased turnover.

Theoretically, there are two reasons why higher turnover rates may produce larger market profits. First, securities prices do not rise and fall linearly or uninterruptedly. Most of their movement is simply backing and filling, in the course of which their price gradually advances or declines. A medium-priced stock may rise and fall a *gross* total of 200 to 300 points in permanently rising 10 points. An investor clever enough to catch the intervening twists and turns could net, even after commissions, much more than he could gain by merely buying and holding the stock until it had risen 10 points.

The second reason theoretically supporting rapid turnover is that stocks often take long resting spells between periods of rapid movement up or down. At any time, only a small minority of stocks may be really active. In principle, a nimble investor could increase his profits by selling out the quiescent stocks and reinvesting his money "where the action is." When action ends on one market front, he could shift his funds to newly active issues.

For several reasons, however, this theory of profiting from accelerated turnover is prone to fail in practice. Most portfolio managers, including experienced professionals, readily demonstrate that they are not nimble enough to catch shorter swings in either individual stocks or the market averages. Most attempts to do this appear to result both in ill-timed purchases and sales and in higher trading costs. It is perhaps a commentary on the specious appeal of increased turnover rates that the major difficulties of the mutual funds—large investor losses and heavy net share redemptions—stemmed from the funds' efforts during the late 1960s to improve performance by trading on the shorter market swings. The point made concerning filters and moving averages applies equally to turnover: while many methods have been proposed to guide switches from one stock to another, simulation tests suggest that none of these techniques is likely to produce long-period returns equal to those attainable by simply holding a well-diversified list of stocks.

EPILOGUE FOR INDIVIDUAL INVESTORS

For individual investors, the alternatives to personal investment management have all been discussed before. The most promising for individual use were (1) reliance on the advice of a securities firm or salesman; (2) dependence upon the "standard portfolios" recommended by financial periodicals or services; (3) employment of an investment counselor; (4) use of investment companies, at least for funds to be invested in stocks; or (5) the use of trusts. Each of these alternatives is acceptable in its proper place, as the preceding discussions have shown, and the discussions leading to this conclusion need not be repeated here. However, one passing remark will bear repetition: The use of trusts to care for property during its owners' old age, and particularly during the ownership by a widow unskilled in business affairs, is a wise expedient too little utilized by American investors. Such trusts may even be created by will, so that they do not come into being unless the exact contingency they were designed to meet—in this instance, the death of the husband while his wife still lives—occurs.

Title and safekeeping Although a discussion of the available methods of taking title to property is beyond the proper scope of this book, the choice of the most convenient method is an essential part of investment management. Each state makes available by statute or common law an extensive collection of tenancies which may be used for real estate and tangible property within its borders and by citizens for intangible property generally. Among these ownership devices will be found separate property, tenancy in common, joint tenancy or tenancy by the entirety, community property, life tenancies, remainder interests, trusts, and tentative trusts. It is well worth an investor's while to study all the ownership devices which are available to him on different forms of property and to include in his plans for investment management the receipt of all titles in the most useful and convenient form. The choice of the most useful and convenient form would be based first of all on the technical fact of ownership, but matters of administrative convenience, estate settlement, and estate and tax planning would all be of high importance. To illustrate: Families making gifts of property to minor children will usually do well to transfer the property to an adult member of the family as trustee rather than directly to the child, for a subsequent desirable sale of the property might be a cumbersome matter with title in the possession of a minor. Most states have recently passed special laws dealing with stock ownership by minors.[12]

Many investors who take title to stocks and registered bonds find it convenient to order dividend and interest checks made payable to and sent to others. This is not an assignment of the money; it simply permits the income to go to the owner's bank for deposit, or to some other person for any purpose, as the owner wishes; and the owner may terminate the arrangement when he wishes. Securities held in trust may in this way be caused to pay income to the beneficiaries directly.

Previous chapters have noted the importance of keeping stock and bond certificates safe from loss or destruction. Savings bonds, insurance policies, and similar documents may be replaced at small cost if lost or destroyed, but even in these instances the effort and trouble would be a burden. Consequently, safekeeping is important. Most of these things are not negotiable by delivery, hence may be conveniently kept at home or in a business office in a fireproof safe—the convenience of having them available for inspection or sale is an argument for this practice—but a safe is a natural target for a burglar, and the investor is therefore driven to choose between storage in an excessively expensive safe, use of a commercial safe deposit vault, or storage of securities with a broker. This is perhaps a minor point, but the investor should be sure of what he is doing when he selects one of these storage plans. In many states, safe deposit boxes are instantly closed by the safe deposit company upon the death of the holder or of any

[12] Under the Uniform Gifts to Minors Act, an adult has full freedom to sell a security on which he is named as "custodian" for a minor.

joint holder and may not be opened, even for inspection, without inheritance tax office or probate court approval. This may take a few days or several weeks. If insurance policies, wills, savings bonds, or the property of others happen to be stored in this way, unnecessary delays may occur. There are many ways of meeting these problems; the investor, after reviewing his own situation, should choose the arrangement best suiting his needs.

Living on principal The pressing investment problem encountered by most investors during their later years is that of managing an estate whose earnings are inadequate to maintain a reasonable standard of living for them. Social security annuities plus retirement pensions plus interest and dividend and rental incomes are not ordinarily enough. The situation seems to call for a program recognizing four definite needs. First, it is necessary to plan for convenient inroads upon principal in ways which will retain the income as long as possible. Second, it will be necessary to maximize income to the greatest degree possible, without taking unnecessary risks. Third, it is desirable to stress safety, income stability, and value stability, in order to have assurance of both income and principal for the needs which will occur. Finally, it must be conceded that the need for price-level protection in this situation is as great as or greater than in the case of the young investor, for here the price-level protection afforded by personal earning power no longer exists.

It would be idle to assume that elderly persons solve their investment problems solely in the light of what they have and what they need, in terms of arithmetic and economics. They do not. Most of them have families to whom they wish to leave property and upon whom, in hard extremity, they could depend. Consequently, the use of life annuities to guarantee an income to the end and the willingness to endow old-age homes generously in return for lifetime care are not so common as good logic would suggest they should be. Instead, a limited use of life annuities is supplemented by grudging and fearful consumption of the principal upon which the bulk of income usually depends.

The ideal solution to the problem would be joint and survivor annuities amounting in value to nearly half the available property, if need be, plus a moderate quick-recourse fund in savings account or savings bonds, with the balance in high-quality, high-dividend common stocks and residential real estate. The common stocks and residential realty would provide price-level protection, and in addition, the real estate would place both its net income and the recovered principal of depreciation allowances in the owner's hands. Needless to say, the stocks should be those of large, stable, low-leverage concerns in stable industries, and the real estate should be free and clear of debt and not located in areas likely to be burdened with assessment for improvements. The stocks could then be liquidated one by one, if need be, to provide the extra money needed for living; but it would be a comfortable situation if the annuities plus the rental income plus the dividends could balance the household budget. In that way a considerable portion of principal—the cost of the annuities plus the depreciation of the real estate—could be consumed during the investors' lifetimes without any shrinkage in their monthly receipts and with a minimum amount of risk taking.

There are, of course, many alternatives to which an investor may resort. Series E bonds purchased at intervals for the last 10 or 15 years preceding retirement provide a convenient and economical postretirement means of consuming principal, as well as emergency reserves. A trust established in a bank which operates a common trust fund can distribute quarterly sums from principal with very little loss of income. Holdings in several balanced mutual funds would serve the same purpose. Savings accounts could be drawn upon at times when shares in the trust or funds were not cashable at good prices.

QUESTIONS AND PROBLEMS

1 Why do all investment policies and portfolio plans imply an economic forecast? Explain. Would it help all investors to write out fully the economic assumptions on which their investment policies are based?

2 Which do you consider more difficult for the average investor: arriving at a satisfactory portfolio policy, or adhering to it through market ups and downs? Why?

3 Do you find any merit for yourself in the idea of a lifetime financial plan? Would such a plan disclose, for example, the adequacy of the planner's provision for a widow at age 35?

4 In view of the steady inflation and rising interest rates over the past three decades, do you think bonds deserve inclusion in a businessman's long-term portfolio?

5 Should an investor concentrate on growth stocks during his younger years, switching gradually to more conservative investments as he nears retirement?

6 Would you approve of stock ownership by a widow of limited means? What kinds of stocks?

7 Can you reconcile the "investment" and "trading" viewpoints toward common stocks into a practical policy? In your opinion, which of the policies studied in this chapter best satisfies this standard?

8 Should young people accept speculative "flyers"? Consider this pro and con.

9 What advantages and disadvantages can you find in a policy of owning 80 per cent bonds and 20 per cent speculative stocks?

10 Is buy-and-hold a better policy for growth stocks or income stocks? Income stocks or bonds? Discuss.

11 What specific guides for timing purchases and sales would you rely on if you were a major-swing investor? What main difficulties would you face, using this policy? How would you attempt to overcome them?

12 Does intrinsic-value investing simultaneously answer both the selection and the timing problems of the investor? Explain. What weaknesses, if any, do you see in this approach?

13 How many stocks should a businessman include in a $100,000 common stock portfolio held for long-term growth? Suppose the portfolio amounts to $1,000,000? To $10,000?

14 How do you think the manager of a stock-trading portfolio can time his purchases and sales to best advantage? Are the methods discussed in this chapter practicable for all stock traders? Explain.

15 If you were manager of a 50-million-dollar mutual fund, what percentage of the fund's value would you expect to turn over in an average stock market year? Why this estimate?

16 What plan of safekeeping do you employ for fire insurance policies, life insurance policies, will, savings deposit passbooks and certificates, savings bonds, other bonds, stocks? Is this entirely satisfactory?

REFERENCES

Badger, Ralph E., and Paul B. Coffman: *Investment Analysis*, McGraw-Hill Book Company, New York, 1967, Chaps. 7–9.

Bellemore, Douglas H., and John C. Ritchie, Jr.: *Investments*, 3d ed., South-Western Publishing Company, Incorporated, Cincinnati, 1969, Chaps. 29–31, 34.

Cohen, Jerome B., and Edward D. Zinbarg: *Investment Analysis and Portfolio Management*, rev. ed., Richard D. Irwin, Inc., Homewood, Ill., 1973, Chaps. 14–19.

Ellis, Charles D.: *Institutional Investing*, Dow Jones-Irwin, Inc., Homewood, Ill., 1971.

Elton, Edwin J., and Martin J. Gruber: *Security Evaluation and Portfolio Analysis*, Prentice-Hall, Inc., Englewood Cliffs, N.J., 1971, Part 2.

Francis, John Clark: *Investment Analysis and Management*, McGraw-Hill Book Company, New York, 1972, Chaps. 13–20.

Fredrikson, E. Bruce (ed.): *Frontiers of Investment Analysis*, International Textbook Company, Scranton, Pa., 1965, Part V.

Graham, Benjamin: *The Intelligent Investor*, 4th rev. ed., Harper & Row, Publishers, Incorporated, New York, 1973.

Hayes, Douglas A.: *Investments: Analysis and Management*, The Macmillan Company, New York, 1966, Chap. 27.

Institute of Chartered Financial Analysts: *C. F. A. Readings in Financial Analysis*, 2d ed., Richard D. Irwin, Inc., Homewood, Ill., 1970, Part 4.

Latané, Henry A., and Donald L. Tuttle: *Security Analysis and Portfolio Management*, The Ronald Press Company, New York, 1970, Chap. 7 and Part 4.

Lishan, John M., and David T. Crary: *The Investment Process*, paperback ed., International Textbook Company, Scranton, Pa., 1970, Part 5.

Loeb, Gerald M.: *The Battle for Investment Survival*, rev. ed., Simon and Schuster, New York, 1965.

Markowitz, Harry M.: *Portfolio Selection*, John Wiley & Sons, Inc., New York, 1959. Also "Portfolio Selection," *The Journal of Finance*, March 1952.

Sauvain, Harry: *Investment Management*, 3d ed., Prentice-Hall, Inc., Englewood Cliffs, N.J., 1967, Part IV.

Glossary

Accelerated depreciation of accounting charge-off of initially large and subsequently diminishing annual sums, to influence taxable or reported net income.

ADR (American depository receipt) a negotiable share in a block of foreign stocks or bonds held in trust by an American bank.

Alpha coefficient the portion of a stock's or portfolio's price movement during some past period that is not "explained" statistically by the general market move. (Technically, the "Y" intercept of the linear regression of a stock's or portfolio's percentage price changes on simultaneous percentage changes in some market average.)

Arbitrage process of buying and simultaneously selling the same or equivalent securities in different markets.

Assessment bond a state or local bond payable from specific levies to be collected from each property in a specified district.

Auction market a market in which the highest bidder buys securities from the seller who offers them at the lowest price, with all bids and offers audible to the "crowd" at the trading place.

Authority state or local agency authorized to conduct a public business, such as a toll road or a water supply project, and to sell bonds payable solely from its business funds.

Average index numbers of stock or bond prices.

Banker's acceptance draft drawn upon a bank and "accepted" (i.e., signed) by it, on behalf of a customer, hence equivalent to a promissory note, usually payable within 90 days.

Bankruptcy Act federal statute whose various sections provide for settlement of the affairs of persons or corporations unable to meet their obligations.

Beta coefficient a statistical measure showing how fast an individual stock or a portfolio has moved up or down relative to the general market over a specific period. (Technically, the slope coefficient calculated by regressing percentage changes in a stock price or portfolio value on simultaneous percentage changes in some market average.)

Bid and ask (or offer) in securities parlance, a bid is a proposal to buy a specific quantity at a named price; an ask or offer is a corresponding proposal to sell.

Blue List title of a daily publication which lists tax-exempt bonds for sale, naming offeror and ask price.

Blue-sky laws state laws prohibiting fraud and imposing regulations on the securities business.

Board lot standard trading quantity in stock exchange transactions, usually 100 shares or one $1,000 bond.

Bond negotiable promissory note of corporation or public body, usually of $1,000 denomination when of corporate origin.

Bond indenture the complete contract for a bond issue, covering the rights and duties of corporation, trustee, and bondholders.

Bond issue the entire block of similar or related bonds sold under one indenture.

Bond (yield) table mathematical table showing average compound-interest returns on bonds bought at various possible prices if capital gain or loss at maturity is regarded as income.

Book value recorded cost price less depreciation and other write-downs.

Book value per share of common stock book value of assets less all debt and preferred stock claims, divided by number of outstanding common shares.

Broker securities firm (or representative of such a firm) which executes customers' securities transactions as agent.

Broker-dealer securities firm which serves as broker and also on occasion trades as principal with customers.

Business risk the hazard of adverse economic developments in a corporation or a community which may cause loss to investors.

Call contract entitling the holder at his option to buy from the signer a specified quantity of a specified security at a specified price within a specified time period. Also, a notice to a bondholder that a debtor is exercising his contractual right to pay off the bond.

Call provisions terms in a bond indenture which govern the debtor's right to pay off all or portions of the issue before maturity.

Capital to an economist, an accumulation of goods useful in productive processes or for future consumption. To a corporation, the excess of net assets over all liabilities.

Capital funds to a bank, the excess of net assets over all liabilities and loss reserves.

Capital gain (loss) gain (loss) when net selling price of investment is more (less) than cost.

Capital gains taxes federal and state income taxes levied on capital gains, usually at lower rates than on ordinary income.

Capital structure the proportioning of various types of stock and debt obligations used to provide funds for a corporation.

Capital-value risk see *Money-rate risk.*

Capitalization the equity portion of a capital structure.

Cash flow the excess of cash receipts from operations over operating expenses paid in cash—often roughly measured as net profits plus depreciation allowances.

Certificate of deposit an interest-bearing time deposit in a bank, usually maturing in 1 to 6 months and usually negotiable; often used for temporary investment of funds.

Charter (corporation) state or federal authority to a corporation to do business.

Chartist one who predicts stock market behavior by means of graphic presentations of stock prices.

Closed-end company (or fund or trust) investment company which operates like ordinary corporation, normally neither redeeming its shares nor selling new ones.

Collateral trust bonds corporation bonds secured by securities collateral held by the trustee.

Commercial paper promissory notes of major corporations, usually maturing within 6 months, sold via dealers to banks and other short-term investors.

Commission, brokerage fee paid by stockholder to a securities firm for buying or selling securities as agent.

Commission, underwriting difference between price paid by underwriters to issuers of a new issue and the retail price to investors.

Common stock the basic ownership equity in a corporation, having no preferences to income or assets.

Common trust fund a pool of investments administered by bank and used as joint diversified investment outlet for small trusts.

Competitive bidding submittal of written bids by underwriting groups for new issues of bonds or stocks, usually municipal or public utility issues.

Concession small discount from public offering price allowed to securities firms that forward orders to offerors of new issues, municipals, or open-end funds.

Conglomerate corporation which operates or controls several business activities in unrelated industries.

Consolidated statement financial statement which combines the affairs of holding company and subsidiaries as though they were one business.

Constant ratio plan an investment management plan which attempts to make market profits by adjusting stock–bond proportions to a planned ratio.

Convertible bond (or preferred stock) a senior security which company will convert at holder's option into stated amount of common stock.

Coupon bond a bond bearing semiannual

interest coupons collectible like checks when due. Usually a bearer bond. Use of the coupon form is diminishing.

Court trust a trust which must make reports and remain indefinitely under court supervision, usually because established by will or court order.

Coverage of fixed charges the number of times available pretax earnings would cover bond interest and related charges.

Credit union a state- or federally chartered association of individuals which receives savings deposits from, and makes loans to, its members.

Current assets business assets, such as cash, inventory, and receivables, which normally will be converted into cash within one year.

Current liabilities outstanding short-term debts, such as merchandise payables, bank loans, accrued taxes.

Current ratio ratio of a firm's current assets to its current liabilities.

Day-to-day movements short-term changes in stock prices or market averages, caused by current news and accidental demand-supply factors.

Dealer securities firm which trades as principal, especially one which "makes a market" by standing always ready to buy or sell certain issues.

Debenture a bond not secured by mortgage or collateral.

Default failure to observe terms of a contract, especially failure to pay bond interest or principal.

Dilution reduction in actual or potential earnings or asset coverage for bonds or stock by issuing more securities or giving options to obtain them.

Disintermediation withdrawal of savings by investors from deposit-type financial intermediaries in order to buy higher-yielding marketable securities.

Diversification making investments of varied types and maturity dates in various industries and localities.

Dividend a corporate distribution to shareholders, usually from earnings and usually in cash.

Dollar-cost averaging technique for buying stocks at satisfactory average prices by investing uniform sums at regular time intervals.

Dow-Jones Averages well-known indexes of stock prices compiled by Dow, Jones & Co.

Dow theory widely quoted theory that the general medium-term direction of stock price change is indicated by certain aspects of short-term price fluctuation.

Earnings per share (EPS) corporate earnings for a stated period, after preferred dividends have been paid, divided by the adjusted average number of common shares outstanding during the period.

Earning power per share earnings per share adjusted to indicate typical periodic earnings.

Earnings yield earnings per share or earning power per share expressed as percentage of stock price.

Equipment obligations notes or certificates which are in effect bonds secured by pledge of buses, railway cars, or other movable equipment.

Estate planning process of planning assets, bequests, and estate disposition to assure liquidity, provide for family needs, minimize confusion, and avoid unnecessary taxes and forced sales.

Estate taxes taxes levied by the federal government and certain states, based on total size of a decedent's taxable estate.

Estate tax privilege a feature of certain long-term government bonds which permits them to be used at par to pay estate taxes, if owned by decedent.

Ex-dividend without the pending dividend. Hence, when stock is sold ex-dividend, seller retains dividend.

Federal agency bonds bonds issued by federal corporations such as Federal Land banks or TVA. Some are guaranteed by the government, some are not.

Federal securities acts eight major acts with many amendments, under which the securities business is regulated by federal authorities.

Finance company paper promissory notes issued by sales finance and personal loan companies for time periods up to one year. An important money-market investment.

Financial leverage tendency for profits to change at faster rate than revenues because of presence of fixed-return elements in company's financial structure.

Fixed assets business assets of a long-term nature, such as land, buildings, and machinery.

Fixed charges expense charges for interest, amortization of bond discount, and in some cases lease rentals.

Fixed dollar-sum plan an investment management plan which attempts to make market profits by adjusting stock–bond proportions so that stock holdings remain at fairly constant dollar value.

Flat quotation bond quotation which covers both principal and interest, implying that no accrued interest will be added.

Foreign Bondholders' Protective Council a private association which negotiates with foreign government agencies when American-held foreign public bonds are defaulted.

Foreign dollar bonds bonds issued by foreign corporate or public borrowers which are payable in the United States in dollars.

Formula plans plans for the making or managing of stock–bond investments through system or formula which is expected to result in market profits.

Franchise (public utilities) a permit, often imposing duties or obligations, granted for a period of years or in perpetuity entitling the utility to operate, sometimes as a monopoly.

General obligation (G.O.) a state or municipal bond which is an unconditional obligation to pay, issued by a government unit with power to levy taxes.

Gift taxes taxes levied by the federal government and several states on donors of noncharitable gifts.

Give-ups controversial practice under which brokers deliver portions of their commissions on large securities transactions to other brokers as compensation for favors they have done for the customer.

Group insurance life or casualty insurance procured jointly with others, usually under a master policy arranged and subsidized by employer.

Growth stock stock whose earnings and price are expected to increase at a much above-average rate.

Guaranteed bond (stock) a bond whose interest and principal payments are guaranteed by a firm other than the issuer, usually a lessee of the issuer's property.

Hedge fund a private investment partnership, exempt from registration as investment company, which uses margin trading, short selling, option writing, and other speculative methods to achieve quick market profits.

Holding company a corporation which owns controlling interest in stock of at least one other corporation.

Income bond a bond on which the interest payment is not mandatory unless earned, though it is usually cumulative when unpaid.

Income risk see *Money-rate risk.*

Indenture see *Bond indenture.*

Industrial (corporation or security) pertaining to a corporation which is not a railroad, public utility, or financial firm.

Industrial aid bond controversial type of municipal bond issued to finance a building for a long-term lessee (usually a business firm employing local labor) whose rental payments are the sole source of funds to serve the bonds.

Industrial Average an index number of industrial stock prices compiled by Dow, Jones & Co.

Inflation hedge an investment whose earnings, dividend payments, and price are expected to rise at least as much as the general price level.

Inheritance taxes state taxes levied on inheritances received by heirs from the estate of a decedent.

Institutions (financial) investment companies, pension funds, bank trust departments, insurance companies and endowments whose large transactions impact sharply on the securities markets.

Intangible drilling costs expenses incurred in drilling for oil, a large item which is immediately deductible for tax purposes and which is variously handled in company accounts.

Internal Revenue Code the federal tax law.

Investment Advisers Act 1940 statute, one of the securities acts, which regulates the sale of investment advice.

Investment analysis the study of investment characteristics and trends and the consequent estimation of values, relative values, or probable market performance.

Investment banking the business of obtaining new securities from issuers and selling them to investors.

Investment company a business organization which sells its own securities to investors and invests and manages its funds in a diversified portfolio of securities.

Investment Company Act a federal securities act, passed in 1940, which subjects investment companies to detailed regulation.

Investment credit a provision in federal tax law since 1963 which subsidizes new plant construction by permitting up to 7 per cent of the cost of certain outlays to be deducted from the year's income tax. Accounting for its impact on net income is controversial.

Joint tenancy joint ownership of securities or property under state statutes which makes the survivor the full owner after the first death. Tax situation is complex.

Last-in-First-out (LIFO) an inventory accounting system which assumes that cost of goods sold is cost of those last purchased. Profits and income taxes may be so computed.

Leasehold mortgage a mortgage on a building and/or fixtures affixed to land leased (not owned) by the debtor.

Legal list a list of bonds approved by state authorities for investment of savings bank or trust funds.

Legal list state a state whose laws restrict investment of certain funds to legal lists of bonds.

Legal opinion written opinion by a qualified attorney that an issue of municipal bonds conforms to law.

Lettered stock unregistered shares which a mutual fund or other holder can dispose of only through private placement or by completing entire registration process before offering them for public sale.

Leverage tendency for profits to change at faster rate than revenues.

Limit order customer's order to buy or sell securities at a stated price "or better."

Liquidity capacity to be sold for cash or borrowed on to full value without delay.

Listed security security which is fully accepted for trading on a stock exchange.

Living trust a trust established by a trustor while he is living and competent.

Margin owner's net equity in a brokerage account. Or owners' initial payment on a margin transaction.

Margin account brokerage account in which the owner furnishes a proper equity and the broker lends him the balance needed to pay for his trades.

Margin trading buying or selling securities in brokerage account which owes a balance to the broker.

Market averages stock or bond price index numbers.

Market order an order to a broker or dealer to buy or sell securities at the best price currently obtainable.

Market risk the risk that a security or property may not be salable or pledgeable at a fair price when money is needed.

Massachusetts trust a business vested in a group of trustees who manage it on behalf of the beneficial owners whose interest is evidenced by transferable shares.

Maturity time of completion, especially the time when the principal of a bond is due.

Merger a combining of two or more firms

into a single entity which retains all the assets and liabilities of the constituent firms.

Minority interest the portion of the common stock (and possibly the preferred) not controlled by a holding company which dominates the firm's affairs.

Money-market securities high-grade short-term securities or notes which are used as temporary investments.

Money-rate risk the risk that income-bearing securities, especially long-term bonds or preferred stocks, may decline in price because of interest-rate increases (capital-value risk), or that the holder of a short-dated debt may be unable to renew it at its former high interest rate (income risk).

Monthly Investment Plan (MIP) plan sponsored by New York Stock Exchange enabling individuals to buy a stock through small periodic payments.

Mortgage a lien on property to secure a debt.

Mortgage bond a bond which is part of a bond issue secured by a mortgage.

Municipal bond a bond issued by a state or lesser governmental unit or authority.

Mutual fund an open-end investment company which characteristically stands ready to issue new shares or redeem existing ones.

Mutual savings bank a bank without stockholders which receives and pays interest on savings deposits but does no checking-account business.

National Association of Securities Dealers (NASD) association formed to develop and enforce standard procedures and ethics in the securities business.

National Quotation Bureau organization which compiles and publishers dealers' bids and offers on thousands of over-the-counter stocks and bonds in a daily service.

Net asset value per share value of a firm's assets, minus liabilities, divided by number of outstanding shares. Term generally applied to firms holding securities and receivables rather than tangible assets.

Nonrecurring item a special gain or expense item, such as a capital gain or a fire loss, which makes an income statement non-typical.

Odd lot a small quantity of shares, usually less than 100, sold or bought by a special procedure on a stock exchange.

Odd-lot dealer a member of a stock exchange who is designated to buy or sell odd lots for customers at prices based on current round-lot prices.

Odd-lot differential a small surcharge added to customer's odd-lot purchase price or subtracted from his selling price to compensate the odd-lot dealer. Usually 12½¢ per share.

Open-end fund see *Mutual fund*.

Open indenture bond indenture under which additional bonds may be issued subject to any self-contained limitations.

Open order an order, good until filled or canceled, to buy or sell a security, usually at a limited price.

Operating leverage tendency for profits to change at faster rate than revenues because of fixed costs in company's operations.

Operating (expense) ratio ratio of operating expenses to gross revenue.

Option in the securities business, a written contract permitting the holder, if he chooses, to buy from, or sell to, the maker a stated quantity of stock at a stated price before a stated date.

Outstanding stock number of shares in stockholders' hands, not including unissued or reacquired shares or any held for future bond conversions or executive stock options.

Over-the-counter market market operated by dealers and brokers by telephone and advertised list, through which securities are traded without use of stock exchanges.

Participating preferred a preferred stock which receives extra dividends under stated conditions, usually when common receives large amounts.

Percentage depletion a tax-accounting device under which extractive companies may deduct as depletion expense a statutory percentage of the market value of the mineral produced.

Performance cash income plus gain in price expressed as a percentage of price at beginning of time period.

PHA (Public Housing Act) bond obligation of a local housing authority whose interest payments are tax-exempt, but on which interest and principal are contractually payable by the federal government.

Philadelphia plan a method for providing chattels security for equipment obligations, under which title is held by a trustee.

Pooling of interests accounting method for mergers and other corporate combinations, under which assets are recorded by acquiring concern at book value.

Portfolio a collection of securities and other assets representing the entire holdings of an individual, trust, or institution.

Present-value tables mathematical tables indicating the present values at compound interest of sums or annuities payable in the future.

Preferred stock ownership shares in a corporation which are entitled to stated priorities as to income or assets ahead of other shares.

Price-earnings (PE) ratio a measure of highness of stock price, computed by dividing a per-share annual earnings figure into price of the stock.

Purchasing power risk the risk that the principal and income from investments will lose their purchasing power because price-level inflation proceeds faster than investment growth.

Purchasing syndicate a group of securities firms which arrange to buy a new issue of securities from the issuing firm or government, for resale to customers.

Put a contract entitling the holder at his option to sell to the signer a specified quantity of a specified security at a specified price within a specified time period.

Ratio analysis a technique of investment analysis which evaluates a firm's position by studying ratios of certain accounting figures to one another and to external data.

Recapitalization a corporate process through which certain securities are retired in exchange for others.

Receivership situation in which a court-appointed receiver takes control of a corporation to conserve its assets until troubles can be resolved.

Registrar, stock agency in a bank or trust company which countersigns stock certificates to assure validity.

Registration (federal securities acts) obligatory process of filing information and data which brings stock exchanges, securities firms, corporations, and securities issues under regulation by the SEC.

Regulated investment company an investment company which meets certain statutory requirements and is therefore exempt from corporate income taxes on income distributed to stockholders.

Reorganization court-supervised process of creating a successor corporation and issuing its securities to securityholders in a bankrupt corporation.

Repurchase agreement contract under which an owner sells securities to another and pledges to repurchase them within a few weeks at a stated price.

Resistance point a price, somewhat above present price levels, at which ample stock offerings may halt a price advance.

Revenue bond a state or local bond whose interest and principal payments come exclusively from a business project such as a toll road or a water system; also, in some jurisdictions, from a specific tax or revenue source.

Rights, stock negotiable privilege, evidenced by salable certificate, to buy securities (usually common stock) from the company at below-market price. Usually distributed to common stockholders, one "right" for each share.

Round lot standard trading quantity in

stock exchange transactions, usually 100 shares or one $1,000 bond.

Savings bond a small- or medium-sized federal obligation sold to individuals either on a discount basis to compound to par or at par to pay semiannual interest.

SBIC see *Small-business investment company.*

SEC (Securities and Exchange Commission) the federal agency which regulates the securities business.

Secondary distribution organized sale by security dealers of a substantial block of existing securities, usually stock.

Secondary movements up or down price trends in a single security or in market indexes, usually of a few weeks' to a few months' duration and not exceeding 15 per cent in scope.

Selling group a group of securities dealers who purchase new securities from a purchasing syndicate and retail them.

Serial bonds bonds which mature in installments over the life of the issue, each bond having its own due date.

Settlement day the day when sold securities or purchase price must be delivered, usually on the fifth business day after a transaction in existing securities.

Short interest the aggregate outstanding amount (in shares) of uncovered short sales in a single stock or in the whole market.

Short sale any sale of a security which is completed by delivery of borrowed shares or bonds.

Sinking fund a periodic payment by the debtor corporation to a bond trustee, usually used to buy in bonds or call them by lot for retirement.

Small-business investment company (SBIC) federally chartered closed-end investment company with special tax privileges and access to government loans; chartered to assist in financing small and medium-sized corporations.

Special offering technique for selling a large block of stock on a stock exchange floor through exchange member brokers.

Special situation a security which promises unusual gains if certain developments occur.

Specialist a stock exchange member who is appointed to handle other brokers' limit orders in certain stocks when so requested, and who is obligated to prevent unnecessary price fluctuations in his stocks by interposing his own bids and offers.

Speculation acceptance of risk in owning or trading unstable securities in the hope of capital gains or large income.

Stock dividend a prorata distribution to stockholders of additional shares of stock.

Stock-of-record day date designated by directors to determine the stockholder list to receive a dividend, rights, voting privilege, or other distribution.

Stock split a process which divides each share into a larger number of shares, usually to reduce the price per share by diluting the equity per share.

Stop (loss) order a stock exchange order to buy or sell which becomes a market order when a transaction occurs at a stated "triggering" price.

Stopping stock a stock exchange specialist's action in earmarking an open order to cover a stop order when the latter becomes effective.

Subordinated bond (note, debenture) a bond which by its terms remains junior in rank to other company debt.

Support point a price, somewhat below present levels, at which numerous bids may halt a price decline.

Tax selling sales made to realize gains or losses for income tax calculations.

Third market an over-the-counter market in listed securities, wherein large blocks are at times bought and sold by dealers.

Transfer process of removing one security-holder's name from the official corporate list of stockholders or registered bondholders and substituting another's.

Treasury bill a type of United States government obligation which is sold at a discount from face, pays no running interest, matures at par in most cases within a year's time, and is traded in great quantities as a liquid money-market investment.

Treasury bond a United States government bond of the usual type which had 7 or more years before maturity at time of first issue.

Trust an arrangement under which a bank or other trustee takes title to and possession of another's property under legal obligation to administer it as directed and pay income or principal to designated beneficiaries.

Trust deed a substitute for a mortgage in corporate bond transactions and personal real estate loans in some states, in which the debtor's property is deeded technically to a trustee instead of to the creditor.

Trustee a bank, a group, or an individual which undertakes administrative obligations under a trust. Or a bank which holds title as security for a bond issue or real estate loan and performs other duties also for a bond issue.

Trust Indenture Act one of the federal securities acts under which bond indentures and trustees are regulated. Enacted in 1939.

Underwriting action by securities firms in agreeing to buy new securities which a projected selling effort does not sell; or, alternatively, the process of buying a block of securities with intent to market them immediately; or, in insurance, agreement to indemnify a possible future loss in return for a cash premium.

Underwriting commission the fee which securities firms get for assuring the success of a securities offering, or their gross markup in a purchase-and-sale transaction.

Unlisted market the over-the-counter securities market for securities not traded on an exchange.

Variable annuity a life annuity whose reserve funds are in whole or part invested in common stocks and whose annuity payments will be based on the value of such reserves.

Variable-ratio plan a mechanical plan for managing a stock–bond portfolio, wherein the percentage of stocks is increased when a formula shows the market price level to be low, and vice versa.

Warrant a long-term certificate evidencing the holder's right to buy an indicated quantity of new stock at a stated price from the corporation.

When-issued contract a contract entered into by investors through securities brokers for the purchase and sale of pending securities, to be completed when and if they are issued.

Working capital net liquid assets with which a firm does business, roughly measured as current assets minus current liabilities.

Yield on stock, the current or prospective dividend rate expressed as a percentage of price; on a bond, the annual interest payment plus amortization of discount or premium to maturity expressed as an average percentage of amortizing principal.

Index